T0178512

Lecture Notes in Computer Science 13520

Founding Editors

Gerhard Goos
Karlsruhe Institute of Technology, Karlsruhe, Germany

Juris Hartmanis
Cornell University, Ithaca, NY, USA

Editorial Board Members

Elisa Bertino
Purdue University, West Lafayette, IN, USA

Wen Gao
Peking University, Beijing, China

Bernhard Steffen
TU Dortmund University, Dortmund, Germany

Moti Yung
Columbia University, New York, NY, USA

More information about this series at https://link.springer.com/bookseries/558

Matthias Rauterberg · Fiona Fui-Hoon Nah ·
Keng Siau · Heidi Krömker · June Wei ·
Gavriel Salvendy (Eds.)

HCI International 2022 – Late Breaking Papers

HCI for Today's Community and Economy

24th International Conference on Human-Computer Interaction
HCII 2022, Virtual Event, June 26 – July 1, 2022
Proceedings

 Springer

Editors

Matthias Rauterberg
Eindhoven University of Technology
Eindhoven, The Netherlands

Fiona Fui-Hoon Nah
City University of Hong Kong
Kowloon Tong, Kowloon, Hong Kong

Keng Siau
City University of Hong Kong
Kowloon Tong, Kowloon, Hong Kong

Heidi Krömker
Technische Universität Ilmenau
Ilmenau, Germany

June Wei
University of West Florida
Pensacola, FL, USA

Gavriel Salvendy
University of Central Florida
Orlando, FL, USA

ISSN 0302-9743 ISSN 1611-3349 (electronic)
Lecture Notes in Computer Science
ISBN 978-3-031-18157-3 ISBN 978-3-031-18158-0 (eBook)
https://doi.org/10.1007/978-3-031-18158-0

© Springer Nature Switzerland AG 2022, corrected publication 2023
Chapter "Investigating End-User Acceptance of Last-Mile Delivery by Autonomous Vehicles in the
United States" is licensed under the terms of the Creative Commons Attribution 4.0 International License
(http://creativecommons.org/licenses/by/4.0/). For further details see license information in the chapter.

This work is subject to copyright. All rights are reserved by the Publisher, whether the whole or part of the
material is concerned, specifically the rights of translation, reprinting, reuse of illustrations, recitation,
broadcasting, reproduction on microfilms or in any other physical way, and transmission or information
storage and retrieval, electronic adaptation, computer software, or by similar or dissimilar methodology now
known or hereafter developed.
The use of general descriptive names, registered names, trademarks, service marks, etc. in this publication
does not imply, even in the absence of a specific statement, that such names are exempt from the relevant
protective laws and regulations and therefore free for general use.
The publisher, the authors, and the editors are safe to assume that the advice and information in this book are
believed to be true and accurate at the date of publication. Neither the publisher nor the authors or the editors
give a warranty, expressed or implied, with respect to the material contained herein or for any errors or
omissions that may have been made. The publisher remains neutral with regard to jurisdictional claims in
published maps and institutional affiliations.

This Springer imprint is published by the registered company Springer Nature Switzerland AG
The registered company address is: Gewerbestrasse 11, 6330 Cham, Switzerland

Foreword

Human-computer interaction (HCI) is acquiring an ever-increasing scientific and industrial importance, as well as having more impact on people's everyday life, as an ever-growing number of human activities are progressively moving from the physical to the digital world. This process, which has been ongoing for some time now, has been dramatically accelerated by the COVID-19 pandemic. The HCI International (HCII) conference series, held yearly, aims to respond to the compelling need to advance the exchange of knowledge and research and development efforts on the human aspects of design and use of computing systems.

The 24th International Conference on Human-Computer Interaction, HCI International 2022 (HCII 2022), was planned to be held at the Gothia Towers Hotel and Swedish Exhibition & Congress Centre, Göteborg, Sweden, during June 26 to July 1, 2022. Due to the COVID-19 pandemic and with everyone's health and safety in mind, HCII 2022 was organized and run as a virtual conference. It incorporated the 21 thematic areas and affiliated conferences listed on the following page.

A total of 5583 individuals from academia, research institutes, industry, and governmental agencies from 88 countries submitted contributions, and 1276 papers and 275 posters were included in the proceedings that were published just before the start of the conference. Additionally, 296 papers and 181 posters are included in the volumes of the proceedings published after the conference, as "Late Breaking Work". The contributions thoroughly cover the entire field of human-computer interaction, addressing major advances in knowledge and effective use of computers in a variety of application areas. These papers provide academics, researchers, engineers, scientists, practitioners, and students with state-of-the-art information on the most recent advances in HCI. The volumes constituting the full set of the HCII 2022 conference proceedings are listed in the following pages.

I would like to thank the Program Board Chairs and the members of the Program Boards of all thematic areas and affiliated conferences for their contribution and support towards the highest scientific quality and overall success of the HCI International 2022 conference; they have helped in so many ways, including session organization, paper reviewing (single-blind review process, with a minimum of two reviews per submission) and, more generally, acting as good-will ambassadors for the HCII conference.

This conference would not have been possible without the continuous and unwavering support and advice of Gavriel Salvendy, Founder, General Chair Emeritus, and Scientific Advisor. For his outstanding efforts, I would like to express my appreciation to Abbas Moallem, Communications Chair and Editor of HCI International News.

July 2022   Constantine Stephanidis

HCI International 2022 Thematic Areas and Affiliated Conferences

Thematic Areas

- HCI: Human-Computer Interaction
- HIMI: Human Interface and the Management of Information

Affiliated Conferences

- EPCE: 19th International Conference on Engineering Psychology and Cognitive Ergonomics
- AC: 16th International Conference on Augmented Cognition
- UAHCI: 16th International Conference on Universal Access in Human-Computer Interaction
- CCD: 14th International Conference on Cross-Cultural Design
- SCSM: 14th International Conference on Social Computing and Social Media
- VAMR: 14th International Conference on Virtual, Augmented and Mixed Reality
- DHM: 13th International Conference on Digital Human Modeling and Applications in Health, Safety, Ergonomics and Risk Management
- DUXU: 11th International Conference on Design, User Experience and Usability
- C&C: 10th International Conference on Culture and Computing
- DAPI: 10th International Conference on Distributed, Ambient and Pervasive Interactions
- HCIBGO: 9th International Conference on HCI in Business, Government and Organizations
- LCT: 9th International Conference on Learning and Collaboration Technologies
- ITAP: 8th International Conference on Human Aspects of IT for the Aged Population
- AIS: 4th International Conference on Adaptive Instructional Systems
- HCI-CPT: 4th International Conference on HCI for Cybersecurity, Privacy and Trust
- HCI-Games: 4th International Conference on HCI in Games
- MobiTAS: 4th International Conference on HCI in Mobility, Transport and Automotive Systems
- AI-HCI: 3rd International Conference on Artificial Intelligence in HCI
- MOBILE: 3rd International Conference on Design, Operation and Evaluation of Mobile Communications

Conference Proceedings – Full List of Volumes

http://2022.hci.international/proceedings

24th International Conference on Human-Computer Interaction (HCII 2022)

The full list with the Program Board Chairs and the members of the Program Boards of all thematic areas and affiliated conferences is available online at:

http://www.hci.international/board-members-2022.php

HCI International 2023

The 25th International Conference on Human-Computer Interaction, HCI International 2023, will be held jointly with the affiliated conferences at the AC Bella Sky Hotel and Bella Center, Copenhagen, Denmark, 23–28 July 2023. It will cover a broad spectrum of themes related to human-computer interaction, including theoretical issues, methods, tools, processes, and case studies in HCI design, as well as novel interaction techniques, interfaces, and applications. The proceedings will be published by Springer. More information will be available on the conference website: http://2023.hci.international/

General Chair
Constantine Stephanidis
University of Crete and ICS-FORTH
Heraklion, Crete, Greece
Email: general_chair@hcii2023.org

http://2023.hci.international/

Contents

HCI for Energy, Environment and Sustainability

Interaction in Automated Vehicles and Mobility

Interacting with Cultural Heritage

Visualizations of Historical Spatial Data as Tools of Exploration and Education

Monika Barget[1,2]([⊠]) [iD]

[1] FASoS, Maastricht University, 90-92 Grote Gracht,
6211 SZ Maastricht, The Netherlands
m.barget@maastrichtuniversity.nl
[2] Leibniz-Institut für Europäische Geschichte (IEG),
Alte Universitätsstraße 19, 55116 Mainz, Germany
https://www.maastrichtuniversity.nl/p70076654

Abstract. Based on pilot studies conducted in the DigiKAR geohumanities project, which analyzes spatial relations in the Holy Roman Empire of the seventeenth and eighteenth centuries, this paper explores the value of iteratively and experimentally visualizing spaces in historical research. Bringing together interdisciplinary researchers as well as heritage professionals and students, the current pilot phase of the DigiKAR project uses maps for high-level data evaluation, data cleaning and educational purposes. At a later stage, more elaborate visualizations as tools of science communication will ensue. Throughout our research process, visualizations are closely linked to historical and contemporary narratives across media genres. Visualizations rely on textual sources and correspond with the academic texts we produce. Our experiences are meant to inspire other humanities projects, especially in historical subject areas, to experiment with visualizations even on a technically basic level, and even when sources are incomplete, fragmented or uncertain.

Keywords: Geohumanities · Spatial history · Visualization

1 Geodata Visualization in Historical Research as an Approximation of Space

Edward Tufte, American statistician and professor of political science, statistics, and computer science as well as a "pioneer in the field of data visualization" [1], has pointed out that visualizations are not only useful for presenting research results, but also serve as supplementary tools of analysis throughout the research process [2,3]. In his opinion, visualizations could make the process

Supported by Leibniz Association, funders of the DigiKAR project. This paper was also made possible through contributions by MA students in Digital Humanities at JGU Mainz: Konstantin Arnold, Sarah Büttner, Viviane Chantal El-Garrahi, Maximilian Michel, Yohan Park, Maren Reeb, Linnaea Charlotte Söhn, Nele Zunker and Robert Zwick.

© Springer Nature Switzerland AG 2022
M. Rauterberg et al. (Eds.): HCII 2022, LNCS 13520, pp. 3–19, 2022.
https://doi.org/10.1007/978-3-031-18158-0_1

of social research more transparent, and the overall aim of visualizations was "the clear portrayal of complexity", giving "visual access to the subtle and to the difficult" [4]. Revealing the complexity of the sources or data behind our research is especially important in historical research projects in which data gathering is often the first major obstacle, and in which many data sets remain fragmented, incomplete or difficult to evaluate. The data that historians work with range from biographic information to numerical data relating, for example, to economic developments. And in many projects, geographic information matters. This paper presents case studies from the early modern geohumanities project Digitale Kartenwerkstatt Altes Reich (DigiKAR, Digital Map Lap Holy Roman Empire) to highlight some of the challenges and opportunities of visualizing spatial data that are linked with political and legal structures as well as people who perform certain functions within these spaces. In line with Edward Tufte's perceptions, DigiKAR uses visualizations in different stages of the project and for different heuristic and narrative purposes. In general, visualizations in historical research evolve from sources in multiple original formats.

The first group of visualizations in DigiKAR is based on structured data gathered from narrative texts, the second group displays textual information that already comes in a (semi-)structured format (e.g. in lists or tables), and the third group relies on historical visualizations (e.g. hand-drawn or printed maps). The DigiKAR project develops workflows for extracting relevant spatial information from all these sources and inter-relates them through data modelling, which entails entity disambiguation and ontological mapping [5]. The visualizations we create often help us compare data from our various sources and are an important tool of data criticism. Moreover, linking different layers of historical information through visualization is a way of "data storytelling" [6,7] that makes sense of the heterogeneous sources we work with. Meaningful visualizations, however, rely on meaningful data modelling and on an active engagement with data representations that preceded our own. As DigiKAR only officially began in summer 2021, the role of visualizations in science communication with a non-expert public cannot yet be covered in this paper. Instead, I am focusing on the value of visualizations in experimentally narrowing down research questions and in enhancing the critical skills of project members, including MA students and interns. Rather than creating one large visualization that presents a homogeneous perspective, we repeatedly create visualizations as approximations to different spatial perceptions. To this end, we go through a complex, often difficult process of data gathering and data cleaning, in which the application of GIS technology is only one step.

2 Explorational Mapping of Early Modern Spaces in DigiKAR

The project Digitale Kartenwerkstatt Altes Reich (DigiKAR, Digital Map Lap Holy Roman Empire), led by the Institute of European History in Mainz and funded by the Leibniz Association from 2021 to 2024, questions established visual representations of a historical space whose legal and political complexity is only insufficiently captured through polygons and line-oriented maps with narrow thematic foci. As a fractured and interwoven territory, the Holy Roman Empire and its individual, often contested regions require multi-modal and multi-perspective visualizations. By proto-typically tracing human, material, and ideational border-crossings and competing spatial conceptions, the project addresses central challenges of both traditional imperial historiography and digital historical research. Rooted in historical research methods, DigiKAR follows the fragmentation (German: "Fraktalität", French: "fractalité") model of the Holy Roman Empire proposed by Falk Bretschneider and Christophe Duhamelle (EHESS Paris) [8,9]. Moreover, we consider existing studies on the Empire's overlapping layers of secular and ecclesiastical power, and the various forms in which principalities could be organized. Bahlcke has described increasing density ("Verdichtung"), territorialization ("Verräumlichung") and institutionalization ("Institutionalisierung") as "fundamental processes" of structural development in the century following the Thirty Years' War [10].

Although clearly defined territories and formal citizenship did not exist before the nineteenth century, a trend towards spatial organisation of government is already visible in the early modern period, and modelling and visualisation efforts can contribute to exploring how these processes played out within individual realms, e.g. in the already well-researched field of clerical contributions to state formation [11]. Two especially important concepts for understanding early modern spaces are "non-secluded territories" ("territoria non clausa" [12]) and "translocality" [13]. In international historiography (covering regions other than the Holy Roman Empire), similar approaches to early modern states have been promoted in so-called "platial" analyses, which likewise stress subjective, multi-layered implications of spatial experiences over objective or merely physical attributes [14,15]. In DigiKAR, we analyze spaces as zones of interaction and thus present places as flexible, ambiguous connections of points. The exact geographic location of these points and their possible representation in areal geographies matter less than their meaning to people at certain points in time, which is why we first and foremost emphasize collecting and structuring political, legal, cultural and biographical place attributes. In this approach, territories emerge from multitudes of points but are not the major focus. We are aware that an individual bridge or an entire city do not have the same geographic extensions, yet both can initially be modelled as relational entities which are only geo-coded at a later stage of the project [16].

In our two thematic and methodological work packages on Electoral Mainz and Electoral Saxony, current developments in cartographic semiotics, data modeling as well as non-cartographic visualization of space are integrated into transparent workflows which can be adapted by other historically oriented researchers. While the central objectives of our two case studies are gradually narrowed down by the project's historians at JGU Mainz and EHESS Paris, I as project co-coordinator and DH advisor have carried out smaller pilot studies with the help of student assistants and student interns in order to identify overarching challenges and themes. The preliminary studies were 1) the identification of key concepts and spatial relations in metadata of maps and text sources (November 2020 to June 2021), 2) the digital edition and visualization of birth and apprenticeship records (October 2020 to February 2021), 3) further analysis of the birth and apprenticeship data by Maximilian Michel (September 2021 to January 2022), and 4) the analysis and visualization of spatial information in an illustrated gazetteer of Mainz published in 1646 (October 2021 to February 2022). The common goals of the pilot studies prior to project kick-off and in the first months of our collaboration were to better assess existing (academic) traditions of spatial visualization, and to develop best practices for visually supported data criticism. Accordingly, we adopted an explicitly humanistic view of spatial relations and always considered visualizations and text as complementary. The fact that MA students in class, a student assistant and two student interns were involved in the process also fostered research-led teaching at the University of Mainz. Through hands-on experimentation with original sources and digital mapping, the students grasped the challenges of visually capturing multiple layers of meaning, selecting the relevant attributes for their research questions, and communicating their findings to colleagues and the public.

3   Tracing Key Concepts and Spatial Perceptions in Archival Metadata of Early Modern Text Sources and Maps

Before embarking on the visualization of historical geodata, it is important to understand the context in which geodata were created and communicated in their own time, especially if textual sources were already combined with visualizations. In the case of early-modern Mainz, such combinations occurred in illustrated gazetteers like the Topographia Archiepiscopatuum Moguntinensis [17] of 1646 and in different hand-written records that contained hand-drawn maps. In order to get an idea of seventeenth- and eighteenth-century territorial representations of Electoral Mainz that we would be able to build on, we collected metadata of 188 maps showing the Electorate or parts of it from two major German archival databases, namely Archivportal-D and Deutsche Digitale Bibliothek. In addition, we collected metadata of early modern textual archival records relating to the spatial structure of Electoral Mainz. Over several months in 2021, research assistants semi-manually imported the metadata of both maps and texts to a ZOTERO library. The text sources were mainly hand-written documents created in administrative or legal contexts. In the bibliography management system ZOTERO, the metadata could be tagged and analyzed via JavaScript and PyZOTERO (a package for Python corresponding with the ZOTERO API, cf. use cases mentioned in [18]). The analysis was based on an automated list of unique words from all collected item title words, adapting a script I had initially compiled for a book index (cf. collection of Python scripts on https://github. com/MonikaBarget/DigitalHistory). The index words could then be written to a spreadsheet and classified further to create a source-driven tagging system for content analysis.

This analysis gave us a preliminary overview of spaces affected by border conflicts, zones of particular economic importance, or regions where refugees settled. Although the original context of the sources was not always clear or may not have been recorded in the metadata, co-occurrences of places, people, and thematic terms in the titles will henceforth serve to refine our project ontology and help us enrich place names with additional attributes. The names of people and places mentioned also function as disambiguation aids in the automated fuzzy matching that we perform on data collected from other sources [5]. The different types of official records ("Akten" or "acta") relating to borders, uses of land, territorial conflicts, movements of people and goods, or the levying of taxes in certain regions also show how important negotiating spaces was to the early-modern administration of Electoral Mainz and the Holy Roman Empire as a whole.

While the metadata of the text sources were mainly tagged automatically, the less detailed metadata of the maps needed to by tagged by hand. This task was predominantly carried out by our student assistant Sarah Büttner [19]. As the titles of the maps were often less telling than the titles of the text sources, she had to check the available digital previews of the maps to adequately define their topics and purposes. In cases where no digital image was published online, we had to rely on scarce archival descriptions to assign classifications, which undoubtedly led to a bias in our own data. Nevertheless, the classification gives us important hints as to why certain types of maps have been preserved, and what cartographic interpretations of Electoral Mainz have shaped historiography. Sarah Büttner found that circa one third of all preserved maps had been crafted in a military context, predominantly dating from the war against Louis XIV of France in the late seventeenth and the French revolutionary occupation in the late eighteenth century. The late eighteenth-century maps often showed individual fortifications. Many maps furthermore covered possession conflicts and possession claims, mainly involving the Electorate of Mainz and neighboring territories, or recorded infrastructural features (e.g. waterways or postal roads). Especially the many hand-drawn maps we traced were clearly linked with specific events and communicational contexts, sometimes only covering one forest or contested meadow.

For instance, a hand-drawn map of "the territory between Wiesbaden, Breckenheim, Flörsheim am Main and Mainz" ("Karte des Gebietes zwischen Wiesbaden, Breckenheim, Flörsheim am Main und Mainz"), created sometime in the seventeenth century, depicted villages and infrastructure in the Rhein area [20]. Such maps were usually meant as legal demarcations of space and produced in moments of territorial conflict. They may thus provide deeper insights into alternative border concepts of their time. For example, four maps of contested woodlands near the river Necker between the Electorate of Mainz and the Rhine-Palatinate were drawn between 1768 and 1772 [21–24]. Most likely, those maps, which are now part of general old map collections in Darmstadt and Wiesbaden, were taken out of context and originally served as evidence or documentation in court trials. All four hand-drawn maps were created when local authorities revisited the area to re-determine the border after incidents of trespassing. In each of them, the border is represented as a slightly curved line with landmarks depicted on either side and border markers such as trees and stones on the line itself. Mapping the identified places on a modern topographic base map, it becomes obvious that the depicted border did not aim to represent the true-to-life geography of the river Neckar and its banks. By contrast, the map is highly symbolic and relational. One of the depicted places, Hirschhorn, is also mentioned in the Mainz topography of 1646, and this description explains why a border conflict may have occurred:

"Hirschhorn/on the Necker/between Eberbach/and Necker-Steinach/above Heydelberg [now: Heidelberg]/a small place/together with a mighty castle/the like of which is not said to be in the Neckerthal; which belonged to those of nobility of this name before; after their death/it came to Chur Mäyntz. It now has a Carmelite monastery there. The last of this ancient noble family was Friderich von Hirschhorn, the hereditary Prince of the Palatinate, who died in 1632 in the 52nd year of his age" [25] [translated by Monika Barget].

According to this text, the extinction of the local noble family had brought Hirschhorn into the possession of the Mainz Electorate ("Chur Mäyntz") in the mid-seventeenth century – an inheritance which did not remain uncontested. Similarly, abstract maps of escort rights kept in the Hessian state archives in Wiesbaden possibly originated from legal conflict among the nobility and resembled a modern mind map more than a topographic representation [26, 27]. These examples show that constructing and communication spatial relations in the early modern Holy Roman Empire was a multi-modal process in which text documents were linked with situationally important (hand-drawn) maps, among them sketch maps ("Augenscheinkarten").

In the DigiKAR project, the spatial attributes and relations revealed by these maps will support the development of a place index for early modern Electoral Mainz which we intend to publish as an interoperable and openly accessible data set in the World Historical Gazetteer (http://whgazetteer.org), one of the leading aggregators of historical spatial information on the web. (Their linked pasts data template is available on https://github.com/LinkedPasts.) The immediate use case in the DigiKAR project will be to create more detailed maps of administrative activities and the careers of leading officials. The spatial data collected in DigiKAR are, therefore, never isolated nor an end in themselves. They are always connected with our overarching research questions relating to the people who experienced and shaped the different spaces throughout time. The historical overlaps between people, institutions, events and places that the top-level analysis of archival metadata revealed will be further explored, and alternative visualizations are needed to sufficiently capture the complexity of the data. Looking at the same data from different angles and highlighting different spatial attributes was also at the heart of our classroom project and the ensuing student internships in autumn 2021.

4   Mapping Metadata – Early Modern Birth and Apprenticeship Records from Mainz

Prior to the official DigiKAR launch in July 2021, teaching at Hochschule Mainz and Johannes Gutenberg-Universität Mainz (JGU) offered the opportunity to explore sources relevant to private and professional mobility in Electoral Mainz with MA students of Digital Humanities. In the course Digitale Editorik Historischer Quellen (Digital Editing of Historical Sources), IEG historian Jaap Geraerts and I transcribed and annotated six birth and apprenticeship records kept at the Mainz City Archive with our class, paying particular attention to the reasons given why people migrated from and to Mainz, and who the officials were that served as witnesses or signatories [28]. Moreover, the available metadata of all 998 letters were used to contextualize our discoveries. For this contextualization, we created maps displaying the different places of origin and education associated with the letter recipients. An interactive map published on GITHUB and our edition website shows the recipients' places of origin alongside their gender. This included letters written for groups of people of mixed gender, e.g. siblings. The map screenshot in Fig. 1) represents the letters to men in red, letters for women in yellow, and letters for groups of both genders in purple. In the interactive map, letters written in languages other than German can additionally be displayed in green. In addition, the students created smaller maps highlighting all place names mentioned in our six case studies. As the students lacked GIS experience, I taught the students to semi-manually create GeoJSON files in geojson.io [29]. These GeoJSON files were then uploaded to our project

Fig. 1. Preliminary map of places of origins, categorised by the recipients' gender, in birth and apprenticeship letters from early modern Mainz. Data processed by digital humanities students at JGU Mainz, map created by Monika Barget, July 2021.

GITHUB repository, where they were automatically rendered as zoom-able web maps.

Using these maps helped the students get a better sense of the distances that early modern people travelled for work or family reasons, and it helped us disambiguate commonplace names. The mapping experience also showed the students how complex spatial identities and border concepts have always been. They came across fragmented territories and territories whose political affiliation in the course of time shifted. Apart from imperial cities like Strasbourg, we came across the Duchy of Limburg and the Prince-Bishopric of Liège as territories which once belonged to the Holy Roman Empire but are located outside present-day Germany. The multi-linguality, which early modern people were able to navigate, was another finding that surprised the students. Our case studies came in German and Latin as well as French, suggesting that border crossing was not only a common physical experience but also a common cultural skill. The Latin birth letters in our collection came from region that were (and still are) Italian- and French-speaking. Latin was used as the pan-European administrative language that officials and potential employers abroad would most likely understand—or be able to understand through the mediation of a scholar or priest.

Two life stories that stood out among our six case studies where Jeanne le Pourceau's and Karl Anton Mayer's. Jeanne le Pourceau was a Catholic woman from present-day Belgium who came to Mainz in 1685. Thanks to genealogy forums, we found that she was going to marry Johann Adam Schmitt, a wealthy cooper and brewer from Mainz. The birth letters for her were written in Latin and French by a priest and a local official, stressing her respectable family background and her Catholic faith. Interestingly, the birth letter by the priest mentioned that her legitimate birth and baptism were certified based on witness statements rather than written evidence as the church records had been stolen by enemy soldiers in the 1670s.

Karl Anton Mayer, for his part, was a mason apprentice who left Mainz to gain professional experience with other masters. Additional notes on his apprenticeship letter, which he carried as proof of his previous training, reveal that he stopped in Strasbourg with stone-mason Georges Christophe Freysinger and received a small allowance from the city's charity fund. Later stops in Burgdorf (Switzerland) and Lindau (today in Bavaria) are also recorded. Although we do not know when Mayer returned to Mainz, his apprenticeship letter is a fine example of the mobility of early modern craftspeople. Mapping the mobility of Jeanne le Pourceau and Karl Anton Meyer, in particular, helped the students understand the problem of disambiguation of places in (digital) historiography as Burgdorf in Switzerland is not the only town of that name, but proved to be the most likely on Meyer's journey south. Jeanne le Pourceau, on the other hand, spent her youth in the culturally diverse borderlands of the Duchy of Limburg and the Prince-Bishopric of Liège. Looking at the recorded place names in general, we find that migration to Mainz was most common from other Catholic areas and included regions in non-German-speaking areas (cf. Latin and French certificates from Switzerland, Italy, present-day Belgium and France). Most letters were, in fact, written in places that belonged to the territorially fragmented Electorate of Mainz or its neighboring territories. Unfortunately, the place index provided by the Mainz City Archive could not be used for data analysis and data visualization as it is merely an alphabetical list of all places mentioned in a letter and does not state how the places relate to each other or the involved human agents. This database index is based on a hand-written index created in the 1930s which occasionally included contemporary place names of the Weimar Republic/the Third Reich that are no longer in use. At the same time, actual historic place names deducted from the sources and modern attributions by the archivist were not distinguished. As a consequence, we had to extract place names from the much more reliable source titles stored elsewhere in the database and manually enrich the data. These problems are by no means unique to DigiKAR but affect many projects working with (older) archival data.

During his student internship at IEG Mainz from September 2021 to January 2022, Maximilian Michel continued editing the information found in all early modern birth and apprenticeship letters (dated 1500 to 1800) kept at the Mainz City Archives [30]. He has further disambiguated the titles, professions and political functions of the record issuers with the help of Florian Stabel (historian at JGU Mainz) and Ingo Frank (information scientist at IOS Regensburg). In this process, mapping relations between places and people mentioned in the birth and apprenticeship letters helped us correct several mistakes in the archive database and refine our previous geo-coding of the recipients' places of origin. First of all, Maximilian Michael double-checked all letters in which the distance between the place of issuing and the place of origin was more than 30 km (see Fig. 2), to identify wrongly attributed original data or geo-coding errors. As even local parish priests could lawfully issue birth letter, it seemed unlikely that the nearest person entitled to sign such a record would be further away than a day's journey by foot. We thus made sure to check all letters with greater distances for metadata or geo-coding errors. In cases where a larger distance between the two places proved correct (see Fig. 3), the letters were, in fact, apprenticeship letters for people who left their home towns to learn a craft or trade far away. This included apprentices from the Eastern Hapsburg dominions. As part of his exploratory visualizations, Maximilian Michel then experimented with different QGIS functionalities to display the data attributes. For instance, he created a heat map showing the areas where most letters were issued as clouds of varying opacity on a modern base map. The advantage of the heat map was that the base map remained more visible whereas his bubble map visualizing the same data (see Fig. 4) highlighted quantitative hierarchies. Both maps confirmed our anecdotal impression formed in the digital editing seminar that a particularly close connection existed between places along the rivers Rhein and Main, between Cologne in the north-west and Würzburg in the south-east. Sixteen birth and apprenticeship letters were issues in Koblenz, which belonged to Electoral Trier. Koblenz is one of the oldest cities in Germany and was a center of Jesuit activities in the seventeenth century. In the late eighteenth century, it also became

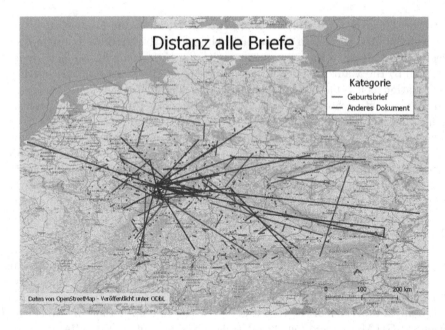

Fig. 2. Distances between recipients' places of origin and places where letters where issued, categorised by document type. Red lines indicate birth letters, blue lines indicate all other documents. Map created by Maximilian Michel, January 2022 (Color figure online)

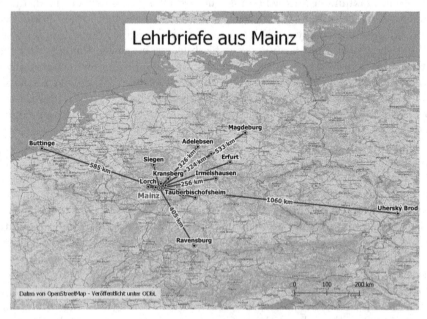

Fig. 3. Apprenticeship letters with greatest distances between recipients' place of origin and place where letter was issued. Map created by Maximilian Michel, January 2022.

a center of exiled French royalists. By contrast, Boppard was a comparatively small but fortified town on the Rhine and jointly governed by a town council and the Archbishop of Trier. Aschaffenburg was an administrative unit within the Electorate of Mainz, governed by a deputy ("Vizedom"). Würzburg was also the seat of a bishop and the center of the Würzburg "Oberstift". In ecclesiastical terms, Würzburg was subject to Mainz as suffragan diocese. Most of the places thus shared a Catholic tradition and the administration of a prince-bishop although Mainz, Trier, Cologne and Würzburg had their own agendas.

In a second step, Maximilian Michel analyzed the issuers of the letters, visualizing their social status and gender. Most issuers turned out to represent secular authority, including professional guilds and individual nobleman. These issuers represented different administrative levels within the nested structure of the Holy Roman Empire. Among the ecclesiastical issuers, Maximilian Michel found Maria Euphrosina, abbess of the convent of Heiligkreuzthal. Like her letter, most other birth and apprenticeship letters were written by unique issuers of whom only one letter has survived. At the same time, issuers representing a city or larger political territory ("Stadt/Territorium") are clearly over-represented (see Fig. 5). Over time, these findings will be matched with our analyses of university records and administrative lists from Mainz to differentiate (fluid) social

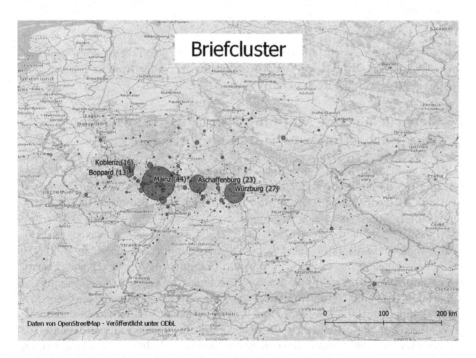

Fig. 4. Clusters of places where early modern birth and apprenticeship letters kept in Mainz were issued. Map created by Maximilian Michel, January 2022.

Fig. 5. Issuers of birth and apprenticeship letters from Mainz categorized by social status. Some letters had more than one issuer. Chart created by Maximilian Michel, January 2022.

networks and their geographic centers. This will also generate insights into religious, economic and political structures within the Holy Roman Empire and early modern Europe more generally.

5   Structuring and Mapping Narrative Information from Early Modern Printed Gazetteers

Another addition to spatial information from Electoral Mainz was made by student intern Nele Zunker from October 2021 to February 2022 when she supported the DigiKAR team in structuring and classifying spatial information from the Topographia Archiepiscopatuum Moguntinensis written by Martin Zeiller and illustrated by Matthäus Merian in 1646 [17]. This book is a narrative description of what the editors deemed to be the most important places in the three ecclesiastical electorates of Trier, Mainz and Cologne. In addition to the descriptive chapters, the Topographia also contains engraved city views, engravings of individual (especially Roman) monuments, and maps of the regions covered. The places detailed in the chapters include larger towns as well as villages, individual castles, churches, monasteries, bridges, gates or antique relics. Although the Topographia is roughly split into chapters for each of the major place names, many other places of different size and function are merely mentioned within these chapters. As such, the information given for the various inhabited places does not follow a fixed pattern and includes presumed historic facts and outright myths as well as descriptions of their physical state. The Topographia also contains cultural and economic information (e.g. on prototypical products of the region such as wine). These anecdotal attributes need to be manually translated into abstract geographic information, and their visualization poses challenges similar to those of "literary mapping", that is the geo-representation of places mentioned in works of fiction [31, 32].

The Topographia's table of contents, place index and most chapters had already been transcribed for Wikisource when Nele Zunker began her work [33]. This allowed us to easily transfer original keywords and dates from the source to a spreadsheet. Alongside original source terminology, the table captured modern categorizations based on the World Historical Gazetteer spreadsheet format, as well as information on political, legal and religious affiliations. Mapping mid-seventeenth-century spatial categories to the World Historical Gazetteer (WHG) terminology, however, proved challenging because the WHG vocabulary follows a Getty ontology of place types that is better suited to post-nineteenth-century history. The Topographia and other early modern gazetteers cover a wide range of place types from bridges, (city) gates, and (ancient) monuments to counties or more culturally defined regions. Such historical differentiations of settlements can hardly be transferred directly to the modern ontologies. We therefore work with two data columns: one contains the historical place term found in the sources, the other one approximates it to the modern (English) terms proposed by the WHG data model. Numerous places mentioned in the Topographia are not classified at all, which makes it necessary to flag unknown settlement types.

As a consequence, not all our entities could be sufficiently described, and we will continue the discussion with the WHG team and other historians how such dichotomies ought to be handled. Based on the preliminary information collected by Nele Zunker, however, we could already address overarching ontological problems of the DigiKAR project and carry out some experimental mapping to see the different early modern and modern spatial categories in context. Apart from the problematic matching of place types, the Topographia is a case in point for the challenges of data disambiguation and normalization. Spellings such as "Dreckhusen" differ from present-day spellings ("Drexhausen" or "Dreckhausen") and make attribution difficult without in-depth knowledge.

Moreover, working with the Topographia draws our attention to the challenge of modeling spatial and functional relationships or even hierarchical dependencies, which we are currently managing via different "neighbour" and "parent" attributes in our data table. Experimenting with maps to better understand dichotomies between spatial distances and functional connections proved a helpful starting point for further data cleaning as many places in our data table required more careful research. The name "Amelburg" (modern: Amöneburg), for instance, can either refer to a modern-day quarter in the Hessian city of Wiesbaden or to a still independent town near Marburg. Only the fact that geocoding APIs could not identify the name itself as a unique location made us aware that more than one place of that name existed as none of us know German geography by heart. Also, many of the mentioned castles and (abandoned) monasteries were at first mislocated by both the Google and Geonames APIs because their names had changed over time, or because the buildings no longer exist.

In order to resolve these errors, we needed to go beyond the spatial information provided in the text itself and include additional spelling variants or location markers found in the historic maps that illustrated the Topographia. In order to extract and process the map information, we did not make an attempt to geo-reference the original maps but used the Transkribus OCR tool to work with the map labels [35]. In this way, our vector layer of point geometries based on the textual information could be directly projected onto the same base map as our new layer of points based on visual information. In cases where the Topographia maps showed borders, it was thus possible to clarify the political affiliation of places that were only briefly mentioned in the narrative. After all, some places in the Topographia chapters on Mainz had never or only temporarily been under the rule of Mainz when the volume was published in 1646. Two territories with complex political geographies were the counties Catzenellenbogen (modern: Katzenelnborgen) and Dietz (modern: Diez). Catzenellenbogen was a county whose male line was extinguished in 1479, and which eventually became part of the Landgraviate of Hesse. The county of Dietz is an even more challenging case. After the death of the last nominal count in 1388, the territory was split and governed by multiple beneficiaries. After 1564, the county was mainly divided between the counts of Nassau-Dillenburg and the Elector of Trier.

Neighbouring territories of the Prince-Archbishopric of Mainz are especially covered in the Topographia's chapter on Hessia Superior and the Lower Rhine Circle of the Holy Roman Empire, which also names the counts of Nassau-Beilstein (here: Nassaw-Beilstein), Reifferschied, Rheinegg am Rhein, Nider-Isenburg (including Salm/Solms) und Neuenar as lords in the region. Other independent territories are the Baley Coblentz, the imperial city of Gelnhausen, and the Probstey Seltz [36]. According to Zeiller, however, details on Gelnhausen and Beylstein-Dyllenberg were provided in his separate geographical volume on Hesse. This hints at spatial classifications widely accepted by seventeenth-century geographic publishers and their audience. Within the Holy Roman Empire, the so-called Imperial Circles (Reichskreise) were an important structural element beyond individual principalities [37]. The selection of places in the Topographia and the diverse political, historical and cultural information given for each of them suggests that the book was written neither for actual navigation on-site nor for a specific scientific purpose, but for the general edutainment of the privileged classes. Such historical narratives of our sources do not completely determine the historiographical narratives into which we integrate them, but they oblige us to offer more than one interpretation of the past not only in what we write, but also in what we visually display.

6   Summary: Metadata, Text and Visualization as Interwoven Analytical Categories

All in all, the process of creating visualizations such as maps for historical research projects is like an iceberg, the visual output being only the uppermost part of the technical and human effort that goes into it. From the analysis of source availability and potential biases in archival collecting to the challenges of extracting data from historical manuscripts or prints to modelling the data, most historians cannot rely on just one tool or methodology. Sources must constantly be analyzed in comparison with others, including sources of entirely different genres. This also requires seeing abstract structures in text and reading historic maps as narratives. Visualizations we create are hardly ever final but reflect work in progress. This is why the DigiKAR project shares data tables, scripts and exemplary visualizations on GITHUB where they can be easily updated and versioned. At the same time, we want our data to be inter-operable and open for re-use, which is why we apply established data models whenever possible.

Beyond the specific research questions of the DigiKAR project, we intend our data modelling and visualization efforts to be samples for similar humanities projects. Our maps are not primarily research output but flexible tools of exploration. Moreover, experienced historians as well as students and interns benefit from making maps themselves as it challenges them to name uncertainties and ambiguities in their research data.

References

1. NT, B.: 30 thought leaders in Data Visualization. https://bigdata-madesimple. com/30-thought-leaders-in-data-visualization. Accessed 5 Feb 2021
2. Tufte, E.R.: The Visual Display of Quantitative Information. Graphics Pr, Cheshire, Conn (1984)
3. Tufte, E.R.: Visual Explanations: Images and Quantities, Evidence and Narrative. Graphics Pr, Cheshire, Conn (2000)
4. Pauwels, L.: Visual Cultures of Science: Rethinking Representational Practices in Knowledge Building and Science Communication. UPNE (2006)
5. Barget, M.: Disambiguating people and places in dirty historical data. https:// insulae.hypotheses.org/333. Accessed 20 Dec 2021
6. Bremer, N.: Using "Data Storytelling" with a chord diagram. https://www. visualcinnamon.com/2014/12/using-data-storytelling-with-chord.html. Accessed 17 Feb 2020
7. Nussbaumer Knaflic, C.: Storytelling with Dta. A Data Visualization Guide for Business Professionals. Wiley, Hoboken (2015)
8. Bretschneider, F., Duhamelle, C.: Fraktalität: Raumgeschichte und soziales Handeln im Alten Reich. Z. Hist. Forsch. **43**, 703–746 (2016)
9. Bretschneider, F.: Étudier la fractalité. Les espaces du Saint-Empire entre pluralité des échelles et liens tarnsversaux. In: Bretschneider, F., Duhamelle, C. (eds.) Le Saint-Empire. Histoire sociale. XVIe-XVIIIe siècle, pp. 147–166. Éditions de la Maison des sciences de l'homme, Paris (2018)
10. Bahlcke, J.: Landesherrschaft, Territorien und Staat in der frühen Neuzeit. Oldenbourg, München (2012). https://doi.org/10.1524/9783486714111
11. Schorn-Schütte, L.: Evangelische Geistlichkeit in der Frühneuzeit. Deren Anteil an der Entfaltung frühmoderner Staatlichkeit und Gesellschaft. Dargestellt am Beispiel des Fürstentums Braunschweig-Wolfenbüttel, der Landgrafschaft Hessen-Kassel und der Stadt Braunschweig. Gütersloher Verlag Haus, Gütersloh (1996)
12. Brachwitz, P.: Territoria (non) clausa. In: Die Autorität des Sichtbaren: Religionsgravamina im Reich des 18. Jahrhunderts, pp. 157–235. De Gruyter (2011) https:// doi.org/10.1515/9783110251876.157

13. Derix, S.: Haus und Translokalität: Orte der Macht - Orte der Sehnsucht. In: Derix, S., Eibach, J., Schmidt-Voges, I., Hahn, P., Harding, E., Lanzinger, M. (eds.) Das Haus in der Geschichte Europas: Ein Handbuch, pp. 589–604. de Gruyter, Berlin (2015)
14. Association for Computing Machinery. Towards platial joins and buffers in place-based GIS. In: Proceedings of The First ACM SIGSPATIAL International Workshop on Computational Models of Place, pp. 42–49. ACM Digital Library, New York (2013). https://doi.org/10.1145/2534848.2534856
15. Westerholt, R., Mocnik, F.-B., Comber, A.: A place for place: Modelling and analysing platial representations. Trans. GIS **24**, 811–818 (2020). https://doi.org/10.1111/tgis.12647
16. Frank, I., Barget, M.: Ontology-based modeling of time, places and agents in the project DigiKAR (Digitale Kartenwerkstatt Altes Reich/Digital Map Lab Holy Roman Empire). Data 4 History Poster Slam (2021). https://doi.org/10.5281/zenodo.4895498
17. Zeiller, M.: Topographia Archiepiscopatuum Moguntinensis, Treuirensis et Coloniensis. Merian, Frankfurt (1646)
18. Barget, M.: Bibliographic data management and data analysis with ZOTERO: Einführung in Methoden der digitalen Geisteswissenschaften. DH Brownbag-Lunch 3, Mainz. https://www.slideshare.net/MonikaRenateBarget/bibliographic-data-management-and-data-analysis-with-zotero. Accessed 21 Nov 2019
19. Büttner, S.: Tagging metadata. https://github.com/ieg-dhr/DigiKAR. Accessed 10 Feb 2022
20. Anon. Karte des Gebietes zwischen Wiesbaden, Breckenheim, Flörsheim am Main und Mainz (1600). https://arcinsys.hessen.de/arcinsys/detailAction.action?detailid=v2650170. Accessed 1 Jan 2022
21. Anon. Karte der Grenze zwischen Kurmainz und Kurpfalz bei Neckarsteinach und Schönau zu den Streitigkeiten mit Kurpfalz wegen Bestrafung des kurpfälzischen Hofbauern von Michelbach wegen Fällung eines Mahlbaums und Durchführung einer neuen Grenzbegehung durch kurmainzische Beamte zu Schönau (1768). https://arcinsys.hessen.de/arcinsys/detailAction.action?detailid=v3216496. Accessed 1 Jan 2022
22. Bürger, A.P.: Kurpfälzisch Geistlicher Administrations-Renovator: Karte der Grenze zwischen den zur Kurpfälzischen Geistlichen Administrations-Pflege Schönau gehörenden Wäldern Neckarhausen und Michelbuch und der Gemarkung der kurmainzischen Stadt Hirschhorn und den kurmainzischen Kameral-Hack-Wäldern (1771), Deutsche Digitale Bibliothek. http://www.deutsche-digitale-bibliothek.de/item/PCMYATRETBAR3E3L6U5HYAT55U4ROLIU. Accessed 1 Jan 2022
23. Bürger, A.P.: Kurpfälzisch-Geistlicher Administrationsrenovator: Karte der Grenze zwischen der Gemarkung der kurmainzischen Stadt Hirschhorn und den zur kurpfälzischen geistlichen Administrations-Pflege Schönau gehörenden Waldungen zu Neckarhausen und Michelbuch (1772), Deutsche Digitale Bibliothek. http://www.deutsche-digitale-bibliothek.de/item/Z47C75VWAMJROB2PXIVB5STJ5KA5P23A. Accessed 1 Jan 2022
24. Hoffmann, D.: Karte der Landesgrenze zwischen der Vogtei Schönau in Nassau-Weilburg und den Orten Espenschied und Wollmerschied in Kurmainz (1782). https://arcinsys.hessen.de/arcinsys/detailAction.action?detailid=v5417572. Accessed 1 Jan 2022
25. Wikisource. Topographia Colonia et al.: Hirschhorn. https://de.wikisource.org. Accessed 1 Jan 2022

26. Hessen-Darmstadt, L., Kurmainz: Vergleich zwischen Hessen-Darmstadt und Kur-mainz über die Ausübung des Geleitrechts an der Bergstraße bei Beendigung der Kaiserwahl zu Frankfurt 1658, Archivportal-D. https://www.archivportal-d. de. Accessed 30 Sept 2021

27. Anon. Karte über die Streitigkeiten zwischen Kurmainz und Hessen-Darmstadt um den Grenzverlauf und die Geleitsrechte bei Diedenbergen 1700. https://arcinsys. hessen.de. Accessed 30 Sept 2021

28. Barget, M., et al.: Frühneuzeitliche Geburtsbriefe aus Mainz: Mobilität in der Frühen Neuzeit entdecken. http://teaching-dhlab.pages.gitlab.rlp.net/ geburtsbriefemainz/home . Accessed 17 May 2021

29. Barget, M.: Geohumanities I: Ortsdaten mit Geojson.io erfassen und bearbeiten. https://dhlab.hypotheses.org/1576. Accessed 10 May 2020

30. Michel, M.: Praxisprojekt 2021. Leibniz Institute of European History (IEG) Mainz. https://github.com/ieg-dhr/Praxisprojekt2021. Accessed 3 Feb 2022

31. Piatti, B., Bär, H.R., Reuschel, A.-K., Hurni, L., Cartwright, W.: Mapping litera-ture: towards a geography of fiction. In: Cartography and Art, pp. 1–16. Springer, Heidelberg (2009). https://doi.org/10.1007/978-3-540-68569-2_15

32. Cooper, D., Donaldson, C., Murrieta-Flores, P.: Literary Mapping in the Digital Age. Routledge, London (2016)

33. Wikisource: Topographia Colonia et al.: Meyntz. https://de.wikisource.org. Accessed 20 Oct 2021

34. Wikisource: Topographia Colonia et al.: Amelburg. https://de.wikisource.org. Accessed 20 Oct 2021

35. Barget, M.: Reading historic maps with optical character recognition (OCR) tech-nology. https://insulae.hypotheses.org/485. Accessed 2 Jan 2022

36. Wikisource: Topographia Colonia et al.: Im Untern Rheinischen Craiß. https://de. wikisource.org. Accessed 1 Jan 2022

37. Sanson, G., Hoffmann, J.: Der Churfürstliche Rheinische Craiß worinnen begrif-fen die dreÿ Erzbist. und Churfürstenthümmer Maintz, Trier und Kölln wie aüch Chur=Pfaltz nebenst noch mehr andern zugehörigen Ländern und Herrschafften. Homann, Nürnberg (1675)

Modified SCQA Framework for Interactive Scenario Design

Yiyuan Huang[✉], Chengbo Ji, and Chun Chen

Beijing Institute of Graphic Communication, Beijing, China
yiyuan.huang@bigc.edu.cn

Abstract. As a branch of digital art, interactive art has typical characteristics, including aesthetics, digitization, and interactivity. Spatial and temporal experiences often accompany the artwork. With the development of digital communication and technology, this form of art has become more and more abundant but more and more challenging to ensure the balance between features. Therefore, this paper proposes a framework named Modified SCQA for interactive scenario creation. This framework is constructed based on the classic SCQA Model and integrates cinematic narrative methods and aesthetic-cognitive models. By combining the interactive art scenario with the Modified SCQA Framework, the article aims to help format temporal and spatial narrative structure and balance between aesthetic, behavioral, and technical elements and symbols, providing continuous high-value experience and accurate communication of concepts and emotions.

Keywords: Modified SCQA framework · Interactive scenario · Interactive art · Experience

1 Introduction

"Participation" in interactive art has become an essential part of the creation. Interactive art is said to be 'created' by the people engaged in the active experience [1]. Artist tries to express their emotions and concepts through interactions between work and audiences. Roy Ascot puts forward that the interactive relationship is the core of the art [2]. Therefore, in interactive artwork, more and more attention is paid to the audience's experience [3]. Thus, "experience" has become another keyword.

In 2018, Edmonds subdivided participation into static, dynamic–passive, dynamic–interactive, and dynamic–interactive (varying). With static art, the art object does not change and is viewed by a person. With dynamic–passive art, the art object has an internal mechanism that enables it to change or it may be modified by an environmental factor such as temperature, sound or light. Note that changes that take place in this category might be predictable or not. If a piece changes in response to environmental temperature but using a complex, non-linear function, this would not necessarily be predictable to a human observer. Likewise, if a piece changes in response to environmental temperature but with some stochastic variation, this would also not be fully predictable. With dynamic–interactive art, the audience has an active role in influencing the changes in

© Springer Nature Switzerland AG 2022

M. Rauterberg et al. (Eds.): HCII 2022, LNCS 13520, pp. 20–38, 2022.
https://doi.org/10.1007/978-3-031-18158-0_2

the art object. Finally, in dynamic–interactive (varying) category, either the human agent or software agent can change the original specification of the art object. This may also include a possibility for learning outcomes from the previous experiences of interaction to automatically modify the specification of the object [4].

In interactive art, the natural experience process and emotional awakening are often accompanied by changes in physiological and psychological events in spatial and temporal dimensions. This dynamic process constitutes the narrative in interactive art [5]. The traditional linear narrative method transforms information directly to the participants. This method is constructed by using long narration to promote and develop. The start, middle, and end of the interactive process are clearly defined, characterizing a linear narrative [6]. As a result, because of boredom, most participants choose to skip. The interactive narrative should be results realized by the interactions and choices of participants during the development of the interactive process [7]. Therefore, a nonlinear interactive narrative is an appropriate design method for interactive art.

Furthermore, the concept of cross-media narration is meaningful for constructing interactive scenario design. Henry Jenkins first proposed this concept, and he mentioned that "an integral element is systematically dispersed in multiple (media) channels to create a unified and coordinated entertainment experience" [8]. Designing with different media, in terms of content or logic, necessarily emphasizes the principle of mutual independence and correlation - intertextuality. In a hypothetical situation, every medium should be irreplaceable.

However, the position of the artist and audience is often unbalanced within complex narrative construction. Regardless of what shape the final product of an artist's activity takes on, an interactive artwork finds its final formation only as a result of participative behavior of the viewers [9]. The artist is concerned with the subjective expressions, while the audience is interested in the experience. The artwork often cannot provide appropriate experiences because of a lack of environmental and cognitive solutions. Unlike traditional art, the interaction between the participant and the art makes the work complete and realizes its value.

At present, there are few narrative models in the interactive art domain. They specifically refer to exploring how to build intuitive interaction based on aesthetic fluency and how to build interactive scenario design based on emotional awakening and cognitive understanding.

Therefore, this paper attempts to introduce the Modified SCQA Framework and help the artist create an interactive scenario. The construction of Modified SCQA refers to the cinematic narrative model and aesthetic-cognitive process, which forms a closed aesthetic loop by controlling four steps: situation, complication, question, and answer. Through the four steps, Modified SCQA suggests participants' emotional and cognitive development. Finally, Modified SCQA provides solutions to complete the concept and purpose of the artwork. The framework ensures the balance between artistic expression, technical support, interactive setting, and participative cognition in the interactive scenario construction. This progress enhances emotional communication effectiveness and optimizes the balance between creative narrative and human-computer interactive experience.

2   Related Works

With user experience research, which is wildly concerned with the system of interactive art, we found many inspiring interactive models.

In the earlier studies, Roger Dannenberg and Joseph Bates (1997) presented an interactive art model with four main components: a human artist, an artistically competent agent, interaction, and an optional audience [10]. This model stresses that computer allows very sophisticated art systems that are qualitatively different from traditional art. This study established a basic framework of a changeable interactive process, enhancing the artistic expressions.

In terms of interactive narrative systems, Marie-Laure Ryan describes four types of interactivities in 2015, which can be split into a 2*2 model: internal/external, exploratory/ontological. Internal/external means if users play a role in the script or from a bystander. Exploratory/ontological means if audiences have the power to take actions which can affect the mainspring of the story [11] (see Fig.1). In the internal mode, users project themselves as members of the fictional world. In the external mode, users are situated outside the virtual world. In the exploratory mode, users navigate the display, move to new observation points, alter their perspective, or examine new objects in order to learn more about the virtual world. In the ontological mode, by contrast, the decisions of the users send the history of the virtual world on different forking paths [12].

	EXPLORATORY Users navigate the display, move to new observation points, alter their perspective, or examine new objects in order to learn more about the virtual world.	ONTOLOGICAL The decisions of the users send the history of the virtual world on different forking paths.
INTERNAL Users project themselves as members of the fictional world	Internal-exploratory interactivity In the texts of this category, the user takes a virtual body with her into the fictional world—to paraphrase but her role in this world is limited to actions that have no bearing on the narrative events.	Internal-ontological interactivity Users are cast as characters situated in both the time and the space of the fictional world. This narrative is created dramatically, by being enacted, rather than diegetically, by being narrated.
EXTERNAL Users are situated outside the virtual world	External-exploratory interactivity The user is external to both the time and the space of the fictional world. Interactivity resides in the freedom to choose routes across a textual space, but this space has nothing to do with the physical space of a narrative setting.	External-ontological interactivity Here the user is like the omnipotent god of the system. Holding the strings of the characters, from a position external to both the time and the space of the fictional world, the user specifies their properties, makes decisions for them, throws obstacles in their way, and creates different destinies for them by altering their environment.

Fig. 1.   Marie-Laure Ryan's 2*2 interactive model

Ryan also proposed five levels of interactivity between interactive art and narrative:1. Peripheral Interactivity. 2. Interactivity Affecting Narrative Discourse and the Presentation of Story. 3. Interactivity Creating Variations in a Partly Pre-Defined Story. 4. Interactivity Leading to Real-Time Story Generation. 5. Meta-Interactivity. The influence of participation on narrative is divided into different levels, guiding the interactive scenario design: the higher the level, the greater the impact of the participant on the story, and the easier the results are to change.

The forms and levels of interactivity proposed by Ryan can be considered as a generalized design and evaluation framework that specify the relationship between participant and interaction system. This theory conducts the interactive scenario and experience design.

Ryan also emphasizes the applicability of narration in different media: story is not tied to any particular medium, and it is independent of the distinction between fiction and nonfiction. A definition of narrative should therefore work for different media (though admittedly media do widely differ in their storytelling abilities), and it should not privilege literary forms [13].

The application of Affective Interface technology in interactive art significantly contributed to the interactive scenario design. The PAD model proposed by Stephen William Gilroy and other scholars based on this technology has been widely used (see Fig. 2). The PAD model measures emotional tendencies and response along three dimensions: pleasure/displeasure corresponding to cognitive evaluative judgement; arousal-non-arousal to levels of alertness and physical activity; and dominance-submissiveness to the feeling of control and influence over others and surroundings [14]. According to the three

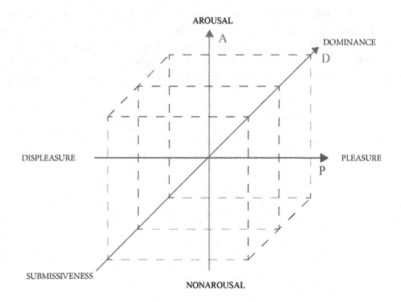

· Pleasure degree P: it reflects the enthusiasm (positive value) and negativity (negative value) of users' emotional state.
· Activation degree A: reflects the activation level and excitement degree of the user's nerve (physiological level) (high excitement is positive and low excitement is negative).
· Dominance degree D: reflects the strength of mutual dominance between users and the external environment (user dominance is positive and external dominance is negative).

Fig. 2. PAD model proposed by Stephen William Gilroy

dimensions, personal emotional changes can be quantified into spatial vectors while experiencing. Those vectors represent the experience quality and determine artworks' dynamic attributes (narrative emotions).

The PAD model assumes that stimuli affect the three primary emotions of individuals and influence the experience with the environment. The PAD model is in line with the widely accepted stimuli–organism–response (S-O-R) paradigm; the model is usually used to explain the influence of stimuli on people's intentions and behaviors [15].

Costello's Pleasure Framework can be used both to support the design and to evaluate playful interactive experiences. The framework comprises thirteen categories of pleasure that can be experienced when interacting. Those categories help the interactive scenario design create the emotional narrative and various experiences [16]. Those thirteen categories of pleasure can be summarized as: Creation, Exploration, Discovery, Difficulty, Competition, Danger, Captivation, Sensation, Sympathy, Simulation, Fantasy, Camaraderie, and Subversion [17].

In *A Study of Interactive Art in the Narrative Form of "Magic Monkey"*, the researchers described a methodology for narrative analysis inspired by *Interactive storytelling techniques for 21st century fiction* by Andrew Glassner: 1) Main-objective; 2) Main action; 3) Obstacle/conflict(competition); 4) Development; 5) Climax and ending [18].

This study skillfully carried out the interactive scenario writing and a framework (see Fig. 3) integrating the dramatic narrative method into the interactive art. The team of Je-ho Oh used the framework realizing a practice: *Magic Monkey*, in which a monkey desires to be a human being. However, this mission is challenging. The participant needs to create a narrative through interaction and play the monkey's role in achieving the goal.

Je-ho Oh's Framework for Interactive art

Factor	Interactive art in narrative forms
Main-objective	The audience wants to be or to do something
Main action	Interactive actions of the audience
Obstacle/conflict (competition)	Obstacles and conflict overcome by audience actions - First / second / third obstacle
Development	Development of a narrative through conflict by the audience - First / second / third development – try to overcome the crisis
Climax and ending	The climax is the peak period of conflict in the narrative as developed by the audience action The ending resulting from the audience's choices

Fig. 3. Je-ho Oh's framework for interactive art

Researchers set up three stages to introduce the whole story. The image of roles was well-shaped. The interactive scenario guaranteed a dramatic experience with conflicts using Je-ho Oh's framework in each stage. After comparison experiment and analysis, significant differences appeared between narrative and non-narrative groups. In conclusion, a detailed and guidable design of the interactive scenario could effectively improve the expression of interactive art, expanding the experience and enhancing communication.

The framework confirmed a methodological orientation for interactive scenario application. However, it lacks detailed narrative writing and aesthetic reflections. The practice was simple - mapping the virtual narrative protagonist to the participant. The dramatic conflict should not be limited to avoiding obstacles by behaviors but a series of "anti-logical" surprises.

In Stephen G. Ware's work, *A Plan-Based Model of Conflict for Narrative Reasoning and Generation*, he emphasized the importance of conflict in the narrative process: conflict is an essential element of interesting stories. It structures the discourse, motivates the story's action, and engages the audience. Conflict can be operationalized in terms of the difficulties that an intentional agent experiences while carrying out a plan to achieve a goal [19].

In summary, we should create a flexible and systematic paradigm for interactive scenario design. This paradigm adapts to various interaction modes, reinforces narrative experience, and guarantees temporal and spatial emotional control.

3   Modified SCQA Framework and Narrative Structure

3.1   Classical SCQA Model and Modified SCQA Framework

SCQA Model is a structured expression tool proposed by McKinsey consultant Barbara Minto in her book Pyramid Principles. The model is widely used in logical thinking training, business, writing and other fields. Its advantage is to divide the event into four parts, and gradually draw a conclusion through the progressive relationship between the four parts [20].

The SCQA Model consists of four parts: S (situation) - introduced by familiar situations and facts; C (complication) - the actual situation often conflicts with our requirements; Q (question) - what to do? A (answer) - our solution is ......

Fabia Ling-Yuan Lin used the SCQA Model as a means of evaluation to examine and classify the narration of informational picture books in her work: *Narrative Rhythm of the Informational Picture Book: A Seed is Sleepy*. This framework was proposed as a tool for structuring information in business documents (e.g., reports, e-mails, proposals, and presentations). It is also helpful for understanding the structure of informational picture books. By adapting the SCQA Framework, we can examine and classify the narration of informational picture books as four elements: Situation (ST), Complication (CO), Explanation (Ex), and Conclusion (C) [21].

The SCQA Model can be used in interactive art and scenario design because its four parts correspond with interactive aesthetic features.

In the Situation module, we mainly state an event widely known and recognized. Such an event aims to bring resonance and a sense of substitution. Concerning the interactive art experience, the Situation can be extended to the environmental and contextual setting. A consensus is needed in this stage.

In the Complication module, we mainly propose a phenomenon, which means that the actual situation is different from our psychological expectations. Concerning the interactive art experience, we set up contradictions, create conflicts to motivate interactive behaviors, and stimulate exploration desires. This process breaks the common understanding outputs and improves expressive variety. Those effects are similar to the cinematic narrative.

In the Question module, we concretize the contradiction, explore the provenance, and find the solutions. Sometimes it is necessary to change the minds from subjectivity to objectivity, rebuild points of view, and reconstruct the understanding modes. In the interactive art experience, the contradictions and conflicts cause continuous reflection and thinking, trying to grasp the logical structure behind the contradictions.

In the Answer module, the interactive scenario provides solutions and possible answers. It means the end of the experience process. Through interactions and thinking, the participant explores the truth and meaning conveyed by the artist.

3.2 Narrative Structure of Modified SCQA

The modified SCQA Framework is based on the classical SCQA Model. The framework also includes four phases with the same names as the classical SCQA Model: Situation (background), Complication, Question, and Answer. Since the modified SCQA Framework is for interactive art experience and dynamic narrative design, it should be a temporal and spatial model similar to film narration. Therefore, we refer to the Three-Act Structure [22] to construct the basic narrative framework of modified SCQA (see Fig. 4). Most films and dramas follow this narrative structure.

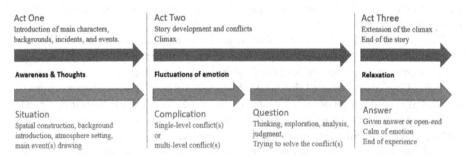

Fig. 4. Three-Act structure VS modified SCQA framework

The Act One is the beginning of the story. The scenario introduces the main characters, backgrounds, incidents, and events. This part corresponds with the Situation stage in the Modified SCQA Framework. It is necessary to construct a spacial narrative, complete the background introduction and setting of the atmosphere, and draw (or divert attention to) the main event. Thus, the construction of Situation stage in the Modified SCQA Framework should arouse participants' awareness and thoughts about the environment and main objects.

The Act Two is the development of the story and the formation of the main conflicts. This part is usually most extended scene. In this stage, the protagonist gets the expected purpose, and the story achieves the climax. For example, the protagonist realizes that he made a big mistake previously. What he has been pursuing is not what he wants. At the highest point of the conflict, the audience's mood fluctuates strongly. This part corresponds with the Complication and Question stage in the Modified SCQA Framework. An essential mission in the interactive scenario design is to carefully detail the conflict construction to arouse questions from the participant. Conflict can seize the participant's interests and cause hierarchical fluctuations of emotion. According to the contents of the interactive scenario and the complexity of temporal and spatial construction, the conflict can be single-level or multi-level.

The Act Three is the extension of the climax and the end of the story. The closer the end is, the more compact the story is. All doubts will be answered. This part corresponds with the Answer stage in the Modified SCQA Framework. However, the answer at this stage may not be exact but open-ended. The participant can interpret the meaning by himself. Besides, the narrative calms the participant's emotion, and the scenario is completed.

4   Cognitive Theories Applied in Modified SCQA

4.1   Mental Flow Model

Unlike film, interactive art is a process of active acceptance, including the participant's decisions and behaviors. A similar paradigm is video games. Therefore, the Mental Flow theory can be studied to help narrative construction with temporal and spatial changes [23]. In the domain of video game, various models and outcomes are based on Mental Flow theory, such as game mechanism, law of motions in mind, educational game creation, game-based learning, etc. [24–27] In addition, some researchers also tried to use the Three-Act Structure to analysis the narrative structure of video games [28].

Mental Flow refers to a mental state focusing on a particular event or task in psychology. It's a feeling that one's cognitive power is wholly invested in a specific activity. The Mental Flow state is usually accompanied by excitement and fullness.

The early Mental Flow Model was proposed by Mihaly Csikszentmihalyi and mainly considered two dimensions of "skills" and "challenges." According to the model, if the participant's skills are more substantial than the difficulty of a series of simple challenges, they will feel bored; if the challenges are more complicated than the participant's skills, they will feel anxious. The participant enters the Mental Flow channel only when "skills" and "challenges" are equal. The difficulty of the task and the ability of the participant change dynamically. If the task's difficulty remains and the participant's ability is improved, the Mental Flow channel will be broken, and the participant will feel bored.

Later, in the book *Flow and the foundations of positive* psychology [29], Mihaly Csikszentmihalyi modified the old Flow Model that only focused on two elements of challenge and skill. With experimental data, it was found that just balancing those two elements was not enough to optimize the experience. For example, when low-level skills correspond to low-level challenges, the Mental Flow state won't occur whether balanced or not.

The Milan group redefined Mental Flow as the balance of challenges and skills when both are above average levels for the individual. In the new model (see Fig.5). Eight zones are distinguished according to difficulty combinations of challenges and skills. The zones mainly correspond to the following different emotional states:

- Arousal: high challenge - medium skill
- Flow: high skill - high challenge
- Control: medium challenge - high skill
- Relaxation: low challenge - high skill
- Boredom: low challenge - medium skill
- Apathy: low challenge - low skill
- Worry: medium challenge - low skill
- Anxiety: high challenge - low skill.

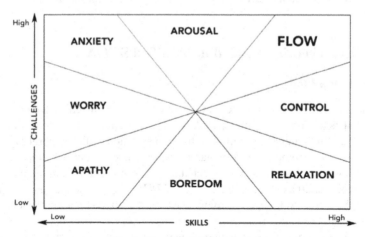

Fig. 5. New mental flow model

The new model has a higher emotional resolution in different states. In addition to the challenges- skills balance, we also need to research the relationship between the levels and the participant's average ability.

Therefore, based on the Mental Flow Model, we need to guarantee that the skills and challenges are carried out in a high-valued and linear progress with each narrative level during the construction with temporal and spatial changes. Keeping the participant in the Flow area is the best solution. However, some offsets are acceptable. For example, in the Situation stage of the Modified SCQA Framework, the participant can also stay in the Arousal area to keep curiosity before entering the narrative. In the Complication and Question stage, some subtasks can be introduced to ensure a sense of control. This design can increase confidence and achievement.

To better orient the participant's emotions and ensure the output of aesthetic symbols corresponding with the Mental Flow structure, we still need to clarify the participant's cognition and confirm appropriate aesthetic and behavioral expressions.

4.2 Unconstrained Cognitive Experience Model

In the design process of Mental Flow, interactions need to be as natural as possible. Therefore, it is necessary to study the audience's attention mechanism. This research helps us determine narrative elements. This paper introduces the Unconstrained Cognitive Experience Model by Laurens Van Calster and his colleagues [30]. This model was obtained from the unconstrained experience reports collected in their study.

In an unconstrained experience environment, the participant's attention is divided into Controlled, Automatic and Diffuse (according to symbolic stimuli). The reaction of attention can be presented by thoughts or perceptions. Thoughts are generally logical and reflected by Controlled attention. In contrast, perceptions are relatively intuitive and reflected by Automatic attention. If the symbolic stimuli are incomprehensible to the participant's cognition, his attention may be unfocused which is Diffuse attention.

Among the attention results, Thoughts are relatively complex. With the participation of logic, the participant can be directly attracted by stimuli from environment or be aroused by some unique thoughts associated with his memory. Then, the output of the Thoughts is determined by participant's cognitive schema (self-relevance, emotion, social, modality, future/past/present). The term schema was introduced by Kant (1781/1929) and widely used in cognitive science. Schemas are units of semantic knowledge, primitives of action and reasoning, rules, concepts, sensory qualia, etc. [31].

Therefore, we need to ensure that we focus on the Stimuli-Dependent relying on aesthetic and behavioral symbols to active some specific thoughts related to the purpose of the narrative (see Fig. 6). We also need to study the schema and aesthetic perception features. This research can help us control the appreciation outcome.

Unconstrained Cognitive Experience Model

▨ Parts involved in Modified SCQA Framework

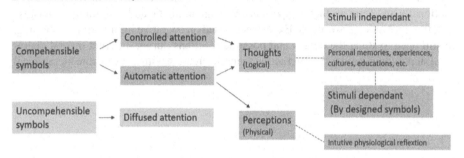

Fig. 6. Unconstrained cognitive experience model involving Modified SCQA framework

Based on the Unconstrained Cognitive Experience model, we emphasize the importance of Stimuli-Dependent. Therefore, the next mission is to clarify the information classification process related to human cognitive features and environmental stimuli, especially in the domain of art.

4.3 Model of Aesthetic Experience

Model of Aesthetic Experience by Christoph Redies [32] is meaningful in this research. The model distinguishes the external information and internal presentations based on the cognitive features in the domain of the art. The design of interactive scenario is a process of creating aesthetic information and provide experience. The Model of Aesthetic Experience guides the choice of aesthetics and behavior symbols. Cognitive processing is automatic, including Stimuli of Form and Stimuli of Content. Stimuli of Form mainly refer to cognitive results decoded directly through sensation and intuition. Those outputs are universal and fast, based on physiological reflections, relying on natural experiences like the fire is warm and the ice is cold. Those cognitive results are usually shared, simple and sensory. In the interactive scenario, although the Stimuli of Form allow us to control the symbolic expression output efficiently, this mechanism can only convey simple and physiological concepts or support the design of sub-element in complex reconstruction. Therefore, in the Modified SCQA Framework, we mainly use Stimuli of Form in the Situation stage. The participant can quickly immerse himself into the environment and context without increasing the cognitive cost.

In contrast, Stimuli of Content are individual and relatively slow, based on the unique culture, logical thinking and memory association, involving the cognitive mastery process in the Cognitive Flow Model mentioned in the next paragraph. Using Stimuli of Content to design aesthetic symbols means studying the participant's cultural and ideological cognitive space, combining personal schema with the concept of the work, and finding appropriate aesthetic elements. This process is complex but can convey complicated, logical and personalized experience content. In the Modified SCQA Framework, Stimuli of Content are usually used in the stage of Complication and Question to create personalized conflict and cultural thinking. The reconstruction of concepts often needs a traceback in memory and depends on individual intelligence (see Fig. 7).

In addition, sometimes, the Stimuli of Form introduce some symbols of a particular experience (memory association). It means a decoding process combined with Stimuli of Form and Stimuli of Content. The two cognitive processes are finally expressed emotionally and form aesthetic experience through aesthetic and cultural mechanisms.

After the Model of Aesthetic Experience based on cognitive information processing, we still need to study the details and possible reactions during different mental operational steps, which guides the interactive scenario creation with an evaluable hierarchical paradigm.

Model of Aesthetic Experience

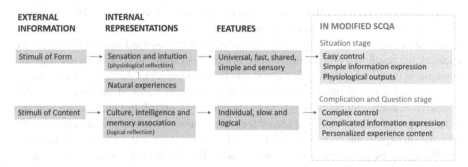

Fig. 7. Model of aesthetic experience involving modified SCQA framework

4.4 Cognitive Flow Model

The Cognitive Flow Model (see Fig. 8) proposed by Matthew Pelowski [33] is a valuable reference for our study. This model manifests aesthetic experience with detailed factors for each cognitive stage, which is capable of guiding the task and symbolic design in Modified SCQA.

Cognitive Flow Model

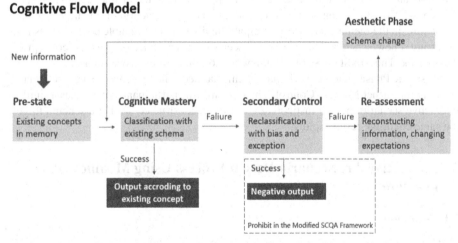

Fig. 8. Cognitive flow model (blue zone) with intervention of modified SCQA framework (red zone) (Color figure online)

The Cognitive Flow is divided into five stages:

Pre-State means everyone's existing schema, including the opinions and interpretations of things. Pre-state is the setup phase of cognition. It corresponds to audience cognitive analysis, which means the symbols corresponding to the existing schema and the other elements associated with the unknown schema, including objects, events, experience, culture, etc.

Cognitive Mastery focuses on classifying the information and judging whether the objective matches the existing schema. If matched, the results in the schema will be output. If not, it means a differentiation, and the process will continue to the next stage. Matching means that the elements of the interactive scenario exist in the participant's schema, and the participant only needs to recall the association mechanism (instinctively) to output the result at a low cognitive cost. Matching design can be used in the stage of Situation in modified SCQA. It is natural and habitual but lacks novelty and attraction.

Secondary Control means reclassification. If the non-matched information in the Cognitive Mastery can be classified in the Secondary Control, the mechanism will try to make a partial interpretation or physiological rejection. The results will be inaccurate information expression, reduced sensitivity, physiological tension, self-worth defense or devaluation. If the reclassification is unsuccessful, the Cognitive Flow passes to the next phase. Secondary control is a dangerous process. During the design, we need to avoid the success of secondary classification. Success means some symbols in the interactive scenario are negative unfamiliar, disgusting and repulsive. Once the secondary classification occurs, the participant needs to face negative experiences. However, in some particular cases, the interactive scenario requires arousing some negative experiences. But it is always risky. It is more common to make the secondary control unsuccessful, which can stimulate conflict, create the Complication stage in Modified SCQA, and let the participant enter the Question stage.

Re-Assessment suggests the participant abandon the initial cognitive expectations and re-examine the schema until constructing a new schema and achieving self-awareness. This stage means that, after continuous reconstruction of cognitive schema and testing in the mental state, the participant finally obtains available cognitive results, exporting a new schema. The interactive scenario successfully outputs the concept of the artwork. The Modified SCQA Framework completes the Answer phase.

Aesthetic Phase means the original schema has been changed, and the new schema is working for further Mastery Control. The next time the participant experiences a similar interactive scenario, he can instinctively use the reconstructed aesthetic schema to get the same cognitive result rapidly.

5 Interactive Art Scenario Design Process Using Modified SCQA Framework

5.1 Situation

In the Situation stage, the interactive scenario is responsible for creating a beginning and introducing the subjects and environment recognized by participants. Pre-cognition arouses interpretations based on memory and experience, which helps the development of the next steps.

According to the Mental Flow Model, the level of skills and challenges should be in the Arousing or Flow area in the initial stage. A medium skill level is accompanied by a medium or higher challenge level. For example, a surreal scene can be presented visually. The environmental elements are easy to understand, but the reconstruction result is attractive. It is better to use artistic symbols encoded by physiology and instinct (rather than logical coding) for environmental structure. This process starts with an easy recognition and ends with a precious information result. The objective is to identify the environment and arouse interest. Therefore, information design could be "large", "tensive", "dreamy", "cherished", or "unforgettable". The information should be simple and easy-coded, providing positive psychological suggestions (avoiding confusion or frustration) (see Fig. 9).

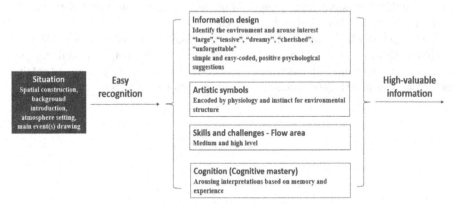

Fig. 9. Situation stage of modified SCQA framework

5.2 Complication

In the Complication stage, the interactive scenario focuses on establishing single-layer or multi-layer conflicts, emphasizing expressiveness.

According to the Mental Flow Model, at this stage, skills and challenges should mainly stay in the Flow area, synchronously improved to a medium and high level. The participant's thoughts are activated through behavioral and logical coding. Cognition for the main objects and events requires the process of accommodation, but the detailed aesthetic symbols (elements or factors within main objects and events) should not confuse. When someone receives a new message that does not match his known message, the new message will not be decoded by any existing schema. To understand this information, the schema must be changed or reconstructed. This is the accommodation process [34]. Therefore, it is best to output the results with cognitive assimilation. Contrary to the accommodation process, when someone receives a new message that matches his known message, the new message will be taken over by the existing schema. Schema uses the results of known information to decode new information, which is the assimilation process [35]. Thus, in the interactive scenario, it is necessary to apply appropriate guiding design and accurate expressions, helping participants resolve the narrative conflict of the main objects and events through assimilation.

Concerning the information design in the Complication stage, interactive scenario design should pay attention to the precision of details. We construct main objects and events in each narrative step and follow the principle of reconstructive conflict. It means that main objects and events need to be artistically deconstructed, and the schema should easily decode the elements after deconstruction. However, the combination of features should be specifically re-designed. The combination may be in conflict and needs a re-consideration and re-exanimation by logic. This process goes through the re-assessment stage and finally forms a new schema output.

The process of re-assessment is not only an improvement of the participant's skills but also a narrative climax and concept exploration. In this part, the perception of the details should be physiological coding, and the reconstruction and combination of the details should be psychological coding (logical).

Participant may feel confused in this stage and arouse the re-assessment mechanism intuitively. However, it should not produce negative cognitive output (or directly give positive cognitive results) - interactive scenario design focuses on suggesting and helping participants complete mental reconstruction under confusion and conflict (see Fig. 10).

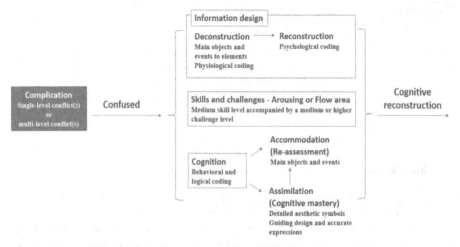

Fig. 10. Complication stage of modified SCQA framework

5.3 Question

In the Question stage, the interactive scenario focuses on the construction of questioning and thinking. According to the Mental Flow Model, the Flow channel enters a higher area at this stage. Therefore, the interactive scenario may require the highest skills and challenges. The participant searches memory and explores possible schema combinations, hoping to resolve conflict and get the artwork concept. Therefore, this stage is mainly controlled by cognitive accommodation. As a continuation of the Compilation, the interactive scenario should help the participant avoid frustration and negative mental output about the information design. Therefore, it is not necessary to introduce new objects or events. Instead, we could import some auxiliary elements (to help the participant understand the main objects or events). Those elements have a low cognitive cost.

At this stage, the psychological coding (logical) is mainly mobilized. Finally, the interactive scenario should conduct the participant's cognitive state from conflict to empathy, arousing an emotional fluctuation and completing cognitive reconstruction (see Fig. 11).

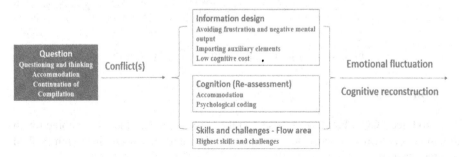

Fig. 11. Question stage of Modified SCQA framework

5.4 Answer

In the Answer stage, the interactive scenario comes to an end. The answer and the concept of the artwork will be given or accompanied by an open-end for further discovery.

About the information design, the scenario can be divided into two different directions:

Given answer - The meaning of objects and events in Complication is published by scenario. The accommodation process is thus interrupted, and the answer is given by artwork instead of the participant's schema change. Thanks to the given solution, the previous conflict details can be understood neutrally. Furthermore, the assimilation mechanism is activated immediately. Finally, the empathy between the concept of the artwork and the participant's cognition is established.

Open-end - The Complication stage continues. Finally, the reconstruction of the new schema is worked out for further assimilation. Then, the participant tries to find the answer by himself. Thus, the solution can differ depending on individual cognition with schema change. Finally, the empathy between concept and cognition is also established personally.

After the answer has been found, the changed schema recognizes previous conflict elements and incomprehensive constructions. Then, when similar events or objects appear, the changed schema will be activated and easily restart the mastery process (see Fig. 12).

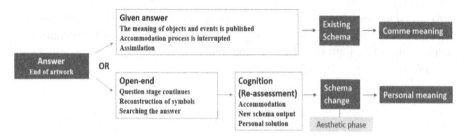

Fig. 12. Answer stage of Modified SCQA Framework

6 Conclusion

The Modified SCQA Framework based on the classical SCQA model, combined with the Three-Act Structure, provides a method for the interactive scenario design applied in interactive art.

Due to the active participation in interactive art, the artwork's construction requires the participant's intervention. Furthermore, the communication of aesthetic concepts and emotions is closely related to cognition. Therefore, the structure of Modified SCQA needs the help of cognitive psychology. Consequently, we combined the Mental Flow Model, the Unconstrained Cognitive Experience model, the Model of Aesthetic Experience and the Cognitive Flow Model in constructing the Modified SCQA Framework.

Through the information processing and aesthetic-cognitive progress, we determined critical points of the Situation, Complication, Question and Answer stage in the Modified SCQA. The framework emphasizes the information and symbolic design strategy, the cognitive process and the outcome during the scenario development.

This research started with the spatial-temporal characteristics and cognitive experience of interactive narrative, developed by combining film narrative structure and a series of cognitive-psychological analyses. However, this study remains in the theoretical stage and has not been analyzed in practice. Therefore, there may be deviations in the application and specific measures.

Next, our work will focus on solving those deficiencies and updating the model. Finally, we hope that this paper can provide some references for designers and researchers for their creation of interactive art.

Acknowledgement. This research is supported by the Initial Funding for the Doctoral Program of BIGC (27170121001/028).

References

1. Candy, L., Amitani, S., Bilda, Z.: Practice-led strategies for interactive art re-search. CoDesign **2**(4), 209–223 (2006)
2. Edmonds, E., Turner, G., Candy, L.: Approaches to interactive art systems. In: proceedings of the 2nd International Conference on Computer graphics and Interactive Techniques in Australasia and South East Asia, pp. 113–117 (2004)

3. Costello, B., Muller, L., Amitani, S., et al.: Understanding the experience of interactive art: lamascope in Beta_space. In: ACM International Conference Proceeding Series, vol. 123, pp. 49–56 (2005)
4. Jeon, M., Fiebrink, R., Edmonds, E.A., Herath, D.: From rituals to magic: Interactive art and HCI of the past, present, and future. Int. J. Hum Comput Stud. **131**, 108–119 (2019)
5. Zimmerman, E.: Narrative, interactivity, play, and games: Four naughty concepts in need of discipline. First person: New media as story, performance, and game 154 (2004)
6. Neto, J.S.D.O., Filgueiras, L.V.L.: Crossmedia application design: exploring linear and non-linear narrative abilities. In: Proceedings of the 26th Annual ACM International Conference on Design of communication, pp.22–24 (2008)
7. Yang, Z.: Cross media narrative analysis of literary IP adapted animation. J. News Res. **12**(03), 143–146 (2021)
8. Schiller, M.: Transmedia Storytelling. Amsterdam University Press, Amsterdam (2022)
9. Kluszczynski, R.W.: Strategies of interactive art. J. Aesthetics & Culture **2**(1), 5525 (2010)
10. Dannenberg, R.B., Bates, J.A.: Model for interactive art (1995)
11. Ogle, G.: Screenwriting for new film mediums: conceptualizing visual models for interactive storytelling. J. Screenwriting **10**(1), 3–27 (2019)
12. Ryan, M.L.: Beyond myth and metaphor: narrative in digital media. Poetics Today **23**(4), 581–609 (2002)
13. Ryan, M.L.: Toward a definition of narrative. Camb. companion to narrative 22-35 (2007)
14. Gilroy, S.W., Cavazza, M., Chaignon, R., et al.: An affective model of user experience for interactive art. In: Proceedings of the 2008 International Conference on Advances in Computer Entertainment Technology, pp. 107–110 (2008)
15. Huang, M., Ali, R., Liao, J.: The effect of user experience in online games on word of mouth: A pleasure-arousal-dominance (PAD) model perspective. Comput. Hum. Behav. **75**, 329–338 (2017)
16. Duarte, E.F., Baranauskas, M.C.C.: Revisiting interactive art from an interaction design perspective: Opening a research agenda. In: Proceedings of the 17th Brazilian Symposium on Human Factors in Computing Systems, pp.1–10 (2018)
17. Costello, B.: A pleasure framework. Leonardo **40**(4), 370–371 (2007)
18. Oh, J., Kim, S., Kim, S., et al.: A Study of Interactive Art in the Narrative Form of Magic Monkey. In: Eighth International Conference Computer Graphics, Imaging and Visualization. IEEE 39–46 (2011)
19. Ware, S.G.: A plan-based model of conflict for narrative reasoning and generation. North Carolina State University (2014)
20. Minto, B.: The Minto pyramid principle: logic in writing, thinking and problem solving. Minto International Inc (1996)
21. Lin, F.L.Y.: Narrative rhythm of the informational picture book: a seed is sleepy. Image Narrative **22**(3), 88–114 (2021)
22. Ismail, N.: Emotional engagement in feature film storytelling: reframing the classical three-act structure. J. Skrin Malaysia **3**, 35–54 (2006)
23. Huang, H.C., Pham, T.T.L., Wong, M.K., et al.: How to create flow experience in exergames? Perspective of flow theory. Telematics Inform. **35**(5), 1288–1296 (2018)
24. Akman, E., Çakır, R.: Pupils' opinions on an educational virtual reality game in terms of flow experience. Int. J. Emerg. Technol. Learn. **14**(15), 121–137 (2019)
25. Chang, C.C., Warden, C.A., Liang, C., et al.: Effects of digital game-based learning on achievement, flow and overall cognitive load. Australas. J. Educ. Technol. **34**(4), 124–137 (2018)
26. Iida, H., Khalid, M.N.A.: Using games to study law of motions in mind. IEEE Access **8**(1), 138701–138709 (2020)

27. Boyan, A., McGloin, R., Wasserman, J.A.: Model matching theory: a framework for examining the alignment between game mechanics and mental models. Media Commun. **6**(2), 126–136 (2018)
28. Pudjoatmodjo, B., Mandasari, R. I. M., Salam, S., et al.: Storytelling Technique Using Three Act Structure and Directed Graph for Virtual Reality Game (case study: UrBandung Legend). In: 7th International Conference on Information and Communication Technology (ICoICT), IEEE. pp.1–5 (2019)
29. Csikszentmihalyi, M.: Play and intrinsic rewards. In: Flow and the Foundations of Positive Psychology, pp. 135–153. Springer, Dordrecht (2014). https://doi.org/10.1007/978-94-017-9088-8_10
30. Van Calster, L., D'Argembeau, A., Salmon, E., et al.: Fluctuations of attentional networks and default mode network during the resting state reflect variations in cognitive states: evidence from a novel resting-state experience sampling method. J. Cogn. Neurosci. **29**(1), 95–113 (2017)
31. Samsonovich, A., DeJong, K.: A General-Purpose Computational Model of the Conscious Mind. In: Processing of the sixth international Conference on Cognitive Modeling, pp.382–282 (2004)
32. Redies, C.: Combining universal beauty and cultural context in a unifying model of visual aesthetic experience. Front. Hum. Neurosci. **9**, 218 (2015)
33. Pelowski, M.: Tears and transformation: feeling like crying as an indicator of insightful or "aesthetic" experience with art. Front. Psychol. **6** 1006 (2016)
34. Yang, Y.F.: Cognitive conflicts and resolutions in online text revisions: three profiles. J. Educ. Technol. Soc. **13**(4), 202–214 (2010)
35. Paolo, E.A.D., Barandiaran, X.E., Beaton, M., et al.: Learning to perceive in the sensorimotor approach: piaget's theory of equilibration interpreted dynamically. Front. Hum. Neurosci. **8**, 551 (2014)

"Anti-space" as a New Approach to Museum design—A Case Study of the Influence of Social Sculpture on the General Art Field

Haoli Huang[✉]

The Academy of Arts and Design, Tsinghua University, Beijing, P.R. China
Hhaolee@163.com

Abstract. The concept of Anti-space is not perceived to be a rebellion against traditional physical space, social space, and spiritual space. Its fundamental purpose is to reshape the space itself. The new space of the art museum is the extension of form, content and meaning, the transformation of field, and finally the realization of new meaning for space design. The concept of anti space corresponds to the transformation of the form of art museum design and the relationship between art works dependencies, even impact on the ready-made art. Through the theory of "Social Sculpture" put forward by Boyce, this paper attempts to urge artists to focus on the field to the whole of all things, and enable art museum design to obtain a new life form. Then, through the concept of Anti-space as a response to spatial reflexivity; Spatial design regeneration of specific field integration; The overall construction of the new style art museum design. This paper discusses the proposal and construction of the new state design of the art museum in the future from three aspects. Finally turns the design of the art museum from the attention of artists, art works and the art museum itself to the space design of the world, history, thought, ecology, education and individual human whole.

Keywords: Anti-space · Social sculpture · Critical regionalism

1 Introduction

The increasing of new-style art gallery space design has attracted much attention in the art world. "Social Sculpture" is becoming a trend of aesthetic experience in contemporary art galleries. In view of this tendency, the current art field and social needs, not only means display and communication, but also expands the boundary of the art gallery space in a larger sense. Therefore, fine art pavilion space design has become a trend under this issue.

Using Boyce's "Social Sculpture" theory, while designing the new-style space of the museum, this concept can better allow more audiences to participate in the design of the museum, follow the generation mechanism of the audience's emotional experience, and realize the viewer's presence. Audience can get the opportunity of emotional experience, participation right and identity equality in the museum.

© Springer Nature Switzerland AG 2022
M. Rauterberg et al. (Eds.): HCII 2022, LNCS 13520, pp. 39–50, 2022.
https://doi.org/10.1007/978-3-031-18158-0_3

In contrast to the "Social Sculpture" theory which opened an era in which everyone is an artist, another important concept is "Anti-space", which does not mean a rebellion against traditional physical space, social space, and spiritual space. Its fundamental purpose is to reshape the space itself, and its form, content and meaning will be expanded in space and field transformation. A new meaning is realized in the process.

New space design and cultural planning in particular explore "the nexus between planning practice, public participation, and place" (Carp, 2004, p. 243). Artworks in the public realm are "reflective of a specific group of people with a shared sense of values and practices based on geographic location and/or identity" (Grodach, 2011, p.74). The concept of Anti-space should be used to transform the type of art museums. Such cultural vibrancy contributes to a thriving democracy, an essential ingredient in the production of the just city (Fainstein, 2010). The dependence between art museums, works, culture, and even the entry of ready-made art cannot be separated from the category of art itself and restricted art space.

This study uses the "Social Sculpture" theory proposed by Boyce to encourage the artist to focus on all aspects of the field and allow the museum to acquire a new life form. "sculpture as an evolutionary process, he thinks everyone is an artist. This is why the nature of my sculpture is undetermined and unfinished. The process continues in most of them: chemical reactions, fermentation, discoloration, decay, and drying up. Everything is in a state of change."(Quoted from C. Tisdal "Joseph Boyus", 1989). Multiple public art expands the conceptual interpretation and meaning presentation of anti-space; the regeneration of space design through the integration of specific fields; the overall construction of human beings under the design of art museums. Three aspects are discussed to discuss the construction of art museums in the future. From artists, works of art, and museums themselves to analysis the global, historical, ideological, ecological, educational, and individual human whole.

In order to enrich the art gallery design on the basis of the above theory, In order to enrich the design of Art Museum on the basis of the above theory, two questions are put forward:

1. Through the three theories of "critical regionalism", "anti-space" and "social sculpture", can the construction and guidance of the current art gallery space design achieve the integration of theories?
2. As a discussion and thinking between design and philosophical concepts, can the extension of art museums in the future public space become the carrier and dissemination area of public art?

2   Anti-space as a Response to Spatial Reflexivity

The spatial construction of the museum itself is based on physics, which is also the basic element that constitutes the practical function of the museum. When the art gallery appears with the most vivid metaphor of the "white box", the physical attributes of its own space also present the most direct and visual expression of the space. With the continuous improvement of physical space, it is necessary to insert more connotative content from the form itself, which means how the space presents "meaning itself".

What follows is the continuous planning of exhibitions inside the art gallery to achieve more content supplements, and at the same time, the physical attributes of the space are continuously expanded within the space, so that the social attributes can be extended. But for a successful art museum, in addition to the exquisite architectural space design and appearance, there is also the most profound and meaningful exhibition content. Even today, major art museums are actively expanding their business sectors. To achieve public aesthetic education and social services, all these actions are constantly raising their own social influence and the industry's benchmark position in the process of practice. But when we look back at the history of art museums and respond to the crises and challenges, all art museums seem to be able to reflect and reform themselves in order to adapt to the changes in this turbulent wave. Among them, whether the construction of the art gallery's spiritual space and the social critical efforts of the space are in place is a problem that all art museums are thinking together at the moment. There is no need to respond urgently to this, nor can it be just a practice. The answer to the case is so simple, it is a lasting and procedural test.

Fig. 1. Antiroom I Photo source: ZaomeDesign @Alexandra Kononchenko

Regarding the art gallery space mentioned above, the concept of "anti-room" is discussed in the general sense of the art gallery's limitation of space. That is, the original must be inside the art gallery. The presented artwork is transferred to the outside of the space. Obviously, this realization is not new. As early as the 1960s, Duchamp's ready-made art to Andy Warhol's Pop Art claimed to be "I am a machine", and then to Bo Locke's Action Painting, Aaron Kaprow's Happenning Art at the end of the 1950s, this type of art has moved the original traditional art exhibition to fine art in an "anti-art" approach and action outside of the pavilion space. For "anti-space", what we need to discuss now is not only how to break through the limitation of physical space, but also how to restore the "specific field", publicity, participation and spirituality of art works. Therefore, anti-space itself does not oppose the physical space attributes of the art gallery

Fig. 2. Antiroom I Photo source: ZaomeDesign @Alexandra Kononchenko

Fig. 3. Antiroom I Photo source: ZaomeDesign @Alexandra Kononchenko

itself. On the contrary, it attempts to expand the present part, the meaning of expression and the possibility of more interpretation on the basis of the original physical space. Therefore, the emergence of the concept of anti-space is an attempt to transcend and method itself for the current construction of a new style of art museums.

Regarding the extension of the concept of "anti-space", a case is used to illustrate the practice and effect of anti-space. The three artists, Elena Chiavi, Karl Ebejer, and Matteo Goldoni, come from the EASA project organization. During the process of artistic practice, they proposed a new concept of Anti-room. This artistic practice is a wooden theater built by the three people instructing students from different European countries. As a result of the 2014 EASA (European Architecture Student Assembly) workshop held in Veliko Tarnovo, Bulgaria, this theater also won the local people of pro gaze. This artistic practice project is divided into two series: the red theater construction project in Bulgaria and floating "islands" on the sea of Malta. Both series of works break through the necessary conditions of the original space setting in a creative way. At the same time, the selection of materials, color images and specific field settings have become the highlights of the project. From the two cases of anti-space works, combined with the contemporary expression of public art, it (Fig. 3) tries to interpret the classics of this project from three aspects: the integration of the field, the regeneration of the space, and the extension of meaning.

From the beginning of its establishment, the purpose of EASA was to promote the viewpoints and cultural exchanges between European architecture students, and to realize the formation of a diverse and sustainable art project between works and space, region, people, and history and culture. Anti-space art creation aims at the most basic form, the most basic structure, the most basic force field, and the formation of an infinitely open and extended space, so that the space has the possibility of regeneration.

3 Spatial Design Regeneration of Specific Field Integration

A more specific way of expressing anti-space is to move towards a mature "special field" in which artists and their works have been integrated into the space itself, and are no longer stereotypical displays. In this way, when Boyce opened the door to artistic creation with the most avant-garde, most inexplicable, and sharpest perspective in the anti-art wave, he proposed that "art is creation, that is, human freedom." He believed that art and life are inseparable. The entire social life is a work of art, and our task is to carry out "Social Sculpture" to transform human society into a perfect work of art.[1] Facing the theory of social sculpture, it can be seen that Boyce's artistic concept has broken through art itself, whether it is material, form, or law, and a breakthrough has been made. How to create and use such a big concept of social life, has been accompanied by his works in response to the public.

Before the concept of "social sculpture" appeared, Boyce himself explained the reasons for this concept:

"My works are to be seen as a stimulant that changes the concept of sculpture, or the whole art. They should reveal the idea of what sculpture can be and how the concept of shaping can be extended to the intangibles used by everyone.

Thinking form-how do we mold our thoughts. Or form of discourse-how do we define our thoughts as words. Social Sculpture-How do we model and determine the world in which we live: sculpture as an evolutionary process; everyone is an artist. This is why the nature of my sculpture is undetermined and unfinished. The process continues

---

[1] Hou Hanru, True Avant-Garde-Art toward People-Joseph Boyus and Social Sculpture, Literature and Art Studies, 1989 (01).

in most of them: chemical reactions, fermentation, discoloration, decay, and drying up. Everything is in a state of change."[2].

From this quotation, we can see that Boyce's social sculpture has a thought form to mold thoughts, and the discourse form defines thoughts as concrete words, while social sculpture uses life and real society as raw materials. Created on this basis, the biggest breakthrough in this process is the clustering of artists, the sacred subject of creation. The subject of creation in social sculpture is no longer a single individual artist, but every viewer or audience. The concept of "everyone is an artist" gives a new subject of artistic creation, and more importantly points out the indeterminate and unfinished meaning of social sculpture itself. This kind of artistic creation is constantly being carried out in the process of continuous creation, and with a continuous attitude to keep its meaning updated and continuous changes. This seems to better interpret that after social sculpture creates a specific field, the space can be regenerated, which not only broadens the physical limits of the space itself, but also continuously enriches the social meaning and social participation of the space in this process.

Fig. 4. Antiroom II Photo source: ZaomeDesign @ Ehmad EI Mad

The spatial design regeneration of the new-style art museum is first of all a break-through in the original concept of limitation, and from the ideological interest of social sculpture, we can find a mixed and rich emotional will, which is similar to the accumulated "social energy". This energy can seem to have two motivations, positive and negative. One is passion, with strong enthusiasm and yearning for enthusiasm and antic-ipatory energy; the other is negative and dull, maintaining the law of reason and weakening enthusiasm and energy. But at the two extremes of emotion and will, Boyce uses artistic creation methods to maintain a balance, so that the two extreme emotions, wills,

---

[2] Quoted from C. Tisdal "Joseph Boyus".

desires and imaginations can maintain a "fluid" state in the process of social sculpture creation. Create a flexible sense of circulation. This is similar to "harmony" in the sense of traditional Chinese aesthetics. The flowing social energy forms a clearer creative state through mutual dredging, transfer, and integration.

Based on two typical cases of anti-space(Figs. 2, 4), the theater space created by wooden materials is a theater that surpasses the previous general perception. Each door made of wood and all the chairs and stools surrounded by circles on the ancient theater create a scene of a new visual experience. And the bright red expresses the original sacredness of the theater with a strong image. The theater art style in ancient Greece and ancient Rome was indeed surrounded by huge stone carvings. The quiet and great sense of solemnity still maintains the original seriousness and heaviness of "theatre". In the attempt of new materials and the use of color images, the work not only strips off the original heaviness of the stone, but also creates a unique red theater with bright red. In this ancient forest, every spectator who walks into this field is awakened with the brightest color quality. In this field, it does not need too much explanation and invitation. This kind of wrap-around wooden material chair and door will automatically allow every audience to enter, shuttle, sit and touch.

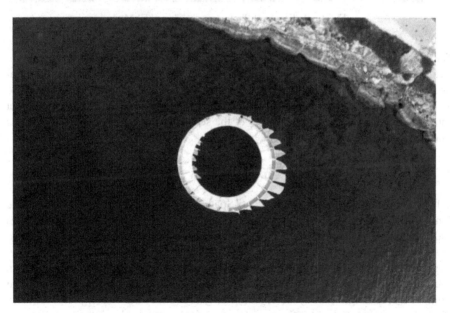

Fig. 5. Antiroom II Photo source: ZaomeDesign @ Ehmad El Mad

In the work of Anti-Space II (Fig. 6), the realizing space has shifted from the original forest theater to the sea of Malta. The vastness and depth of the sea are both fascinating and challenging. On the one hand, the artist has to overcome the difficulty of placing and presenting the work on the sea level that is difficult to fix with a bracket, and on the other hand, the work itself must be integrated into the sea without any sense of violation. This is not only a test of technical difficulty but also an innovation of aesthetic methods.

Fig. 6. Antiroom II Photo source: Ehmad EI Mad

Therefore, the team members chose to continue to use wood as the basic material to create a ring-shaped "island". The white plastic film around the ring is used as a curtain-like decoration, making it no longer a "monotonous wood" "Small island" can also make this transparent white substance and the deep blue of the deep sea form a perfect combination, and float it on the surface of the sea. This work also excellently forms a dual fusion of vision and beauty between the field and the work.

4   The Overall Construction of the New Style Art Museum Design

In fact, in the wooden theater built by Anti-Space I, the works are naturally rooted in the dense forest in the form of an ancient open-air theater. The repeated component modules make the whole structure dynamic and can be regenerated indefinitely. The single red dissolves the physical attributes of the space and creates a unified space like a paradise, complementing the greenery of the forest. The wind passes through the wooden pavilion that awakens the sleeping between the components, and the door leaves move with the wind, as if breathing. In the sense of immortality brought by the theater place, the form of the theater transcends the influence of any particular style and points to eternity.

The floating island on the sea in Anti-Space II does not have too many decorations and complicated functions. It is also very important that the center of the circle is a vacant place. This vacant part is just integrated into the sea, and people can jump, go down to swim and float, or walk and rest on the "island" in the middle of the circle. The spatial reproduct ability of this work breaks through the limitations and stereotypes of fixed space, allowing people to stay attached to the "island" without being trapped by the island. This is a free space, but also a good connection between the sea, man-made islands and people, so that the space can glow with new vitality.

Fig. 7. Basalt and oak trees are placed in front of the Kassel art gallery. Photo source: Phoenix art

Fig. 8. Boyce is implementing the art creation scene of 7000 oak trees. Photo source: Phoenix art.

In the creation of social sculpture, the creative materials have broken through the original explicit material media materials. Boyce transformed the materials into actual abstract objects, such as sound waves, air, animals, and popular cultural concepts. Therefore, as a medium of artistic creation, social sculpture has taken a big step forward, even completely "de-territorializing" the attributes of "things" in this sense. Therefore, this process can be interpreted as the development logic of "chaos (potential)-movement (transformation)-order (crystallization)". This also means that the creation of social sculpture seems to be chaotic, differentiated or illogical, but in fact it contains a very deep and secret internal generation logic. This is undoubtedly an inspiration for the shaping of the new style of art museums, but also reflects the publicity of art museums in the future, and public art as an important link in the process of constructing new styles of art museums.

The concept of anti-space is not an absolute connection with the original space, but a kind of thinking presentation that breaks the space limitation and innovative design under the law of form and inherent concepts. This new design method and new creative concept move the city into the forest and move the land to the sea. In this artistic practice, all artists are creating and thinking about how to construct a work of art in universal norms, and works full of inner meaning. For the current process of constructing a new style of art museums, this cannot be accomplished overnight. It is a long-standing process, and it is an expansion of the medium to the world of society, nature, animals, and even the sacred world, and it also takes the artist away from the world. The transformation of the original single individual into the group public, and even the continued social energy in the social sculpture, is used as the multiple possibilities of artistic creation to continuously realize the meaning itself in this process.

Fig. 9. The work "Wasteland wolf: I Love America, America loves me" Photo source: The Beijing News http://epaper.bjnews.com.cn/html/2013-10/09/content_469706.htm?div=-1

From "7000 Oak Trees" to "Wasteland Wolf: I Love America, America Loves Me", a series of works by Boyce, in addition to the new social significance he proposed or demonstrated, focused on expressing strong political implications. But if the work is limited to this topic, he will lose the fundamental meaning of his own transfer of social sculpture. Therefore, in this process, Boyce's artistic concept points to the advancement of human beings to a greater extent, and regards social energy as a kind of flowing energy constructed by humans as a whole, allowing water, air, sound waves, Nature, animals, environment, cultural symbols and people to form a whole together, and continue to grow in this process. "With a sense of mission as the bearer of human destiny, we can insight into the relationship between art and life and strive to seek humanity through artistic creation." The way out for the future."

[3]This concept can be said that it has gone beyond the artistic ideas of individual artists in the past, and has upgraded to a kind of ultimate concern of human nature. In the future construction process of a new type of art museum, it should also be operated by such a holistic construction model. In addition to the function of the exhibition itself, it is a brand new attempt to grasp the spiritual core and use the space as a whole.

5 Conclusion

Social sculpture has taken a big step forward, and even completed "Deterritorialization" the attribute of "things" in this sense: "Chaos (potential) - movement (transformation) - order (crystallization)". This development logic means that the creation of social sculpture seems to be a chaotic, divided or illogical formal state, but in fact it contains a very deep and secret internal generative logic. Therefore, three levels of cognition can be proposed: Firstly, "anti-space" is the proposal and practice of an idea. Secondly, "social sculpture" is the reflection and innovation of current art itself. Finally, "critical regionalism" is a concept expansion and life care of human design itself.

According to the discussion of the paper, three aspects can be summarized:

1. The anti space concept makes the art museum take space as a new reform point. This innovation challenge is another application of the established space.
2. Social sculpture has moved from the original practical "sculpture" of physical objects to the "sculpture" of people, thought, morality, ethics and even spirit, which is also the core part of this theory. It emphasizes that art should have dialogue and contact with the current society by participating in social life.
3. Boyce's theory continues with "critical regionalism". From the perspective of politics, art, art education, democracy, environmental protection, nature, ecology, peace and politics, these seemingly unrelated themes finally form a whole process of human beings. His ideas, behaviors and events are expressing these contents and forming the final works.

The reuse of social sculpture is actually a sobering agent in the design of modern art museum, which can transform art into life form, life state and spiritual territory. In Argentina, the space design of the local hospital (Fig. 10) is a successful case of "social sculpture". It not only meets the needs of medical treatment and residence in function, but also integrates into the local culture in aesthetics, and changes people's impression of fear and resistance to the hospital. In this process, human beings connect all things and form an integrated whole. Through the use of the concept of Anti-space, we can turn from artists, art works and art galleries to the world, history, thought, ecology, education and individual human whole, and give birth to a regenerative space with unlimited meaning.

---

[3] Lu Chuan. Who is Powys——A Critical Biography of German Artist Joseph Powys .Northwest Art, 2005(01), pp. 34-35.

Fig. 10. Design of smf-tu social medical facilities in Argentina Photo source: https://www.dou ban.com/note/559924872/?_i=4511496-tgiyOq

References:

1. Nagy Attila B., András, K.: Acoustic Design of a New Museum. J. Acoust. Soc. America **141**(5), 3598-3598 (2017)
2. Lord, B.: Museum origins: readings in early museum history and philosophy. In: Museum Management and Curatorship, 25(1) (2010)
3. Baoping, Y.: Research on dynamic generation of 3D lines in city rail transit simulation system J. Syst. Simul. **28**(10), 2607–2612 (2016)
4. Shufen, W., Jie, R.: Study on the impact of elevated rail traffic on the urban landscape and the response measures China Explor. Design **2**, 57–60 (2011)
5. Peiyun, Y.: For the investigation of the public indoor space design in urban rail transit Design **21**, 111–113 (2015)
6. Ming, H., Sisi, J.: The exploration of public device art in the transportation construction—taking Wuhan rail Transit subway line 2 Art design engineering as an example. Urban.Architect. **20**, 223–224 (2013)
7. Hanru, H.: True avant-garde-art toward people-Joseph Boyes and social sculpture. Lit. Art Stud. **01**, 68–75 (1989)
8. Park, E.J., Kang, E.: Sublime Experience for sustainable underground space: integration of the artists' works in Chichu art museum. Sustainability **13**(12) 6653–6653 (2021)
9. Liakou, M., Odysseas, K.: Analyzing museum exhibition spaces via visitor movement and exploration: the case of white worth art gallery of Manchester. J. Phys. **1391**, 12171 (2019)
10. Guo, J.: The space design of the contemporary art museums. Int. Sci. Cult. Acad. Contacts **12** 43–48 (2019)
11. Research on Visual Guidance Design of Ethnology Museum Taking the Museum of South-Central University for Nationalities as an Example. Wenzhen Nie. In: Proceedings of the 7th International Conference on Art, Design and Contemporary Education (ICADCE 2021) (2021)
12. Contemporary Museums of Japan: New approaches to the shaping of architectural and artistic image. Nina Konovalova. In: Proceedings of The Third International Conference on Architecture: Heritage, Tradition and Innovation (AHTI2021) (2021)
13. Kenney, E., Spaces, I.: The metropolitan museum of art's 'Damascus Room' reinstalled. Int. J. Islamic Architect. **7**, 305–323 (2018)

Interaction Design of Museum Displays in the Digital Age-Taking British Museum as an Example

Min Ma[✉]

Academy of Arts and Design, Tsinghua University, Beijing, China
52200343@qq.com

Abstract. Interaction design now jostles for attention of museum display design in the digital age. Such design concerns interactions between visitors and computers, visitors and space, and also interpersonal correlation in the space. The museum, accordingly, underlined interactive experience from aspects given above. This paper attempts to induce features displaying interactive designs of art museum, and probes into its design significance and law of development, thus to provide certain reference for continuous study and exploration in the field referring to digital management and case analysis of the British Museum.

Keywords: Digital age · Interaction design · British museum

1 Introduction

This kind of design owes to rapid advance of information technology, changes to people's cognitive and thinking modes, and crucially, great attention paid to digital education by countries in the world in the digital era. Digital technology "provided access to information, networks of communication and fresh approaches of presenting learning", stated the 2011 UNESCO report on education (http://www.unesco.org/new/en/). China clearly requested to act out the "Digital Education 2020 Action Plan", and make progress in emerging education mode by promoting and applying information technologies such as computers, communications, and networks. Coincidentally, similar measures were seen in the reform of educational informatization by the United States, the United Kingdom, and Japan. Art museums, responding to such development tide, as public education institutions largely themed art cultivation, are witnessing varying interactive display designs emerging in large numbers. Inevitable is the interaction design awaiting displays of art museums in the information age. As a result, most of them begun to infuse interactive thinking into display designs, such as offering exclusive exhibits, installations or visiting routes in accordance with needs of visitors; in the meantime, some are bending themselves to enhance the interestingness and participation of the display and augment visual, auditory, tactile and other stimulation making the best of diverse media resources and interactive technologies, while others focus on guiding visitors to the theme spirit of exhibits in a subtle way. Display content now is rich and form is flexible and versatile.

© Springer Nature Switzerland AG 2022
M. Rauterberg et al. (Eds.): HCII 2022, LNCS 13520, pp. 51–61, 2022.
https://doi.org/10.1007/978-3-031-18158-0_4

The comprehensive British Museum, one of the world-famous museums and the first national museum open to the public, now houses over 100 exhibition halls, and exhibits more than 8 million pieces of cultural relics, books, natural history specimens, sculptures, coins, badges, prints, sketches, etc., covering collections of ancient Central Asia, Islamic world, Africa, Egypt, China, Japan, Korea, South Asia, Oceania, Renaissance and modern Europe, medieval Europe, modern Europe, Greece and Roman Empire, and playing a decisive standing. More than 1.5 million objects out of the 8 million pieces in the British Museum are listed in the collection database at length, attracting more than 35 million virtual audiences. Digital construction facilitated visitors and scholars, and also offered a sound platform for museum staff to raise efficiency. For the first time visitors can access to the museum on their mobile phones and computers since the official release of online catalogue in 2007. That is, they now can view nearly 4.5 million objects and 1.9 million artwork images uploaded in the British Museum's online database anytime, anywhere. This paper attempts to induce features displaying interactive designs of art museum, and probes into its design significance and law of development referring to digital management and case analysis of the British Museum.

2 Display Features of Interactive Design in Art Museums

Digital age reinterprets and enrich definition of artworks, showing flexible and varying presentation forms. Traditional exhibition method now losses its shining of displaying. Collection management, a basic function accompanying museums, bases all works of museums. This complex process wants scientific methods and professionals, [1]and needs to be done according to specific categories of museum collection. Aided by digital technology, traditional museums have to change from the perspective of experts to that of audiences. They should reveal the nature of collections in all rounds through digitalization, thus to enable visitors to understand the deep relationship of collections in art, society and life. British Museum, of course, and also designers of major art museums are rethinking the relationship between visitors, exhibits, and the space environment in the museum, and are busy with distinguished interactive creations. Consequent artistic expressions and emerging design concepts provided museum exhibition design research with a brand-new perspective, largely seen in following three aspects.

1. Man-machine interaction that follows interplay between visitors and computers values the mutual influence and interaction. Designers sort out and integrate vast quantities of artwork information into the computer, and output interactive installation of different sizes and shapes. Visitors, on the other hand, are allowed to access, consult, view corresponding information or stories behind through easy-to-learn operations such as touch, voice, gestures, etc. They even can customize exclusive visiting modes and visiting routes. Simply put, efforts were invested to delve into possibilities of interaction between visitors and display forms, so as to achieve the final goal of interactive experience. General display screens equipped in the Capitoline Art Museum in Rome expound information about art works to visitors; the 12.2-m-long electronic screen in the Cleveland Museum in the United States displays 4,100 artworks, which enable viewers to click on the screen to check the detailed information of each piece; while sensors installed

outside the Perception Art Museum in New York, USA, change shapes and colors to mirror emotions and feelings of visitors in real time, in accordance with their overall mood index collected through connecting to their mobile phone APP or Twitter.

The British Museum rolled out alike moves in man-machine interaction. For instance, an international itinerant exhibition——Egyptian Mummy: Discover life in ancient Egypt started in September 2020, which offered visitors a chance to join its research team, and presented six mummies that lived and died in Egypt between 3,000 and 1,800 years ago. The museum, following the development of the times, applied a new generation of CT scanner to clear confusions of curious visitors. This fresh device guides question-raisers to view intricate human remains and objects beneath mummy wraps, and is capable of accurately determine key information such as the gender, age, and health status age at the time of death. Such exhibition of ancient Egyptian mummies gives us a glimpse into the unusual burial traditions of the forefathers prepared for the afterlife. These fascinating conventions allure us to explore lives happening on banks of the Nile thousands of years ago (Fig. 1).

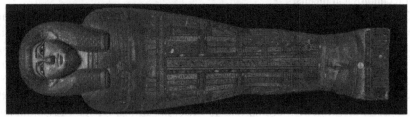

Fig. 1. Egyptian mummy (Discover life in ancient Egyptian · International Itinerant exhibition exhibits)

Aforesaid interaction method expands static display and vivifies the interaction process. Cooper Hewitt National Design Museum in the United States made an advanced innovation of a mobile device digital pen named "The Pen" out of this display method. Visitors, with the pen, can interact with the capture interactive projection in any interactive area inside the museum. Cases in point are that they can check detailed information of artworks through scanning labels of exhibits, or design and outline furniture styles and wallpaper patterns on the screen at will. These improvisational works, aided by the perfect presentation of interactive technology, can be projected on the wall for further appreciation. Creators may even list them in their own virtual collection at any time. Each participant will get a URL path to view the favorite exhibits and data reserved anytime by the time of returning the digital pen at the end of the visit. This transtemporal and transspatial experience enhanced communication between individuals and the museum by encouraging visitors to actively explore, discover and feel the entire exhibition hall. Information preset by the computer unfolds gradually in an accurate, orderly and impressive manner as visitors operate. Interaction display lies in stimulating users' participation, enhancing interactions between users and exhibits, integrating into the display environment and taking the initiative to seek for the best learning mode, in addition to boosting the audience's sense of experience through media equipment and virtual interactive technology. Interactive exhibitions, compared with traditional style, highly value initiative and participation of visitors, and acquire new knowledge through exploration and discovery, thus to realize effective information dissemination.

3   Interaction Between Visitors and the Space Environment

Interactive experience labels the most prominent feature of the interaction between visitors and the space environment, which essentially stresses experience needs of visitors. It highest realm is "long-lasting impression, inner resonance, knowledge reserve, and life construction". The museum evolves into a place triggering interactive behaviors. Artists wait for visitors to supplement and perfect "blanks" intentionally left during the creation, thus to inspire visitors to actively participate, realize real interactive experience, and satisfy their participation, integration and self-worth fulfilled needs. Most display interaction designs now achieve the human-space interaction by stimulating visitors' visual, tactile, auditory and other sensory. For example, "Infiltration", the exhibit at the Museum of Modern Art in Montreal, Canada, shapes a lively biological world making use of technological means.

Visitors wearing electronic equipment step into a virtual display environment, and integrate into the space surrounded by creatures, light spots, dewdrops, insects, etc., triggering interaction with the virtual space with strong sense of individual belonging. They actively receive information from sensory stimuli and behavioral activities which speaking to the space. This experience breaks through the unilateral constraints of human behavior and senses, and enables viewers to experience different feelings even in the same space.In the exhibition of missions to Mars, the British Design Museum allows visitors to see the clothes and equipment designed to wear on Mars in the future, and uses tactile, visual and auditory ways to interact with people, so that people can truly understand and feel the power of science and technology (Fig. 2).

Fig. 2. The design museum missions to mars

Computer technology offers more possibilities for space generation in today's information age. Computers and external devices picks up and sorts out spatial information, edit, process and synthesize them according to display requirements. Space environment then is like an organic structure that promotes the human-space interaction. The space that evolves dynamically affected by behaviors of visitors, in turn, exerts counteractive impacts. The entire NOX Water Exhibition Hall is a display platform. Its interior space is characterized in flow and uncertainty, as the ground, wall and top surface are blended and transformable. The spatial environment is coordinated by sets of microprocessors.

Movement, speed and density of people activate computer software embedded in the building structure, which in turn fans visual and auditory effects. Such "smart" building is designed with perception ability that reacts differently targeting behaviors of visitors. Visitors integrate into the architectural space like living organisms. "It is not a water show. On the contrary, visitor becomes part of the water, and experience changes to their behaviors in the constantly changing surroundings". While being "immersed" in the space, visitors also act on and create spaces, which constitutes a part of the display. They perceive and receive information from the interactive and emotional experience, triggering visitors' imagination and active exploration.

British Museum initiated a world roving exhibition - Ancient Greeks: Athletes, Warriors and Heroes between June 12 and November 7, 2021. Ravishing Greek sculptures, jewelry, armor, vases and ancient sports equipment were exhibited, mirroring competitive consciousness of ancient Greece, whether they were athletes, warriors or heroes. People of varying fields, including politics, sports, theater, or war, were world-renowned for their competitive spirit. Such awareness gave birth to thriving cultures and exchange of ideas of great value, despite accompanying conflicts. The exhibition supported necessary adjustments to support concomitant educational program, thus to closely integrate top-notched academic contents with the exhibition. In that case, children, the young generation, and people of different ages are able to participate in varying thematic activities launched by the exhibition. For instance, historical events, art and design and literacy activities were designed to re-play the drama life (Fig. 3).

A fresh lecture and discussion on "Beyond Bridgeton" was unveiled by British Museum in March 2021. Inspired largely by the well-known Netflix show "Bridgerton", the lecture followed true stories of Africans and people of African descent in Regency Britain and beyond. Bridgeton, Netflix's most successful show so far, joined the online event by the British Museum that was watched by 82 million people worldwide. Discussions were unfolded talking about why the series was a hit, the real life behind Bridgeton's fantasy, and whether the British Museum can bridge the gap between fantasy and reality, thus to deepen our understanding on complex history. Author and historian Oliver Otele, author and broadcaster Bonnie Greer, and Hartwig Fischer, the curator, delivered speeches. The event revealed that the British Museum has been endeavoring to establish interaction and communication between its collections and visitors. The Museum has made a sound decision integrating collections or historical time with online publicity.

New stimulus shapes up as the display space guides visitors to change the form of the space or display, which constitutes another method of interactive experience. Guggenheim Virtual Museum designed referring to the "progressive line composition" has been used on displaying virtual artworks and hosting rich cultural and commercial activities. Visitors are capable of shaping and restricting the space according to their own wishes and needs, and accessing to ideal viewing methods, processes and even virtual display places for distinguished activities, enabling visitors to have a deeper understanding and experience of the display theme. Such a display method exhibited features of exhibits and serves visitors to the greatest extent.

To attend this online event

Book now to secure your place. We're hosting the event on Zoom – a free video conferencing system that requires users to register in advance. If you do not already use Zoom, you can sign up using this **registration link**.

If the event is fully booked, or you don't wish to use Zoom, you can also watch the event streamed live – as well as other events in the series – on the Museum's **live events YouTube channel**.

This event includes live captioning delivered by **Stagetext** and delivered by **MyClearText**.

Read our **booking form privacy policy**.

Fig. 3. Announcements of lectures and discussions and online meetings beyond "Bridgeton"

4 Interpersonal Interaction

The first refers to the interaction between designers and visitors. University of Reading's KBF system enables space users to intervene in the entire design and manufacturing, and designers, fabricators and space users to compare solutions in real time. Virtual reality technology offered a new set of standards for the design, production and construction, making it possible for designers and space users to test the designing scheme through a virtual "walkthrough" before the official completion. The second is Museums of China and the UK share commonalities in certain construction and can learn from each other despite disparate systems and national conditions, and discrepancy of organizational structure, funding sources, collection categories, etc. How to manage and utilize collections reasonably and effectively, serve the broad masses, and make the full use of exhibition and social education functions constantly perplex every worker of museum business. Digital technology gifted human society a novel approach of communication. Interpersonal interaction and exchange T involved in the space gradually form a systematic entirety. Essential is interpersonal interaction in museum exhibitions, of which that between designers and visitors constitutes one of its manifestations. Designers exchanges ideas with visitors, solicit their opinions, and guide them to participate in design creation. Supreme is the British Museum in disseminating knowledge and educating the public. Every year, the Museum holds hundreds of lectures and seminars, publishes a large selection of books and albums of painting, and even specific education department and program for the large visiting group of primary and secondary school students. Educational events rolled out for these young participants are classified according to four groups of 3–6 years old, 7–11 years old, 12–16 years old, 16 years old and older. Educational program for the youngest group emphasizes inspiration of numbers, colors, shapes and graphics, and works with the basic curriculum set by the state, offering a surprising journey of discoveries. Programs for the older group involve certain cultural, historical, religious and social content, and are designed with relevant themes, such as activities corresponding to festivals, God and spirit, sculpture, symbols, etc., as well as cultures and arts of Egypt, China and Islam.

The interaction between visitors and visitors is another important manifestation of human-human interaction. The defamiliarization of interpersonal relationships in modern society is already an established fact. During the visit, visitors communicate with their peers and even strangers, which can meet individual emotional needs and social communication needs, deepen visitors' understanding of exhibits, and realize knowledge sharing.. One of the cultural and art projects of the British Museum is mainly designed for fourth grade students. After they come to the museum, they will visit and appreciate the exhibition halls of China, Africa and India up close. Under the guidance of teachers, in addition to learning and understanding these In addition to the history and characteristics of the country's cultural artworks, I will also draw some sketches and take photos to record my new discoveries. After returning to school, I will use the information I have recorded to make five handicrafts. Crafts should include elements such as African masks and textiles, Chinese calligraphy and pottery, and Indian henna and patterns.

5   Significance of Interaction Design in Art Museum Display

Interactive designs reshaped people's cognition and thinking patterns, and hastened fresh design thinking and methods. Visitors can view and experience according to their own wishes and needs, and stimulate their creativity, equipping the space with plenty of fun and unlimited energy. Meanwhile, visitors are surprised by spatial changes caused by their own behaviors, which induces their stronger interest and enthusiasm to explore all the possibilities in the space. Only exhibitions intriguing audiences to participate achieve knowledge dissemination, believed Oppenheim. In addition, the display space cannot be expressed perfectly by any form and expression method, and can only be perceived through direct experience. Architect Anthony said: "Only by experiencing the spaces in person, walking through them, and viewing them with pleasure, can you experience their intrinsic qualities." Interactive design display of Art Museum enriches spaces, deepens emotional experiences and spaces cognitive, for which it is more real and profound.

The British Museum's Image Licensing Service is the authoritative source for high-quality images from the British Museum's collection, offering a wide range of images for both commercial and non-commercial use. In addition to simple flat images, the image service also provides 3D images of collections, video recordings, custom photography of designated collections, and more. About 50,000 images are available online, which is only the tip of the iceberg in the British Museum's collection. Shooting prices for selected collections not available online range from £60 to £85 per flat image, £85 per 3D image and £350 per panoramic image (Fig. 4).

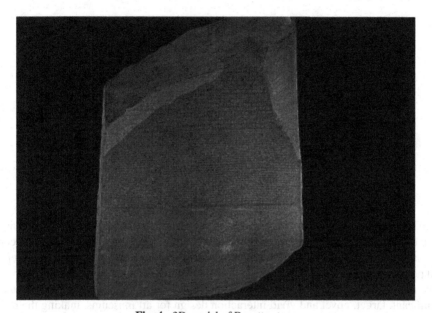

Fig. 4. 3D model of Rosetta stone

Image studies categorize collections into different themes. The British Museum shines on one of the largest collections of Rembrandt's manuscripts. In 2019, the 350th anniversary of Rembrandt's death, the British Museum has used this as the theme to authorize some of its manuscripts for a fee (Fig. 5).

More creative ideas and open imagination await museum businesses in the new era. Assistance of technology, warmth of humanity, and transparent management process will output greater value, "enliven" antiquities of tens of millions of years, and shape the museum into a cultural card of the city and a beacon of world civilization. Judging from the development of the entire museum, the modern museum is at a critical moment in the new century. The museum must demonstrate its exact social value, and even further develop smoothly in the new century. In other words, it is to empower museum collections and deepen the interaction between museums, society and people.

Fig. 5. Part of rembrandt manuscript licensed for a fee

Although some cases are in need of general promotion, its transformative significance of space and design concepts exudes multi-round cultural meaning. Interaction between visitors and computers (man-machine interaction), visitors and the space environment, and people make the viewing process more comprehensive and profound. We, however, must rationally identify, analyze and apply this tide, thus to create subject-appropriate, significant, target, novel and vivid interaction design for art museums, making the best of technology and media and starting from the function and meaning of design.

References

1. Xiangyang, X.: Interaction design: from physical logic to behavioral logic, decoration. Issue. **1**, 58–62 (2015)
2. Guobin, W.: Analysis of concept of interactive museum in exhibition design. Packag. Eng. Issue **8**, 26 (2015)
3. Gossel, P., Leuthouser, G.: Architecture in the 20th Century (Volume 2) , koln: TASCHEN, p. 550
4. Wei'an, L.: Exploring display design under multimedia interactive technology. Packag. Eng. Issue **6**, 132 (2014)
5. http://www.unesco.org/new/en/
6. Oppenheimer, F.: The exploratorium: a playful museum combines perception and art in science education. Am. J. Phys. Issue **7**, 2–3 (1972)
7. Shiyi, P., et al.: Commune at the Foot of the Great Wall, p. 92. Tianjin Social Science Press (2003)
8. Hooper-Greenhill, E.: Museums and Their Visitors, p. i. Routledge, London (1994)

9. Museum, B.: Treasures of World Civilization: 250 Years of British Museum Collection, edited by Capital Museum, p. 3. Cultural Relics Press, Beijing (2006)
10. Hauser, A. (Amold Hauser), translated by Ju Yanan, Sociology of Art, Shanghai, Xuelin Publishing House (1987)
11. Young, L.: Globalization, Culture and Museums, Museum Newsletter, Issue 19, translated by Tang Jingguang. Taiwan Museums Society (2002)
12. Gang, C.: Analysis of Concept, Characteristics and Development Mode of Digital Museum, China Museum, March 2007

The Road of "Bie-modern" of Periodization of Chinese Design Modern History

Wenzhi Wu[✉], Jingyuan Wang, and Xiaoyu Hu

Shanghai University of Engineering Science, Shanghai 216020, China
wendy04115027@163.com

Abstract. In the western theoretical system of "Modernity", terms such as "pre-modern", "early modern", "modern early ", "modern", "post-modern", and "modern and contemporary" are very popular. In addition, although the interpretation system established by the academic circles for the research of "modernization" and "Modernity" provides a broad and solid thinking paradigm, it seems to be unable to match with China's national conditions. The theory of "Bie-modern" put forward by Professor Wang Jianjiang was an original concept in the field of aesthetic modernity. The three backgrounds of this theory are not only unique in the field of aesthetics. Today's Chinese society integrates "highly modern", "pre-modern" and "post-modern", which is applicable to such a background for any subject field. China's academic field is facing the problem of "Bie-modern", rather than the problem of modernity and post modernity in the West academics. On the one hand, the theory of "Bie-modern" provides original thinking for China to construct modernity theory based on its own development logic; On the other hand, it also provides another "modern vision" for the whole modern world. The development of Chinese modern design history is also in such a diversified modernity. It is extremely unbalanced in region, different in system, diverse in development path and continuous in depth. The research on the periodization of Chinese modern design history has encountered the embarrassment of unclear distinction between "modern" and "contemporary". In fact, the discipline of design history may follow the growth path of "bie-modern". The development of design in modern history has encountered a very complex reality. Xiaoou Cao once argued that "Chinese modern design was born in modern China", and academician Shiling Zheng also pointed out that "modern architecture in Shanghai itself includes modern architecture". This kind of "awkward" expression in the field of design history shows that the "dislocation" and "discord" in Chinese modern design and Chinese modern design history showing the form of "bie-modern". The introduction of "Bie-modern" theory into the study of Chinese modern design history is an appropriate return of local theory. It is the interpretation and application of a creative theory aimed at China's special "Bie-modern" social form and institutional culture in the staging of design history. By borrowing the "Bie-modern" theory, the paper firstly analyzed the reasons for this situation, and then summarizes three important reference principles for the periodization of Chinese modern design history through the historical review, research and discussion of the breaking limit of the periodization of Chinese modern architectural history: the staging difference between general history and special history The non antagonistic relationship between "China Centered Theory" and subject ontology, as well as modern architecture and modern

© Springer Nature Switzerland AG 2022
M. Rauterberg et al. (Eds.): HCII 2022, LNCS 13520, pp. 62–88, 2022.
https://doi.org/10.1007/978-3-031-18158-0_5

architecture. Clearly put forward three basic assumptions about the stages of Chinese modern and modern design history. One is to take the Central Academy of Arts and crafts established in 1956 as the beginning of Chinese modern design. The other is to turn the design history before 1949 into modern design history, followed by Chinese modern design history. The third is to divide modern, modern and modern design history into three independent stages. The staging of Chinese modern design history can provide a reference framework for its research towards clearer, accurate and in-depth research.

Keywords: Bie-modern · Chinese modern design history · Modern architecture design history · Periodization

1 Periodization: A Problem on Hold

The study of Chinese modern and contemporary design history has shown a sign of "activity", but it is far from establishing a "paradigm" and becoming an independent discipline. Most of the existing studies on the history of Chinese modern design generally refer to "modern" and "modern" as "modern" (or "modern", the content includes "modern and modern"), resulting in a state of confusion. When we face the awkward expression that "the birth of Chinese modern design should begin with the beginning of Chinese modern history", we really feel the difficulty of discussing the breaking stages of Chinese modern and modern design history. However, it is necessary to further explore this problem and seek a solution. "For contemporary historians, historical periodization is also an important field of research and reflection. Due to its existence, the way of human organization and evolution in time and time has become clear." Therefore, the division of Chinese modern design history is also an inevitable requirement for the deepening and specialization of Chinese design history research. Why did Chinese design historians put this issue aside for a long time? Investigating its subjective and objective reasons, the author attempts to summarize it into the following three aspects.

1.1 "Impure" Design and Design History

In the 1970s and 1980s, there began to be a belief that the contents that could be revealed by the historical study of design, especially the design itself, and then, as is now well known, it was mainly a non reflective practice. At the same time, it was also recognized (although never fully recognized) in the early days that if the design provided the "truth". It is also an extremely chaotic truth. There is no purity in the design. Even one foot should seek autonomy. Even within a certain critical distance, the other foot always falls into the mire of Commerce or rights. But participation in this chaotic life is also part of the attraction - this is one of the reasons for its political interests… "Compared with traditional disciplines, design is not a pure, clear and clear discipline, and design history is not a long, orthodox and fully recognized historical category. It has considerable flexibility and extensibility.

Design history is a very flexible subject, which can change with completely different philosophical concepts and actual conditions. However, the flexibility of design often leads to widespread misunderstanding, and more efforts are needed to recognize its essence. The history of design is not only the history of things, but also the history of evolving ideas. Designers' conception, planning and production of physical objects are also the expression of their design ideas. Some people even think that the history of design history should also be the history of the ideas of design historians, including what themes they think can become the object of design Every science related to design regards design as a specific application of its own knowledge, methods and principles. They also believe that design is one of the examples of their research object, and take design as a practical demonstration of the scientific principles of their theme. Therefore, we often encounter the following adventures, that is, design is misunderstood as "applied" natural science, "applied" social science, or "applied" art. No wonder designers encounter great difficulties in communicating with people in these fields. The different understandings encountered by the design history make its research present a "colorful" appearance. There is no boundary extension and still unclear noumenon, which leaves many practical problems to be solved in the study of Chinese modern design history. In analyzing the current situation of the research on the history of Chinese modern design, Shen Yu mentioned, History of Chinese modern design "This research is still on the edge, and the accumulated research results are very few. The reason may be that the research on the history of western modern design concepts is very mature, and the introduction of their research results is relatively safe and not easy to make mistakes; perhaps Chinese researchers believe that there is no design activity in modern sense in China, and there is no design concept at all, Let alone history; Perhaps Chinese scholars have realized the importance of the study of the history of ideas in theory, but in order to avoid spending a lot of energy on extensive data accumulation, many research topics use the extension of the history of Chinese arts and crafts to 'replace' the study of the history of Chinese modern design, or simply use magazines in the field of mass media in the development stage of capitalist economy in the 20th century Calendar advertising, logo design, packaging design to replace. Of course, these all contain elements of "modern design", and the final results also point to the "design concept", but what is the role of this "design concept" in expressing the process of Chinese modern design and discovering new knowledge points? You can only be vague."

The current situation of "entanglement" between Chinese modern and modern design history and other related historical disciplines leads to the obvious uncertainty and randomness of the connotation and extension of Chinese "modern design history" and "modern design history". It is not just China, but also around the world. First, "There are many ambiguous interpretations of the concept of 'design' for a variety of reasons. Design practitioners often find it difficult to define their own work and explain to others what design is. On the contrary, most people have some understanding of the work of architects and the qualification requirements of mechanical engineers II. Designers may be familiar with the way of this industry, but the problem is often that the audience of design, whether the general public or potential customers, often have a very different understanding of what design is or what state design should be. [6] Secondly, there are a lot of research on the history of modern design in the world, and there is no definite scope guidance and content screening. The root of this problem may also lie in the rapid evolution of the word "design", which seems that theoretical research can not keep up with the speed of practical development. People's understanding of design is so, which will inevitably lead to "thousands of differences" in the understanding of design history. In a broad sense, the history of design can be regarded as the history of the development and evolution of all design disciplines. At this level, facing the serious challenges of other disciplines with a long history and strong disciplinary status, such as architectural history, garden history, clothing history, arts and crafts history, engineering history and science and technology history, it is impossible to be actively "recruited", and most of the researchers of these special histories will not change their course and think they are "design history" researchers. In a narrow sense, the study of design history is an extremely short-lived special study, which can not be compared with the above-mentioned special history in terms of breadth, depth and systematicness. At the same time, because "design" itself is difficult to define and normalize, the object of design history is not as clear as many historical disciplines. When studying the history of modern design, most researchers often include all the traditional graphic design, sculpture and mural, industrial products, clothing, interior design, architectural design and garden design, forming a mixed and neutral face. The specific aspects are completely subject to the author's own professional knowledge background and the perspective of choice. This approach is undoubtedly based on the limitations of the current professional division of design disciplines (at present, China's design majors include environmental design, visual communication design, product design, digital media and background education).

1.2   The Challenge of Convention Breakthrough and Paradigm Reconstruction

The research history of ancient and modern design is too light, while the research history of modern design is too light. Specifically, the main dilemma of the study of Chinese design history lies in the long cultural and artistic tradition and the relatively conservative and stable national cultural psychology. Coupled with the twists and turns of the concept of modernity and the process of modern academic acceptance since modern times, part of the research in the field of Humanities and social sciences is still greatly affected and constrained by the comprehensive inertia composed of traditional thinking, traditional disciplines and traditional foundation. For the research of design history, researchers mostly linger on how to coordinate the concept of "design" between tradition and modernity, and how to use the materials they have mastered to put them on the hat of "design history", carry out surface "technical" treatment and word conversion, so as to create a mummy like illusion of "design history". Among them, the most common is to "drift", "transfer" and "misappropriate" the previous research on art history, art history and arts and crafts to the "hat" of design history. There is no doubt that this is a relatively easy job. After all, "at first, people set the agenda of design history according to the conventions of art history and architectural history. Art historians and architectural historians built their words around famous artists and masters, and many design historians followed suit, and set the correct research object of the discipline as designers or design products (or both)."

Over the past 40 years of reform and opening up, the development of the discipline of design history in China has also followed the path of evolution from art history, pattern, decoration, arts and crafts history and other related fields. A large number of design history researchers and design educators have been trained from such an educational tradition. Of course, they are better at writing "design history" in this way. Since entering the 21st century, especially in the past 10 years, with the continuous emergence and translation of foreign research achievements in design history to China, the "new generation of design research" that has really grown and developed from the new and systematic system of design education and design history has gradually broken away from the shackles of the traditional routine of "art history and arts and crafts history", which also shows us that China's recent The great development of modern design history and the hope of updating "upgrading". Nevertheless, the research of design history still faces many challenges. For example, the problem framework, discipline attributes, research objects and research methods of design history, as well as the diversity of design history research and the relationship between life style, consumption, acceptance and interest are all problems that must be faced and solved by the field of design history, and there is a premise to solve these problems, That is, we must understand the history of the formation of disciplines in China's modern sense.

The formation of most disciplines in modern China is composed of two reasonable aspects: one is the vertical axis, which represents the force of Chinese history; One is the horizontal axis, which represents the force of external influence. Under the joint

Top 21 Keywords with the Strongest Citation Bursts

Keywords	Year	Strength	Begin	End	1990 - 2022
Installment	1990	1.445	1998	2002	
Art history	1990	1.7473	2004	2009	
Painting	1990	0.8269	2004	2009	
The theory of evolution	1990	1.1675	2004	2008	
Modern buildings	1990	0.73	2008	2012	
Styles	1990	0.8394	2009	2012	
History of Chinese art	1990	1.4919	2009	2013	
Zhengxu	1990	0.7379	2009	2013	
Staging criteria	1990	0.8394	2009	2012	
History of Chinese Art	1990	0.7379	2009	2013	
Modern Chinese Architecture	1990	0.9254	2010	2014	
Image study	1990	0.8316	2012	2015	
Art historian	1990	0.8316	2012	2015	
Art history stages	1990	1.0582	2013	2015	
The fine arts history	1990	1.3604	2014	2017	
The research methods	1990	1.0972	2015	2016	
Art history study	1990	1.1441	2016	2017	
Calligraphy	1990	0.7514	2016	2020	
History of Chinese Art	1990	0.9566	2016	2018	
Historical stage	1990	0.807	2017	2020	
History of Chinese painting	1990	0.98	2018	2020	

Fig. 1. Key words in stages of Chinese modern art history and architectural history

action of the two forces, new disciplines in modern times came into being, or the process of reorganizing new disciplines. [7] China's design science and design history are also produced in the process of alternating strength, balanced growth and decline, but always intertwined. Based on the above judgment, when we stage the history of modern architecture or design, we need to properly deal with the relationship between the two forces. From the discussion on the breaking limit of stages in the history of modern Chinese architecture, the following points have important guiding significance for the stages of the history of modern Chinese design.

For the study of Chinese modern and contemporary design history, there are still many differences in the interactive mechanism and development theory of "East" and "West", "he" and "I", which is also difficult to distinguish and coordinate. Fei Zhengqing's theory of "impact response", Ke Wen's idea of "China Centered orientation" and Yu Yingshi's theory of "internal reasoning" are all seeking different historical perspectives. Yu Yingshi once said, "I hope to find an internal way to connect tradition and modernity. If there is transformation, it should also be based on internal transformation. Without internal transformation, things outside can't come in. What many people have done in the past is to sort out modern elements from tradition, which is not enough. Transformation at the literal level alone can't come out." [8] What Yu said is a reversal of the "impact response" model, but this reversal may also highlight and even amplify the meaning of "internal reasoning". Therefore, there are two tendencies in analyzing history. One is to start from the outer edge and believe that "external causes are the reasons for change". Taking the history of modern thought as an example, it is the introduction and impact of Western knowledge, thought and belief that changes have taken place in modern China; One is to argue from the inner edge, "the internal cause is the basis of change". Without the evolution of China's own thought, external influence may not make traditional China move towards modern times. In other words, due to the evolution of Chinese knowledge and thought, it has gradually become as modern as the West. However, theories always have regrets. Emphasizing external causes and highlighting internal causes and emphasizing external influence and highlighting internal reasoning are actually one-sided, profound and tenacious expressions of an insight. However, is there a more suitable and plain writing method? I think this way of exploring historical memory and acting as ideological resources and reinterpretation of meaning seems to be able to comprehensively influence and choose the interaction. [9] 82–83 history can be full of vitality only through contemporary interpretation, and history can "live" for itself and the construction needs of the real world.

1.3 Lack of Landmark Staging Events and Objects

In the study of Chinese modern and contemporary design history, it is difficult to find typical events (objects) as a clear symbol of limit stages. We can see that most of the studies of Chinese modern and contemporary design history have made great efforts to build a complete chain and framework of "modern and contemporary design history", such as the excavation and use of materials and the selection and screening of cases. In order to form a narrative system, researchers have racked their brains and made many attempts. However, from the current general situation, the construction of narrative framework presents a "system" that is somewhat patchwork, complex and "matchmaking". Roughly speaking, there are three main lines in the occurrence of "splicing" and "borrowing": one is the tireless derivation of the concept and background of various prefixes and suffixes of "modern". For example, it is inspired by many historical concepts, such as pre modernity, early modernity, germination of modernity, modernity, modern enlightenment, modern consciousness, industrialization, modernization and so on. This cross-border "subject reference" and "concept misappropriation" not only constitute the basic context of modern design history research, but also too much tracing and questioning (other humanities and social sciences have already had systematic, in-depth and mature discussions). To a certain extent, is it not a "Representation" of hesitation and aphasia of the research noumenon? The misunderstanding and misuse of the concepts of industrialization, modernization and Modernity in the academic circles are also ignored. Specifically, these concepts include western (European and American) influence, industrialization process, national industry, citizen culture, economy and trade, business communication, enlightenment, new culture movement, science and democracy, etc.; The second is to trace the orthodox gene of art design (Design Art) such as pattern, decoration and arts and crafts, including various professional categories under modern disciplines such as sculpture, architecture, city, industrial design, film set, book design, graphic design (visual design), fashion design and so on. Third, learn from the research results of other historical disciplines such as ideological history, technological history, economic history, political history, social history, art history and aesthetic history. In short, most of the research on the history of Chinese modern and contemporary design is convergent or divergent from the above three paths. In the limited research results, the face of Chinese modern design history is also magnificent and different.

The view of Chinese modern and contemporary design history held by the author is clear: the primary task at the current stage is to clarify their own research objects, find their own research methods and establish their own research paradigm from the numerous "design" understanding and "design history" research. The most basic and primary step is to divide them by stages. Only after completing this task can we move forward in the state of "interdisciplinary" and "interdisciplinary" as emphasized now. Looking back on the development of modern design history, since Gropius founded Bauhaus, the "cross-border" design consciousness of breaking boundaries and boundaries has been mentioned to a programmatic and important position. Today, we do not want to make the research of design history an isolated research of "painting the ground as a prison", but hope to establish an open (boundary) and clear research subject (object) in art, architecture, technology and broader technology, science and life. With the development of the times, the boundary of the subject is clear, and the research object is inevitable. Indeed, this effort is a dynamic process full of contradictions. The value of further in-depth study of design history will also move towards a more "self confirmation" legitimacy in this dynamic contradiction. Of course, to explore the staging of Chinese modern design history is not to touch the elephant with the blind. The existing research on the staging of other special history can provide enough powerful reference evidence. For the history of design, the first thing is the relatively mature staging of architectural history and art history.

2 Periodization of Architectural History: A Valuable Sample

Why take the research on the stages of architectural history as the key object of the stages of design history? In fact, for the origin, development and evolution of the history of Chinese design, the category of design and the connotation of main disciplines, architecture and art (Art) are the two most important sources, and there is a close relationship between architecture and art itself. The concept of architecture as art developed under the background that Cai Yuanpei advocated replacing religion with aesthetic education. After the beginning of the Republic of China, art schools were established everywhere. Among them, the design department and Architecture Department of Beijing art school and the National Academy of art in Hangzhou are related to architectural education. The establishment of the architecture department in the art school marks the gradual emergence of the art characteristics of architecture. This is closely related to the background of China's art movement. The "art movement society" led by Lin Fengmian launched China's Renaissance art movement based on the National Academy of art, and began a revolution affecting the fate of Chinese painting in the field of painting. At the same time, the representative of the art movement in architecture is Liu jipiao. He expressed the art movement with "Art Architecture" and further demonstrated it with the help of nationalism. Here, take Liu jipiao's West Lake Expo as an example to investigate the problems of art architecture. The understanding of the dual attributes of "Engineering" and "art" of architecture has become the basis of China's understanding of architecture. [7] Due to the limited space, the periodization limit of Chinese modern art history is omitted temporarily. This paper mainly discusses the periodization of Chinese modern

Fig. 2. Keyword Atlas of Chinese modern art history and architectural history

architectural history, so as to provide reference for the periodization of Chinese modern design history.

The discussion on the stages of architectural history has been put on the agenda in the 1980s and 1990s. Gong Deshun, Yang Bingde, Yang Hongxun, Liu Tuo, Chen ganglun, Zou Denon, Zheng Shiling, Sha Yongjie, Xu Subin and others have specially discussed the stages of modern architectural history. The research of the above scholars has two common characteristics. First, compare the field of vision. Looking for reference coordinates in the stages of world modern history and making judgments in combination with China's national conditions and historical development; Second, specific judgment. In the special field of architectural history, a more targeted discussion is carried out in combination with the main line of China's architectural development. Of course, although the consensus has been basically reached, its views are not completely consistent.

2.1 The Stage Difference Between General History and Special History

There is an idea that universal history (General History) is higher than special history. This kind of history is called the history about the history of various doors. For example, one can be regarded as real history, which includes political history, economic history, institutional history, moral history, emotional history, ethical ideal history, poetry and art history, thought and philosophy history. But if so, there is dualism, and with the usual result of dualism, two indistinguishable words look empty. In this case, or the general history seems empty, when the special history completes their tasks, the general history has nothing to do; Or special history seems empty. When the feast is wolfed down and swept away by general history, special history can't even get bread crumbs. Or adopt a temporary expedient to give the content of a special history to the general history, and the rest of the special history is put aside by the general history: at most, this classification can only be said to be purely literal, without indicating a logical distinction and opposition; The worst that can happen is to give it a real value, because in this case, a level of fabrication is established, which makes the real development of facts incomprehensible. Almost no special history has not been raised to general history, sometimes identified as political and social history, and takes the history of literature and art, philosophy, religion and other secondary aspects of life as an appendix; Sometimes it is defined as the history of ideas or the history of ideological development, which reduces the social history and all other history to a subordinate position; Sometimes it is identified as economic history, and all other history appears as "superstructure" history or chronicle. In the final analysis, it has become the appearance and illusion of economic development. The economic history does not know in what way and by what force. It has no thought and will, but it produces thought and will, or mainly imagination and fantasy, just like bubbles floating on the surface of its process. Those who oppose general history need to insist on excluding special history and there is no other real thing, because when thinking about facts, they must recognize their special features and always constitute conceptual, imaginary, political activities, apostolic mission and similar history. [10] 69–70 The intertwining and differentiation between general history and special history is a pair of twin contradictions, which nourish and restrict each other. In this process, the stage difference between Chinese modern architectural history and Chinese general history is regarded as the primary problem.

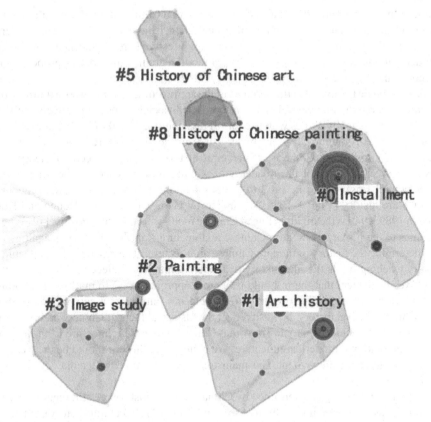

Fig. 3. Clustering map of stages of Chinese modern art history and architectural history

Gong Deshun, Zou Denong and Dou Yide once wrote that "the stages of Chinese modern architectural history are inconsistent with those of modern general history, but the stages of western modern architectural history are also inconsistent with that of Chinese modern architectural history." this inconsistency is not a problem, that is to say, we do not need to have any sense of discord about the inconsistency between special history and general history. "We have no reason to think that the stages of Chinese and Western architectural history should be completely consistent, but we have reason to doubt whether the history of Chinese modern architecture should start in 1949? Although Chinese architecture before 1949 was in a complex environment of semi feudal and semi colonial, there have long been important traces and examples of western modern architecture." The author explains the core meaning of the word "modern architecture", which refers to the modern architectural movement produced by the development of modern industry and technology and the needs of modern society since the middle of last century. It is the product of industrial revolution and specific historical conditions, and has some recognizable common characteristics. However, the question is "does the history of Chinese" modern architecture "since 1949 have this meaning?" Gong (Deshun), Zou (Denon) and Dou (Yide) further pointed out, "The trend of thought of

Western 'modern architecture' had a certain impact on China before 1949. Although its development has been slow or even stagnant since then, it has been on the road of 'modern architecture'. Therefore, the Chinese 'modern' architecture here has the meaning of both 'modern' in the era and 'modern' in western modern architecture, but its proportion is different Just. " [11]2–3.

Yang Bingde believes that the opinions of the architectural community on the division of Chinese modern architectural history according to social forms are relatively unified, and everyone basically agrees with the cut-off division from 1840 to 1949. For example, from the second volume of "brief history of Chinese architecture" compiled by the Editorial Committee of Chinese architectural history of the architectural theory and History Research Office of the Academy of Architectural Sciences of the Ministry of Architectural Engineering in 1962 to the publication of "outline of Chinese modern architecture history (1949 ~ 1985)" compiled by Gong Deshun, Zou Denon and Dou Yide in 1989, 1949 is the dividing line of Chinese modern architecture history. [12] When it comes to the history of modern Chinese architecture, can Zou de Nong's analogy of 1–2 determine the history of modern Chinese architecture? The practice of architectural history teaching holds that the history of modern Chinese architecture began in 1949. But "We always feel that there should be a more appropriate era to mark the beginning of Chinese modern architecture: this era should not only have a certain relationship with China's general history, but also reflect the historical facts of Chinese architectural activities. In particular, it should show that Chinese modern architecture is an integral part of international modern architecture. We believe that this era should be the western modern architecture movement The mainstream is determined after the "end of the 1920s" or the 1930s. [13]6.

To sum up, the stages determined by China's general history are still regarded as an important basis for breaking the limit of special history (Architectural History), but there are also opposite views. Facing the discussion of "modern" elements here, although we can not provide the exact answer and staging path, we can still judge from this that there are two inconsistent reference answers to the staging of Chinese modern architecture from the late 1920s to the 1930s and after 1949. Some scholars, based on the "China Centered Theory" and architectural ontology, support the former phased approach.

2.2   "Chinese Ontology" and "Discipline Center"

According to Chen ganglun, "it's best to set a position before making a theory on governing history. If we talk about the history of modern Chinese architecture, our position is: China Centered Theory and architectural ontology." "The so-called 'China Centered Theory' emphasizes that the study of modern Chinese architectural history should not be 'Eurocentric'", "The so-called 'architectural ontology' emphasizes that the investigation of modern Chinese architectural history does not need to be bounded by political events. Architecture is not an isolated phenomenon, but must be the product of social politics, economy, culture, religion, science and technology. In particular, social form and political system have always been the most important, the most important, and sometimes even the first decisive factor It reflects the face of the building. " These two principles and understandings have important guiding significance for the phased research of Chinese modern design history. Wang further analyzed the relationship between architectural events and social forms and political events. "Some major architectural events are often directly triggered by major social and political events in a certain place. However, social forms and political events are only the conditions for the emergence and development of architecture, not the architecture itself. Only architecture, architectural events and their development are the research objects of architectural history. Therefore, social history can not replace architectural history. Of course, both Is closely related. In order to find the reasons for the development of modern Chinese architecture, we can go deep into the research of modern Chinese architecture. " Wang gave a brief explanation of the difference between Chinese modern architectural history and Chinese modern architectural history. In short, the history of Chinese modern architecture is the history of Chinese "modern architecture". "Modern architecture is obviously a transitional form of architecture that is different from both ancient architecture and modern architecture. The process of its evolution is the history of modern architecture. Ancient architectural forms are different in different countries; modern architectural styles are similar in the world. Therefore, the history of modern architecture in all regions of the world is bound to go the same way." [14]162–163.

Yang Hongxun and Liu Tuo think it is necessary to fully discuss what is the staging standard? It is considered that this is an important academic problem to be solved urgently. "One view holds that the development of modern Chinese society should be divided into different stages… But the essence of the problem lies in whether the buildings and their basic forms and characteristics appear in different stages of social history? If not, what is the significance of such architectural history staging? Obviously, what we want is the organic combination of the relationship between architectural development and social development, rather than mechanically arranging the corresponding points. Another view is that it is divided into stages according to the form and evolution of the building itself. This understanding has its inherent rationality, because architecture itself is a very complex phenomenon. On the one hand, it is directly related to the development of productivity and production relations; On the other hand, it was influenced by superstructure, social thoughts and aesthetic views. I am afraid that adopting this method of staging is more practical than adopting the method of social and historical staging, but it is much more difficult. In short, the division of architectural history is an important topic of modern architectural academic theory and has a lot to do. " [15] 51–52 Yang and Liu then pointed out that "it is necessary to make a multi-disciplinary and multi angle architectural comparison of modern architecture, that is, to study in a larger architectural cultural background and comprehensively analyze and compare architecture with history, philosophy, art, religion, psychology and other related disciplines." "For the study of modern Chinese architecture, it is to always take Chinese architectural culture as the basic comparative body, understand the essence of introducing or transplanting foreign things through comparison with other relevant countries and national buildings, and find out the" similarities in differences "and" differences in similarities ". In this way, we can more deeply identify the value, advantages and disadvantages of our own traditional architecture, Summarize the experience and lessons of architectural development, and provide the direction and reference of architectural development and evolution for the current architectural creation and practice. I think this should be one of the main purposes of studying modern Chinese architectural theory. For the investigation of important typical buildings, in addition to the characteristics of the building itself, it is also necessary to investigate the author's creative environment and basic creative mentality, and explore its significance and characteristics from the actual factors of specific social economy, history, culture and environment, so as to grasp the research purpose of comparing Chinese and Western architecture In short, the study of Chinese modern architectural theory and history must stand at the height of history, not only explore problems across national boundaries, but also explore the cross and horizontal relationship between architecture and other cultures, arts and other related disciplines, and find out a regular thing through the comparison methods of China and foreign countries, so as to improve the research level of modern architecture. " [15]52–53.

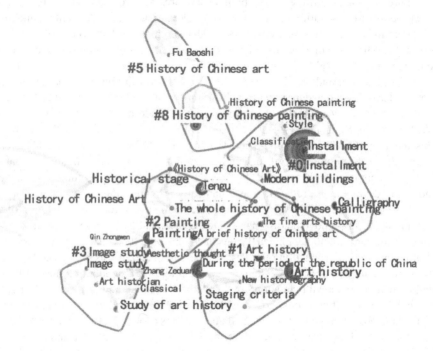

Fig. 4. Wireframe of clustering by stages of Chinese modern art history and architectural history

Li nan ming put forward that the staging of architecture must be based on the reality of China. "We should put the study of modern architectural history 'in the rapidly changing social, economic and cultural background of modern China, and examine the emergence and development of modern Chinese architecture as the result of the development and change of modern Chinese social, economic and cultural background'," 110 years (1840–1949) After roughly scanning the history of modern Chinese architecture, we will find that the development of modern Chinese architecture is very uneven. It developed slowly before 1900. After the outbreak of the Anti Japanese war in 1937, the construction activities stagnated due to the war. The period of real rapid development is only a short period of more than 30 years from 1900 to 1937 '. Therefore, a modern Chinese architectural history can be divided into three periods: the initial period from 1840 to 1900; The prosperous period from 1900 to 1937; And the withering period from 1937 to 1949. There are two important milestones: the war of aggression against China by the Eight Power Allied forces in 1900 and the war of resistance against Japan in 1937. These two wars had a great impact on Chinese society and also made a sudden change in the development process of China's modern architectural history. " [16] This is also the consensus of many architectural history scholars on the issue of staging.

There is no problem in adopting the two basic principles of China Centered Theory (based on China's reality) and architectural ontology in the staging of Chinese modern architectural history. The consideration of major political events, although not the only basis for staging, is still regarded as an important standard. Social form, multi-disciplinary perspective and greater architectural cultural background are also the reference standards for defining the stages. In addition to the research on the overall stages of Chinese modern architecture, the regional stages of modern architecture also provide us with a different perspective.

2.3 Non Antagonistic Relationship Between Modern Architecture and Modern Architecture

There is a view that emphasizes the non antagonistic relationship between modern architecture and modern architecture. The staging of modern architecture mentioned by Zheng Shiling in his book "Shanghai modern architectural style" is meticulous and thoughtful, which is of great reference value. Zheng believes that according to the view generally agreed by the current historical circles, the dating of China's modern history is from the Opium War in 1840 to the founding of the people's Republic of China in 1949 China's modern architecture should not only be included in the category of world modern architecture, but also have the characteristics of national conditions and regions in dating. It is generally agreed that the stages of modern Chinese architecture are the same as those of modern Chinese history. For modern architecture in Shanghai, the dating should be from the opening of the port in 1843 to the founding of the people's Republic of China in 1949. Using "modern" to define the architecture of this period is mainly from the perspective of history, not from the perspective of architectural style. Although some scholars have questioned: "is the history of modern Chinese architecture the history of modern Chinese architecture or the architecture of modern Chinese history?" Some scholars even advocated "pushing the end of modern history to 1977". In fact, the definition of "modern architecture" is not a definition of architectural style or "modern architectural movement" relative to "modern architecture". Modern architecture in Shanghai itself includes modern architecture that became popular in the 1930s. "Shanghai modern architecture" is a concept of the times, and its definition itself has the characteristics of pluralistic symbiosis. At the same time, the modern Shanghai defined in this book is a regional concept, not a historical concept of administrative division. As mentioned earlier, although the buildings in this historical period from 1843 to 1949 are called "modern architecture", they contain a wide range of architectural styles and architectural systems, and also show the development towards modern architecture. Many studies on modern architecture in Shanghai are related to modernity, modernism and modern transformation. The modern architectural style of Shanghai is not a certain architectural style, which can not be classified into the same category as the Byzantine style, Gothic style, Renaissance style, Baroque style and other architectural styles related to historical stages in the world architectural history, but an expression of the overall architectural style, an architectural style that almost integrates all kinds of styles. This period has a total history of 106 years. The diversified architectural styles and architectural systems presented in modern architecture in Shanghai can only be described by a revolution in Shanghai architectural culture. It almost covers from early Christian architecture, Roman architecture, Gothic architecture, Renaissance architecture, Baroque architecture, neoclassical architecture to modern architecture, And the evolution of various styles in the revival of Chinese tradition in about 2000 years. With regard to the stages of modern architecture in Shanghai, the division by age can more accurately reflect the reality, avoid label analysis, and focus on its connection with the world architectural culture, as well as the creative activities of foreign architects in Shanghai, the evolution of architectural stage, architectural types and styles between Chinese architects and Shanghai. Therefore, according to the age, the modern architecture in Shanghai can be roughly divided into four periods: early modern (1843–1900), middle modern (1900–1920), prosperous modern (1920–1937) and late modern (1937–1949). The dating of these four periods is only for the convenience of discussion. The relationship between them can not be simply expressed by a certain era or style, and the architectural style also has a process of continuation and penetration. [17]8.

The core point of Zheng's discussion on the stages of modern Shanghai Architecture is not to regard "modern architecture" as the architectural style of "modern architecture" or "modern architectural movement", and put forward the opinion that "modern architecture in Shanghai itself includes modern architecture prevailing since the 1930s". The internal logic of the expression is easy to understand, But it still makes people feel "awkward". It is precisely because of such a thoughtful consideration that the confusion and difficulties in the staging of modern Chinese architecture have been exacerbated. Modern Shanghai in the sense of general history has a historical stage. In fact, it is a period of vigorous development of Chinese modern design.

3   Stages of Modern Chinese History: Three Key Issues

With the vigorous development of Chinese design discipline and the deepening of the research on design history, it is time for Chinese modern design history and Chinese modern design history to seek a clear cut-off and stage. Why is it possible to divide the stages of Chinese modern and contemporary design history? First, the cut-off stage of general history gives a macro reference framework, and the stage of relevant special history (such as architectural history and Art History) provides a more detailed and specific demonstration model, which provides a major premise for the solution of this problem. Second, distinguish "modern" as a transitional social form between ancient and modern times, highlight the characteristics of "hybridity", "intermediation" and "diversity" in the history of Chinese modern design, and compare it with the "mechanization and batch" of the conceptual core of "modern design" originated in the West in the context of the development and evolution of Chinese design history. Finally, with the advancement of the study of Chinese modern and contemporary design history, more and more relevant materials can provide "evidence" and case support for stages. Following the above, we can give a relatively reasonable and clear answer to the staging of Chinese modern and contemporary design history. In addition, of course, we also face some specific difficulties. We need to further follow up the continuous extension and change of the connotation of design concept, and define the object of Chinese modern and modern design history more clearly. Rezman, a design historian, once mentioned the "two difficulties" in modern design research (it is not easy to distinguish design from engineering, and it is not easy to strictly distinguish commercial motivation from artistic motivation) [18] preface 11–12 also gives us an important enlightenment, that is, we should fully consider the dynamic interactive relationship between design engineering and business art.

3.1 Key Words of Chinese Modern Design History

Modernity, modernization and industrialization are three important key words for staging the history of Chinese modern design. They have both close connections and great differences, which are often confused in some studies. Generally speaking, modernity has the connotation of modernization and industrialization, and is also related to rational enlightenment and capitalism. Among the definitions of the concept of modernity, the more famous ones are the following three viewpoints. First, Giddens regards modernity as the abbreviation of modern society or industrial civilization from the perspective of sociology. It includes a set of structures from world outlook (attitude towards the relationship between man and the world), economic system (industrial production and market economy) to political system (nation-state and democracy). He focused on "understanding modernity from the institutional level", so his concept of modernity mainly refers to the behavioral system and model established in post feudal Europe and increasingly becoming a world historical influence in the 20th century. In this sense, modernity is roughly equivalent to "industrialized world" and "capitalism", including its competitive product market and the commodity production system in the commercialization of labor force. Second, Habermas regards modernity as an "unfinished design" from a philosophical point of view. It aims to replace the disintegrated models and standards in the middle ages with new models and standards to construct a new social knowledge and era, in which individual "freedom" constitutes the era characteristics of modernity, and the principle of "subjectivity" constitutes the principle of self confirmation of Modernity Reason has become the source of truth and value, and thus the place for modernity to settle down. In addition, Foucault understands modernity as "an attitude", not a historical period, not a concept of time. "The so-called attitude, I mean the mode connected with contemporary reality; a voluntary choice made by a specific people; finally, a way of thinking and feeling, that is, a way of behavior and behavior, which marks a relationship of belonging and expresses it as a task at the same time. Undoubtedly, it is a bit like what the ancient Greeks called society Will have a good spirit. " [19]4–5.

Looking back, Cao Xiaoou once put forward three basic judgments about the concept of "modern design": first, generally, "modern design" is not a concept of time. For example, ancient Chinese design refers to the Chinese handicraft design before the opium of the Qing Dynasty; Contemporary design refers to the current and ongoing, although contemporary design includes the characteristics of both modern design and post-modern design. Second, although the term "modern design" has timeliness, its significance lies in that it is a complete design system, which usually refers to the overall design of modern countries after the completion of the French Revolution and the British Industrial Revolution. The so-called modernization refers to the transformation of the country's political and economic system, that is, from the agricultural society to the industrial society, or from the traditional society to the modern society. Third, the time of "modern design" in various countries and regions is inconsistent. At first, it only happened in a few Western countries, and then it gradually expanded to the "late rising" society of the third world. Therefore, China's modern design is nearly a century later than that of western countries. [1] 2–3 Cao's judgment is undoubtedly influenced by Foucault's view of modernity. However, Foucault talks about it from the perspective of philosophy, and it is only an opinion on modernity. Whether it is appropriate to replace the concept of modernity from the perspective of philosophy with "modern design" is still debatable. The author believes that the first focus of history is time. Time is one of the important attributes of the concept of "modern design", which corresponds to the overall transformation of social form in a certain social period. "Modern design" is not only a concept of time, but also a process of evolution. The division of history is to find the events with special historical significance and take the time period of their occurrence as the symbol. It is crucial to clarify this point. Because, what kind of "modern design concept" has what kind of "modern design history".

Will introducing the controversial concept of "Modernity" into the phased discussion of modern and contemporary Chinese history "add chaos to chaos" and make the problem more complex and difficult to clarify? In essence, modern China is a transitional period between ancient and modern times. If the "Modernity" of Chinese design originated from heavy industrial products - such as guns, ships and production machinery, the real birth of Chinese modern and modern design is mainly based on light industrial daily necessities - such as cosmetics, toothpaste, mosquito repellent incense, condiments, light bulbs, flashlights, electric irons, electric fans Refrigerator, stove, etc. This is from the focus of production and life. Secondly, from the essential characteristics of Chinese modern design, we should return to the core representation of "mechanization and batch".

Kong Lingwei, a scholar of art history, also talked about this issue, "The basic discourse on modernity, modernity and modernization comes from the West... According to the master of Western cultural strategy, modernization and modernism are a closed structure. They are not China's endogenous forms of civilization, but fundamentally changed China's appearance and ended China's imperial form of more than 2000 years. Modern China's material facilities, social system Customs, even the way of thinking and language expression have deeply left the brand of western modern culture since the 19th century. Following the western style, China launched a series of large-scale national consciousness movements and industrialization movements, and finally established a modern democratic government. Such a period of history has completely reversed our cultural concepts. Modern China has become "China of the world". Accordingly, modern Chinese culture is also a complex of Chinese and Western cultures, which poses a challenge to all traditional or Western values. " About the stages of modern art history, Kong believes that: "If we regard Chinese history since the mid-19th century as a conflict between tradition and modernity, then the history of modern art should be

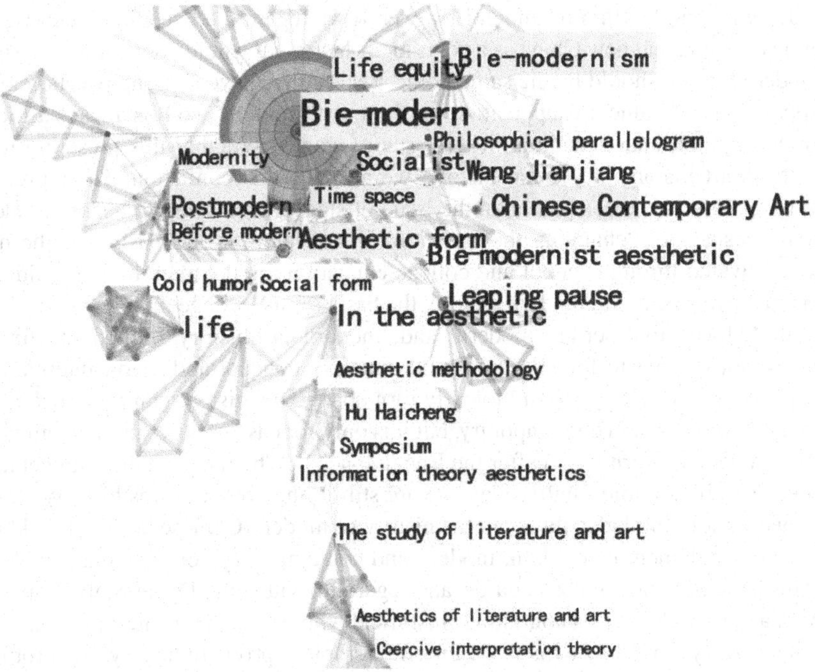

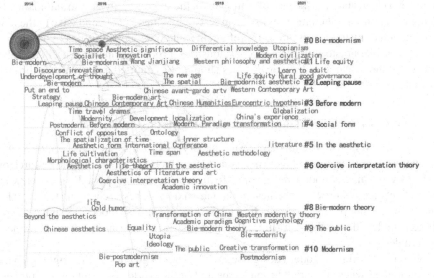

Fig. 5. Frequency of "Bie-modern" keywords

Fig. 6. "Bie-modern" timeline map

divided from the May 4th movement. However, if we regard the late Qing Dynasty, the Republic of China and new China as a continuous historical whole, then modern history and modern history should be the same point. Because we have a strong psychological presupposition and value presupposition for the word 'modern', so It is always difficult to obtain a unified understanding on the issue of stages. Whether this presupposition comes from art history or general history, we all have this confusion. Therefore, we can only retain a vague consensus on the issue of staging according to historical facts: the consciousness of "changing the situation" in the late Qing Dynasty and the new culture cultivated through school and college education are the main body of Chinese modern consciousness and modern culture, the basis for us to stage modern history, and the foothold for us to describe "modern" and "modern" art history. In modern Chinese society, various opposite forces - spirit and material, concept and merit, internal and external forces have always been violently torn apart. This history can also be divided into modern, modern and contemporary, but it is only for ease of description. Compared with the modern western world after the Renaissance or China before the 19th century, the three are still a whole - until today, we are still in the vortex of this history. Therefore, if we want to think deeply about the history of modern Chinese art, we should put aside the entanglement of modern, modern and contemporary concepts, get rid of the problems of stages and value standards, and regard the late Qing Dynasty, the Republic of China and new China as a continuous historical whole, outside the narrative mode of "Dynasty history" and "style history", Present complex 'problem history' or 'problem consciousness' through the material itself." [20]21–22.

Kong's proposition not only combs the main context of relevant issues, but also emphasizes the coherence and Modernity of history. However, the concept is not clear, the stage is not clear, and even the idea of getting rid of the stage is equivalent to automatically giving up an important content of historical research, which is not conducive to the new construction of historical research. Therefore, the author supports the idea of presenting complex problem history or problem consciousness through the material itself, and also insists that the research of historical stages should be supported and promoted through the material.

3.2 New Construction of Ontology of Design History Research

On the research of Chinese modern design history, Guanzhi's "modern" achievements are relatively few, and most of them are named after "modern". However, the research on the history of Chinese modern design often focuses on the modern period. This somewhat "forced" choice also reveals the hesitation and anxiety of researchers in staging. This compromise is adopted in works such as the history of Chinese modern design concept, Chinese modern design thought - life, enlightenment and change, and the birth of Chinese modern design.

When will Chinese modern design begin? We should go back to the origin, go back to the moment when modern "design" appeared in the world, and find out the process of its eastward spread. This is the first step. The second step is to fully understand and absorb the internal logic of western modern design concepts, return to the reality of China, and find the appropriate positioning from the "internal logic" of Chinese society itself. In the west, although the English word 'design' existed earlier than the European

Renaissance to describe the budding process of artists' ideas before artistic creation, as a word to describe a full-time professional, it did not officially appear until the beginning of the western industrial revolution in the 19th century' "Modern design" is clearly defined for the first time in this modern trend of introspection (as opposed to Morris's definition of counterpart Technology: namely "mechanism", "large quantity", "standard" and "mass"). We believe that we can understand the true meaning of "the birth of modern design" according to this meaning. Through the above simple description of the "birth of modern design" in the west, we can learn that the modeling culture highlighted by "modern design" is very different from the modeling culture of previous dynasties and other contemporary utensil manufacturing techniques (handicrafts). The birth of modern design is more closely related to the context of Chinese and western economy. After the industrial revolution began, the manufacturing industry produced in large quantities. Therefore, on the one hand, there was a large demand for raw materials, on the other hand, there was a surplus of products, so it was necessary to expand the market. This situation made western countries involved in an unprecedented business competition, and began to expand rapidly from Europe to the world in order to find resources, markets and cheap labor. Therefore, from the beginning to the middle of the 19th century, almost European and American countries have sent steamships to Asia... [21] 6–7.

The transformation of social form generally includes the overall characteristics of modern design separated from the previous design. "History is a rich totality with many regulations and relationships, and history as an ideology 'changes with the changes of people's living conditions, people's social relations and people's social existence'. To summarize the achievements of history and measure its social background and social effects, we cannot be separated from the socio-economic conditions and political struggle in various historical periods Potential and ideological and cultural conditions, as well as the interrelationship and interaction between them." [22] page 11 of the preface to the Chinese Translation.

The definition of design and design history needs a new ontological view that breaks through the inherent cognition as a guide. With the continuous expansion of design research group, design research has developed rapidly in all aspects, and new achievements emerge one after another, constantly refreshing people's new cognition of design. At the same time, we also feel that the design concept is developing in a very uncertain direction, which provides a variety of possibilities for research. If we still examine design research according to the existing discipline classification framework, many questions can not find a corresponding answer. That is to say, the existing division of disciplines can not make design show a clear face to some extent. Design researchers often borrow theories and methods from other disciplines for research. The reason is not only that design lacks its own "meta theory", but that the discipline nature of design itself determines that it does not have a clear ontology in the sense of traditional disciplines, In this paper, this discipline attribute and discipline state are called "infiltrated viscosity" - corresponding to the interdisciplinary, marginal and comprehensive discipline attribute of design. Based on this, the discipline attribute of design can no longer be framed by the traditional discipline concept, and in fact, it can not be achieved. This provides the most effective possibility for the new paradigm of discipline in the future. The noumenon of design is no longer fixed, invariable and tangible. It has turned to a diffuse, integrated and infiltrated direction, which will build a strong inclusion and coverage on the basis of the existing discipline classification. This judgment involves the solution of many related problems, such as design object, design method, design element theory, design boundary and so on. It is reasonable to believe that design will play an important role in the establishment of a new discipline paradigm in the future. The study of design history and design theory is bound to make more positive and fruitful achievements in the development of this new paradigm.

3.3   Tentative Ideas on the Stages of Chinese Modern Design History

Among the existing literature on the research of Chinese modern design history, few scholars have discussed the staging of modern and contemporary design history. Most studies include modern times and Modernity in an overall framework, and use relatively flexible words such as the origin/germination/birth of modern design, modern design consciousness and design in the modern sense to describe the development and development of the overall design history of modern times. The following will discuss the discussion of modern design stages (stages) by two scholars in the field of design history. The difference is that Li Yanzu talks about the stages of Chinese modern design history; Correspondingly, Xu Ping is thinking about the western modern design thought (Design History) by stages (not by stages). Finally, the author will put forward his own thoughts and ideas on the stages of Chinese modern and modern design history according to the three basic propositions of "don't be modern" theory.

Li Yanzu discussed Chinese modern design in stages. He believes that the beginning of China's modern design or modern design culture should be traced back to the birth of the concept of Arts and crafts and pattern at the end of the 19th century and the beginning of the 20th century. However, as a modern discipline, the real construction and becoming a professional modern discipline should be from the 1980s to today. I personally understand that this period of history can be divided as follows: before the 1950s as the first stage, after the 1950s to the reform and opening up in the 1980s, these three decades can be used as the second stage of modern design and Chinese design education. From 1980s to today, it can be regarded as the third stage of design development. I think these three stages are completely continuous. From the late 19th century to today, the relationship between design and culture can also be understood as the process of the development of Chinese design modernity, that is, the process of cultural modernity. The modernity of design is closely related to the modernity of culture. When we understand the relationship between design itself and culture, it is developed from a historical point of view. The development of modern design has a history of more than 100 years. Our industrial production and all aspects of development and progress can be reflected through design. [23]42–44.

In the process of discussing the practical development and theoretical development of western modern design, Xu Ping divided this distinctive corresponding feature into "seven steps". Specifically, the first step: excellent craft design (roughly corresponding to the "art and handicraft movement" and "new art" movement from the three British islands and the European and American mainland from the second half of the 19th century to the early 20th century). The second step: rational design (roughly corresponding to the German manufacturing alliance, Bauhaus and Dutch "style" design from the early

20th century to the 1930s). The third step: merchandising design (roughly corresponding to the climax of commercial design in the world economic crisis from 1929 to 1933, which led to the presentation of American professional designers and commercial design system). The fourth step: brand value design (roughly corresponding to the rise of brand design and visual identity design around the 1950s). The fifth step: psychological design (directly related to the rise of postmodern cultural thought after the 1960s). The sixth step: Green Design (roughly corresponding to the green environmental protection movement and the wave of ecologism around the 1980s). The seventh step: non materialistic design (roughly corresponding to the "non materialistic" design trend since Europe at the end of the 20th century). Xu believes that the distinction of these "steps" can be regarded as the "method" or "clue" to interpret modern design and its ideological development, but it is not the standard of historical segmentation. In fact, the category renewal of each "step" does not mean a negative substitution relationship. More precisely, when a new category appears, the original design content and objectives often still exist, but the emergence of a new category may be a hint to find an updated solution after discovering a new "problem". In this sense, the century old "category history" is also the "problem history" of modern design academia. It is these constantly adjusted phased trends that change the direction of design development and, to some extent, affect the quality of the development of modern product economy and consumer culture. [24]12–16.

Li Yanzu and Xu Ping put forward their own clear ideas from the stages of modern design in China and the west, and coincidentally put forward the important concept of "continuity", which also provides important enlightenment for the stages of modern and modern design history in China. The formation of most disciplines in modern China is composed of two reasonable aspects: one is the vertical axis, which represents the force of Chinese history; One is the horizontal axis, which represents the force of external influence. Under the joint action of the two forces, new disciplines in modern times came into being, or the process of reorganizing new disciplines. There are many variations in the process of reorganization, marking the difference between "ancient" and "modern", which can be said to be a sign of the beginning of modern times. [7]7. We have to consider the influence of Japan, France, the former Soviet Union, the United States, China, Taiwan and China Hongkong on the mainland's modern and contemporary history. In today's context, of course, we need to face up to the motivation of the complex development of this period of history, but we should "understand history and increase trust" from this historical process. In contemporary academic research, whether for the research of Chinese modern design history or the development of contemporary design, Of course, we should move towards the construction of China's own research system of design history. The research on the history of Chinese modern design is far from enough, and the external research is far from forming a certain level and scale. In the long run, "Historical research is an inexhaustible subject. It is more and more necessary to try to thoroughly understand the old materials, return the enthusiasm of the soul to its object, and yearn to think about things as they are, because no one has been able to think about it before. With the growth of experience, every new foothold obtained, with the rise of spirit To a more perfect life, there is another view of the distant past from a higher and new level and a new corresponding change in the characteristics of the recognized object." [25]14.

The sporadic appearance of a social phenomenon cannot represent the overall change of the whole social form. The birth of Chinese modern design consciousness and the case of star point modern design can not become the symbol of Chinese modern design in the strict sense. The development of history is a gradual process from quantitative change to qualitative change. Whether the local quantitative change and prosperity of Chinese modern design (special history) in modern China (General History) has opened the symbolic and well deserved prelude of Chinese modern design is still worth going deep into its interior to do more empirical research. Of course, I can't agree with the conclusion that "the real Chinese modern design began after 1980" (Zhao Nong). In the numerous historical events, the author discusses the stages of Chinese modern and contemporary design history, and thinks about three possible ideas for academic criticism.

The first way of thinking about the staging of modern Chinese history can refer to the birth symbol of modern design in the world - the establishment of Bauhaus in 1919. Historical staging is to find a recognized major landmark event as a node. It is the most important joint point for the development of things to qualitative change. It is not only for the convenience of historical writing and historical cognition, but also a recognition necessary for historical research and historical cognition. The first design college in China's modern history is the Central Academy of Arts and crafts established in 1956, which can be regarded as the beginning of Chinese modern design. House's judgment is based on the reality of China's development. The history of Chinese modern design is bounded by this. It was called the history of modern design before, and then the history of modern design. Doubts about this stage probably still exist. Because before the Central Academy of Arts and crafts, the orphan craft factory in Tushanwan (including painting, sculpture, printing, woodcarving, metalworking, photography and other workshops), Fuzhou shipping school, Hubei technology school, Zhili higher industry school, etc. [26] 70 in a sense, the Beijing art school, Sichuan Art School and Shanghai Art College in the period of the Republic of China all had "modern" characteristics, Why is the Central Academy of Arts and crafts a symbol of staging? We turn our attention to the design of the era before Bauhaus. As early as after the industrial revolution, there have been a large number of design colleges, design works and design institutions with modern characteristics, but the birth of modern design is defined as the birth of Bauhaus. This is the same truth, that is, based on the influence on world design and the formation of comprehensive and mature ideas of modern design. From this point of view, taking the Central Academy of Arts and crafts as the beginning of the history of Chinese modern design, the author believes that there is not much discord and discomfort.

The second idea, combined with the general history of China and referring to the stages of architectural history, art history and other special history, is also an appropriate choice to turn the design history before 1949 into the history of modern design, and then the history of modern design in China. This involves a problem of how to deal with modern design ideas and modern conceptual design of local areas. In fact, it is not worth bothering. Zheng Shiling's discussion on the issue of architectural staging in modern Shanghai has had a more convincing explanation. As for the series of stagnation and retrogression after 1949, there is no need to worry about it. Because there is no smooth road to modernity. Under the framework of the times, a series of problems can be regarded as a "alienation" phenomenon at this stage, and they are still not divorced from the overall trend of the times.

The third consideration is to divide modern times, modern times and modern times into three independent stages, in which "modern times" as a combination of the other two stages highlights the "transition" connecting the preceding and the following. "Modern" as a stage of Chinese design history, on the one hand, it refers to neither modern nor modern, but the historical continuity of intermediate state and transitional tense; On the other hand, it includes not only part of modern times, but also part of modernity, that is, the integration of modern times and modernity. This staging considers two aspects. First of all, in terms of independence, it is mainly considered from the staging of the time dimension, giving a clear staging cut-off point; Secondly, inclusiveness emphasizes the blending and interlacing of modern and contemporary design in content and phenomenon. When we make the above conclusion on the staging of Chinese modern design history, They try to abandon the kind of "removing the rich, complex and inexhaustible individual and collective experience from practice; they always want to depict the human history full of contradictions, oppression, discontent and dreams as a quantitative and mechanical time process, as if there is only more time behind time, as if history is just a rosary of a series of demonstrable isolated events." [27]116.

4 Conclusion

Jacques Le Goff, the third generation leader of the Amnales School, once wrote a book entitled "Must we divide history?" The book discusses in detail many views and research cases on historical stages, including the old historical stages, the middle ages, the Renaissance, historical stages and globalization. Final, he puts forward a clear view on the division of history: "we can - I think we should - retain the division of history. Two major movements run through the current historical thought, and history is in a long period of time and Globalization (mainly from the general history of the world in the United States), there is no incompatibility for its use... There are quantitative time periods and quantitative time that can coexist. Historical staging can only be used in a limited field of civilization, and globalization needs to find the relationship between these whole ". [2] Preface, 132–133 The author also believes that historical stages are not only necessary and feasible, but also have limitations in the field of civilization. The division of Chinese modern design history is a feasible and necessary proposition. Historical staging itself represents a value orientation rather than value neutrality. It is a universal ideological and cultural concept. It is people's specific understanding and judgment in the process of historical transformation. "Historical stages show human activities at a certain time, and emphasize that such stages are not neutral. The reasons why people cut time into periods often come from some definitions, which emphasize the significance and value given to these periods by people. Therefore, we should highlight these self-evident reasons here." [2] The history of Chinese modern design is not only faced with the complex situation of iterative evolution of the ontology words of "design", "modern design" and "modern design", but also often discussed in the intertwined and confused realistic academic context of "Industrialization", "Modernization" and "Modernity". These two extremely complex staged discussion premises are inseparable from the specific form evolution of

China's social development, and must also be firmly established in the specific context of China's modern design development. Therefore, the "force" of Chinese modern history and the "force" of western modern history are two closely related and mutually different "forces". In particular, the result of this "resultant force" should and must be Chinese in essence, not western. This is why I think it is more appropriate to use the theoretical core of "don't be modern" to discuss the staging of Chinese modern design history.

When we put forward the idea of staging the history of Chinese modern and contemporary design, we do not expect to be widely recognized by the academic circles immediately. Because, "identification is not only a matter of defining and struggling, but also understanding and cognition. Therefore, these dual factors must be themed in the historical discourse." [25] the embarrassment we face is, "Design does not have its own special theme. In a certain range, design theme has potential universality, because design thinking can be applied to any field of human experience. However, in the process of application, designers must jump out of various problems and specific situations to find and create special themes. This characteristic is formed between natural science disciplines In a strong contrast, the latter has fixed principles, laws, rules and structures, and these elements are inevitably covered in the existing topics The designer conceives the theme at two levels: generality and particularity. At the general level, designers start from concepts or known assumptions and consider the attributes of products or the characteristics of man-made world. Its significance is entirely the designer's personal perspective, not as good as the relationship between "man-made" and "nature", and so on. In this sense, designers have a wide range of perspectives on the nature of design and its scope of use. " [4] Therefore, when people ask whether design has its own theory (meta theory), it is always difficult for us to answer positively. In addition to the difficult identification of design stages, there are still many obstacles to the identification of design disciplines. "Every kind of identity of discipline exists because of the recognition of the other, and the tension between various cultural concepts of identity or identity, even the struggle or conflict, have to be understood as a cognitive requirement. What makes the other different? Without understanding this, cognition can not be realized. In this way, we must understand the strong cultural elements and mistakes in the differences of the other Cheng. Furthermore, without the comprehensibility principle of this difference, cognition is impossible. At the level of academic discourse, these universal elements and dimensions are essentially related to the discourse characteristics of professional historical thinking when subjecting historical identity to become an example of difference."

References

1. Cao, X.O.: Chinese modern design thinking, p. 01. Shandong Fine Arts Publishing House (2018)
2. Jacques, L., Yang, J., (trans.): Faut-il vraiment découper l'histoire en tranches?, p. 01. East China Normal University Press (2018)
3. Clive, D., Wu, Z., (trans.): Design history economics: a John Heskett Reader, p. 10. Jiangsu Phoenix Fine Arts Publishing House (2018)
4. Margolin, V., Buchanan, R., Li, Z., (trans.): The Idea of design: a design issues Reader, p. 04. Jiangsu Fine Arts Publishing House (2018)

5. Shen, Y.: History of Chinese modern design concept, p. 01. Shanghai People's Fine Arts Publishing House (2017)

6. Heskett, J., Dinote, C., Boztepe, S., Translated by Yin, H., Zhang, L.: Design and the creation of value, p. 11. Jiangsu Phoenix Fine Arts Publishing House (2018)

7. Xu, S.: The birth of modern Chinese architecture, p. 02. Tianjin University Press (2010)

8. Chen, Z.: Interview with Yu Yingshi, p. 03. Zhonghua Book Company (2012)

9. Ge, Z.: Introduction to the history of Chinese thought. Fudan University Press, Shanghai (2001)

10. Croc, B.: Translated by Tian, S.: Theory and history of history, p. 08. China Social Sciences Press, Beijing (2005)

11. Deshun, G., Denong, Z., Yide, D.: History of modern Chinese architecture 1949–1985, p. 05. Tianjin Science and Technology Press, Tianjin (1989)

12. Yang, B. (ed.) Modern cities and architecture in China, Ed. codern Chinese cities and architecture 1840–1949, p. 06. China Architecture and Architecture Press, Beijing (1993)

13. Zou, D.: History of Chinese modern architecture, p. 05. Tianjin Science and Technology Press, Tianjin (2001)

14. Wang, T.: The third Symposium on Chinese modern architectural history, 07. p. 162 China Architecture and Architecture Press, Beijing (1991)

15. 汪坦主编，《第三次中国近代建筑史研究讨论会论文集》，中国建筑工业出版社，1991年.陈纲伦《从"殖民输入"到"古典复兴"——中国近代建筑的历史分期与设计思潮》一文。

16. Yang, H., Liu, T. (eds.): Architectural History Branch of Architectural Society of China, Architectural History and Theory, vol. 5, p. 50. China Architecture and Architecture Press, May 1997

17. 杨鸿勋 刘托，《建筑历史与理论 第5辑》，中国建筑工业出版社，1997.王绍周《正视中国近代建筑的研究价值》一文。

18. Nan, L.: The rise of a modern summer resort in Moganshan, p. 01. Tongji University Press, Shanghai (2011)

19. Zheng, S.: Shanghai modern architectural style, p. 09. Tongji University Press, Shanghai (2019)

20. Reitzman, D., Ang, L., Li, C., (trans.): History of modern design 2nd edn. China Renmin University Press, Beijing (201)

21. Chen, J.: Fifteen lectures on modernity and post-modernity, p. 04. Peking University Press, Beijing (2006)

22. Kong, L.: Modernism and Modernity in modern Chinese art history. Fine Arts Observ. (12), 21–22 (2020)

23. Guo, E., Su, J.: The Birth of Chinese Modern Design. Sanlian Bookstore, Hong Kong (2007)

24. Gooch, G.P., Translated by Geng, D: History and Historians in the 19th Century. The Commercial Press, Beijing (1989)

25. Li, Y.: Culture and historical responsibility of design-Li Yanzu on "design and culture" Design 02, 42–46 (2020)

26. Xu, P., Zhou, B.: Design Truth, p. 01. Jiangsu Fine Arts Publishing House, Nanjing (2010)

27. Bradley, F.H., Translated by He, Z., Zhang, L.: The Presuppositions of Critical History, p. 25. Peking University Press (2007)

28. Yan, X.: Fuzhou ship administration school and Chinese modern design education. Decoration (01), 70 (2008). https://doi.org/10.1007/978-90-313-6596-8_70

29. Zhang, X.: Traces of Criticism: Cultural Theory and Cultural Criticism 1985–2002, p. 08 Life, Reading, New Knowledge Sanlian Bookstore, Beijing (2003)

30. Wang, J.: Difference in the Bie-mordern. Jiangxi Soc. Sci. 39(06), 82–90 (2019)

31. Wang, J.: Bie-modernism: doctrine and noumenon – response to the discussion of Bie-modernism in China J. Northwest Norm. Univ. (Soc. Sci. Edn.) **55**(05), 53–61 (2018)
32. Xie, J.: What's the future of "Bie-modern"-preliminary study on Wang Jianjiang's "Bie-modern" theory. Guizhou Soc. Sci. **02**, 49–54 (2019)

A Study on the Back and Forth Manzai of Milkboy by Focusing on Embodied Motions and Actions for Liven-Up

Hong Zhang[1]($\boxtimes$) (ID), Haruka Shoda[2] (ID), Saizo Aoyagi[3] (ID), and Michiya Yamamoto[1] (ID)

[1] Kwansei Gakuin University, Gakuen 2-1, Sanda, Hyogo, Japan
cyoukou1008@gamil.com, cbl81936@kwansei.ac.jp
[2] Ritsumeikan University, Nojihigashi 1-1-1, Kusatsu, Shiga, Japan
[3] Komazawa University, Komazawa 1-23-1, Setagaya, Tokyo, Japan

Abstract. *Manzai* is a form of comedy, and there have been reported attempts to make robots perform *manzai*. On the other hand, it captures the essence of human communication, such as interactions in live performances. In this study, we extracted the basic units that make up *manzai* and analyzed the changes in these units to elucidate the laughing mechanism of the characteristic story progression called the "back and forth *manzai*" of Milkboy. As a result, it was revealed that the story itself is the object of *tsukkomi*; the comedy is generated by clever story progression; and the comedy is enlivened by embodied motions and actions.

Keywords: *Manzai* · Human communication · Embodied motions and actions

1 Introduction

The entertainment style that can be achieved with an audience is changing drastically due to the influence of the COVID-19 pandemic. According to Wikipedia, *manzai* is "a form of entertainment or narrative art performed mainly by two people, providing laughter through the comical interaction of their conversations." Through the Taisho, Showa, Heisei, and Reiwa eras, various kinds of performances have been established and enjoyed by many people. Researchers have tried many new attempts, such as Robot Manzai. In this study, we focused on the *manzai* of the Milkboy.

Milkboy is a *manzai* (Japanese double act comedy) duo with Takashi Komaba of *boke* (a funny man) and Takashi Utsumi of *tsukkomi* (a straight man). They are known for scoring the highest score ever in the 15th M-1 Grand Prix 2019 [1], which was hosted by the M-1 Grand Prix Secretariat, produced by ABC TV [2], and broadcasted on December 22, 2019. One of the judges, Hitoshi Matsumoto, called the characteristics of the Milkboy's *manzai* "back and forth *manzai*." Komaba brings up various topics (mainly names and characteristics that mommy [*okan* in Osaka] has forgotten). In response, Utsumi alternates between affirmation and denial with strong opinions. Finally, as a punchline, Komaba gives an answer that is completely different from the topic by other people (mainly daddy [*oton* in Osaka]), and Utsumi says, "Absolutely different!" (Wikipedia)

© Springer Nature Switzerland AG 2022
M. Rauterberg et al. (Eds.): HCII 2022, LNCS 13520, pp. 89–103, 2022.
https://doi.org/10.1007/978-3-031-18158-0_6

[3]. This style, which follows the traditional *manzai* method, is so fascinating that it has been analyzed by so-called stray researchers on the Internet [4–6].

On the other hand, focusing on academic study on *manzai*, Kawashima et al. [7], Hosoma [8], and Okamoto et al. [9] conducted multimodal analysis that is widely used in communication research. We have also conducted analysis on *manzai* Combi Knights' topics. Here, we proposed an analysis method by defining a "basic sub-topic unit" and by understanding the structure of the entire topic by analyzing the changes in its parameters [10].

In this study, based on the previous studies' methods of extracting the basic units that make up Milkboy's *manzai* and analyzing the parameter changes, the characteristic topic progression of "back and forth *manzai*" is made clear.

2 Extraction of Basic Units

2.1 Analysis Target

The flow of typical *manzai* dialogue consists of *furi* (a preface phase by talking mainly about daily topics), *boke* (a phase that mainly spoken by the *boke* role), and *tsukkomi* (a phase that mainly spoken by the *tsukkomi* role) [11]. In our previous study about Knights' *manzai*, we focused on the speedy repetition of *boke* and *tsukkomi*, based on the analysis by Hosoma. We clarified that Knight's manzai has the characteristic topic progression through the repetition of *boke*, correction, and follow keywords. Based on this, we defined "basic sub-topic unit" as a feature of repetition to analyze their *manzai*. On the other hand, the *manzai* of Milkboy does not progress quickly with keywords alone. Therefore, to extract the basic unit, we transcribed the utterances of the first-round topic "Cornflakes" and the final topic "*Monaka*" at the 15th M-1 Grand Prix 2019 (Fig. 1).

First, we find that the topic's overall structure, which consists of *tsukami* (hook), *hon-neta* (main dialogue), and *ochi* (punchline), as Mashimo et al. claimed [12], is obvious. For example, "Mommy forgot the name of XX that she liked" is *tsukami*, and "What mommy said is not XX" is *ochi*. Here, the part of XX is "Cornflakes" or *Monaka* (which is a Japanese sweet made of red bean paste sandwiched between two thin crisp wafers), and the *manzai* dialogue can be clearly understood as the repeated keyword. Based on this, the "back and forth," which is the *hon-neta* of Milkboy's *manzai*, was chosen as the analysis target to be described in the basic unit.

2.2 Utterance Analysis

When we reviewed *hon-neta*, we found the dialogue begins with the utterances of the *boke* role and ends with utterances of the *tsukkomi* role. First, the *boke* role makes utterances of "introduction," such as "sweet and crunchy" and "suitable for the last meal of life." In response, the *tsukkomi* role makes utterances of Yes or No, such as "Is it XX?" or "Isn't it XX?" Hereafter, we describe these attributes as YN. Afterward, the *tsukkomi* role's conversation continues. What we noticed here is that the *boke* role agrees with the *tsukkomi* role's utterance by nodding or saying, "that's right, that's right." This

JANPANESE	ENGLISH
. . .	. . .
B: うちのオカンがね、好きな朝ごはんがあるらしいんやけど	B: My mom says she has a favorite food for a breakfast.
T: あー、そうなんやー	T: Uh, yes.
B: その名前をちょっと忘れたらしくてね、	B: She seem to have forgotten that name.
T: ほー、朝ごはんの名前すすれてもうてー、どうなってんねんそれー	T: Oh, She forgot the name of the food for a breakfast...what's happened?
B: でま色々聞くんやけどな、全然わからーへんねんな	B: I asked her a lot of questions, but I don't get it.
T: わかれへんの、ほな俺がね、おかんの好きな朝ごはん、ちょと一緒に考えてあげるから、ど	T: You don't get it? I'll help you to think your mother's favorite food for a breakfast.
んな特徴言うてたか、教えてみてよー	so you just tell me what feature of food she said about.
. . .	. . .
B: 甘くてカリカリしてて、で、牛乳とかかけて食べるやつやっていうねんな	B: She said that it's sweet and crunchy, and you eat it with milk.
T: ほー、コーンフレークやないか	T: Oh,It's cornflakes.
B: （うなずき）	B: Hum
T: その特徴はもう完全にコーンフレークやがな	T: That feature is totally cornflakes.
B: コーンフレークな	B: cornflakes ?
T: すぐわかったやんこんなんもう	T: It's too easy.
B: ちょっと分かれへんのよな	B: But i'm a little confusing.
T: 何がわからーへんのよ	T: What are you confusing about?
B: 俺もコーンフレークと思てんけどな、	B: I also thought it was cornlakes,but..
T: いやそうやろー？	T: Is that right?
B: オカンがいうには、死ぬ前の、最後のごはんもそれでいいて言うねんな	B: My mom said it could even be the last meal before she died
T: ほな、コーンフレークとちがうかー	T: So, it is not cornflakes...
B: （納得した感じで）おー	B: Oh
T: 人生の最後がコーンフレークでええわけないもんねー	T: It's impossible to eat cornflakes at the end of our life
B: そやねん	B: That's right
T: コーンフレークはね、まだ寿命に余裕があるから食べてられんのよ、あれ	T: We can eat cornflakes because we have plenty of life left
B: そやんな、おー	B: That's right
T: コーンフレーク側もね、最後のご飯に任命されたら荷が重いよ、あれ	T: If cornflakes are appointed as the last meal,it will be a burden for cornflakes.
B: そやねん、そやねん	B: Yes, that's right.
T: コーンフレークてそういうもんやから、ほなコーンフレークちゃうがな	T: That's what cornflakes are, so it's not cornflakes your mom is talking about
B: そやねん	B: that's right.
T: ほなもうちょっと詳しく教えてくれるー？	T: So can you talk about a bit more ?
. . .	. . .
B: 食べるときに、誰に感謝してええか分からんらしい	B: We don't know to whom we should thank when we eat them.
T: コーンフレークやないかい。コーンフレークは生産者さんの顔が浮かばへんのよ	T: Then it's not cornflakes. We can't imagine the producer's face at all when eating cornflakes.
B: ほー（深くうなずき）	B: Oh
T: 浮かんでくるのは腕組んでるトラの顔だけ	T: All that comes to mind is the face of a tiger clutching its arms.
B: そやねんそやねん	B: Yes, that's right.
T: 赤いスカーフのトラの顔だけ	T: Only the face of a tiger wearing a red scarf.
B: そやねん	B: That's right
T: コーンフレークに決まりそんなん	T: It is just cornflakes
. . .	. . .
B: でも分かれへんねん	B: But I don't know.
T: 分かれへんことない、オカンの好きな朝ごはんはコーンフレークもう	T: You know.Your mom's favourite the food for breakfast is cornflakes.
B: でもオカンが言うには、コーンフレークではないって	B: But my mom said it was'n cornflakes.
T: ほな、コーンフレークちゃうやないかい。オカンがコーンフレークではないといえばコーンフレークちゃうがな	T: So,It's not cornflakes because your mom said it wasn't cornflakes.
B: そやねん	B: That's right
T: 先言えよ、	T: You should have said so before
B: おー	B: Oh
T: 俺がトラの真似してるときどう思っててん	T: What did you think when I was posing a tiger?
B: 申し訳ない	B: Sorry
T: ほんまに分かれへんがな	T: I don't really understand
. . .	. . .

Fig. 1. Transcript of "Cornflakes" (Source: M-1 Grand Prix 2019, ABC TV, 22.12.2019).

means that the *boke* role agrees with the *tsukkomi* role; in other words, the *boke* role also makes jokes. Therefore, it is not the *boke* role's speech but the topic itself, which are the cornflakes in this case, that is roasted. Then, no matter if it is Yes or No, both roles continue to roast cornflakes and *monaka*. Finally, the *tsukkomi* role moves on to the next *furi*. In other words, the *boke* role of Milkboy is not a typical *boke* and only makes utterances of *furi*.

To confirm this, we analyzed the topics of Milkboy using the ELAN software, as shown in Fig. 2. As a result, the *boke* role's ratio of nodding or agreeing during *tsukkomi* utterances was 100%. In addition, the *boke* role's agreement ratio reaches 71% (Fig. 3).

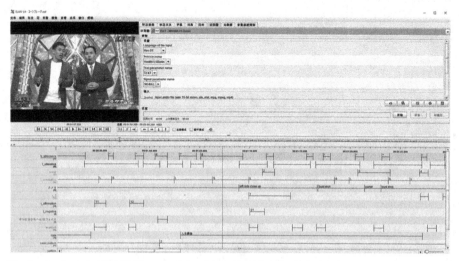

Fig. 2. Analysis in ELAN (Source of the video part: M-1 Gr. (Prix 2019, ABC TV, 22.12.2019).

■ Number of agreement of the boke role

■ Number of other utterances of the boke role

Fig. 3. The agreement ratio of the *boke* role.

2.3 Multimodal Analysis

As for nonverbal information, we observed characteristic movements while the topic was in progress. Here, we focused on the fact that the *boke* role's movements were not large, but the *tsukkomi* role performed various movements. Among them, the most characteristic ones were rubbing his hands and putting his hands on his waist (Fig. 4).

Rubbing hands   Putting hands in waist

Fig. 4. The actions of rubbing his hands and putting his hands on his waist.

Table 1. The degree of laughter

1	Less than 1 s
2	Less than 1.5 s
3	More than 1.5 s

Table 2. The degree of clapping hands and laughing

1	2–3 persons
2	More than a few people
3	Clapping hands

As Okamoto proposed, *manzai* is "open" communication. Because it is scripted on the assumption that the audience enjoys it, the element of laughter is also important. Therefore, we defined the degree of laughter based on our discussion about criteria of laughter by time, as shown in Table 1. Furthermore, the laughter that provides a sense of unity between the *manzai* duo and the audience is a feature of the M-1 Grand Prix. In this study, we focused on the importance of the audience's hands clapping to analyze this situation, which is laughing with clapping in a very funny situation. In both "Cornflakes" and "*Monaka*," only when laughter continued did a few people clap their hands. As the number of clapping people increased, it became clear that some people clapped their hands and laughed (Table 2). Moreover, in a very humorous situation, the number of people clapping hands increased, and people began to clap their hands as applause. Figure 5 shows the relationship between the degree of laughter and the number of claps in the topic of "Cornflakes" and "*Monaka*". In other words, we found that there were many clapping sounds when the topic was very funny.

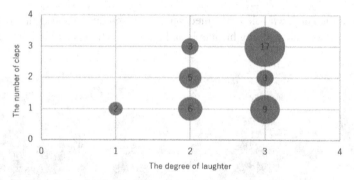

Fig. 5. The relationship between the degree of laughter and the number of claps.

2.4 Extracted Basic Unit

Based on the discussions in 2.2 and 2.3, we decided to analyze Milkboy's *manzai* with the basic unit, as shown in Fig. 6. First, the utterance is in the order of the *furi* of *boke* (B), Yes or No of *tsukkomi* (T), *tsukkomi* 1, *tsukkomi* 2, and then *furi*. The number and types of actions are extracted, such as B's nodding, T's actions of rubbing hands and putting hands on his waist, and so forth. For the audience, we extracted the number, timing, and degree of laughter (W) and the number, timing, and degree of clap sounds (H).

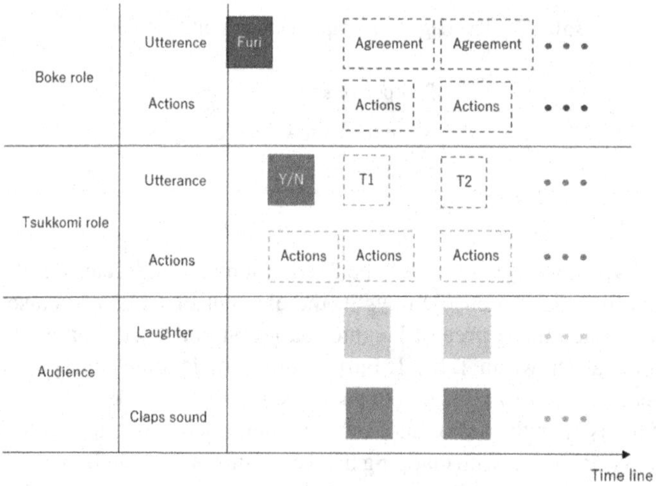

Fig. 6. The basic unit.

3   Analysis by Change in Basic Unit

3.1   Analysis Policy

Based on the extracted basic unit, we exported the annotated data of ELAN by csv files and analyzed it using Python. Just like a structure in a programming language, we stored the characteristics of each basic unit as if they were member variables. In addition, we described *hon-neta* as a collection of multiple basic units, and we stored them in an array in programming.

When analyzing through this method, we first examined how the YN proceeded (Fig. 7). Here, we found that the YN of the basic unit before *ochi* is always "Yes." In other words, to finish a topic with the phrase "Mommy said it is not XX," the YN of the unit before *ochi* must be "Yes." This is one of the charms of Milkboy's *manzai*.

However, it is difficult to make fun with "Yes" because the typical *tsukkomi* consists of "No." We can see this from the fact that *Pekopa*, the other finalist of the 2019 M-1 Grand Prix, gave notice of "non-denying *tsukkomi*." Therefore, we analyzed changes of the basic unit in terms of how elaborately Milkboy designed a topic procedure so that they could end with "Yes" in a raised atmosphere.

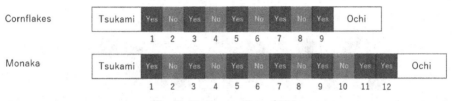

Fig. 7. The proceeding of YN.

3.2   Changes in Utterences Duration and Laughter

First, we extracted the duration per unit, as shown in Figs. 8 and 9. In both cases, the duration per unit tends to be shorter as the topic proceeds, meaning the unit becomes quicker at the end. However, just before the *ochi* of "*Monaka*," a series of two "Yes" units appeared, and the duration per unit becomes longer. The family tree of "*Monaka*" is explained to raise the atmosphere and to connect to *tsukkomi*, "*Monaka*'s twins are *Monaka*."

Next, we calculated the percentage of the *tsukkomi* utterance and laughter durations per unit. Both tend to increase as topics progress, as shown in Figs. 10 and 11. We can see the audiences continue to laugh as *tsukkomi* continues.

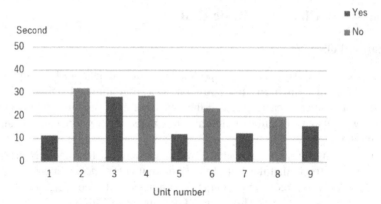

Fig. 8. The duration per unit for "Cornflakes."

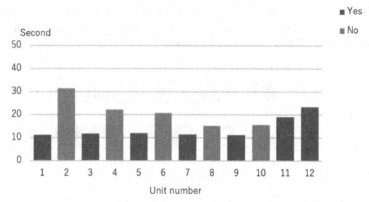

Fig. 9. The duration per unit for "*Monaka.*"

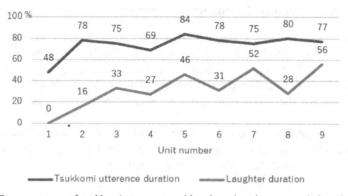

Fig. 10. The percentage of *tsukkomi* utterance and laughter durations per unit for "Cornflakes."

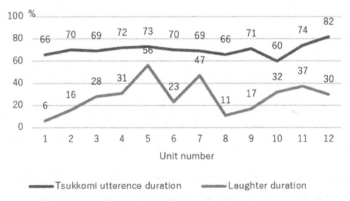

Fig. 11. The percentage of *tsukkomi* utterance and laughter durations per unit for "*Monaka.*"

3.3   Changes in Motions and Actions

In terms of actions and motions, we counted the number of *tsukkomi's* total movements and the characteristic movements of rubbing hands and putting hands on his waist, as *tsukkomi's* movements are characteristic, as shown in Figs. 12 and 13. The number of movements tends to increase. In the former, the increased hand rubbing makes the audience feel humble, but the latter shows strong *tsukkomi* by putting his hands on his waist.

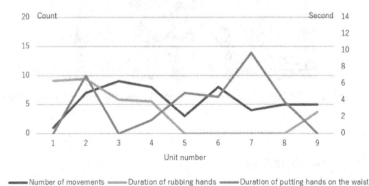

Fig. 12. The changes in movements of *tsukkomi* for "Cornflakes".

Looking back at Figs. 12 and 13, the aforementioned movement characteristics of the units, in which laughter leads to applause, was not seen as often. Therefore, we reexamined how motions and actions occurred in those units. For example, the part "We don't know to whom we should thank when we eat them." in Fig. 1 corresponds to unit 7. In the unit, the *tsukkomi* role folded his arms and said, "I remember only the face of the tiger with his arms folded" (Fig. 14). In this way, the movements that correspond to Ekman's illustrator classification were observed in all the units that had applause. In other

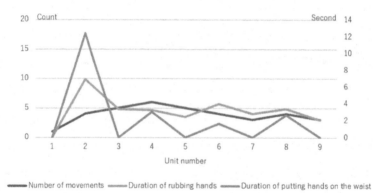

Fig. 13. The changes in movements of *tsukkomi* for "*Monaka*."

words, in most units, Milkboy performed with the regulators classified by Ekman, but in the most critical units, they encouraged the audience by intentional physical actions in a way that emphasized the fun of the topic.

Fig. 14. The actions of folding his arms while saying, "I remember only the face of the tiger."

3.4 MILkboy's Laughing Trick

From the extraction of basic units and the analysis of their changes, we can summarize the characteristics of Milkboy's *manzai* as follows.

- Milkboy's *boke* role is not a typical *boke* and only makes utterances of *furi*. The *boke* role and *tsukkomi* role continue to make fun of *tsukkomi*.
- To finish with the unique *ochi*, the unit before *ochi* is necessary to make fun through affirmation, rather than denial, which is the typical *tsukkomi*.
- Specifically, Milkboy shortens the unit duration, increases the utterance percentage of the *tsukkomi* role, the number of actions, and the actions of putting hands on his waist and decreases the rubbing hands action.
- In a way that emphasizes the fun of the topic, the *tsukkomi* role performs with the motions of an illustrator. This leads to the laughter with claps.

• In addition to the above, the audience increased the laughter duration and clapping with laughter later in the topic.

4 Verification

We verified whether the above findings could be applied to other topics. We selected four topics: "Sea Lion, Steller Sea Lion, Walrus, or Fur Seal" ("Steller sea lion"). This was broadcast on Fuji Television's "ENGEI Grand Slam" on May 22, 2020, and "Umaibo's Guy" ("That guy") broadcast on Fuji Television's "THE MANZAI 2021" in December 2021. Moreover, JR Tokai's original commercial *manzai* film "N700S x Milkboy" ("N700s") [13], and "Milkboy" by another *manzai* duo, Kamaitachi, were broadcast on Yomiuri TV's "Downtown DX" on February 20, 2021. Although "Steller sea lion" and "That guy" are comedy topics, "N700s" is a commercial topic produced for advertising purposes, and we considered that the commercial composition does not have *boke*. "Milkboy" is performed by a different comic duo, so there is a high possibility that the characteristics of "Milkboy" cannot be seen.

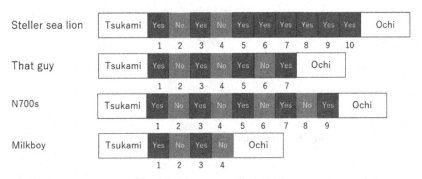

Fig. 15. The proceeding of YN.

First, the composition of the units is shown in Fig. 15. Next, the results of extracting changes in unit duration are shown in Figs. 16, 17, 18 and 19. In the former, the material is sped up. However in the latter, the unit duration is lengthened, and the pacing is slowed. In terms of laughter, the former shows an increase in the percentage of time spent laughing before the punchline, including hand-clapping laughter, whereas the latter shows a lower percentage overall and no increase in laughter.

The results of the extracted movement changes are shown in Figs. 20, 21, 22 and 23. The former has characteristics similar to those of "Cornflakes" and *Monaka*," while the latter has a continuous action of rubbing hands until the end, which is completely different from the typical *manzai*. In this way, we found that, although the laughter mechanism in M-1 shown in 3.4 can be seen in other laughter topics, the feature is not seen in the topics made as commercials.

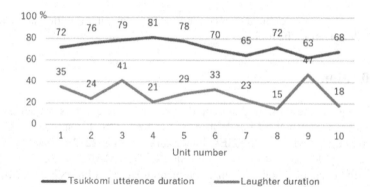

Fig. 16. The duration per unit for "Steller sea lion."

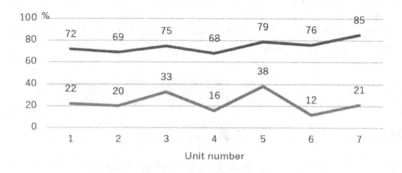

Fig. 17. The duration per unit for "That guy."

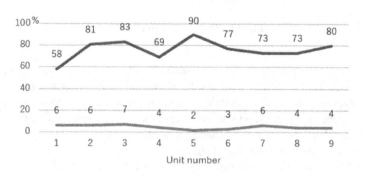

Fig. 18. The duration per unit for "N700s."

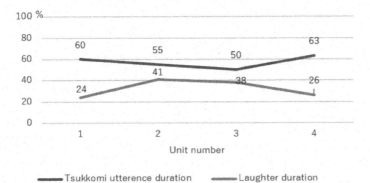

Fig. 19. The duration per unit for "Milkboy."

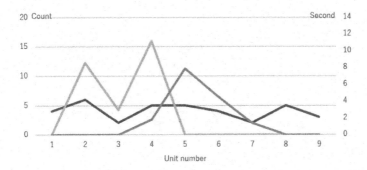

Fig. 20. The changes in *tsukkomi* movement for "Steller sea lion."

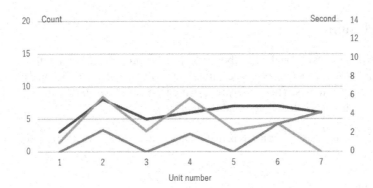

Fig. 21. The changes in *tsukkomi* movement for "That guy."

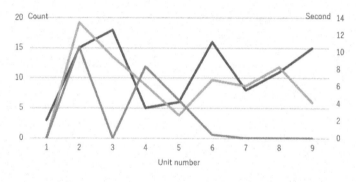

Fig. 22. The changes in *tsukkomi* movement for "N700s."

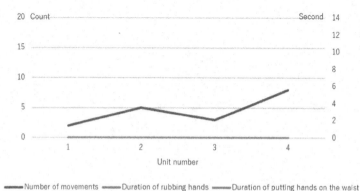

Fig. 23. The changes in *tsukkomi* movement for "Milkboy."

5   Conclusion

In this study, by focusing on the Milkboy's *manzai*, we proposed a method for analyzing their *manzai*. We extracted the basic units that make up *manzai* and analyzed their changes in various topics. These analyses clarified the attractive and skillful mechanism of laughter's progress called "back and forth *manzai*."

Acknowledgement. This research was partially supported by JSPS KAKENHI 20H04096, etc.

References

1. M-1 Grand Prix official Homepage, https://www.m-1gp.com/archive/2019/. (Accessed 19 Feb 2021). (in Japanese)
2. ORICON NEWS Homepage. https://www.oricon.co.jp/news/2151696/full/. (Accessed 19 Feb 2021) (in Japanese)
3. Toyokeizai Net Homepage. https://toyokeizai.net/articles/-/322518. (Accessed 19 Feb 2021) (in Japanese)

4. Akashishoten WebMedia Homepage. https://webmedia.akashi.co.jp/posts/3620. (Accessed 19 Feb 2021) (in Japanese)
5. Haranomachi   Homepage.   https://www.haranomachi.com/entry/2019/12/25/235020. (Accessed 19 Feb 2021) (in Japanese)
6. Note Homepage. https://note.com/ash3/n/n6034c2854d5f. (Accessed 19 Feb 2021) (in Japanese)
7. Hiroaki, K., Levi, S., Takashi, M.: Analysis of the dynamic structure of Manzai: toward a natural utterance-timing control. Trans. Human Interf. Soci. **9**, 379–390 (2007) (in Japanese)
8. Hiromichi, H.: Performative awareness of the tsukkomi role in Manzai talks and skit performances, IEICE technical report, vol. HCS2011–42, pp. 83–86 (2011) (in Japanese)
9. Masashi, O., Masato, O., Mika, E., Hitoshi, I.: Multimodal analysis of Manzai dialogue toward constructing a dialogue-based instruction agent model. Japan Soc. Fuzzy Theory Intell. Inf. **20**(4), 526–539 (2008) (in Japanese)
10. Michiya, Y.: Why "Hitori Knights" is Fun? ~ from the viewpoints of multimodal analysis. Trans. Human Inter. Soc. **21**(3), 73–78 (2019) (in Japanese)
11. 安倍 達雄, 漫才における「ツッコミ」の類型とその表現効果, 国語学研究と資料, (Originally written in Japanese. Can be translated as: Tatsuo, A.: Types of "tsukkomi" in comics and their expression effects. Japanese Lang. Res. Mater. **28**, 48–60 (2005)
12. 真下 遼, 梅谷 智弘, 北村 達也, 灘本 明代, つかみ・本ネタ・オチから構成される漫才ロボット台本自動生成手法の提案
(Originally written in Japanese. Can be translated as: Ryo, M., Tomohiro, U., Tatsuya, K., Akiyo, N.: Proposal of a manzai robot script automatic generation method consisting of Tsukami, Hon-neta, and Ochi. ARG SIG-WI2 **4** 14 (2014)
13. Central Japan Railway Company, https://recommend.jr-central.co.jp/n700s/_thichbox/movie2.html. (Accessed 19 Feb 2021) (in Japanese)

Participatory Practices in a Miniature Community Museum Based on Interaction Design Approaches

Lili Zheng⬥, Geng Huang⁽⊠⁾⬥, and Pei Wang⬥

Donghua University, Shanghai 200051, China
1310632056@qq.com

Abstract. Interaction design makes designs based on human behavior and user experiences. From the perspective of social innovation and ecological sustainability, design activities can become the main drivers of social change if they are effective, long-lasting, easy to disseminate, and help accelerate social innovation. Interaction designers, with their expertise in optimizing user experience through innovative design, provide solutions to social problems such as poverty, the hollowing out of communities, and an aging population. Designers achieve these goals through conveying more accurate information in their works, and they put innovative design elements into traditional communities to help those communities improve and update themselves. One project form of these innovative efforts by interaction designers is the emergence of miniature community museums. With compact space, these miniature museums can perfectly fit the needs of antiquated communities, which usually have limited vacant spaces. Despite their small space, these museums, equipped with all the essential functions of museums in traditional forms, can become part of the more significant effort to revive community culture. Furthermore, they can encourage co-governance through participatory activities and thus help enrich community culture.

Keywords: Interaction design · Miniature community museums · Co-governance by multiple parties

1 Introduction

1.1 Introducing the Research Question

As social innovation becomes a new tool for exploring social transformation, the drive from the community prompts a bottom-up cultural renaissance and its regeneration. At present, China's community culture construction is in the initial emerging stage, and the accelerated flow of community residents and immature practice methods have exacerbated the homogenization of community culture, making it increasingly difficult for residents to empathize with community culture. The *Technical Guidelines for Community Living Circle Planning* [1] issued by the Ministry of Natural Resources of China in 2021 set new standards for the organization of community functional spaces, which

© Springer Nature Switzerland AG 2022

M. Rauterberg et al. (Eds.): HCII 2022, LNCS 13520, pp. 104–118, 2022.
https://doi.org/10.1007/978-3-031-18158-0_7

include multiple types of cultural and experiential shared spaces. This is in extreme contrast to the current scarcity of physical dimensions in public areas. The discovery of the housing stock and the creation of humanized cultural experience spaces is a major difficulty in developing public spaces in communities today. During the 14th Five-Year Plan period, the residential stock will be fully utilized to promote the pace of urban renewal. Community participatory museums have come to the forefront as the development of diverse communities stimulates awareness of the value of living in a community in a better cultural context.

The concept of "participatory community museums" comes from Nina Simon's description of participatory museums as "a place where audiences can create, share, and communicate with others around their content" [2]. This concept of participatory community museums, when taking root in communities, can deliver a whole new operating model for communities. A miniature museum is a place for providing comprehensive services for residents, showcasing the artistic and historical culture of a community, reflecting the collective consciousness of residents, and serving as a cultural bond connecting community residents. It also turns passive consumers into active participants, contributors, and even decision-makers as community governance shifts into a new model characterized by the voluntary organization by the people through power transformation and shared governance. However, most community museums in China have directly transplanted the layout and operation model of traditional museums, so some of these museums end up merely "eye candies" because they have poor interactive designs and thus lack resident participation. In addition, the physical size and operating costs of the museums are in conflict with the resources available in the community. This field project intends to correct these deficiencies by connecting residents with the community environment through better interaction design and the introduction of diverse and engaging media (i.e., products, projects, spaces, etc.). This paper therefore applies the fourth dimension of interaction design (i.e., how to design places where environmental interactions take place [3]) and uses the participatory interaction model to conduct a series of experiments in the community, such as starting participatory activities and building miniature museums to ignite a sense of cultural belonging to the community among residents. This paper will then evaluate the results of this project with the triangle product feature model (Fig. 1).

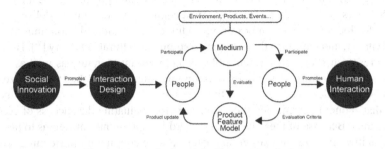

Fig. 1. Theoretical model of interaction design

1.2 Research Background

Social innovation is a process of delivering change, and it reaches socially accepted goals in new manners. To accommodate the transition towards sustainable development, the attributes of interaction design have changed in recent years, with the research focus gradually shifting more towards "perceptual interaction" and "interpersonal interaction." Richard Buchanan, former dean of CMU's School of Design, has interpreted the concept of interaction design in this way: "interaction is how one person connects with another through the medium of a "product" [3]. A "product" is not limited to an artifact: a product can be a law, a plan, an organization, a piece of software, and all the other man-made things. As the understanding of the term "product" becomes more diverse, the value of interaction design shifts from information dissemination to interpersonal connection, and the interaction model gradually switches from the traditional human-object and object-to-object interaction model to a participatory interaction model. The participatory interaction model refers to applying social interaction to transform users from mere participants to co-builders, and the essence of this model meets the need for a bottom-up community-based participatory museum.

Museums are spaces to showcase collections of cultural artifacts and works through permanent exhibitions or special exhibitions. The public, as viewers, has to be present in the exhibition space all along and engage in the whole process. In 1992, media scholar Henry Jenkins proposed a contrast between "passive" viewing in the past and "engaging" participation in modern media. Nina Simon further proposed the idea of "participatory museum based on the concept of Web 2.0, aiming to restore connections with the public and emphasizing the importance of participation from the audience [4]. The world's first community museum serving the public is the Anacostia Community Museum, which was built in 1967 [5]. John Kinard, founding director of the museum, believed that community museums should meet the challenges of social problems through new ways of thinking, and the local community members should be the planners and decision-makers. Miniature participatory museums can promote sharing in communities and encourage cultural output. They also transform residents from mere passive participants into active co-builders of the community, asserting citizens' rights to be involved in the governance of community matters.

In the 1980s, the idea of community museums was first introduced to China, providing new ways of thinking and new methods to preserve and popularize local culture in China. Scholars in the field of Museology treat community museums as delivering new lifestyles for local residents, empowering traditional or "outdated" communities with cultural vitality, and they have the potential to stimulate cultural creativity [6]. However, based on research studies on current policies and relevant literature as well as related cases, it is found that most community museums are small in size: they vary in size from 5 m^2 to 500 m^2. Generally speaking, they are not very well-known, and most people assume that economic profits are the key criteria for evaluating the success of community museums. Because of these factors, it is hard for community museums to take root in communities. In terms of exhibition contents, these community museums also have certain deficiencies. Many exhibitions are outdated in forms with no updates for years, and the contents are not properly adapted to fit in with the local culture. The result is that community museums are mistakenly regarded as "enemies" who take away public resources from the community. It is clear that the museums for the community should have an effective operation and win empathy from residents to ensure their survival in the long run and the sustainability of successful events.

1.3 Research Significance

Social innovation creates changes at a local scale in various perspectives, and it depends on the complex interplay among measures from disparate areas [7]. Community culture reflects the cultural mentality of local organizations and includes both explicit and implicit components, from material culture and spiritual culture to institutional culture [8]. By applying the interaction theory in a practical case, the authors of this paper intend to verify how human-computer interaction shifts towards interpersonal interaction and assist more miniature community museums in taking root in communities and maintaining effective operation in the long run in the following aspects:

Preserving and Revitalizing Community Culture. Community culture creates a platform for people across social classes to communicate with each other and offers a shared vision for high-quality public life, which accommodates both differences and similarities. Community culture also helps individuals from all social classes to find meaning in their lives [9]. As community museums emerge, people begin to reflect on how cultural development lacks behind when urbanization is taking on a rapid speed. They have also realized that community vitality can be a crucial driver of economic and cultural development. In China, museums for the community are just getting started, and there are even fewer theories on community museums, especially those targeting their local specialties, level of integration with community culture, and sustainable value generation in the long run.

Updating and Utilizing Community Micro-spaces. The definition of micro-space scales is based on the standard area determined for different functional spaces as specified in the *Technical Guidelines for Community Life Circle Planning* [1] issued by the Ministry of Natural Resources of China in 2021. At present, small and medium-sized old communities constitute the major part of Chinese communities, many of which suffer from poor planning, low construction standards, inadequate supporting facilities, and lack of effective management [10]. With increased community population density and non-standard construction projects, community public space is decreasing. Miniature community museums bring new vitality when community resources are under enormous pressure. They are able to meet the basic demands of community revitalization with limited inventory space and at the same time to educate and entertain local residents.

Transforming and Improving Participation from Community Residents. As early as 2012, the Party's 18th National Congress Report proposed that "we should focus on building a socialist social management system with Chinese characteristics and accelerate the formation of a social management system led by the Party committee, responsible by the government, coordinated by the society, joined by the public, and guaranteed by the rule of law [11]. "Public participation" is a method used to govern communities in recent years and has achieved positive results and feedback in practice. Its essence is a way to deliver governance "driven by the will of the residents" and to safeguard the rights of the public will. It also plays an important role in enhancing community cohesion and promoting harmonious development in communities.

Applying interaction design methods in the context of revitalizing community culture, this paper sets up a new framework integrating the elements of cultural regeneration, commercial markets, and community services. Based on this framework, this paper further explores how participatory community museums can have the potential to regenerate local community culture and thus offers first-hand experience and shed new light on the preservation, regeneration, and sustainable development of local and community cultures in China.

1.4 Research Methodology

This paper combines theoretical and practical approaches to the design and operation of miniature community museums by connecting interactive activity designs with observations, interviews, and questionnaires in communities. The following research on behaviors has obtained the informed consent of the participants.

Community Observation: Based on our review of existing literature, we conducted research and analysis of the community environment. We collected information, including the cultural characteristics of the community, the power structure and relationship of community figures, as well as major community events and folk stories, to have a more comprehensive understanding of community history and culture; We also tracked the flow of people and timing and investigated existing and missing services, which can help facilitate site selection and make adjustments to services in the later stage.

Interviews and Questionnaires: The community members were categorized into children, young people, older adults, and staff members, and through questionnaires and specific interviews targeted at certain individuals with their own unique roles in the community, we were able to understand the community situation from different perspectives and summarize the issues in the community, residents' needs, residents' expectations, community culture awareness, and willingness to participate in the community. Through role analysis, we can accurately determine the most urgent needs of different groups so as to design effective participatory activities and encourage the co-building of the miniature museum.

Participatory Design Activities in the Whole Process: Through scenario orientation and catalyst events [12], we brought together multiple interest groups and set common goals for them to complete specific activities, including surveys and construction activities. We also assigned residents the right to execute and supervise these activities throughout the process to improve their experience. In this process, we could obtain fair, impartial, and professional research results and thus transition towards the construction and operation of the miniature museum.

Model Validation: Richard Buchanan, while teaching at CMU, proposed that a well-designed product should be "useful", "usable", and "desirable". In this paper, this product model will be used as the evaluation criteria, and resident participation and feedback will be used as a reference to assess the feasibility and effectiveness of the practice.

2 Exploring Design Methods for Miniature Community Museums

2.1 A General Introduction of the Selected Community

The site for this participatory project is located at Hongqiao Airport New Village, Changning District, Shanghai, and this community is near the Shanghai Hongqiao International Airport. Hongqiao Airport New Village was built-in 1978, and the village covers an area of around 160,000 m^2. It is an extra-large community with a resident population of over 10,000 people and a professional community staff of approximately 50 people. With its unique population structure and geographic location, the village has witnessed Shanghai's reform and opening-up as well as the changes in China's civil aviation. Hongqiao Airport New Village is also home to many old-generation aviators. In the early years, the houses there were allocated as welfare housing to employees working in China Eastern Airlines, Shanghai Airport, and the Aviation Administration. The village carries many memories and stories, and until today, many people working in the aviation industry still live there.

With accelerated population movement in Shanghai, the structure of the community has also changed dramatically, and the cultural landscape of the new village has become more diverse, while the original airport community culture has gradually been lost, and community cohesion is gradually declining. Under the goals set by policy guides in "the Shanghai 14th Five-Year Plan Vision" and "Creating a 15-min living circle for community residents", Hongqiao Airport New Village Committee decided to build a miniature participatory museum with community culture and aviation theme as one of Chengjiaqiao Street's "One Street, One Way" projects. It invited the Shanghai Big Fish Community Development Center (later referred to as "Big Fish") as a third-party organization to link together residents and social resources to create the community's own culture brand featuring the theme of aviation. Inviting a professional third-party organization can make the project more professional and fairer.

2.2 Conducting Community Observations, Interviews, and Questionnaires

Launching a new community project is a step-by-step process, and mapping up the human environment of the community is the first task. In the early stage of the project, in-depth and comprehensive research work was carried out through communicating with the community committee, holding interviews with experts and typical users, giving lectures, and opening "Small White Houses" (bases for conducting research work). A total of 7 research activities were held, with about 3,500 participants, six on-site meetings for renovation plans, two hearings for residents, ten interviews with typical users, more than 20 field visits, 140 valid questionnaire responses, 50 aviation stories, and 26 opinion polls on color choices for the museum. And based on the above research results, the following conclusions were reached:

In terms of physical space: If the target of establishing "a 15-min living circle" was applied as criteria, then the following facilities at Hongqiao Airport New Village reached the target by meeting the needs of children, young people, elderly people, and these facilities included kindergartens, schools, parks, supermarkets, life service points, chess, and card rooms, etc. However, other facilities failed to meet the target, and they included community restaurants, cultural activity rooms, and places for entertainment activities. Most of the facilities are outdated, which is not in line with the growing needs of the residents.

In terms of community relations: currently, millennials constitute a large part of the total population (75%) at the Hongqiao Airport New Village. The constant flow of residents and increased mobility of tenants make it challenging to promote community culture because residents there show huge differences in their level of belonging to the community and their connection with the culture. Because of these latest trends, the local cultural identity is gradually in decline, and the problems of social exclusion and group conflicts begin to emerge.

2.3   Holding Full Process Participatory Activities

The preliminary surveys and research gave residents an initial understanding of participatory museums, laying the foundation for the later scenario orientation and catalyst events. After holding follow-up activities and discussions, the "Little White House" became a temporary shared space for managing office work, holding activities, and encouraging resident participation. According to the statistics, "Little White House" has held 15 participatory activities co-organized by the Big Fish and the residents' committee, with about 950 people participating. The initial activities were led by the Big Fish, and the main purpose was to attract the attention of residents of all ages and to find out what residents truly wanted from the community and their visions for the museum. Some of these activities included "Community Day", "Flying Chess Competition", and "Family Photo for Soy Sauce". After the initial activities, residents became aware of their rights in the community and saw new possibilities for the future. They were inspired to become part of the community project and began to organize their own community activities, such as "storytelling", "children's chess tournament", and "mobile phone class for the elderly".

A variety of targeted theme activities were held to stimulate the interest of and participation of many residents, many of whom began to provide community stories and valuable cultural collections to the museum voluntarily. They also helped link together available resources, creating favorable conditions for the construction of a multicultural, democratic, and collaborative community-based participatory museum (Fig. 2).

Fig. 2. Photos of participatory community activities [15]

2.4 A Summary of the Demands for Miniature Community Museums

Meeting the Cultural Needs for Community Brands. China is in the era of the "image economy", i.e. an economy where value and profits are derived from images and their effects [13]. As one of the community's brand images, community museums represent not only the cultural diversity of different communities but also the innovative capacity of communities. Based on the principle of brand systematization and linkage, the community museum can attract the attention of both social enterprises and public welfare organizations, allowing the community to absorb more community capital and funds within a short period of time. In this way, it can make up for the lack of initial operating funds. Establishing a community brand enables community residents to become founders of the brand as well as the service providers of the brand, enjoying profits from the brand as well as gaining better service experiences.

Meeting the Needs for the Democratization of Community Arts. The popularization of art education has always been one of the national measures to cultivate "all-rounded talents". In recent years, museums have also been discussing the democratization of art or the popularization of public art education in museums. The integration of museums into the community has promoted the democratization of art while at the same time subconsciously enhancing the popularity of art education in the community, allowing residents to understand the aesthetics and beauty of art from a distance, thus stimulating public creativity artistic innovation, and alleviating solidification.

Meeting the Needs for Expressing "Locality" in Community Cultures. Community "locality" includes community styles, living habits, management systems, unique resources, cultural styles, literature, and art. While traditional museums focus on history, artifacts, documents, and photographs, the appeal of community museums is that they not only share valuable collections with academic value but also focus on the "common culture" created by residents of the community. According to Paul Wills, "common culture" refers to lifestyles that give meaning to our lives and it educates people, and adds a touch of beauty to people's lives in their daily living space and social practices [14]. The museum is also an expression of the local nature of the museum, in the form of interesting stories from the neighborhood, displays of talents, and residents' visions for the future of the community, and it is also a place where the stories of people's lives are woven together in a community.

Meeting the Needs for Multi-dimensional Space Utilization. Miniature community museums often have limited physical space, so some of their functions have to be superimposed upon each other. From the physical dimension, community museums consist of rooms for storing collections, displaying collections, offering a socializing space for residents and office space for staff members; from the human dimension, community museums need to meet people's spiritual and cultural needs while also serving their functions for education and entertainment and holding public activities such as residents' meetings and parent-child interaction activities; from the operational dimension, community museums, aside from displaying and selling cultural products, should also serve other functions including managing the flow of visitors, planning inner spaces, and setting up regulations for visitors.

Meeting the Needs for Multifaceted Participation and Shared Governance. On the one hand, "multifaceted participation" guarantees the rationality, integrity, and sustainable revitalization of the community's cultural output. On the other hand, "multifaceted participation" provides the opportunity to express itself and create value for each participating member, ensuring fairness in the development process. The transparency of information and self-awareness in the participation process creates a good communication platform for different parties, which is of practical significance to alleviating neighborhood conflicts and promoting community development. Space Functions.

2.5 Space Functions and Exhibition Strategies

Based on our research of the inventory space in Airport New Village, we finally selected Room No.1 on the first floor of the Community Activity Center, which was formerly the office address of Oriental Information Center, with an area of about 88 m². This room is an old building with a series of problems including outdated facilities and construction violations because of its old age and poor maintenance. The site is located at the center of the Airport Village, with the Hongqiao Airport New Village Committee to its north, the Lotus Pond Park to its south, and the activity plaza and community business areas to the east. High foot traffic and levels of activity make it a more suitable site for community miniature museums (Fig. 3).

Fig. 3. Photos of the original building [15]

Space Functions. Based on collected information and data from preliminary participatory workshops and field research, the renovation takes place in the following aspects. First, the museum facade color is chosen to match the airport's properties of blue and gray, and the original red brick finish on the roof is removed and replaced with pure white, while the billboards, pipes, air conditioning units, and other illegal and disorganized equipment are removed and renovated. Also, the images of airplanes drawn by children during community activities are processed with parametric designs, and they are then used as patterns on the handrails on the second floor of the building. These designs intend to add more "airplane" elements to the museum. For the facade of the museum (Room No. 1), white aluminum panels are used to outline the doors, windows, and public notice boards on the periphery of the museum, highlighting the presence of the museum while administering effective information interactions between the public and the museum. Considering the complexity and varied age groups of the museum's users, its interior facilities and equipment need to offer a variety of interactive experiences. After discussions, it was agreed that the facade area would be used as a community cultural display area, and the display area would be enlarged by adding mobile partitions, such as "mobile panels" and "rotating windows". This renovation work can retain more free ground area as a temporary activity carrier in the future. Functional partitions would be divided into a foyer, an area for creative culture, an activity area, a screening room, and a temporary studio. Except for the creative area, the rest of the space can be easily set up for multiple uses to improve operational flexibility for the museum in the later stage (Fig. 4).

Fig. 4. Photos of the exterior of the renovated community museum [15]

Exhibition Strategies. As the first participatory miniature community museum in Hongqiao Airport New Village, the theme of its first exhibition needs to highlight the special "spirit of aviation culture" and the collective memory of the Hongqiao Airport New Village. It should also reflect how local residents of the past three generations feel about the community as well as the impressions and expectations of the people who study, work, and live around the community. After deliberations, the theme of the first exhibition is set as "we are all airport people", which aims to bring the community members together, to awaken the memory of "airport people", to share the unique sentiment of this community to new residents and community members, and to build a sense of trust and to belong among residents.

The first exhibition is divided into five sections: (1) "The Seal of the New Village" section introduces the history of civil aviation and the community's cultural history, and it is jointly created by scholars, designers, and residents in collaboration with the residents' committee. It features memories and stories from the past to the present, taking community development and changes in residents' lives as the starting point; (2) The second section, named "I was present at the major events" tells the history of community development recorded by Luo Keping, a former civil aviation journalist and resident of Airport New Village. The display items include old photos of the community, work certificates, old objects, and old magazines; (3) The section named "Micro-documentary of Three Generations of Airport People" mainly records the new outlook of the new airport village and the new ideas of the diversified community in the new era, as well as the blessings and expectations of the community for the new airport village; (4) The "Community Ecology" section shows that the rich vegetation and beautiful natural environment are important parts of a good community life, so this section places specimens of the vegetation in the community in the display window to show the diversity of the community ecology; (5) The "Interactive Co-creation" section features the work uniforms of the airport personnel jointly created by the village committee, residents, Hongqiao Airport primary school students, and New Century Hongqiao Kindergarten students. They co-designed these uniforms to form vivid, lovely cartoon signs for display in windows, showing respect for the airport staff and the praise for their dedication to their work (Fig. 5).

Fig. 5. Indoor exhibition photos of the reconstructed community museum [15]

2.6 Operation and Shared Governance

Miniature community museums need to prioritize costs in their operations, so a "1 + 2" approach is adopted, whereby community management teams take a leading role in daily operations with the help of community residents and third-party organizations. Community management teams are mainly responsible for managing the operating funds, rules and regulations, and review exhibition themes; third-party organizations can serve as auxiliary parties to relieve the community's financial pressure while providing professional and reliable strategies and methods for museum operations to minimize the risk of operational failure; local residents can work as museum volunteers and temporary curators to make museum exhibitions and activities more local, helping to utilize the potential and talent within the community. Currently, the community museum has a daily traffic of about 400 people per day, and has conducted activities such as "community yoga classes" and "community governance meetings".

The key to the continued success of the museum is strengthening its core competencies. In order to take advantage of the "culture of the airport ", after deliberations by both designers and community residents, "Mini White Cloud" cartoon image was designed as the IP of the community museum and the village's own publications, as well as cultural and creative products, were also produced for sale and promotion. In the future, the museum would cooperate with outside museums and invite artists to hold participatory art creation activities in the community so as to enrich the cultural and educational contents of the community museum and enhance the brand value of the community.

Fig. 6. The cultural and creative products of the community museum [15]

3   An Evaluation of the Results

3.1   Community-Level Evaluation

Community museums are evaluated by the triangle model of usefulness, usability, and desirability; the actual output and resident feedback are used as the judging criteria. The evaluation is illustrated as follows (Figs. 6 and 7).

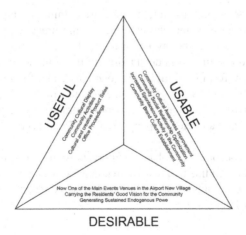

Fig. 7. Triangular model of community achievement evaluation

Being Useful: The community museum is equipped with the functions of displaying community culture, holding group activities, selling creative culture products, providing space for office proceedings and so on;

Being Usable: The community museum has improved recognition for community culture, upgraded community social relations, and established a cultural brand for the community;

Being Desirable: Since the completion of the community museum, it has become one of the main activity places in the New Airport Village, carrying the residents' vision of a better community, and it shows that the community itself can regenerate its culture in a sustainable manner.

The Airport New Village Museum thus demonstrates a good balance of these three features, thus proving the effectiveness of the practical project.

3.2 Social-Level Evaluation

The birth of the participatory miniature museum in the Hongqiao Airport New Village community has attracted enthusiastic attention and feedback from the community, as well as the attention of many media and scholars, and about 30 news media have reported on the museum so far. Academic exchanges have been held with Shanghai Visual Institute, Jiangnan University, Shenzhen University, and other universities. It has become a demonstration and visiting the site for outstanding cases of community renewal in Shanghai, providing valuable experience for the preservation of domestic community cultural and sustainable innovation.

3.3 Limitations and Outlook

This project is the first attempt to build a miniature community museum in Shanghai, so there are many difficulties and shortcomings in the practice and operation of the museum. In the early stage of the project, it took a lot of time for us to integrate into the community due to insufficient understanding of the community. Also, "community participation" is a new form of community governance and the majority of residents have little understanding of this new governance model, which makes it difficult to carry out participatory activities. The majority of people attracted by participatory activities are children, middle-aged and elderly people, so the social needs of young people are still unexplored.

As COVID-19 has become normal, in the future, the community museum will extend the "online service" branch line to assist the maintenance of interpersonal relations and information sharing of community residents under the pandemic through the internet and human-computer interaction.

4   Conclusion

Miniature participatory museums can be seen as an innovative application of interaction design methods in the context of social innovation, and they adjust the relations among people and culture through building an interactive space. With this space, community museums gathered together the government, community residents, third-party organizations, and social resources to carry out participatory survey activities, and they are all involved in the build-up and operation of the museum. The museum would also help establish a series of procedures for optimizing the community's cultural environment that is compatible with local culture, encourage innovative thinking, and increase emotional cohesion, tolerance, and openness. These procedures would promote the sustainable development of the community, increase the cultural literacy of the public, and foster public awareness of shared governance among community residents.

Acknowledgments. Our work would be impossible without the support from the Chengjiaqiao Street Community, Changning District, Shanghai. We want to thank them for providing the site and financial support for the project. We also express our gratitude to the Chengjiaqiao Street Airport New Village Committee for providing the staff and information support for the project. Our thanks also go to the Big Fish Community Development Center, Xinhua Road Street, Changning District, Shanghai, for providing technical and theoretical support for the project and providing the data and images for the whole project process.

References

1. TD/T 1062-2021 Technical Guide for Community Life Circle Planning (Submitted for Approval). Ministry of Natural Resources of China (2021)
2. Hu, K.: Research on the Significance and Application of Dialogue in Museum Exhibitions. Zhejiang University (2017)
3. Buchanan, R.: Former Dean of CMU Carnegie Mellon School of Design Richard Buchanan Explains the Four Dimensions of Interaction Design. https://zhuanlan.zhihu.com/p/364374848
4. Tong, F.: A study of museum participation culture in the context of digital technology. Art Panorama **12**, 118–120 (2020)
5. Qiao, X.: Community Museums: Going to the World. China Culture Daily, 16 Feb 2011 (006)
6. Pan, S.: The Chinese experience of ecological (community) museums and academic critical reflection. Southeast Cult. **6** (2017)
7. Manzini, E., Xin, X., Sun, Z.: The creation of things: social innovation and design. Creativ. Design **3**, 4–8 (2017)
8. Song, W.: Research on Residents' Willingness to Participate in the Construction of Urban Community Culture. Suzhou University (2013)
9. Yan, Y.: Cultural confidence and collaborative community cultural governance innovation. Magaz. Study Explor. **2**, 48–53 (2019)
10. Yu, Y., Jiang, L.: Research on micro-renewal design of public facilities in antiquated urban communities. Furnit. Interior Decorat. **10**, 107–111 (2021). https://doi.org/10.16771/j.cn43-1247/ts.2021.10.020
11. An, M.: Modernization of rural governance (Pencil talk II). J. Hubei Minzu Univ. (Philos. Soc. Sci. Edn.) **38**(2), 1–27 (2020). https://doi.org/10.13501/j.cnki.42-1328/c.2020.02.001

12. Buchanan, R., et al.: Design Problems-Innovation Patterns in Interactive Thinking, vol. 10, p. 86. Tsinghua University Press (2017)
13. Gao, C.: Introduction to the Economics of Fashion Industry. Economy and Management Publishing House, vol. 5 (2011)
14. Mu, X.: Research on the participation of self-organization in community cultural governance in Chinese urban communities. Chinese National Academy of Arts (2019)
15. Images are cited from the Big Fish Community Development Centre, Xinhua Road Street, Changning District, Shanghai

A Study on the Virtual Delivery of Cultural Courtesy: AR Services for Packaging

Ye Zhou[1]([✉]) and Sunghee Ahn[2]

[1] IDAS HongIk University, Seoul, Korea
zhouye202109@163.com
[2] School of Design Convergence, HongIk University, Sejong, Korea

Abstract. For a long time, gift packaging has been a means of conveying the sender's feeling and message just as important as the gift itself. This has been a part of social communication mean for a long time especially in East Asian societies. Therefore, packaging used to be a form of cultural communication which carries much personal and social meaning by using all kinds of material. In the twenty-first century, under the social atmosphere of sustainability, such cultural communication is regarded as vain, and the use of recycled packaging materials or the omission of packaging itself is increasingly common. Also, due to the COVID-19 pandemic, it is even more difficult to meet face-to-face and convey thankful and beloved feelings.

The aim of this research is to study how non-material communication can contribute to people's emotional satisfaction within the object exchange. The purpose is to develop a virtual packaging service using augmented reality (AR) technology, while reflecting people's cultural and personal needs, as a sustainable user experience (UX) approach. This research analyzes user perceptions and attitudes towards virtual packaging through a quantitative study of 200 participants and evaluates users' acceptability and cultural needs for immaterial packaging. Based on this, a new AR packaging service is developed which can bring psychological and spiritual satisfaction to people, unlike virtual messages and material packaging which have simple delivery purposes.

This research will promote the use of AR technology as a cultural bridge between physical packaging and virtual communication delivering people's hopes and cheerful minds, as well as a factor for sustainable development and the green economy.

Keywords: Virtual packaging · AR UX · Cultural sustainability

1 Research Background

From the social and cultural perspectives, gift wrapping and packaging is not only a layer of protection for presents with a short-lived value and function. It also reflects givers' intentions, as well as the time and energy they spent. Although several definitions for 'emotional behavior' can be found, all existing approaches refer to 'human-like' agents when speaking about software systems that mimic human behavior biased by emotions

© Springer Nature Switzerland AG 2022
M. Rauterberg et al. (Eds.): HCII 2022, LNCS 13520, pp. 119–127, 2022.
https://doi.org/10.1007/978-3-031-18158-0_8

[1]. From human experience research perspective, the maximal courtesy process on social communication is more less related with this emotional side satisfaction. Therefore, in order to enable people to express their affection and accept gifts in a greener and more innovation way, the design aims to create an AR application, through which people can design packaging online by using AR technology and more diverse elements like sounds and GIFs.

In this study, people's emotional satisfaction was considered, and the positive cultural characteristics of giving and receiving gifts as an expression of heart was reflected as far as possible [2]. Purpose of this study is to reduce wasteful consumption of packaging materials, which is a severe problem due to the expansion of delivery and takeout in the context of the recent pandemic. An alternative method was proposed to address the issue.

2   Design Insight and Hypothesis

Ultimate goal of this research is to develop an AR application with which can make personal virtual wrapping, decorate his (her) package and send it to recipients. In this research, participants creating the AR gift packaging can prepare the unique and fantastic packaging by themselves, and creators can sell their own designs on this platform. A recipient of the gift can interact with the giver based on the gift in a more interesting way after the receipt. Through the AR application, stakeholders can emotionally engage and fulfil the lack of materiality in object-related communication, especially in gift handout. In addition, it is more fun and meaningful in preparation. The main design concept in the development of this application rests upon "No recycle, no waste, more sustainable, more interesting". In order to provide users with better experience and make hypothesis visible and feasible, quantitative research questionnaires followed by qualitative research tools, such as persona and development of a user journey map, were conducted in this paper. In this process, design insights for the application and a designed wireframe including the user interface were extracted in this research. AR technology becomes a bridge between virtual digital culture and personal communication in real world.

3   AR Application Development

3.1   Questionnaire Architecture

The existing mobile UX design approaches can be applied to mobile–based AR application development. However, AR application design has different context. In AR application people engaged both physically and mentally by the process of using application and mobile phone [3]. With this reason, this research has been conducted on-line questionnaire as a quantitative research stage which gives ground for hypothesis. In order to understand consumers' needs and attitudes towards immaterial packaging, a questionnaire was made by the authors. The main question is about gift packaging and acceptance of the technology. A total of 200 questionnaires were distributed on the Internet, with 6 related questions.

The survey includes the following aspects:

(1) Basic information on people giving gifts and packaging.
(2) Consumers' preference for packaging.
(3) Consumers' attention to technology.
(4) Acceptance and reasons for AR packaging.

3.2 Analysis of Research Results

1. Analysis of basic information: 82% of the subjects will give gifts to their beloved ones, of which 78% will choose to wrap gifts and 22% will not do so. In this case, reasons that people do not wrap gifts were found. The main reason is that they think the packaging is just for decoration and fails to express their wishes and alike, so they do not care about it (76.5%). Some do not take hand-made gifts into consideration (65.5%) and suggest that the traditional wrapping is tedious for a recipient (42%). The analysis shows that there are still many people who are willing to prepare gifts for others in order to express their affection and prefer to packaging them. However, the cumbersome and boring process of traditional packaging may stop them physically and mentally.
2. Consumers' preference for packaging: based on the questionnaire results, compared with the traditional packaging (35.9%), most consumers prefer the packaging with sounds (54.49%) and electronic packaging (51.28%). 43.59% of the subjects said if the packaging offering much more interaction is preferable, which indicates that, with the development of the entertainment industry, most people are no longer just satisfied with traditional material packaging, and are willing to embrace strong sensibility and interaction, even immaterial packaging.
3. Attention to the AR technology: most of the subjects(74.5%)usually pay attention to technological information and products, and also experience AR or VR.
4. In the questionnaire, 'Pokémon Go' game was mentioned which was a smash hit in 2016. This game leverages AR effectively and millions of users could play it on their smart phones, which is a successful project bringing AR technology into people's life and enable more people to familiarize and access to AR. The data from the survey shows 71% of the users played the game before and 41.5% of them loved it. 16.5% of the subjects said they never played it before, but they have heard of this game and think it is interesting. This demonstrates that the AR technology has been gradually permeated into people's daily life and accepted by more people who are willing to apply new technology and enjoy the changes in life brought by the technology.
5. Acceptance and reasons for AR packaging: firstly, users who chose to accept AR packaging instead of the traditional one account for 76% of the total. The main reason is that AR packaging is more novel, creative, and eco-friendly than the traditional one. Meanwhile, this proves the advancement of the technology. Secondly, 24% of the consumers choose not to accept AR packaging mainly because they worry that immaterial packaging has less sense of ceremony and cannot be preserved. From this question, it can be concluded that most people can accept and use AR technology to change the traditional packaging method, but there are still some issues to be considered.

Based on the analysis of the survey results, consumers regard gifts as a bond to convey their emotions, and gift packaging can indirectly express more affection. With the advancement of technology, people have accepted the changes brought by technology, and it is trendy that surging number of products will transform from the material form to the immaterial one. Users prefer a more interactive and creative form than the traditional packaging. However, in the design process, it is also crucial to thinking about how to enable users have the sense of ceremony brought by wrapping.

3.3 Persona Development for AR Application

In order to find target users and better understand some behavioral habits of different consumers to optimize the design, user portraits were analyzed with the data that had been collected to analyze their pain points and demands. In this persona, 2 different types of users were summarized: the giver and the receiver. (Fig. 1).

Persona of the giver: Lens, a 28-year-old woman, is an office lady and stress-free at work. She likes to buy souvenirs, and always prepares gifts for friends and colleagues around her. Beautiful and trendy items suit her taste, and sometimes, she participates in public welfare activities. In the analysis of Len's user portrait, Len buys numerous decorations every time when she wraps a gift. These decorations are usually sold in a set, but she only uses a few decorations each time and the rest will be idle. However, the style of decorations she grows fond of are changing due to the rapidly changing trend. Len feels that this has caused waste and is unsustainable. Benny is a 31-year-old man who is a teacher. He has many friends who are not in the same city. He delivers gifts to friends on important festivals, but he never packs a present since he is too busy to prepare these things, such as purchase of materials and delivery of gifts to a post office, which will be a waste of time. On the other hand, he finds that crafting is troublesome, although he is creative. Therefore, he usually purchases gifts online and delivers them directly.

Persona of the receiver: Jane is a 22-year-old student. She usually receives gifts from others. In this case, she will be attracted and amazed for a few seconds when she notices the beautiful packaging, but she is more looking forward to the gift than the packaging. Hence, after receiving the gift, she will quickly open the packaging and throw it away, and she will not be impressed with the prepared packaging. She thinks the traditional packaging is normal and unattractive. Charles, a 23-year–old man, is a product manager. He is interested in technological products and will pay attention to contemporarily trendy topics and news. He is fond of electronic products, and is more willing to try the AR packaging than the material one, for he thinks the virtual wrapping is more interesting than the traditional one, which is more creative and environmentally friendly.

It can be analyzed from the user personas that gift givers will spend much time and energy in the process of inconvenient gift wrapping and sending. After receiving gifts, recipients care more about the gifts than the material packaging, and some of the decorations are not recyclable, which is not environmentally friendly. The target users are the people who are obsessed with trendy culture, technology, surprises and sharing. They are willing to try and apply new technology to make life better, which indicates the direction of design.

Fig. 1. Persona

3.4 Journey Map

A user journey map helps better discover the details of users' behaviors, emotions and thinks for preparing a flow chart of the application. From the journey map, (Fig. 2) there are four stages that may take place in the entire process. In the preparing stage, users purchase gifts and look for decorations for packaging, but at this step, users become annoyed. There is an application to help them make the AR packaging on smart phones and they can download the application. Then, in the packaging process, they can decorate the gifts online and there are many types of elements for them to use and edit, which interests them. After decoration, the platform will create a QR code and in the process of delivery, users stick the QR code on a box and then sent the gift. At last, in the receiving process, the recipient scans the QR code and saw the decoration effect that designed by their friends and will be surprised.

Giving and receiving of gifts are both-way behaviors, we should enable both the giver and the recipient to access to the equal level of emotional value in the process. For gift givers, they do not want to be bound by some traditional forms and hope to be more

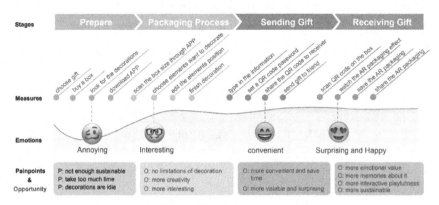

Fig. 2. User journey map

creative. For gift recipients, their interactivity with the packaging rather than the simple and same opening process is increasing.

3.5 Flow Chart Development

A flow chart features better logic and explanation of the application. When a user starts to operate the application and first of all, he/she needs to log in to it. Henceforth, it comes to the main page and there are four first-level functions: box function; decoration function; store function and myself information.

Firstly, under the box function, gift givers can choose the box size which they will decorate and receivers can scan the QR code they have received. Secondly, under the decoration function, gift givers can choose the preferable elements, such as, sounds, dynamic effects and GIFs. They could edit the position and size of the elements. When they finish, the platform will create a QR code and users can set passwords, and then share the code to recipients. Thirdly, under the store function, users can search for the themed elements they prefer and download or buy them. Meanwhile, if the users are people who have plenty of ideas and obsessed with design, the users can upload their original work on the application so that to earn money. Finally, under myself function, the users can check all the packaging they have designed and received, and they can also edit the information. This is the entire flow of this AR packaging application (Fig. 3).

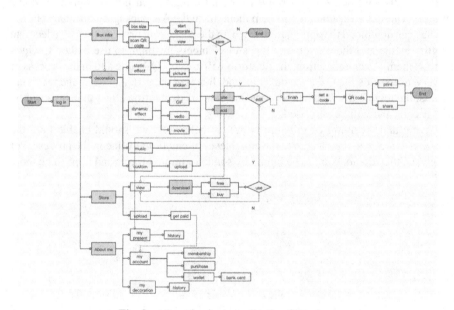

Fig. 3. AR packaging's application flow chart

3.6 Wire Frame Design

In order to sort out the correct structure of content logic and display every module clearly on smart phones, a wire frame was made. (Fig. 4) The wire frame shows the basic layout of the application, the functional hierarchy of the page, the function buttons and the jump logic of pages. Considering the pain points of users which were analyzed in the previous, some details were designed to be more user-friendly.

Firstly, users need to log in and then start decoration. This AR packaging application only has one main page, namely the homepage, and the design aims to enable users to use the application easily and figure out their needs clearly. Due to this application without complicated page jumping and functions that are not frequently used, it is suitable for middle-aged and elderly people as well. There is also a guide book to teach users how to leverage this application. Under the homepage, there are four functions: box, decoration, gallery, and mine. Users can choose any of them and different functions have diverse layout and contents. Secondly, after a recipient scans the QR code, there will be a pop-up box designed as a gift card. Users need to open the card and they can watch the designed effects. The design aims to make users get the sense of ceremony.

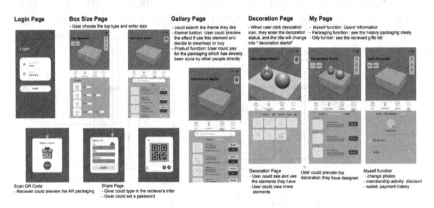

Fig. 4. AR packaging's application wire frame

4   AR Graphic User Interface

Theme color of the interface is green, which represents environmental protection, and safety. The color in the secondary concern of the interface is yellow, which represents happiness in Eastern countries. After users log in, it comes to the homepage of the application where users commence their operation. There are four functions in the homepage: box function; decoration function; gallery function and my function. When users click the "box" icon, they can choose the top's style and input the size of their boxes or they can click the "camera" button to scan their boxes to confirm the size of decorations. After the confirmation of size, the title of homepage will change from "Let's start" to "Decoration Starts" to remind users to start decoration. Then, when users click the "decoration" icon, the homepage jumps to the edit mode and there are different types of elements, such as stickers, GIFs, sounds, and pictures. Under this function, people can use the elements they have already had. At the same time, if users want to add more elements, they can click 'view more' button and the page will jump into "gallery". When users finish decoration, click "done" button, the homepage will end the edit mode and jump to the original mode. In addition, the title of homepage will change from "Decoration Starts" to "Decoration Done". In this case, users can click the "display" button to preview the effects they have designed. When they click the "share" button, there will be a box popping up which shows the information they should fill in (name, content, password). While this step is completed, there will be a QR code and users can share it to recipients. When users click the 'gallery' icon, they can see different types of elements and preview the effects to decide whether to download or buy an element. Besides, they can search for the theme they prefer. Under this function, people can directly pay for the packaging made by other users.

When users click the 'my' icon, there are functions of my gift, my packaging and myself. When they click my gift or my packaging, they will see the history of the AR packaging they have received or made. Time line of the history is from the present to the past. Under the function of myself, people can edit their profile, and when they click the 'my wallet' button, it will show the payment records and they can upload their original designs to earn some money. When users click the 'membership' button, they can buy a membership to get a discount when purchasing elements. (Fig. 5).

Fig. 5. AR packaging's application graphic user interface

Down below shows the user scenario of mobile AR application working process. It contains both side of sender and receiver of gift box. People would use their own mobile phone with the downloaded AR application. As Dowell et al. [4] see, the cultural context is very complicated and locally specific, unified package outfit cannot create happiness of gift receiving. This AR application may re-bring up humane quality of satisfaction and make the mundane delivery event to cultural communication and exchange (Fig. 6).

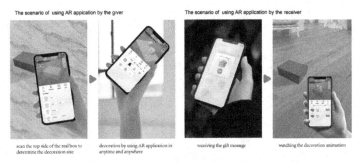

The scenario of using AR application by the giver   The scenario of using AR application by the receiver

scan the top side of the real box to determine the decoration site   decoration by using AR application in anytime and anywhere   receiving the gift message   watching the decoration animation

Fig. 6. The scenario of AR packaging application

5   Conclusion

Technology is developing rapidly, many of which are applied in people's daily life. This phenomenon influences people's lifestyle and the public is satisfied with these changes. In the future, the transformation of materiality to immateriality will become a trend. The AR virtual packaging will become a new approach of cultural output as well. Meanwhile, with the impact of COVID-19 around the world in the past two years, people cannot conduct face-to-face activities conveniently. Therefore, online models have become more frequently seen and accepted, such as online education, working and shopping.

In this study, the needs and pain points of users were analyzed through questionnaires and persona. The user journey map simulates the behaviors and emotional changes of consumers in the process of gifts preparation and packaging, so as to take into the specific functions and requirements of the application into consideration. The flow chart and the wire frame determine the structure and logic of the application that helps perfect the application. Compared with the physical packaging, the AR packaging brings creativity and participation to increasing number of users. The application is user-friendly and has little limitation about age, and people can make unique packaging for others and further the process to become more environmentally friendly.

This project aims to leverage technology to improve people's ways of life, and promote the use of AR technology as a cultural link between the physical and the virtual worlds, conveying people's affection. What's more, more people were suggested to be involved in sustainable activities in this study, and more people can do something that benefits to the environment.

References

1. Acosta, R., Esteve, J.M., Mocholí, J.A., Jaén, J.: Ecoology: an emotional augmented reality edutaiment application. In: International Conference on Cognition and Exploratory Learning in Digital Age (CELDA), pp. 19–26 (2006)
2. Wang, Q., Razzaque, M., Keng, K.: Chinese cultural values and gift-giving behavior. J. Consum. Mark. **24**(4), 214–228 (2007)
3. Dirin, A., Laine, T.H.: User experience in mobile augmented reality: emotions, challenges, opportunities and the best practices. Computers **7**, 33 (2018)
4. Dowell, D, Garrod, B., Turner, J.: Understanding value creation and word-of-mouth behaviour at cultural events. Serv. Ind. J. **39**(7-8), 498–518 (2019)

eCommerce, Business and Innovation

Human-Computer Interaction Activities as a Basis in the Development of Innovations in Process: The Case of the Colombian Exporter SMEs

Eduardo Chang Muñoz[1]([✉]) [iD], Andrés Felipe Guarín García[1] [iD],
Alpha Nieto Parejo[1] [iD], Nohora Mercado-Caruso[1] [iD],
José Fernando Gallego-Nicholls[2] [iD], and Aida Patricia Huyke Taboada[1] [iD]

[1] Universidad de la Costa, CUC, Barranquilla, Colombia
{echang1,aguarin,anieto6,aguarin,ahuyke}@cuc.edu.co
[2] ESIC Business Marketing School, Valencia, España
josefernando.gallego@esic.edu

Abstract. The incorporation of best technological practices or components guides the development of processes and promotes transformations with new approaches in organizational structures. In this regard, it is necessary to increase productivity and competitiveness levels of SMEs. However, having greater knowledge about the type of activities to be implemented for the development of innovations in process is one of the main difficulties usually hindering the growth potential of Small and Medium-sized Enterprises (SMEs). Among the key factors leading to innovation, we find the Human-Computer Interaction (HCI) activities entailing cooperation and the pursuit of R&D activities based on that increase productivity and competitiveness. Nevertheless, several young or small firms do not have those capabilities, and it is paramount for them to know which type of HCI activities they must undertake to allocate their innovation resources adequately to obtain outstanding results.

For this purpose, this paper aims to determine the effect of diverse HCI innovation activities on the deployment of innovations within exporter SMEs' processes. First, we carried out a survey for collecting data on different innovation variables encompassing both activities and processes of 56 exporter SMEs. The data analyzed in this study derive from a structured questionnaire with 21 questions, out of which 16 measured orientations to process innovation, production and distribution methods, techniques, teams and technologies for production whin improve quality; and 5 questions measure the type of innovation activities, such as R&D, links to information sources, cooperation on innovation, scientific, technological, organizational and financial actions. The main economic sectors of these firms are chemical products, fertilizers and pesticides, pharmaceutical and medications, plastic and its manufactures, iron, steel and its manufactures, minerals, oils, vegetal and animals.

The model proposed in this study through correlation tests and factorial analyses will allow companies in these economic sectors to know which are the different HCI innovation activities that should be pursued and allow them to devise strategies focusing their efforts and resources in innovative processes.

© Springer Nature Switzerland AG 2022
M. Rauterberg et al. (Eds.): HCII 2022, LNCS 13520, pp. 131–148, 2022.
https://doi.org/10.1007/978-3-031-18158-0_9

Then, correlation tests and factor analyses were undertaken to identify the main HCI drivers of process innovations in these companies. The results revealed the association between the ease of the technological component through the development of scientific and technological activities with: the number of new or significantly improved processes, techniques, equipment and computer programs to optimize production (p-value $= 0.005 \, \chi 2 = 12.67$); with the implementation of a significant and improved distribution method (p-value $= 0,001 \, \chi 2 = 15,59$) and the implementation of a new production method (p-value $= 0,030 \, \chi 2 = 7,014$). Likewise, it is evinced a significant positive association between the investment on Research, Development and Innovation (RDI) and the number of significantly improved product distribution methods (p-value $= 0.019 \, \chi 2 = 9.9$).

These results make it possible to identify the main drivers and the main HCI activities that have an effect on the deployment of process innovations that will benefit the activities of these companies in the long term and boost economic growth. This study serves as a guideline for countries where the required levels of productivity and competitiveness have not been achieved due to the low level of investment in innovation activities and technologies.

Keywords: Human-Computer Interaction (HCI) · Process innovation · Small and medium-sized enterprises (SMEs) · Innovation activities · Competitive advantage

1 Introduction

In recent years, due to the new coronavirus, economic activity and trade has significantly in the global, regional and local context with dramatic impact on supply, demand and economic performance of companies in general and MSMEs in particular, triggering the closure of productive units [1]. In the first quarter of 2020, 78% of MSMEs in Colombia reported a reduction of more than 50% in their revenues, affecting their operations and installed capacity, with a significant deterioration in their economic situation affecting operating margins [2]. This segment of companies has been forced to adopt digital transformation strategies, alliances with suppliers and partnerships with other companies and entities with practices that guide the development of processes and promote transformations with new approaches and structures [3] allowing them to overcome barriers to international markets with intensity in innovation and human talent skills [2]. According to the latest National Competitiveness Report Colombia 2021, 21% of companies in the manufacturing sector were classified as innovative, showing a certain level of maturity, background and previous experience in this aspect [1]. One of the sectors that exports the most is the manufacturing of chemical substances and products (21.3%) [4].

Among the key aspects of innovation are cooperation and the development of R&D activities. Many small or early-stage firms do not have these capabilities and for them it is essential to know what type of activities to develop in order to focus their innovation resources and obtain superior results [1]. The importance of innovation as an engine for boosting productivity and promoting the competitiveness and economic growth of countries and companies is becoming increasingly evident, allowing them to adapt to the new global reality [3].

The objective is to deepen our knowledge about the type of activities that MSMEs should implement to carry out process innovations, and to guide them to focus their efforts and resources on the search for superior results, thus overcoming the limited barriers of the quantities of innovation produced. On the other hand, it seems that companies learn to overcome knowledge, market or regulatory obstacles more easily [1]. According to ECLAC, the GDP of Latin American SMEs in 2022 will be in the order of 3.75%, reaching pre-pandemic levels, and within the framework of the necessary actions for the economic reactivation of this type of company, science and technology activities stand out, where innovation activities are fundamental [3].

Innovation, as a key determinant of productivity and value creation in economies and long-term growth, is closely related to the capacity for business innovation. Colombia has not yet reached the levels of business innovation due to the low level of investment in innovation activities with indicators below the country's target and the average for the region. Despite these results, in recent years the participation of the private sector in R&D investment in the country has increased significantly, from 40.2% of investment in 2010 to 56% in 2019, with an increase in real terms of 178%, but still below the countries of the Organization for Economic Cooperation and Development (OECD) where the private sector executes 66.7% of investment in R&D or innovation activities [1].

The expectations of this type of companies to be on a recovery path in the short and medium term depend to a large extent on the return of demand to pre-pandemic levels, but in the same sense, on the supply of new products and services and effective key processes [4]. Therefore, it is important to study and analyze the type of activities that companies in this subsector must implement and to identify the main drivers and the effect that these activities have on the deployment of process innovations and achieve potential economic growth. On the other hand, SMEs can create value and obtain benefits through the implementation of innovation activities, which provide the effective use of market innovation to sell different products and services in complex environments and their performance through process innovation [5].

2   Methodology

The data analyzed come from the application of a structured questionnaire with 21 questions, of which 16 measure the orientation to process innovations and 5 measure the type of innovation activities that these companies perform; the questionnaire was applied to the management personnel related to innovation management of a sample of 56 exporting SMEs in the Colombian Caribbean; the sample was selected by size, income level and by ordinary activity of the manufacturing macro-sector (Decree 957, 2019). The main economic sectors of these companies are Chemicals, fertilizers and pesticides, pharmaceuticals and medicine, plastic and its manufactures, Iron and steel and its manufactures, Minerals, Oils, Vegetables and animals, and Bituminose materials [6] (Table 1).

The proposed model will allow companies in this sector to know which are the different innovation activities they should develop and will allow them to direct strategies, focusing their efforts and resources. All this by means of correlation tests and factorial analysis. The rest of this document is organized as follows: In Sect. 2, a review of the

Table 1. Firm size

Size	Income level	Sample	%
Small	From 811 up to 7.027	18	32.3%
Medium	From 7.027 up to 59.527	38	67.7%
Total		56	

Source: authors

* Figures of Income from Annual Ordinary Activities in millions of Colombian pesos of 2019 in accordance with decree 957 of June 05, 2019.

literature and related studies is presented Sect. 3. The case of small and medium-sized enterprises is described. Finally, Sect. 5 presents conclusions and future work.

Among the key factors leading to innovation, we find the Human-Computer Interaction (HCI) activities entailing cooperation and the pursuit of R&D activities based on that increase productivity and competitiveness. Nevertheless, several young or small firms do not have those capabilities, and it is paramount for them to know which type of HCI activities they must undertake to allocate their innovation resources adequately to obtain outstanding results.

3   Related Studies

The HCI (Human Computer Interaction) aims to analyze the different degrees of interactions between humans and machines, being an approach widely used at the enterprise level by the ability to produce information, data and actions between a human (user) and the computer, and vice versa.

New technologies are becoming increasingly complex and require a process of interaction to get the maximum benefit at the enterprise level. The rise of new technologies and HCI activities are fundamental for the development of research and its implementation at the operational level in order to improve processes and achieve incremental and disruptive innovations.

HCI (Human Computer Interaction) allows organizations to generate technologies that facilitate the development of scientific and technological activities, such as software development, new inventions, development of research activities, incorporation of new technologies, creation of interactive designs, technological surveillance processes and scaling of technologies to improve competitiveness indexes in SMEs.

In this study it is important to analyze how human–computer interaction is a basic input for the implementation of interactive systems that converge in the development of activities in SMEs to improve export management in the Colombian Caribbean and innovation levels.

Thus, innovation is a process that involves the creation or transformation of new knowledge into products, processes or services that meet changing consumer needs, combined with aspects such as systematic learning, linkages with external actors and investments in resources [7]. Technological innovation (product and/or process) and non-technological innovation (organization and/or marketing) play a crucial role in affecting the performance of companies in terms of productivity and even profitability, since the innovation process influences the internal allocation and use of resources, allowing companies to respond better to the changing market. For innovation to be efficient, it must be persistent over time so that it generates an increase in productivity ranging between 13.4% and 6.2% and the companies obtain an underlying premium that fluctuates between 5.1% and 2.8% with respect to their peers that do not act accordingly [8]

The literature has argued that investment in R&D per se cannot guarantee the success of innovation; therefore, coordination, integration and knowledge transfer within and between industries are vital for the innovative performance of companies. The combination of internal and external knowledge sources is the best alternative when seeking improvements in process innovation performance [5]. External knowledge input (suppliers, customers, competitors, universities and government agencies) has a direct effect on product and process innovation through the absorptive capacity (AC) of small and medium-sized enterprises (SMEs), customers and government agencies contribute to improve the capacity of companies, so that they can focus on developing and managing effective sources, also incoming knowledge from universities and government agencies have a significant impact on process and product innovation respectively [12].

Among the actors involved in R&D activities we can find trade associations, virtual networks, university research centers, associations, government programs, government organizations, incubators and suppliers, actors that make up the innovation ecosystem. Once the innovation network is built, including the key actors or innovation bridges, a monitoring system should be implemented for each sub-process to ensure adequate supervision of the activities, resources, interactions and internal and external actors involved [11].

Cooperation with suppliers in the different links of the value chain makes it possible to increase the sustainability of manufacturing processes, becoming a fundamental basis for collaboration and customer orientation [11]. For process innovation, SMEs require both the learning of advanced technologies and production methods and the collaboration of employees; leadership style also plays a role in communicating and sharing an assertive vision of innovation, which stimulates and drives employees to promote process and product innovation. However, it appears that transformational leaders have a greater impact on process innovation than on product innovation [16].

One of the important innovation activities in the current competitive times is concerning technological learning, which influences the innovation strategies of companies because it facilitates indirect knowledge of foreign competitors or customers with cutting-edge technologies; while the effect of external demand increases the production of companies and, therefore, the profitability of introducing process innovations [13]. Most digital tools focus on the initial stages of innovation processes, which include especially ideation and idea management, and to some extent concept development, in addition these tools are usually equipped with the innovation radar method, which allows managing new market opportunities and trends, often with the support of artificial intelligence mechanisms [14].

On the other hand, the size of companies, their cooperation in R&D activities, the use of public financial support, patent protection and the use of market information sources (customers, suppliers) are significant factors when making investment decisions in innovation activities; The level of investment and patent protection is more relevant in manufacturing sector companies, since these companies innovate more through technological innovations, thus allowing the increase of productivity especially in low technology sectors, on the contrary in the service sector non-technological innovations take more strength, since knowledge is less tangible and codified, their activities are less formal and more ad-hoc and their productivity is reflected particularly in Non-KIBS services vis-à-vis KIBS [9].

Regardless of the size of the company, innovation is considered a crucial factor in the internationalization process; access to new technologies, resources and R&D activities is considered a fundamental factor as important as the favorable growth prospects of an industry for entering new markets or a customer follow-up strategy. There are statistically significant differences in the degrees of importance of the factor access to new technologies or resources and it is closely linked to those sectors with a greater propensity to innovate [16].

The performance of less innovative companies is lower compared to those that carry out process innovation activities and, as a result, obtain higher competitive advantages. However, these activities must be carried out with caution because they cannot be above a certain threshold that affects the performance of SMEs and generates an increase in costs that exceeds the benefits. Therefore, it is important for these companies to perform a break-even analysis, while maintaining an internationally oriented vision and preparing internally for emerging challenges [7]. Process innovation positively impacts the development of SMEs' sustainable performance and sustainability, creating value, benefits and important elements in market innovation to sell different products and services in complex environments [5]. In the design of an organizational policy, technological innovation (product and/or process) and non-technological innovation (organizational and/or marketing) should be considered together to avoid counterproductive effects on business productivity [6].

The degree of persistence in performing R&D and technological innovation may be different in each country, in the sense that it may be related to the distinction of their industries; taking into account the Spanish productive structure, the probability of performing R&D activities in the current period is higher than 20% for companies that also performed it in the previous period, in relation to technological innovation the probability is higher by 28% for companies that innovated in a previous period; When technological innovation is disaggregated into product and process innovation, there are also differences in the persistence patterns considering that process innovation has a higher persistence [18].

Small and medium-sized enterprises in Colombia represent more than 90% of the nation's total production, with 35% of GDP, generating 80% of employment. Particularly in Colombia's Carib-bean Region, they represent close to 10% of the country's total SMEs, with sales of close to US$7.8 billion, accounting for 37.2% of the country's total exports. The region's exports are mainly concentrated in Minerals, Oils, Vegetable and Animal Products, and Bituminous Materials with 52%, Iron and Steel and their manufactures with 16%, Plastics and their manufactures with 10%, Chemical products, fertilizers and pesticides, pharmaceuticals and medicines with 8%, and Others with 14% [18].

The literature has argued that investment in R&D per se cannot guarantee the success of innovation; therefore, coordination, integration and knowledge transfer within and between industries are vital for the innovative performance of companies. The combination of internal and external knowledge sources is the best alternative when seeking improvements in process innovation performance [5]. External knowledge input (suppliers, customers, competitors, universities and government agencies) has a direct effect on product and process innovation through the absorptive capacity (AC) of small and medium-sized enterprises (SMEs), customers and government agencies contribute to improve the capacity of companies, so that they can focus on developing and managing effective sources, also incoming knowledge from universities and government agencies have a significant impact on process and product innovation respectively [12] (Table 2).

Table 2. Related studies.

Year	Study	Objective	Methodology	Conclusions
2020	Institutional Quality, Bank Finance and Technological Innovation: A way forward for Fourth Industrial Revolution in BRICS Economies	Investigate the effects of bank finance and institutional quality, on the technological innovation, in the presence of other important control variables such as high technology exports, and the GDP for BRICS countries	The basic model used in this study is given as: $TI_t = \lambda 1 BF_t + \lambda 2 GDP_t + \lambda 3 HTE_t + \lambda 4 INS_t + \eta t$ (1) Where TI is the technological Innovation, BF denotes the bank financing, GDP represents the gross domestic product, HTE shows the High-technology Exports	The results show that bank finance, institutional quality, high technology exports, and GDP are positively associated with technological innovation
2020	Technological innovation and the demand for labor by firms in expansion and recession	Model and estimate the demand for labor by profit-maximizing firms, as a dynamic function of variables that capture the propensity of these firms to innovate introducing only product, only process and product and process innovations together, in a time period	The sample data includes annual firm-level information for several thousand firms of all sizes, ages, and economic sectors (industrial and service firms), from the CSI-PITEC (Panel de Innovación Tecnológica)	These results are broadly consistent with product and process innovations shifting firms' demand and production functions upwards, but differentially in expansions (less product market competition) than in contractions (more competition)

(continued)

Table 2. (*continued*)

Year	Study	Objective	Methodology	Conclusions
2020	Digitalising and visualising innovation process: comparative analysis of digital tools supporting innovation process in SMEs	This paper aims to explore the level to which such digital tools reflect the complexity and fuzzy nature of innovation process in the context of SMEs	The study involved qualitative analysis of available digital tools, aimed at supporting management of innovation process. Firstly 20 most popular innovation management tools were selected	The conclusions provide insights into usability of existing innovation digital tools for SMEs and their supporting potential for small business innovation processes. It is concluded innovation management digitalization has the potential to affect modifications in innovation behaviors in the nearest future
2020	A possible relationship between internationalization and innovation strategies: an analysis of Portuguese SMEs	Investigate the influence of internationalization on innovation, by exploring whether Portuguese entrepreneurs consider innovation as an important factor or a motivation in the internationalization process	The data used in this research was gathered through an online questionnaire survey. It was sent to all companies registered in the AICEP database of Portuguese internationalized firms. Answers collected were processed by IBM SPSS Statistics 26.0 software through a quantitative approach based on descriptive and inferential analysis	Predictive and prescriptive BDA bring product and process innovation in SMEs' business operations. Similarly, product and process innovation lead to attaining the best SMEs' performance
2020	Together or separately? Direct and synergistic effects of effectuation and causation on innovation in technology-based SMEs	Analyze the potential of direct and ambidextrous application of the decision-making logics on the innovation results of technology SMEs, focusing on product innovation and process innovation	Our hypotheses were tested on a sample of Spanish technology-based SMEs. Sample selection followed International Standard Industrial Classification criteria in the SABI database. A telephone questionnaire was administered using the CATI system	The results provide evidence that not just one path, but rather a pool of alternatives, supports product and process innovation development. If firms also seek to develop process innovations, however, they may obtain better results with an ambidextrous approach

(*continued*)

Table 2. (*continued*)

Year	Study	Objective	Methodology	Conclusions
2021	Transformational leadership and employee voice for product and process innovation in SMEs	Investigate the impact of transformational leader-ship on the innovation of small and medium enterprises (SMEs) through employee voice behaviors. It is hypothesized that employee voice is the mediating mechanism through which transformational leadership affects the process and product innovation in SMEs	Data was collected from 169 SMEs of Pakistan through an online self-administered questionnaire. The proposed hypotheses were tested using partial least squares structural equation modeling (PLS-SEM)	Findings confirm that transformational leadership positively affects both process and product innovation in SMEs and employee voice behavior mediates between these relationships
2021	Green together? The effects of companies' innovation collaboration with different partner types on ecological process and product innovation	Analyze the impact of firms' innovation collaboration with different partner types (i.e., science-based collaboration, supplier collaboration, enterprise customer collaboration, and consumer collaboration) on process-EI and product-EI	It was created a time-lagged dataset based on the 2008 and 2009 waves of the MIP. For the 2009 CIS, a total of 35,197 companies were contacted. We limited analysis to companies in manufacturing sectors to provide a clear sectoral	Collaboration with consumers is associated positively with both process- and product-EI, whereas collaboration with universities and suppliers is associated positively only with process-EI. Collaboration with enterprise customers and competitors is neither associated with process-EI nor product-EI
2021	Spinner Model: Prediction of Propensity to Innovate Based on Knowledge-Intensive Business Services	Represent a global model, to assess prediction of propensity to innovate through KIBS in the service sector, called the Spinner model presenting three interacting dimensions: knowledge creation, knowledge transfer, and innovation, similar to the three axes of dynamic interaction of a fidget spinner with KIBS being at the center	In order to achieve the research goal, we carried out three logistic regression models, one for each dimension: knowledge creation, knowledge transfer, and innovation. KIBS were divided in p-KIBS (professional KIBS) and t-KIBS (technological KIBS), according to the analysis carried out in 71 small, medium, and large firms	The findings contribute to theory development on knowledge intensive solutions, by revealing the relationship of knowledge creation and transfer with innovation in KIBS, and their relationships in the assessment prediction of propensity to innovate

(*continued*)

Table 2. (*continued*)

Year	Study	Objective	Methodology	Conclusions
2021	SMEs and the Innovation Management Process: A multi-level process conceptual framework	Propose a conceptual framework to manage the innovation process in small businesses. It is based on research from 11 case studies in the Montreal software industry using contingency and resource dependency theories	Research from eleven (11) small businesses in the Montreal software industry, from an exploratory study that targeted 83 small businesses. Using open-ended questions around these themes: Description of the business, type of innovations, innovation intensity, and a description of the innovation process, actors, interactions, challenges, and resources	This conceptual framework provides a view of the innovation process that differs from the linear approach often used in many studies to investigate innovation in SMEs. Successful mobilization of innovation resources at all key points determines the success or failure of SMEs' innovation processes
2021	Innovation in Small & Medium Enterprises in São Paulo	Diagnose and contribute with innovation recommendations for the processes of twenty SMEs in the manufacturing segment of the southern area of the São Paulo city	The Radar of Innovation was applied to support the model of the diagnostic method tool, to perform data analysis with the needs of each organization. Analyzing the 12 Dimensions of Innovation for a sample of 20 SMEs in the manufacturing segment, in the south region of São Paulo, is used for the research fieldwork	The role was to promote recommendations and collaboration, to improve the opportunities to be replicated in other organizations with similar challenges. They all found the need to differentiate themselves from their competitors

(*continued*)

Table 2. (*continued*)

Year	Study	Objective	Methodology	Conclusions
2021	Fostering growth patterns of SMEs through business model innovation. A tailored dynamic business modelling approach	Explore how a Dynamic Business Modelling approach complies with inherent SME characteristics and serves as a lean strategy design tool for innovating associated business models	Consists of four steps. Literature review on BMs in an SME to draw the DBM framework. Then, case-study was selected and investigated. Two main data sources were used. Company website and specialized newspapers articles through five semi-structured interviews with entrepreneur and three executives. Face-to-face interviews for additional information about the decision to involve Giglio.com in a BMI process	This paper aims to explore how a Dynamic Business Modelling approach complies with inherent SME characteristics and serves as a lean strategy design tool for innovating associated business models
2021	Effects of Total Quality Management (TQM) Dimensions on Innovation—Evidence from SMEs	Study and identify which dimensions of TQM influence and support innovation strategies within the Portuguese SMEs, in the context of products or services' innovation and process innovation and analyze the extent to which this relationship occurs	A multiple linear regression analysis was chosen, and an eight-predictor multiple linear regression model was proposed. The total sample consisted of 946 companies and 287 completed questionnaires were received, which accounted for 30.34%	This research study allows to conclude that several dimensions of TQM, such as benchmarking, quality/conception and product design, and continuous improvement, have a significant and positive association with product innovation

4   Results: The Case of Small and Medium-Sized Companies in Colombia in the Chemical Products Sector

Technological Component

Competitive advantage is the result of investments in technological capabilities, development of improved human–machine interaction and increased demand, which will allow the generation of strategies to increase productivity levels and technological scaling. The study carried out in the 56 exporting companies of the Colombian Caribbean analyzes how the technological component facilitates the development of scientific and techno-logical activities and how it could improve the processes and techniques in the companies in the last year.

Type of variable	Applied test	Results
One quantitative and one qualitative variable	Mood median test	Pearson's Chi-square = 12,67 Degrees of freedom = 3 P-Value = 0,005; Individual 95,0% CIs Overall Median = 2,00

The results show that the incorporation of scientific and technological activities is associated with the number of processes, techniques, equipment and software that SMEs must optimize their production, where the p-value is 0.005. This agrees with the authors [20], where knowledge management is a key factor for the development of technological innovations, applied research and the generation and dissemination of new technologies. The application of technologies to processes allows faster identification of market needs and the capabilities of companies to meet them [21].

One of the keys to take advantage of technology through HCI (Human Computer Interaction) is the treatment of information, since the incorporation of new technologies is fundamental for the improvement of processes. Through the incorporation of computer programs, information automation activities and data analytics, costs and process time are improved, and a broader vision of the information is achieved for decision making at the managerial and operational level.

Type of Variable	Applied test	Results
Qualitative of dichotomic type	Pearson's Chi-square and the likelihood ratio Chi-square	• *Pearson's Chi-square = 7,014; Degrees of freedom = 2; P-Value = 0,030* • Likelihood ratio Chi-square = 7,284; Degrees of freedom = 2; P-Value = 0,026

Note: For this association, the data for the response options "Neither agree nor disagree" and "Disagree" for both variables were eliminated as they invalidated the Pearson Chi-square test.

The results of the previous table evidenced that implementing technologies in SMEs facilitates the development of scientific and technological activities and is associated with the implementation of a new production method during the last year, given that p-value (0.030) is less than the α level (0. 05); it is important to consider that production methods in companies allow developing projections and coordinating activities for the manufacture of products at lower cost; the scientifically supported elaboration of short-, medium- and long-term plans of structured processes for continuous improvement, establish a roadmap at the operational level and strategies to expand their markets. This is associated with the companies' commitment to invest in technological improvements and applied research [22].

Type of variable	Applied test	Results
One quantitative and one qualitative variable	Mood median test	Pearson's Chi-square = 13,34 Degrees of freedom = 3 P-Value = 0,004; Individual 95,0% CIs Overall Median = 1,00

When analyzing the results of the previous table, the p-value (0.004) is lower than the α level (0.05). Therefore, it was evidenced that implementing technologies in SMEs facilitates the development of scientific and technological activities and is associated with the number of new production methods implemented during the last year. This is evidence that SMEs, by having methods to correctly produce goods at an effective cost and in a timely manner, increase operational performance and the speed of the manufacturing cycle. Implementing different methods throughout the production life cycle and improving existing ones can have great benefits for companies such as quality, customer satisfaction and technological improvements [23].

Type of variable	Applied test	Results
One quantitative and one qualitative variable	Mood median test	Pearson's Chi-square = 8,00 Degrees of freedom = 3 P-Value = 0,046; Individual 95,0% CIs Overall Median = 1,50

In the above table, since the p-value (0.046) is less than the α level (0.05) it is established that implementing technologies in SMEs facilitates the development of scientific and technological activities and is associated with the implementation the number of improved production methods implemented during the last year.

This result highlights a decisive factor of any company: continuous improvement. When applied, the improvement in production methods and techniques involves the reduction of lead time, cycle costs, physical efficiency of processes, energy loss, control of unit consumption of raw materials, control of water loss in the process and any improvement in the processes that allows to achieve the desired results.

Establishing continuous improvement plans must be done in an efficient and adaptable way to meet customer and business needs. Therefore, management has an important commitment to the operational activities of SMEs. Moreover, the development of investments and commitment to technological improvements is directly related to process improvements. The levels of uncertainty in the business value chain must be evaluated in terms of costs, deadlines and quality. It is important to have control metrics, establish production capacity and processes, as well as strategies for their optimization.

It should be noted that continuous improvement is based on the monitoring of activities to resolve deviations and optimize performance. The introduction of HCI (Human Computer Interaction) increases the capacity of software implementation and data analysis that SMEs require to make decisions in manufacturing systems.

Organizational Culture Component

Type of Variable	Applied test	Results
Qualitative of dichotomous type	Pearson's Chi-square and the likelihood ratio Chi-square	• *Pearson's Chi-square = 5,528; Degrees of freedom = 1; P-Value = 0,019;* • Likelihood ratio Chi-square = 5,622; Degrees of freedom = 1; P-Value = 0,018

The results of the previous table showed that the organizational culture tending to develop innovative ideas through the establishment of cooperation mechanisms with different levels is associated with the implementation of new or substantially improved practices to increase the efficiency of the information, production and logistics systems during the last operational period. This demonstrates the importance of a management that seeks to empower employees, to achieve continuous improvements in various dimensions of the companies and keep them competitive and with an immediate response capacity [24].

Type of variable	Applied test	Results
Qualitative of dichotomous type	Pearson's Chi-square and the likelihood ratio Chi-square	• *Pearson's Chi-square = 8,440; Degrees of freedom = 2; P-Value = 0,015* • Likelihood ratio Chi-square = 8,652; Degrees of freedom = 2; P-Value = 0,013

Note: For this association, the data for the response options "Neither agree nor disagree" for the variable "cooperation mechanisms" and "Disagree" for both variables were eliminated because they invalidated Pearson's Chi-square test.

The results of the previous table showed that the organizational culture tending to develop innovative ideas through the establishment of cooperation mechanisms with different levels is associated with the implementation of new or substantially improved practices to increase the efficiency of the distribution systems during the last operational period. Employees play an important role in product and process innovation [12].

Type of Variable	Applied test	Results
One quantitative and one qualitative variable	Mood median test	Pearson's Chi-square = 8,36; Degrees of freedom = 3; P-Value = 0,039; Individual 95,0% CIs Overall Median = 2,00

The results of the previous table showed that the organizational culture tending to the development of innovative ideas through the establishment of cooperation mechanisms with different levels is associated with the number of new or significantly improved processes, techniques, equipment and computer programs to optimize production, developed in the last year. Therefore, for process innovation, SMEs require learning advanced technologies and production methods [12].

Type of variable	Applied test	Results
One quantitative and one qualitative variable	Mood median test	Pearson's Chi-square = 16,33; Degrees of freedom = 3; P-Value = 0,001; Individual 95,0% CIs Overall Median = 1,00

The results of the previous table showed that the organizational culture tending to the development of innovative ideas through the establishment of cooperation mechanisms with different levels is associated with the number of new production methods implemented during the last year. Organizational ambidexterity has a positive effect on the development of product and process innovation [25].

In summary, in the organizational culture component, according to the results, a correlation was found with the following variables:

- Increased efficiency of information, production and logistics systems.
- Improved efficiency of distribution systems.
- New or significantly improved processes, techniques, equipment and software to optimize production.
- New implemented production methods.

Commitment to Invest Resources for the Development of R&D Activities

Type of Variable	Applied test	Results
One quantitative and one qualitative variable	Mood median test	Pearson's Chi-square = 9,90; Degrees of freedom = 3; P-Value = 0,019; Individual 95,0% CIs Overall Median = 2,00

This type of periodic investment allows SMEs to build innovation networks that include key actors or innovation bridges, and to implement a monitoring system for each sub-process to ensure adequate supervision of the activities, resources, interactions and internal and external actors involved [9]. This type of periodic investment allows SMEs to build innovation networks that include key actors or innovation bridges, and to implement a monitoring system for each sub-process to ensure adequate supervision of the activities, resources, interactions and internal and external actors involved [12].

Similarly, having a mechanism for acquiring knowledge from external sources is associated with the number of significantly improved distribution method implemented during the last year, as the p-value (0.004) is less than the α level (0.05); and it is associated with the number of new production methods implemented during the last year, as the p-value (0.001) is less than the α level (0.05). The results evidence the importance for this type of organizations to seek to increase revenue levels through different channels and distribution methods, and in the same sense to make the companies more responsive to the changing market [8]. For innovation to be efficient, it must be persistent over time in order to generate an increase in productivity [8].

Type of variable	Applied test	Results
One quantitative and one qualitative variable	Mood median test	Pearson's Chi-square = 8,13; Degrees of freedom = 3; P-Value = 0,043; Individual 95,0% CIs Overall Median = 1,50

The results in the table above show a Pearson's Chi-square = 8.13, with Degrees of Freedom = 3 and a P-Value = 0.043; with an Individual 95.0% CIs and an Overall Median = 1.50. These results show companies in this sector that have a clear definition of organizational and financial aspects to facilitate the development of technological innovation activities, is associated with the improved number of production methods. Indirect or direct knowledge of competitors or external customers, and the effect of external demand increases the production of enterprises and thus the profitability by introducing process innovations [13], which requires new or significantly improved processes, techniques, equipment and software to optimize production. To develop innovation processes, SMEs require learning advanced technologies and production methods. The voice of employees plays a mediating role and is used by leaders to communicate a vision that stimulates and drives employees to promote process and product innovation. Transformational leaders have a greater impact on process innovation than on product innovation [15].

5 Conclusions and Future Work

With the above results, it is possible to conclude some important aspects that will allow SMEs to make better decisions on innovation management.

- The present study was related to SMEs in Colombia; in future works, the present model could be used to evaluate the correlation of the variables in another country, understanding that the correlation may vary depending on the environment and conditions of the National Innovation System of each country.
- The present study was related to Colombian SMEs in the chemical products sector. In future works, the present model could be evaluated to assess the correlation of variables in other sectors such as manufacturing, IT companies, services, food, among others, understanding that the correlation may vary depending on the conditions present in each sector.
- Periodic investments in R&D allow SMEs to build innovation networks that include key actors. Implementing a system for monitoring activities, resources, interactions and the internal and external actors involved allows for greater results.
- These types of companies seek to increase revenue levels through different channels and distribution methods by responding better to market changes.

- SMEs require learning advanced technologies and production methods; here the human factor is important, but the responsibility of the leaders in communicating the vision to stimulate and encourage employees to promote process and product innovation is fundamental.
- The technological component factor is analyzed in SMEs through their capacity to generate knowledge through automated processes and procedures, improvement of existing technologies, development of product innovation and improvement of technical characteristics in recent years. For those SMEs that are in the process of growth and want to expand into new markets, technological development is a fundamental tool for optimizing industrial and logistic processes.
- For SMEs, the development of technologies and scientific activities is associated with the implementation of better production methods, with continuous improvement being key to the operation of production plants, establishing real indicators and on-site decision making.

References

1. National Competitiveness Council 2022: "National Competitiveness Report Colombia 2020–2021," National Competitiveness Council (2022)
2. Pollster, F.: Big, and SMEs. National reading Results Report great SME survey"
3. "ECONOMIC-PERSPECTIVES-2021".
4. Chamber of Commerce Barranquilla 2021: Atlantic economic analysis and perspectives
5. Haryati, R., University, E., Yasri, Y.: Development of small, micro enterprises based (SMES) on innovation and environmental sustainable development in west sumatera (2021)
6. Chamber of Commerce Barranquilla 2021: Economic and Social Document Department of Atlántico (2022)
7. Ukpabio, M.G., Adeyeye, A.D., Oluwatope, O.B.: Absorptive capacity and product innovation: new evidence from Nigeria. Innov. Dev. 6(2), 213–233 (2016). https://doi.org/10.1080/2157930X.2016.1215801
8. Bartoloni, E., Baussola, M.: Driving business performance: innovation complementarities and persistence patterns. Ind. Innov. 25(5), 505–525 (2018). https://doi.org/10.1080/13662716.2017.1327843
9. Serrano-Bedia, A.M., López-Fernández, M.C., García-Piqueres, G.: Complementarity between innovation knowledge sources: does the innovation performance measure matter? BRQ Bus. Res. Q. 21(1), 53–67 (2018). https://doi.org/10.1016/j.brq.2017.09.001
10. Technology Innovation Management Review (2021)
11. Kobarg, S., Stumpf-Wollersheim, J., Schlägel, C., Welpe, I.M.: Green together? The effects of companies' innovation collaboration with different partner types on ecological process and product innovation. Ind. Innov. 27(9), 953–990 (2020). https://doi.org/10.1080/13662716.2020.1713733
12. Rasheed, M.A., Shahzad, K., Nadeem, S.: Transformational leadership and employee voice for product and process innovation in SMEs. Innov. Manag. Rev. 18(1), 69–89 (2021). https://doi.org/10.1108/inmr-01-2020-0007
13. Fassio, C.: Export-led innovation: the role of export destinations. Ind. Corp. Change 27(1), 149–171 (2018). https://doi.org/10.1093/icc/dtx028
14. Zaverzhenets, M., Łobacz, K.: Digitalising and visualising innovation process: comparative analysis of digital tools supporting innovation process in SMEs. Procedia Comput. Sci. 192, 3805–3814 (2021). https://doi.org/10.1016/j.procs.2021.09.155

15. Aboal, D., Garda, P.: Technological and non-technological innovation and productivity in services vis-à-vis manufacturing sectors. Econ. Innov. New Technol. **25**(5), 435–454 (2016). https://doi.org/10.1080/10438599.2015.1073478

16. Azevedo, M., Azevedo Lobo, C., Santos Pereira, C., Durão, N., Maldonado, I.: A possible relationship between internationalization and innovation strategies: an analysis of portuguese SMEs. Polish J. Manag. Stud. **23**(1), 74–90 (2021). https://doi.org/10.17512/pjms.2021.23.1.05.

17. Bagheri, M., Mitchelmore, S., Bamiatzi, V., Nikolopoulos, K.: Internationalization orientation in SMEs: the mediating role of technological innovation. J. Int. Manag. **25**(1), 121–139 (2019). https://doi.org/10.1016/j.intman.2018.08.002

18. Altuzarra, A.: Are there differences in persistence across different innovation measures? Innovation **19**(3), 353–371 (2017). https://doi.org/10.1080/14479338.2017.1331911

19. Camara Comercio Barranquilla 2021: Annual growth of Barranquilla's GDP

20. Aquilera Diaz, A.: Cost-benefits as a decision tool for the investment in scientific activities (2017)

21. Darío, M., Serna, A., Ruiz Moreno, S., Ortiz Vásquez, L.F., Andrés, J., Cortes, Z.: Performance indicators for logistics enterprises: an approach from the land freight transport sector (2017)

22. Vergara Portela, R.: Development of production planning and scheduling processes in the manufacturing sector of small and medium-sized companies in BOGOTÁ (2006)

23. Ibujés Villacís, J.M., Benavides Pazmiño, M.A.: Contribution of technology to the productivity of SMEs in the textile industry in Ecuador. Econ. Noteb. **41**(115), 140–150 (2018). https://doi.org/10.1016/j.cesjef.2017.05.002

24. Antunes, M.G., Mucharreira, P.R. Justino, M.R., Texeira-Quirós, J.: Effects of Total Quality Management (TQM) Dimensions on innovation—evidence from SMEs. Sustainability **13**(18) (2021). https://doi.org/10.3390/su131810095

25. Alzamora-Ruiz, J., del Mar Fuentes-Fuentes, M., Martinez-Fiestas, M.: Together or separately? Direct and synergistic effects of effectuation and causation on innovation in technology-based SMEs. Int. Entrep. Manag. J. **17**(4), 1917–1943 (2021). https://doi.org/10.1007/s11365-021-00743-9

The Impact and Countermeasures of the "Two Pillar" Scheme for Mobile Digital Enterprise Taxation

Xiaochen Cheng[(⊠)] and Peiyan Zhou

Jilin University, 5988 Renmin Street, Changchun, Jilin, China
sunshinecxc@163.com

Abstract. Twenty-First Century, digital economy has been a tremendous development and become the main economic forms of the world. However, mobile digital enterprises mostly provide services through the use of new platform models, advertising models, etc. and rely on the Internet as commercial interaction channel. Their virtuality and liquidity have brought huge challenges to the existing International Taxation System. The international taxation rules based on "taxable entity" as the basis of authority of taxation venue have been divorced from the current era. The international taxation rules based on "taxable entity" as the basis of authority of taxation venue have been divorced from the current era. In October 2021, 136 members States of the OECD inclusive framework issued <Statement on a Two Pillar Solution to Address the Tax Challenges Arising from the Digitalization of the Economy> . The "pillar one" formulates new connectivity recognition rules and double-layer profit distribution mechanism under the digital economy, so as to minimize the complexity of international tax. The "pillar two" aims to solve the problem of profit transfer and tax base erosion of multinational corporations. The innovative content of the "Two Pillar" program has a direct impact on mobile digital companies in terms of profit distribution, corporate income tax collection and the applicability of preferential policies, etc. In this regard, we should improve the information exchange mechanism, expand the data sources of mobile digital enterprises, unblock the channels of information sharing, and strive to establish a modern international tax governance system.

Keywords: Business models for mobile communications · Mobile taxing · Two Pillar

1 Foreword

With the rapid development of mobile Internet, big data, cloud computing, artificial intelligence and other new generation information technologies, countries are actively competing and cooperating around a new round of technology and industrial commanding heights. All kinds of new technologies, new business forms and new models are emerging one after another. The digital economy has entered a new stage of vigorous development and become a driving force for stimulating economic vitality an important

© Springer Nature Switzerland AG 2022
M. Rauterberg et al. (Eds.): HCII 2022, LNCS 13520, pp. 149–157, 2022.
https://doi.org/10.1007/978-3-031-18158-0_10

engine to promote the new round of global economic growth. As an emerging economic mode, digital economy has played a positive role in Entrepreneurship and innovation, promoting upgrading, transforming kinetic energy and improving factor productivity. But at the same time, the digital economy also has a profound impact and great challenge on the tax rules and system based on the traditional economy. <The 2019 digital economy report> released by the United Nations Conference on Trade and Development shows that a global digital value chain with digital platform as the carrier, digital data as the element and digital drive as the core has been formed. However, the openness, virtuality, liquidity and other characteristics of the digital economy also make the traditional tax connection rules and the distribution of tax rights invalid, which has brought an unprecedented impact on the current international tax rules. At the same time, many countries and regions have taken unilateral tax measures against the digital economy in expanding the application of the withholding income tax collection mechanism and levying digital service tax, so as to safeguard their own interests. Such "separate policies" are not only detrimental to the healthy development of the digital economy, but also to the stability of the international tax order. In this context, it is urgent to actively and effectively respond to the tax challenges brought by economic digitization and build a unified, standardized and inclusive international tax cooperation framework that keeps pace with the times. In recent years, the formulation of solutions to the challenges of economic digital taxation led by the G20 and undertaken by the OECD is accelerating, which is also the largest substantive reform in the development history of the current international tax system in recent 100 years, and will have a far-reaching impact on the distribution of international tax benefits and even the reconstruction of international tax rules. Since the 2013 G20 summit in St. Petersburg commissioned the OECD to launch the base erosion and profit shifting (BEPS) initiative, the OECD has been promoting international tax reform on a global scale. On 2021, the OECD issued a statement on its "Two Pillar"approach to the digital tax challenge for the economy on July 1, and again on October 8, 136 of the 140 members of the BEPS inclusive framework agreed on a "Two Pillar" scheme.

2   Contents of the "Two Pillars" Scheme

2.1   Core Content of "Pillar-One" Scheme

In order to minimize the complexity of international tax and solve the international allocation of taxing rights in the digital economy, the OECD has made the "Pillar-One" scheme, which takes into account the significant differences in tax policies of different countries. The scheme applies to large multinationals with annual revenues of more than 2 billion euros and profit margins of more than 10%. As a result, the latest program is no longer focused solely on the digital economy, but on super-sized multinationals. The core content of Pillar-One includes the object of tax right distribution, the mechanism of profit distribution and the mechanism of dispute settlement.

The Object of Tax Right Distribution. As far as the allocation of taxing rights is concerned, taking into account the impact and challenges that the new types of business models derived from the digital economy have on existing international tax rules, The "pillar-One" scheme introduces "market jurisdiction" in addition to the original local tax collection jurisdiction and resident tax jurisdiction of income source. If multinational enterprises are continuously and significantly involved in economic activities in the market, for example, by selling consumer-oriented products to a market jurisdiction for a period of time, or providing targeted advertising to users in market jurisdictions in a highly digital business model, it can be argued that the business activities of multinational enterprises are closely related to market jurisdictions. Therefore, the market jurisdiction has the right to tax the multinational enterprise's participation in the economic activities in the market.

The Mechanism of Profit Distribution. As far as the distribution of profits is concerned, "Pillar-One" scheme proposes the elimination of amount C from the previous "harmonized approach" in order to adjust the three-tier profit distribution mechanism to two-tier. And it has introduced a "Marketing and distribution profit safe port" mechanism in the amount-A, which is different from the traditional "safe harbor". "Amount-A": It is different from the traditional transfer pricing method used by the independent entity, amount-A is measured by pre-tax profit in the consolidated financial statements of the multinational enterprise as the preferred indicator, the portion of pre-tax profit that exceeds a certain level of profit is the residual profit. The overall assumption is that pre-tax profits are multiplied by a fixed percentage to arrive at the residual profits to be distributed to the market jurisdictions. On this basis, a portion of the residual profit is divided into amount-A in a fixed proportion, or different weights are given depending on the degree of digitization of the various business models, the sum of the residual profit is weighted to obtain the amount-A. After determining the size of amount-A, the OECD measures the distribution of amount-A among different market jurisdictions based on a fixed percentage of business model sales and possible additional factors at different levels of interconnectedness. The OECD also suggests setting a minimum threshold for pre-tax profits and breaking down the different areas of the digital economy, taking into account regional differences in policies, regulations, accounting standards and the profitability of multinational companies in different regions. Amount-B: When a distributor establishes a link with a market jurisdiction through a subsidiary or a traditional permanent establishment, "Pillar-One" scheme will establish a fixed return to the distributor based on the principle of independent dealing B, with the purpose of standardizing the benchmark activities of marketing and distribution. The establishment of amount-B will help tax authorities to simplify transfer pricing rules, reduce taxpayers' tax payment costs and improve the tax certainty of transaction pricing. Of note is the proposal to introduce a "Profit safe harbor for marketing and distribution"rule in amount-A. Under this rule, if a multinational group has a taxable entity in a market jurisdiction, the group will first determine the return on the performance of its marketing and distribution functions in relation to the revenue within the scope of the tax, in accordance with the existing rules on the distribution of profits, the return is then compared to the "Safe Harbor Return"(that is, amount-A + amount-B). If the "Current marketing and distribution return" exceeds the "Safe Harbor Return", the amount-A is no longer allocated to the market jurisdiction, to minimize the risk of double taxation.

Subject to Tax Rule. The rule is limited to certain types of payments made between members of the controlled group, that is, if the agreed types of income are not taxed at the minimum rate in the jurisdiction of the payee or beneficial owner, the minimum tax objective will be achieved by imposing withholding income tax, limiting or denying tax treaty preferences.

In general, the "Pillar-One" scheme fully takes into account the significant differences in tax policies between countries, and has formulated practical and feasible rules for the connectivity determination rules and the allocation of taxing rights in the digital economy, to minimize the complexity of international taxation. The redistribution of taxing power will help to improve the certainty of international tax rules and give enterprises more stable expectation of foreign investment and trade. In addition, the establishment of a more binding tax dispute prevention and settlement mechanism can effectively ensure the implementation of the overall program in place to protect "backtracking" of tax revenue in the tax jurisdiction where the income originated.

2.2   Core Content of Pillar-Two Scheme

The core of Pillar-Two scheme is embodied in the Global Anti-Base Erosion plan, which consists mainly of three rules.

Income Inclusion Rule. The rule is based on a minimum effective tax rate of 15%. If the effective tax rate on the income from the operations of the multinational enterprise is lower than the minimum effective tax rate, the business will pay a fixed percentage of top-up tax to resident tax jurisdictions. At the same time, the income inclusion rules would also explicitly calculate the tax-jurisdictional mix of the actual minimum tax rates, as well as the key contentious issue of how to create exclusion rules for substantive economic activities. Income inclusion rules can ensure that income from multinational enterprises is taxed at a minimum rate and reduce the incentive for multinational enterprises to transfer profits to low-tax countries or regions through branches or subsidiaries.

Switch-Over Rule. The rule applies to countries and territories that have mutually established tax exemption provisions in bilateral tax treaties to ensure the universality of the GLoBE program. If the profits of foreign branches of multinational enterprises or income from foreign real estate are subject to the tax exemption provisions of bilateral tax treaties, the effective tax rate of such profits or income is lower than the minimum tax rate. According to the rule of income inclusion, the resident tax jurisdiction should tax the part of profits or income, which gives rise to the contradiction between bilateral tax agreement and the rule of income inclusion. To solve this problem, the GLoBE established a conversion rule. Through this rule, the resident country can "close" the application of the tax treaty with tax exemption provisions between it and the source country, and switch to the credit method to exempt the tax of this part of profits or income.

Under-Taxed Payments Rule. Theoretically, the low tax payment rule can be regarded as the "Backing" rule of the income incorporation rule. The income inclusion rule is that when the effective tax rate of the overseas branch or subsidiary is lower than the agreed minimum tax rate, the overseas branch or subsidiary will be subject to supplementary tax to increase the tax income of the resident tax jurisdiction, while the low tax payment rule aims to tax the low tax rate entity by refusing pre tax deduction.

Generally speaking, the OECD has drawn on the experience of the United States on the Global Invisible Low Tax Income(GILTI) policy, and formulated the "Pillar-Two"program, which aims to systematically address the problem of base erosion and profit transfer of the remaining tax base outside the "Pillar-One"program. From the analysis report of the economic impact assessment of the "Two Pillar"program of Taxation in the Digital Economy, the goal of Pillar-Two is to reduce the transfer of profits from multinational enterprises by reducing bottom-up competition in income taxes between different tax jurisdictions, which is expected to significantly increase overall global corporate income tax revenues.

3   The Influence of OECD'S "Two Pillar" Scheme on China

The calculation of the amount-A in the "Pillar-One" scheme relies on the fixed proportion formula method, which is a new challenge to the enterprise income tax. At present, the enterprise income tax is calculated on the basis of individual tax liability, while "Pillar-One" needs to calculate the total profit and residual profit at the level of enterprise group or business line. The current <Enterprise Income Tax Law> has relevant provisions on the profit rate of construction, design consulting, management service and other business models. However, it lacks the determination of the average profit margin of non-resident digital enterprises, which hinders the application of the comparable analysis rule under the principle of independent transaction to a certain extent. And the corporate income tax on non-resident enterprise permanent establishment defined the expression is relatively broad. For example, the <Enterprise Income Tax Law> stipulates: "A non-resident enterprise means an enterprise that is established in accordance with the laws of a foreign country (region) and whose actual administrative organ is not in China, but has an establishment or place in China, or an enterprise that does not have an establishment or place in China but has income from sources within China."The "establishment or place"here belong to the category of traditional permanent establishments, and there is a lack of relevant identification of non-resident digital enterprises. Corporate income tax laws and regulations fail to clearly define the scope of taxation in the digital economy, so it is urgently needs to cover the two types of taxable products and services proposed in the "two pillar" scheme: automated digital services and consumer oriented business model.

The impact of the "Pillar-Two" scheme on the existing preferential policies of Chinese enterprise income tax. the nominal rate of Chinese enterprise income tax is 25%, however, the actual tax rate may be lower than the nominal tax rate after the enterprise applies the preferential tax policies. For example, R & D fees are deducted, high-tech enterprises have low tax rates, software integrated circuit enterprises are exempted or halved, etc. Under the income inclusion rule, parent companies are required to pay back income tax in their country of residence if the actual effective tax rate charged by the controlled foreign enterprise is lower than the minimum tax rate. For Operating entities within the territory that enjoy various enterprise income tax preferences, if their parent company is found to be outside the territory, they will be required to pay the difference between the actual tax burden and the lowest tax rate to the location of the parent company. This means that the tax breaks that China gives to companies do not actually benefit them, but also the tax relief will flow abroad. In addition, under the low tax payment rule, If the payment made by the overseas payer to the domestic related party is not taxed at the lowest tax rate, the payer shall not deduct the payment before tax. Therefore, the "Pillar-Two" plan will bring the enormous challenge to the existing enterprise income tax preferential policy of China.

The impact of the "Two Pillar" program on the existing tax collection and management capacity. The orderly progress of the "Two Pillar" scheme depends on the tax authorities' access to relevant tax information. For example, when calculating the actual effective tax rate, it is necessary to merge all income taxes and fees in the jurisdiction that meet the definition of Globe and adjust the financial statements, as well as determine the ownership structure. At this time, tax authorities need to collect more information than tax-related information. It even involves the collection and judgment of enterprise structure and real business operation data. While the national reporting system and the tax information exchange system already in place can reduce the tax administration burden of tax authorities under the "Two Pillar" program, at the international level, the existing country reports and tax information exchange mechanisms do not provide for this. The information exchanged still requires extensive analysis by the tax authorities before it is possible to extract valuable content. Within digital enterprises, data resources are its core assets. The obligation of the platform to provide information is not clearly defined in the current law, and digital enterprises lack the power to provide tax related information. Tax Authorities must have clear evidence before they can get information about such enterprises, which seriously hampers the effectiveness of tax collection and management in the digital economy. Therefore, if there is no multi-dimensional and full coverage of data resources, we cannot solve the "Two Pillar" program on tax collection and management challenges.

The impact of the "Two Pillar" scheme on China's foreign-invested digital enterprises. The "Pillar-One" scheme has included online intermediary platforms, streaming media, online games and so on into the scope of taxation, while China's cross-border e-commerce transactions are still dominated by exports. In 2019, China's cross-border e-commerce market totaled 10.5 trillion yuan, and the export cross-border e-commerce transactions totaled 8.03 trillion yuan, accounting for 76.48% of the total. Therefore, if the "Two Pillar" scheme is finally implemented, the long-term development of China's cross-border e-commerce business will be affected to some extent. From the analysis of enterprises of different sizes, the "Two Pillar" scheme may lead to new market barriers. Small and medium-size enterprise investing abroad will face more severe competition challenges in the process of development. As for China's foreign-invested digital enterprises, because some countries are implementing unilateral tax measures such as expanding the scope of permanent establishment and levying digital service tax, in the short term, these "Going-out" enterprises will bear heavier tax burden, facing the uncertainty of international taxation and the challenge of double taxation.

4   China's Response Measures

As the world's second largest economy and an OECD observer, China is hardly immune from the torrent of international economic development. Therefore, China should actively participate in the formulation of international tax rules in an open, inclusive and fair manner and contribute Chinese wisdom. Use international rules to effectively protect China's tax sovereignty and safeguard the legitimate rights and interests of Chinese enterprises.

4.1   Support the New Connectivity Rule and Actively Participate in the Rule of Global Profit Sharing

Breaking through the original regional existence and giving the tax authorities of market countries the power to levy taxes is essentially to participate in the global profit division of multinational enterprises, which can be divided into two specific situations: for "Going Out" enterprises, taking the overseas process of Alipay and WeChat payment as an example, credit cards are widely used in overseas developed countries, and it is difficult to open up the market. Therefore, most of their overseas destinations are economically underdeveloped countries and region. The main overseas target group is still Chinese tourists traveling abroad. Although there may be consumer markets in Europe, the United States and other Southeast Asian countries, user is all Chinese and value is created for Chinese tourists. Under the current "Pillar-One" scheme, countries will generally levy global taxes on Alipay and WeChat accordingly. In this case, whether market consuming countries still have the right to tax is debatable. For "Imported" enterprises, such as Amazon, Google, no matter whether the business is carried out by "no physical existence" or "physical existence", it is finally participated by Chinese users in the Chinese market, for which China should enjoy the right to tax. Market consumer, user participation and value creation are particularly important in the new connectivity rule. China should pay more attention to the improvement of the "user participation" rule and emphasize the application of the user location rule. The new connectivity rule can be applied only if local users in the market consuming country participate and value is created by local users in the market consuming country. The new connectivity rule is the premise of the application of amount-A. It is also a tax rule that gives due consideration to global fairness under the current complex international tax situation. Therefore, It is suggested that China can accept and adopt it on a sound basis and actively participate in global profit segmentation.

4.2   Introduce the Recognition Standard of Permanent Establishment and Revise the Rules for Determining the Source of Income

The new rules require China to revise the current criteria for identifying permanent establishments, and to make user participation, marketing intangible assets and significant economic presence the criteria for identifying permanent establishments of Chinese digital economy enterprises, taking into account factors such as "Continuous Revenue Generation" "User Location" "User Data" and "Local Partner Business Activity". For non-resident taxpayers who have not established institutions or places in China, their income obtained from China through cross-border transactions in the form of remote assistance and cooperation with domestic third parties shall be taxed in accordance with the new association rules. China should have a tax basis for "non-entity" high-tech enterprises and levy taxes accordingly. On this basis, the identification standard can be appropriately extended to other fields in order to solve the bottleneck problems existing in the current identification process of permanent establishments of non-resident enterprises. For example, the same project is divided into different periods and different operations are carried out, how to determine the number of days to provide labor services in China in order to avoid enterprises artificially splitting the overall project into several small projects or commercial activities, and then using non-resident exemption clauses to avoid tax obligations. The introduction of this recognition standard, the collection of taxes according to law, and the administration according to law are the first and most crucial step for China to start levying taxes on the digital economy. In the early stage, it is an important prerequisite to widely solicit public opinions, collect data and calculate the impact.

4.3 Reasonably Determine the "Minimum Tax Rate" of the "Pillar Two" Scheme to Maintain the Security of China's Tax Base

The "pillar two" scheme can better solve the problem of large amount of foreign payments by foreign-funded enterprises in China. Unilateralism is on the rise in the field of international taxation, and some countries are "cleaning up their own affairs". China advocates strengthening international tax cooperation, but at the same time, we will not give up the right to tax multinational enterprises. The acceptance of "Pillar Two" is conditional on the determination of the minimum tax rate. This suggestion can be based on the investigation of foreign enterprises in China, build relevant models to calculate the "break-even point" of corporate tax, so as to determine the final lowest tax rate, rather than passively accept the final tax rate determined by OECD. At present, China's preferential withholding income tax rate is 10%, according to the tax arrangements between the mainland and the Hong Kong Special Administrative Region and China's tax agreements with some countries, enterprises can enjoy a preferential withholding tax rate of at least 5%, although they will not be able to enjoy the preferential tax agreement as a punishment under the "pillar two" scheme, however, there is still a significant gap between the 10% withholding income tax and the 25% preferential tax rate, which cannot deduct related expenses before tax. The "Pillar Two" scheme does not specify the specific application situation, but only states that the amount can be subject to "withholding income tax" or "pre tax deduction is not allowed". China clearly stated in the Announcement No. 6 that when the enterprise pays the royalties and "non beneficial labor services" that "do not bring economic benefits and do not conform to the principle of independent trading" to the related parties, The tax authorities can implement special tax payment in full according to the amount deducted before tax, which shows that China has an adjustment method of "no pre tax deduction", and ultimately, whether China adopts no pre tax deduction or levying withholding income tax or both will have a significant impact on the tax burden of enterprises. Therefore, it is suggested that China should carefully choose the "adjustment method" when choosing the "Pillar Two" scheme, so as to avoid higher tax burden on enterprises and crack down on the investment power of "imported" enterprises, resulting in negative impact.

4.4 Improve the Information Exchange Mechanism and the "Global One-Family" Risk Assessment Mechanism

The implementation of the "Two Pillar" scheme puts forward higher requirements for the modern and scientific collection means of tax authorities in various countries, and the information exchange mechanism is one of the better choices at present. We should improve the information exchange mechanism for enterprises in the Digital Economy. By specifying the form, frequency, mode and specific application of specific exchange, we can deal with possible tax disputes and better serve "going global" enterprises and manage "bringing in" enterprises. The transactions of "Highly Digital" companies are more hidden and difficult to master. Countries all over the world are seeking to establish a "Global one-family" risk assessment mechanism, so as to have a comprehensive grasp of all the transactions of multinational enterprises and the latest trends, but at present China still lacks the corresponding evaluation mechanism and the policy basis. Even if the relevant information is obtained, there is no response means to manage it. It is suggested to introduce the mandatory disclosure rules of multinational enterprises, explore the establishment of a "Global one-family" risk assessment response mechanism. China can Implement the same standard and the same caliber of countermeasures for specific risk points to minimize international tax disputes.

References

1. OECD: Tax Challenges Arising from Digitalisation: Interim Report 2018. OECD, Paris (2018)
2. Shi, Y.Y.: A study on the countermeasures to the tax challenges arising from the digitalisation of an economy——from the perspective of enterprise income tax (论我国经济数字化的税收应对——基于企业所得税视角). Tax. Res. (3), 108–111 (2020). https://www.doi.org/10.19376/j.cnki.cn11-1011/f.2020.03.018
3. Andreas, P, Alessandro, T.: Global Minimum Taxation? An Analysis of the Global Anti-Base Erosion Initiative, pp. 315–355. IBFD, Amsterdam (2021).
4. Cui, X.J., Liu, Y.: OECD pillar two proposal: challenges and responses (OECD支柱二方案：挑战与应对). Int. Tax. China (9), 51–64 (2021). https://doi.org/10.19376/j.cnki.cn10-1142/f.2021.09.007
5. OECD: Statement by the OECD/G20 Inclusive Framework on BEPS on the Two Pillar Approach to Address the Tax Challenges Arising from the Digitalisation of the Economy[EB/OL], 31 January 2020. http://www.oecd.org
6. Zhang, Z.Y., Li, H.L.: A digital economy, value creation and wealth distribution: an analysis from tax perspective (数字经济、价值创造和财富分配). Int. Tax. China (9), 3–14(2021). https://doi.org/10.19376/j.cnki.cn10-1142/f.2021.09.001.
7. Jorgenson, D.W., Wu, K.M.: The ICT revolution, world economic growth, and policy issues. Tele-commun. Policy **40**(5), 383–397 (2016). https://doi.org/10.1016/j.telpol.2016.01.002
8. Qiu, D.M.: The latest progress in the formulation of international rules on income taxation in digital economy and China's response (数字经济所得课税国际规则制定的最新进展及中国应对). Tax. Res. (10), 63–72(2020). https://doi.org/10.19376/j.cnki.cn11-1011/f.2020.10.009

Research on China's Mobile Commerce Value Added Tax Under DEPA

Hanhan Han[✉] and Peiyan Zhou

Jilin University, Jilin, China
1785712561@qq.com

Abstract. With the rapid development of modern information technologies such as big data, artificial intelligence and 5 g, global digitization will be an inevitable trend in the future. It can be seen that the situation of digital trade is irreversible, and only compliance can survive, which has an energy that can not be underestimated for the future economic growth of the country. Depa was born in June 2020, and many countries are interested in it, as is China. In early November this year, China officially applied for the "group". By analyzing the characteristics and current situation of depa, this paper analyzes that China's accession to depa will have a significant impact on China's future economic development, then analyzes and summarizes the current value-added tax system for mobile commerce in OECD and EU, and then proposes to establish a rapid value-added tax information automatic exchange platform, focus on tax exemption and tax refund with retention, building a tax credit system and other measures to strengthen the collection of value-added tax.

Keywords: DEPA · Mobile commerce · Value added tax

1 Current Situation and Characteristics of DEPA

In June 2020, Singapore, Chile and New Zealand jointly signed depa online. At present, the volume of depa is small, but depa is a comprehensive and forward-looking agreement. Through DEPA, parties can use technology to consolidate existing trade agreement commitments. At the same time, depa can enable contracting parties' enterprises and consumers to better participate in the development of digital economy and make full use of and share more opportunities and dividends brought by trade digitization. It represents a new trend, that is, in addition to the existing trade and investment agreements, it puts forward a separate special agreement on the digital economy. It is the first important rule arrangement on the digital economy in the world and provides a template for the institutional arrangement of the global digital economy. In the future, with the development of the agreement and the increase of its members, DEPA will have more and more influence and voice in the global digital economy governance system.

The most prominent feature of depa is its modular protocol. DEPA consists of 16 thematic modules, including business and trade facilitation, dealing with digital products and related issues, data issues, broader trust environment, business and consumer

© Springer Nature Switzerland AG 2022
M. Rauterberg et al. (Eds.): HCII 2022, LNCS 13520, pp. 158–166, 2022.
https://doi.org/10.1007/978-3-031-18158-0_11

trust, digital identity, emerging trends and technologies, innovation and digital economy, cooperation of small and medium-sized enterprises, digital inclusion, transparency and dispute settlement, which cover the implementation of paperless trade Strengthen network security, protect personal information, strengthen cooperation in the field of financial science and technology and other issues of social concern. DEPA's modular protocol allows parties to add only a few modules without having to agree to all of them. The flexible and modular accession mode breaks the rule monopoly of the digital economy power to a certain extent and provides a more inclusive institutional framework for intergovernmental digital economic cooperation to all international parties.

2 Impact of Joining DEPA on China

At present, China has become a big digital economy country, but its influence on the global digital trade pattern still needs to be improved. According to China Internet development report 2021, the scale of China's digital economy will reach 39.2 trillion yuan in 2020, accounting for 38.6% of GDP, maintaining a high growth rate of 9.7%, becoming a key driving force for stable economic growth. Among them, the transaction volume of e-commerce reached 37.21 trillion yuan, a year-on-year increase of 4.5%, and the operating revenue of e-commerce service industry reached 5.45 trillion yuan, a year-on-year increase of 21.9%. DEPA is a high-level digital trade agreement. If China joins, it can connect with the international rules of high-level Digital Trade and provide new development space for the development of digital economy and digital trade.

Among the 16 theme modules of DEPA, "business and trade facilitation" and "data issues" are the core and focus. The relevant rules and requirements will have an important impact on China's digital trade development, data cross-border flow, personal information protection and network security industry. DEPA business and trade facilitation module requires each party to provide electronic trade management documents, and each party shall accept the electronic version as the legal equivalent of paper documents, so as to promote paperless trade. This rule will greatly accelerate the paperless process of China's trade, improve the docking efficiency and interoperability of trade between China and DEPA member countries, optimize the customs clearance approval process with other countries, promote the international development of cross-border e-commerce platform enterprises, expand the scale of cross-border e-commerce and other digital service trade, and greatly improve the facilitation and competitiveness of China's foreign trade Degree of digitization.

China's cross-border data flow management and services will be upgraded and optimized. DEPA proposes to allow enterprises doing business in Singapore, Chile and New Zealand to seamlessly transmit data across borders, that is, to allow the free flow of data across borders, on the premise of complying with the necessary regulations. Joining depa will encourage China to strengthen the review of cross-border data, improve the cross-border data security assessment system, optimize the hierarchical and classified management of cross-border data, improve the rules of cross-border data flow, promote the certification of cross-border data flow with DEPA Member States, and improve the quality of cross-border data flow and the level of corresponding cross-border data flow services.

In addition, DEPA defines the principles of strengthening the protection of personal information, including collection restrictions, data quality, purpose norms, use restrictions, security, transparency, personal participation and accountability, and requires parties to establish a legal framework to protect personal information in accordance with these principles. The existence of this principle will promote China to further improve personal information protection laws and regulations, improve the compatibility of personal information protection rules with relevant international rules, speed up the mutual recognition process between personal information protection rules and other countries, regions and international organizations, and further deepen the exchanges and cooperation between China and DEPA Member States in the field of personal information protection.

3 Tax Management Practice Related to Value-Added Tax in the International Community

Digital economy, e-commerce and mobile commerce have brought great challenges to the traditional tax system, and the international community has issued relevant countermeasures. International organizations, especially OECD (Organization for economic cooperation and development), actively explore the coping strategies of tax management in digital economy. Therefore, this paper mainly analyzes the relevant practices of OECD and EU on value-added tax under the digital economy.

At present, 35 OECD countries are composed of 22 EU countries and 13 countries from other continents (Europe, America, Asia, etc.). Most countries implement the traditional value-added tax system (VAT) based on EU value-added tax, and a few countries (Canada, Australia, New Zealand, etc.) levy a goods and services tax (GST) called modern value-added tax.

(1) OECD Value Added Tax Related Tax Management Suggestions. Value added tax, also known as goods and services tax. Value added tax belongs to turnover tax, which is not ultimately borne by enterprises, but by consumers. The tax principle of value-added tax is that taxpayers in the supply chain have the responsibility to pay value-added tax according to a certain proportion in a specific tax period. At present, the international mainly adopts the method of invoice deduction, so as to ensure that only the value-added part is taxed.

There are two principles for the collection of value-added tax: the source tax principle and the destination tax principle. Under the principle of destination, the tax payable related to sales belongs to the country of final consumption, which helps to maintain tax neutrality. Under the principle of place of origin, part of the tax returns to the place of origin, which is inconsistent with the country where the final payer of value-added tax is the destination country. Therefore, at present, the international community mainly adopts the principle of destination.

When the principle of destination is adopted, the export tax rebate and import tax are paid. According to whether the goods collected are tangible or not, value-added tax can be divided into tangible goods value-added tax and intangible goods value-added tax. For the value-added tax on goods, considering the tax cost, the imported low-value goods will be exempted from value-added tax under the traditional tax system. However, in the digital economy environment, the increase in the number of goods imported and the increase in the use of value-added tax import threshold for tax planning will lead to the problem of national tax loss. For intangible goods, including services and intangible assets, due to the concealment of digital economy, it is difficult for the destination country to effectively judge the tax location.

(1) For the value-added tax mode of imported tangible goods, there are four tax collection modes: traditional collection mode, buyer collection mode, seller collection mode and intermediary collection mode. Their respective features are:

1) Traditional collection mode. Goods can be imported through express carriers and postal services. It is transported by express carrier. When it is imported through the customs, the relevant data information is transmitted to the customs of the importing and exporting country in electronic form. Generally, paper materials are mainly used for postal transportation, and there is a lack of electronic data transmission system. With the increasing popularity of electronic postal transportation, the efficiency of the traditional collection mode will be improved.

2) Buyer collection mode. There are three forms of buyer's collection mode - pre registration, self-evaluation when goods arrive and evaluation after release. These three buyer collection modes require the buyer to conduct self-evaluation, so the success of this collection mode depends on the buyer's tax compliance, and this mode is unlikely to achieve satisfactory tax collection effect. At the same time, adopting this tax collection method may produce higher tax costs.

3) Seller collection mode. The seller's collection mode requires non resident enterprises to collect and pay value-added tax in the country where the market is located, which will improve the collection efficiency of value-added tax on low-value imported tangible goods and give the government the opportunity to cancel or reduce the threshold of import value-added tax. However, the seller's collection mode will increase the burden on the seller of non resident enterprises. At the same time, the core of this collection mode is to ensure the tax compliance of non resident enterprises.

4) Intermediary collection mode. The intermediary collection mode can be divided into postal operator collection, express operator collection, e-commerce platform collection and financial intermediary collection.

Collection by postal operators; At present, postal operators mainly transmit information in paper form. Therefore, if it is necessary to collect taxes by using postal operators as intermediaries, it is necessary to electronize relevant information and develop corresponding electronic systems.

Collection by express operators: for goods higher than the threshold of import value-added tax, it has become a practice to collect taxes through express operators. If the express operator needs to be used as an intermediary for tax collection, it may be necessary to develop a new VAT declaration and collection system for low-value tangible goods.

Collection through e-commerce platform: collection through e-commerce platform requires a certain degree of adjustment to the current e-commerce system and customs procedures, which may involve additional costs.

Collection by financial intermediaries: if taxes are collected and paid through financial intermediaries, the data collection and processing system needs to be reformed because the current financial intermediaries do not have the corresponding system for collecting information and collecting and paying taxes. Therefore, financial intermediaries are unlikely to effectively collect taxes.

Taxation through intermediary can ensure the neutrality, efficiency, flexibility and fairness of taxation. Among them, express operators can ensure the simplicity and effectiveness of taxation because they have more comprehensive supply chain related information and electronic systems. For financial intermediaries, the transformation of relevant systems is more difficult, which will affect the simplicity and effectiveness of taxation.

(2) For the confirmation of the tax payment place of the value-added tax on imported intangible goods, the tax payment place is easy to judge for the value-added tax on goods. However, when the goods are intangible goods or services, it is difficult to judge the tax location. In cross-border trade, VAT generally adopts the principle of destination to determine the tax payment place.

B2B has the right to tax the intangible assets in the place where the e-commerce service is operated and only one party has the right to tax the intangible assets in the place where the e-commerce service is received. When the service recipient has more than one place of business and tax payment location, the following three methods can be used: (1) direct use method, which is more applicable when the use of services or intangible assets by an organization is obvious; (2) direct delivery method, which is more applicable when services or intangible assets need to be provided on site, such as catering services: (3) re charging method, When the provider of services or intangible assets has the right to re charge an institution of the purchaser, the location of the institution of the purchaser is the place of tax payment.

In the traditional economic environment, because consumers generally buy goods, services or intangible assets from local suppliers, and generally can expect the services to be consumed in the place where the services occur, the tax location is usually easy to judge. In the digital economy environment, when the buyer is an individual, the services or intangible assets consumed by consumers may be provided by suppliers all over the world. In the context of digital economy, OECD suggests that the tax location of B2C e-commerce where goods are services and intangible assets can be determined according to the following two principles. (1) When services or intangible assets are consumed, both the supplier and the recipient are present: when these three conditions are met at the same time, the actual consumption place can be regarded as the tax payment place: (2) when the above conditions are not met, the tax payment place is the regular residence of the consumer.

In the mobile commerce tax environment, the above judgment of tax payment location is also applicable. The difference is that in the B2C e-commerce environment, consumers' habitual residence is used as the basis for judging the tax location.

In the mobile commerce environment, due to the characteristics of "location relevance" embodied by the combination of Commerce and "mobile terminal", habitual residence can be combined with the place of frequent use of mobile network, or the location of mobile terminal can be used to judge the habitual residence.

(2) The Practice of Value-Added Tax Related Tax Administration in EU Countries.
The EU is the first region in the world to levy e-commerce value-added tax, creating a precedent for e-commerce taxation. Its value-added tax system is a tax system of great significance to the digital economy. In order to meet the challenges brought by the digital economy and promote the development of small and medium-sized enterprises, the EU has gradually tried to establish a simple, sound and effective value-added tax system for the single market to eliminate the value-added tax obstacles of cross-border mobile commerce, and prevent value-added tax fraud by strengthening administrative cooperation and information cooperation, so as to promote the modernization and upgrading of the value-added tax system in line with the digital economy. The main measures include:

1) **Implement the "European Union's one stop shop scheme".** OSS system means that the seller only needs to register in one EU member state and fill in a VAT tax return to declare and pay the VAT tax to be paid in all EU member states at one time, without separately registering and reporting in the EU member states with sales activities. The new decree issued by the EU also requires the e-commerce platform to be responsible for withholding and paying value-added tax on goods and services sold by non EU e-commerce providers on the platform. One stop taxation, platform withholding and other systems ensure that sellers pay value-added tax in the country where the final consumer is located, so as to make the tax distribution among EU Member States more equitable and contribute to the formation of EU single digital market strategy.

2) **Support the development of small and micro enterprises.** On January 18, 2018, the EU put forward a proposal to support the development of small and micro enterprises: first, open the small enterprise exemption policy to all enterprises meeting the EU conditions; The second is to determine the maximum threshold of national tax exemption; Third, establish a temporary transition period for small enterprises. When small enterprises temporarily exceed the tax exemption limit, they can still continue to enjoy the exemption policy; Fourth, further simplify the VAT obligations of tax-free and non tax-free small and medium-sized enterprises, including simplifying registration, simplifying record keeping and extending the tax period, reducing the frequency of filing VAT, etc. On November 8, 2019, the European Commission reached a provisional agreement on simplifying the VAT rules for small enterprises, further reducing the administrative burden and compliance costs of small enterprises. First, the provision of an exemption of 10000 euros/year for micro enterprises. The second is to simplify the collection and management procedures for small and medium-sized enterprises with online cross-border sales of less than 100000 euros.

3) **Promote VAT invoicing rules.** The EU introduced the relevant provisions of electronic invoices in the 2006 VAT directive. In 2010, the EU also revised the content of electronic invoices in the directive, which was fully implemented from January

1, 2013. The EU e-commerce value-added tax package rules adopted on December 5, 2017 proposed that from 2019, the invoicing will gradually adopt the principle of place of supply rather than place of consumption. All enterprises have the right to choose the value-added tax invoice solution that best suits their needs. Electronic invoices have the same basis as paper invoices, and the standards apply to both. The tax authorities of Member States should not impose certain preconditions, such as electronic signature. The VAT invoice requirements of the whole EU are unified, which provides legal certainty and ease of operation for cross-border enterprises. At the same time, even if the original is recorded on paper, it is allowed to store the invoice electronically, and the storage period of both is the same.

4) **Strengthen information cooperation and tax cooperation obligations.** The European Court of auditors pointed out that the administrative cooperation tools between tax administrations have not been fully utilized. Therefore, the EU needs to shift from the existing cooperation mode based on the exchange of information among Member States to a new mode of sharing and jointly analyzing information and acting together. In the action plan on the establishment of a single EU value-added tax zone and the draft regulations on strengthening administrative cooperation in value-added tax, the European Commission proposed to further strengthen the construction of the "EU rapid exchange of value-added tax fraud information network". With the support of the European Commission, the competent officials of the European Commission can have direct access to relevant information from different Member States, so that Member States can exchange, share and analyze key information and launch joint audits.

4   Response to China's Mobile Commerce Value-Added Tax Under DEPA

(1) Establish a Rapid Automatic Exchange Platform for Value-Added Tax Information. One belt, one road tax collection and management cooperation mechanism, is established for the purpose of achieving digital tax collection and administration of value-added tax. The platform mainly has two functions: first, multinational tax authorities can exchange value-added tax information related to cross-border transactions in time and automatically through the platform, change the previous pure information exchange mode on the basis of information exchange, and realize information sharing and joint analysis functions such as real-time communication, joint audit and comparison of tax related information content of cross-border transactions through the platform; Second, the platform integrates and automatically links to the VAT taxpayer identification number database of all Member States, which is open to all the public for sharing, so that overseas sellers can find and confirm whether the purchaser is qualified as a VAT taxpayer through the database, so as to prevent the purchaser from deliberately concealing its true identity. When the system is used for search, the search engine system will automatically retrieve data from the value-added tax database of each member state. In addition to the information that needs to be kept confidential, the platform can recommend that all alliance member states establish a unified format of VAT taxpayer identification number database, which can include the taxpayer's VAT taxpayer identification number, business address, website address, email and other main information.

This will one belt, one road to improve tax collection and management capacity in all countries, and better to build an open, equal, inclusive and sustainable tax collection and management cooperation mechanism. It will play an important role in improving the business environment of the "one belt and one way" country and region and promoting a more fair and reasonable international tax order.

(2) Focus on Tax Exemption and Tax Refund with Retention. In the digital economy, how to better connect the tax exemption and tax rebate of taxpayers' export business has become an important issue. The tax authorities should actively publicize the enterprises that meet the tax refund conditions, actively guide the taxpayers to complete the tax refund declaration online, and improve the tax refund efficiency. As a turnover tax, value-added tax should theoretically maintain a complete deduction chain, so as to avoid double taxation and tax evasion. As a tax preferential measure, tax exemption breaks the special turnover mechanism of value-added tax, which may lead to the imbalance of tax burden among taxpayers. Therefore, we should further clarify the scope of tax exemption for tax-free items that may increase the difficulty of collection, such as grain, oil, agricultural materials and other tax-free items that need to list taxpayers and limit sales objects. At the same time, we should also simplify the listing method of tax-free items. In addition, with China's economic development and changes in the international economic environment, as a macro-control policy, the export tax rebate rate has dynamic adjustment, which undoubtedly increases the complexity of the VAT tax rate structure and the tax compliance cost of cross-border e-commerce. Therefore, in the face of the frequently changing export tax rebate policy, we should further optimize the tax rebate rate structure on the basis of adhering to the principle of differentiation, strengthen the level of tax collection and management, and crack down on export tax fraud.

(3) Build Tax Credit System. In the past reform practice, the construction of tax credit system was mainly carried out from the single perspective of tax collection and management. In the face of many challenges brought by the digital economy to tax collection and management, we should further deepen the reform of certificates and licenses, build a tax credit platform based on the taxpayer identification number, use the big data network to form a social supervision, reward and punishment mechanism for the taxpayer's credit, and carry out targeted compliance incentives and illegal punishment according to the "concealment" characteristics of e-commerce.

At the same time, we should also improve the channels and mechanisms for the settlement of value-added tax disputes, improve the coordination and communication mechanism between tax collectors and payers, improve the scientificity of relevant legislation, improve the tax verification provisions and anti tax avoidance rules, and avoid damaging the trust and interests of taxpayers due to the abuse of administrative discretion. In addition, on the premise of strengthening information cooperation, we should also pay attention to protecting the privacy rights of taxpayers, standardize the confidentiality obligations of tax authorities and third-party tax partners, and establish and improve the legal accountability mechanism for violating the obligation of information confidentiality.

References

1. Einav, L., Knoepfle, D.T., Levin, J., et al.: Sales taxes and internet commerce. Soc. Sci. Electron. Publ. **104**(1), 1–26 (2014)
2. Jones, R., Basu, S.: Taxation of electronic commerce: a developing problem. Int. Rev. Law Comput. Technol. **16**(1), 35–51 (2002)
3. Lv, G., Chen, W., Chen, X., Ghannouchi, F.M., Feng, Z.: A fully integrated 47.6% fractional bandwidth GaN MMIC distributed efficient power amplifier with modified input matching and power splitting network. IEEE Trans. Microw. Theory Techniq. **69**(6), 3132–3145 (2021). https://doi.org/10.1109/tmtt.2021.3067034
4. OECD: International VAT/GST Guidelines, p. 2017. OECD Publishing, Paris (2017)
5. Cai, W.: Comparison of China's value-added tax system with Britain, France, Germany and Japan. Mall Moderniz. **19**, 214–215 (2016). https://doi.org/10.14013/j.cnki.scxdh.2016. 19.131.(蔡文莹.我国增值税制与英国,法国,德国,日本的比较.商场现代化. **19**, 214–215 (2016). https://doi.org/10.14013/j.cnki.scxdh.2016.19.131)
6. Gong, T.: The dilemma and outlet of value-added tax taxation for cross-border B2C digital transactions -- a review of the policy recommendations of the OECD international value-added tax guide. Int. Tax: 2021–2025. https://doi.org/10.19376/j.cnki.cn10-1142/f.2021. 03.004.(宫廷.跨境B2C数字化交易增值税课税的困境与出路——对OECD《国际增值税指南》政策建议的检思. 国际税收 **3**, 25–35 (2021). https://doi.org/10.19376/j.cnki.cn10-1142/f.2021.03.004)
7. Ma, X.: Research on cross-border service value-added tax policies in some countries. Int. Tax. **5**, 58–63 (2018). https://doi.org/10.19376/j.cnki.cn10-1142/f.2018.05.013. (马晓鸣.部分国家跨境服务增值税政策研究. 国际税收 **5**, 58–63 (2018). https://doi.org/10.19376/j. cnki.cn10-1142/f.2018.05.013)
8. Sun, X.: Depa and global digital economic governance. China Financ. **23**, 79–80 (2021) (孙晓.DEPA与全球数字经济治理. 中国金融 **23**, 79–80 (2021))
9. Zhou, M.: China's accession to depa: promoting global digital economy innovation cooperation. World Knowl. **22**, 62–63 (2021). (周密.中国加入DEPA:推动全球数字经济创新合作. 世界知识 **22**, 62–63 (2021)
10. Wu, D.: On the tax development of China's digital economy from the EU e-commerce value-added tax scheme. China Financ. **18**, 28–30 (2019). https://doi.org/10.14115/j.cnki. zgcz.2019.18.008 (吴东明.从欧盟电子商务增值税方案看我国数字经济税收发展. 中国财政 **18**, 28–30 (2019). https://doi.org/10.14115/j.cnki.zgcz.2019.18.008)
11. Guan, Y., Wu, J., Jia, C.: Value added tax system and characteristics of OECD countries and Its Enlightenment to China. Friends Account. **1**, 62–66 (2018). (管永昊,吴佳敏,贾昌峰.OECD国家增值税制度, 特点及对我国的启示. 会计之友 **1**, 62–66 (2018))
12. He, F.: Discussion on international taxation under the environment of e-commerce. Contemp. Financ. Econ. **11**, 28–29 (2002). (何飞云. 电子商务环境下的国际税收问题探讨. 当代财经 **11**, 28–29 (2002))
13. Ma, X.: Problems and countermeasures of e-commerce development from the perspective of tax law. People's Forum **A12**, 74–76 (2015). (马秀玲. 从税法角度看电子商务发展问题及对策. 人民论坛 **A12**, 74–76 (2015))
14. Wang, H.: EU promotes Taxation on digital economy and its impact on China. Macroecon. Manag. **415**(7), 88–94 (2018). https://doi.org/10.19709/j.cnki.11-3199/f.2018.07.017. (王灏晨. 欧盟推动对数字经济征税及对我国的影响. 宏观经济管理, **415**(7), 88–94 (2018). https://doi.org/10.19709/j.cnki.11-3199/f.2018.07.017)

Digital Advertising Literacy in Gastronomy Brands. The Case of the Spanish Chef Dabiz Muñoz

Pedro Hellín Ortuño[✉], Antonio Raúl Fernández Rincón,
and Onésimo Samuel Hernández Gómez

University of Murcia, Murcia, Spain
{phellin,antonioraul.fernandez,onesimosamuel.hernandez}@um.es

Abstract. In this study, our aim is to contribute to the debate around the possibility of building a brand through creating content of a pedagogic nature. Immersed in the digital ecosystem, transmedia storytelling offers wide-ranging options for corporate socialization, whether through personal identity or through business identity. Our study centers on the sector of haute cuisine, utilizing as a case study the construction on social media of the identity of Spanish chef Dabiz Muñoz, someone of significant media interest who, moreover, was named the best chef in the world in 2021. Following a mixed methodological model, we analyze his social media posts from 2017 to 2021 to reveal how his more pedagogic content achieves greater visibility on social media and contributes more efficiently to constructing a personal identity which also extends to the businesses he runs. This pedagogic approach can be studied from an advertising literacy perspective as an example of a brand/person who disseminates their discourse through formats which are not formally advertising formats.

Keywords: Digital literacy · Advertising pedagogy · Brands · Gastronomy · Dabiz Muñoz

1 Branding, Personal Branding and New Narratives

The digital ecosystem generates among brands, today more than ever, an imperative need for them to create firm and lasting bonds with their audiences. Over and above strategies focusing on driving transactions, the challenge is to build relationships, generate trust, and foster loyalty. To that end, digitalization –in a broad sense– and social media –in a strict sense– offer a wide array of options that corporations, institutions, and individuals have to be aware of and know how to manage. In this context, the strength of the brand is a major strategic requirement. Defining and consolidating the axiological universe in which the brand exists and is developed is essential in order to identify the profiles, groups, and territories in which it must act, as well as the content to be promoted depending on these [44].

© Springer Nature Switzerland AG 2022
M. Rauterberg et al. (Eds.): HCII 2022, LNCS 13520, pp. 167–180, 2022.
https://doi.org/10.1007/978-3-031-18158-0_12

Together with corporate strategies for digital media content creation, one of the major aspects under consideration nowadays is the work around personal branding, an aspect which takes on particular significance in our study. Personal branding as an autonomous concept was given a major boost in the late 1990s [31, 35]. Although for some authors the origin of the term is found in Goffman's work on the concept of "self" in the 1960s [19, 25, 36] or in the 1980s with market research [46], today the terms "personal branding" and "self branding" [14] appear to be the accepted terminology to emphasize the importance of the image and identity of individuals. Image refers to the sphere of external perception –how we are perceived by others- whereas identity is understood to be the self-definition of the individual at an existential level -"who am I?" [2]. Thus, personal branding is created at an individual level and, in this respect, the concept is linked both to image and to identity. The need to create and manage a personal brand has traditionally been related to the professional sphere, that is, people's identity and image in the job market [8]. Hence, the aim is to convey the value that the individual can provide [18].

The context of the digital society emerged as a driving force for personal branding, transforming managing these brands into a complex, multivariate process that involves actions both in real life and on online platforms –essentially, social media- as they obtain greater reach and enable continual updates. Likewise, the proliferation of touchpoints between brands –whether personal or corporate- and their audiences requires them to act in a more agile and coordinated manner in order to build rapport. According to Llorens [24], any digital branding strategy should take into account 10 key principles: 1) Consolidating a clear strategic focus; 2) Greater speed in any strategic adjustments; 3) Working based on a coherent approach, centralizing management and decentralizing resources; 4) Combining online (digital touchpoints) and offline (physical touchpoints) elements in the funnel; 5). Handling the data efficiently; 6) Immediacy and personalization; 7) Building based on experience; 8) Brand and business should go hand-in-hand more than ever; 9) Creating spaces for collaborative management; and 10) Constant monitoring. Digital branding is the personality of our organization, service, or product, created through the sum of all the experiences an individual has with it. While it still includes things such as visual identity, now it also contains far more important and influential touchpoints, such as interactions on social media and online reviews [39]. Digital branding has been associated with the corporate environment of companies and institutions; however, the ubiquitous nature and ease of use of digital media and devices has also given rise to the term "digital personal branding", to refer to a collection of efforts which seek to showcase an individual's professionalism through digital media.

The fragmentation of the communicative space generated by interactive digital communication has a decisive influence on the stories or narratives that circulate and how these are consumed. With regard to the content circulating in the digital ecosystem, the most widespread reference is the consolidation of transmedia storytelling. This concept, which has been adopted almost across the board by the content industry, goes back to the early 21st century, specifically to the article "Transmedia Storytelling" by Henry Jenkins from 2003. These narratives involve going beyond the notion of narrative as a story to encompass a social practice. Scolari [41] defines transmedia storytelling as an experience arising out of the fragmentation of audiences which encompasses different media and devices, all of which are linked together by a common narrative thread. Therefore, it combines storytelling as creation and as social practice as, among the people who participate in it, it fosters engagement and interaction, from a media perspective. Transmedia discourse transforms the audience into users and consumption into a participatory act [11].

2 Advertising Pedagogy and Literacy

The paradox of advertising discourse is that in spite of its omnipresence in our lives, of its desire to penetrate into every corner of the community, it is practically invisible and that is precisely where its brilliant success lies [32]. Its ubiquitous nature generates a perceptual overload which has multiplied exponentially since the introduction of digital media. Its effectiveness lies in the "pedagogic action" of messages which are simultaneously informative and evaluative, as well as guiding conduct [38], incorporating semiotic (semanticized objects), ideological (instructing behavioral guidelines), and economic (such as financing media structures) practices [16]. Advertising as pedagogic discourse incorporates three modes of practice: a semiotic practice, through the proposition of a social model founded on a specific framework of production, circulation, and consumption of messages; an ideological practice with the essential aim of orienting audiences toward the market, deploying before these audiences a specific configuration of the world, talking to them about objects while at the same time perpetuating the social system of which it is both guarantor and defender; and, lastly, an economic practice, from the moment when the advertising discourse has assured its omnipresence in the public sphere, the place where the true products of the media reside, transformed into exchange value: the audiences [10].

Advertising literacy is defined as the ability to recognize, evaluate, and understand advertising [26]. Historically, research has focused on cognitive literacy [40, 42] and on conventional advertising formats [29], even though literacy with regard to advertising should be understood as the acquisition of skills to analyze, evaluate, and create persuasive messages in a variety of contexts and media [23]. Immersed in a digital society, we receive a large volume of information through new ways of accessing and processing that demand new capabilities in order to access, analyze, and evaluate images, texts, and sounds that utilize multimedia resources [1]. Its citizens themselves, backed by technological advances, have assumed their ability to participate and control some of the advertising communication mechanisms, modifying the traditional unidirectional model and presenting themselves as builders of content and experiences linked to products and brands [27].

As regards brands [12, 28], advertising literacy is the ability to be able to understand and transfer the meanings emitted by the brands, but also the ability to use these meanings within the social context of existence. It thus becomes an important factor used by many consumers to locate and reposition their social groups and their identity. Brands can be used by the consumer as resources for the symbolic construction of the self and help establish and communicate some fundamental cultural aspects such as social status, gender, age, family, tradition, and authenticity.

3 Objective and Methodology

The objective of this work is to reflect on the ability to build a brand by generating content of a pedagogic nature through digital media, specifically through social media. We focused our study on one of the sectors which has used this content and these tools most profusely over recent months: the sector of haute cuisine, the personal branding of internationally famous chefs, and corporate branding (in this case, restaurants). The study looks at the particular case of Spanish chef Dabiz Muñoz. This top professional was named the best chef in the world in the The Best Chef Awards 2021. Muñoz has owned the restaurant DiverXO, located in Madrid (Spain) and boasting three Michelin stars, since 2007. At the current time, he is also the owner of the StreetXO premises located inside a department store in the Spanish capital and inspired by international street food; GotXO, an offering of imaginative home-cooked food for home delivery, representing one of the leading examples of food delivery for haute cuisine; and the project currently under way, RabioXO. Muñoz is the present and future of Spanish gastronomy, "his cooking is filled with flare, tastes, textures. It has products and craftsmanship, it is delectable and lacks nothing" [37]. He is a leading exponent of what has come to be called "Brand Spain". The gastronomy sector in Spain represents 33% of its GDP (EUR 388 billion) and employs 3.73 million workers (18%) [20].

In light of the crisis triggered by the COVID-19 pandemic in the hospitality industry, those in the sector of haute cuisine have reacted by implementing considerable changes in work processes and in the way they relate to their audiences, changes which, more than suggesting a temporary reaction, could be marking a shift in paradigm in the sector. The "recipes" to alleviate the recession in the sector include:

- The reappraisal of the figure of the chef as an agent to promote education and food systems.
- The role of chefs as agents for educating and promoting healthy eating [43].
- The digital transformation of the chefs and their brands to generate new communication channels and improve consumers' knowledge in order to segment and personalize products and strategies [5, 9, 21, 34].

Our choice of Dabiz Muñoz satisfies a two-fold purpose, which, on one hand, has to do with him being the leading figure at the current time in Spanish haute cuisine and, on the other hand, is due to his status as one of the most active chefs on digital media in recent years, primarily during the initial months of the pandemic and lockdown for the population in Spain. The use of digital communication is an attitude which has become widespread in the haute cuisine sector in recent months. For the Barcelona Culinary Hub (BCH), it is one of the six post-COVID-19 trends in the restaurant sector, together with sustainability, adaptability, efficient management, innovation, and humanization. An analysis (not included here) conducted prior to this study revealed that out of the Spanish restaurants currently with three Michelin stars, Dabiz Muñoz and his restaurant DiverXo have a higher overall number of followers on social media that the rest (Jordi Cruz, "AbaC"; Martín Berasategui, "Lasarte"; Josep Roca, "Celler Can Roca"; Quique

Dacosta; Elena and Juan Mari Arzak, "Arzak"; Ángel León, "Aponiente"; Pedro Subijana, "Akelarre"; Eneko Atxa, "Azurmendi"; and Jesús Sánchez, "Cenador de Amos"). In this respect, it is of interest to highlight that both the chefs' personal profiles 'and the restaurants' corporate profiles have greater visibility and impact on Instagram than on Facebook.

The mixed methodological design contains an element of a qualitative nature in which we performed a content analysis [4, 22, 33] of the videos to extract the thematic resources used and classify them into various categories and subcategories. The quantitative element relates to a numerical analysis of the videos regarding the impact achieved. In this respect, we recorded the two key variables: interactions (the amount of comments or reactions obtained by the videos) and views (the number of times the video has been viewed by users). The study focused on the period between December 2014 and December 2021. A total of 217 videos were located which were posted in this period from the chef's personal accounts on Facebook (dabizdiverxo) and Instagram (dabizdiverxo). He generates and disseminates this content with the help and supervision of his partner, the Spanish presenter and influencer Cristina Pedroche (CristiPedroche).

Based on this design, our aim is to progress further in understanding the mechanisms through which brand content is generated in transmedia storytelling. The themes, the methods and the tools used by the chef can serve to reflect on identity expressed through positioning. All this is in the context of a sector of such particular social and economic relevance as that of haute cuisine and such a unique period of study as that of the COVID-19 pandemic.

4   Results

After viewing the videos, we performed an initial classification of the videos into two general categories which we named Brand Identity (BI) and Product (P). The former category consists of videos focusing on working on the chef's personal brand in a broad sense (134 videos) and the latter category contains videos centering on the product, his style of cooking, influences, the recipes he offers, the ingredients, and how to cook them (see Fig. 1).

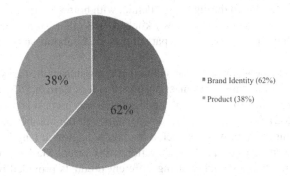

Fig. 1. Percentage of videos per category

Within these general categories, we were able to establish a series of subcategories which show the activity by theme. We therefore differentiated between the various, more personal, videos through which Dabiz Muñoz creates his identity by largely showing his interests, hobbies, and personality. In this group we included: "Gastronomy/Travel" (58), "Sport" (40), "Promotional" (16), "Humor" (10), "Love/Humor" (5), "Travel/Humor" (4) and "Corporate" (2). In the Product category, we differentiated between "Cooking/Recipes" (33), "Promotional" (11), "Cooking/Demonstration" (16), "Cooking/Tasting" (11), "Cooking/Corporate" (7) and "Corporate" (4) (see Fig. 2).

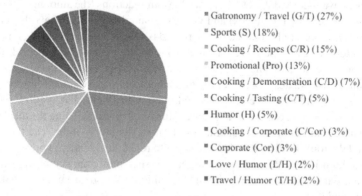

- Gatronomy / Travel (G/T) (27%)
- Sports (S) (18%)
- Cooking / Recipes (C/R) (15%)
- Promotional (Pro) (13%)
- Cooking / Demonstration (C/D) (7%)
- Cooking / Tasting (C/T) (5%)
- Humor (H) (5%)
- Cooking / Corporate (C/Cor) (3%)
- Corporate (Cor) (3%)
- Love / Humor (L/H) (2%)
- Travel / Humor (T/H) (2%)

Fig. 2. Percentage of videos per subcategory

As we can see, the most prominent subcategories are: "Gastronomy/Travel" (G/T), in which the chef showcases the different restaurants that he visits on his travels around the world, describing the dishes he tries and thus demonstrating how important it is to know other cultures and ways of doing things so as to build his product and, thus, his brand identity; "Sport" (S), which consists mainly of the early years of the period studied, in which the chef carries out his collaboration with the Nike brand with the hashtag #RunWithDabiz and where he displays his personality and character, conveying traits such as effort, tenacity, and personal growth; and "Cooking/Recipes" (C/R), a category which essentially developed during the pandemic, with home-made videos in which the chef prepares personal recipes in his own kitchen, and other, similar videos he made in the post-lockdown period which are part of a paid collaboration with Spanish firm Correos Market.

Analysis of the videos for each year shows that it was during the first year of the pandemic (2020), and coinciding with a mass posting of videos from the "Cooking/Recipes" (C/R) subcategory, when the amount of videos posted was highest and their length was the greatest. In 2021 (the year after lockdown), although the number of videos posted dropped considerably, there was not such a marked reduction in length, since some of the videos were born out of the paid collaboration with Correos Market whereby the chef made recipes in his home's kitchen using different products provided by the supplier (see Table 1.).

Table 1. Duration of videos per year and average in seconds

Year	No. of videos	Time (sec.)	Average time (sec.)
2014	2	29"	14.5"
2015	2	23"	11.5"
2016	11	279"	23.36"
2017	28	1155"	41.25"
2018	34	1625"	47.8"
2019	53	3265"	61.06"
2020	61	16038"	262.91"
2021	26	4316"	166"

For the purposes of this study, it is interesting to observe the evolution in number of views both on Facebook and on Instagram. As we can observe in Fig. 3, in 2020 there was an exponential increase in views of the videos, particularly on the Facebook social network, which decreased in 2021. As regards Instagram, we can see that there is also an increase, albeit not as significant as on Facebook; however, the interesting thing about Instagram is that the number of views was maintained in 2021, giving an idea of the level of fame achieved by the chef in the previous year which helped him to consolidate his account on that social network.

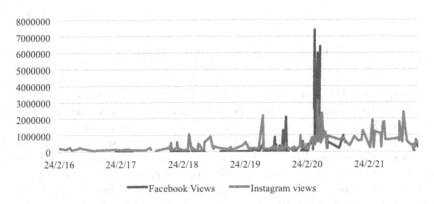

Fig. 3. Performance of views on Facebook and Instagram

As regards interactions by users with the videos (likes, comments and different reactions) (see Fig. 4), we can see a similar pattern to that of views, being representative of reactions being maintained on Instagram following the first year of the pandemic.

If we observe views for each of the social networks in detail (see Fig. 5), we see that most views are on Instagram; however, in 2020 we can see that the amount of views on Facebook exceeds, for the first and only time, the amount of views on Instagram.

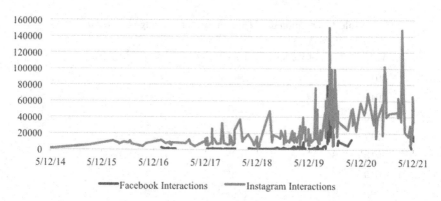

Fig. 4. Performance of interactions on Facebook and Instagram

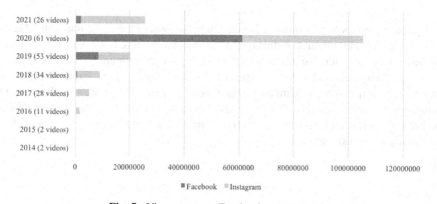

Fig. 5. Views per year Facebook + Instagram

As regards number of interactions (see Fig. 6), we observe that Instagram is a social network on which there is more interaction with the content than on Facebook. Despite this, in 2020 Facebook posts fostered a notable increase in interactions.

In addition to these data, we considered it appropriate to classify the data by number of views and interactions on Facebook and Instagram with the aim of determining which were the most successful videos on the different social networks (see Table 2.).

As we can see in Table 2., of the 10 most-viewed videos on Facebook, nine belong to the "Cooking/Recipes" (C/R) subcategory of the "Product" (P) category, and their posting coincides with the lockdown period. The only video which does not belong to this category but was ranked among the top 10 most-viewed videos, and was posted some months later, belongs to the subcategory of "Love/Humor" (L/H) included in the "Brand Identity" (BI) category.

As regards Instagram, six of the most-viewed videos belong to the "Product" category, of which five fall within the "Cooking/Recipes" subcategory and one within "Cooking/Demonstration". Three of these videos were published during lockdown and a further three in the post-lockdown period (two of these as part of the paid collaboration

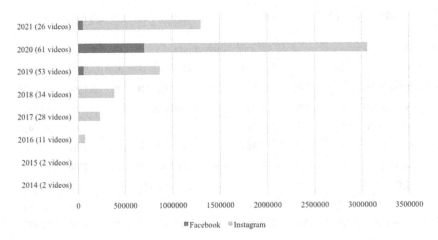

Fig. 6. Interactions per year Facebook + Instagram

Table 2. Top 10 most-viewed videos on Facebook and Instagram

Facebook					Instagram				
	Date	Cat	Sub	Views		Date	Cat	Sub	Views
1	09/04/2020	P	C/R	7400000	1	26/04/2020	P	C/R	3110903
2	10/05/2020	P	C/R	6400000	2	16/09/2021	BI	Pro	2400000
3	26/04/2020	P	C/R	6000000	3	24/05/2020	P	C/R	2312180
4	10/04/2020	P	C/R	5500000	4	11/06/2019	BI	G/T	2182019
5	24/04/2020	P	C/R	4900000	5	10/05/2020	P	C/R	2068678
6	01/05/2020	P	C/R	3500000	6	14/03/2021	P	C/D	1900000
7	07/04/2020	P	C/R	2600000	7	22/05/2021	P	C/R	1809529
8	29/04/2020	P	C/R	2200000	8	22/08/2021	BI	G/T	1800000
9	05/05/2020	P	C/R	2200000	9	15/05/2021	P	C/R	1767400
10	24/10/2019	BI	L/H	2100000	10	17/01/2021	BI	H	1300000

with Correos Market). The four remaining videos belong to the "Brand Identity" category, within the "Gastronomy/Travel" (G/T) (2), "Promotional" (Pro) (1) and "Humor" (H) (1) subcategories.

It is noteworthy that the company Correos Market saw an opportunity in this type of pedagogic content and entered into a paid collaboration with the chef to raise the visibility of its brand. It is significant that this campaign (two of the videos of which are part of the top 10 most-viewed videos and also among the 10 videos with the most interactions) was only rolled out on Instagram. We can deduce from this the importance and impact of this type of content, its suitability for reaching a certain audience, and the opportunity it represents.

Table 3. Top 10 videos with the most interactions on Facebook and Instagram

Facebook					Instagram				
	Date	Cat	Sub	Interact.		Date	Cat	Sub	Interact.
1	26/04/2020	P	C/R	84344	1	26/04/2020	P	C/R	150368
2	09/04/2020	P	C/R	78904	2	16/09/2021	BI	Pro	147321
3	10/05/2020	P	C/R	74671	3	15/05/2021	P	C/R	101956
4	10/04/2020	P	C/R	54594	4	06/06/2020	BI	L/H	98584
5	24/04/2020	P	C/R	37217	5	10/05/2020	P	C/R	98048
6	01/05/2020	P	C/R	35677	6	22/05/2021	P	C/R	84111
7	07/04/2020	P	C/R	32961	7	18/01/2020	BI	L/H	75484
8	03/05/2020	P	C/R	30898	8	24/05/2020	P	C/R	74552
9	19/04/2020	P	C/R	30560	9	17/01/2021	BI	H	68838
10	29/04/2020	P	C/R	29559	10	30/11/2021	BI	H	65164

Another table was created to rank the number of interactions in each social media network (Table 3.). We can observe that the 10 videos which received the most reactions on Facebook all belong to the "Product" (P) category, in the "Cooking/Recipes" (C/R) subcategory. On Instagram, five videos fall within that subcategory, four of which were posted during lockdown and one after lockdown. The other five videos belong to the Brand Image (BI) category, two of which fall within the "Love/Humor" (L/H) subcategory, another two in "Humor" (H), and one in the "Promotional" (Pro) subcategory. As we have observed, we can deduce there are differences between the two social networks: Facebook, a social networking site on which the chef's audience has an older age range and a clear interest in more educational videos, and Instagram, a social media platform with a younger audience on which content related to "Humor" becomes more important, even though the videos containing recipes are also of importance.

5 Discussion

Following our analysis of the full period of social media posts by the chef Dabiz Muñoz, we can state that, thanks to him beginning to post on social media practically from the time their popularity began, we have been able to observe the increase in use and interaction typical of any user, highlighting the following features:

- The number of posts has been increasing from year to year, in correlation with the general increase in the Western world in use of social media.
- The duration of the posts and interactions have increased in the same way, most probably due to the same cause.

The most significant item of data as regards posts and interactions is from 2020, specifically in the period coinciding with lockdown. This was the time during which most videos were posted and the length of the videos increased considerably. In addition, this audiovisual content was the content obtaining the most views and interactions. This rebuts the generalized belief that shorter videos are more likely to go viral. The time available to the population undoubtedly has an influence on this fact, as during the lockdown period they were obliged to remain at home, on a compulsory basis, and decided to occupy their leisure time by consuming online content.

In line with the objectives set in this study, we can highlight that the themes obtaining the highest number of views and interactions are those of a notably pedagogic nature: that is, videos in which the chef opts to disseminate his own recipes in an educational manner so that his followers can enjoy watching how the dishes were made or even make his recipes themselves.

From our study, we can see that during the initial years of the chef's activities on social media he was interested in showing aspects linked to his personality and his own particular philosophy of life, many of which were related to his sports interests and his keenness to learn about manifold gastronomic cultures. These initiatives undoubtedly contributed to building a very well-defined personal brand identity, based on effort, personal growth, knowledge, and creativity.

As can be drawn from the study we have performed and although the content we have just mentioned is of a pedagogic-promotional nature, since the lockdown caused by COVID-19 advertising pedagogy has become more patent in audiovisual content. With the explosion of social media, there has been a quantitative leap, reaching broader and more diverse segments of the population. We can confirm this based on the success obtained by Dabiz Muñoz's profile on Instagram, where the age range of its users is very young to be the audience for his messages.

In the social media sphere, there are also differences in this respect as, despite the success of some content of a pedagogic nature on Instagram, most of the more popular content is of a more social nature and linked to either Humor or Love. However, on Facebook, where the user profile is of an older age range, recipe cooking is the subcategory dominating the 10 top positions. If we examine our Product and Brand Image categories, the winning content on Facebook is related to product, while on Instagram, it is related to brand image. The audience on Facebook, being a more adult audience, already has a consolidated picture of Dabiz Muñoz as a benchmark in cuisine, as well as being the chef's potential customers.

The discursive mechanisms used in the different videos include the technical and linguistic treatment characterized by the intention of showing a natural, improvised and domestic aesthetic, lacking artifice or great technical skills. The same is true with the language the chef uses to address his audience, showing a natural style and affinity with his viewers, signaling the values of his brand and his positioning in the world of chefs.

We can therefore conclude that the use of advertising pedagogy for building personal brands in the haute cuisine sector both works and is accepted by social media audiences. We can also conclude that (according to the example analyzed in this study) it can follow different strategies, related to the type of social network and the associated audience, although always offering content that is in demand among the audience. This includes educational content and personal opinions with a friendly approach and which can be quickly consumed by viewers, who thus feel that they are the ones choosing to view and hence accept the advertising content.

References

1. Aguaded, I.: Media programme international support for media education. Comunicar **40**, 07–08 (2013). https://doi.org/10.3916/C40-2013-01-01
2. Alvesson, M.: Knowledge Work and Knowledge-Intensive Firms. Oxford University Press, Oxford (2004)
3. Barcelona Culinary Hub. https://www.barcelonaculinaryhub.com. Accessed 3 Jan 2022
4. Bardin, L.: El análisis de contenido. Ediciones Akal, Madrid (2002)
5. Batat, W.: How Michelin-starred chefs are being transformed into social bricoleurs? An online qualitative study of luxury foodservice during the pandemic crisis. J. Serv. Manage. **32**(1), 87–99 (2020). https://doi.org/10.1108/JOSM-05-2020-0142
6. Best Chef Awards. https://thebestchefawards.com. Accessed 2 Dec 2021
7. Bueno, P.: Un cuarto de siglo en la cocina Española. https://www.revistadelibros.com/juan-mari-arzak-y-ferran-adria/. Accessed 20 Nov 2021
8. Cassinger, C.: Personal branding. In: Dahlgaard-Park, S.M. (ed.) The SAGE Encyclopedia of Quality and the Service Economy, pp. 490–491. Sage, Thousand Oaks (2015)
9. Clarke, T.B., Murphy, J., Adler, J.: Celebrity chef adoption and implementation of social media, particularly Pinterest: a diffusion of innovations approach. Int. J. Hosp. Manag. **57**, 84–92 (2016). https://doi.org/10.1016/j.ijhm.2016.06.004
10. Correa, R.I., Guzmán, M., Aguaded, I.: La mujer invisible. Una lectura disidente de los mensajes publicitarios. Huelva, Grupo Comunicar (2000)
11. De la Fuente Prieto, J., Lacasa Díaz, P., Martínez-Borda, R.: Adolescentes, redes sociales y universos transmedia: la alfabetización mediática en contextos participativos. Rev. Lat. Comun. Soc. **74**, 172–196 (2019)
12. Elliott, R., Wattanasuwan, K.: Brands as symbolic resources for the construction of identity. Int. J. Advertising Rev. Mark. Commun. **17**(2), 131–144 (1998). https://doi.org/10.1080/026 50487.1998.11104712
13. Food and Agriculture Organization of the United Nations: Chefs as Agents of Change. http://www.fao.org/3/ca3715en/ca3715en.pdf. Accessed 20 Sept 2021
14. Gandini, A.: Digital work: self-branding and social capital in the freelance knowledge economy. Mark. Theory **16**, 123 (2016). https://doi.org/10.1177/1470593115607942
15. Goffman, E.: The Presentation of Self in Everyday Life, 1st edn. Anchor Books, New York (1959)
16. Hellín, P.: Publicidad y valores posmodernos. Siranda, Madrid (2007)
17. Hellin, P., Trindade, E.: Latin-American perceptions on definitions and arguments about crossmedia and transmedia in advertising. El profesional de la Información (EPI) **28**(4), e280408 (2019)
18. Johnstone, T.: Without personal branding your career is dead. Ottawa Bus. J. **18**(16), 19 (2015)
19. Khedher, M.: A brand for everyone: guidelines for personal brand managing. J. Glob. Bus. Issues **9**, 19–27 (2015)
20. KPMG, La gastronomía en la economía española. https://assets.kpmg/content/dam/kpmg/es/pdf/2019/01/gastronomia-en-economia-espanola.pdf. Accessed 18 Dec 2021
21. Kuwonu, F.: Stranded chef's online cuisine classes help beat COVID-19 lockdown blues Africa Renewal. United Nations (2020). https://www.un.org/africarenewal/magazine/may-2020/coronavirus/stranded-chef%E2%80%99s-online-cuisine-classes-beat-covid-19-loc kdown-blues

22. Laurence, C.: How do I calculate my engagement rate on Instagram? (2017). https://bit.ly/2jOEkXW

23. Livingstone, S., Helsper, E.J.: Does advertising literacy mediate the effects of advertising on children? A critical examination of two linked research literatures in relation to obesity and food choice. J. Commun. **56**(3), 560–584 (2006). https://doi.org/10.1111/j.1460-2466.2006.00301.x

24. Llorens, C.: Retos de la gestión de la marca en el entorno digital (2018). https://www.marketingnews.es/investigacion/opinion/1119040031605/retos-de-gestion-de-marca-entorno-digital.1.html. Accessed 11 Jan 2022

25. Lorgnier, N., O'Rourke, S.: Improving students communication skills and awareness online, an opportunity to enhance learning and help personal branding. Paper Presented at the 5th International Technology, Education and Development Conference, Valencia (2011)

26. Malmelin, N.: What is advertising literacy? Exploring the dimensions of advertising literacy. J. Visual Literacy **29**(2), 129–142 (2010)

27. Martínez Pastor, E., Nicolás Ojeda, M.A.: Publicidad Digital. Esic, Madrid (2016)

28. McCracken, G.: The value of the brand: an anthropological perspective. In: Aaker, D., Biel, A. (eds.) Brand Equity and Advertising. Lawrence Erlbaum Associates, Hillsdale (1993)

29. Meeus, W., Walrave, M., Van-Ouytsel, J., Driesen, A.: Advertising literacy in schools: evaluating free online educational resources for advertising literacy. J. Media Educ. **5**(2), 5–12 (2014)

30. Michelin Guide. https://guide.michelin.com. Accessed 13 Dec 2021

31. Montoya, P., Vandehey, T.: The Brand Called You. Nightingale Conant (2002)

32. Nacach, P.: Las palabras sin las cosas. Lengua de trapo, Madrid (2004)

33. Neuendorf, K.A.: The Content Analysis Guidebook. SAGE Publications LTD, Los Angeles (2002)

34. Perez, J.: Virtual cooking lessons during the COVID-19 pandemic. CTV News Ottawa (2021). https://ottawa.ctvnews.ca/virtual-cooking-lessons-during-the-covid-19-pandemic-1.5389424. Accessed 13 Dec 2021

35. Peters, T.: The Brand Called You. Fast Company, vol. 10(83) (1997). http://www.fastcompany.com/28905/brand-called-you. Accessed 13 Dec 2021

36. Philbrick, J.L., Cleveland, A.D.: Personal branding: building your pathway to professional success. Med. Ref. Serv. Q. **34**, 181–189 (2015). https://doi.org/10.1080/02763869.2015.1019324

37. Poncini, H.: Dabiz Muñoz, la madurez del chef rebelled. https://elpais.com/eps/2021-11-28/dabiz-munoz-la-madurez-del-chef-rebelde.html. Accessed 20 Sept 2021

38. Prieto Castillo, D.: Discurso autoritario y comunicación alternative. Premia Editora, México (1987)

39. Rowles, D.: Digital Branding. Kogan Page, London (2018)

40. Rozendaal, E., Lapierre, M.A., Van-Reijmersdal, E.A., Buijzen, M.: Reconsidering advertising literacy as a defense against advertising effects. Media Psychol. **14**(4), 333–354 (2011). https://doi.org/10.1080/15213269.2011.620540

41. Scolari, C.A.: Narrativas transmedia. Cuando todos los medios cuentan. Deusto, Barcelona (2013)

42. Spielvogel, J., Terlutter, R.: Development of TV advertising literacy in children. Int. J. Advertising Rev. Mark. Commun. **32**(3), 343–368 (2013). https://doi.org/10.2501/IJA-32-3-343-368

43. Steno, A.M., Friche, N.: Celebrity chefs and masculinities among male cookery trainees in vocational education. J. Vocat. Educ. Training **67**(1), 47–61 (2015). https://doi.org/10.1080/13636820.2014.927901

44. Summa: Branding digital, más branding que nunca (2022). https://cdn2.hubspot.net/hubfs/3318473/Ebooks/SUM-ebook3-brandingdigital.pdf. Accessed 12 Jan 2022

45. The World's 50 Best Restaurants. https://www.theworlds50best.com. Accessed 2 Dec 2021
46. Vallas, S.P., Cummins, E.R.: Personal branding and identity norms in the popular business press: enterprise culture in an age of precarity. Organ. Stud. **36**, 293–319 (2015). https://doi.org/10.1177/0170840614563741

Interface Experience, Brand Experience. On How Interface Design Models the Relationship with the Brand

Audrey Moutat[(✉)]

CeReS, Limoges University, 87000 Limoges, France
audrey.moutat@unilim.fr

Abstract. Based on a corpus of websites from various brands, this conference will aim to show how UI/UX design models the relationship that the Internet user will build with brands. To do so, we will discuss the contributions of experiential marketing in order to show the new ways in which digital technology can create links between the Internet user and the brand. The aim is to highlight the semiotic functions of the graphic and interactive choices made by designers. We will see that the different sensitive meanings at stake (sensory, emotional, even somatic) build a reflexive relationship with the brand that integrates the lifestyle of the Internet user/consumer.

Keywords: UX design · Brand digital experience · Experiential marketing

1 Introduction

Aware of the mistrust, even defiance, of some consumers towards them, brands have renewed their approaches in order to propose a lasting link with their audiences. Placing the consumer-subject at the heart of their communication strategy, they have developed new orientations with the aim of creating a link with them and producing a real experience. Because self-esteem depends on the value of its consumers, brands today propose interpersonal discourses, in a one-to-one communication mode, a trend that has developed notably with the advent of web 2.0. Indeed, the Internet never ceases to offer opportunities to express oneself in a renewed way and to innovate in the strategies of interactions with the targets. If the participative web, micro-blogging and social networks have allowed to weave close links between consumers and brands, the design of websites has also considerably evolved in order to produce real browsing experiences and, with them, different ways of understanding brands and institutions. Thus, since the 2000s, new web design practices have been developed, giving rise to an innovative design methodology: UX design or user experience design, which consists of designing interactive products by focusing not on the product but on the experience of its use. By "practicing" the site, the user "practices" the brand itself and gets to know it in a different way.

Among the possibilities offered by UX, emotional design proposes to optimize these interpersonal relationships by designing interfaces as people. The construction of a

© Springer Nature Switzerland AG 2022
M. Rauterberg et al. (Eds.): HCII 2022, LNCS 13520, pp. 181–195, 2022.
https://doi.org/10.1007/978-3-031-18158-0_13

brand's identity is then based on the affirmation of an authentic personality that is embodied in character traits and the assertion of an ethos that make it unique. The link that the consumer can then forge with the brand operates according to the same principles as everyday interpersonal relationships: the recognition and sharing of deep values as well as an accounting of character become the vectors of a feeling of euphoria, conducive to the establishment of a lasting relationship. It is in this sense that Simon Sinek recognizes that what people buy is not so much the products manufactured by a brand, but what drives and motivates the brand to produce them. People are more inspired by why brands create their products than by the products themselves. Shared values and principles as well as self-recognition through the brand, a reflexive level as Donald Norman would say, are the main drivers of what Bergkvist and Bech-Larsen (2010) call brand love. "This brand love is the foundation for the development of brand loyalty and active engagement. In other words, brand love is formed by positive emotional responses that generate brand loyalty." It is usually expressed through adherence to the theme (in other words, the ethos and core values) so embodied and is usually conveyed through symbolic devices.

It is in this service-dominant context (Ford and Bowen 2008) with a strong symbolic charge, where the sharing, or even the co-creation, of value between a brand and its targets is paramount (Vargo and Lusch 2004), that we propose to highlight the strategies underlying experience design. In this work, we will study the way in which emotional branding exploits the potential offered by digital interfaces to establish an affective link between a brand and its consumers. Our objective is not to measure their efficiency with the public, which would require further investigations based on interviews and observation of the uses of Internet users, but to highlight the functioning of the discursive structures of digital interfaces in the creation of an experiential context and to typologize them into strategic types implemented by the brands.

2   From Experience to UX Design

"Complex and protean" (Boutaud 2021), the concept of experience raises varied problems inscribed in a vast inter-disciplinary network, going from literature to communication, passing by philosophy, sociology and marketing, to quote only these few examples. However, it is in phenomenology that this concept finds its true anchor: the lived experience of the world consists in perceiving and feeling the whole of the sensitive phenomena which constitute it.

Understood as "knowledge acquired either by the senses, or by the intelligence, or by both, and opposed to the innate knowledge implied by the nature of the mind" (CNRTL), experience is thus presented as the articulation of three dimensions: sensitive, pragmatic and cognitive. Experiencing one's environment is thus based on a perceptive act that variably engages the sensoriality of a subject towards the different aspects of the world in which he or she is immersed (Bordron 2011 and Moutat 2015, 2019). Simultaneously, this experience is felt and experienced, engaging the subject in a perpetual thymic evaluation of its experience, very often polarized between pleasure and displeasure, euphoria and dysphoria, depending on the feelings and affects experienced (Greimas and Fontanille 1991). However, the environment in which the subject evolves is neither simply lived, nor passively experienced. The subject is an actor who touches, manipulates and uses the objects and products that surround him. It is notably as he practices them, that he manages to experience them and learn more about them and their use (Guibourgé and Moutat 2017). It is in this sense that experience constitutes a "mode of acquiring knowledge based on direct contact with realities and phenomena" (Laing cited by Lochard 2007, p. 82).

However, these three dimensions should not be considered as the three successive moments of a necessarily ordered sequence from perception to cognition. Indeed, we have shown (Moutat and Sekhniachvili-Komperdra 2021) that these three dimensions constitute places of emergence of experiential meanings (called "semiosis" in semiotics), which vary according to the subject. Let's take the example of any showcase website. At the sight (sensitive dimension) of the interface's graphic design, an Internet user can immediately be seduced, in the mode of wonder and admiration (affective dimension), and continue his or her navigation (pragmatic dimension) to learn more about the advertiser-brand (cognitive dimension). However, the capture of information (cognitive dimension) can increase the user's adhesion to the brand (affective dimension) and his desire to interact with the site (pragmatic dimension) or, on the contrary, lead to disinterest or even rejection. In other words, each dimension can model the others in a reinforcing or diminishing way, concomitantly or successively, and this according to sequences specific to each individual.

A similar approach can be found in Roederer (2012), who recognizes the existence of four dimensions of experience: 1. Praxeological, which concerns the consumer's actions and activities with the consumer good and other people, 2. Hedonic-sensory, which refers to the physical and sensory aspects of the experiential context, 3. Rhetorical, which corresponds to the meanings attributed to the experience, and 4. Relationship to time, in terms of duration, rhythm, and sequence. These dimensions constitute, according to Roederer and Filser (2015, p. 56) "an experiential system activated by the subject as he or she interprets a given experiential context." For as Sylvie Daumal (2012) points out, experience is subjective and singular, varying over time and contexts. Therefore, if these dimensions offer strategic levers in the experiential promise, they do not allow us to model the subjects' experience but the conditions of its production, the latter being dependent on the subjects themselves.

2.1 Marketing Through Experience

This modeling of the conditions of experience has been widely explored in management science since the beginnings of experiential marketing. Schmitt (1999) identified all the experience providers as action levers to be used to create conditions conducive to the experience, which can fall under distinct experiential strategy modules (sense, feel, think, act, relate). Filser (2002) proposes to model the experience according to the theatrical device where the decor creates an environment favorable to the unfolding of a story about the brand or the product, addressed to the consumer. The concretization of the experience takes place through the actual realization of the actions planned by the device.

From then on, the consumer's performative acts are fundamental because they are the only ones that guarantee the experience itself. In this respect, Pine and Gilmore (1999) have defined the domains of experience (Entertainment, Educational, Aesthetic and Escape), articulated according to the degree of participation of the consumer and the relationship that he/she weaves with the experiential environment, and according to which the consumer is assigned variable roles, oriented towards specific actions and behaviors.

Beyond the simple role prescribed by the advertiser, the consumer is endowed with a real empowerment that authorizes different forms of collaboration. Antéblian et al. (2013) distinguish three hierarchically ordered forms of collaboration as follows: 1. Interpretative collaboration, which consists of identifying the meanings conveyed by the brand or company through its different stimuli and giving emotional responses 2. Directed self-production, which takes shape in the actual performance of the actions that the brand has planned for the consumer to carry out and 3. Creative co-production which actively mobilizes the consumer in the construction of the meaning of the experience within which he/she has a certain autonomy.

Experiential marketing has thus made it possible to typologize the different forms that experiential contexts can take, as well as the underlying strategies that underlie them, allowing for a variable degree of consumer participation. However, it has not managed to determine concretely how experiential processes work and how the signifying structures should be configured to engage the consumer and generate the expected meanings. This is what we propose to do in this semiotic study, which will allow us to determine the conditions of production of experiential meanings. In other words, it will be a matter of highlighting the way in which signs are structured in terms of expression in order to configure the conditions conducive to an experience of the digital interface of a brand.

2.2   The Experiential Process

In this respect, a step has recently been taken in Information and Communication Sciences with the figurative expansion of the experiential sequence formulated by Jean-Jacques Boutaud (2021). Indeed, for the researcher, the figurative dimension plays a determining role in the structuring of the experience:

> [...] the figurative dimension has always appeared to us as determining, at all levels of experiential elaboration with: the sensory and synesthetic imprint (Moutat et al. 2019); the epoch, rupture or parenthesis: the moment detaches itself from the background of ordinary activities; the reflexive position of the subject, at the same time actor and spectator of his situation and of the transformation that it operates on him; the unity of action, dramatic unity immersed in the hic et nunc of the experience and dramaturgical unity which assigns a role in situation; the affective coloration favorable or not, that the subject wishes above all to share with others, through multiple springs and resources of communication. (2021, online)

This figurative primacy of experience operates according to two registers of manifestation: (i) a plane of expression that takes the form of "figurative semiospheres" (micro, meso, macro). Using the example of the meal experience borrowed from Filser (2002), Boutaud associates the micro figurative cue with the product and the emotions sought, the meso with the restaurant setting and the macro with the social image of the self. (ii) an experiential sequence, between "prefiguration" (anticipation, organization and prepa-ration of the experience), "configuration" (discovery of the setting, of the experiential device), "figuration" (entry into the device, living the experience) and "reconfiguration" (return on the experience by putting it into a narrative).

Thus, each element of the experiential framework is presented as a figurative stratum that participates in the structuring of the overall experience. Moreover, this experiential genesis follows an aspectuality organized in four moments, which also constitute points of articulation of the experiential event:

Prefiguration: anticipate, prepare, organize, imagine;

Configuration: discovering the setting, the experiential device;

Figuration: entering the device, living the experience, putting oneself on stage;

Reconfiguration: returning to the experience, sharing it, extending the narrative, highlighting certain aspects, including through memory (Flacandji 2017).

And in order for the experiential proposal to keep its full meaning, without eroding, Boutaud proposes to configure the process through the combination of three factors: the "predisposition to live the experience ("the expectation of the unexpected"), [the] device (configuring the experience) and [the] availability of the subject (openness and freedom of appropriation), actor of a phenomenal experience that takes on meaning as a life expe-rience" (*Ibid.*). Better yet, building on Badot and Lemoine's (2009) considerations, he advocates a compromise between modeling the workings of the experience and config-uring a performative device. This compromise would be based on an experiential motif, a stabilized structure regardless of the variations in the subject's sensitivity, according to the form of life (Fontanille 2015 and Macé 2016) that is specific to him or her.

2.3   Designing Experience

"Too strategic to be only the business of marketing" (Roederer and Filser 2015, p. 2), experience concerns all levels of brand discourse, which we can equate with levels of semiotic relevance (Fontanille 2007): 1. Signs correspond to the set of graphic, lexical, and sound codes, etc. that characterize the physicality (Kapferer 1988) of the brand, 2. Texts are diverse compositions resulting from the arrangement of these signs (adver-tisements, publications on social networks, websites, for example), 3. Objects can be both the products manufactured by the brand and the goodies it offers to its consumers, 4. Practices take various forms such as the actions performed by the brand or those it prescribes to its consumers, 5. Strategies consist of an accommodation, an adjustment, between practices according to spatial and temporal circumstances, and 6. Life forms are the values and ethics of the brand which, in the best case, correspond to those of the consumer, engaging a kind of reflexivity (or mirror effect).

From then on, the experience also becomes the business of communication, com-merce, design… The latter can variably concern the space, the graphics or the digital devices deployed by the brand. In this respect, the 2000s saw the emergence of new web design practices based on an innovative design methodology: user experience design or UX design. Popularized by Donald Norman at the end of the 80's, UX design proposes an innovative approach no longer focused on the product but on the experience of its use and integrates users at the heart of the product development process (co-design principle). It is a sensitive approach to man-machine interactions, sometimes involving users emotionally. UX design thus concerns.

> all aspects related to the way people use an interactive product: the sensation of the product in their hands, the understanding of its functioning, the feeling during the use, the achievement of their goals but also its adequacy with the global context in which they use it. (Alben 1996, p. 11)

Applied to the web domain, UX design cannot operate without the mediation of interface design (UI Design), which consists of composing the pages of a website by adopting specific graphic styles (colors, typography, iconography, animations, page flow) and a particular spatial organization.

Thus, in the same way that experiential marketing has made it possible to model the conditions conducive to shopping experiences, interface design (UI) makes it possible to create the context of a digital experience specific to each user, according to his or her navigation path (UX). Therefore, if the UX designer can set up an environment that prefigures the user's experience, he can't control the actual realization of it, because of the diversity of the public, their motivations or their usual practices and usage strategies implemented according to the circumstances.

It is in this sense that we can bring the UI/UX design strategy closer to Benveniste's propositions on enunciation, with the difference that here, the enunciative stakes are not only cognitive but also sensitive and pragmatic. Understood as an individual linguistic activity, enunciation consists in producing a discourse by drawing on the syntactic and semantic resources of the language in order to act on an enunciator. In UI/UX design, this device allows the enunciator, in this case the brand, to assert its singularity and generate cognitive, pragmatic and affective effects on Internet users by variably combining graphic, typographic, semantic and interactive elements. The enunciation will be fully realized once the user has grasped the true meanings conveyed by the brand and acted in accordance with the interaction program it had initiated for him. It is thus concretized in the experience produced by the navigation, the various interactions and the use of the functionalities, during which the user produces a sensorial, emotional and hedonic judgment resulting in a symbolic valorization of the brand.

Within this framework, our research consists in studying the way in which the websites of certain brands are structured in order to prefigure a future experience. The aim is to reveal the way in which the experiential promise of the interface is constructed, in other words the way in which the user experience of the site proposes an experience of the brand itself.

3 The Brand's Digital Experience

3.1 The Brand Experience

According to Amic Garfield Ho (2017), emotional branding is a consumer-centric approach that involves adopting communication based on creating connection through brand storytelling:

"It aims to build up in-depth and affective connections among consumers for brands. (Roberts 2004) Senses and emotions are the main channels involved to form an in-depth, long-lasting and emotional connection to the brand. In other words, brand transcends material satisfaction during the design consumption (Morrison and Crane 2007 and Rahinel and Redden 2013)."

This emotional satisfaction is based on the satisfaction of the subject's need for rapid and two-way interaction. The latter then becomes a consumer-actor who no longer simply experiences the content proposed by the brand but shares and co-constructs it with it. In this perspective, Amic Garfield Ho (*Ibid.*) recognizes the existence of four axes for creating emotional branding: 1. Personality, where the positioning of the brand stems from its ideology and values, in accordance with the social needs of the intended targets, 2. Appeal, which consists of designing branding according to the effects that the characteristics of the brand produce on subjects, 3. The senses, whose solicitation through interactions with the various elements of the brand generates a deeper emotional commitment, and 4. Navigation, which involves communicating directly with consumers via social networks.

3.2   The Brand's Digital Experience Strategies

After defining the general conceptual framework within which we situate ourselves, we propose to analyze some examples of online experiential enhancement strategies adopted by brands. Aware of the richness of today's devices made possible by constantly evolving technologies, renewed trends and the creativity of designers, we have selected a sample which, although not exhaustive, allows us to highlight some of the strategic levers deployed by brands to create a link with consumers. The examples we have selected are recognized and awarded by a consortium of designers who evaluated them for their ergonomics, design, creativity and content. Each website will be the subject of a brief presentation followed by an analysis of the devices put in place so that the user can experience the brand.

Gamification

In a hyper-competitive market where every player is trying to occupy a place of choice on the web, it is very difficult to attract and retain the attention of the Internet user. For a few years now, we have seen the development of marketing and communication strategies based on the principle of gamification. The latter consists in borrowing the codes and principles of video games (scenario, gameplay) in order to provide the Internet user with a fun and interactive experience. Gamification is an emotional design strategy that allows to satisfy several communication objectives: 1. to improve the image of the brand, which is then perceived as "friendly" by the public; 2. to increase its visibility by creating a buzz to go viral; 3. to maintain the relationship with the consumer by relying on co-production and cooperation between the brand and the Internet user Through the scenario built by the brand, the Internet user transcends himself by forging a new identity, that of the hero of the adventure in which the brand engages him. But beyond the realization of the Internet user, the brand seeks to present a new product or to communicate its values. The game allows to divert attention from its Brand centered strategy by subjecting the

Internet user to other stimuli. This is the principle of priming which, according to Walter (2012), consists of exposing a person to a stimulus with the aim of influencing his or her response to another stimulus (in this case, the commercial stimulus). Thus, Renault (https://www.experience-nouvelletwingo.renault.fr) offers to experiment with driving the new Twingo on different obstacle courses or trajectory control courses. The SNCF offers Internet users the possibility of practicing the Ouigo pinball machine (http://let splay.ouigo.com). Users control the pinball machine with their keyboard and try to keep a ball thrown by an Ouigo train in the middle of a setting of different places served by the train. The game, in the colors of the Ouigo brand, offers a metaphor for travel.

Estée Lauder (https://www.esteelauderanrcade.com/en-us/game-3) has also been tempted by gamification to promote its Advanced Night Repair serum. In a futuristic site, largely inspired by Star Wars settings, the brand proposes to let the user enter the brand's technological universe, the ANRcade, to play four arcade games: Beauty Bounce, Serum Quest, Repair Racer and Smooth Satisfaction. The entrance to the site begins with a call-to-action "Slide up" that immediately immerses the user in the interface in a sensory-motor mode. To the soundtrack of a science-fiction adventure, similar to an American blockbuster, the animations transport the user into space, into the heart of the solar system, with the difference that the sun is embodied by Estée Lauder serum, then into the heart of the illuminated city of London, to finally enter a building with a modern architecture, in the shape of a sphere, the ANRcade. This luminous and modern place with its feminine curves becomes emblematic of the brand and its serum, and is presented as an autonomous place (Pignier and Drouillat 2008). The communication strategy here is based on concealing the brand's commercial objectives in favor of the user's gaming experience. The discourse is immediately oriented towards the consumer benefit of the serum in order to present the interest that the internet user may have in interacting with the brand: "Play our games to win youth points". However, it is in the performance of the game itself that the brand's advertising strategy takes place, as each arcade mini-game is actually a demonstration of the serum's actions on the consumer's skin. Thus, by playing Beauty Bounce, the Internet user plumps and moisturizes the skin, which becomes radiant. With Serum Quest, a game deeply inspired by the narrative arc of space invaders, they participate in the anti-oxidant protection of the skin and its defense against the effects of pollution. Repair Racer allows him to participate in the reduction of fine lines while Smooth Satisfaction engages him in the reduction of wrinkles. By playing the game, the user uses each product benefit to become a co-actor in the product's action on the skin. The interface created by Estée Lauder engages a co-driven experience (Carù and Cova 2007) that gives the Internet user the impression of being in control and working for the benefit of the consumer. The cognitive objective of the brand's communication is therefore not served by a long demonstration of the product's effectiveness but by the performative act of the Internet user-player. And it is because it hides its cognitive objectives under gamification that this site borrows from the media genre of the serious game, "computer application, whose objective is to combine serious aspects (Serious) such as, in a non-exhaustive way, teaching, learning, communication, or even information, with ludic springs coming from the video game (Game)" (Alvarez 2007). More precisely, the ANRcade is an advergame, a serious game with a promotional aim which consists in conveying a marketing or communication message. Indeed, the purely advertising traces are essentially camouflaged by the playful actions, sometimes subtly present within the interface. A light scroll or a discreet "Explore" button allows to obtain more formal information about the serum at the end of each game. Here, Estée Lauder exploits with relevance and efficiency all the components of gamification: 1. an epic story in the middle of space with an immediate immersion thanks to the sensory-motricity (absorption within the interface); 2. The call to action: each arcade game has a specific gameplay that engages the web user in a different way 3. Feedback and virality: by inviting users to share their score with their friends via social networks, it is to talk about the brand and encourage the community to interact with it. The principle of variable rewards with the score and random congratulatory messages to the user-player, allows him to satisfy emotional and psychological needs and, therefore, to strengthen his emotional bond with the brand and share it with his community.

Aesthetic and Multi-sensory Enhancement
The sensoriality is a dimension very often employed by the marks to develop the organoleptic properties of the products which it markets. The strategies of communication then adopted engage specific modes of organization of the digital interface, which rest on the central concept of aesthetics, "symbolic configurations of sensitive knowledge" (Ouellet 2000, p. 21). By referring to sensory experiences previously lived and memorized by the subjects, the aesthetics used on the websites are figurative strategies that orient the interpretative paths (Rastier 1987) of the Internet users and allow them to experience the products of the brand. The idea here is to make the experience of the digital statement, configured by the aesthetics, analogous to the real experience of these products.

Thus, to celebrate the launch of its new fragrance, Gucci (https://florafantasy.gucci.com/) has created an immersive experience based on the principle of aesthetics, through which users can discover Gucci Flora Gorgeous Gardenia eau de parfum and its ingredients. The website opens in the middle of a blooming flower garden, populated by cats and a perfectly groomed poodle, facing a pink, dollhouse-like house. The floating effects, the sounds of wind and glitter and the swirl of flower petals at each sequence of discovery produce a dreamlike universe inspired by Japanese anime. This enchanted parenthesis (Hetzel 2002) transports the subject to a fantastic universe by awakening his different senses: sight but also touch (through the manipulation of the interface to move in the represented space), hearing (solicited by the cat's meows, the dog's bark, the birds' song and the ambient music) and smell (in the mode of synesthetic games with the representation of jasmine flowers). The internal movements of the interface ensure the passage from one place to another (from the garden to the porch of the house and then from the porch to the beach) thanks to sound effects and to a floral swirl which is concretized in a luminous white halo. These animations produce sensory-motor effects that seem to draw the user into the heart of the interface. The subject leaves the here and now towards an elsewhere assimilated to a dream and within which he can discover the components of the perfume by interacting with the elements of the interface. The result is somatic effects of quietude and appeasement, a suspension of time in the image of the objects floating on the screen that make the Internet user forget that he is navigating in the Gucci universe, despite the presence of the Gucci Flora perfume bottle.

This digital interface offers a co-driven experience (Carù and Cova 2007) of the brand by offering interactions that the user is free to perform or not, and in the order he or she wishes. Thus, the user experience that allows the discovery of the garden and the beach allows the user to experience the fragrance indirectly. The story told here is that of the user, who co-constructs it with the brand by navigating through this magical world. There is no doubt that this emotional branding, based on the senses and the creation of a personality, will speak to Japanese anime fans. The kawaii aesthetic approach, imbued with innocence and vulnerability, is based on a culture of adorableness to satisfy young women in search of enchantment and dreams, but with a strong personality, as evidenced by the rock'n'roll notes of the soundtrack, the electric guitar on the beach, and the muse of the fragrance, Miley Cyrus.

If the figurative strategy adopted by Gucci is based here on synesthesia and polysensoriality, other modes of aesthetic valorization can be engaged. Thus, the Distillerie des 3 lacs (https://distillerietroislacs.ca/product/limonade-rose/) oscillates between figurative abstraction of a metaphorical or metonymic nature and hyperesthesia (Boutaud 2016). Indeed, the site opens with the appearance of three successively black drops and waves of flat colors that represent respectively the distillation of spirits and the movement of each product served in a glass: the Lemon Sunflower Gin in yellow, the Grapefruit Rosemary Gin in pink, The Lime Basil Gin in green, etc. This figurative abstraction, which adopts a substantial mode of representation (Boutaud *Ibid.*) proceeds to a valorization of the material of the spirits. It is opposed to the hyperesthetic staging of each gin: for each product presentation, the scroll of the page makes the different ingredients appear in order to simulate their organoleptic properties. A sort of gustatory sequence appears before the eyes of the Internet user, in the mode of hypotyposis. The valorization then becomes analytical by proceeding to a decomposition of the image of the flavor (Boutaud, 2005) of the various gins: the contrast between the sharp and the blurred models this image, by referring to the degree of presence of the aromas and the flavors which constitute it. The figurative strategy culminates in the situational representation of the gin, which offers an enhancement of its context of use, in cocktails. We can thus see that the brand experience, through the product experience, proceeds to a deployment on the different expressive levels of the gustatory valorization. The Distillerie des 3 lacs adopts an openly Brand centered strategy, which concentrates its discourse on the brand and its products, leaving little room for maneuver to the Internet user. The experience thus offered to the consumer is more of a company-driven device (Carù and Cova 2007).

Artification of the Brand

Still following a Brand centered strategy, but in an indirect way, the brand can propose an experience on the mode of artification. This technique consists in using cultural scenography devices to promote the brand's values and products.

For the Frieze London Art Fair, the Ruinart brand (https://unconventionalgallery.ruinart.com/#/) put online an interactive museum, The Unconventional Gallery, which offers an immersive exhibition of David Shrigley's works. From one work to the next, the British artist recounts the wine-making techniques that are characteristic of Ruinart Champagne wines and presents the environmental issues of the vineyard.

With this museum site, the brand adopts an oxymoronic discourse strategy: by proceeding with an enunciative desacralization of itself (welcoming the Internet user with heady music, playful typography and pink earthworms in 3D that snake to orient the Internet user) the Ruinart brand defends sacred values.

Here, the digital interface takes up all the codes of the conventional museum, from the scenography of the works (presentation cartridges) to the signage addressed to visitors (a "do not walk this line" cordon). The adoption of a common place, familiar to the Internet user, facilitates guidance and orientation in the interface, which can be easily explored. The actions prescribed by the structure of the interface are identical to those performed by a visitor to a physical museum: following the instructions for discovering the work, moving towards it, and stepping back to better appreciate it are all levers that invite the Internet user to participate in the mode of an experiential as well as interpretative journey. Indeed, if the Ruinart brand seems to fade away in favor of the artist's voice, it sends a subliminal message to the Internet user by implicitly promoting its identity, its know-how and its history:

"This poetic drawing from David Shrigley is an evocation to the art of blending and know-how of Maison Ruinart cellar master. Representative of the blue bird, he selects the best quality of grapes for wines. An ode to preserve the essential: life and nature.

"In the regulations of champagne making, the grapes must arrive in bunches at the press. Harvesting is therefore necessarily done by hand. A robot or machine cannot do it. The hands of this robot look particularly not adapted to a subtle harvest."

Ruinart adopts here a strategy of depublicitarization (Berthelot-Guiet and de Montety 2009) by using the tactics of masking and euphemization. While the cultural form of the museum is presented as a means of promoting the brand, David Shrigley becomes the enunciator in charge of promoting Ruinart's values, particularly those of eco-responsibility. The messages conveyed by the artist's work are intertwined with the brand's subliminal messages about the values it defends:

"This poetic drawing reminds us with humor that worms also work in the champagne production. "Worms are important. They help create the soil that is vital for all life. We take the soil for granted and we take worms for granted but we should remember how vital they are. In terms of saving the planet you could say quite unequivocally that worms work harder than us" David Shrigley "

This detachment of the brand from the strictly commercial one also holds in this principle of media hybridization (Berthelot-Guiet and de Montety, *Ibid.*) adopted by this digital device. By presenting the creations of an artist dedicated to Ruinart Champagne, this interactive museum is not specifically perceived as advertising. Indeed, the elements of identity enhancement of the brand are discrete during the navigation. The various works by David Shrigley are offered as fragments of Ruinart's identity that the journey within the interface structure allows to reconstruct.

Nevertheless, the brand still indulges in a few classic communication processes. Indeed, rare implicit connections between Ruinart and the consumer can be observed, always through the mediation of the artist. This is the case of the awards with the download of wallpapers of the artist's productions or the work "You are the bottle, I am the glass" whose cartridge maintains a speech on the consumption of Champagne:

"An unmissable couple: the bottle and the glass. Opposites attract each other. The glass is very important for Maison Ruinart because it retranscribes all the aromatic notes of its cuvées. Thus, the cuvée cannot express itself without the glass.

Through this unconventional museum, Ruinart succeeds in lifting the suspicion of the internet user by building a more engaging and emotionally engaging identity.

Velvet Rope, Elevation and Sense of Exclusivity

Some brands have chosen to reverse the polarization of their strategy by becoming more consumer-centric. The aim is to give a special place to the Internet user, so that he feels privileged and unique. Thus, on the occasion of a new collaboration with Jack Daniel's, Shoe Surgeon (https://www.finely-crafted.com/) has put online an interactive visit site of its studio. The Internet user is then welcomed by a video of Dominic Cambrione, founder of Shoe Surgeon, on an urban music specific to the sneakers' universe. The brand creates the illusion of a limited access to its workshop, creating a feeling of exclusivity and elevation for the Internet user, a privilege that responds to his need to belong to a community and to self-esteem.

The visit to the workshop begins at the bar with the discovery of cocktails made with Jack Daniel's. It then continues in three separate parts of the workshop to learn more about the secrets of sneaker making and previous collaborations with the whisky brand. However, this information is not delivered in an obvious way and requires the help of the Internet user. Indeed, the visit of the workshop is made according to a cognitive quest program (to learn more about this collaboration) but also modal (to collect bee cells in order to obtain an exclusive gift). These beehives are scattered throughout the interface and "unlocked" in the manner of easter eggs when the user has completed the actions programmed on the interface. This participative navigation, which operates on the principle of the double quest, integrates the user into the story unfolded in the interface by giving him a narrative role, that of an investigator. The sanction of this quest, namely the collection of all the alveoli, is concretized in the retribution: a new Instagram filter, inviting to share with the community and marking a return to the advertising and commercial ambitions of the brand.

Eric Bompard (https://experience.eric-bompard.com/) is aiming for these same goals by exploiting the potential of augmented reality. Thanks to its mobile application, the Internet user can exclusively attend the behind-the-scenes photo shoot of the Fall-Winter collection: sets, technical team, models… All the details of the session are accessible to him. This "velvet cord" (Walter 2012) reduces the distance between the brand and the Internet user, who then experiences a feeling of elevation and perceives the brand differently. They no longer perceive the brand's commercial attributes, but rather a team at work, a professional rigor with a sense of detail that does not prevent them from being friendly. Once integrated into this atmosphere, the mobile user will be more inclined to learn more about the brand's design secrets and the products worn by the models. Call-to-actions of varying shapes are scattered across the interface, discreetly reminding the user of the application's marketing objectives. Indeed, if the affective semiosis has taken hold, the mobile user can be redirected to the brand's website where he can buy the product(s) he likes.

We can see that, although Eric Bompard and Shoe Surgeon both adopt a consumer-centered strategy, the discourse remains oriented towards the brand that the web user is invited to discover, as a VIP. This is a "centripetal" approach which aims to make the communication axes converge towards the brand, in order to rally the Internet users. Ikea, on the other hand, proposed the opposite strategic orientation with its interactive experience created for its 25th anniversary (https://www.family.ikea.es/25aniv-demo-version/). "Centrifugal", the discourse emanates from the brand to focus on its Ikea family members and put them in the foreground. This interface, based on the metaphor of an amusement park, is a true celebration of its most loyal customers, who appear as "chosen ones". To do this, the narrative concedes to the latter the role of actant (Greimas 1966) without whom the brand's narrative program could not have been realized. The site offers a personalized experience for each Ikea family cardholder in the mode of cognitive and pragmatic sanction. Indeed, Ikea recognizes the accomplishment of its actions ("You've spent 21 h assembling our furniture") but also its qualities ("Way to go handyman! You're a real wiz with our Allen key! The consumer is presented as a hero who accomplishes "feats" for the brand and is given a place of honor in the "hall of fame. The Ikea experience thus creates a kind of filiation with the consumer through shared memories that the brand recalls, like a family album. The objective is to create surprise and delight for the consumer ("Incredible! I never knew I'd bought so many"), which will influence the pragmatic and cognitive semiosis to come.

Thus, whether it is directed towards the brand or the consumer, this velvet cord strategy revalues the consumer and makes it possible to condition him or her in a situation that is more favorable to the brand's discourse. Its effectiveness lies essentially in the fact that it meets half of the potential needs of consumers identified by Packard (1957), namely reassurance of value, ego gratification, feelings of power and rootedness. Linked to emotions, these strategic levers allow consumers to self-actualize by subconsciously touching their affect.

4 Conclusion

In this brief study, we have outlined the first elements of a typology of strategies deployed by brands to create engaging experiences with their users: gamification, aesthetic and polysensory enhancement, artification and velvet cord. Sometimes focused on the brand, sometimes on the consumer, they engage the latter's participation in a variety of ways, with the aim of creating diversified relationships and making sensitive, pragmatic and cognitive sense. Although digital technology opens up new potentialities thanks to con-stantly renewed technologies, we note that the processes at the basis of these strategic orientations are not new. Indeed, we find here the principles raised by the pioneers of experiential marketing: the domains of experience (Pine and Gilmore 1999), experiential packaging (Filser 2002) or the categories of experience (Carù and Cova 2007). Media hybridization also proves to be a powerful engine of de-publicitarization (Berthelot-Guiet and de Montety 2009) which, by diverting the attention of audiences from the real motivations of brands, makes it possible to re-establish links with them and facilitate their adhesion.

Given these observations, it would seem that a further step can be taken in the creation of experiences. A step that brands would like to take and which is feeding the thoughts of digital giants: the metaverse. Metaverse combines virtual reality with augmented reality in order to decompartmentalize the real and virtual worlds and to immerse users without the need for screens. The experience will also be "meta": evolving in the metaverse will allow consumers to experience the brand, to integrate its universe but also to co-create value with other consumers. A shared, real-time living experience, the metaverse proposes to revolutionize the act of purchasing by transforming consumers into collaborators and contributors. The brand experience will no longer be a simple access to the Internet but a real digital integration. Metaverse is the key to the war of the biggest names in digital, and tends towards a hyperesthesia that superimposes several domains of experience at the same time and combines new forms of participation in the experience. If it has been feeding imaginations for more than 40 years, its concept is now taking shape and is only waiting for the technological evolutions necessary for its advent. On your marks!

References

Alben, L.: Quality of experience: defining the criteria for effective interaction design. Interactions **3**(3) (1996)

Alvarez, J.: Du jeu video au serious game, approaches Culturelle, pragmatique et formelle. Université de Lille, Thèse (2007)

Antéblian, B., Filser M., Roederer, C. : L'expérience du consommateur dans le commerce de détail. Une revue de littérature. Recherche et Applications en Marketing **28**(3), 84–113 (2013)

Badot, O., Lemoine, J-F.: La ritualisation du parcours-client chez Build-a-Bear. In: Workshop, Phénoménologie et enseignements, Actes des 14èmes Journées de Recherche en Marketing de Bourgogne (2009)

Bergkvist, L., Bech-Larsen, T.: Two studies of consequences and actionable antecedents of brand love. J. Brand Manag. **17**(7), 504–518 (2010)

Berthelot-Guiet, K., de Montety, C.: Hyperpublicitarisation et dépublicitarisation : métamorphoses du discours des marques et gestion sémiotique. Revue du CIRCAV, vol. 20, pp. 63–78. L'Harmattan, Paris (2009)

Bordron, J.-F.: L'iconicité et ses images. PUF, Paris (2011)

Boutaud, J-J. : Le sens gourmand. De la commensalité, du goût, des aliments. Jean-Paul Rocher Editeur, Paris (2005)

Boutaud, J.-J.: L'esthésie et l'épiphanique : Traces figuratives de la saveur. In : Semiotica, de Gruyter Mouton **2016** 211), 203–229, (2016)

Boutaud, J-J. : L'expérience d'un concept. Vers un nouvel âge post-expérientiel ? REFSICOM (2021). http://www.refsicom.org/966

Carù, A., Cova, B.: Consuming experience: an introduction. In: A. Carù, B. Cova (eds.) Consuming Experience, 3–16, Routledge, Abingdon (2007)

CNRTL Homepage. https://www.cnrtl.fr. Accessed 23 Feb 2022

Daumal, S.: Design d'expérience utilisateur. Principes et méthodes UX. Eyrolles, Paris (2012)

Filser, M.: Le marketing de la production d'expérience : statut théorique et implications managériales. Décisions Marketing **28**(4), 13–22 (2002)

Flacandji, M. : Le souvenir de l'expérience vécue en magasin physique. Les apports de l'analyse de réseaux. Décisions Marketing **88**, 71–87 (2017)

Fontanille, J.: Textes, objets, situations et formes de vie. Les niveaux de pertinence du plan de l'expression dans une sémiotique des cultures. In : Alonso Aldama, J. Bertrand, D. Costantini, M., Dambrine S. (eds.) Transversalité du Sens. PUV, Paris (2007)

Fontanille, J. : Formes de vie. PULg, Liège (2015)

Ford, R., Bowen, D.: A service-dominant logic for management education: It's time. Acad. Manag. Learn. Educ. **7**(2), 224–243 (2008)

Greimas, A.-J.: Sémantique structurale. PUF, Paris (1966)

Greimas, A.-J., Fontanille, J.: Sémiotique des passions : des états de choses aux états d'âme. Seuil, Paris (1991)

Guibourgé, J., Moutat, A.: Comment le design intuitif communique-t-il ? In : Darras, B. Vial, S. (eds.) MEI Médiation et Information, vol. 40, pp. 185–196. L'Harmattan, Paris (2017)

Hetzel, P.: Planète Conso. Editions d'organisation, Paris (2002)

Ho, A.G.: Explore the categories on different emotional branding experience for optimising the brand design process. In: Marcus, A., Wang, W. (eds.) DUXU 2017. LNCS, vol. 10289, pp. 18–34. Springer, Cham (2017). https://doi.org/10.1007/978-3-319-58637-3_2

Kapferer, J-N. : Maîtriser l'image de l'entreprise : le prisme d'identité. Revue Française de Gestion, 76–82 (1988)

Lochard, Y.: L'avènement des « savoirs expérientiels ». Revue de l'IRES **3**(55), 79–95 (2007)

Macé, M.: Styles : critique de nos formes de vie. Gallimard, Paris (2016)

Morrison, S., Crane, F.G.: Building the service brand by creating and managing an emotional brand experience. J. Brand Manag. **14**(5), 410–421 (2007)

Moutat, A. : Du sensible à l'intelligible. Pour une sémiotique de la perception. Lambert-Lucas, Limoges (2015)

Moutat, A.: Son et sens. Presses Universitaires de Liège, Liège, Sigilla (2019)

Moutat, A., Sekhniachvili-Komperdra, E. : Expériences d'achat in situ et on line, modélisation comparative des parcours marchands. REFSICOM (2021). http://www.refsicom.org/970

Norman, D. : Design émotionnel : Pourquoi aimons-nous ou détestons-nous les objets qui nous entourent ? De Boeck, Bruxelles (2012)

Ouellet, P. : Poétique du regard : littérature, perception, identité. PULIM, Limoges (2000)

Packard, V.O.: The Hidden Persuaders. David McKay Company, Philadelphia (1957)

Pignier, N., Drouillat, B.: Le webdesign. Sociale expérience des interfaces web. Hermès-Lavoisier, Paris (2008)

Pine II, B.J., Gilmore, J.H.: The Experience Economy. Work is Theatre & Every Business a Stage. Harvard Business Press, Boston (1999)

Rahinel, R., Redden, J.P.: Brands as product coordinators: matching brands make joint consumption experiences more enjoyable. J. Consum. Res **39**(6), 1290–1299 (2013)

Rastier, F.: Sémantique interprétative. PUF, Paris (1987)

Roberts, K.: Lovemarks: The Future Beyond Brands. Powerhouse Books, New York (2004)

Roederer, C.: Contribution à la conceptualisation de l'expérience de consommation : émergence des dimensions de l'expérience au travers de récits de vie. Rech. Appl. Mark. **27**(3), 81–96 (2012)

Roederer, C., Filser, M.: Le marketing expérientiel : vers un marketing de la cocréation. Vuibert, Paris (2015)

Schmitt, B.: Experiential Marketing: How to Get Customers to Sense, Feel, Think. Act and Relate to Your Company and Brands. The Free Press, New-York (1999)

Sinek, S.: Commencer par Pourquoi – Comment les grands leaders nous inspirent à passer à l'action. Broché, Paris (2015)

Vargo, S.L., Lusch, R.F.: Evolving to a new dominant logic for marketing. J. Mark. **68**(1), 1–17 (2004)

Walter, A.: Design émotionnel. Eyrolles, Paris (2012)

Research on Financial Restatement of Listed Companies in China—Based on Internal Control and Risk Management Database (DIB)

Xiaoyan Niu[1(✉)] and Yuping Jia[2]

[1] Shandong University of Finance and Economics, No. 7366 Er Huan Dong Road, Jinan, Shandong, China
20059464@sdufe.edu.cn

[2] Department of Accounting, Frankfurt School of Finance and Management, Frankfurt, Germany

Abstract. Financial restatement is a kind of accounting behavior of listed company to correct the accounting errors in the financial report. The true and fair financial accounting information is one of the important conditions to guarantee the healthy development of the capital market. The purpose of establishing the financial restatement system is to improve the quality of accounting information of listed companies, improve market transparency, and effectively reduce the negative impact of accounting errors on the decision-making of users of financial reports through timely correction of accounting errors, restore the confidence of market participants. However, since 2003, the number of financial restatements has increased year by year, and there is a tendency that financial restatements are abused. Listed companies wantonly correct accounting errors and use financial restatements as a shield to cover up corporate losses, the financial restatement system has deviated from its original intention, caused huge property losses to investors, and had a very bad impact on the operation of the capital market.

On the basis of sorting out the relevant literature and theory, this paper first sorts out the financial restatement data through the DIB database, and analyzes the financial restatement of listed companies in China from 2011 to 2019 from three areas: numbers of restatement, frequency of occurrence and type; second, the motive or cause and economic consequences of financial restatement of listed companies are studied and analyzed in turn; finally, suggestions are proposed to modify the financial restatement behavior of listed companies and improve the quality of information disclosure of listed companies.

Keywords: Financial restatement · DIB database · Listed companies · Information disclosure

1 Introduction

In recent years, there have been more financial restatement incidents of listed companies in China's capital market, and listed companies have actively or passively released

This paper is funded by the International Exchange and Cooperation Project of the International Office of Shandong University of Finance and Economics.

© Springer Nature Switzerland AG 2022
M. Rauterberg et al. (Eds.): HCII 2022, LNCS 13520, pp. 196–207, 2022.
https://doi.org/10.1007/978-3-031-18158-0_14

corrected or supplemented financial restatement reports through financial fraud or intentional omission of key information in the later stage. This kind of financial restatement violates the original intention of financial restatement to provide more authentic and reliable financial information, and causes great losses to listed companies, investors and capital markets. Through reviewing and combing the relevant theories and literature research on financial restatement, this paper analyzes the current situation, financial restatement causes and economic consequences and finally puts forward relevant countermeasures and suggestions.

2   Theoretical Basis for Financial Restatement

A financial restatement is an act of correcting or supplementing a disclosed financial report and is essentially an ex post remedy. The financial restatement may be voluntarily taken by the listed company, or it may be carried out passively at the request of the regulator, and it is necessary to correct or supplement the error, untruth, omission or misleading information disclosed in the financial reports that were disclosed in previous years, so that the financial reports can be more reliable and truly reflect the financial situation of the enterprise. Theories related to financial restatement are as follows:

2.1   Principal-Agency Theory

Principal-agent theory is a contract theory, the principal gives a certain share of remuneration and rights to the agent, then a principal relationship is formed between the principal and the agent. The principal-agent relationship in listed companies is mainly the principal-agent relationship between shareholders and managers. The shareholders are the owners and the principal party of the enterprise, who entrusts the management of the company's affairs to the operator and regularly accepts the operator's report to know the company's operating performance; the managers act as the agent to manage the enterprise, and have more corporate resources and information than the shareholders. The difference in goals has led to a different focus: shareholders are primarily concerned with maximizing the value of the business, while managers are primarily concerned with maximizing personal compensation and benefits. The difference in concerns between the two has led to a certain degree of conflict of interest between shareholders and managers. This difference will prompt managers to maintain information asymmetry in order to protect their legitimate rights and interests, and even more to choose to sacrifice the interests of investors. For the principal, how to strengthen the supervision of the agent's behavior in all aspects of the operation to protect their own interests is the key focus (Fig. 1).

Fig. 1. Principal-agent relationship (source: the author)

2.2 Information Asymmetry Theory

There has always been a serious phenomenon of information asymmetry between enterprises and investors, and this asymmetry is mainly manifested in two aspects: first, investors mainly rely on various types of data disclosed by listed companies to make judgments when making investment decisions; second, listed companies have multiple considerations when disclosing information: such as in order to create a good image of enterprise development, conceal some information that is unfavorable or unsafe to the development of enterprises when disclosing information, etc. These behaviors result in information asymmetry between listed companies and investors. In the case of information asymmetry, reverse selection problems are prone to occur, which leads to market failure, reduces market operation efficiency, and triggers moral hazard (Ying 2016).

In recent years, financial restatements in the capital market have occurred frequently, such as some listed companies choosing to issue temporary announcements to supplement or correct errors or deficiencies in disclosed financial reports; or some listed companies deliberately take advantage of the information asymmetry between companies and investors to carry out accounting fraud through financial restatement, so as to seek more benefits for enterprises. In this context, the financial restatement behavior of listed companies has greatly hit investors' confidence, aggravated the negative impact of information asymmetry, and in the long run is not conducive to the development of enterprises themselves and the sound stability of the capital market. Therefore, in the process of information disclosure, high-quality information is particularly important, true and reliable financial information can completely and truly reflect the operating conditions of enterprises, which also puts forward higher requirements for the self-discipline and integrity of listed companies and the supervision and punishment of listed companies (Fig. 2).

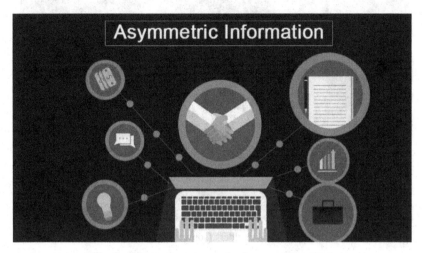

Fig. 2. Information asymmetry (source: the author)

2.3 Stakeholders Theory

Freeman proposed the stakeholders theory in 1984, and a broad sense of stakeholders refers to those individuals or groups that can influence or be affected by the achievement of corporate goals, including shareholders, creditors, employees, suppliers, consumers, government departments, relevant social organizations and social groups, and members of surrounding society. Stakeholders in the narrow sense refer to individuals and groups that have made a certain degree of investments in the enterprise and assumed certain risks, and whose activities can affect the realization of the company's goals or be affected by the process of the enterprises achieving their goals (Chen and Jia 2004). Theoretical research believes that there is a close correlation between the development of enterprises and the behavior of stakeholders, and when considering the pursuit of interests, the stakeholder collective should be considered rather than a certain group, and different methods should be used to coordinate the interest needs of different stakeholders. The interest needs between the shareholders and the operators of the enterprise are mainly reflected through the disclosure and use of financial information. If the operator has a significant profit reduction behavior in the process of financial restatement, this behavior deviates from the overall goal of maximizing the wealth of shareholders, so supervision and incentive measures can be used to coordinate between the two parties. And the target needs of stakeholders can be effectively realized under the effective institutional supervision of the operators and the continuous improvement of the corporate governance structure (Fig. 3).

Fig. 3. Stakeholders (source: the author)

3   Literature Review

The empirical research on financial restatement by domestic and foreign scholars mainly focuses on the following aspects:

3.1   Market Effects of Financial Restatements

Anderson and Yohn (2002), Desai et al. (2006) found that for financial restatements of listed companies due to revenue recognition errors, the initial announcement will cause the company's stock price to fall, and at the same time lead to a decline in the trust of outside investors in the company, but when the restatement announcement is issued for a period of time, the problem of incorrect information will be alleviated to a certain extent, but the damage to corporate reputation caused by financial restatement has not decreased over time. Outside investors have always been skeptical of the company's earnings.

Almer et al. (2007) and Wilson (2008) both believe that once a financial restatement occurs, its financial report will be questioned by investors for a long time, and the prestige of the enterprise will drop significantly.

A study by Zhou and Zhou (2012) using the 2004–2010 surplus restatement as a sample found that the "offsetting effect" or "exacerbation effect" of the negative impact of the annual good news or non-positive news on the negative impact of the surplus restatement was significant, and the restatement of the retrospective adjustment range, profitability, financial risk and debt level could significantly affect the degree of market reaction at the time of the restatement announcement.

Wei and Li (2009), Chen and Hu (2011) found that financial restatement announcements have a weak negative effect on the entire securities market, especially the impact on the same industry.

3.2 Financial Restatement and Surplus Management

Richardson (2002) studied the restatement announcements issued between 1995 and 1999, in which 403 restated announcements, executives with higher expectations of the company's future surpluses adopted a risky accounting policy to increase the company's disclosed surplus amounts, and excessive surplus amounts caused the gap between the statements and the actual figures, which led to financial restatements.

Zhang and Wang (2004) studied A-share listed companies that corrected accounting errors between 1999 and 2001 and found that 402 listed companies had financial restatements of their previous annual statements, of which 343 companies had overstated surpluses in previous years.

Lei et al. (2006) conducted a study and analysis of 1109 restated samples between 1999 and 2003, and the results showed that the scope of supplementary corrections of listed companies was very extensive, and more than half of the corrections had a potentially significant impact on profits, and the large fluctuations in profits before and after corrections also showed that some listed companies were likely to deliberately whitewash their financial statements.

Callen's (2008) study found that companies that are not doing well and may continue to lose money in the future are more likely to manipulate their earnings than well-run and profitable companies that are financially restated.

Based on accrual surplus manipulation and authenticity surplus manipulation, Xie (2015) found that restated companies that included accrued content and increased profits had a higher level of surplus management.

3.3 Financial Restatement and Executive Motivation

In terms of executive compensation incentives, executive compensation incentives were originally intended to alleviate proxy conflicts and eliminate conflicts of interest between management and shareholders. However, while solving the agency problem, it has also become a motivation for management to manipulate the surplus and push up the stock price in the short term to meet its own desires. When management avoids legal liability for manipulating surpluses, it restates the financial report by correcting errors.

Burns and Kedia (2006) found that management pushed up and profited from the company's financial statements by whitewashing the company's financial statements, and that the gains received by management correlated positively with the probability of the financial restatement of the company.

Niu and Xu (2010) argue that when management is unable to drive stock prices up through good performance reporting, in order to benefit themselves, it is possible to use non-compliant methods to beautify financial reports, thereby increasing the frequency of financial restatements of enterprises.

Research by Ishak and Yusof (2014) also shows that the age of a company's general manager is also linked to financial restatement. When the retirement bonus of the general manager of the company is performance-related, the general manager of the company near the retirement age will tend to beautify the statement to get a more substantial retirement bonus.

Gao (2016) believes that equity incentives, as the most common incentive method at present, although they can make the interests of shareholders and managers tend to be consistent and promote the enthusiasm of managers to improve the company's performance, may also prompt managers to use aggressive accounting policies or other non-compliant methods to push up stock prices in order to meet personal self-interest, thus triggering financial restatement of the company.

3.4 Financial Restatement and Internal Control

Scholars generally believe that higher the quality of internal controls, lower the probability of financial restatement in a company. Doyle et al. (2007) argues that weaker internal controls in companies can lead to poor quality of accounting information and thus increased likelihood of financial restatements. Liu et al. (2011) conducted a correlation test between the company's internal control deficiencies and the company's financial restatement behavior, and concluded that there is a large correlation between the two, that is, the more significant the internal control defect, the higher the possibility of the company's financial restatement. Liu et al. (2012) analyzed the data of listed companies from 2007 to 2009, and concluded that the quality of internal control of enterprises can have a negative effect on financial restatement, and the higher the quality of internal control, the lower the probability of financial restatement, so it can be done by strengthening internal control to prevent financial restatement. Wang et al. (2015), Zhang and Zhang (2018) found that the effectiveness of corporate internal controls can significantly inhibit financial restatement.

4 Overview of Financial Restatements of Listed Companies on the Main Board in Chinese Mainland

This paper takes the A-share companies listed on the Shenzhen stock exchange and the Shanghai Stock Exchange on main board from 2011 to 2019 as the research object, analyzes the situation of their financial restatement reports, excludes the listed companies in the financial industry and the samples with incomplete data, and defines the financial restatement year by the date of the first announcement of disclosure. The relevant data are derived from the DIB (Internal Control and Risk Management Database).

4.1 Overview of the Financial Restatements

Table 1. Statistical table of financial restatements of the listed firms (source: DIB)

Date (in year)	Numbers of financial restatements	Sample restate firms	Numbers of listed firms in total	Proportions of restate firms
2011	147	134	1393	9.6%
2012	154	133	1416	9.4%
2013	432	364	1412	25.8%
2014	417	311	1453	21.4%
2015	404	270	1540	17.5%
2016	373	237	1642	14.4%
2017	477	281	1854	15.2%
2018	423	350	1906	18.4%
2019	388	237	1956	12.1%

As we see from Table 1, the number of financial restatements of listed companies in 2011–2019 showed an overall upward trend, and the financial restatement behavior of listed companies increased sharply in 2013, which was the highest proportion of financial restatements in 2011–2019, and the number of financial restatements reached 364 companies in that year, and the number of financial restatements reached 432, and the proportion of restate companies doubled compared to the previous year, which may be related to the revision of corporate accounting standards in 2013. After 2013, the proportion of financially restated companies stabilized and declined slightly. The proportion of restatements tends to be around 15% since 2013. But in general, the absolute and relative numbers of financial restatements are not low, indicating that it is a common phenomenon of financial restatements of listed companies on the main board.

4.2 Frequency Analysis of Financial Restatements

According to Table 2, we found that there is an overall increasing tendency of financial restatements in 2011–2019. And the number of listed companies that restated for two or more times was also increasing. Even more, there have even been listed companies that have been restated for more than ten times a year, which is particularly noteworthy.

Table 2. Table of financial restatement frequency (source: DIB)

Frequency of financial restatement	Numbers of restated firms									Total
	2011	2012	2013	2014	2015	2016	2017	2018	2019	
1 time	122	115	308	241	188	168	188	301	154	1785
2 times	11	16	47	49	55	42	53	32	51	356
3 times	1	1	7	15	14	11	22	12	19	102
4 times	0	1	1	0	6	8	3	3	6	28
5 times and above	0	0	1	6	7	8	15	2	7	46

4.3 Financial Restatement Type Statistics

Table 3. Table of financial restatement types (source: DIB)

Types of financial restatement	Year of financial restatement									Total	Percentage
	2011	2012	2013	2014	2015	2016	2017	2018	2019		
Accounting problems	13	15	21	107	113	154	165	30	122	740	23.0%
Technical issues	55	62	109	96	107	144	153	113	149	988	30.7%
Sensitive issues	43	22	79	58	56	17	53	22	0	350	10.9%
Requirements of legal and regulatory exchanges	34	48	208	142	124	47	88	255	63	1009	31.4%
Accounting fraud or accounting scandals	0	0	10	5	4	11	9	3	0	42	1.3%
Other issues unknown	2	7	5	9	0	0	9	0	54	86	2.7%
Total	147	154	432	417	404	373	477	423	388	3215	100.0%

Table 3 above shows the statistical results of the types of financial restatements. The numbers of financial restatement that occur in response to the requirements of legal and regulatory exchanges, technical issues, accounting problems, sensitive issues and major accounting errors, accounting fraud or accounting scandals decreases sequentially, 31.4%, 30.7%, 23%, 10.9% and 1.3% respectively. Among the types of financial restatements, due to technical problems and in response to the requirements of legal and regulatory exchanges account for the largest proportion. Accounting issues, sensitivities and significant accounting errors in financial restatements, while not accounting for fraud or accounting scandals, should also be of greater concern because such reports are likely to involve with corporate profits or cause serious consequences.

5 Analysis of the Causes and Economic Consequences of Financial Restatement of Listed Companies

5.1 Causes of Financial Restatements

Information Asymmetry. In the capital market, the management of a company with more timely, comprehensive and accurate financial information is the information superior party. While the external investors with less financial information are the information inferior party. In order to maximize their own interests, the information superior party deliberately delays the time of information disclosure, conceals some financial information, and falsely reports financial information to induce the information inferior party to make wrong decisions, which cause huge loss to their wealth.

Increase Expected Earnings

1. The perspective of the company's managers - the motivation of executive compensation

   The remuneration incentive system aims to link the personal interests of the managers with the company's performance, and when the company's performance does not meet its expected remuneration standards, the managers may take illegal or non-compliant means to whitewash the financial statements in order to obtain a more generous compensation.

2. The perspective of listed companies - corporate financing pressure

   The expansion of enterprises creates financing needs, but regulators will conduct a strict review of the operation and profitability of financing enterprises. As a result, companies have an incentive to use profit manipulation to meet regulatory requirements. Moreover, China's accounting standards stipulate that when an enterprise adopts the retrospective adjustment method for financial restatement, it tacitly applies the corrected method to the enterprise when the transaction or event is first processed. In order to beautify financial indicators, many companies deliberately use various means to inflate profits in the early stage, and then use financial restatement as a "mine clearance tool" to evade legal punishment in the later stage, and the method will not have an impact on the current report.

Reduce the Tax Pressure of Enterprises. Some enterprises will choose to increase costs and expenses through "negotiation" with cooperative units in terms of costs, and at the same time tamper with actual profits to reduce corporate profits to manipulate taxable income, so as to achieve the purpose of reducing the amount of tax paid in the current year, which increases the risk of financial restatement of enterprises.

Internal Control Defects. In practice, financial statements are misstated due to employees' lack of awareness of internal control or accounting and working errors. These types of misstatements composed of a considerable proportion of financial restatements. The occurrence of such errors often means that there are problems with the internal controls of the enterprise, and the reasons for such financial restatements are most likely to be used by management as an excuse for financial restatements.

Lack of External Supervision. According to article 193 of the Securities Law, the maximum penalty for errors in information disclosure is only 600,000 yuan, while the mild punishment is only 300,000 yuan. When the profit brought by fraudulent financial data is much greater than the upper limit of the fine, the top management of the enterprise may deliberately break the law and manipulate the surplus to achieve the purpose of profitability, which resulting in an increase in the frequency of financial restatements.

5.2 Economic Consequences of Financial Restatements

The economic consequences that may result from financial restatement of listed companies are mainly reflected in the following aspects:

Penalties Imposed by the CSRC. For listed companies that violate the rules and carry out improper financial restatements, the CSRC (China Security Regulatory Commission) will issue corresponding penalties according to the types of regulations.

The Stock Price Falls. The increase in the market value of listed companies is inseparable from good performance, and when there is a performance thunderstorm, the stock price is the first to be hit hard. Empirical studies by numerous scholars have found that the market reaction due to accounting problems or financial restatements caused by suspected fraud is very significant, and generally causes a sharp decline in stock prices.

Cause Litigation. Listed companies through financial restatement fraud often cause huge economic losses to investors, after the CSRC issued an administrative penalty decision, investors will choose to file a lawsuit, and the huge compensation that may result from litigation will further worsen the company's financial situation.

Push Up Market Costs. In order to revitalize market confidence, listed companies may change management, and these measures may also be counterproductive, aggravating market doubts, thereby pushing up the financing costs of listed companies and increasing audit fees.

6 Governance Measures for Financial Restatements of Listed Companies

6.1 Improve Relevant Laws and Regulations on Financial Restatement

The current financial restatement system is still not perfect, for example, there are no strict standards for the conditions for financial restatement, retrospective adjustment methods, and disclosure formats, resulting in a situation where financial restatement in the capital market is common, frequent and arbitrary.

6.2 Strengthen External Supervision and Increase Penalties for Improper Financial Restatement

In terms of supervision, we can learn from the experience of the recent Zhangzidao case and jointly investigate and punish companies that disclose false information through various means. According to the 2020 revised Securities Law, the maximum fine for false information disclosure can reach 10 million yuan, but compared with the financial fraud benefits or losses, the relevant penalties are still not enough to deter false information disclosure, so further increasing the cost of violating the law will help deter the relevant listed companies. At the same time, the regulator should also strengthen supervision and punishment for certified public accountants who have not fulfilled their duty of diligence to reduce the risk of information disclosure; in addition to increasing the upper limit of the penalty amount, External investors who make a wrong judgment due to false financial statements should be given civil compensation.

6.3 Establish Incentive Inspiring Mechanisms for Enterprise

According to the quality of information disclosure in corporate financial statements, a certain degree of rewards can be given to enterprises with qualified information disclosure, so as to encourage enterprises to take the initiative to improve the quality of financial statements.

6.4 Strengthen the Construction of Audit Teams

Certified public accountants need to issue audit reports on the financial reports of listed companies, in a sense, the standard unqualified opinion is an endorsement of the financial reports of listed companies, in order to maintain the independence and objectivity of the audit, the audit institution and the signatory accountants should be rotated regularly; the certified public accountants should ensure their professional ethics, improve their own auditing business capabilities, and check well to reduce the improper financial restatement of the listed company.

References

Zhang, W., Wang, X.: Analysis of the driving factors of accounting errors of listed companies in China. Account. Res. 4, 24–29 (2004)

Wei, Z., Li, C.: Study on the effect of restatement announcement in annual reports of Chinese listed companies. J. Account. Res. 08, 31–39 (2009)

Zhou, X., Zhou, Q.: Study on market response and its influencing factors of surplus restatement. Secur. Mark. Her. 03, 20 (2012)

Wang, Z., Xiao, H., Li, W.: Internal control, executive compensation and financial restatement: an empirical study based on Chinese listed companies. J. Field Actions 05, 30–32 (2014)

Luo, J.: A study on the financial restatement of listed companies in China: motivations, influencing factors and economic consequences. Jiangxi Normal University (2020)

What is Stopping You from Using Mobile Payment? A PLS-SEM Approach

Hao Rui, Garry Wei-Han Tan[✉], Eugene Cheng-Xi Aw, Tat-Huei Cham, and Keng-Boon Ooi

UCSI Graduate Business School, UCSI University, Kuala Lumpur, Malaysia
1002059230@ucsiuniversity.edu.my, garrytanweihan@gmail.com

Abstract. Mobile payments are rapidly taking over the market with their convenience and speed, creating new payment and profit models for consumers and organizations. While they are beneficial the adoption is still at the infancy. On this basis, this study combines consumers' perceived risk (e.g., affective risk and performance risk) and consumers' perceived value (e.g., economic value, emotional value, function value, social value) as second-order constructs with ease of use to study on the willingness of consumer to use mobile payment. Results indicate that all the hypotheses are supported in this study. The research enriches the literatures of mobile payment and deepens the understanding of mobile payment usage from a developing country perspective.

Keywords: Mobile payment · Perceived ease of use · Perceived value · Perceived risk · PLS-SEM

1 Introduction

Mobile payment has changed the way we live in recent years and has become an indispensable part of our lives [3, 26]. With the continuous development of mobile payment, however there is no standard definition of mobile payment [39]. Generally mobile payment is an innovative way of payment, with the mobile internet helping to achieve the transfer of payments between individuals, between individuals and organizations, and between organizations [38, 46]. The adoption of mobile payment has helped to enhance the consumers' information experience, create new business models, and improve mobile commerce's market revenue. However, different factors are limiting the effectiveness of mobile payment usage. According to [24], mobile payment involves four parties namely consumers, banks, payment companies, and merchants. The system is therefore complex and prone to security issues such as the exposure of password. Moreover, due to the mobile devices' portability, the reliability and information confidentiality are inherently worse than the conventional internet environments. As an essential payment method for online consumption, mobile payments should first ensure the security of funds, and the endless online consumption fraud casts a shadow on consumers' mobile payments [13, 40]. For a long time, scholars focused on the traditional models emphasizing the function and fluency of the technology, while ignoring the consumers' perception of value and

© Springer Nature Switzerland AG 2022
M. Rauterberg et al. (Eds.): HCII 2022, LNCS 13520, pp. 208–220, 2022.
https://doi.org/10.1007/978-3-031-18158-0_15

risks in the process [19, 21, 27, 31]. A theoretical model of the factors influencing the willingness of consumers to use mobile payment is therefore constructed in this paper, based on the theory of perceived value and perceived risk. Mobile commerce in China is in a period of rapid development. Mobile payment has rapidly occupied the market with its convenient and fast advantages, which creates a new payment and profit model for consumers. Although the mobile payment market has an extensive user group, it has not been widely accepted by all walks of society. Therefore, it is of practical value to understand mobile payment acceptance from users' perspectives, identify the driving factors, and consider the strategies to improve consumers' willingness to use. Practically, this study provides essential references to stakeholders such as mobile commerce companies and mobile payment system designers. Theoretically this study summarises a large number of existing scholars' theoretical research on mobile payment, proposes the influencing factors of mobile payment based on the theory of value and risks. In general, this study adds to the research content of mobile payment from a developing country perspective.

2 Literature Review

2.1 Theory of Perceived Value

The overall evaluation of a product or service is based on the customer's perceived utility vs the cost of receiving it [51]. [18] put forward the intention to use a model in a specific mobile Internet environment based on integrating the existing research and found that the user-perceived value significantly impacts the adoption intention. At present, the multi-dimensional structure of perceived value has been generally recognized by scholars, but there are different opinions on its dimensions. Perceived value is separated into functional, emotional, social, cognitive, and situational values, according to [36]. These five values will influence consumers' choice behaviour at the purchase level. In addition, many scholars put forward different ways to divide perceived value according to different research objects. [23] divides perceived value into social price, content, interactive and interface design value. [52] divides perceived value into social, information, and emotional value and find that perceived value positively affects consumer satisfaction. [34] divided perceived value into functional value, emotional value, and social value.

2.2 Theory of Perceived Risk

Perception of risk is thought to be a multifaceted items. When making a purchasing decision, [33] claims that the consumer bears the risk of loss, which includes loss of time, danger, self, and money. [47] believe that consumer perceived risks include privacy risk, financial risk, operational risk, psychological risk, and time risk for consumers of mobile value-added services. [17] conducted regression analysis and correlation analysis on 12 products according to the five risks and overall risk proposed. The results showed that the five risks explained 74% of the variance of the overall risk. [29] looked into perceived risk in more depth. Financial risk, performance risk, physical danger, psychological risk, and social risk are the dimensions of perceived risk in this study, which are based on

Jacoby and Kaplan's research progress. Financial risk is composed of venture capital related to money and property. Performance risk may occur when the product function is executed, and the requirements are met. Physical risk refers to the risk related to the loss of physical strength, health, and energy. Social risk is the potential damage to the respect, respect, and friendship of other members of society caused by the purchase or use of a product. Psychological risk is due to purchasing or using personal image and connotation damage. Based on the principal component analysis of perceived risks in these five aspects, [4] extracted two factors: financial and operational risk performance, and physical risks; and emotional risks, which are social and psychological.

3   Hypotheses Development

When consumer thinks that it is easier to use mobile payment and does not need to spend too much energy and time, his perceived value of this new technology will improve [1]. For mobile payment, when consumers think that mobile payment is convenient and straightforward, it will improve the product's perceived quality and reduce the uncertainty surrounding it [8]. With the development of mobile internet, mobile applications are increasingly pursuing user's experience. On the premise of fast payment, function design becomes easy to understand, and the operation is more smoother [16]. Good user experience improves users' perceived ease of the use of mobile payment, which indirectly affects the perceived value and perceived risk. Thus, it is hypothesised that:

H1: Perceived ease of use has a positive impact on perceived value.

H2: Perceived ease of use has a negative impact on perceived risk.

Users' perceived ease of use has a major impact on consumers' propensity to adopt mobile commerce, according to [42]. Perceived ease of use relates with the simplicity of learning to use mobile payment system and the easy way of handling payment. Consumer confidence will increase when using mobile payment system is convenient, as well as free from time, place, and transaction condition limitations. Therefore, it can be assumed that.

H3: Perceived ease of use has a positive impact on willingness to use.

Consumers' perceived value is the main basis of consumers' willingness to use [5]. The study revealed factors that contribute to the perceived values, which are: effort involved in the use of the technology, which is considered beneficial, time spent on the use of technology, which is considered worthwhile to the consumers, reduction of the financial management costs, as well as the technology delivery of good value in terms of meeting expectations of the consumers; therefore, the study showed the significance of perceived value in the adoption of the payment technology. The study also revealed that not only monetary but also non-monetary value is associated with perceived value. Financial costs are included in the monetary component. Therefore, it is hypothesised that:

H4: Consumers' perceived value has a positive impact on willingness to use.

With regard to the impact of perceived risk on willingness to use, it is generally accepted that perceived risk undermines willingness to use. [11] explored the relationship between perceived risk and continuous use intention and found that perceived risk negatively affects users' continuous use intention. Consumers still place a high value on the risk of transaction failure or information leakage in mobile payments, despite the fact that they benefits from the adoption [32]. Obviously, consumers' perceived risk of mobile payment business inhibits their willingness to exchange, while consumers' perceived value of mobile payment business improves their willingness to exchange [37]. Thus, it is hypothesised that.

H5: Perceived risk has a significant negative impact on willingness to use.

4   Research Methodology

This paper is a cross-sectional and the primary purpose is to study on the relationship between variables in the model. According to previous scholars, the age of consumers using mobile payment is concentrated between 20 and 40 years old [35]. Simultaneously, according to the national Internet Network Information Centre survey, the people born in the 1980s grow up under the background of the internet, have the inherent Internet gene, and are easier to accept and quickly learn emerging technologies internet-related products. Based on two reasons, this study mainly takes this age group as an example to study consumers' willingness to use mobile payment. 377 samples were put forward in this study by using the convenience sampling technique. The specific definition content is shown in Table 1. The analysis will be conducted using PLS-SEM.

Table 1. Definition of constructs

Constructs	Definitions	Sources
Perceived ease of use	Perceived ease of use refers to the degree that consumers think it is easy to use a certain system, reflecting the quickness of consumers learning to use mobile payment easily	[7, 31]
Perceived value	Perceived value is the overall evaluation of a product or service based on a trade-off between benefits and costs perceived	[51, 36]
Perceived Risk	Consumers perceive the loss expectation they may suffer from using mobile payment	[6, 28]
Willingness to use	As a rational actor, users will not be interfered with by the external environment. When they use or consume, they will make consumption behaviour according to their nationality or preliminary plan, which is mainly affected by their behaviour. When they have the behaviour will, they will pay the actual user behaviour	[2]

5 Data Analysis

5.1 Background of Respondents

According to Table 2, of the 307 effective respondents, there are more male respondents (52.4%) than female respondents (47.6%). The age group with the highest frequency is 26 to 30 years old (25.7%). More than half of the respondents (54.7%) earn between RMB2000-RMB6000 per month and 42.7% holds a bachelor's degree (42.7%). A large percentage of the respondents have more than 3 years of using mobile devices to make payment (70.1%). Also, nearly half of the respondents (45.9%) use smart mobile devices to make payments every day.

Table 2. Descriptive statistics

Demographic characteristic		Frequency	Percentage (%)
Gender	Male	161	52.4
	Female	146	47.6
Age (years old)	18 and below	46	15.0
	18–25	69	22.5
	26–30	79	25.7
	31–40	70	22.8
	41 and above	43	14.0
Current education level	Primary or secondary education	81	26.4
	High school/advance diploma	61	19.9
	Bachelor degree	131	42.7
	Postgraduate (e.g., Master, Doctorate)	34	11.1
Monthly income	Below or equal to RMB2000	51	16.6
	RMB2001-RMB4000	86	28.0
	RMB4001-RMB6000	82	26.7
	RMB6001 and above	88	28.7
Frequency of using mobile payment	Every day	141	45.9
	Every week	94	30.6
	Every month	72	23.5
Experience of using smart mobile devices specifically to make payment	Less than 3 years	92	30.0
	3 to 5 years	108	35.2
	More than 5 years	107	34.9

5.2 Statistical Analysis

Measurement Model Evaluation. Reliability is a measure of the stability or consistency of test scores. The results of Dijkstra Henseler (rho_A) and composite reliability (CR) are presented in Table 3. All constructs record values within 0.778 to 0.905 and 0.869 to 0.936, which shows that all the constructs are reliable [9, 14, 45]. All average variance extracted (AVE) are above 0.50 and each construct had external loadings above 0.70 [43, 12, 30] indicating convergent validity.

Table 3. Composite reliability, Dijkstra Henseler and average variance extracted.

Constructs	Number of items	Dijkstra Henseler (rho_A)	Composite reliability (CR)	Average Variance Extracted (AVE)
Affective risk	3	0.856	0.912	0.775
Consumers' willingness to use	5	0.905	0.928	0.72
Economic value	3	0.778	0.869	0.689
Emotional value	3	0.889	0.931	0.818
Function value	3	0.872	0.921	0.796
Perceived ease of use	5	0.885	0.915	0.683
Performance risk	3	0.898	0.936	0.83
Social value	3	0.804	0.884	0.718

All HTMT first-order and second-order values in Tables 4 and 5 are less than 0.8 indicating discriminant validity [9, 20, 41].

Table 4. Hetero-Trait-Mono-Trait assessment (HTMT.85) for first order constructs

Affective risk	Consumers' willingness to use	Economic value	Emotional value	Function value	Perceived ease of use	Performance risk	Social value
Affective risk							
Consumers' willingness to use	0.638						
Economic value	0.558	0.558					
Emotional Value	0.362	0.586	0.823				
Function value	0.461	0.610	0.755	0.730			
Perceived ease of use	0.792	0.760	0.654	0.562	0.582		
Performance risk	0.791	0.698	0.406	0.331	0.378	0.719	
Social value	0.483	0.540	0.839	0.783	0.766	0.671	0.362

Table 5. Hetero-Trait-Mono-Trait Assessment (HTMT.85) for second order constructs

	Consumers' perceived risk	Consumers' perceived value
Consumers' perceived risk		
Consumers' perceived value	0.528	

Structural Model Evaluation. The SRMR values are between 0.075 and 0.079 indicating fitness of model. VIF values range from 1 to 2.381 why implies that there is no issue of multicollinearity as all exogenous constructs' VIF values are lower than 5.0 [12]. The results of the structural model evaluation is shown in Fig. 1.

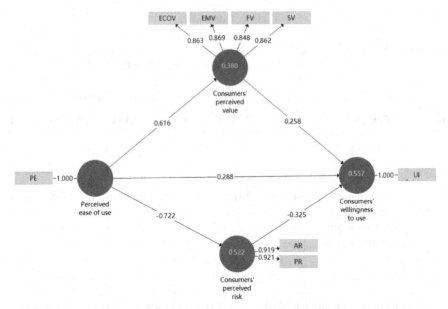

Fig. 1. Structural model evaluation

Table 6. Outcome of structural model evaluation

Hypothesis	PLS paths	Original sample (O)	T Statistics (IO/STDEVI)	P values	Bias corrected confidence intervals		Remarks
					2.50%	97.50%	
H1	Perceived ease of use -> Consumers' perceived value	0.616	10.233	0.000	0.479	0.711	Supported
H2	Perceived ease of use -> Consumers' perceived risk	−0.722	19.06	0.000	−0.789	−0.641	Supported
H3	Perceived ease of use -> Consumers' willingness to use	0.288	3.088	0.002	0.107	0.466	Supported

(*continued*)

Table 6. (*continued*)

Hypothesis	PLS paths	Original sample (O)	T Statistics (IO/STDEVI)	P values	Bias corrected confidence intervals		Remarks
					2.50%	97.50%	
H4	Consumers' perceived value -> Consumers' willingness to use	0.258	4.21	0.000	0.138	0.372	Supported
H5	Consumers' perceived risk -> Consumers' willingness to use	−0.325	3.867	0.000	−0.49	−0.169	Supported

As can be seen from Table 6, all the proposed hypotheses in this study are supported. Table 7, showed that the R^2 is 0.522, 0.380 and 0.557 for consumer's perceived risk, value and willingness to use respectively. R^2 values of 0.75, 0.50, and 0.25, respectively, strong, medium and weak, indicating that the interpretation of this study is medium and weak [12, 25, 48].

Table 7. R^2

Variable	R^2
Consumers' perceived risk	0.522
Consumers' perceived value	0.380
Consumers' willingness to use	0.557

According to [44], 0.020 to 0.149, 0.150 to 0.349 and 0.350 indicates small, medium or large effects. The results in Table 8 showed that the constructs f^2 ranges from small to large effects. All Q^2 in Table 9 shows that the value is >0 indicating sufficient predictive relevance [15].

Table 8. Effect size (F^2)

	Consumers' perceived risk	Consumers' perceived value	Consumers' willingness to use
Consumers' perceived risk			0.114
Consumers' perceived value			0.093
Perceived ease of use	1.091	0.613	0.070

Table 9. Effect size (Q^2)

	SSO	SSE	$Q^2 (= 1 - SSE/SSO)$
Consumers' perceived risk	614	346.699	0.435
Consumers' perceived value	1228	885.822	0.279
Consumers' willingness to use	307	142.312	0.536

6   Discussion and Implications

There is a positive significant relationship between perceived ease of use and consumers' perceived value, thereby H1 is supported. This result shows that mobile payment platform is simple and easy to use and thus will lead to consumers realizing the perceived value of mobile payment. There is a negative significant relationship between perceived ease of use and consumers' perceived risk and also a positive relationship between ease of use and consumers' willingness to use, thereby H2 and H3 are supported. When consumers find that mobile payment is easy to use, their perception of risk is reduced [50]. This result shows that mobile payment ease of use improve the user's shopping experience, improve shopping efficiency, and make shopping more convenient and fast [31] and thus helps to increase consumers' willingness to use. There is a positive significant relationship between consumers' perceived value and consumers' willingness to use, thereby H4 is supported. This result shows that mobile payment can bring more promotional activities to consumers and allow them to perceive more profits [22], which facilitates consumers' overall planning of their wealth and greatly enhances the convenience of managing their finances and generating greater value. Lastly there a negative significant relationship between consumers' perceived risk and consumers' willingness to use it. Therefore, H5 is supported. Mobile payments often require consumers to submit some basic information, which usually involves some private information, including consumers' mobile phone numbers, names, etc. The use of this information often leads to many consumers' insecurity, fear of what negative consequences might occur [31]. The research model used in this study was able to provide useful findings as the model can explain 55.7% of willingness to use. This paper is based on the theory of perceived value and risk and therefore contributes to the literatures of mobile payment in the developing country. Practically, in the promotion of mobile payment, businesses and marketers should comprehensively consider the perceived ease of use, consumers' perceived risk and consumers' perceived value brought by mobile payment to consumers.

7   Limitations and Future Directions

First, the study was conducted from a Chinese perspective. As a result, the results of the study may not accurately reflect the adoption of mobile payments in other countries. This is because cultural differences affect the adoption of mobile payments [49]. In other words, technology use behaviour depends to some extent on culture. Future studies should therefore be conducted on a transnational basis and should be extended to include data from developing and developed countries for comparative studies. The consumers' perceived risk in this study was studied from only two dimensions, while the risk-theory indicates that there are seven different risks [10]. Therefore, it is recommended to adopt the seven dimensions of risk as a whole or to conduct a more comprehensive study on risk. Last, this study emphasises the willingness to use mobile payments which is evolving and changing rapidly. Consumers' willingness to adopt mobile payments will change over time. Therefore, future researchers should consider using a longitudinal method to analyse and compare data.

References

1. Bailey, A.A., Pentina, I., Mishra, A.S., Mimoun, M.S.B.: Mobile payments adoption by US consumers: an extended TAM. Int. J. Retail Distrib. Manage. **45**(6), 626–640 (2017)
2. Bhattacherjee, A.: Understanding information systems continuance: an expectation-confirmation model. MIS Q. Manage. Inf. Syst. **25**(3), 351–370 (2001)
3. Brem, A., Viardot, E., Nylund, P.A.: Implications of the coronavirus (COVID-19) outbreak for innovation: Which technologies will improve our lives? Technol. Forecast. Soc. Chang. **163**, 120451 (2021)
4. Chaudhuri, A.: A macro analysis of the relationship of product involvement and information search: the role of risk. J. Market. Theory Pract. **8**(1), 1–15 (2000)
5. Chen, Q.: Research on Influencing Factors of mobile payment willingness based on perceived value (Master's thesis, Beijing University of Posts and Telecommunications) (2015). https://kns.cnki.net/KCMS/detail/detail.aspx?dbname=CMFD201502&filename=1015583501.nh
6. Cunningham, S.M.: The major dimensions of perceived risk. In: Cox, D.F. (ed.) Risk Taking and Information Handing in Consumer Behavior. Harvard University Press, Boston (1967)
7. Davis, F.D.: Perceived usefulness, perceived ease of use, and user acceptance of information technology. MIS Q. Manage. Inf. Syst. **13**(3), 319–339 (1989)
8. De Kerviler, G., Demoulin, N.T., Zidda, P.: Adoption of in-store mobile payment: are perceived risk and convenience the only drivers? J. Retail. Consum. Serv. **31**, 334–344 (2016)
9. Dijkstra, T.K., Henseler, J.: Consistent partial least squares path modeling. MIS Q. **39**(2), 297–316 (2015)
10. Featherman, M.S., Pavlou, P.A.: Predicting e-services adoption: a perceived risk facets perspective. Int. J. Hum. Comput. Stud. **59**(4), 451–474 (2003)

11. Forsythe, S., Liu, C., Shannon, D., Gardner, L.C.: Development of a scale to measure the perceived benefits and risks of online shopping. J. Interact. Mark. **20**(2), 55–75 (2006)
12. Hair, J.F., Hult, G.T.M., Ringle, C., Sarstedt, M.: A Primer on Partial Least Squares Structural Equation Modeling (PLS-SEM), 2nd edn. Sage Publications, Thousand Oaks (2017)
13. Hansen, J.M., Saridakis, G., Benson, V.: Risk, trust, and the interaction of perceived ease of use and behavioral control in predicting consumers' use of social media for transactions. Comput. Hum. Behav. **80**, 197–206 (2018)
14. Hew, J.J., Leong, L.Y., Tan, G.W.H., Ooi, K.B., Lee, V.H.: The age of mobile social commerce: an Artificial Neural Network analysis on its resistances. Technol. Forecast. Soc. Chang. **144**, 311–324 (2019)
15. Hew, J.J., Tan, G.W.H., Lin, B., Ooi, K.B.: Generating travel-related contents through mobile social tourism: does privacy paradox persist? Telematics Inform. **34**(7), 914–935 (2017)
16. Hsiao, K., Chen, C.: What drives smartwatch purchase intention? Perspectives from hardware, software, design, and value. Telematics Inform. **35**(1), 103–113 (2018)
17. Kaplan, L.B., Szybillo, G.J., Jacoby, J.: Components of perceived risk in product purchase: a cross-validation. J. Appl. Psychol. **59**(3), 287–291 (1974)
18. Kim, H.W., Chan, H.C., Gupta, S.: Value-based adoption of mobile internet: an empirical investigation. Decis. Support Syst. **43**(1), 111–126 (2007)
19. Lee, V.H., Hew, J.J., Leong, L.Y., Tan, G.W.H., Ooi, K.B.: Wearable payment: a deep learning-based dual-stage SEM-ANN analysis. Expert Syst. Appl. **157**, 113477 (2020)
20. Leong, L.Y., Hew, T.S., Ooi, K.B., Lee, V.H., Hew, J.J.: A hybrid SEM-neural network analysis of social media addiction. Expert Syst. Appl. **133**, 296–316 (2019)
21. Lew, S., Tan, G.W.H., Loh, X.M., Hew, J.J., Ooi, K.B.: The disruptive mobile wallet in the hospitality industry: an extended mobile technology acceptance model. Technol. Soc. **63**, 101430 (2020)
22. Wei, L.: Research on the influence of consumer perceptional factors on the intention to use mobile payment technology in Peru-Based on Technology Acceptance Model. Chang'an University (2020)
23. Li, W.: The impact of perceived value on e-book reading client customer satisfaction and loyalty. J. Libr. Sci. China **06**, 35–49 (2017)
24. Liébana-Cabanillas, F., Munoz-Leiva, F., Sánchez-Fernández, J.: A global approach to the analysis of user behavior in mobile payment systems in the new electronic environment. Serv. Bus. **12**(1), 25–64 (2018)
25. Loh, X.K., Lee, V.H., Loh, X.M., Tan, G.W.H., Ooi, K.B., Dwivedi, Y.K.: The dark side of mobile learning via social media: how bad can it get? Inf. Syst. Front., 1–18 (2021)
26. Loh, X.M., Lee, V.H., Tan, G.W.H., Hew, J.J., Ooi, K.B.: Towards a cashless society: the imminent role of wearable technology. J. Comput. Inf. Syst. **62**(1), 39–49 (2022)
27. Loh, X.M., Lee, V.H., Tan, G.W.H., Ooi, K.B., Dwivedi, Y.K.: Switching from cash to mobile payment: what's the hold-up? Internet Res. **31**(1), 376–399 (2021)
28. Morais Watanabe, E.A., Alfinito, S., Curvelo, I.C.G., Hamza, K.M.: Perceived value, trust and purchase intention of organic food: a study with Brazilian consumers. Br. Food J. **122**(4), 1070–1184 (2020)
29. Murray, K.B., Schlacter, J.L.: The impact of services versus goods on consumers' assessment of perceived risk and variability. J. Acad. Mark. Sci. **18**(1), 51–65 (1990)
30. Ng, F.Z.X., Yap, H.Y., Tan, G.W.H., Lo, P.S., Ooi, K.B.: Fashion shopping on the go: a Dual-stage predictive-analytics SEM-ANN analysis on usage behaviour, experience response and cross-category usage. J. Retail. Consum. Serv. **65**, 102851 (2022)
31. Ooi, K.B., Tan, G.W.H.: Mobile technology acceptance model: an investigation using mobile users to explore smartphone credit card. Expert Syst. Appl. **59**, 33–46 (2016)
32. Rauschnabel, P.A., He, J., Ro, Y.K.: Antecedents to the adoption of augmented reality smart glasses: a closer look at privacy risks. J. Bus. Res. **92**, 374–384 (2018)

33. Roselius, T.: Consumer rankings of risk reduction methods. J. Mark. **35**(1), 56 (1971)

34. Sánchez, J., Callarisa, L., Rodríguez, R.M., Moliner, M.A.: Perceived value of the purchase of a tourism product. Tour. Manage. **27**(3), 394–409 (2006)

35. Sekaran, U., Bougie, R.: Research Methods for Business: A Skill-Building Approach, 7th edn. Wiley, New Jersey (2016)

36. Sheth, J.N., Newman, B.I., Gross, B.L.: Why we buy what we buy: a theory of consumption values. J. Bus. Res. **22**(2), 159–170 (1991)

37. Singh, S., Zolkepli, A., Cheah, W.: New wave in mobile commerce adoption via mobile applications in Malaysian market: Investigating the relationship between consumer acceptance, trust, and self-efficacy. Int. J. Interact. Mobile Technol. **12**(7), 112–128 (2018)

38. Sun, Z., Sun, L., Strang, K.: Big data analytics services for enhancing business intelligence. J. Comput. Inf. Syst. **58**(2), 162–169 (2018)

39. Tew, H.T., Tan, G.W.H., Loh, X.M., Lee, V.H., Lim, W.L., Ooi, K.B.: Tapping the next purchase: embracing the wave of mobile payment. J. Comput. Inf. Syst., 1–9 (2021). https://doi.org/10.1080/08874417.2020.1858731

40. Wan, S.M., Cham, L.N., Tan, G.W.H., Lo, P.S., Ooi, K.B., Chatterjee, R.S.: What's stopping you from migrating to mobile tourism shopping? J. Comput. Inf. Syst., 1–16 (2021)

41. Wang, G., Tan, G.W.H., Yuan, Y.P., Ooi, K.B., Dwivedi, Y.K.: Revisiting TAM2 in behavioral targeting advertising: a deep learning-based dual-stage SEM-ANN analysis. Technol. Forecast. Soc. Chang. **175**, 121345 (2022)

42. Wang, H.Y., Wang, S.H.: Predicting mobile hotel reservation adoption: Insight from a perceived value standpoint. Int. J. Hosp. Manag. **29**(4), 598–608 (2010)

43. Wong, C.H., Tan, G.W.H., Loke, S.P., Ooi, K.B.: Mobile TV: a new form of entertainment? Ind. Manag. Data Syst. **114**(7), 1050–1067 (2014)

44. Wong, C.H., Tan, G.W.H., Loke, S.P., Ooi, K.B.: Adoption of mobile social networking sites for learning? Online Inf. Rev. **39**(3), 762–778 (2015)

45. Wong, L.W., Tan, G.W.H., Lee, V.H., Ooi, K.B., Sohal, A.: Unearthing the determinants of Blockchain adoption in supply chain management. Int. J. Prod. Res. **58**(7), 2100–2123 (2020)

46. Yan, L.Y., Tan, G.W.H., Loh, X.M., Hew, J.J., Ooi, K.B.: QR code and mobile payment: the disruptive forces in retail. J. Retail. Consum. Serv. **58**, 102300 (2021)

47. Yongqing, Y., Jinlong, Z., Nan, L., Guang, Y.: An Empirical Study on the antecedents of perceived risk of mobile value-added service consumers. Manage. Rev. **03**, 115–123 (2012)

48. Yuan, Y.P., Tan, G.W.H., Ooi, K.B., Lim, W.L.: Can COVID-19 pandemic influence experience response in mobile learning? Telematics Inform. **64**, 101676 (2021)

49. Yuen, Y.Y., Yeow, P.H., Lim, N.: Internet banking acceptance in the United States and Malaysia: a cross-cultural examination. Mark. Intell. Plan. **33**(3), 292–308 (2015)

50. Zang, X.: Research on Influencing Factors of Perceived Risk of Mobile Payment Users. Nanjing Normal University (2018)

51. Zeithaml, V.A.: Consumer perceptions of price, quality, and value: a means-end model and synthesis of evidence. J. Mark. **52**(3), 2–22 (1988)

52. Wenjun, Z., Ming, Y., Xuedong, W.: An Empirical Study on consumers' willingness to participate in social Q & A platform from the perspective of perceived value. Inf. Sci. **02**, 69–74 (2017)

Consumers' Perceived Benefits and Costs for Amazon Go Based on Social Media Data Using Text Mining

Jaehye Suk[1] , In-Hyoung Park[1] , Cheol Lee[1] , Youmin Park[1] ,
and Jae-Eun Chung[2(✉)]

[1] Convergence Program for Social Innovation, Sungkyunkwan University, Seoul, South Korea
[2] Department of Consumer Science, Convergence Program for Social Innovation,
Sungkyunkwan University, Seoul, South Korea
jchung@skku.edu

Abstract. This study aims to identify the perceived benefits and costs of Amazon Go, the first unmanned store with advanced technology, based on the value-based adoption model using a text-mining technique. We collected 15,435 documents posted on Twitter from January 21, 2018, to September 1, 2021, employing "Amazon Go" and "#Amazon Go" as keywords. Frequency analysis, clustering analysis, CONCOR, and semantic network analysis were conducted using Python and R programming. The major results are as follows. First, we extracted 20 attributes of Amazon Go, which are classified into four dimensions (functionality, no humanity, privacy risk, and self-service). Second, overall, consumers perceived greater benefits than costs of Amazon Go. Consumers perceive "automation" as the most beneficial attribute of Amazon Go, and attributes referring to "frictionless payment," "tracking of past purchase history," "no humanity," and "no cash acceptance" were also observed positively. However, negative perceptions regarding each of these attributes, such as "hard," "bad," and "worried," were also detected. Third, we found concerns about privacy infringement, indicating that consumers may resist new technologies due to privacy concerns. In addition, consumers' worries about "shoplifting" were extracted as costs. Finally, terms related to price perceptions were not extracted, reflecting that the concept of Amazon Go is still new to consumers and its users are still at the trial stage. This study offers implications that may help unmanned retailers with the advanced technology to deliver services that correspond to consumer values and expectations, thus increasing consumer utility and satisfaction.

Keywords: Amazon Go · Perceived benefits & costs · Semantic network analysis

© Springer Nature Switzerland AG 2022
M. Rauterberg et al. (Eds.): HCII 2022, LNCS 13520, pp. 221–236, 2022.
https://doi.org/10.1007/978-3-031-18158-0_16

1 Introduction

Retailers have been increasingly using cutting-edge technology, such as artificial intelligence (AI), to improve profitability and consumer shopping experiences [1, 2]. As a result, many human tasks have been replaced by machines, transforming traditional retail-service models into unmanned stores [3]. These retailers enable consumers to avoid having to wait for salespeople and cashiers [3] and eliminate workers to reduce costs [4]. They can also collect consumers' purchase histories and behavioral data more accurately, consequently predicting demand more precisely [5]. Amazon Go is the first unmanned store using AI. Since it opened a pilot store in Seattle, the U.S., in 2016, it has introduced an entirely new shopping environment that relies on a "just walk out" concept that utilizes AI-based technology. Amazon Go is not only a cashier-free convenience store but also a provider of a new smart service. This smart retail service is expected to create new values by generating considerable convenience, accessibility, control perception, and time efficiency for consumers [6, 7]. When consumers install and use the Amazon Go application on their smartphones, the automatic sensor recognizes their in-store movements, automatically checks their purchase lists, and pays through one of their registered payment methods. However, new services often face barriers in terms of consumer resistance to adaptation [8–10]. Therefore, retailers must decide how to overcome inexperienced consumers' aversion to using Amazon Go, focusing on critical factors that affect consumer intentions. Consumer evaluation of the benefits and costs of using such technology services does not depend entirely on the usefulness of the technology itself. Therefore, it is important to understand consumers' perceptions of Amazon Go and how they form particular attitudes toward these types of services. According to the value-based adoption model, consumers adopt a particular technology by balancing its perceived benefits and costs [11]. Therefore, to examine the consumers' acceptance of Amazon Go, it is necessary to understand how consumers perceive its benefits and costs.

Studies on consumer awareness and acceptance of smart retail services [1, 12–14] were mainly conducted on the basis of surveys. However, this type of approach requires a lot of labor and material resources and cannot obtain large amounts of information and to promptly reflect consumers' opinions. Furthermore, sampling is also prone to bias [15]. In order to overcome the limitations of such research methods, many recent consumer studies have instead analyzed consumer-generated online data [16–18]. These data include various opinions, such as those of consumers who use the service, consumers who are considering using it, and consumers who refuse to use the new service. Therefore, this study aims to analyze consumer-generated online data using text mining, which can derive meaningful information from text data and grasp even complex relationships and structures between contents. The purpose of this study is to examine consumers' perceived benefits and costs of Amazon Go that may have direct effects on their acceptance of the innovative store based on social media data. Specifically, this study focuses on the following research questions:

RQ1: What are the keywords that consumers refer to about Amazon Go?
RQ2: What kinds of benefits and costs do consumers perceive of Amazon Go?
RQ3: What is the overall structure of consumers' perceptions of Amazon Go?

This study enhances the understanding of consumers' perceptions of unmanned stores by extracting insights from consumer-generated social data using text mining. In addition, the study's findings will shed new light on the use of AI stores and have practical implications for unmanned retailers.

2   Literature Review

2.1   Unmanned Stores and Amazon Go

Unmanned stores are creating unique user experiences by innovative technologies such as AI, big data, and the Internet. Some unmanned stores use self-service detection and tracking systems to capture and track every movement of consumers in the store to provide more personalized services and consumption experiences. However, unmanned stores are still in the early stages of exploring advanced technology and understanding user experiences [3].

Amazon Go is the most representative unmanned store with using advanced technology. In order to enter the store, consumers must first install an app on their smartphones and scan personalized QR codes that can identify them as they pass throung electronic gates. When entering the store, items that consumers take from the display, put in a bag, or take outside the store are automatically recorded in the app. Consumers can take products directly through the electronic gate without interacting with any cashiers or scanning their items at a automatic register. Every store has a high ceiling to accommodate cameras and sensors, which are used to carefully track the movements of goods and consumers in the store.

2.2   Value-Based Adoption Model (VAM)

For this study, we adopted the theoretical framework of the value-based adoption model (VAM) [19] According to the VAM, which was derived from the technology acceptance model (TAM), consumers decide whether to adopt a particular technology by balancing the perceived sacrifice associated with its use, including technicality and anticipated fees, with its the perceived benefits, including usefulness and enjoyment. In other words, when consumers earn greater benefits than the pay in vasious types of costs, they perceive the value of products and services to be higher, and this perceived value drive consumers to accept the products and services [11, 19]. Accordingly, this study focuses on identifying various benefits and costs consumers perceive of Amazon Go based on the VAM.

2.3   Consumers' Perceived Benefits and Costs of Unmanned Stores

Innovative developments in the retail industry improve consumers' access to the services [20, 21] but may induce negative attitudes toward retailers and technology [22]. The perceived value of the new technology is determined by two dimensions: benefit and cost [23]. Further, there are two types of benefits: utilitarian and hedonic. Utilitarian benefits refer to functional and practical benefits that are associated with performance improvement (e.g., high-quality products, conventional shopping environments), while hedonic benefits indicate sensory and aesthetic benefits (e.g., pleasure) [24, 25]. Similarly, two types of costs are identified: non-monetary sacrifices, such as time and efforts spent on purchasing goods, and monetary sacrifices, including the price paid for products by consumers [26, 27].

Researchers have found the following perceived benefits and costs for smart unmanned stores. First, the perceived usefulness and ease of use were identified as functional benefits [2, 12, 28]. Perceived usefulness refers to the consumers' perception of the efficience and effectiveness with which they can purchase items in a store. Ease of use refers to how easily consumers perceive that they can use the services of smart unmanned stores. Second, perceived enjoyment, a hedonic benefit, was crucial in determining the acceptance of smart unmanned stores.

Regarding perceived costs, consumers are concerned about using stores without clerks and potential problems accessing stores due to facial recognition system malfunctions, and especially financial losses resulted from service malfunctions [29]. In particular, privacy concerns were the most frequently presented factor [13, 14]. Advances in retail technology increase consumer concerns about ways their personal information could be abused [30]. Meanwhile, Kazancoglu and Yarimoglu [28] found that consumers who have greater anxiety about using new technologies were less likely to use self-service stores.

3 Research Methods

We employed the following data analysis procedures. First, from January 21, 2018, to September 1, 2021, 15,435 documents were collected from Twitter using "Amazon Go" and "#Amazon Go" as keywords to examine consumers' opinions about Amazon Go.

Second, texts not related to the research topic were excluded, and we unified terms with the same meaning into the same words. Documents containing keywords like "advertising/marketing" and "reporter/news" were excluded. Accordingly, a total of 11,287 data points were used for the final analysis.

Third, capital letters were changed to lowercase using Python after tokenization based on spaces and punctuation. Subsequently, lemmatization was performed to transform the words into lemma. Finally, in addition to removing stopwords, unnecessary words, such as "Amazon," "Amazon Go," and "consumer," which are commonly used in the data of this study, were removed. Through this process, we identified 2,376 terms.

Fourth, we performed a word frequency analysis to identify the general responses toward Amazon Go. A frequency analysis was conducted on terms that appeared more than 20 times among the extracted terms. We selected 69 words (30 nouns, 8 verbs, and 31 adjectives) out of the top 100 terms suitable for research purposes based on the frequency analysis results. To ensure reliability, we cross-checked the results among researchers.

Fifth, we conducted a hierarchical cluster analysis using the cluster package in the R program to find common themes and summarize the data of the 38 words (30 nouns and eight verbs) out of 69 previously selected terms. Specifically, we intended to extract core themes reflecting attributes of Amazon Go that consumers perceive as either benefits or costs by grouping words with similar meanings into clusters (i.e., themes or attributes).

Adjectives were excluded in the cluster analysis because they are irrelevant to attributes. As a result, 20 clusters were derived, and each cluster was named as an attribute of Amazon Go.

Finally, a CONCOR (CONvergence of iterated CORrelations) analysis was conducted using Ucinet6 for the 20 clusters derived earlier to identify the sub-dimensions of Amazon-Go attributes. A CONCOR analysis divides highly relevant nodes into one dimension in the entire network structure [31]. After that, a semantic network analysis was performed using 20 attributes and 31 adjective words as nodes. When two words appear simultaneously in one document, an edge that connects two words appears as part of this analysis. We determined whether each attribute was seen as a benefit or a cost by examining the sentiments (positive or negative) of the adjectives that were paired with it from the edge lists [32]. In addition, based on the following four centralities, we identified the role of specific keywords in the network structure.

Degree centrality characterizes how nodes are connected to other nodes in the network and measure the number of connections [33]. Betweenness centrality measures the frequency of a given node on the shortest path to all other connected pairs [33, 34]. Closeness centrality, on the other hand, measures closeness, calculating the sum of the shortest paths between nodes to all other nodes in the network [33], in which a node with a short path has greater closeness and is interpreted as a more important concept than a node with a longer path [35]. Lastly, eigenvector centrality helps find the most influential nodes in the network by assigning the relative scores to all concepts in the network based on the number and the quality of their relationships [36]. Because it considers the number of directly connected nodes and the influence of other connected nodes, it is efficient in screening influential nodes across the entire network [37].

4 Results

4.1 Word Frequency Analysis

A word frequency analysis was conducted to examine the overall consumer perception of Amazon Go. The results of the top 100 words in the order of frequency of appearance are shown in Table 1.

Amazon Go's technology that allows consumers to "just walk out," appeared the most frequently. In addition, words such as "no lines" and "automation" were noticeable, and terms indicating negative aspects of Amazon Go, such as "privacy" and "no humanity," were also extracted.

In addition, it can be seen that words such as "fast," "easy," and "exciting" represent consumers' positive perceptions of Amazon Go, and words that show negative perceptions, such as "hard" and "hateful," are also extracted.

Table 1. The results of term frequency

No.	Keyword	Freq	No.	Keyword	Freq	No.	Keyword	Freq	No.	Keyword	Freq
1	justwalkout	3963	26	track	223	51	credit card	58	76	curious	35
2	retailtech	3329	27	scan	220	52	future of retail	57	77	recognition	35
3	grocery store	1756	28	feel	194	53	privacy	56	78	accurate	32
4	seattle	1449	29	amazing	188	54	nice	53	79	hateful	32
5	nolines	1388	30	fast	184	55	pickup	51	80	qrcode	32
6	automation	1186	31	city	181	56	facial	50	81	ceiling	31
7	cashless	964	32	account	159	57	checkout	49	82	wrong	31
8	convenient	863	33	easy	158	58	evolution	49	83	fascinating	30
9	e-commerce	683	34	trendy	155	59	bad	48	84	tired	30
10	innovation	637	35	exciting	148	60	meal	48	85	unique	30
11	app	603	36	accept	137	61	snack	47	86	essential	29
12	AI	488	37	receipt	134	62	surprise	47	87	impressive	29
13	payment	478	38	mobile	128	63	control	46	88	different	28
14	cash	364	39	bigdata	115	64	cx	46	89	access	26
15	launch	389	40	downtown	104	65	security	46	90	touch	26
16	smartphone	344	41	experience	102	66	simple	46	91	not close	26
17	brick&mortar	309	42	fresh product	97	67	tried	46	92	worried	24
18	sensor	287	43	seamless	84	68	beverage	45	93	efficient	23
19	shoplift	284	44	covid19	81	69	hard	45	94	preventive	23
20	staff	284	45	funny	81	70	concerned	43	95	capture	21
21	camera	244	46	awesome	79	71	threatful	43	96	monitor	21
22	cool	243	47	mom&pop	76	72	enjoy	39	97	spread	21
23	love	238	48	replace	66	73	use	39	98	dashcart	20
24	frictionless	237	49	iot	64	74	surveillance	39	99	no_humanity	20
25	disruption	223	50	desirable	63	75	selfservice	38	100	virtual	20

Note: The 69 words selected for the final analysis were shaded

4.2 Hierarchical Cluster Analysis

As mentioned above, a hierarchical cluster analysis was conducted on 38 terms out of 69 total terms to identify various attributes of Amazon Go, yielding 20 clusters, as shown in Fig. 1. Each cluster was named as an attribute of Amazon Go. For example, an "account," "receipt," and "credit card" cluster was named *account*[1]. In the case of a cluster including the terms "facial" and "recognition," it was called *facial recognition*, describing the ability to recognize consumers directly. In particular, the attribute of *automation*, consisting of "cashless," "no lines," and "automation," is the most significant characteristic of Amazon Go, as it shows the highest frequency of appearance. A cluster of "ceiling" and "monitor," which describe technology installed on the ceiling to identify consumer and product movements, was identified as *ceiling monitor*. A "capture" and "accurate"

---

[1] The names of attributes (clusters) are italicized, and terms (words) are in quotations.

cluster was named *capture* to describe whether the products purchased by consumers are accurately registered. A cluster containing "app" and "track" was named *tracking*, meaning that smartphone apps can track purchase details. A cluster of "payment" and "frictionless," which describe frictionless payments are possible, was identified as *frictionless payment*. Finally, a cluster containing "account," "receipt," and "credit card" was named *account*, meaning that an account must be created to use Amazon Go. Consumers need to enter their credit card information in their accounts and can check their receipts there.

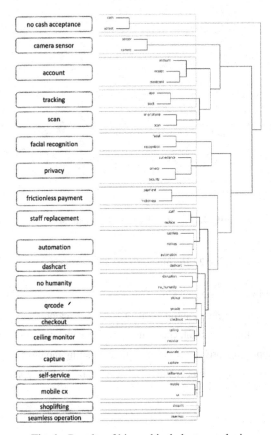

Fig. 1. Results of hierarchical cluster analysis

4.3 CONCOR Analysis

To determine the sub-dimensions of the Amazon Go attributes, a CONCOR analysis was conducted on the 20 clusters derived earlier. The results are shown in Fig. 2.

Four dimensions were extracted and named as follows. The first dimension including *tracking, automation,* and *QRcode*, is called "Functionality." The second dimension was formed with *frictionless payment, staff replacement,* and *no humanity,* so it was named "No Humanity." The third dimension comprises *shoplifting, privacy, facial recognition,* and *ceiling monitor,* named "Privacy Risk." The last dimension was "Self-Service," consisting of *seamless operation, capture,* and *self-service.* Table 2 summarizes the dimensions of the Amazon-Go attributes shown through the CONCOR analysis results.

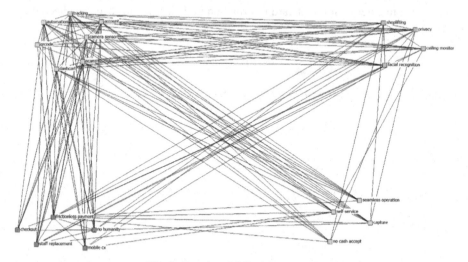

Fig. 2. Results of CONCOR analysis

Table 2. Results of CONCOR analysis

Dimensions	Attributes of Amazon Go
Functionality	Tracking, account, automation, qrcode, scan, camera sensor, dashcart
No Humanity	Frictionless payment, checkout, staff replacement, mobile cx, no humanity
Privacy Risk	Shoplifting, privacy, facial recognition, ceiling monitor
Self-service	Seamless operation, capture, self-service, no cash acceptance

4.4 Semantic Network Analysis

A semantic network analysis was conducted on 20 attributes (clusters) and 31 adjectives to examine the contents and the structure of the perceived benefits and costs of Amazon Go. The visualization of the network is shown in Fig. 3. The larger the node's size, the higher the degree centrality is. The node color represents the betweenness centrality, from high to low in the order of red, orange, and yellow. In addition, as the number of documents mentioned by the two nodes simultaneously increases, the edges (i.e., lines) between the nodes are more thickly expressed. Finally, the four types of centrality of the networks are presented in Table 3.

The results of degree and eigenvector centralities indicate *automation, tracking*, and "convenient," as the three most central words. Thus, these terms are essential consumer responses to Amazon Go because they most frequently appear along with other responses in the documents.

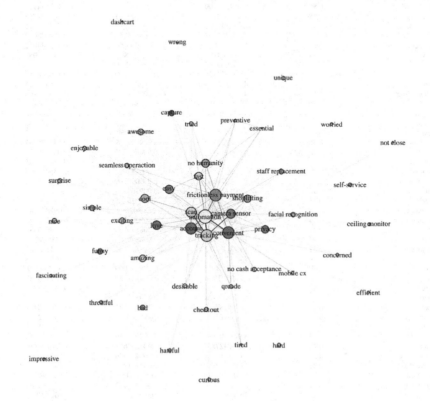

Note: The larger the node's size, the higher the degree centrality is. The node color represents the betweenness centrality, from high low in the order of red, orange, and yellow.

Fig. 3. Results of semantic network analysis

Perceived Benefits of Amazon Go. The edge lists of attributes paired with positive adjectives are shown in Table 4. We found 31 types of benefits (17 utilitarian and 14 hedonic). Specifically, first, utilitarian benefits such as *automation* and *account* were identified as they were frequently related to the word "convenient" (127 times, 21 times, respectively). In addition, *tracking, frictionless payment, no humanity*, and *no cash accpetance* were also detected as benefits. Second, interestingly, all the attributes mentioned above were also extracted as hedonic benefits. For example, *automation, account*, and *tracking* were related to "love" and "cool."

Table 3. Results of centrality

Node.	Degree centrality (Average: 0.398431373)	Betweenness centrality (Average: 27.03195095)	Closeness centrality (Average: 0.008424461)	Eigenvector centrality (Average: 0.148534004)
automation	1	3.781818182	0.006060606	1
frictionless payment	0.9	52.01424655	0.009615385	0.396544848
convenient	0.88	62.38824309	0.008474576	0.603634761
tracking	0.88	17.92952593	0.008403361	0.867999365
account	0.84	64.50843601	0.009009009	0.533758911
scan	0.76	25.81235431	0.008695652	0.754078042
camera sensor	0.68	57.47404987	0.009009009	0.412784802
love	0.64	63.67544123	0.009090909	0.148559983
cool	0.62	38.82265137	0.00877193	0.176973168
easy	0.62	53.62673854	0.009090909	0.136598241
no humanity	0.6	42.51136841	0.00990099	0.145436425
shoplifting	0.56	46.73106975	0.009009009	0.143106908
fast	0.56	18.84109918	0.008849558	0.248434423
privacy	0.56	61.24055362	0.009708738	0.12738444
amazing	0.5	11.76774614	0.008695652	0.094156345
exciting	0.44	18.74649353	0.00862069	0.075075747
awesome	0.44	32.58221329	0.009090909	0.042325887
funny	0.4	52.86996476	0.009803922	0.038009575
capture	0.4	81.11295942	0.009708738	0.054351835
simple	0.4	33.43253691	0.009433962	0.055210908
staff replacement	0.36	38.91079460	0.009090909	0.062717663
nice	0.36	35.01725135	0.009708738	0.033241564
bad	0.36	49.60662501	0.009615385	0.042197769
facial recognition	0.34	35.51163085	0.00862069	0.092854245
seamless operation	0.34	7.242399267	0.007692308	0.077201058
no cash acceptance	0.32	13.63327901	0.008849558	0.093919335
surprise	0.32	18.13480947	0.008849558	0.03594025
enjoyable	0.32	13.73623337	0.008695652	0.021589463
desirable	0.3	7.423196248	0.0078125	0.099855193
checkout	0.3	16.5276621	0.008547009	0.07654369
tried	0.3	17.23587981	0.008196721	0.052574557
qrcode	0.28	2.924145299	0.0078125	0.167794021
hard	0.28	12.66118326	0.008547009	0.023946151
unique	0.26	20.7628352	0.008130081	0.023058415
threatful	0.24	26.5990698	0.00862069	0.031232963
selfservice	0.24	19.65119186	0.007874016	0.030751035
curious	0.24	8.941046454	0.008064516	0.024260135
hateful	0.24	12.5242785	0.008695652	0.036135183
mobile cx	0.22	14.33493173	0.008474576	0.086234714
concerned	0.22	11.07251623	0.007751938	0.037144263
worried	0.22	16.07895468	0.00877193	0.020736206
ceiling monitor	0.22	24.73342111	0.008264463	0.031882748
fascinating	0.2	16.51823218	0.00862069	0.030993953
preventive	0.2	19.13539377	0.006993007	0.077610490
impressive	0.18	32.12227674	0.008547009	0.010184675
efficient	0.18	6.188034188	0.008064516	0.024109775
tired	0.14	3.329365079	0.007246377	0.05096939
not close	0.14	27.38500389	0.007575758	0.018522524
wrong	0.12	0.225	0.005747126	0.021730538
essential	0.1	0	0.004587156	0.074266893
dashcart	0.1	10.59334734	0.006535948	0.010610705

Note: The centrality values of nodes above the average were shaded

Perceived Costs of Amazon Go. The edge lists of attributes paired with negative adjectives are shown in Table 5. We identified only non-monetary costs: two types of cognitive costs and 13 different emotional costs, reflecting that emotional costs outweigh the cognitive costs for Amazon Go. Specifically, the cognitive costs include *automation*, which was related to "hard" and "not close." Consumers experienced difficulties in opening an account to shop in an Amazon Go store. Further, some consumers indicated the inaccessibility of the store itself. On the other hand, the most problematic emotional costs of Amazon Go were the "Privacy Risks" dimension as they showed the highest level of frequency. In particular, attributes such as *automation, tracking, no humanity*, and *no cash acceptance*, appeared as both emotional costs and perceived benefits. For example, negative feelings, expressed by terms like "bad," "hateful," and "concerned," emerged in connection with *automation*, in contrast to the extraction of "convenient," which is regarded as its functional benefit. Thus, consumers seem to have both positive and negative attitudes toward certain features of Amazon Go.

Structures of Consumers' Perceptions of Amazon Go. The average value of degree centrality was 0.39843, and nodes such as *automation, frictionless payment*, and "convenient" showed the three highest values. The average eigenvector centrality value of all nodes was 0.14853. *Automation* and "convenient" showed the highest eigenvector centrality, indicating that they were the most influential words in the entire network. Finally, the average betweenness centrality of all nodes was 27.03195, and *capture* was identified as the node with the highest betweenness centrality. From the edge list, we see that *capture* is associated with nodes, such as *automation, camera sensor, privacy*, "worried," "concerned," and "wrong." These findings imply the lack of consumer confidence in accurately recognizing purchased items scanned through the automated system and protecting personal information in this process.

Table 4. Edge list for perceived benefits

Utilitarian benefits				Hedonic benefits			
Dimension	Edge type		Freq.	Dimension	Edge type		Freq.
Functionality	Automation	Convenient	127	Functionality	Automation	Love	26
		Fast	46			Cool	23
		Essential	16			Exciting	12
		Easy	13			Amazing	11
		Efficient	5			Funny	7
	Account	Convenient	21		Account	Love	15
		Desirable	7			Amazing	11
		Fast	6			Cool	10
		Simple	5		Tracking	Cool	19
	Tracking	Desirable	12			Love	8
	Scan	Fast	13				
		Easy	10				
No Humanity	Frictionless payment	Fast	21	No Humanity	Frictionless payment	Cool	8
		Essential	18			Awesome	6
	No humanity	Fast	10		No humanity	Exciting	8
Self-service	No cash acceptance	Fast	4	Self-service	No cash acceptance	Fascinating	4
		Efficient	3				

Table 5. Edge list for perceived costs

Cognitive cost			Emotional cost			
Dimension	Edge type		Freq.	Dimension	Edge type		Freq.
Functionality	Account	Hard	7	Functionality	Automation	Bad	10
		Not close	5			Hateful	9
						Concerned	7
						Threatful	6
						Tired	5
					Tracking	Tired	10
				No Humanity	Staff replacement	Hateful	3
					No humanity	Worried	6
				Privacy risks	Shoplifting	Concerned	29
						Worried	8
					Privacy	Concerned	23
				Self-service	Capture	Worried	10
					No cash acceptance	Bad	9

5   Discussion and Conclusions

Retailers have been rapidly integrating cutting-edge technology to improve consumers' shopping experiences [38]. The emergence of unmanned stores based on AI technology can be considered the most innovative outcome of such efforts [1]. However, retailers must examine consumers' perceived benefits and costs of the such novel, high-tech services in order to counter their potential resistance. Thus, this study identified the perceived benefits and costs of Amazon Go by analyzing consumer-generated social data using text mining. These data are useful for extracting meaningful insights into consumers' candid opinions and attitudes. The results and implications of this study are discussed as follows.

First, we extracted 20 attributes of Amazon Go, which are classified into four dimensions (functionality, no humanity, privacy risk, and self-service). Further, eleven attributes out of 20 (automation, account, tracking, scan, frictionless payment, no humanity, and no cash acceptance, staff replacement, shoplifting, privacy, and capture) were identified as those associated with consumers' perceived benefits and costs of Amazon Go. Comparing these attributes of Amazon Go to the findings of previous studies on unmanned stores [2, 12, 28], *frictionless payment*, *no cash acceptance*, *capture*, and *shoplifting* are newly detected in this study, uncovering consumers' particular attention to payment and shoplifting issues.

Second, the existent studies have mainly focused on consumers' perceived "pleasure" or "anxiety" related to the use of unmanned stores [13, 14, 29]. However, the present study revealed a variety of mixed, positive, and negative emotions that consumers felt about Amazon Go, such as "amazing," "cool," "exciting," "hateful," "threatful," or "tired." These emotions inform consumers' intricate responses toward unmanned stores that survey research methods cannot detect.

Third, overall, consumers perceive greater benefits dominantly than costs of Amazon Go based on the comparison of the number of edge types and the frequency level between benefits and costs. In particular, consumers perceive *automation* as the most beneficial attribute of Amazon Go, and its relevant attributes, such as *frictionless payment, tracking, no humanity*, and *no cash acceptance* were also perceived positively. However, negative perceptions regarding each of these attributes were also detected. For example, some consumers used words like "hard," "bad," and "worried" when describing a situation in which no employees are around while they perform the entire process of purchasing in the unmanned store. They also state feeling "bad" when cash payments are impossible and finding it "hard" to open an account. These *automative and frictionless payment* retailing systems provide consumers not only convenience but also stress due to the inherent complexity of smart retail technology [1, 39] and the absence of human-generated services [40]. Thus, Amazon Go needs to work on reducing consumer discomfort caused by the complexity of technology, such as the account opening process.

Fourth, similar to the findings of the previous studies [13, 14], we identified concerns related to privacy infringement, indicating that consumers may resist new technologies due to privacy concerns. Further, some consumers perceived automation as threatful, confirming the previous finding that official surveillance in unmanned stores can make honest consumers nervous and even increase their sense of the store being a hostile environment in stores [41]. Interestingly, however, consumers' concerns about *shoplifting* were also extracted as costs, implying that such a surveillance system is not an efficient measure in preventing shoplifting.

Finally, according to previous studies, operating unmanned stores with new technologies is inexpensive, resulting in lower prices for the products sold in them (e.g., Zheng and Li [42]). This finding implies that consumers may perceive the economic benefits of using unmanned stores. However, terms related to price perceptions were not extracted. This may reflect that the concept of Amazon Go is still new to consumers and that its users are still at the trial stage.

The present study contributes to the smart retailing literature by identifying consumers' candid and intricate perceptions about various attributes of Amazon Go using text mining with a large amount of social media data. These attributes and consumer perceptions can be utilized to build theoretical models for better consumer behavior prediction in unmanned stores like Amazon Go. Managerially, the findings of perceived benefits and costs of Amazon Go provide practical implications for unmanned retailers. Because consumers perceive costs regarding the innovative features of Amazon Go such as *automation, frictionless payment, no humanity, capture* and *tracking*, unmanned retailers need to make greater efforts to reduce psychological rejection due to these newly perceived costs. For example, consumers perceive that automation is "threatful" and "concerned" and that account use is "hard." Thus, unmanned stores may consider providing consumer education on how to shop in their stores using YouTube or other social media platforms to lower consumers' psychological barriers to patronage.

This study has a couple of limitations that become venues for future studies. First, the generalization of the findings of this study should be cautioned because this study analyzed consumer-originated online posts mentioning Amazon Go. Amazon Go is the first unmanned store based on AI technology. However, as other retailers continue to launch unmanned stores, comparative research on various types of unmanned stores is necessary. Second, since this study analyzed SNS data, extracting the demographic characteristics of the authors of the tweets analyzed is difficult. As young people mainly use SNS, future research should examine consumers' perceived benefits and costs of unmanned stores with advanced technologies across various demographic characteristics using surveys.

References

1. Adapa, S., Fazal-e-Hasan, S.M., Makam, S.B., Azeem, M.M., Mortimer, G.: Examining the antecedents and consequences of perceived shopping value through smart retail technology. J. Retail. Consum. Serv. **52**, 101901 (2020)
2. Roy, S.K., Balaji, M.S., Quazi, A., Quaddus, M.: Predictors of customer acceptance of and resistance to smart technologies in the retail sector. J. Retail. Consum. Serv. **42**, 147–160 (2018)
3. Park, H.J., Zhang, Y.: Technology readiness and technology paradox of unmanned convenience store users. J. Retail. Consum. Serv. 102523 (2022)
4. Denuwara, N., Maijala, J., Hakovirta, M.: The impact of unmanned stores' business models on sustainability. SN Bus. Econ. **1**(10), 1–27 (2021). https://doi.org/10.1007/s43546-021-001 36-8
5. Chandramana, S.: Retail analytics: driving success in retail industry with business analytics. Res. J. Soc. Sci. Manage. **7**, 159–166 (2017)
6. Polacco, A., Backes, K.: The amazon go concept: implications, applications, and sustainability. J. Bus. Manag. **24**(1), 79–92 (2018)
7. Türegün, N.: Impact of technology in financial reporting: the case of Amazon Go. J. Corp. Account. Finance **30**(3), 90–95 (2019)
8. Lin, C.Y., Chao, Y.C., Tang, T.W.: Why not be 'smarter'? Examining the factors that influence the behavioral intentions of non-smartphone users. Ind. Manag. Data Syst. **117**(1), 32–49 (2017)
9. Mani, Z., Chouk, I.: Consumer resistance to innovation in services: challenges and barriers in the internet of things era. J. Prod. Innov. Manag. **35**(5), 780–807 (2018)
10. Gonçalves, L., Patrício, L., Grenha Teixeira, J., Wünderlich, N.V.: Understanding the customer experience with smart services. J. Serv. Manag. **31**(4), 723–744 (2020)
11. Zeithaml, V.A.: Consumer perceptions of price, quality, and value: a means-end model and synthesis of evidence. J. Mark. **52**(3), 2–22 (1988)
12. Chuawatcharin, R., Gerdsri, N.: Factors influencing the attitudes and behavioural intentions to use just walk out technology among Bangkok consumers. Int. J. Public Sect. Perform. Manage. **5**(2), 146–163 (2019)
13. Shaw, N., Sergueeva, K.: The non-monetary benefits of mobile commerce: extending UTAUT2 with perceived value. Int. J. Inf. Manage. **45**, 44–55 (2019)
14. Chouk, I., Mani, Z.: Factors for and against resistance to smart services: role of consumer lifestyle and ecosystem related variables. J. Serv. Mark. **33**(4), 449–462 (2019)

15. Chang, J.-R., Chen, M.-Y., Chen, L.-S., Chien, W.-T.: Recognizing important factors of influencing trust in O2O models: an example of OpenTable. Soft. Comput. **24**(11), 7907–7923 (2019). https://doi.org/10.1007/s00500-019-04019-x

16. Gunasekar, S., Kumar, D.S., Purani, K., Sudhakar, S., Dixit, S.K., Menon, D.: Understanding service quality attributes that drive user ratings: a text mining approach. J. Vacat. Mark. **27**(4), 400–419 (2021)

17. Shankar, A., Tiwari, A.K., Gupta, M.: Sustainable mobile banking application: a text mining approach to explore critical success factors. J. Enterp. Inf. Manag. **35**(2), 414–428 (2021)

18. Zhang, J.: What's yours is mine: exploring customer voice on Airbnb using text-mining approaches. J. Consum. Mark. **36**(5), 655–665 (2019)

19. Kim, H.W., Chan, H.C., Gupta, S.: Value-based adoption of mobile internet: an empirical investigation. Decis. Support Syst. **43**(1), 111–126 (2007)

20. Pantano, E., Naccarato, G.: Entertainment in retailing: the influences of advanced technologies. J. Retail. Consum. Serv. **17**(3), 200–204 (2010)

21. Weijters, B., Rangarajan, D., Falk, T., Schillewaert, N.: Determinants and outcomes of customers' use of self-service technology in a retail setting. J. Serv. Res. **10**(1), 3–21 (2007)

22. Reinders, M.J., Dabholkar, P.A., Frambach, R.T.: Consequences of forcing consumers to use technology-based self-service. J. Serv. Res. **11**(2), 107–123 (2008)

23. Sweeney, J.C., Soutar, G.N.: Consumer perceived value: the development of a multiple item scale. J. Retail. **77**(2), 203–220 (2001)

24. Van der Heijden, H.: User acceptance of hedonic information systems. MIS Q. **28**(4), 695–704 (2004)

25. Holdack, E., Lurie-Stoyanov, K., Fromme, H.F.: The role of perceived enjoyment and perceived informativeness in assessing the acceptance of AR wearables. J. Retail. Consum. Serv. **65**, 102259 (2022)

26. Cronin, J.J., Jr., Brady, M.K., Hult, G.T.M.: Assessing the effects of quality, value, and customer satisfaction on consumer behavioral intentions in service environments. J. Retail. **76**(2), 193–218 (2000)

27. Dodds, W.B., Monroe, K.B., Grewal, D.: Effects of price, brand, and store information on buyers' product evaluations. J. Mark. Res. **28**(3), 307–319 (1991)

28. Kazancoglu, I., Yarimoglu, E.K.: How food retailing changed in Turkey: spread of self-service technologies. Br. Food J. **120**(2), 290–308 (2018)

29. Wang, I., Liao, C.W., Lin, K.P., Wang, C.H., Tsai, C.L.: Evaluate the consumer acceptance of a IoT-based unmanned convenience stores based on perceived risks and technological acceptance models. Math. Probl. Eng. **2021** (2021)

30. Inman, J.J., Nikolova, H.: Shopper-facing retail technology: a retailer adoption decision framework incorporating shopper attitudes and privacy concerns. J. Retail. **93**(1), 7–28 (2017)

31. Weng, C.S., Chen, W.Y., Hsu, H.Y., Chien, S.H.: To study the technological network by structural equivalence. J. High Technol. Managem. Res. **21**(1), 52–63 (2020)

32. Lee, Y.L., Jung, M.J., Kim, A.Y., Park, I.H., Chung, J.E.: Smart watch consumers' perceived benefits and costs from product experience using semantic network analysis: focused on Apple Watch. Consum. Stud. Res. **30**(6), 195–225 (2019)

33. Freeman, L.C.: Centrality in social networks conceptual clarification. Soc. Netw. **1**(3), 215239 (1978)

34. Stanley, W., Faust, K.: Social Network Analysis: Methods and Applications. Cambrigdge University, Cambridge (1994)

35. Raad, E., Chbeir, R.: Socio-graph representations, concepts, data, and analysis. In: Alhajj, P.R., Rokne, P.J. (eds.) Encyclopedia of Social Network Analysis and Mining, pp. 1936–1946. Springer, New York (2014)

36. Heymann, S.: Gephi. In: Alhajj, P.R., Rokne, P.J. (eds.) Encyclopedia of Social Network Analysis and Mining, pp. 612–625. Springer, New York (2014)

37. Bonacich, P.: Some unique properties of eigenvector centrality. Soc. Netw. **29**(4), 555–564 (2007)
38. Renko, S., Druzijanic, M.: Perceived usefulness of innovative technology in retailing: consumers' and retailers' point of view. J. Retail. Consum. Serv. **21**(5), 836–843 (2014)
39. Lee, H.J., Jeong Cho, H., Xu, W., Fairhurst, A.: The influence of consumer traits and demographics on intention to use retail self-service checkouts. Market. Intell. Plann. **28**(1), 46–58 (2010)
40. Bulmer, S., Elms, J., Moore, S.: Exploring the adoption of self-service checkouts and the associated social obligations of shopping practices. J. Retail. Consum. Serv. **42**, 107–116 (2018)
41. Lin, B., Hastings, D.A., Martin, C.: Shoplifting in retail clothing outlets: an exploratory research. Int. J. Retail Distrib. Manage. **22**(7), 24–29 (1994)
42. Zheng, Y., Li, Y.: Unmanned retail's distribution strategy based on sales forecasting. In: 2018 8th International Conference on Logistics, Informatics and Service Sciences (LISS), USA, pp. 1–5. IEEE (2018)

When Do People Purchase a Product of Color Which They Do Not Like?

Naoki Takahashi[1]([✉]), Yuri Hamada[2], and Hiroko Shoji[1]

[1] Chuo University, Bunkyo-ku, Tokyo, Japan
naoki@kc.chuo-u.ac.jp
[2] Aoyama Gakuin University, Fuchinobe, Kanagawa, Japan

Abstract. This study aimed to analyze the effects of color preferences and personality traits on peoples' product selection, particularly choosing other colors over one's favorite color. The results showed that the desire to purchase products in favorite colors depended on the product category and the favorite color. Despite the evaluations of favorite colors being high, the desire to purchase products in them is low in case of expensive products and in cases where bright colors such as blue and green are preferred. Contrarily, people who favored black or white, in most cases displayed an increased desire to purchase products in these colors as these are considered safe colors for expensive products that are difficult to replace. In terms of personality, for the extraverted and emotional group, the influence of the product category on the color selection seemed to be relatively less as compared to the delicate and shy group, as well as the cautious and forward-thinking group. Hence consumer preferences may not always be directly reflected in their behavior.

Keywords: Color preference · Purchasing behavior · Personality traits

1 Introduction

Individual differences as well as differences in gender and culture cause diversity of impressions and preferences for certain colors. To meet the demand for variety in colors, variations in colors are often introduced in product design. However, even if consumers have the choice to choose a product in their favorite color, they may not always exercise that choice. When and why do we choose a product in a color that may not be our favorite?

People often choose colors that they may not like because they are concerned about color harmony with other items and their perception by others. This is a form of conflict between personal kansei (sensitivity) and the environment. From the perspective of color harmony, vivid colors are generally used as accents on small objects, while low-saturation colors are used as base or main colors. Such color schemes can make it easy to change the impression of the entire by changing the colors of small items; in addition, it is economically reasonable. It can therefore, be hypothesized that products in favorite colors can be used as accents or inexpensive items that are easy to replace.

© Springer Nature Switzerland AG 2022
M. Rauterberg et al. (Eds.): HCII 2022, LNCS 13520, pp. 237–245, 2022.
https://doi.org/10.1007/978-3-031-18158-0_17

In this study, we conducted an experiment under various conditions to determine whether consumers choose their favorite color from among the color variations and to examine the patterns. Participants were surveyed on their personalities, regarding their favorite colors, and purchasing behavior. Thereafter, ten different color variation images were created for ten different products, and the participants were asked to subjectively evaluate their impressions of each image.

2 Related Works

2.1 Product Preference and Purchasing Behavior

It is consider that the reason for the existence of color preferences is due to the emotional reactions to objects with which colors are associated [1]. The impact of color on marketing is diverse, and its findings have been widely incorporated in product and space design [2, 3]. Huang and Lu showed that the color of a food package influences the evaluation whether the product is hedonic or utilitarian [4].

In product design, the consumers' color preferences are considered to be vital. However, whether they affect their product choices remains controversial. An earlier study of automobile, clothing, and furniture has shown that consumers' product color choice was not related to their individual color preferences [5]. Further, some studies have found that consumers' color preferences not only affect their perception and attitude toward products, but also influences purchase decisions. A study of personal care products has shown that for products such as toothbrush in particular, consumers are more inclined to choose products that cater to their individual color preferences [6]. For automobiles, a study has shown that color preference is one of the determinants of consumers' choice as consumers were more inclined to purchase cars that match their color preferences [7]. A recent study that focuses on household products (kitchen and bathroom) found that color preference is not the primary factor affecting consumers' purchase decisions; color functionality, color performance, and color culture may be more crucial factors [8]. A study of children's learning space furniture concluded that the color design of such furniture should be based on the character of children's color preferences [9]. This underlines the importance of children's color preferences for furniture design.

In an experiment to test the idea that adolescents choose products in their favorite colors, Jiang et al. [10] found that their color preferences influenced their choice of furniture, however, the degree of influence varied depending on the category of furniture. In addition, the furniture preference differed slightly depending on the functional space.

2.2 Personality Traits and Purchasing Behavior

Various methods have been proposed to assess personality traits quantitatively. The most famous is the Big Five Personality test [11, 12], which expresses personality by scores on five factors: openness, conscientiousness, extraversion, agreeableness, and neuroticism. Gosling et al.'s [13] Ten-item personality inventory (TIPI) is a questionnaire developed to calculate scores for five factors in ten questions. Oshio et al. [14] developed a Japanese version of the TIPI, TIPI-J, which can be used in experiments with the Japanese participants. On the contrary, the Five Factor Personality Questionnaire (FFPQ), which corrects the five-factor structure of the big five, has been developed to explain the personality of Japanese people. Furthermore, Fujishima et al. [15] developed the FFPQ-50 that is a short form of FFPQ comprising only 50 questions.

In a study of the relationship between personality traits and purchase behavior, Tsao and Chang [16] investigated the relationship between purchase behavior and the big five personality traits in e-commerce by means of a questionnaire experiment, and found that hedonic purchase motivation is positively influenced by three of the big five traits: neuroticism, extraversion, and openness to experience. When consumers have higher degrees of these three traits, they tend to be utility-motivated to shop online. Utilitarian purchase motivation is a key factor that invokes the search intention in consumers, unlike the hedonic motivation. Lissitsa and Kol [17] added a generational perspective to their analysis of the relationship between personality factors and purchase behavior in mobile shopping. According to them, all five middle level traits, i.e., innovativeness, need for cognition, trust, value consciousness, and buying impulsiveness, are related to online purchase intention. The elemental traits of openness to experience, conscientiousness, need for arousal, and need for materials are related to one or two middle level traits respectively.

3   Methods

The target product categories of product images were a bag, car, curtains, microwave, mug, outer wall of house, pencil case, smartphone case, t-shirt, and toothbrush. For each product image, ten different color variations were created. The colors were red, orange, yellow, green, blue, violet, pink, brown, black, and white; the tones were adjusted for a natural look. Figure 1 shows color variations of a bag and curtains as examples of product images.

Fig. 1. Examples of product images used in the experiment (First row: red, green, and blue bags. Second row: red, green, and blue curtains). (Color figure online)

The participants in the experiment were 65 students between the ages of 18 and 25. Each participant answered questions about (a) his or her personality, (b) purchasing behavior and habits, and (c) his/her favorite colors.

For the question about one's personality, we used the FFPQ-50, which is a simplified version of the five personality factors for Japanese people. For the questions about purchasing behavior and habits, nine questions were asked to be answered on a 6-point scale. Regarding their favorite color, participants were asked to choose one color from red, orange, yellow, green, blue, violet, pink, brown, black, and white. The participants then viewed images of ten different color variations of ten different products and rated their desire to purchase on a 6-point scale (from "desire to purchase" to "do not desire to purchase").

After the experiment, the means of the ratings for the favorite color and the ratings for the other colors for each product were calculated and compared. A t-test at 5% level of significance was used to examine the difference between them. To divide the participants into groups with similar personalities, clustering was performed using the ward method, which is a type of agglomerative hierarchical clustering that can create dendrograms. In this study, we used the ward method, which can determine the appropriate number of clusters from the shape of the dendrogram. For each personality cluster, the mean values of the desire to purchase products of favorite and non-favorite colors in each product category were calculated. Finally, to examine the relationship between personality and color selection behavior, we conducted a qualitative analysis of the relationship between personality traits and desire to purchase, for each cluster.

4   Results and Discussion

4.1   Desire to Purchase for Each Product and Color Category

We calculated the average of the magnitude of each participant's desire to purchase the product images of their favorite color as well as of other colors, and thereafter calculated

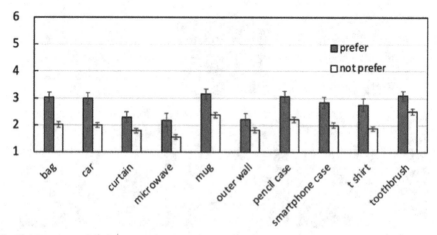

Fig. 2. Averages of desire to purchase products of preferred and not preferred color. Error bars indicate standard errors.

the average for all participants and all color variations. Figure 2 shows averages of desire to purchase products of preferred and not preferred color in each category. In addition, a two-sided t-test at a 5% significance level was conducted to see if there was a difference in purchase desire between the favorite color and other colors. As a result, the purchase desire was higher for images of the favorite color in all product categories, and there was a significant difference in all categories except for outer wall of house.

When we compared the results for each color variation, we found that those who expressed that black or white were their favorite colors, had an extremely high desire

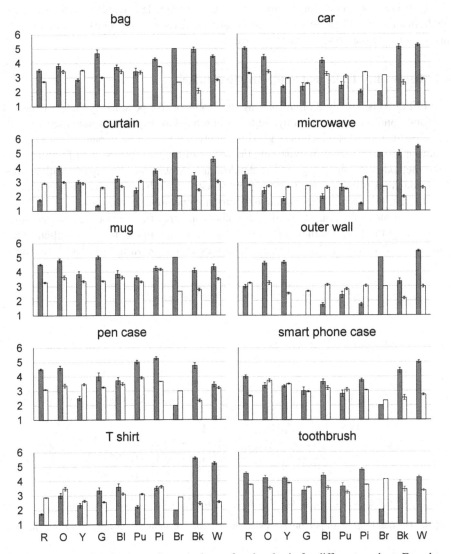

Fig. 3. Averages of desire to purchase products of each color in for different products Error bars indicate standard errors. Abbreviation codes on horizontal coordinates are red, orange, yellow, green, blue, purple, pink, brown, black and white respectively. (Color figure online)

to purchase products in black or white, while in many cases those who preferred other colors did not have a high desire to purchase products in their favorite colors (Fig. 3). In addition, the purchase desire for microwave and outer walls of the house in favorite colors of those who answered that they liked green, blue, or pink was lower than the average purchase desire for products in colors other than their favorite. The outer wall and microwave are relatively expensive products and are relatively large in size among the product categories used in this study.

The results show that though the purchase desire for favorite colors is high in most cases, those who prefer chromatic colors may have a higher purchase desire for large or expensive products in colors other than their favorite. This result is in line with the prediction that people are less likely to choose their favorite color for expensive products that they have little opportunity to replace.

4.2   Personality Traits and Subjective Evaluation

The FFPQ-50 is a method of calculating the scores of five personality factors using 50 questions, and is characterized by the fact that it has fewer questions than the Big Five, and the structure of the factors is good for expressing Japanese personality traits. The dendrogram of the result of clustering the scores of the five factors of FFPQ-50 by the ward method is shown in Fig. 4. The dendrogram shows how participants with similar scores on the personality factors are combined with each other. Based on the shape of the dendrogram, we divided the participants into three personality clusters:1) the "delicate and shy" group as they rarely stand up for others and are often nervous; 2) the "cautious and forward-thinking" as they think carefully before acting and try to plan their work, and 3) "highly extroverted and emotional," as they are lively, warm and friendly to others.

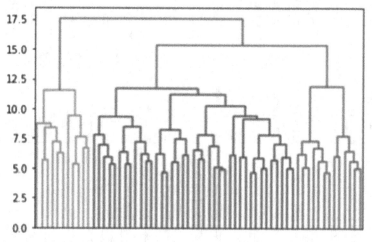

Fig. 4. The dendrogram of personality clusters: vertical axis indicates distance between clusters.

For each cluster of subjects, we compared their desire to purchase their favorite color and other colors in each product category. In the delicate and shy cluster, only the mug with the preferred color was rated high, while other products were rated low. In the cautious and forward-thinking cluster, the exterior wall with the preferred color and the microwave oven were rated low. Both cautious and forward thinking cluster as well as highly extraverted and emotional cluster gave lower ratings to their preferred color exterior walls and microwave ovens despite the fact that these two groups have different characteristics. This is consistent with the theory that people are likely to choose their preferred color for inexpensive products and not for expensive products. On the contrary, in the highly extraverted and emotional cluster, there is little difference in the evaluation of the different product categories. Comparing the personality traits, the delicate and shy cluster had a negative attitude toward the evaluation by others and their own preferences, while the cautious and forward-thinking cluster prioritized harmony with other items and the surrounding environment. The highly extraverted and emotional cluster may be more concerned with their own preferences, values, and self-expression, and tend to prioritize their own preferences irrespective the situation (Fig. 5).

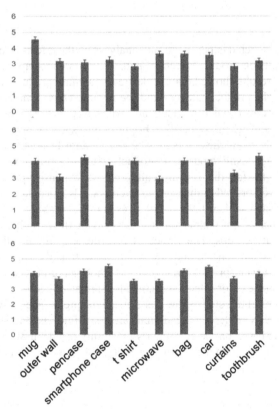

Fig. 5. Averages of desire to purchase products of preferred color in each personality cluster. Top: 1st cluster ("delicate and shy"), middle: 2nd cluster ("cautious and forward-thinking"), and bottom: 3rd cluster ("highly extraverted and emotional")

This study does not take into account the influence of personality traits on color preference. Matsuda et al. [18] reported the correlation between personality scores with "a favorite color," "the color of clothing which people want to wear," and the color of clothing they often wear." It was suggested that, by mediating the emotional meaning of color (image of color), people like colors with images similar to their personality and that tend to wear clothes of such colors. In this study, however, we did not focus on this relationship to examine the effects of personality and color preference separately. More precise data and analysis methods will be needed to construct a model that represents the conflict between preference and other factors.

In this study, the color of each image was considered to be a single color, but some products had multiple colors or constituted a color scheme with surrounding objects. In actual products, color coordination may be more complex, and it is more difficult to predict color preferences for color schemes than in the cases of a single color. Moreover, the participants were instructed to choose only one of their favorite colors, considering their ease of responding. However, for detailed analysis, it is necessary to have data that evaluates the degree of preference for all the color choices.

5   Conclusion

In this study, we conducted experiments and analyses on the effects of color preference and personality traits on product selection, particularly in choosing a favorite color or another color. The results showed that the desire to purchase products in one's favorite colors depends on the product category and the favorite color. Evaluations of favorite colors are high; however, when products are expensive, such as house exteriors and microwave ovens, and when people like bright colors such as blue and green, their desire to purchase their favorite colors may be low. Contrarily, people who prefer black or white, had a higher desire to purchase products in their favorite colors in most cases. This may be due to the fact that it is difficult to replace expensive products and people tend to choose safe colors rather than eccentric colors. Also, people who originally like black or white can choose their favorite colors even in such cases.

Based on the analysis of the personality survey data, the participants were divided into three personality groups. The choice of favorite or safe color depended on the product category for the delicate and shy group, as well as the cautious and forward thinking group. However, for the extraverted and emotional group, the influence of the product category on the color selection seemed to be relatively less.

Hence, the results of this study show that consumers' preferences may not be directly reflected in their behavior. Recommendations are sometimes used to suggest products with favorite colors based on the consumer's sensibility profile, however, this function is inappropriate depending on the product category, color, and user's personality.

References

1. Stephen, P.E., Karen, S.B.: An ecological valence theory of human color preference. Proc. Natl. Acad. Sci. 107(19), 8877–8882 (2010)
2. Singh, S.: Impact of color on marketing. Manag. Decis. 44(6), 783–789 (2006)

3. Priluck, G.R., Joseph, W.Z.: What we know about consumers' color choices. J. Market. Pract. Appl. Market. Sci. **5**(3), 11 (1999)

4. Huang, L., Lu, J.: The impact of package color and the nutrition content labels on the perception of food healthiness and purchase intention. J. Food Prod. Market. **22**(2), 191–218 (2016)

5. Holmes, C.B., Buchanan, J.A.: Color preference as a function of the object described. Bull. Psychon. Soc. **22**(5), 423–425 (1984). https://doi.org/10.3758/BF03333865

6. Westland, S., Shin, M.J.: The relationship between consumer colour preferences and product-colour choices. JAIC-J. Int. Colour Assoc. **14** (2015)

7. Funk, D., Oly, N.N.: Colour and product choice: a study of gender roles. Manag. Res. News **29**(1/2), 41–52 (2006)

8. Yu, L., Westland, S., Li, Z., Pan, Q., Shin, M.J., Won, S.: The role of individual colour preferences in consumer purchase decisions. Color Res. Appl. **43**(2), 258–267 (2018)

9. Kim, J.K., Sun, W.M.: An analysis on the color characteristics for improving childhood children's learning spaces and furniture design. J. Korea Furniture Soc. **28**(4), 294–304 (2017)

10. Jiang, L., Cheung, V., Westland, S., Rhodes, A.P., Liming, S., Lei, X.: The impact of color preference on adolescent children's choice of furniture. Color Res. Appl. **45**(4) 754–767 (2020)

11. Goldberg, L.R.: An alternative description of personality': the big-five factor structure. J. Pers. Soc. Psychol. **59**(6), 1216 (1990)

12. Goldberg, L.R.: The development of markers for the Big-Five factor structure. Psychol. Assess. **4**(1), 26 (1992)

13. Samuel, GD., Rentfrow, P.J., Swann Jr, W.B.: A very brief measure of the Big-Five personality domains. J. Res. Person. **37**(6), 504–528 (2003)

14. Atsushi, O., Shingo, A.B.E., Cutrone, P.: Development, reliability, and validity of the Japanese version of Ten Item Personality Inventory (TIPI-J). Japanese J. Person. **21**(1) (2012)

15. Fujishima, Y., Yamada, N., Tsuji, H.: Construction of short form of five factor personality questionnaire. Jpn. J. Pers. **13**(2), 231–241 (2005)

16. Tsao, W.-C., Hung-Ru, C.: Exploring the impact of personality traits on online shopping behavior. African J. Bus. Manage. **4**(9), 1800–1812 (2010)

17. Lissitsa, S., Kol, O.: Four generational cohorts and hedonic m-shopping: association between personality traits and purchase intention. Electron. Commer. Res. **21**(2), 545–570 (2019). https://doi.org/10.1007/s10660-019-09381-4

18. Matsuda, H., Natori, K., Hatano, T.: The relationship between color preferences and personality traits - Consideration from the emotional meaning of color. J. Color Sci. Assoc. Jpn. **43**(2), 69–80 (2019)

Luxury and Digital, Hindered Narratives?

Didier Tsala Effa[(✉)] [ID]

Université de Limoges, 87036 Limoges Cedex, France
didier.tsala-effa@unilim.fr

Abstract. Previously exclusive, because of a rather too quick assimilation of social classes to a particular access to wealth, luxury, in parallel with the blossoming of mass consumption, has been democratized, with a particularly intense acceleration due to the development of virtual means of communication.

We wanted to show how these forms of communication operate. We have established the notion of semiosic alteration as the organizing principle of luxury communication on the Internet, with the constraint of control defined as what allows us to preserve its exclusivity. While we should have expected the rhetoric of luxury to operate as forms of expression, it becomes the form of content: the legend, the documentary, the praise, the chronicle. In the end, we retain luxury not what concretely translates it, i.e. the substance of the brands or products, but the spectacle held around these translations. This seemed to us to be the essential issue; under the model of theatricalization. While the Internet medium offers the widest latitude to highlight in all its forms what usually constitutes the essence of luxury, i.e. its substance, all the rhetorical games operate precisely to postpone it. The tactic is quite visible: it is a question of subtly putting away recognizable signs for the sole benefit of a prior decoding operation. The paradox of the luxury is played thus, like a discriminatory order.

Keywords: Luxury brands websites · Enaction · Narratives · Data · Singularity

1 Introduction

The subject we are considering is about "transmediation", applied in the specific field of marketing and communication. According to Marjorie Siegel[1], teachers at Columbia College, which sees it in the particular perspective of education,

"The term "transmediation" was first introduced by Charles Suhor (1984) as part of his development of a semiotics-based curriculum. Suhor, a language educator interested in integrating media and the arts across curriculum, defined transmediation as the "translation of content from one system into another" (p. 250) and characterized it as a syntactic concept since deals with the structure of sign systems and the relationship between different sign system".

---

[1] Siegel M., *More than Words: The Generative Power of Transmediation for Learning,* Canadian Journal of Education / Revue canadienne de l'éducation, Autumn, 1995, Vol. 20, No. 4, Cultural Psychology and Semiotics (Autumn, 1995), p.460.URL: https://www.jstor.org/stable/1495082, last access, 15th March, 2022.

© Springer Nature Switzerland AG 2022
M. Rauterberg et al. (Eds.): HCII 2022, LNCS 13520, pp. 246–259, 2022.
https://doi.org/10.1007/978-3-031-18158-0_18

If this definition is clear, it is especially useful for its processual dimension. Transmediation is not just a simple transposition of a content. As a syntactic concept, it concerns mainly the schematic contingencies that allow this transposition. In other words, we are dealing here with content in between two media, that is to say, between two systems of signs. The transmediation operates when inside this double system, it's seen like an re-organisation or an invention which, while maintaining it, gives it new conditions of perception. The problem we have to solve is then what really happens inside this "in between", and, perhaps mainly, what do we mean by talking about that.

2 The Websites of Luxury Brands

The websites of luxury brands surprise by the fact that they are able to immediately configure the idea of luxury even though, like many other websites, they also present products, in particular, various commercial information, prices, order spaces, collections, descriptions, and stagings of usual situations, with mannequins or various environments. It is therefore difficult to rely on this level of data to identify what constitutes its singularity. However, something always invites us to perceive effects of exceptional magnification: we are dealing with stories rather than information, with muses rather than advertising figures, with art objects rather than products. In the same way, the emitted discourses literally take control over our sense of reading, by imposing constrained paths, with consequently an unpredictable narrative rationality and an obliged access to passionate effects of meaning. How can we identify the conditions of such unexpectedness?

Our hypothesis is that everything is played out in the dynamic interaction between the in vivo presentation of these data and the conditions that accompany the possibility to perceive something in them. According to the theory of enaction, defined as the theory of perceptual interactions (Varela[2]), these interactions would take the form of salience, i.e. of perceptual discontinuity. They are, for example, such insistent catchphrases in the discourse; they would also be, for example, such diagrams or such graphic biases on a configuration. In other words, as such, these saliencies are the fact of the discrepancies between the apparent data of the discourse and the final model that singularize the latter, as a signifying form and as a sensible form. They operate in fact as hindrances, when a first level look would have led to the banality of the data in vivo. Our proposal consists in questioning them from this point of view. By observing the specific case of luxury brand websites, we pose these hindrances as the primary basis of the narratives that singularize them as specific sites, far from the banality risked by the indistinct format of the website.

2.1 An Ambiguity: Democratization vs Distinction

Addressing the issue of luxury communication almost always comes down to an ambiguity, and with a great gap, between on the one hand the concern to preserve the necessary line of distance that gives luxury its distinction, among other products intended for consumption, and on the other a perfectly legitimate desire for democratization. Indeed,

---

[2] Varela F., Thompson E., Eleanor R., *L'Inscription corporelle de l'esprit. Sciences cognitives et expérience humaine,* (trad. Veronique Havelange), Paris, Seuil, (1997).

we can no longer pretend to ignore this other dimension of luxury, which makes it also and even more and more a priority market share. To put it bluntly, while the nostalgia for luxury as an exclusive reflection of chivalry still remains, the need to democratize it has definitely imposed itself, not so much to allow the greatest number of people to have access to it, but because the very survival of the idea of luxury depends on it. It is a question of economics: no one would dream of disputing that luxury has always been, including in the past, underpinned by economic constraints. Nowadays, economic power is no longer what is reserved for a few, but at least what everyone is able to accumulate in order to afford something exceptional. This is the case of the modes of consumption of luxury, for example this description proposed by Benoît Heilbrun[3] in an eminently marketing orientation, which envisages luxury as "what one can afford in an exceptional way". In other words, if we had to look for a reason for the communication of luxury, it would certainly be of this order. Previously exclusive, due to a rather too quick assimilation of social classes to a particular access to wealth, luxury, in parallel with the blossoming of mass consumption, has been democratized, with a particularly intense acceleration due to the development of virtual means of communication. This is our starting point.

2.2 Luxury on the Internet

While it has always been endowed with specific and exclusive supports (particular boutiques, specific magazine pages, specific advertising codes), apart from other more generic media supports, the communication of luxury brands must now also build its specificity to continue to hold its own in virtual supports, starting with its presence on the Internet. The constraint is to avoid banality and to continue to cultivate the exception. Not that it is necessary to invent new contents, "luxury is luxury", but obviously, it is a question of appropriating the Internet in its particularity, in order to say always luxury without confusion. A paradox.

However, if there is a space that accommodates confusion, as the creative possibilities are so extensive, it is indeed the Internet. Not only are luxury products disseminated through various generic sites (promotional sites, distribution sites), but luxury brands, in order to ensure their presence on this medium, must also deal with the need to occupy this space as a place of sale. This constraint constitutes a second rupture, given the requirements of exclusivity of luxury; one does not sell a luxury product like any other product. From the outset, the question that arises is that of the strategies used?

Through our text, the result of an observation of more than 150 websites of luxury brands, all products included, fashion, jewelry, watches, luxury cars as well as wines and spirits, our idea is to make a small point on the existing.

3 Luxury: A Discriminatory Order

Our hypothesis is synthetic, to say the least. Today, no one can question marketers' offensives to blur the boundaries between luxury and mass-market brands. Nevertheless,

---

[3] Heilbrun B., « Le luxe est mort, vive le luxe ! Le marché du luxe à l'aune de la démocratisation», in Assouly O., *Le luxe. Essai sur la fabrique de l'ostentation*, Paris, Édition du regard, (2005), p. 365.

luxury, in addition to being aspirational, is distinguished above all in that it is always driven by a discriminatory order. In reality, one can only access it if one knows its true codes: a real issue and a real debate maintained by the creators themselves. For example Pierre Bergé, President of the prestigious Yves Saint-Laurent Foundation, who firmly believes in this exclusive part: "Assigning luxury a history that is its own, means conceiving other expressions without abandoning luxury to the anarchy of unmeasured creators or unimaginative commercialism"[4].

This is our position, in order to question the way in which luxury brands proceed in order to continue to maintain their efficiency on a medium of communication as democratized as the Internet.

3.1 The Clichés of an Exceptional Magnification

From the outset, when one begins an exploration, even the most minimal, of the websites of luxury brands, one cannot escape the most obvious clichés of what it is usual to imagine of a luxury brand: an exceptional magnification, the negation of banality and the commonplace. The information is not simple statements to present and describe the products or the brand, they are small stories; the models, when they are present, operate as muses rather than as simple advertising figures; as for the products, they are mostly objects and even art objects. The technique also participates by its prowess, with sites in flash and dynamic parades. In short, on these websites, everything that is offered to the Internet user is justified only because it gives the impression that it is justified by an extra (soul?). The same is true of the modalities that underlie the expression of these brands as data to be seen. Everything operates under the prism of a magnifying mirror, with effects of scale; the argument is laudatory, with hyperbolic terms, which belong to the marvelous, the fantastic, with enlarged objects, "XXL" illustrations. In the end, where any other site would have taken advantage of this to aim for the most realistic access to its products, allowing the greatest number of people, thanks to the Internet, to discover, at last! What luxury really is, we observe for this communication, a desire to always add an additional media layer.

3.2 A Semiosic Alteration

What is at stake in signification is what could be called a semiotic alteration, with a view to finding a real way of controlling any signifying manifestation in question. In other words, the question is that of the inscription of a particularity in the semiotic device. We are not far from what Hjelmslev invites us to consider as "connotative semiotics" or as "metasemiotics". Unlike the usual semiotics, where the plane of expression and the plane of content are defined only by opposition and relative to each other, connotative semiotics, according to Hjelmslev, is a semiotics in which, even before entering the semiotic process, the plane of expression and the plane of content are already semiotics:

"By [denotative semiotics] we mean those in which neither plane is a semiotic. It remains for us to demonstrate, by broadening our perspective, that there are also semiotics whose expression plane is a semiotic and others whose content plane is a semiotic. We

---

[4] Bergé P., « Préface», in Assouly O., op. Cit. p. 11.

will call the former connotative semiotics and the latter metasemiotics. Since the plane of expression and the plane of content can only be defined in opposition to and relative to each other, it follows that the definitions of connotative semiotics and metasemiotics proposed here are only provisional 'realistic' definitions to which we cannot even give an operational value"[5].

Of course, there is room for further discussion of the additional considerations set forth here by Hjelmslev. What stands out is the predominance, indeed the intrusion in each form used to carry the discourse of luxury, of an element that always already presupposes its idiomatic bias. For example, this is visible as soon as the site is accessed. When it does not open on a page of which one does not know which path to take for the navigation, it generally imposes an order of accessibility, with a mode and a rhythm that cannot be controlled a priori. Very often, figures appear and impose themselves on the visibility, and for certain sites, the Internet user is subjected to a musical listening without possibility of regulating the flow. It occurs thus as a phenomenon of desubstantialization. What is given to see is not for its own sake, but because it is dispossessed of its supposed substance.

But the most revealing translations of the semiosis are those that can be observed when one undertakes to explore the very substance of the discourse emitted by these sites to speak of luxury. From the outset, we are obliged to resort to a cognitive device that invites us to solicit more than a purely interpretive skill intended to provide access to a meaning constructed and placed there to be interpreted or co-produced by an enunciator. Continuing the parallel with Hjelmslev, this cognitive device would in fact operate as a connotator, in other words an indicator which, faced with the particularity of a given text or discourse, would ensure its translatability. This is the case, as we have just seen, of the takeover of the navigation on a website by its transmitter, at the place where we would expect the most instantaneous access.

4   Four Forms of Contents: The Legend, the Documentary, the Praise, the Chronicle

The discourses held by the websites of luxury brands are characterized by a set of information that concerns two types of referential data. A first one refers to the particularities of the products, their ranges, their characteristics, their uses, their commercial indications; and the other one concerns the life of the brands, their history, their position on the market and their specific codes. At the level of their manifestation, that is, when we try to identify their content, as specifically dedicated to expressing luxury, the analysis allows us to identify four forms of expression for these manifestations whose discursive functioning induces essentially rhetorical modes of articulation. Either the discourse proceeds through rhetorical flights of fancy, the modes of articulation solicited are thus for the brand the legend, and for the products the praise; or the discourse resorts to a certain form of rationalization, by injecting distance into it, the mode of articulation is then for the brand, the chronicle; and for the products, the documentary. We would have the following representation, in the form of a Klein group:

---

[5] Hjelmslev L., *Prolégomènes à une théorie du langage*, Paris, Minuit, (1971), p. 144.

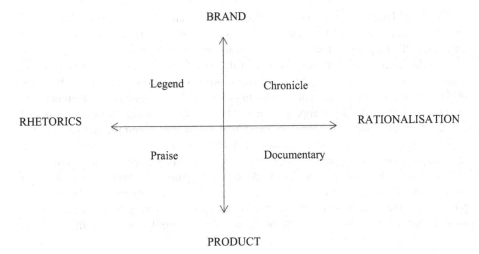

However, even though one would expect that by their very nature these modes of articulation would serve as media supports to organize the whole of the discourses of what is said about luxury, the observation is quite different. These forms become the object of discourse. More clearly, we are not dealing with a semiological rationality, where what is given to be seen would be linked by isomorphism to what is given to be understood. These modes of articulation operate in the form of already constituted signifying sets, that is, as "semiotics"[6]. From then on, they owe their discursive scope only to the mediation of a third instance, in the sense in which Eric Landowski[7] defines it. It is about this interpretative competence that makes the signifying object not a structure already there, but a spectacle to which one can only access because one has interpreted its meaning.

4.1 The Third Instance as "In Between"

Incidentally, we find one of the central arguments, often convened, to underline the consubstantial exclusiveness of the luxury, in front of the other universes of consumption, as what we can reach only because we know the codes of it:

"There is the idea that luxury must be really exclusive, almost intimidating. If it's too accessible, it kills the dream and the luxury dimension. So brands need to put consumers back in that spirit, to recreate barriers",

---

[6] Hjelmslev, op.cit.

[7] Landowski E., *La société réfléchie*, Paris, Seuil, (1989).

Stéphane Truchi[8], Chairman of the Board of the French survey institute Ifop, interviewed by Relaxnews, a French leisure information agency, emphasized in this sense during the 2014 review of the state of the luxury market in France.

For the discourse, everything will then depend on what this third-party instance chooses to translate, that is, to reveal of the show. It is indeed the reading to be made of these identified modes of articulation. In other words, the legend, the documentary, the praise and the chronicle appear in the end as the effect of the rhetorical games of this third instance, which, rather than translating the substance and the efficiency of the brands and the products to which it has access, chooses to express only the reliefs or the reflections of them. This guarantees the conditions of luxury's inaccessibility, as reserved exclusively for those who know how to decode. Everything results from the effects of sorting, specific to each of the four modes of articulation thus identified. The semiosic process is a sum of rhetorical games, which consists in postponing the substances of the expression, as well as the substances of the contents perceptible at first sight.

4.2 Rhetorical Games

The legend

According to the definition that we have of it, that is to say as "a story of a marvelous character, where historical facts are transformed by popular imagination or poetic

---

[8] Voir http://www.ladepeche.fr/article/2013/11/25/1760439-exclusivite-savoir-faire-patrimoine-combinaison-gagnante-grands-luxe.html, Last access the 12th february 2022.

invention" (Larousse), the legend is indeed distinguished by semiosic jumps. A narrative structure unfolds and, at the same time, as this unfolding takes place, the story told incidentally loses substance, to let appear only facts of articulation, that is to say the reliefs that continue to give the illusion (in the cognitive and Cartesian sense of the term) of a positive logic of history, "transformed historical facts", says the definition. The same is true of the various discourses held on websites, in general of the stories told about the life of brands, where the narrative is only worthwhile insofar as it makes every aspect of the brand an obvious fact that can only be understood in terms of its status, its history, its use, its characteristics, its inspiration, etc. Thus, for example, everything that precedes, everything that has surrounded and defined the brand since its birth is only of interest as a means of justifying its prestige, strength and luster. It is from this point of view that we should understand the obvious exception of the Ferrari luxury car brand, defined as being consubstantially linked to the personal life of Enzo Ferrari. In fact, according to the information provided on the Ferrari website, Enzo Ferrari's life, even the most banal, was never anything but exceptional, starting with his birth. Born on February 18, 1898, contrary to what we are used to, his birth was not declared until two days later because of a heavy snowfall (Exceptional!); "At the age of 10, Enzo and his brother Alfredo attended a race with their father on the Via Emilia motor racing circuit in Bologna. Felice Nazzaro won the race, but Vicenzo Lancia made the fastest lap of the circuit. The young Enzo is totally captivated by this spectacle[9]. (Exceptional!), etc. And so it is with John Galliano, pioneer of a revolutionary fashion and whose whole life has been legendary. Galliano was born in Gilbraltar, lived in London, studied fashion at Saint Martin's and named the theme of his graduation diploma "The Incredibles", inspired by the French Revolution, thus announcing his own revolution: the new messiah of fashion was born. Quite a story!

The semiotic alteration is justified insofar as no other deviation is possible with regard to the content inferred from each aspect of the story. The meaning is entirely under the control of a content (a connotator) that is already installed as self-evident. From then on, it is no longer a question of constructing a sign, of articulating a meaning; it is a question of testifying to the manifestation of something, that is to say, of a "semiotic" already installed.

In more concrete terms, this is the way the content of the "About Us" tab of the Montblanc pens website is graphically configured, for example. While the page displays different pictures, indifferently in black and white, it imposes itself as a reading constraint that leads to see it mainly as a novelistic sequence. The series of visible photos do not count either individually, or as a strictly constituted whole. We are forced to infer a minima an interpretative form, disconnecting as well from the photos as from the luxury stricto sensu. This form would proceed from the syntactic dynamics induced between these photos because of the spatializing potential offered by the website as a media. We can arrange the photos opposite each other according to specific characteristics (B/W), we can arrange them close to or far from each other, which allows us to access them by scrolling, we can vary the sizes, the shots, etc. For the tab thus concerned, this opens the access to a zone of contingency, which thus makes it possible to invent new contents or

---

[9] http://www.ferrari.com/french/about-us/histoire-de-ferrari/Pages/enzo_ferrari.aspx,   Last access the 12th february 2022.

more specifically imaginary ones, up to poetry. For example between the two pictures of signs[10], the simple black and white street sign and the same sign displayed in a large luxury building.

The induced syntax, especially associated with the environment imposed by the other photos on the page, leads to all possible contents: a saga, a performance, an exploit, etc. This is how the imaginary takes place here. It is not the result of the intrinsic contents associated with the photos; it's more the results of the multiple analogies constructed by the syntactic forms that underlie their display. Thus operates the transmediation here.

The praise

The process is almost identical for the praise, although with a different terms. It is a form of content that by itself gives the impression of ostentatious access to the substance of the products. They finally appear to be displayed, accessible to all. The staging takes advantage of the various processes of theatricalization or exhibition, recourse to halos of light, construction of aesthetic cases to magnify the products, appeal to emphatic speeches. In general, the style is laudatory, eulogistic, with a use of absolute superlatives and a strong focus on the essence of the products. However, it is precisely here that a paradox operates, which leads to the postponement of this substance. By dint of this theatricalization and exhibition, in the end, we observe that although benefiting from this ostentation, or at most precisely because of it, the products tend to be worth nothing more than for that, that is to say, they lose their substance. It is a question of theatricalization, of exhibition, but whose objective is to put under silence what would belong to the schemes which would define the products of luxury as the fact of semiotic causality. It is the theater, the exhibition as such that counts and not what is given to be seen instantaneously.

Thus is justified the semiotic alteration. Expected however as a form of expression to manifest the meaning inferred to the brand and the product, the praise becomes the plane of the content. We do not see the product, which would make it commonplace, we see the aura, "what makes it luxurious": it is the constraint, the control.

The more explicit example could be the one of Bulgari[11] website, a huge jewelry brand. The website opens on a series of stagings, where while everything is ostensibly offered to the eye, nothing seems clearly graspable. The models appear in formats that make them elusive: no sooner do they reveal themselves in the mini-films, than they immediately turn away from the camera; and their portraits are in perpetual motion on the site's visual page. And it is the same for the products, they are presented under scales which it is difficult to grasp the right proportions. Thus is built the narrative alteration. Like the legend, the effects of meaning result here not directly from the content of the information (visual and even textual) given to see, but from these games of disruption or iconic or semantic derealization, while everything is ostentatious. Only the aura remains, i.e. the atmospheric effects that surround this data.

---

[11] https://www.bulgari.com/fr-fr/.

The documentary

The purpose of the documentary is not to say or show elements in bulk, but to start from data that seem to be scattered to build and assert a point of view, the most convincing; the idea in the end being to persuade that the best possible interpretation is the one presented. For our statements, it is generally a matter of talking about the backstage of brands and products to confirm their excellence, to show the underside of the products, which operates on the other side of the mirror. But here too, because of the very discursive definition of documentary, we observe that everything only manages to mean something because it is constrained: the workshops, research and development, expertise, know-how, manufacturing secrets, etc. are only summoned insofar as, together, they contribute to the perfection of the brand and the products, without needing to say more. It is through this process that the third instance manages to manifest what emerges from the expression of the products as the site of a spectacle, in the Athenian sense of the term. This is a fairly recurrent process in the world of watchmaking, for example, with an insistence that is very often based on the world of research and creation. In general, the discourse focuses on the staging of the creative process, highlighting expertise, exposing the creative part of the product, and using special staging of the worker or engineer. Often also, a design office is put forward, or the behind-the-scenes of the artistic choices are highlighted, etc. In short, this is the reign of the analytical narrative. What is important is not so much the content of the signals chosen to concretely represent the substance of luxury as the effects of discourse that allow the elements of rhetoric proper to documentary to be inscribed: slowness, sequentization, investigation, but also rationalization and evaluation, etc. The control operates by the form, less by the substance of the deployed contents.

Let's take for example the page "Advanced research"[12] of Patek Philippe, a very luxury brand of watches. Various available data present the products from several angles, mainly with a particular focus on the technological innovations of which they are the object. We insist on the inspirations that led to it, on the research that brought them, and as well as on all the improvements to which these innovations have made it possible to lead, for Patek watchmaking and by extension in this specific universe.

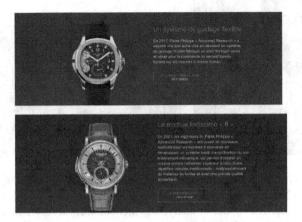

The interest of transmediation concerns the content conferred on these data. On the page, they are represented in the form of chapters which are accessed gradually. By being each presented in the form of exclusivity (a visual, a specific text), each chapter gives each detail selected as an effect of exception, and even of total perfection. For the information delivered, it is no longer a question of simple data to be read, but of real exclusive documents to be kept, almost to be classified with prestigious descriptors. In this case, not only is each chapter surmounted by a title, but above all, a technical reference (like in a library) is assigned to each innovation selected.

---

[12] https://www.patek.com/fr/entreprise/savoir-faire/advanced-research.

The chronicle

Finally the chronicle. It completes to install us in the heart of the most evident scenography of what is in question in the semiotic process to be ratified. It is a question of spectacle, we say. The model of analysis is then all seen. It refers in many points to the Athenian dramaturgy of which Eric Landowski gives a schematization in his book La société réfléchie to describe the semiotic structure of the opinion. According to him, finally, the opinion is never that the fact of a process of transformation, to short-circuit the word of the public, indistinct, heterogeneous, in short banal. The word of the public finds value only taken again and translated by the chorus which observes the peripatetic ones of it to comment them to the attention of the spectators. It is thus of the chronicle. By its format, it operates insofar as at the same time as one leans on it to develop a mark, one overdetermines it of fact by an opportune topicality.

Here, the staging uses the present time, current events, and the stars of the moment to create display effects and to show the brand's existential interest. This is done by opportunistically exploiting recognizable images or facts that have already been established: news stars, charities, celebrities, guarantors, testimonials.

We will cite the example of various civic actions of the Montblanc pen brand in connection with Unicef for the benefit of educational actions throughout the world; or even such a particular evening of such a brand. The idea is to build up topical effects. The acts of presence, the blows in the air of time, the strong punctual facts is thus what becomes central. They are the ones that guarantee the constraints of the control: any element summoned is so because it contributes to the writing of a constantly renewed scenario and it is this particular scenario that constitutes the object of the discourse, with the consequence, as for the other rhetorics, of the postponement of the substance of the brand and the product.

5 Conclusion

Previously exclusive, because of a rather too quick assimilation of social classes to a particular access to wealth, luxury, in parallel with the blossoming of mass consumption, has been democratized, with a particularly intense acceleration due to the development of virtual means of communication.

We wanted to show how these forms of communication operate. We have established the notion of semiosic alteration as the organizing principle of luxury communication on the Internet, with the constraint of control defined as what allows us to preserve its exclusivity. While we should have expected the rhetoric of luxury to operate as forms of expression, it becomes the form of content: the legend, the documentary, the praise, the chronicle. In the end, we retain luxury not what concretely translates it, i.e. the substance of the brands or products, but the spectacle held around these translations. This seemed to us to be the essential issue; under the model of theatricalization. While the Internet medium offers the widest latitude to highlight in all its forms what usually constitutes the essence of luxury, i.e. its substance, all the rhetorical games operate precisely to postpone it. The tactic is quite visible: it is a question of subtly putting away recognizable signs for the sole benefit of a prior decoding operation. The paradox of the luxury is played thus, like a discriminatory order.

References

1. Assouly, O.: Le luxe. Essai sur la fabrique de l'ostentation, Paris, Édition du regard (2005)
2. Courtés, J.: Analyse sémiotique du discours. De l'énoncé à l'énonciation, Paris Hachette (1991)
3. Fontanille J., Sémiotique du discours, Limoges, Pulim, (1998)
4. Fontanille, J.: Pratiques sémiotiques. Puf, Paris (2008)
5. Hjelmslev, L.: Prolégomènes à une théorie du langage. Minuit, Paris (1971)
6. Jolles, A.: Les formes simples. Seuil, Paris (1972)
7. Landowski, E., La,: société réfléchie. Seuil, Paris (1989)
8. Landowski, E.: Passions sans nom. Puf, Paris (2004)
9. Siegel, M.: More than words: the generative power of transmediation for learning. Canadian J. Educ./Revue canadienne de l'éducation, Autumn, Cultural Psychology and Semiotics, **20**(4), 460 (1995). https://www.jstor.org/stable/1495082
10. Varela, F., Thompson, E., Eleanor, R.: L'Inscription corporelle de l'esprit. Sciences cognitives et expérience humaine, (trad. Veronique Havelange), Paris, Seuil (1997)

Research on Interactive Experience Design of E-Commerce Livestreaming Based on Interaction Ritual Chains—Taking Taobao Livestreaming Platform as an Example

Ziyuan Wang[✉] and Hong Chen

East China University of Science and Technology, Shanghai, China
609823908@qq.com

Abstract. With rapid development, e-commerce livestreaming has become the largest type of livestreaming in China. As multiple live streaming platforms enter e-commerce livestreaming, the interactive experience of e-commerce livestreaming platforms is also facing the problem of high homogeneity. How to interact well with users and improve user experience has become the primary goal. In order to strengthen user stickiness, better promote the transaction rate of e-commerce livestreaming, and create a better livestreaming shopping experience. Starting from the interactive ritual chain theory of sociology theory, this paper focuses on e-commerce livestreaming and analyzes the interactive ritual within e-commerce livestreaming by taking Taobao livestreaming platform as an example. This paper explores the underlying reasons of interactive experience in livestreaming rooms, analyzes user experience in combination with emotional design theory, and summarizes pain points and user needs. Finally, the interactive experience design strategy of e-commerce livestreaming is proposed, which provides a new design idea and design method for the design and optimization of e-commerce livestreaming platform.

Keywords: E-commerce livestreaming · Interactive ritual chain · Experience design · Interactive design

1 Introduction

With the development and popularization of the mobile Internet, the public can access the Internet more conveniently, and the Internet has become an indispensable part of people's lives. As a representative industrial form of my country's Internet industry, webcasting has developed rapidly. According to the 48th "Statistical Report on Internet Development in China" released by the China Internet Network Information Center (CNNIC), as of June 2021, the number of online livestreaming users in my country has reached 638 million, accounting for 63.1% of the total Internet users. Among them, e-commerce livestreaming has developed rapidly and has become the livestreaming category with the largest user scale among online livestreaming, with a user scale of 384 million.

© Springer Nature Switzerland AG 2022
M. Rauterberg et al. (Eds.): HCII 2022, LNCS 13520, pp. 260–267, 2022.
https://doi.org/10.1007/978-3-031-18158-0_19

E-commerce livestreaming is a form of livestreaming to display and sell products by means of online livestreaming platform. The content is produced by the Internet celebrity anchor, and the user interacts with the user through the introduction of the product and the provision of real-time customer service, thereby realizing commercial realization. According to the report data, the scale of China's e-commerce livestreaming market will reach 1.2 trillion yuan in 2020, and it is expected that the scale of e-commerce livestreaming will exceed 4.9 trillion yuan in 2023. Livestreaming has become a normalized marketing method and sales channel in the e-commerce market. In February 2019, in order to lay out the e-commerce livestreaming market segment, Alibaba separated the livestreaming module in Taobao APP and officially entered the e-commerce livestreaming. With the rapid rise of e-commerce livestreaming business on multiple platforms, e-commerce livestreaming platforms are also facing the problem of homogeneity. How to interact well with users and improve user experience has become the primary goal. Therefore, this article will take Taobao livestreaming platform as an example, and introduce the theory of interactive ritual chain of sociology theory to analyze the interactive experience of e-commerce livestreaming.

2   Interactive Ritual in E-commerce Livestreaming

2.1   Interactive Ritual Chain

Beginning with the classical sociologist Émile Durkheim, sociology has attached great importance to the study of ritual. Randall Collins put forward the theory of interactive ritual chain on the basis of summarizing previous theories [1]. He pointed out that "interactive ritual" is a process in which participants form a common focus, generate emotional resonance and form feedback. According to Randall Collins, there are four elements that need to be fulfilled to achieve an interactive ritual: the presence of two or more people, the restriction of outsiders, the focus of the participants on a common object, and the sharing of a common emotion or emotional experience. When the conditions are met, the elements are effectively combined, and short-term emotional stimulation will be transformed into long-term emotional energy, which will achieve group excitement and produce the following experiences: group solidarity, individual emotional energy, symbols representing the group or "sacred objects", maintain the group, and respect the moral sense of group symbols.

2.2   Elements of Interactive Ritual in E-commerce Live Streaming

"Common presence" is a prerequisite for the completion of the entire interactive ritual. In the Internet livestreaming environment, e-commerce livestreaming has broken through the time and space limitations of the traditional shopping environment. Webcasting uses its own characteristics to help users use the network to transmit information on terminal devices such as computers and mobile phones. Although users are in different physical environments, they all gather in a virtual situation through the mobile network and conduct interactive exchanges. The livestreaming platform creates a virtual situation where the anchor and the viewer are in the same situation at the same time, achieving the group gathering that Randall Collins refers to. Compared with the traditional shopping environment, users only need to open the mobile phone software to reach the host's livestreaming room, and communicate and discuss with the host or other users through barrage, comments, etc. The host also transmits product information to users in real time through the live screen. Efficiently meet the shopping needs of users.

"Setting restrictions on outsiders" is one of the important elements of the interactive ritual chain. Due to its own attributes, the livestreaming room of e-commerce has formed a natural barrier. The audience of the livestreaming room completes the registration and chooses to enter the livestreaming room that they are interested in, which naturally forms a situation of setting restrictions on outsiders. The interest in livestreaming also enables the audience in the livestreaming room to have the same focus. In such an environment, members of the group will gain a more stable sense of identity, which also helps the group to form group unity.

People need to focus their attention on a common object or activity, and by communicating that focus to each other, each other is aware of the focus. In the e-commerce livestreaming room, the anchor and the products they sell are the focus of users' attention. At the same time, the focus of the audience's attention is constantly changing, and the audience and the anchor will repeatedly remind each other of these focuses. For example, when an anchor introduces a product and conducts a lottery event, the audience's attention will be shifted from the product to the lottery event. During this process, the audience will also remind each other through comments and consolidate the relationship between groups. Which drives users to engage in continuous interaction.

The common focus enables the audience in the e-commerce livestreaming room to interact and stimulate some emotional energy. Viewers will express their emotions by sending comments, concerns, likes, etc., in order to attract the attention of the anchor, and the anchor will also respond to the comments and read the user's nickname to interact accordingly. In this process, the emotional state is shared between users and other users or streamers. In order to maintain this relationship, users will continue to repeat the above interactive behaviors to achieve the continuation of their emotional energy.

3   Interactive Experience in E-commerce Livestreaming

User experience is an important design principle of user-centered design philosophy when the user's experience with the product or service is discussed or evaluated. American cognitive psychologist Donald Arthur Norman proposed three levels of experience in his book "Emotional Design" [2], namely, the instinctive, behavioral and reflective levels. Both the interactive ritual chain and emotional design recognize the impact of emotional energy on user experience, and this impact is based on interactive behavior. The connection between the two provides the basis for the experience design research of e-commerce livestreaming platforms. In the following, from the perspective of the interactive ritual chain, we will analyze which interactive designs in e-commerce livestreaming help customers gain emotional energy and continue to affect customers' shopping experience.

The interactive ritual in the e-commerce livestreaming is also an experience of the live audience. The process of the interactive ritual is divided into experience levels. The early stage is the instinct layer - the gathering before the experience, the middle stage is the behavior layer - the ritual interaction in the experience, and the later stage is the reflection layer. - Experience the finished result. Among them, the instinct layer in the early stage of the interactive ritual is the user's instinctive awareness and thinking, the interface appearance and layout of the e-commerce livestreaming room is the basis for the formation of the first impression; the behavior layer in the middle stage is in the process of the interactive ritual. The satisfaction brought by the user; the later reflection layer user consciousness, emotion and other more advanced experience feelings, including this feeling brings reflection at the level of thought and meaning.

Instinct Layer - Gathering Before Experience. When the audience opens the Taobao livestreaming platform, they can enter the e-commerce livestreaming room page by recommending livestreaming or clicking on the livestreaming they follow. After entering the livestreaming room, "XXX entered the livestreaming room" will appear in the comment area of the screen in real time. Users with privileged status will also have special customized entrance effects. When the audience enters the venue, some anchors will also make a welcome speech broadcast to the joined audience. This form not only makes the audience realize that they have joined this group, but also is more friendly to the entire live room group. In the livestreaming room, the host's screen is the content of the entire livestreaming room. The upper part of the livestreaming room screen dis-plays the livestreaming room information, including the current popularity, the number of fans, and the number of people in the livestreaming room. In the middle of the screen, the image of the anchor and the products it sells will appear. Comments sent by other users will appear at the bottom of the screen, and a variety of elements are gathered together to form a virtual presence situation and a preliminary sense of identity.

Behavioral Layer - Ritual Interaction in Experience. The interaction in e-commerce livestreaming can be divided into three types of interactive behaviors: information interaction, emotional interaction, and marketing interaction according to the purpose of the behavior. Most of the information interaction is concentrated in the comment area, which carries the broadcast of the audience's communication with the anchor or other audience, as well as other interactive behaviors. Emotional interaction refers to the interactive behaviors that users perform after generating emotional energy in the interactive ritual, including likes, attention, and joining fan groups. Marketing interaction refers to the purchase behavior of users and the marketing functions launched by the plat-form, such as spike kills, grab red envelopes, join members, and receive coupons. Some anchor teams will also conduct some other forms of interaction in the livestreaming room, such as screenshots of screen lottery, likes Send coupons etc. In the livestreaming room, the products sold are the focus of the audience, and the audience interacts with the anchor around the products. Viewers can send comments to express questions about products or activities like the host, the host will answer the questions about the comments, and other viewers in the livestreaming room will also respond to the comments. When your questions are answered by the anchor, the audience will feel a certain sense of satisfaction and will participate more actively in the next interaction. Before the product is put on the shelves, the anchor will use a countdown method to attract the attention of the audience, and the purchase button of the product will appear at the bottom of the screen in the livestreaming room. With the continuous purchase of viewers, the words "Hot Sale" will appear above the product link, and the real-time transaction volume will be updated in real time. At this time, the atmosphere in the livestreaming room reaches its peak, which stimulates the user's desire to buy and causes the user to generate consumption behavior. The audience achieves what Randall Collins calls an emotional bond of shared concern, which is also the climax of the experience.

Reflection Layer - The Result of Experience Completion. The audience in the livestreaming room will have a certain sense of identity after going through this series of interactive ceremonies. The anchors usually say words such as "family", "my fans", "fan group" in the livestreaming, which is a kind of affirmation of the audience's identity, which also continuously strengthens this sense of identity. On e-commerce livestreaming platforms, the form of fan groups provides a basis for group unity. Under the guidance of the anchor, the audience follows the livestreaming room, joins the anchor's fan group, and then obtains coupons for the products sold. When commenting, there will also be a corresponding fan card before the user's nickname, which will enhance the identity of the audience. The audience has a certain sense of superiority. And this group of people will spontaneously guard this group, and will consciously maintain irregular behaviors such as inappropriate remarks in the livestreaming room, and pro-mote the healthy development of the entire livestreaming room environment.

4 Analysis of Pain Points of E-commerce Live Streaming Experience

Based on the analysis of the interactive ritual experience in the e-commerce livestreaming, the interactive ritual experience in the e-commerce livestreaming is divided into three stages: the gathering before the experience, the ritual interaction during the experience, and the result of the completion of the experience. Users will have different behaviors and emotions at different stages, but users will also face some pain points at each stage. For example, in the gathering stage before the experience, the audience opens the livestreaming room and has certain emotions about the content of the livestreaming room. Because the focus of the livestreaming room is chaotic, the screen of the livestreaming room is full of various discounts and activity information, and the information exchanged also has insufficient concentration, It is difficult to quickly understand the problem of selling goods, which causes the audience to stop watching the livestreaming; in the ritual interaction stage of the experience, the audience concentrates on participating in the livestreaming. Due to the complicated gameplay rules and unreasonable rights system in the livestreaming room, the audience will learn costs when watching. High, it is difficult to immerse yourself in the livestreaming; after the experience is completed, the anchor will immediately introduce the next round of other products. Therefore, it is difficult for viewers who have made purchases to share emotions, and their sense of identity with the livestreaming room will weaken over time.

Based on the above pain points, the needs of users in three experience stages can be summarized. In the gathering stage before the experience, it is difficult for users to invest due to the unclear focus of the livestreaming room. Therefore, it is necessary to create a good atmosphere for shopping in the livestreaming room, focusing on the products sold; in the ritual interaction stage of the experience, the activities are complicated and the user It is difficult to immerse, so it is necessary to establish a rhythmic interactive form to gradually stimulate the user's emotional experience; in the post-experience stage, the audience has a weak sense of belonging to the livestreaming, so they need to participate in emotional interaction to enhance their sense of belonging.

5   E-commerce Livestreaming Experience Design Strategy

Taking the Taobao livestreaming platform as an example, this paper analyzes how audiences, anchors or other audiences influence each other in e-commerce livestreaming from the three aspects of the experience process: the gathering before the experience, the ritual interaction during the experience, and the results of the experience completion. Generate emotional energy. This provides a basis for the interactive experience design of e-commerce livestreaming, and therefore summarizes the design strategy of e-commerce livestreaming interactive experience from the perspective of the interactive ritual chain.

5.1   Instinct Layer: Building an Immersive Group Carnival Scene

For e-commerce livestreaming whose main purpose is to sell goods, it is extremely important to give viewers an immersive viewing experience. In the early stage of the audience entering the livestreaming room, the lively and lively atmosphere of the livestreaming room creates a feeling of being in a store. At this time, they will become curious about the products sold in the livestreaming room. Whether the content of the livestreaming room meets the expectations of customers will directly affect audience experience. However, when entering the Taobao livestreaming room, the system will pop up a modal pop-up window for receiving red envelopes and coupons. This type of pop-up window directly interrupts the user's access to the live room information. Therefore, in the design of the livestreaming room, it is necessary to simplify the interaction process of the livestreaming room, reduce the modules unrelated to the products sold and the pages that interfere with the user's viewing experience, so that users can quickly obtain the information they want to know in the initial aggregation stage.

At the same time, we use design methods to design elements such as icons and dynamic effects in the interface of the livestreaming room with keywords such as popularity and panic buying. For example, in the Taobao livestreaming room, the constantly flashing likes and the continuously refreshed purchase information give people an atmosphere of being in a shopping mall, which can stimulate the emotional energy of customers, and gather in groups when users have just entered the livestreaming room. Stage, enhance their enthusiasm for participating in the interaction and the fun of using the product.

5.2   Behavior Layer: Set up Clear and Smooth Interactive Functions

First, the communication efficiency of information interaction should be improved. In the livestreaming room, the products sold are always the common focus of the audience. Therefore, information interaction should be reduced and marketing information unrelated to the product, such as "XXX users followed the anchor", "XXX shared the livestreaming room". At the same time, the existing intelligent question-and-answer function in the livestreaming room can only answer customer service questions such as recommendation, order, and after-sales. Goods have a clearer understanding.

Design clear and smooth marketing interactions. A livestreaming event usually lasts several hours, and the marketing interaction in the livestreaming room will be carried out at the same time, which will continuously consume the emotional energy of the audience and cause a burden to the users. Therefore, users should be provided with controllable and transparent marketing activities, such as providing the audience with a visual marketing process and time, prompting the user's current operation progress so that the user can have a sufficient sense of security.

Set a variety of emotional expressions. After the audience has emotional resonance in the livestreaming, they need to use emotional interaction to release their emotions. However, there is only one way of expressing emotions in text comments, so it is necessary to design a variety of expressions. For example, by using expressions with lower thresholds such as expressions and voices, it can shorten the operation time and process, reduce the obstacles in the process of emotional expression, make it more operable, and ensure that the audience can complete it independently and coherently.

5.3 Reflection Layer: Constructing Emotional Group Symbols

The construction of group symbols can bring vitality to the group, and the group symbols in the livestreaming room should be embodied. For example, in the livestreaming room of anchor Li Jiaqi, if you join the fan group, you will get a "fan medal" such as "2 + 7". "2 + 7" is the homonym of "Love Jiaqi", and the medal will be displayed in front of the nickname when making comments. This is a symbolic expression of fans' love for the anchor. Such identity symbols can be quickly recognized and remembered by users, and a sense of identity can be generated by giving individuals identity. However, in the current livestreaming room, users usually have multiple identity symbols, such as "fan medal", "favorite medal", "anchor special medal", etc. in the livestreaming room, so many identities will cause certain cognitive confusion for the audience. Therefore, it is necessary to establish a priority display mechanism for the correlation between the group symbol and the livestreaming room, appropriately reduce the displayed identity information, give priority to the most relevant identities, help individuals continue to gain emotional energy, and thus strengthen group unity.

6 Conclusion

The participation and interaction of the audience in the e-commerce livestreaming is the key to the entire livestreaming room. This paper analyzes the emotional energy generated by audiences in the same scene in the same scene through the interactive ritual chain theory, and combines the emotional design theory to analyze the user experience. From the three aspects of instinct layer, behavior layer and reflection layer, it is proposed that the interactive experience design of e-commerce livestreaming can be optimized by building immersive group carnival scenes, setting clear and smooth interactive functions, and constructing emotional group symbols to optimize the interactive experience design of e-commerce livestreaming. The experience design in the commercial livestreaming provides a certain reference.

References

1. Collins, R.: Interaction Ritual Chains (2004)
2. Donald, A.N.: Emotional design. Ubiquity (2004)

Purchase Intention in Agricultural Products Live-Streaming Commerce: A S-O-R Model

Suting Yang, Lili Liu[✉], Jiujiu Jiang, and Shanjiao Ren

College of Economics and Management, Nanjing University of Aeronautics and Astronautics, Nanjing, China
{yst1122,llili85,joy9971}@nuaa.edu.cn

Abstract. Agricultural products live-streaming commerce (APLC), a new form of e-commerce with unique features sinking to villages and towns, has significantly promoted the sales of agricultural products in China during COVID-19. However, limited research has explored how the unique and common live-streaming commerce features affect customer behavior in APLC. Drawing on stimulus-organism-response (S-O-R) model, this study develops a research framework to examine how the stimuli (practicality, interactivity, preferential, and commonweal) affect consumers' purchase intention through the mediation of organism factors (perceived trust and perceived value) in ALPC context. 216 valid samples were collected via an online survey. SmartPLS3.0 was used to verify the research model and hypotheses. Findings indicate: perceived trust and perceived value positively affect purchase intention; practicality, interactivity, preferential, and commonweal are positively associated with perceived value; practicality and commonweal positively influence perceived trust; interactivity has no significant effect on perceived trust. Potential theoretical and practical contributions are discussed.

Keywords: Agricultural products live-streaming commerce · S-O-R model · Practicability · Interactivity · Preferential · Commonweal · Purchase intention

1 Introduction

E-commerce live-streaming is a business model, based on e-commerce, using live broadcast as a media to associate users with merchandise sales [26]. Agricultural products live-streaming (APLC), a new form of e-commerce sinking to villages and towns, has significantly promoted the sales of agricultural products in China during COVID-19. In the first quarter of 2020, online retail sales of agricultural products grew against the trend, reaching 93.68 billion CNY, indicating a year-on-year increase of 31.0% [24]. Besides, on September 23rd 2021, daily sales of the first global agricultural product live-streaming festival exceeded 200 million CNY [5]. In a nutshell, agricultural products live-streaming has shown strong power in practice, providing brand-new patterns and ideas for public welfare and poverty alleviation.

As a vertical form of live-streaming commerce, APLC exhibits not only attributes of live-streaming but also several unique features of itself. For instance, its charitable

© Springer Nature Switzerland AG 2022
M. Rauterberg et al. (Eds.): HCII 2022, LNCS 13520, pp. 268–279, 2022.
https://doi.org/10.1007/978-3-031-18158-0_20

nature is rarely available or highlighted in traditional live-streaming commerce. However, limited research has explored how the unique and common live-streaming commerce features affect customer behavior in APLC. To fill this gap, this study develops a conceptual model to investigate purchase intention in the context of agricultural products live-streaming on the basis of S-O-R model. The S-O-R model explains and predicts the impact of different environmental stimuli on people's cognition, emotion and behavior [19], Specifically, four characteristics have been identified (practicality, interactivity, preferential, and commonweal) as external stimuli; consumers' inner emotional state (perceived trust and perceived value) has been recognized as organism; consumers' purchase intention has been considered as response. In short, in order to promote agricultural product sales, this study explores and verifies the key determinants that foster consumers' intention to buy agricultural products, then provides practical suggestions to APLC market.

2 Theoretical Background

2.1 S-O-R Model

Mehrabian and Russell propose the Stimulus-Organism-Response (S-O-R) model, stating that the user would response to the physiological and psychological changes caused by certain external stimulus [19]. S-O-R model has been widely adopted to explain online purchase behavior, prove that the sum of environmental online shopping factors act as stimuli (S), affects consumers' internal emotions and perception (such as perceived pleasure, etc.) (O), which in turn results in consumer satisfaction and related behaviors responses (R) [6]. In addition, S-O-R model has been integrated with other theories, in order to further investigate consumer behavior in e-commerce or live-streaming commerce. For instance, combining S-O-R model and theories of relationship marketing, Hu et al.'s study demonstrates that social and structural bonds positively affect consumer engagement directly and indirectly via affective commitment [9]. Moreover, findings of Kang et al.'s research show that interactivity has dynamic effect on consumer engagement behavior in live-streaming e-commerce [13]. To sum up, SOR model is an overarching theory that explains how environmental cues in e-commerce triggers consumers' cognitive and emotional responses, as well as their subsequent behavioral responses.

Therefore, in light of S-O-R model, we propose that characteristics of APLC (practicality, interactivity, preferential, and commonweal) (S) may influence consumers' perceived trust and perceived value (O), which in turn affect consumers' purchase intention (R). In other words, consumers' perceived trust and perceived value are intensified by the unique attributes of APLC, which then directly affect consumers' purchase intention.

2.2 Perceived Trust and Perceived Value

The concept of trust originates from the discipline of psychology, in which trust has been described as a belief or attitude tendency that an individual or a group expects others to bring benefits to them. Despite an individual cannot supervise or control others' behavior, he/she is willing to take possible risks and consequences that do not conform to expectations [17]. It is worth noting that theories of trust have been extensively applied to social commerce research. For example, findings imply that consumers' perceived trust significantly affect their purchase intention in social e-commerce [25]. Besides, e-commerce virtual communities members may form trust toward products that have been discussed or recommended in the communities, and turn into buyers [16].

Similarly, from the perspective of consumer psychology, Zeithaml defines perceived value as "the overall evaluation of products and services by consumers after weighing what they get and how much they pay" [31]. In marketing literature, perceived value has been verified as the primary predictor of purchase intention and behavior. For instance, Childers et al. find both perceived hedonic value and utilitarian value enhance consumer engagement in retail shopping [4]. Moreover, in the context of live-streaming commerce, Ying et al. have proved that perceived value directly affects consumers' purchase intention [30].

As discussed above, multiple studies have examined how perceived trust and value affect purchase behavior. Therefore, in our research, perceived value and perceived trust are regarded as organism factors in S-O-R model, we then explore how the external stimulus affect consumers' purchase intention in APLC via the two mediators.

3   Research Model and Hypotheses

The research model is shown in Fig. 1. Corresponding assumptions are discussed in detail as followings.

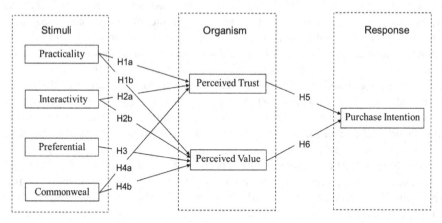

Fig. 1. Research model

3.1 Practicality, Interactivity, Preferential, and Commonweal

Practicality refers to the ability to fulfill consumer's needs for the functionality, utility and effectiveness of goods or services [14]. When more information about the recommended product is provided in live-streaming commerce, consumers are more likely to build trust towards it [34]. Liu et al. also demonstrate the positive effect of practicality on purchase intention in the context of live-broadcasting [14]. In APLC, the broadcasters will precisely introduce the agricultural products (e.g., how to cook them) and display the them in all directions, meanwhile, consumers are able to send comments (e.g., questions) and communicate in real time through the bullet screen, in order to obtain more information about the products. The more information the consumers learn, the more they trust the products and believe the products are valuable. We thus hypothesize:

H1a. Practicality has a positive effect on perceived trust.
H1b. Practicality has a positive effect on perceived value.

Interactivity is defined as various forms of online real-time communication among different participants [33]. In online shopping, research has found that interaction between buyers and sellers will strengthen buyers' trust toward sellers and products, as well as the value of products [33]. Similarly, McKnight et al. have proven that improvement of the interactivity in online shopping platforms, will greatly enhance consumers' trust toward products and sellers [18]. During live-streaming, the more frequent broadcasters and consumers interact or communicate with each other, the stronger perceived trust or value towards the broadcasters and products they can develop [15]. For example, in the context of APLC, interactive information related to products can help to enhance consumers' perceived trust and value. Therefore, we propose:

H2a. Interactivity has a positive effect on perceived trust.
H2b. Interactivity has a positive effect on perceived value.

Preferential refers to promotional methods such as discounts, limited-time purchases, and hunger marketing [28]. Price is a vital factor determining consumers' online purchases. According to Sweeney et al., price directly affect perceived value in retailing [11]. In the context of APLC, broadcasters would offer additional preferential (e.g., discount coupon, gifts) to audiences, comparing with common online shopping. In this case, APLC consumers are able to buy the same products at lower price or given more gifts, which makes them feel the products more cost-effective and worthwhile to purchase. Thus, we assume:

H3. Preferential has a positive effect on perceived value.

Commonweal in APLC reveals that sellers will donate part of the profits obtained from the transaction to farmers, in order to support them [8]. Based on theory of moral emotion, Xu et al. have investigated the reaction mechanism of consumers in public welfare marketing, and concluded that morality has positive effects on perceived trust and value [29]. APLC is essentially a charity event, aiming at selling products for farmers.

When the audiences are informed that their purchase of agricultural products is doing charity and helping others, they will not only easily build trust towards APLC, but also believe in the value of products. Therefore, we propose:

H4a. Commonweal has a positive effect on perceived trust.
H4b. Commonweal has a positive effect on perceived value.

3.2 Perceived Trust, Perceived Value, and Purchase Intention

Perceived trust describes a belief or attitude tendency that consumers expect for benefits when shopping, which can reduce the uncertainty and risk in the transaction process and save transaction costs [17]. Extensive research has found that perception of trust is a strong predictor of online shopping intentions [1, 10]. Perceived value indicates consumers' perception of the overall paid value by evaluating their gains and losses. Scholars have proved that perceived value also has significant impact on consumers' purchase intention [21, 23]. For example, when consumers trust APLC and believe that the recommended products are valuable, they are more willing to buy. Therefore, we assume:

H5. Perceived trust has a positive effect on purchase intention.
H6. Perceived value has a positive effect on purchase intention.

4   Research Methodology

4.1   Measurements

We designed an online survey to collect data. The questionnaire includes demographic questions and measurement items of 7 variables. We used a 7-point Likert scale to measure each item (1 = strongly disagree, 7 = strongly agree). We designed all items following previous studies, with minor changes for each item to fit our research context (see Table 1.). For instance, items of practicality were adapted from Ji et al.'s study [12, 14], while items for interactivity were derived from the study of Zheng et al. [33].

Table 1. Constructs and measures

Constructs	Items	Measures	References
Practicality (PRA)	PRA1	APLC can give me a comprehensive understanding of agricultural products	[12, 14]
	PRA2	By APLC, I can easily find the agricultural products that I like	

(continued)

Table 1. (*continued*)

Constructs	Items	Measures	References
	PRA3	APLC cannot improve the efficiency of my purchase for agricultural products	
Interactivity (INT)	INT1	The broadcaster of APLC often communicates and interacts with me	[33]
	INT2	When watching APLC, I can communicate with the broadcaster by posting comments	
	INT3	When watching APLC, I can understand other consumers' thoughts form the time-sync comments	
Preferential (PRE)	PRE1	I think the price of agricultural products in APLC is very affordable	[7]
	PRE2	In APLC, the promotion of agricultural products is very strong	
Commonweal (COM)	COM1	APLC can help farmers solve the problem of slow sales	[33]
	COM2	In APLC, the broadcaster will publicize the area where the agricultural products are located	
	COM3	After watching APLC, I will continue to pay attention to the sales of agricultural products	
Perceived Trust (PET)	PET1	Based on the broadcaster's recommendations, I am sure that the agricultural products will look good on me as I expect	[20, 32]
	PET2	I believe that the goods and services purchased through APLC will get good after-sales	
	PET3	Even if there is a certain risk in purchasing agricultural products in APLC, I am willing to take it	
Perceived Value (PEV)	PEV1	I think that agricultural products in APLC are cost-effective	[2]
	PEV2	The introduction information obtained in APLC can meet my decision-making needs	

(*continued*)

Table 1. (*continued*)

Constructs	Items	Measures	References
	PEV3	Buying agricultural products from APLC will leave a good impression	
	PEV4	Purchasing agricultural products from APLC gives me a sense of satisfaction or accomplishment	
Purchase Intention (PUI)	PUI1	I will consider APLC as my first shopping choice of agricultural products	[3]
	PUI2	I am willing to recommend to others the agricultural products in APLC	
	PUI3	I expect that I will purchase products or services through APLC	

4.2 Data Collection

The questionnaire was developed on the Sojump website (https://www.wjx.cn/, one of the largest professional data collection websites in China) and then distributed to audiences of APLC. In total, we received 216 valid responses. Table 2 presents demographic information of the respondents. In general, 55.1% of the respondents were female while 44.9% of them were male. Majority of the samples aged between 21 and 40 and held bachelor's degree (76.39%). Besides, respondents' monthly income ranged from 2000 to 8000 CNY. Over 90% respondents spent less than 500 CNY to buy agricultural products via APLC.

Table 2. Demographics of respondents

Item	Options	Frequency	Percentage (%)
Gender	Male	97	44.9
	Female	119	55.1
Age	Under 18	7	3.24
	18–30	173	80.09
	31–45	24	11.11
	Above 45	12	5.56
Educational level	Secondary school or below	11	5.09
	Junior college	14	6.48
	Bachelor	165	76.39

(*continued*)

Table 2. (*continued*)

Item	Options	Frequency	Percentage (%)
	Master's	19	8.8
	PHD	7	3.24
Monthly Income	Less than 2000 yuan	84	38.89
	2000–4000 yuan	58	26.85
	4001–6000 yuan	36	16.67
	6001–8000 yuan	20	9.26
	More than 8000 yuan	18	8.33
APLC purchase consumption	Less than 100 yuan	125	57.87
	101–500 yuan	70	32.41
	501–1000 yuan	18	8.33
	More than 1000 yuan	3	1.39

4.3 Data Analyses and Results

SmartPLS3.0 was used to analyze data and a two-step method was used to analyze the research model respectively: the measurement model and structural model. In general, the reliability and validity of all latent models can be evaluated by checking Cronbach's α value (>0.7), factor loadings (>0.7), and composite reliability (>0.7). Moreover, the average variance extracted (AVE) should exceed 0.5 [27]. As shown in Table 3 and 4, all the four index values were greater than the acceptable value. In summary, our measurement model had sufficient reliability, convergence validity and discriminant validity.

Table 3. Item reliability

Construct	Item	Loadings	Cronbach's Alpha	Composite reliability	AVE
Practicality (PRA)	SY1	0.929	0.798	0.843	0.703
	SY2	0.897			
	SY3	0.711			
Interactivity (INT)	HD1	0.847	0.805	0.899	0.683
	HD2	0.710			
	HD3	0.910			
Preferential (PRE)	YH1	0.917	0.931	0.964	0.857
	YH2	0.957			

(*continued*)

Table 3. (*continued*)

Construct	Item	Loadings	Cronbach's Alpha	Composite reliability	AVE
Commonweal (COM)	GY1	0.893	0.742	0.854	0.698
	GY2	0.871			
	GY3	0.706			
Perceived Trust (PET)	PT1	0.885	0.799	0.837	0.789
	PT2	0.823			
	PT3	0.774			
Perceived Value (PEV)	PV1	0.827	0.719	0.846	0.681
	PV2	0.777			
	PV3	0.724			
	PV4	0.778			
Purchase Intention (PUI)	PI1	0.851	0.836	0.899	0.721
	PI2	0.805			
	PI3	0.818			

Table 4. Discriminant validity

Construct	INT	PRE	COM	PRA	PEV	PET	PUI
Interactivity	**0.826**						
Preferential	0.652	**0.926**					
Commonweal	0.627	0.638	**0.830**				
Practicality	0.501	0.517	0.468	**0.838**			
Perceived value	0.607	0.599	0.776	0.681	**0.825**		
Perceived trust	0.458	0.618	0.576	0.495	0.629	**0.888**	
Purchase intention	0.697	0.483	0.552	0.685	0.328	0.503	**0.849**

Note: INT = Interactivity; PRE = Preferential; COM = Commonweal; PRA = Practicality; PEV = Perceived Value; PET = Perceived Trust; PUI = Purchase Intention

We then tested the structural model and hypothesis. As shown in Fig. 2, perceived trust was positively affected by practicality and commonweal ($\beta = 0.219$, $p < 0.01$; $\beta = 0.326$, $p < 0.001$) while interactivity had no significant impact on perceived trust, H1a and H4a were thus supported. Perceived value was positively affected by practicality, interactivity, preferential and commonweal ($\beta = 0.255$, $p < 0.01$; $\beta = 0.157$, $p < 0.001$; $\beta = 0.240$, $p < 0.001$; $\beta = 0.157$, $p < 0.05$), thus supposing H1b, H2b, H3 and H4b. In addition, perceived trust and perceived value were both positively associated with purchase intention ($\beta = 0.273$, $p < 0.001$; $\beta = 0.455$, $p < 0.001$), H5 and H6 were therefore supported. In addition, 43.5% variance of perceived trust and 41.8% variance of perceived value were explained, which in turn explained 55.7% variance of purchase intention.

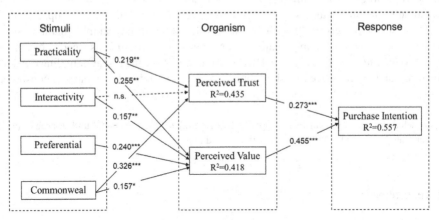

Fig. 2. Structural model

5 Conclusions

In recent years, livestreaming e-commerce has been booming in China and attracted increasing attention from scholars, especially during the epidemic. However, there is a lack of empirical exploration on agricultural products live-streaming, which is beneficial for targeted poverty alleviation and agricultural development, thus of great practical significance and value. To fill above-mentioned gap, this study integrated stimulus-organism-response (S-O-R) model, perceived trust theory and perceived value theory, in order to develop a comprehensive research framework and examine how the stimulus factors (practicality, interactivity, preferential, and commonweal) ultimately affect consumers' purchase intention through the mediation of organism factors (perceived trust and perceived value) in agricultural products live-streaming context. The results supported most of the hypotheses (except H2a) and strongly supported the proposed model, indicating that practicality, interactivity, preferential, and commonweal were positively associated with perceived value; practicality and commonweal positively affected perceived trust; while interactivity had no significant effect on perceived trust.

Our study makes contributions to both theory and practice. Theoretically, this is one of the first empirical study that explore the determinates of purchase intention in agricultural products live-streaming and extend the S-O-R model to the context of APLC, which provides a theoretical basis for future studies. Additionally, it is worth pointing out that this paper identifies and tests the influence mechanism of commonweal, which is rarely considered in traditional e-commerce live-streaming. We advance the existing livestreaming research by adding a new angle for APLC. Practically, our findings yield useful suggestions from different aspects for agricultural products live-streaming operators and sellers, even platforms, who are expected to maximize the effectiveness of targeted poverty alleviation in China.

Our study also has some limitations. APLC combines various attributes of livestreaming, agriculture, and e-commerce. In our model, we identified four important influencing factors, thus might fail to fully capture other related variables, which could be further investigated in future studies. And this study might fail to reflect the comprehensive views of all consumers, with limited samples. In addition, the sample characteristics were imbalanced. For example, majority of respondents were students, aged between 18 and 30 years old, which could affect the generalizability of the research findings. Additional research could solve this shortcoming by collecting data from massive consumer base.

Acknowledgment. This study was supported by the Fundamental Research Funds for the Central Universities No. NR2021003 awarded to the second author.

References

1. Bauer, R.: Consumer Behavior as Risk Taking. Dynamic Marketing for a Changing Word Chicago: America Marketing Association, pp. 389–398 (1960)
2. Bai, L., Chen, Q.: Research progress on the driving factors of customer perceived value. Foreign Econ. Manage. **7**, 39–45 (2006)
3. Chen, Y.S., Chang, C.H.: Enhance green purchase intentions: the roles of green perceived value, green perceived risk, and green trust. Manag. Decis. **50**(3–4), 502–520 (2012)
4. Childers, T.L., Carr, C.L., Peck, J., Carson, S.: Hedonic and utilitarian motivations for online retail shopping behavior. J. Retail. **77**(4), 511–535 (2002)
5. Deng, Y.: Good products from the country are competing for beauty online! 923 Global Agricultural Products Live-streaming Festival Brings Online "Carnival" of Harvest Festival. China Jiangsu Net (2021). https://baijiahao.baidu.com/s?id=1712067574964059400&wfr= spider&for=pc
6. Eroglu, S.A., Machleit, K.A., Davis, L.M.: Empirical testing of a model of online store atmospherics and shopper responses. Psychol. Mark. **20**(2), 139–150 (2003)
7. Feng, Y.F., Chen, Y.P.: Research on the information traceability of fresh agricultural products supply chain and analysis of the influence of fresh agricultural products price information on consumers' purchase intention. Price Theory Pract. **05**, 153–156 (2019)
8. Huang, L.Y.: Research on the persuasive effect of public welfare e-commerce live broadcast. Zhejiang University (2020)
9. Hu, M., Chaudhry, S.S.: Enhancing consumer engagement in e-commerce live streaming via relational bonds. Internet Res. **30**(3), 1019–1041 (2020)
10. Jarcenpaa, S., Tractinsky, N., Vitale, M.: Consumer trust in an internet store. Inf. Technol. Manage. **1**(1/2), 45–71 (2000)
11. Sweeney, J.C., Soutar, G.N.: Consumer perceived value: The development of a multiple item scale. J. Retail. **77**(2), 203–220 (2001)
12. Ji, M., Zhuo, X.Z.: The influencing factors of consumers' purchase intention in e-commerce online live broadcasting environment based on SOR model. J. Huaibei Normal Univ. (Philos. Soc. Sci. Edn.) **41**(04), 49–57 (2020)
13. Kang, K., Lu, J., Guo, L., et al.: The dynamic effect of interactivity on customer engagement behavior through tie strength: evidence from live streaming commerce platforms – ScienceDirect. Int. J. Inf. Manage. **58**, 102251 (2020)

14. Liu, F.J., Meng, L., Chen, S.Y., Duan, S.: Research on the influence of online celebrity live broadcast on consumer purchase intention and its mechanism. Chin. J. Manage. **09**, 94–104 (2020)
15. Liu, P.S., Shi, Y.D., Lin, B.K.: The influence of community interaction information on users' purchase intention under the background of e-commerce live broadcast. Manage. J. **09**, 72–79 (2020)
16. Lu, Y.B., Zhao, L., Wang, B.: From virtual community members to C2C e-commerce buyers: trust in virtual communities and its effect on consumers' purchase intention. Electron. Commer. Res. Appl. **9**(4), 346–360 (2009)
17. Mayer, R.C., Davis, J.H., Schoorman, F.D.: An integrative model of organizational trust. Acad. Manag. Rev. **20**(3), 709–734 (1995)
18. Mcknight, D.H., Choudhury, V., Kacmar, C.: Developing and validating trust measures f-or e-commerce: an integrative typology. Inf. Syst. Res. **13**(3), 334–359 (2002)
19. Mehrabian, A., Russell, J.A.: An Approach to Environmental Psychology, vol. 7, issue 1, pp. 132–133. MIT Press, Cambridge (1976)
20. Pan, Y., Zhang, X., Gao, L.: A study on factors affecting consumers' purchase intention in online retailing—based on the analysis of trust and perceived risk. China Indust. Econ. **07**, 115–124 (2010)
21. Parasuraman, A.: Reflections on gaining competitive advantage through customer value. J. Acad. Mark. Sci. **2**, 154–161 (1997)
22. Parsons, A.G.: Non-functional motives for online shoppers: why we click. J. Consum. Mark. **19**(5), 380–392 (2002)
23. Petrick, J.F., Backman, S.J.: An examination of the construct of perceived value for the pre-diction of golf travelers' intentions to revisit. J. Travel Res. **1**, 38–45 (2002)
24. Shang, W.: E-commerce live broadcasts exceeded 4 million in the first quarter. People's Daily (2020). http://paper.people.com.cn/rmrb/html/2020-05/06/nw.D110000renmrb_2020 0506_3-19.htm
25. Shao, B. J., Gao, Z.X., Shi, L.: An empirical study on influencing factors of consumers' shopping attitudes on social networking sites. J. Intell. **29**(08), 203–207+135 (2010)
26. Tan, Y.L.: The, "live broadcast + e-commerce" model from the perspective of communication science—take Jumei Youpin's live broadcast business as an example. J. Beijing Inst. Graph. Commun. **1**, 20–26 (2017)
27. Tenenhaus, M., Vinzi, V.E., Chatelin, Y.M., Lauro, C.: PLS path modelling. Comput. Stat. Data Anal. **48**(1), 159–205 (2005)
28. Wang, E.P., Ni, Z.Y.: Research on the preference characteristics of agricultural products online consumers—based on the analysis of "Jingdong" sales apple online review data. Price Theory Pract. **02**, 120–123 (2020)
29. Xu, G.W., Lu, D., Xu, X.X.: Consumer response mechanism to public welfare marketing: an explanation based on moral emotion. Marketing **15**, 54–56 (2017)
30. Ying, H.B., Lv, W., et al.: The impact of e-commerce livestreaming service quality, perceived value of commodity on customer purchase intention. J. Distrib. Manage. Res. **25**(2), 99–111 (2022)
31. Zeithaml, V.A., Berry, L.L., Parasuraman, A.: Communication and control processes in the delivery of service quality. J. Mark. **52**(2), 35–48 (2001)
32. Zhao, D.M., Ji, S.X.: An empirical study of trust and perceived risk on consumers' online purchase intention. Math. Stat. Manage. **29**(02), 305–314 (2010)
33. Zheng, X.B., Men, J.Q., Xiang, L., Yang, F.: Role of technology attraction and parasocial interaction in social shopping websites. Int. J. Inf. Manage. **51**, 102043 (2020)
34. Zhou, Y.S., Tang, S.H., Xiao, J.: A study on consumers' purchase intention of e-commerce live broadcasting platform—based on the perspective of social presence [J/OL]. Contemp. Econ. Manage. **01**, 1–11 (2021)

HCI for Energy, Environment and Sustainability

Assurance Cases as Foundation Stone for Auditing AI-Enabled and Autonomous Systems: Workshop Results and Political Recommendations for Action from the ExamAI Project

Rasmus Adler[(✉)] [iD] and Michael Klaes

Fraunhofer IESE, Kaiserslautern, Germany
{rasmus.adler,michael.klaes}@iese.fraunhofer.de

Abstract. The European Machinery Directive and related harmonized standards do consider that software is used to generate safety-relevant behavior of the machinery but do not consider all kinds of software. In particular, software based on machine learning (ML) are not considered for the realization of safety-relevant behavior. This limits the introduction of suitable safety concepts for autonomous mobile robots and other autonomous machinery, which commonly depend on ML-based functions. We investigated this issue and the way safety standards define safety measures to be implemented against software faults. Functional safety standards use Safety Integrity Levels (SILs) to define which safety measures shall be implemented. They provide rules for determining the SIL and rules for selecting safety measures depending on the SIL. In this paper, we argue that this approach can hardly be adopted with respect to ML and other kinds of Artificial Intelligence (AI). Instead of simple rules for determining an SIL and applying related measures against faults, we propose the use of assurance cases to argue that the individually selected and applied measures are sufficient in the given case. To get a first rating regarding the feasibility and usefulness of our proposal, we presented and discussed it in a workshop with experts from industry, German statutory accident insurance companies, work safety and standardization commissions, and representatives from various national, European, and international working groups dealing with safety and AI. In this paper, we summarize the proposal and the workshop discussion. Moreover, we check to which extent our proposal is in line with the European AI Act proposal and current safety standardization initiatives addressing AI and Autonomous Systems.

Keywords: Assurance cases · AI · Autonomous systems · Safety

1 Introduction

Autonomous systems are systems that achieve predefined goals in accordance with the demands of the current situation without recourse to either human control or detailed

© Springer Nature Switzerland AG 2022
M. Rauterberg et al. (Eds.): HCII 2022, LNCS 13520, pp. 283–300, 2022.
https://doi.org/10.1007/978-3-031-18158-0_21

programming [1]. The market prospects of these systems are promising. For instance, the global autonomous mobile robots market is projected to grow from $2 billion in 2021 to $8.7 billion in 2028 [2] and the global autonomous construction equipment market is expected to grow from $8.5 million in 2020 to $16.9 million in 2025 [3]. According to various roadmaps [1, 4], an autonomous system can be composed of several collaborating systems, like an intralogistics system that autonomously controls a fleet of various autonomous mobile robots and forklifts.

To put such systems on the European market, the Machinery Directive 2006/42/EC [5] has to be considered. The Machinery Directive is applicable for systems composed of several physical systems as it defines that "machinery" can be "assemblies of machinery". However, the Machinery Directive does not consider the term "autonomous" and thus not take into account that methods other than "detailed programming" are used to develop software. It demands only that a fault in the software of the control system should not lead to a hazardous situation. Safety standards that are harmonized with the Machinery Directive help practitioners to show that their systems are compliant with the Directive, giving them more detailed advice for specific aspects or types of machinery. They do consider software but focus on classical "detailed programming" and do not consider machine learning and other AI methods. Consequently, it is hardly possible to show compliance with a functional safety standard when AI is used to realize safety-relevant functionality. Autonomous systems with AI-based safety-relevant functions might thus not enter the European market even though they would increase safety and the efficiency of workflows.

Closing this gap is challenging for two reasons. First, it is challenging to develop suitable solutions for assuring the safety of autonomous systems and the correctness of their AI-based safety-relevant functions. Second, it is challenging to update the current normative and regulatory framework with respect to these solutions.

We propose the use of assurance cases to solve the first challenge, as these enable building up the required body of knowledge. We also propose integrating assurance cases into the current normative and regulatory framework. The two proposals are not novel, but we will derive them systematically from challenges with respect to the safety assurance of AI and autonomous systems. Moreover, we provide an overview of current research and standardization activities. One contribution is the formulation of the challenges that is intended to create awareness of pitfalls that may be encountered when enhancing the current normative framework based on the concept of Safety Integrity Levels (SIL), as currently applied in many safety standards. A second contribution is a discussion and evaluation of how assurance cases can help to avoid these pitfalls. The challenges and discussion presented in this paper are founded on a workshop where the problem statement was presented and assurance cases were proposed as a solution [6], as well as on a related whitepaper with policy recommendations [7].

The paper is structured as follows. First, we clarify core terms like "autonomous" or "AI" and provide some background on safety regulations and standards. Second, we state why the current safety standardization framework is in conflict with autonomy and AI. Third, we introduce assurance cases as solution. Fourth, we present to which extent this solution is being considered already in research, practice, standardization, and regulation. Fifth, we discuss and evaluate the solutions based on our workshop results. Finally, we present our conclusions and an outlook on future work.

2 Terminology and Background

2.1 Terminology on AI and Autonomous Systems

Because commonly accepted definitions are still missing – even though governments and companies are investing a lot in the topic of "AI" – it is quite unclear what actually belongs to the topic and whether the topic should not rather be called "autonomous systems". The German AI Standardization Roadmap [8] mentions the difficulties in defining AI and states that "in view of the difficulties in finding a generally accepted definition, this will not be done in this document". In the collection of definitions, the document presents five definitions of AI that are strongly related to the definition of an autonomous system in [1], which we presented in the beginning of the introduction.

To discuss challenges and solutions with respect to safety assurance, we need a term for systems that (1) behave in a very situation-specific way in a complex environment to achieve predefined goals, (2) do not or only partially depend on an operator to handle critical situations, and (3) are based on some software parts that can hardly be interpreted like software based on machine learning. In the following, we will use the term "autonomous system" for such systems, and we will use the term "AI" in order to refer to software parts that are not explicitly programmed and hard to interpret.

Our notion of AI as a special kind of software is in line with the AI definition of the European AI Act proposal. However, it emphasizes interpretability as the main aspect, thus we would not consider an interpretable expert system as AI, whereas the AI Act explicitly mentions expert systems in Annex 1, where it lists AI techniques and approaches.

Our notion of autonomous systems is in harmony with the definition we presented in the introduction. However, it supports the idea of having degrees of autonomy by being more or less dependent on an operator and by having more or less interpretability.

2.2 Background on Safety and Compliance

The Machinery Directive defines Essential Health and Safety Requirements (EHSR) that apply to all manufacturers who wish to put their products on the European market. Standards that are harmonized with the Machinery Directive support the demonstration of compliance with the ESHR. Of particular importance is EN ISO 12100, which provides a comprehensive list of different types of hazards and proposes the following three steps to address them.

The first step is called **inherently safe design.** In this step, hazards are avoided or related risks are inherently limited. For instance, inherently safe design could result in a design that avoids sharp edges in an engine with less power to inherently limit the speed of some machinery or some moving parts of it in order to limit the severity of a potential collision. In the second step, **technical protection mechanisms** are introduced. If the mechanisms are implemented by electric, electronic, or programmable electronic (software) means, a functional safety standard like IEC 61508 shall be applied to address potential malfunctions. For instance, a light barrier that triggers a shutdown is such a mechanism. In the third step, **user information about the intended use and the residual risk** is provided. For instance, warning signs are attached to the machinery in order to avoid critical deviations from the intended use.

These three steps shall be applied with an order of precedence. For instance, removing a hazard in step 1 has preference over addressing it with a protection mechanism in step 2. Similarly, a protection mechanism that detects and handles critical deviations from the intended use is better than a warning sign.

The application of the three steps results in a safety concept that needs to be enhanced with respect to critical malfunctions. A critical failure mode of any protection mechanism is obviously an omission because the protection mechanism cannot achieve the intended risk reduction if it omits acting as intended. However, other failure modes of a protection mechanism can also be safety-critical. For instance, a shutdown could be critical if it occurs in the wrong situation. Furthermore, malfunctions of functionalities other than protection mechanisms could be safety-critical.

The safety concept resulting from the 3-step method may prevent that these malfunctions lead to a hazardous situation, but this needs to checked. Thus, it is reasonable to assess every functionality with respect to safety. If it might be safety-critical, then every failure mode needs to be evaluated with respect to the risks that exist if the failure mode occurs. The higher the risks, the more safety measures should be applied to avoid the occurrence of the failure mode. In order to implement this relationship between risk and safety measures, functional safety standards define risk parameters, a mapping from possible parameter values to Safety Integrity Levels (SILs), and a mapping from SILs to safety measures to be applied (cf. Fig. 1).

The latter mapping is intended to give safety engineers some freedom when choosing safety measures; that is, one SIL can be realized by applying different combinations of safety measures.

Software Engineering Steps
(Requirements, Architecture,...)

Technique/Measure	SIL 1	SIL 2	SIL 3	SIL 4
Traditional Safety measure 1	-	Recommended	Highly Recommended	Highly Recommended
Traditional Safety measure 2	Recommended	Recommended	Highly Recommended	Highly Recommended
measure 2	Recommended	Recommended	Recommended	Recommended

Fig. 1. Illustration of tables for SIL-dependent selection of safety measures

3   Key Challenges in Assuring AI and Autonomous Systems 1

In this section, we will explain why the 3-step method and the SIL concept are generally not sufficient for autonomous systems and AI-based safety functions.

Inherently safe design is a reasonable approach for autonomous systems as long as it does not overly limit the utility of an autonomous system's situation-specific behavior. Unfortunately, this is very often the case. For instance, the inherent limitation of the speed and force of a gripper of a collaborative robot (cobot) reduces risks but lowers the performance of the cobot. Technical protection measures can act in a situation-specific manner in order to optimize the trade-off between safety and performance. For instance, a protection measure could limit the speed only if a human is close to the cobot. However, traditional protection measures are quite simple and not very situation-specific. Considering a mobile robot, a traditional measure would be a simple emergency stop rather than a situation-specific evasion maneuver. In many situations, situation-agnostic behavior typically results in unnecessarily low performance or availability. Situation-specific behavior can overcome this disadvantage. However, it is **challenging to assure safety if the safety concept comprises less inherently safe design, but some safety functions act in a very situation-specific manner in a complex context (problem 1)**. Situation-specific safety functions perceive the current situation and anticipate possible scenarios in order to perform in the best possible way from a safety perspective. The perception and anticipation capabilities go hand in hand with many implicit assumptions concerning the usage context, due to sensor limitations and calculation assumptions. For example, to conduct a successful evasion maneuver, the speed and direction of the human and other obstacles in the given context need to be anticipated, as must possible occlusions or other limitations in perception. It is **challenging to identify all these context assumptions and assure that they are fulfilled (problem 1.1)**. Another challenge stems from the open context. If the concrete operational context is not known or not constrained, safety engineers can hardly foresee and test all relevant operating conditions and scenarios. It is hard to assure that safety is achieved when the situation-specific safety functions act as specified, because the specified behavior might be unsafe in some **unforeseen edge cases (problem 1.2)**. For instance, autonomous mobile robots shall support various use cases and environments like open work yards with bicyclists and many other moving objects that need to be considered. If safety engineers are not aware of some types of moving objects, then the robots' evasive maneuvers might be inadequate for these kinds of objects.

Another issue is that **AI is not considered in functional safety standards and the related SIL-based selection of safety measures for software (problem 2)**. AI supports the implementation of situation-sensitive safety functions. For instance, data-driven models like deep neural networks for object classification are a powerful means for implementing the required perception capabilities. The development steps for such models differ significantly from the development steps for traditional software. In addition, the measures for fault avoidance, fault removal, fault tolerance, and fault forecasting also differ significantly. Consequently, the tables in safety standards like IEC 61508 that define which safety measures shall be applied in a certain development step depending on the SIL of the safety function are insufficient. As illustrated in Fig. 2, a conceivable option could be to enhance the SIL concept by introducing development steps for a particular kind of AI and related tables that define which safety measure shall be applied depending on the SIL of the safety function.

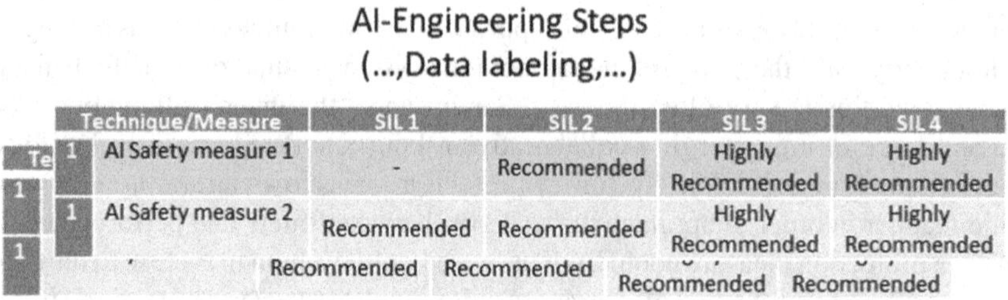

AI-Engineering Steps
(...,Data labeling,...)

Technique/Measure	SIL 1	SIL 2	SIL 3	SIL 4
AI Safety measure 1	-	Recommended	Highly Recommended	Highly Recommended
AI Safety measure 2	Recommended	Recommended	Highly Recommended	Highly Recommended
	Recommended	Recommended	Recommended	Recommended

Fig. 2. Illustration of a possible SIL-dependent selection of safety measures for AI

In doing so, the selection of new AI safety measures should be as effective for AI as the traditional ones for programmed software if the SIL is the same. This intuitive requirement is hard to fulfill for at least two reasons. First, there is **no explicit claim concerning the effectiveness of safety measures for software that has to be achieved (problem 2.1)**. Safety standards do not define metrics for measuring the effectiveness. There are probabilistic target values for safety functions depending on the SIL, but these values are only considered for dealing with random hardware faults, not for dealing with systematic faults, and all software faults are considered systematic faults. The second reason is that general **SIL-oriented claims concerning effectiveness can hardly be fulfilled for AI in practice (problem 2.2)**. For instance, the target failure probability of an SIL 4 safety function is 10^{-4} to 10^{-5} per demand. Data-driven models for common classification tasks generally have a likelihood of misclassification of between 10^{-1} and 10^{-3} (depending on the specific task), even if many state-of-the-practice measures have been applied to minimize the failure likelihood.

4   Advanced Assurance Cases for Autonomous Systems and AI

We propose assurance cases to deal with the presented challenges. In the following, we will present our proposal and discuss to which extent it solves or avoids these problems. First, we will introduce assurance cases as a general approach. Second, we will explain how assurance cases can support the systematic identification of context assumptions (problem 1.1). Third, we will present how assurance cases can be enhanced to deal with the problem of unknown edge cases (problem 1.2). Fourth, we will propose solutions to overcome the problem that there are no explicit claims concerning the effectiveness of safety measures (problem 2.2) and that SIL-oriented claims are hardly achievable (problem 2.2).

4.1   Assurance Cases

According to ISO/IEC/IEEE 15026, an assurance case is a reasoned, auditable artifact that supports the contention that its top-level claim (or set of claims) is satisfied, including systematic argumentation and its underlying evidence and explicit assumptions that support the claim(s). Figure 3 illustrates the general structure of an assurance case and the relationships of its key concepts. The left side shows that it basically comprises three elements: (1) some top-level claims saying that some objectives or constraints are fulfilled, (2) an argument or argumentation supporting the top-level claims, and (3) some evidence on which the argument is based.

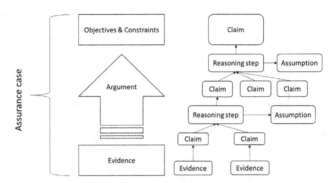

Fig. 3. Illustration of an assurance case

As shown in the right part of Fig. 3, the argument can be structured by means of reasoning steps. In other words, the argumentation can be decomposed into different hierarchically structured arguments. However, we will use the terms "argument" and "reasoning step". Each reasoning step connects some sub-claims (or premises) with a higher-level claim (or conclusion). The reasoning step denotes that the higher-level claim is fulfilled if the sub-claims are fulfilled and if related assumptions hold.

In this paper, we focus on assurance cases where the top-level claim(s) relate to safety. In the case of a supplier of a safety component, the top-level claims refer to some safety properties of the component. In the case of a manufacturer of an autonomous system like a driverless transport system consisting of a fleet of autonomous mobile robots and other elements like cameras on the ceiling, the top-level claim refers to an acceptable level of safety for the intended use of the autonomous system. In the case of an operating company, the top-level claim refers to an acceptable level of safety for the concrete usage of the autonomous system.

Furthermore, we will focus on an approach that modularizes assurance cases and makes them composable. By means of this approach, a manufacturer can build their assurance case based on the assurance cases of their suppliers. The left part of Fig. 4 illustrates such a modular assurance case. For instance, we consider a component that provides information on whether a worker is in a certain area. A top-level claim could be that the information is always correct if some assumptions hold. Some assumptions could refer to the absence of some failure modes of the input information. As illustrated in the right part of Fig. 4, these assumptions create a link to the assurance case of the component that provides the required information. The manufacturer can ensure that the guarantee and demand interfaces of the different components fit to each other.

The red circles in Fig. 4 refer to assumptions that cannot be fulfilled by other components and constrain the usage. For instance, if a worker is detected by means of an infrared camera, then a fundamental assumption is that the worker has a certain temperature and this temperature is detectable by an infrared camera in spite of any clothes that the

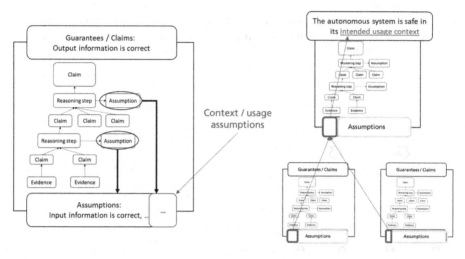

Fig. 4. Illustration of the modularization of an assurance case

worker might wear or other circumstances. Accordingly, some restrictions concerning the clothes that the workers are allowed to wear could limit the intended usage.

A concrete solution that implements this modular approach is shown in Fig. 5.

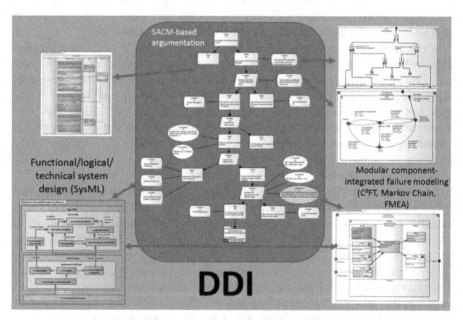

Fig. 5. Illustration of a Digital Dependability Identity (DDI)

It illustrates a Digital Dependability Identity (DDI). The core of a DDI is a formalized assurances case. This core links to several models that are necessary to understand the safety argumentation; e.g., the hazard and risk assessment (HARA), the architecture including a functional, a logical, and a technical perspective, and different error-propagation models like component fault trees. By means of these models, a DDI describes in detail how assumptions have been derived, e.g., from a fault tree analysis. In addition, arguments for getting confidence in the completeness of the assumptions can be provided. Accordingly, these arguments are referred to as confidence arguments in [9].

4.2 Identifying Context Assumptions with Assurance Cases

Assurance cases are a means to explain how context assumptions have been derived and to provide arguments for their completeness. This enables assessing the argument and reasoning about its completeness. This kind of assessment differs from checking the requirements of a safety standard, which demands techniques for identifying context assumptions, because the argument that the implementation of some requirements leads to a complete set of assumptions is implicit. It is not based on the concrete results of the techniques demanded by the standard. An auditor can check all the work products of a safety standard, but the argument why these work products demonstrate the achievement of safety is implicit. This becomes a problem when fundamental assumptions that have been made when the standard was developed are no longer met; an example is the assumption that safety functions are rather simple and do not act in a very situation-specific manner in a complex environment. ISO 26262 uses the term safety-related function for a function that has the potential to contribute to the violation of a safety goal. The naming "safety-related" hints at functions that are not introduced for safety purposes like steering but that are safety-related. These functions have typically higher complexity than dedicated safety function that have been introduced in the second step of the 3-step method of ISO 12100.

However, functions comprising high situational awareness are not sufficiently addressed by the requirements of ISO 26262. Instead, the safety standard ISO/PAS 21448 (SOTIF – Safety of the Intended Functionality) has been developed in order to address performance limitations and insufficient situational awareness. The scope of ISO/PAS 21448 includes Advanced Driver Assistance Systems (ADAS) providing a low level of automation (i.e., SAE levels 1 and 2 according to SAE J3016), but the standard mentions that higher levels of automation might need additional measures. This means that the implicit argument would have some gaps. It would be hard to identify these gaps without making the implicit argument explicit. As illustrated in Fig. 6, this can be done by means of an assurance case that uses the concrete outcomes from the requirements that have been implemented as evidences. We believe that such an assurance case can help to identify and address fundamental gaps of existing standards as well as gaps that are specific to the way the standards have been applied. In particular, it can help to access the completeness of the context assumptions by checking whether the manufacturer has considered all relevant aspects of the concrete usage context and whether the supplier has considered all relevant aspects of how their component is integrated into the autonomous system of the manufacturer.

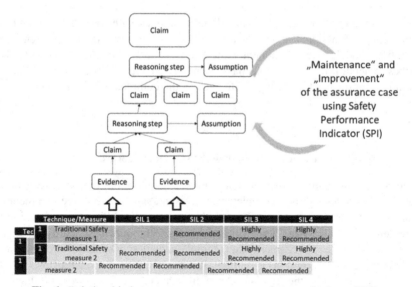

The following table appears within the figure:

Technique/Measure	SIL 1	SIL 2	SIL 3	SIL 4
Traditional Safety measure 1	-	Recommended	Highly Recommended	Highly Recommended
Traditional Safety measure 2	Recommended	Recommended	Highly Recommended	Highly Recommended
measure 2	Recommended	Recommended	Recommended	Recommended

Fig. 6. Relationship between an assurance case, safety standards, and SPIs

4.3 Identifying Unknown Edge Cases with Safety Performance Indicators (SPIs)

Figure 6 also illustrates the approach for attaching Safety Performance Indicators (SPIs) [10] to claims and assumptions in order to check after deployment of the system if they are true in application. For example, assumptions or claims concerning the frequency of situations could be measured by SPIs. This would contribute to the effectiveness of market surveillance. Furthermore, it would support the identification of unknown edge cases. An edge case that is relevant for a claim but that was not known and thus not considered in the underlying argumentation can be identified when measuring the fulfillment of a claim with SPIs. This approach is explained in more detail in [11] and considered in the ANSI/UL 4600 Standard for Evaluation of Autonomous Products [12]. The challenge of dealing with unknown edge cases or "unknown unknowns" is well known in the context of automated driving of road vehicles [13] because they operate in complex environments like cities. However, we see no reason why this approach should not be adopted for many kinds of machinery that are in the scope of the Machinery Directive [5] or the upcoming regulation on machinery products [14]. One example is autonomous mobile machinery that operates in open work yards where it is hard to foresee all possible harmful scenarios. The current draft of the regulation [15] already defines the Essential Health and Safety Requirement that "the risk assessment that manufacturers must carry out before the machinery is placed on the market/put into service will need to include also the risks appearing after the machinery is placed on the market due to its evolving and autonomous behavior". We see the use of assurance cases with SPIs as one powerful means for implementing this requirement.

4.4 Claims and Argument Structure for AI-Based Safety Functions

Figure 6 does not show tables with SIL-dependent safety techniques/measures for AI as illustrated in Fig. 2. Instead of introducing such tables, we propose developing a generic argument structure that can be instantiated or adapted. We provide various kinds of guidance encoded in this generic structure. First, we propose demonstrating that data-driven models are avoided as far as reasonably practicable. This means that it has to be argued that a data-driven model can hardly be replaced with traditional safety-critical software. Second, the consequences of failures of the data-driven model have to be reduced as far as reasonably practicable, e.g., by means of architectural measures such as fault tolerance mechanisms and plausibility checks. If these prerequisites are fulfilled, we propose arguing over the different elements of the autonomous system so that a claim for every data-driven model is established.

As illustrated in Fig. 7, we would start with the claim that the data-driven model is sufficiently safe [37]. In the next step, we would make more concrete what we mean by "sufficiently" by means of two claims considering complementary risk acceptance criteria. The first claim is that the probabilities of the critical failure modes have been reduced as far as reasonably practicable. The second claim is that this reduction satisfies target failure probabilities. The first claim relates to safety measures during the lifecycle phases "Specification", "Construction", "Analysis", and "Operation", because in these

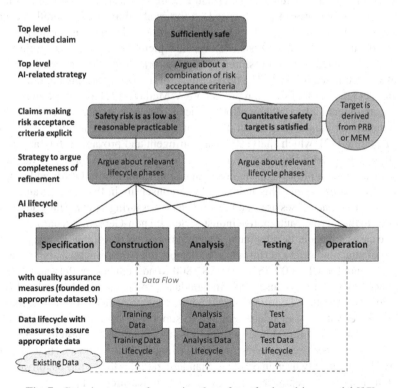

Fig. 7. Generic structure for arguing the safety of a data-driven model [37]

phases, the failure probabilities can be reduced. The second claim relates to safety measures during the lifecycle phases "Specification", "Testing", and "Operation", because these phases are relevant to assuring that the residual failure probability is determined correctly. Because different phases rely on different datasets with different qualities, we also need to argue about the data used in these phases. Figure 7 illustrates only the general idea and not the argumentation with reasoning steps and concrete safety measures for data-driven models, as this is not relevant for discussing the role of assurance cases in regulation and standardization for AI systems and autonomous systems.

5   Assurance Cases in Research, Practice, Standardization, and Regulation

In the previous section, we sketched how the presented challenges concerning the safety assurance of AI and autonomous systems can be handled by means of assurance cases. We presented this sketch [16] in a workshop [17] in order to discuss it with relevant stakeholders and derive policy recommendations. Before summarizing the discussion and the recommendations in the next section, we will reflect on some activities and work in research, practice, standardization, and regulation that we considered when coming up with the proposal for focusing on assurance cases.

The solution sketch is related to German research projects focusing on automated driving. The Pegasus project [18] focused on the establishment of generally accepted quality criteria, tools, and methods as well as scenarios and situations for the release of highly automated driving functions. The overview picture of the Pegasus project illustrates that the complete testing and simulation framework is only for generating evidences for a safety argumentation [19]. The development of this safety argumentation was part of the project [20]. In the follow-up project V&V Methods [21], the work on this overall safety argumentation continues. Both projects did not consider in detail the safety argumentation for data-driven AI models. This challenge is considered in the project KI-Absicherung [22], which shall establish a stringent and provable safety argumentation with which AI-based functions can be secured and validated for highly automated driving. In all of these projects, the majority of German automotive OEMs and suppliers are part of the consortium. This indicates large consensus in the German automotive industry that assurance cases are a suitable means for assuring safety. This consensus is not limited to the German automotive industry. Several non-German standards for safety assurance cases are under development. The first one was UL 4600 [12]. The presented approach of attaching safety performance indicators to elements in an assurance case is already presented in UL 4600. ISO/NP PAS 8800 Road Vehicles - Safety and Artificial Intelligence [23] provides industry-specific guidance on the use of safety-related Artificial Intelligence/Machine Learning (AI/ML)-based functions in road vehicles. Its scope includes the derivation of evidence required to support an assurance argument for the overall safety of the system. This scope highlights the importance of arguing safety in an assurance case. Our projects with the automotive industry have shown us that assurance cases are already heavily used in practice. Standardization is thus a reasonable next step for documenting this acceptance of assurance cases in research and practice.

In aeronautics, assurance cases are also seen as a major solution approach for dealing with increasingly autonomous systems. The authors of the technical report "Considerations in Assuring Safety of Increasingly Autonomous Systems" from NASA believe that "an assurance case is the most suitable method to formalize the arguments and evidence … - providing a basis for assurance and certification of increasingly autonomous systems." The authors of another NASA report claim that assurances cases "address modern certification challenges" (cf. Sect. 5.5) and explicitly mention "Managing Certification of Innovative Technology" (cf. Sect. 5.5.4) as one challenge [24]. However, the European Union Aviation Safety Agency does not explicitly mention assurance cases in its guidance for machine learning applications [25] or its AI roadmap [26].

In the nuclear, railway, and medical industries, safety assurance cases are also well-known and established [24]. Furthermore, assurance cases are considered in defense, for example, in the DARPA Assured Autonomy Program [27] and in the assurance case framework from the Institute for Defense Analyses [28].

To tackle the challenges of autonomy, Asaadi et al. propose dynamic assurance using assurance cases that can be executed and evaluated during operation [29]. In the DEIS project [30], such machine-readable assurance cases called runtime DDIs are also considered. As we found several research activities in this and related fields, we initiated a workshop called Dynamic Risk managEment for AutonoMous Systems (DREAMS) in order to structure this new research field and create synergies [31]. As many of the solutions in this research field are, however, still in their infancy, we did not include them in our solution sketch.

Considering domains that are related to the Machinery Directive, like mining, agriculture, or manufacturing, assurance cases are considered in research but almost completely neglected in practice and standardization. The reason for this might be that (1) safety criticality is generally lower, (2) system complexity is lower, and (3) there is less need to use AI for realizing safety-critical functions compared to domains where assurance cases are already heavily used. The NASA/CR–2017-219582 report mentions these three challenges of modern certification that can be handled by means of assurance cases [24].

Autonomous systems that are in the scope of the Machinery Directive are addressed by the German application rule VDE-AR-E 2842-61 "Development and trustworthiness of autonomous/cognitive systems" [34]. This application rule has assurance cases as one of its key concepts but refers to them as trustworthiness assurance cases because the application rule considers not only safety but also other trustworthiness aspects.

To the best of our knowledge, assurance cases are not considered in regulation for AI and autonomous system. In particular, they are not considered in the current version of the European AI Act proposal [35]. We can only speculate why this is the case even though the goal-based nature of assurance cases is generally suitable for regulation, because regulation is more technology-neutral and more abstract than standardization. One reason could be that it would be too generic to demand only the development and auditing of assurance cases. However, an assurance framework like the Zenzic safety case framework [32] could introduce more concrete requirements concerning the development and auditing of assurance cases. Moreover, regulation could fix the first reasoning steps of the overall assurance case and define the resulting high-level claims as regulatory requirements that have to be shown. For instance, the AI Act follows a risk-based approach by defining three risk classes for AI systems and related measures for each class. An implicit argument or assumption here is that the measures are effective and do not lead to unnecessarily high effort that could be better used for other tasks to reduce risks. The authors of [33] put this into question; they propose more risk levels and a VCIO model that provides traces between Values, Critera, Indicators, and Observables. The VCIO model has similarities with an assurance case, as the traces between Observables and Values are similar to the traces between evidences and top-level claims or objectives.

6   Discussion About Issues with Assurance Cases for Certification

In context of the ExamAI project, we discussed the proposal of using assurance cases as a basis for the certification of autonomous machinery and AI-based safety functions with relevant stakeholders. We focused on machinery with smart manufacturing use cases due to the scope of the project. The discussion was, however, not limited to this focus and considered the horizontal regulation of AI with the European AI Act proposal. The results of the discussions in ExamAI have been published in a policy paper [7]. In the following, we will summarize the findings of the discussion in which we were involved.

A first finding concerns the issue of auditing an assurance case and coming up with objective criteria for assessing its acceptability. Ideally, different auditors would always arrive at the same results when assessing an assurance case. A process-based approach as presented in the Zenzic safety case framework [32] cannot solve this issue, as it defines only how the case is assessed but not under which conditions it is accepted. Research proposes some techniques for quantifying confidence in assurance arguments but the work in [36] concludes that there is "no plausible justification for relying on one of these techniques in making decisions about which critical systems to deploy or continue to operate".

A related issue is that there are different guidelines for developing and structuring an assurance case. The proposal shown in Fig. 7 and published in [37] does, for instance, differ from the AMLAS approach [38]. One goal of a current research project [39] is to achieve consensus on the relationship between the approaches and integrate them. It is currently being evaluated to which extent the approach shown in Fig. 7 can be seen as an instantiation of the AMLAS approach, and to which extent the top-level claims in Fig. 7 could be used as generic objective criteria for an assessment.

Another issue concerns the impact on industry and their concerns. One general concern is intellectual property (IP). As illustrated in Fig. 4, our proposal implies that supplier, manufacturer, and operator work together on an integrated end-to-end assurance case. One could try to use modularization for IP protection purposes and hide the inner part of a modular assurance case. However, this approach has its limits. Different organizations have different knowledge and thus different capabilities for reviewing arguments and finding counterarguments. The conflict between IP protection and safety is a fundamental issue, but assurance cases suggest a solution that focuses on support for safety. In general, assurance cases are a very flexible and cost-efficient solution as one can really focus on what contributes to safety. However, a checklist-based approach requires less reasoning and can thus be faster and cheaper.

A related issue is the necessary level of expertise. Developing and auditing an assurance case for an AI-based safety function requires a high level of expertise with respect to safety assurance and data science. A skilled labor shortage exists in both areas and people that have a rich background in both areas are extremely rare. Thus, some guidance explaining what an assurance case for autonomous machinery should look like is necessary, not only for the purpose of objective assessment. Developing such guidance is a research task that has to consider acceptance by all relevant stakeholders, including industry, notified bodies, and public authorities like market surveillance authorities.

7 Policy Recommendations and Conclusions

In the ExamAI project, policy recommendations [7] have been derived to address the issues concerning certification based on assurance cases. In the following, we will summarize these three recommendations and draw conclusions.

The first recommendation is to create experimental spaces in which the solution approach can be applied and evaluated. The recommendation is in line with the "regulatory sandboxes" being considered in the European AI Act proposal in order to evaluate applications of AI systems. In the automotive domain, areas have been chosen where a specific infrastructure for automated driving is to be introduced, and many pilot projects are trying to introduce autonomous shuttle buses [40]. Such projects are essential to building the necessary body of knowledge for the safety assurance of autonomous systems. However, unlike in the automotive domain, there are only few projects in the smart manufacturing domain.

Assurance cases can be seen as a tool for building and communicating the body of knowledge. They help deal with empirical evidences but cannot generate them. On the one hand, autonomous machinery supports use cases that contribute to sustainability, well-being, and economic growth. On the other hand, building up the required body of knowledge for their safety assurance is very elaborative, expensive pioneer work. For this reason, means such as financial support have to make sure that all relevant stakeholders support this pioneer work even if they do not profit directly from the use cases.

A second recommendation concerns standardization support. AI-based safety functions and autonomous systems will be regulated and standards can significantly ease the task of triggering the presumption of conformity. However, it takes time and effort to achieve consensus on normative requirements for developing, monitoring, improving, and auditing assurance cases. Not all organizations can invest this time and effort. It is generally easier for large organizations than for small organizations. Furthermore, not all organizations that could contribute have sufficient incentives. For instance, some universities and research institutes with valuable expertise may struggle to find concrete benefits. Support for standardization should thus include means for accelerating the process and incentives for organizations to contribute with high expertise.

A third recommendation concerns a transculturation for many stakeholders. Safety culture is an established term that also hints at a certain mindset. As the AI research community and the safety research community have traditionally worked in isolation, their mindsets are different. However, both communities have to work together and find a consensus in order to develop solutions for the safety assurance of autonomous systems and AI-based safety functions. We see assurance cases as a suitable means for this collaboration because it demands explanatory power. It harmonizes with the high level of rigor in safety assurance but also with the empirical aspects of data science. The change in the safety community concerns the transition from checklist-based approaches to assurance cases. The change in the AI community concerns the introduction of a safety culture, related higher levels of rigor in engineering, and the representation of the level of rigor in an assurance case.

Please note that the policy paper [7] presents exactly these three recommendations but the descriptions differ. For instance, it considers industry, standardization organizations, and authorities of market surveillance when presenting transculturation with respect to assurance cases. The policy paper is in German and addresses politicians. The final report addresses a larger audience but is also in German. Our intention was to share the discussions within the ExamAI project and its conclusions with the growing Safety and AI research community.

We conclude that assurance cases are state of the art for assuring the safety of autonomous systems and AI-based functions, but this consensus in research is currently not reflected in relevant regulation and standardization. UL 4600, VDE-AR-E 2842-61, and ISO/NP PAS 8800 do consider assurance cases, but these standards are novel or under development and their acceptance by industry is currently unclear. Also, only ISO/NP PAS 8800 is at the international level, and its scope is limited to road vehicles. The technical report ISO/IEC AWI TR 5469 "Artificial intelligence - Functional safety and AI systems", which is related to the international basic functional safety standard IEC 61508, is currently rather going in the direction of a rule-based approach.

Acknowledgments. Parts of this work have been funded by the Observatory for Artificial Intelligence in Work and Society (KIO) of the Denkfabrik Digitale Arbeitsgesellschaft in the project "KI Testing & Auditing" (ExamAI) and by the project "LOPAAS" as part of the internal funding program "ICON" of the Fraunhofer Society. We would like to thank Sonnhild Namingha for the initial review of the paper.

References

1. Fachforum Autonome Systeme im Hightech-Forum: Autonome Systeme – Chancen und Risiken für Wirtschaft, Wissenschaft und Gesellschaft. Langversion, Abschlussbericht, Berlin (2017)
2. Fortune Business Insights. https://www.fortunebusinessinsights.com/autonomous-mobile-robots-market-105055. Accessed 19 Jan 2022
3. Global Autonomous Construction Equipment Opportunities and Strategies Market Report. https://www.thebusinessresearchcompany.com/report/autonomous-construction-equipment-market. Accessed 19 Jan 2022
4. Brand new roadmap: Safety, Security, and Certifiability of Future Man-Machine Systems. https://www.safetrans-de.org/en/Latest-reports/brand-new-roadmap-%22safety%2C-security%2C-and-certifiability-of-future-man-machine-systems%22/286. Accessed 19 Jan 2022
5. Machinery directive. https://eur-lex.europa.eu/legal-content/en/ALL/?uri=CELEX%3A32006L0042. Accessed 19 Jan 2022

6. KI Testing & Auditing - Gesellschaft für Informatik e.V. https://testing-ai.gi.de/meldung/workshop-zu-ki-in-der-industrieproduktion-zwischen-potenzial-risiko-und-regulierung. Accessed 19 Jan 2022
7. KI in der Industrie absichern & prüfen – Was leisten Assurance Cases? https://www.stiftung-nv.de/sites/default/files/ki_in_der_industrie_sichern_und_prufen.pdf. Accessed 19 Jan 2022
8. German Standardization Roadmap on Artificial Intelligence. https://www.din.de/resource/blob/772610/e96c34dd6b12900ea75b460538805349/normungsroadmap-en-data.pdf. Accessed 19 Jan 2022
9. Hawkins, R., Kelly, T., Knight, J., Graydon, P.: A new approach to creating clear safety arguments. In: Dale, C., Anderson, T. (eds.) Advances in Systems Safety, pp. 3–23. Springer London, London (2011). https://doi.org/10.1007/978-0-85729-133-2_1
10. A More Precise Definition for ANSI/UL 4600 Safety Performance Indicators (SPIs). https://safeautonomy.blogspot.com/2021/06/a-more-precise-definition-of-ansiul.html. Accessed 19 Jan 2022
11. Keynote: A Safety Case plus SPIs Metric Approach for Self-Driving Car Safety" DREAMS Workshop at EDCC 2020. https://www.youtube.com/watch?v=FsKbCV7MWmk. Accessed 19 Jan 2022
12. Presenting the Standard for Safety for the Evaluation of Autonomous Vehicles and Other Products. https://ul.org/UL4600. Accessed 19 Jan 2022
13. Bounding the open context - Specifying safety requirements for automated driving. https://assuringautonomy.medium.com/bounding-the-open-context-26cf01da2e1c. Accessed 19 Jan 2022
14. Webpage: Proposal for a REGULATION OF THE EUROPEAN PARLIAMENT AND OF THE COUNCIL on machinery products. https://eur-lex.europa.eu/legal-content/EN/ALL/?uri=COM:2021:202:FIN. Accessed 19 Jan 2022
15. Proposal for a REGULATION OF THE EUROPEAN PARLIAMENT AND OF THE COUNCIL on machinery products - 21.4.2021. https://eur-lex.europa.eu/resource.html?uri=cellar:1f0f10ee-a364-11eb-9585-01aa75ed71a1.0001.02/DOC_1&format=PDF. Accessed 19 Jan 2022
16. Workshop zu KI in der Industrieproduktion – zwischen Potenzial, Risiko und Regulierung. https://testing-ai.gi.de/meldung/workshop-zu-ki-in-der-industrieproduktion-zwischen-potenzial-risiko-und-regulierung. Accessed 19 Jan 2022
17. Assurance Cases als Prüf- und Zertifizierungsgrundlage von KI. https://testing-ai.gi.de/fileadmin/GI/Projekte/KI_Testing_Auditing/Assurance_Cases_als_Pruef-_und_Zertifizierungsgrundlage_von_KI_final_Draft_offcial.pdf. Accessed 19 Jan 2022
18. Pegasus project homepage. https://www.pegasusprojekt.de/en/home. Accessed 19 Jan 2022
19. Pegasus method picture. https://www.pegasusprojekt.de/en/pegasus-method. Accessed 19 Jan 2022
20. Pegasus Safety Argumentation. https://www.pegasusprojekt.de/files/tmpl/pdf/PEGASUS%20Safety%20Argumentation.pdf. Accessed 19 Jan 2022
21. V&V project homepage. https://www.vvm-projekt.de/en/. Accessed 19 Jan 2022
22. KI-Absicherung project homepage. https://www.ki-absicherung-projekt.de/en/. Accessed 19 Jan 2022
23. ISO/TC 22 N 4142, ISO/NP PAS 8800 Road Vehicles -- Safety and Artificial Intelligence. https://standardsdevelopment.bsigroup.com/projects/9021-05782#/section. Accessed 19 Jan 2022
24. Understanding What It Means for Assurance Cases to "Work". https://core.ac.uk/download/pdf/83530236.pdf. Accessed 19 Jan 2022
25. EASA First usable guidance for Level 1 machine learning applications. https://www.easa.europa.eu/newsroom-and-events/news/easa-releases-its-concept-paper-first-usable-guidance-level-1-machine-0. Accessed 19 Jan 2022

26. EASA AI roadmap. https://www.easa.europa.eu/downloads/109668/en. Accessed 19 Jan 2022
27. DARPA Assured Autonomy Program. https://www.darpa.mil/program/assured-autonomy. Accessed 19 Jan 2022
28. David, M.T.: T&E of Cognitive EW: An Assurance Case Frame-work (Conference Presentation). Institute for Defense Analyses (2020). http://www.jstor.org/stable/resrep25251
29. Asaadi, E., Denney, E., Menzies, J., Pai, G.J., Petroff, D.: Dynamic assurance cases: a pathway to trusted autonomy. Computer **53**(12), 35–46 (2020). https://doi.org/10.1109/MC.2020.302 2030
30. DEIS Project homepage. https://www.deis-project.eu/. Accessed 19 Jan 2022
31. DREAMS workshop homepage. https://www.iese.fraunhofer.de/en/seminare_training/edcc-workshop.html. Accessed 19 Jan 2022
32. ZENZIC Safety Case Framework Report. https://zenzic.io/content/uploads/2020/03/Zenzic-Safety-Framework-Report-2.0-final.pdf. Accessed 19 Jan 2022
33. From Principles to Practice - An interdisciplinary framework to operationalize AI ethics. https://www.ai-ethics-impact.org/resource/blob/1961130/c6db9894ee73aefa48 9d6249f5ee2b9f/aieig---report---download-hb-data.pdf. Accessed 19 Jan 2022
34. VDE-AR-E 2842-61. https://www.vde-verlag.de/standards/0800738/vde-ar-e-2842-61-1-anwendungsregel-2021-07.html. Accessed 19 Jan 2022
35. A European approach to artificial intelligence. https://digital-strategy.ec.europa.eu/en/pol icies/european-approach-artificial-intelligence. Accessed 19 Jan 2022
36. Graydon, P., Holloway, C.M.: An investigation of proposed techniques for quantifying confidence in assurance arguments. Safety Sci. **92**, 53–65 (2017)
37. Kläs, M., Adler, R., Jöckel, L., Gross, J., Reich, J.: Using complementary risk acceptance criteria to structure assurance cases for safety-critical AI vomponents. In: AISaftey 2021 at International Joint Conference on Artifical Intelligence (IJCAI), Montreal, Candada (2021)
38. AMLAS.   https://www.york.ac.uk/assuring-autonomy/news/news/amlas-published/. Accessed 19 Jan 2022
39. LOPAAS. https://www.iese.fraunhofer.de/en/press/current_releases/pm_2021_10_18_para digmenwechsel-se.html. Accessed 19 Jan 2022
40. Innovationslandkarte "Autonomes Fahren im ÖPNV". https://www.vdv.de/innovationsland karte.aspx. Accessed 19 Jan 2022

AI Application in Architecture in UAE: Optimization of Parametric Structure as a Retrofit Strategy of a Mid-rise Residential Building in Downtown Abu Dhabi

Anwar Ahmad[⊠] and Lindita Bande

United Arab Emirates University, Abu Dhabi, UAE
{202070051,lindita.bande}@uaeu.ac.ae

Abstract. Artificial intelligence is a phenomenon that influences every aspect of our life. AI applications already started to change the methods in different disciplines. Architecture is one of the disciplines that is highly affected by the developments of AI technologies. With the UAE heading to employ the new technology to lead the country and region development, it is important to explore and develop the application of AI in the strategic disciplines at the country in which the built environment is essential. This study aims to explore and develop the application of AI in UAE architecture by developing an intelligent system that can generate an optimum parametric structure as a retrofit strategy of a mid-rise residential building in downtown Abu Dhabi. A mixed qualitative, quantitative, and experimental method will be applied on the different stages of this study, The study is divided into four stages: starts with exploring AI progress in architecture, then AI Application in Architecture in UAE at this stage the system will develop, Grasshopper software will be used to develop the system, after that Building stock analysis to get the parameters, and finally apply the system on 3 chosen case study. The results for the first two stages came out and the other tow stages are still in progress. However we get primary results for the later mentioned.

Keywords: Artificial intelligence · Parametric architecture · Building retrofitting

1 Introduction

1.1 Background and Motivation

With the beginning of the Fourth Industrial Revolution, whose pillars are based on the adoption and use the modern high technology and artificial intelligence in most aspects of life at the present time and in the future, and In line with the strategic vision of UAE leadership and government to push all sectors to develop and employ the high modern technology to shape the future and solve the problems [1]. This study aims to explore how we can apply the artificial intelligence to the architectural engineering sector in UAE to facilitate, increase and reduce the cost of solving problems associated with this

© Springer Nature Switzerland AG 2022
M. Rauterberg et al. (Eds.): HCII 2022, LNCS 13520, pp. 301–313, 2022.
https://doi.org/10.1007/978-3-031-18158-0_22

sector such as energy efficiency, climate change, and problematic impact on the natural environment.

Artificial Intelligence is a high technology mechanical system that can perform any task but needs a few human efforts like visual interpretation or design-making etc. AI works and gives the best results possible by analyzing tons of data, and that's how it can excel in architecture [2]. One of the most important tools of AI that relevant to Architecture engineering is the parametric system which used and applied on the architecture on what we called parametric architecture [2]. Parametric architecture when connected with AI tool allows the architect to change specific parameters to create various types of output designs and create structures [3].

Abu Dhabi is a hot and humid region where the energy demand for the cooling load is high [4]. However, based on the site observation, the facade of the midrise buildings in downtown Abu Dhabi are not designed as per local sustainable standards that help addressing the problem of high heat, The architectural openings are not designed and not treated to reduce heat entry into the buildings, which makes the dependency of the building on energy for cooling remarkably high. In this context, there is a need to use Facades retrofit strategies that are efficient in reducing the cooling load of the buildings. This research will focus on the parametric shading structures as a retrofit strategy, this structure will design and generated using AI and machine learning application.

1.2 Research Goal and Objectives

The aim of this study to Develop and evaluating intelligent system using Artificial intelligence and machine learning. This system is to be used to Optimize an X parametric shading structure (As midrise building façade retrofitting strategy) to reach the most energy efficient design based on the building parameters. The system can be applied to any mid-rise building in Abu Dhabi city and generate the optimum parametric shading structure (see Fig. 1).

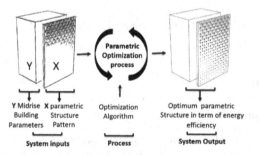

Fig. 1. Optimization system design

2   Literature Review

2.1   Artificial Intelligent

Definition

Artificial intelligence is defined as "A system's ability to interpret external data correctly, to learn from such data, and to use those learnings to achieve specific goals and tasks through flexible adaptation" [5]. If machine or system can imitate one or more of human mind functions, they will be able to called intelligent machines, systems [6].

AI is one of most important field of study in the 21st century. Different disciplines such as marketing, medicine, engineering, economy. Approach AI as a supporting force for their innovative work [5]. AI will become a part of daily life in our future, the important question to be asked here is how the AI will progress on the different disciplines especially those that depend on creativity and innovation, such as architecture and design? and which role the AI systems it will play?

AI Application in Architecture

At the middle of 1980s, programs and software designed to help architects, began to be used to generate 2D drawings and 3D models using the computers [3]. Since then, computers have been used in the realm of architecture for different purposes such as 3D modelling, animations, simulations related to the quality of space in different aspects such as ventilation, heating, durability, cost, time, form generation. After the 1990s, AI development open the door for ideas based on the application of AI to different disciplines such as architectural design. These ideas emerged in the field of architecture as creating more intelligent and interactive environments, programmable, autonomous, and informative spaces, supporting architects in such areas as decision making and optimization [6].

AI influencing architecture in many ways from different aspects and at the different phases of design and construction such as: Data collection and processing, creating design options, Building performance analysis in term of energy and structure [2]. The advantages of applying AI in architecture can appear on different aspects. Firstly, AI provides architecture with enormous amount of data and processing speed to create analytical information that have significant influence on decisions in any phase of design. Secondly, computer-aided design (CAD) programs and algorithmic or parametric design tools can generate forms that could not exist without computation [7]. Furthermore, AI makes fast, effective, and alternative methods for visualization and prototype production possible [2]. The AI have been applied on Architecture in different methods such as Evolutionary computation, Artificial neural network, Fractals, Swarm intelligence and Cellular automata [8].

2.2   Parametric Architecture

Definition
"Process of developing a computer model or description of a design problem. This representation is based on relationships between objects controlled by variables. Making changes to the variables results in alternative models. Selection of a solution is then based on some criteria which may be related to performance, ease of construction, budget requirements, user needs, aesthetics or a combination of these" [9].

AI Role in Parametric Architecture
A variety of fundamentally new parametric and compositional design methodologies are introduced because of artificial intelligence and modern computer technologies. The junction of interdisciplinarity is where natural morphogenesis and innovative parametric modeling collide. Parametricsm's mathematical algorithms are encased in an aesthetic shell, an ideological essence shaped by human intellect [10]. Generative, algorithmic, and Parametric, Architecture is primarily an efficient technique of expressing and creating geometry through scripting, which is a method of linking geometry.to decision variables [11]. There are four different types of parametric modeling techniques: procedural, associative, object modelling, and data flow, they primarily differ in terms of their capacity to facilitate iteration [12].

Visual Programming (VP) systems were created to assist designers in the process of developing scripts to construct parametric models considering different parameters such as climatic conditions, energy consumption systems defined as "any system that allows the user to specify a program in a two-(or more)-dimensional fashion". [13] non-programmers can use VP systems to construct complicated programs with minimal expertise. VP systems have come a long way since then, with software like Grasshopper, Dynamo, and Generative Components making parametric modeling more accessible to designers [11].

Parametric Architecture and Sustainability
Parametric Architecture applications can reduce the time in the design development process. Many factors in sustainable buildings, such as thermal comfort, solar radiation, energy use, can be considered design parameters in architecture. Grasshopper and other parametric design applications are used to quickly change and improve the design by combining and coordinating design elements and sustainable buildings parameters at the same time [14]. Through the development process of an energy efficient building, the designer cannot control the weather at the construction site, but he may make judgments about the structure's attributes (each of which has a different impact on its thermal performance), such as (but not limited to): The thermophysical qualities and thickness of the envelope's materials, General layout, and form (shape and orientation) (walls, roof, floor, windows etc.), Location and size of doors and windows x Shading of openings and envelope, Ventilation rate, Internal partition wall thickness and material, and Electronic and electromechanical systems (heating, cooling etc.) [14].

2.3 Optimization in the Architectural Design

By applying the Darwinian theory of evolution to the design options, one can determine the ideal combination of values for a given set of variables using Genetic Algorithm solvers as the Galapagos Evolutionary Solver24 (plugin for Grasshopper). After multiple iterations and the rejection of unsuitable solutions, the result is a pool of optimized design options that satisfy the set of objective functions [15].

There are 6 typical steps that can be used in an iterative way as building optimization procedures [16]:

1. Determine the variables and constraints of the design.
2. Choosing a simulation tool and building a baseline model
3. Choosing the objective function (s).
4. The optimization algorithm must be chosen.
5. Continue to run simulations until the optimization converges.
6. Data interpretation and presentation.

2.4 Abu Dhabi Building Stock

UAE Climate
The daily average temperature in Abu Dhabi, the capital, ranges from 18 °C in January (so we're in the transition between subtropical and tropical climates) to around 35 °C in August [4] Fig. 2.

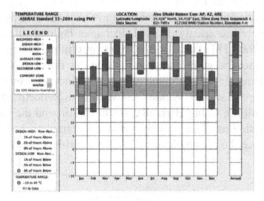

Fig. 2. Abu Dhabi temperature rang.

Energy Consumption
Buildings in the United Arab Emirates (UAE) utilize about 90% of the country's total electricity. Any level of energy retrofit for existing building assets can be successful in cutting UAE carbon emissions and reducing energy consumption and peak power demand. When applied to existing UAE building stock, a simple energy retrofit program

may save 7550 GWh/year in power consumption, 1400 MW in peak electricity demand, and 4.5 million tons/year in carbon emissions [17].

Abu Dhabi Building Stock Elevations

Based on the site observation the facade of the midrise buildings in downtown Abu Dhabi are not designed as per local sustainable standards that help addressing the problem of high heat, the architectural openings are not designed and not treated to reduce heat entry into the buildings, which makes the dependency of the building on energy for cooling very high Fig. 3.

Fig. 3. Mid-rise buildings elevations in Abu-Dhabi downtown at the sun radiation beck hours taken through site visit.

Building Retrofitting Strategies

Retrofitting is: Applying modifications to existing buildings to achieve sustainability aspects by the addition of new technology or features to older systems that may improve energy efficiency, decrease energy demand, increases building life cycle or increase indoor thermal comfort [18]. There are different retrofitting strategies applied to the buildings to achieve several goals and objectives on this research the focus will be on reduction cooling demand and improving energy efficiency. However, many strategies used to achieve these goals such as: Window Louvres, Solar Reflective materials. Shading trees around the buildings, Using High albedo surfaces around the buildings, Thermal insulation of the building envelope A study reported that implementing insulation in the UAE region can reduce the cooling load by 23.6%. Multi-layered glazing [18].

3   Methodology

Investigation Criteria

A mixed qualitative, quantitative, and experimental method will be applied on the different stages of this study, there are many requirements to build the proposed intelligent system defined based on the literature review Figs. 4 and 5.

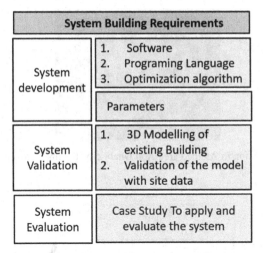

Fig. 4. System building requirements.

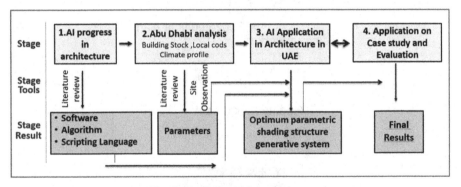

Fig. 5. Study methodology stages.

Case Study Selection for the Study Validation

The chosen existing building for the primary stages of this study is an one bed room apartment which repeated on all the floors except the ground and roof floors, we choose this case due to the availability of the drawing data and annual electricity consumption Figs. 6 and 7.

For the case study details:

Building Typology: Mid-rise Residential Buildings.

Fig. 6. Case study location in Alethad area Abu Dhabi city, the image token from googles earth website.

↓ Repeated floor plan

| Living Room | kitchen | W.C / Bath | Bed Room |

Repeated apartment

Fig. 7. Case study floor plan

Fig. 8. Case study southern elevation.

Number of the floors: 4 main floors + Ground, Mezzanine, and Roof floors (Fig. 8).

Tools and Resources
We require software that uses a programming language that is adaptable to architecture

to produce the best parametric architecture generating system. To create parametric structures, a variety of software packages and plugins are utilized, including:

Rhino's Grasshopper: It is a plug-in software that uses a visual programming language to allow architects to extract the design's driving parameters and tweak them iteratively. It lowers the barrier to entry for using complicated parametric tools [14]. Many plug-ins for studying the parametric structure can be attached to Grasshopper, such as Ladybug for environmental analysis and Karamba for structural analysis. It's compatible with Rhinoceros. Ladybug analyzes weather data in Grasshopper. This includes climatic geo studies such as shade analysis and radiation analysis [14]. However, Honeybee is a plug-in that connects Grasshopper3D to simulation engines like Open Studio and energy plus [14].

Case Study Simulations

The apartment into study are modelled thru Rhino and then investigated using grasshopper, lady bug and hoonybee. The case study data collected through site measurements and the annual electricity bills. The first simulation was to assess the sun radiation levels into the case study the. The second one was for energy modeling to compare the real case energy consumption and the model energy consumption to validate the study. 2021 Climate zone file (.epw) used in both simulations.

4   Preliminary Results

The results of the first 2 stages came out as tools and resources to be used in the main stage of the study which is developing and evaluating the final intelligent system script Figs. 9 and 10.

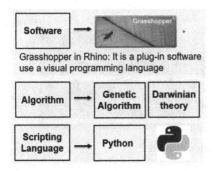

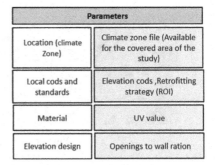

Fig. 9. Study stage 01 results   **Fig. 10.** Study stage 02 results

To develop the optimization system script Many secondary scripts Developed to be considered in developing the final system the Figures below refer to the scripts and their results Figs. 11, 12, 13, and 14. While Tables 1 and 2 refer to the bas case energy modeling results.

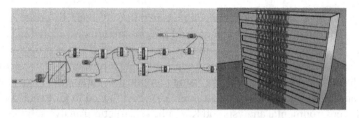

Fig. 11. Parametric structure script

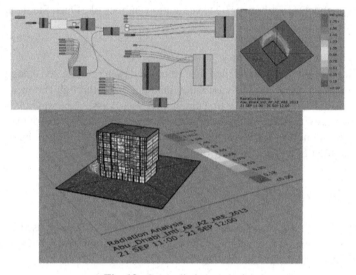

Fig. 12. Sun radiation analysis

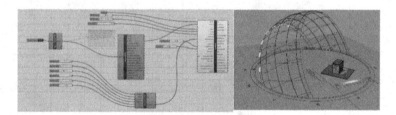

Fig. 13. Sun radiation analysis

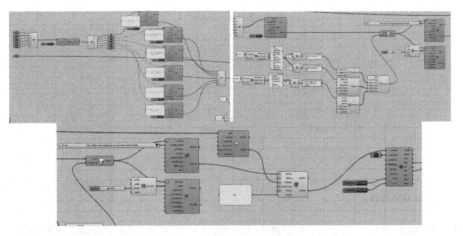

Fig. 14. Base case energy simulation script

Table 1. Site and source energy

	Total energy [GJ]	Energy per total building area [MJ/m^2]	Energy per conditioned building area [MJ/m^2]
Total site energy	26.54	678.08	678.08
Net site energy	26.54	678.08	678.08
Total source energy	86.91	2220.03	2220.03
Net source energy	86.91	2220.03	2220.03

Table 2. End use energy

	Electricity [GJ]
Heating	0.64
Cooling	8.75
Interior lighting	0.48
Exterior lighting	0.00
Interior equipment	5.42
Exterior equipment	0.00
Fans	2.49
Pumps	1.82
Heat rejection	0.59
Humidification	0.00

(continued)

Table 2. (*continued*)

	Electricity [GJ]
Heat recovery	0.00
Water systems	0.00
Refrigeration	0.00
Generators	0.00
Total end uses	20.18

5 Discussion

The focus of this study was to Explore the application of the AI in architectural sector in UAE through applying the AI tools in solving one problem related to this field which is energy consumption. The AI tools applied to optimize parametric structure as retrofit strategy for the med rise building to reduce the energy consumption. This study divided to 4 stages the first 2 stages done and the second 2 are on the progress to reach the result. Conducting this study was challenging due to the lack of available free data. Also collecting material on the base case was challenging. The used software was RHINO/Grasshopper. The modelling and analysis of the case was challenging due to the complexity of the python language. However, the primary results are promising in reach the final target of this study which is the intelligent system.

6 Conclusions

The results from the first two stages came out and the needed tools and resources for stage 03 defined based on the literature review. Stage 03 still in the progress. However paramilitary results came out, as we developed different secondary scripts that are needed for Developing the final optimization intelligent script.Future work is needed Further development for the system to be done at the next stages of this study.

References

1. Bande, L., et al.: Parametric design structures in low rise buildings in relation to the urban context in UAE. Sustainability **13**(15), 8595 (2021). https://doi.org/10.3390/su13158595
2. Ceylan, S.: Artificial Intelligence in Architecture: An Educational Perspective, vol. 1, no. Csedu, pp. 100–107 (2021). https://doi.org/10.5220/0010444501000107
3. Soltani, S., Gu, N., Paniagua, J.O., Sivam, A., McGinley, T.: Investigating the social impacts of high-density neighbourhoods through spatial analysis. In: Lee, J.-H. (ed.) CAAD Futures 2019. CCIS, vol. 1028, pp. 264–278. Springer, Singapore (2019). https://doi.org/10.1007/978-981-13-8410-3_19
4. Abu Dhabi climate: Average Temperature, weather by month, Abu Dhabi water temperature - Climate-Data.org. https://en.climate-data.org/asia/united-arab-emirates/abu-dhabi/abu-dhabi-3217/. Accessed 30 Sept 2021

5. Haenlein, M., Kaplan, A.: A brief history of artificial intelligence: on the past, present, and future of artificial intelligence. Calif. Manag. Rev. **61**(4), 5–14 (2019). https://doi.org/10.1177/0008125619864925
6. Kartal, H.B., Kartal, A.N.: Swarm intelligence in architectural design As a technique of Ai. J. Archit. Eng. Fine Arts **2**(2), 122–129 (2020)
7. Wright, S.: Why architecture and artificial intelligence? XRDS Crossroads ACM Mag. Stud. **24**(3), 16–19 (2018). https://doi.org/10.1145/3187013
8. Artificial intelligence applied to conceptual design. A review of its use in architecture | Elsevier Enhanced Reader. https://reader.elsevier.com/reader/sd/pii/S0926580521000017?token=FA900B2046CC8C742AC80A51B9F523F47DDDEE6BFC6A807446ACACBBEBD325E4A27AC441C50805A390265D718C8009EE&originRegion=eu-west-1&originCreation=20220218085819. Accessed 18 Feb 2022
9. Hudson, R.: Strategies for parametric design in architecture
10. Sohatskaya, D.G.: Parametric architecture and artificial intelligence as a way of modeling three-dimensional environment. In: Popkova, E.G., Ostrovskaya, V.N., Bogoviz, A.V. (eds.) Socio-economic Systems: Paradigms for the Future. SSDC, vol. 314, pp. 33–39. Springer, Cham (2021). https://doi.org/10.1007/978-3-030-56433-9_4
11. Agkathidis, A.: Book review: parametric design for architecture. Int. J. Architect. Comput. **11**(4), 465–468 (2013). https://doi.org/10.1260/1478-0771.11.4.465
12. Ikeda, Y., Herr, C.M., Holzer, D., Kaijima, S., Kim, M.J.: Types of parametric modelling. In: Emergency Experience Past, Present Future Digital Architecture. Proceedings of the 20th International Conference on Association Computer Architecture Design Research Asia (CAADRIA 2015)/Daegu 20–22 May 2015, pp. 157–166 (2015)
13. Myers, B.A.: Taxonomies of Visual Programming P and rogram Visualization g Taxonomies of Visual Programmin and n Program Visualizatio (1989)
14. Muen, Z.: IOP Conference Series: Earth and Environmental Science The Applications of Parametric Design in Green Building. https://doi.org/10.1088/1755-1315/567/1/012033
15. Zani, A., Andaloro, M., Deblasio, L., Ruttico, P., Mainini, A.G.: Computational design and parametric optimization approach with genetic algorithms of an innovative concrete shading device system. Proc. Eng. **180**, 1473–1483 (2017). https://doi.org/10.1016/J.PROENG.2017.04.310
16. Touloupaki, E., Theodosiou, T.: Optimization of building form to minimize energy consumption through parametric modelling. Proc. Environ. Sci. **38**, 509–514 (2017). https://doi.org/10.1016/J.PROENV.2017.03.114
17. Alkhateeb, E., Abu-Hijleh, B.: Potential for retrofitting a federal building in the UAE to net zero electricity building (nZEB). Heliyon **5**(6), e01971 (2019). https://doi.org/10.1016/j.heliyon.2019.e01971
18. Bande, L., et al.: A building retrofit and sensitivity analysis in an automatically calibrated model considering the urban heat island effect in Abu Dhabi, UAE. Sustainability **11**(24), 6905 (2019). https://doi.org/10.3390/su11246905

Design and Implementation of an Eco Electric Vehicle Energy Management System

Qiang Cao[1], Puxi Wang[2], and Shaoyi (Stephen) Liao[1(✉)]

[1] City University of Hong Kong Shenzhen Research Institute, Shenzhen, China
qiangcao2-c@my.cityu.edu.hk, issliao@cityu.edu.hk
[2] BYD Auto Engineering Research Institute, BYD Auto Industry Company Ltd.,
Shenzhen, China

Abstract. Nowadays, electric vehicles have become a prevalent transportation mode for their low cost and zero exhaust gases. Although it reduces air pollution significantly, the range anxiety makes many consumers hesitant about buying a new electric car because the low-energy density of batteries is inconvenient for a long trip. Facing this problem, how to apply advanced technologies to design a new energy management system to alleviate the range of anxiety is a research interest of many researchers. This research designs a new sustainable energy management system and develops a prototypic software for the evaluation. We demonstrate an extended energy informatics framework. Two algorithms, the shortest path problem (SPP) algorithm, and the vehicle routing problem (VRP) algorithm are built to support the decision of our energy management system. We also build a prototype software to demonstrate our new framework.

Keywords: Range anxiety · Electric vehicles · Energy management system

1 Introduction

Energy is the lifeline of modern society. Electric vehicles (EVs), smart cities, and other new businesses usually require a new energy management system (EMS) [1, 2]. How to make use of energy in a clean, efficient way is a challenge for our society. Nowadays, electric vehicles have become a prevalent transportation mode for their low cost and zero exhaust gases. Although it reduces air pollution significantly, the range anxiety makes many consumers hesitant about buying a new electric car because the low-energy density of batteries is inconvenient for a long trip [3]. Facing this problem, how to apply advanced technologies to design a new energy management system to alleviate the range of anxiety is a research interest of many researchers.

Thanks to the development of information technology, modern logistics contribute to the development of electric vehicle energy management systems. Designing an eco-routing system could help save energy and then reduce the range of anxiety. Usually, logistics activities include the forward and reverse flows of goods between origin and destination. Integrating logistics with electric vehicles could help the efficient operation and management of energy batteries. In this research, we mainly focus on the following questions:

© Springer Nature Switzerland AG 2022
M. Rauterberg et al. (Eds.): HCII 2022, LNCS 13520, pp. 314–323, 2022.
https://doi.org/10.1007/978-3-031-18158-0_23

1) How to reduce the range of anxiety of electronic vehicle drivers using new IT methods in energy management systems?
2) How do achieve the energy-saving strategy by optimizing the vehicle dispatching and routing schedules?
3) How to balance the time consumption demand and energy limitation by taking both pre-scheduling and real-time information into account?

To answer these questions, this research designs a new sustainable energy management system and develops a prototypic software for the evaluation. We first discuss the phenomenon of range of anxiety, research on energy informatics, and the theoretical foundations of our system design. And then, we demonstrate an extended energy informatics framework. Two algorithms, the shortest path problem (SPP) [4] algorithm, and the vehicle routing problem (VRP) [5] algorithm are built to support the decision of our energy management system. Based on a generally recognized energy consumption model, our energy-saving strategy could be achieved very well. We also develop a prototypic software for the demonstration. The prototypic software consists of a database, data processing backstage, and a user interface window. Using the traffic and geographic data collected from Google Maps, the logistics operational status, and routing strategies are presented to satisfy various stakeholders' requirements.

The contributions of this paper can be summarized in two aspects: theoretical contributions and methodological and practical contributions. From the theoretical and methodological perspective, this study should be recognized as the application, combination, and extension of energy informatics research and green business process redesign. We design the system and specify the methodology to guide the research in green logistics and addressed some business questions in this specific field. We propose the eco electric vehicle energy management systems with two constructed core models, namely, eco SPP and eco VRP, to support the decisions of stakeholders on routing issues. From the practical perspective, we further extract knowledge for routing strategy generation and build a prototype software.

2 Literature Review

2.1 Range Anxiety

There are three main problems for developing EVs: charging infrastructure, power supply, and driving range [3, 6]. For the limitation of the battery materials, people are usually worried about low battery over a long time. Concerning EV, it is recognized as range anxiety. It refers to EV users' psychological pressure on the uncertainty of sufficient energy for fixed trips.

Some studies are focusing on estimating the range based on the performance of electric vehicles' batteries in different environments [7, 8]. Some research focuses on the factors that may lead to range anxiety as well as this anxiety's impact on user behaviors [3, 9]. Other literature is interested in relieving range anxiety using the strategy design or scheduling [10, 11].

2.2 Eco-routing Research

Eco-routing research has two branches. The first branch focuses on the routing problem for an individual vehicle. Its trip usually has a fixed origin and destination. It is recognized as a solution for eco SPP [12]. SPP uses the energy factor to optimize the routing result. The second branch is based on VRP modeling and solving [13]. VRP is an organizational scheduling and operation process. The current study pays more attention to the first branch for its inter-disciplinary property. However, some technique innovation-centered disciplines, such as computer science and electronic engineering, have contributed to the development of eco-routing from the basic hierarchy.

Current energy management system design focus on analyzing the problem from the individual users' perspective. However, organizational-level users require a more complex system. They would like to can have a system that can match their requirement on the side of corporations or organizations. The current business research is more interested in the aspect of sustainability and green IT. Hence, it should be proceeded around system design to enable better operation in the logistics from the aspect of energy consumption. This study proposes a framework that provides the design guidelines for the energy management system, and the prototype software is also demonstrated.

3 Methodology

The framework of the Eco Electric Vehicle Energy Management System framework is illustrated in Fig. 1. The system is based on a design of three-layer architecture. The first layer focuses on multi-source data storage and process, including GPS (global positioning system) that provides the location-related data, GIS (geographic information system) that provides the geographic data, ITS (intelligent transportation system) that provides the real-time traffic data, EMS (energy management system) that provides the energy consumption data and the LMS (logistics management system) that provides the orders' data. In the second layer, we build two core models for eco-routing, namely, the eco SPP and eco VRP models. These two models are established for solving the following business problems: 1) the information dissemination; 2) the decision support for individual users; 3) the corporation of managers. User interfaces (UIs) constitute the third layer of the system architecture.

A sensor network consists of smart devices and systems used for information loading. It links the input of the eco SPP and eco VRP models. The information flows are transmitted through the network. The flow is visualized in the eco SPP and eco VRP models. The routing strategies are applied to support couriers' decisions on route selection. The scheduling strategies can help the managers arrange the dispatching tasks.

Figure 2 presents the details of the proposed framework with the software and hardware architecture. The hardware consists of a cloud server and several eco routing client modules. They can be conveniently equipped on logistics vehicles. The server works as the computation and storage platform for models, algorithms, and databases. The eco-routing client module has several major components, namely, GPS, EMS, the communication module, the computing module, and the memory module. GPS is used as the location information collector. It records the location of the vehicle at different time points. EMS provides real-time energy consumption information. The communication

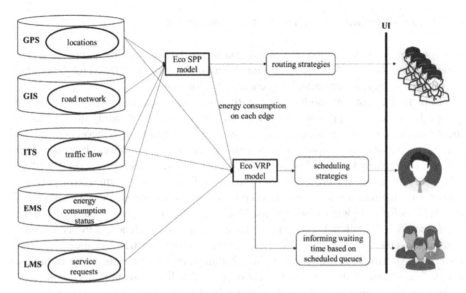

Fig. 1. Proposed framework

module collects all the local data. It sends local data to a server and asks for further strategies and decisions that support the execution of logistics activities. The computation module executes the local computation tasks requested by the software of an eco-routing client. Moreover, the memory module store the instant information from each module until the current routing mission is completed.

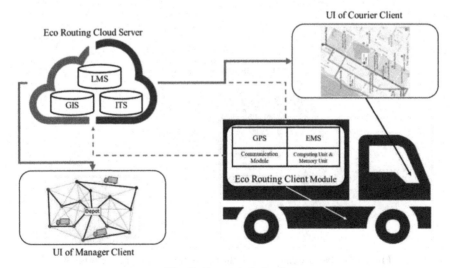

Fig. 2. Framework details

4   Data Collection and Prototypic System Design

In this study, we collected the geographic and traffic data through the application programming interface (API) of web mapping. A simulation approach is used for generating the logistics data, real-time remaining energy, and locations.

To better integrate the models and algorithms into the comprehensive IT artifact of this study, we develop a prototype software. By applying and extending the two-factor theory (motivation-hygiene theory) to the web user satisfaction, a theoretical model with three contributing components [14], namely, features in the web environment, user information-seeking tasks, and information seeker characteristics is proposed. We adopt this theory to guide our prototype software design. Couriers and managers play the role of information seekers in the prototype software. They have different characteristics and missions in logistics operations. Managers consider logistics routing from the macroscopical, operational, and organizational perspectives. Hence, a PC is a proper terminal designed for the overall operational status of the logistics activities. Logistics includes the locations of each courier, the schedule of each vehicle, the status of orders, and real-time traffic information. The couriers are the direct executors of the parcels' pickup/delivery activities. The SSP routing-enabled navigation is designed to ensure the selected route can handle the requirement of the time window and remaining energy. The sequence of pickup/delivery, the selected route between each customer as well as the selected route between the customer and the depot, are provided to couriers (Fig. 3).

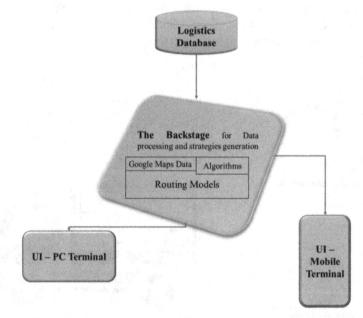

Fig. 3. The basic architecture of the eco-routing prototype software

The eco-routing prototype software consists of three major components, namely, a logistics database, a core backstage, and the UI. The eco-routing logistics database has the typical relational database structure. It includes four tables: order table for order data storage, customer table for customer information management, vehicle table that specifies the vehicle status, and Order_Route table that integrates the routing relevant data stored in order and vehicle tables and the information generated by the backstage. Figure 4 presents the entity-relationship (ER) model of this database.

Other than the three elementary tables, the Order_Route table is a composite table that directly interacts with the core backstage and UI. The value of field Sequence_Ranking of each record is filled by the strategies developed backstage, and it would be presented with the routing result visualizations in PC terminal UI.

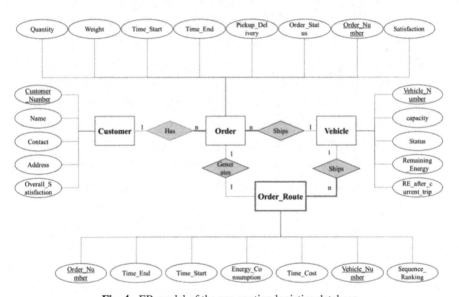

Fig. 4. ER model of the eco-routing logistics database

Eco-routing backstage is the platform that integrates the routing models and algorithms for logistics data processing and routing strategy generation. We implemented this module in the second layer by applying the MATLAB coder to transfer the mathematical programming language algorithms to other common computer language formats, such as C# and Java codes. Then, they can interact with the logistics database and UI through additional intermediate programs.

UI is a design of human-computer interaction of a system, which decides the intuitive sense of users to some extent. To improve user experience, the development of UIs is required to take information-seeking tasks, working environment, and other influential factors into account. Therefore, we developed the PC version client for managers and a mobile version for couriers, respectively. The UI of the PC version software is shown in Fig. 5. Figure 5a is the main menu of a PC version software and it links to the other two sub-interfaces for further information seeking. Managers can browse the database information to learn about the specific status of each order, each vehicle, and routing

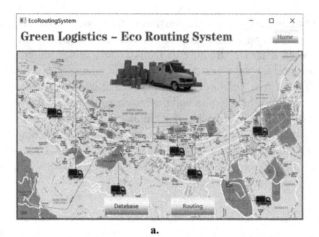

a.

EcoRoutingSystem   − ☐ ✕

Green Logistics – Eco Routing System   Home

| OrderRoute | Order | Vehicle | Customer |

ID	OrderNumber	VehicleNumber	OrderStatus	TimeStart	TimeEnd	EnergyConsumption	TimeCost	Sequ
1	201807251452	1	ing					3
2	201807271456	3	ing					5
3	201807271033	1	ing					2
4	201807261812	3	ing					1
5	201807261127	1	ing					1
6	201807271613	3	ing					2
7	201807271211	3	ing					4
8	201807251311	2	ing					1
9	201807251612	3	ing					3
10	201807261716	3	ing					2

b.

c.

Fig. 5. PC version client of the eco-routing prototypic software

sequences with the sub-interface reflected in Fig. 5b. In the other sub-interfaces that are presented in Fig. 5c, the routing result is visualized on the web map. It helps managers get orders and routing.

Furthermore, we also develop a mobile software. The mobile version has a similar frame to the PC version. We can start the operations with the home page shown in Fig. 6a and 6b that links to the other two sub-modules. The first sub-module provides detailed information about customers. The basic information of the next service recipient and the estimated energy consumption from the current location to the customer's location are also displayed. The disseminated information can help couriers better manage their

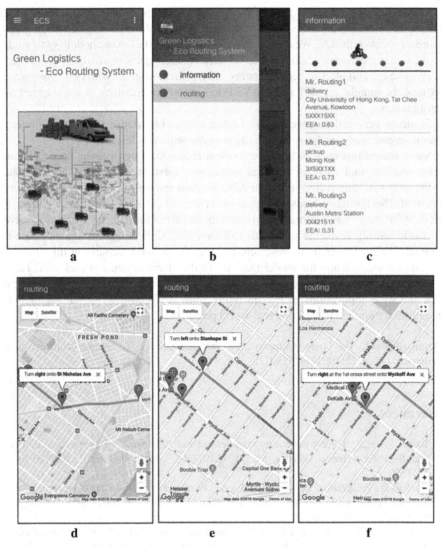

Fig. 6. Mobile version

logistics activities. The second sub-module is a navigation panel between the vehicle's current locations and the customer's locations. It is displayed on Google Maps based on the routing result of the eco SPP model. The two sub-modules are shown in Fig. 6d–f.

5 Conclusion

In this study, we proposed a new sustainable energy management system with eco SPP and eco VRP algorithms. We build a prototype software to enable real traffic and geographic data collection and the energy management system's application in the real world.

From the theoretical and methodological perspective, this study should be recognized as the application, combination, and extension of energy informatics research and green business process redesign. We design the system and specify the methodology to guide the research in green logistics and addressed some business questions in this specific field. We propose the eco electric vehicle energy management systems with two constructed core models, namely, eco SPP and eco VRP, to support the decisions of stakeholders on routing issues.

From the practical perspective, we further extract knowledge for routing strategy generation and apply the knowledge to a prototype software design.

Some limitations exist in this study, which leaves the improvement space for our future research, and they are itemized as follows. First, traffic and geographic data are the only real data collected by the API, whereas the logistics and energy data are simulated. This limitation leads to the evaluation issue of the prototype system. Although the proposed algorithms perform well on the simulation platform, their capability to solve real-world routing problems still needs to be verified. Collecting real logistics data is a crucial mission in our future research. Second, the applied scenario in this study is not complex enough and the model may not fit the characteristics of real data. Thus, real-world situations should be much more difficult to model. To achieve high practical value and wide applications, important future work is to construct systematic models that are strong enough to describe real-world problems.

Acknowledgment. This study is supported by Shenzhen Science, Technology and Innovation Commission (JSGG20170822145318071).

References

1. Tushar, W., et al.: Three-party energy management with distributed energy resources in smart grid. IEEE Trans. Indust. Electron. **62**, 2487–2498 (2015). https://doi.org/10.1109/TIE.2014.2341556
2. Doukas, H., Patlitzianas, K.D., Iatropoulos, K., Psarras, J.: Intelligent building energy management system using rule sets. Build. Environ. **42**, 3562–3569 (2007). https://doi.org/10.1016/j.buildenv.2006.10.024
3. Rauh, N., Franke, T., Krems, J.F.: Understanding the impact of electric vehicle driving experience on range anxiety. Hum Fact. **57**, 177–187 (2015). https://doi.org/10.1177/0018720814546372

4. Broumi, S., et al.: Shortest path problem in fuzzy, intuitionistic fuzzy and neutrosophic environment: an overview. Compl. Intell. Syst. **5**(4), 371–378 (2019). https://doi.org/10.1007/s40 747-019-0098-z
5. Asghari, M., Mirzapour Al-e-hashem, S.M.J.: Green vehicle routing problem: a state-of-the-art review. Int. J. Prod. Econ. **231**, 107899 (2021). https://doi.org/10.1016/j.ijpe.2020. 107899
6. Dong, J., Wu, X., Liu, C., Lin, Z., Hu, L.: The impact of reliable range estimation on battery electric vehicle feasibility. Int. J. Sustain. Transp. **14**, 833–842 (2020). https://doi.org/10. 1080/15568318.2019.1639085
7. Ou, S., Lin, Z., He, X., Przesmitzki, S., Bouchard, J.: Modeling charging infrastructure impact on the electric vehicle market in China. Transp. Res. Part D: Transp. Environ. **81**, 102248 (2020). https://doi.org/10.1016/j.trd.2020.102248
8. Bi, J., Wang, Y., Sai, Q., Ding, C.: Estimating remaining driving range of battery electric vehicles based on real-world data: a case study of Beijing, China. Energy **169**, 833–843 (2019). https://doi.org/10.1016/j.energy.2018.12.061
9. Yuan, Q., Hao, W., Su, H., Bing, G., Gui, X., Safikhani, A.: Investigation on range anxiety and safety buffer of battery electric vehicle drivers. J. Adv. Transp. **2018**, e8301209 (2018). https://doi.org/10.1155/2018/8301209
10. Xu, M., Yang, H., Wang, S.: Mitigate the range anxiety: siting battery charging stations for electric vehicle drivers. Transp. Res. Part C: Emerg. Technol. **114**, 164–188 (2020). https:// doi.org/10.1016/j.trc.2020.02.001
11. Faraj, M., Fidan, B., Gaudet, V.: Multi-module range anxiety reduction scheme for battery-powered vehicles. In: 2018 IEEE Intelligent Vehicles Symposium (IV), pp. 904–909 (2018). https://doi.org/10.1109/IVS.2018.8500370
12. Jaballah, R., Veenstra, M., Coelho, L.C., Renaud, J.: The time-dependent shortest path and vehicle routing problem. INFOR: Inf. Syst. Operat. Res. **59**, 592–622 (2021). https://doi.org/ 10.1080/03155986.2021.1973785
13. Zhang, H., Ge, H., Yang, J., Tong, Y.: Review of vehicle routing problems: models, classification and solving algorithms. Archiv. Comput. Methods Eng. **29**(1), 195–221 (2021). https:// doi.org/10.1007/s11831-021-09574-x
14. Zhang, P., Small, R.V., von Dran, G.M., Barcellos, S.: Websites that satisfy users: a theoretical framework for Web user interface design and evaluation. In: Proceedings of the 32nd Annual Hawaii International Conference on Systems Sciences, 1999, HICSS-32. Abstracts and CD-ROM of Full Papers, p. 8 (1999). https://doi.org/10.1109/HICSS.1999.772668

Blockchain-Based Smart Energy Communities: Operation of Smart Legal Contract

Marta Chinnici[1]([⊠]), Luigi Telesca[2], Mahfuzul Islam[2], and Jean-Philippe Georges[3]

[1] ENEA- C.R Casaccia, Via Anguillarese 301, 00123 Rome, Italy
marta.chinnici@enea.it
[2] Trakti Ltd., Trento, Italy
{luigi,mahfuzul.islam}@trakti.com
[3] Université de Lorraine, CNRS, CRAN, 54000 Nancy, France
jean-philippe.georges@univ-lorraine.fr

Abstract. The Blockchain paradigm applied to energy communities represents both a challenge and an opportunity. Indeed, it introduces a new framework to manage the communities' services and, in the meantime, guarantees the traceability of the energy produced and consumed, informing consumers of the origins and costs of their supply, making tariffs more transparent with the result of promoting energy flexibility. Blockchain enables a real digitalization of the energy sector. The security of the transaction and the guarantee that the platform on which an energy network is based cannot be tampered with has prompted energy communities to start a blockchain-based system. The paper proposed a blockchain-based open and transparent ecosystem for smart energy communities within, different and several actors interfacing thanks to blockchain system and its services interact in a natural and disintermediate way. It allows, in a peer to peer (p2p) way, to implement participatory logic aimed at reducing and self-consumption of energy and direct participation citizens to the electricity system. A proof of concept is created and tested using the Trakti blockchain platform (scalable) that, through an end-to-end approach, implement a new dynamic smart legal contract with real data for the local marketplace within a smart energy community. The results show that the new smart Legal Contract makes it possible to define an energy token, which allows remunerating the energy exchanges in communities between producers and consumers within a smart grid and converting the energy into community services.

Keywords: Blockchain · Energy communities · Energy market · Energy flexibility · P2P

1 Introduction

Energy communities provide flexibility for the electricity system and provide energy efficiency for the citizens by organizing the energy actions. It mainly sets out new regulations that help consumers produce, use, and exchange or trade electricity [1, 6]. With micro-generation, we refer to the small-scale generation of electric power by energy communities composed of citizens, small businesses and public administration to meet

© Springer Nature Switzerland AG 2022
M. Rauterberg et al. (Eds.): HCII 2022, LNCS 13520, pp. 324–336, 2022.
https://doi.org/10.1007/978-3-031-18158-0_24

their own needs as alternatives or supplements to traditional centralized grid-connected power. The concept of the energy community is indeed a pivotal point in the design of the future European energy infrastructure. It implies the strict collaboration of market players (utilities), "energy designers", policymakers and citizens all aiming together to develop smart energy delivery, fostering the use of renewable sources and technology innovation in distributed generation. This to gain benefits on economy, sustainability and energy security [2]. The success of the energy community paradigm relies on several factors like renewable sources and generation system availability, innovative technological solutions, normative regulation, political, psycho-social and cultural dimensions. Those conditions need to be sustainable for all community members. According to this novel approach and in particular referred to security aspect, using a blockchain for energy representation and exchange provides several advantages. According to this novel approach and, in particular, to reference the security aspect, using a blockchain for energy representation and exchange provides several advantages. Blockchain offers a trusted technology that can be used as an Information and Communication Technology (ICT) backbone for an open energy market [6, 7]. The security of the transaction and the guarantee that the platform on which an energy network is based cannot be tampered with has prompted energy communities to start a blockchain-based system. The paper proposed a blockchain-based open and transparent ecosystem for smart energy communities within, different actors interfacing thanks to the blockchain system and its services interact in a natural and disintermediate way. It allows, in a peer to peer (P2P) way, to implement participatory logic aimed at reducing and self-consumption of energy and direct participation citizens to the electricity system. A proof of concept is created and tested using the Trakti blockchain platform (scalable) [5] that, through an end-to-end approach, implement a new dynamic smart legal contract with real data for the local marketplace within a smart energy community. The results show that the new smart Legal Contract makes it possible to define an energy token, which remunerates the energy exchanges in communities between producers and consumers within a smart grid and converts the energy into community services.

The paper is organised as follows: Sect. 1 – Introduction; Sect. 2 – Background: Energy Communities and Blockchain; Sect. 3 – Methodology: Blockchain-Based Smart Energy Communities; Sect. 4 – Results Discussion; Sect. 5 – Conclusions and Future Works.

2 Background: Energy Communities and Blockchain

This section presents our proposal's essential points; we discuss fundamental concepts like energy communities and blockchain to blend these ingredients to create a blockchain-based open and transparent ecosystem for smart energy communities.

Micro-generation is the capacity for consumers to produce electrical energy in-house or in a local community. The concept of "market" indicates the possibility of trading the electricity that has been micro-generated among producers and consumers. User acting both as a producer and consumer is called a "prosumer". Traditionally, this market has been served by pre-defined bilateral agreements between prosumers and retail energy suppliers. This means that electricity-generating prosumers have not had real access to the energy market, which remains a privileged field for institutionalised energy suppliers. So far, this fact has heavily impacted the actual diffusion at a large scale of micro-generation due to the limited economic advantages this energy generation approach would bring to the prosumers. Indeed, the main options considered so far by the technical literature were completely centralised, and their viability (under a prosumer perspective) was in general challenged as they introduced additional management fees and costs and assumed the intervention of a trusted third party, reducing once again the potential gains of end-users [2]. New approaches should be developed, enabling end-users to have free access to the energy market. In this context, the advent of distributed ledgers, i.e., blockchains, can be considered beneficial. In particular, using a blockchain for energy representation and exchange provides several advantages. First of all, it gives the possibility to have a trusted and decentralised direct exchange between two parties. No intermediaries or third parties are needed to fulfil transactions. The data on the blockchain is public, easily verifiable by interested parties, consistent, and always available. Even if the data are available, the users remain pseudonymous; as for the transactions, blockchain addresses and not personal data are used. Moreover, due to their decentralised nature and lack of a central point of failure, blockchains are very resistant to denial of service attacks. Finally, data on the blockchain are immutable, meaning that once inserted in the blockchain, it cannot be altered, providing a reliable point of reference. By having these features, blockchain provides a trusted technology that can be used as an ICT backbone for an open energy market. According to this approach, self-generated electricity could usually be consumed within the house, accumulated in batteries for later use, or simply returned to the grid. Thanks to the distributed and pervasive nature of the blockchain, the produced energy could be redeemed elsewhere. For example, when charging an electric vehicle abroad, or sold through the blockchain to the best buyer, according to a mechanism similar to that of a stock-exchange market. To sum, for its nature, the blockchains presents some interesting advantages:

- Disintermediation and trustless model: exchanges (or transactions) do not require intermediaries or trusted third parties; moreover, the parties have full guarantee that the transactions will be executed as expected
- User empowerment: transactions and data are in control by the users' community
- Resilience: due to their decentralised nature, blockchains do not have a central point of failure
- Transparency and immutability: every modification in public blockchains is visible to everybody, moreover, the transactions stored in a blockchain cannot be altered or deleted.

For these reasons, blockchain can be used to implement other decentralized services apart from currency transactions in which trust is built-in based on blockchain intrinsic properties. Furthermore, blockchain is supported with additional functions to enhance confidence. One of the most promising is smart contracts.

A smart contract is a computer program capable of executing or enforcing a prede-fined agreement using a blockchain, when and if specific conditions are met. Its main goal is to enable two or more parties to perform a trusted transaction without needing intermediaries. Moreover, smart contracts inherit the characteristics of blockchains and thus have no downtime, censorship or third party interference.

Exploiting and applying the potentialities of blockchains to energy communities is a step forward to providing a novel ecosystem for smart energy communities.

In the following, we underline those elements as critical factors for the success of every technological paradigm [2]:

1. Community aspects: sense of community, energy consumes, community renewables project;
2. Digital competencies: digital skills, knowledge, digital divide, niche market;
3. Energy citizenship: social, civic and politic participation, social capital, engagement;
4. Attitudes: conservatives, enthusiastic, techno scepticism, innovators, trust in progress;
5. Motivations: costs reduction, environment, grassroots' actions, mainstream energy policy, hedonic.

In this perspective, microgeneration through innovative digital paradigms should consider the stratification of users' digital competencies. This aims to open Digital Single Market and Society, enhance collaborative and participatory practices to different skilled citizens, and minimize the digital divide. Consequently, the EC in [2] argues that tailor-made micro-generation resources addressing other citizen skills can be more effective for supporting and spreading the communities that called energy communities. However, since the energy community building as an incentive to citizen participation in the micro-generation market can be enumerated among the intrinsic nature of blockchain paradigm – e.g. the use of smart contracts for energy exchange and the services exchange – we define this community as smart energy community.

In this paper, it is a real-case implementation, demonstrating the proper functioning of the entire chain, up to the actual generation of rewards and bonuses, thus validating as a proof of concept the opportunity of smart energy communities.

3 Methodology: Blockchain-Based Smart Energy Communities

Using a mature blockchain platform (Trakti) and real data coming from ENEA, we create an open and transparent relationship ecosystem for smart energy communities. Within this ecosystem we can find different actors that interfacing through the blockchain and its services interact in a peer to peer way (P2P). The eco system envisions the share of the energy services in more secure and transparent way between different end users aimed to encourage better use of electrical resources, distributed production, and self-consumption using blockchain technologies to build smart contracts (see Fig. 1).

This goal will be achieved by creating a Local Energy Market on smart legal contracts using "Smart energy tokens" as a participation incentive for the actors of the designed eco system to trade community services, making all the players in the supply chain active actors. The negotiation among the shareholders and orchestration of the community services in the smart community is facilitated by implementing Smart Legal Contracts in the blockchain system. The Smart Legal Contracts are modelled and implemented

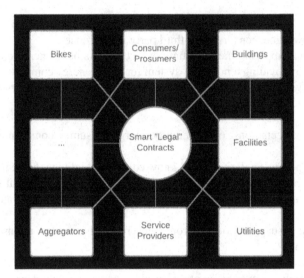

Fig. 1. A sketch of pivotal elements in smart energy community.

in the Trakti platform using dynamic blockchain to support the onboarding procedures and negotiations among the actors. In this way, it will be guaranteed the intra-ecosystem agreements between the various stakeholders and facilitate the initial validation of the Local Market Place of Community Services. The energy token will be used in the Local Market Place to buy community services with the goal of involving and making all supply chain players active actor. The energy tokens are used to remunerate the energy exchanges among prosumers, producers and consumers and reward the users based on their provided services.

3.1 Trakti Blockchain Platform

Trakti [5] is a unified platform for smart, self-executing and compliant contracts running on a private and public blockchain, streamlining the contracting process of medium-large enterprises, financial, insurance and regulated market operators. This platform offers all the tools needed to securely facilitate the acquisition and negotiation flows and manage all corporate contracts in a unique infrastructure.

The objective of Trakti is to assist companies from the beginning right up to the signing and monitoring of the contract in a fully compliant way, combining multi aspects of Fintech, Regtech and Lawtech. The infrastructure can support both traditional contracts and smart contracts with blockchain implementations. Trakti operates on the English and Italian markets. It works with medium and large companies, optimizing the management and facilitating the automation of their contracts. The platform's core is the smart contract because it represents the vital elements in relationship management and process automation. Contract management has slowly become more digital with the rise of the contract lifecycle management (CLM) market. However, the same cannot be said of contracts and, in some ways, traditional CLM vendors. Trakti, in contrast, is a step toward CLM that is digital native—that is, agreements modelled and managed in a fully electronic format. Via a combination of contract management expertise and targeted use of blockchain technology, Trakti offers smart contracts functionality in an end-to-end CLM system it has applied across enterprise use cases, at real customers, at supply chain scale. Those familiar with standard contract lifecycle management solutions may be sceptical of this description. Most CLM vendors excel at digitizing contracts and obligations or streamlining negotiation but rarely do they venture into true automation powered by smart contracts. Trakti does live up to the standard of actually automating CLM processes. And we think the vendor is developing a solid position from which to scale its marketability as an enterprise-grade CLM.

3.2   Case Study: Blockchain-Based Smart Energy Communities

Using the real generated database of data riding system from building within ENEA R.C Casaccia (Rome) - it reads and analyses the data from energy sensors making consumption and production reading - the communities services exchange (e.g. babysitting, car sharing, etc…) in smart energy communities can be investigated using Trakti blockchain-system. Data are sent to the blockchain through a software layer equipped with APIs that can be called up from the outside, which it sends to the blockchain and records copies of them in the relational DMBS for analysis. Considering the Energy Tokens produced by the blockchain and the related readings, a further group reward logic has been implemented instead of the individual. This is because the tokens issued in the various cycles could be used as a proxy for defining the contribution in terms of energy efficiency that the energy micro-energy community, on the whole, could get based on collective behaviour. Based on the tokens assigned, the facilitator stakeholder, in the event of signing a contract made through the Trakti platform, recognize the members of the micro-community, identified through the wallet list acquired during an onboarding procedure, an additional bonus equal to the bonus received divided the number of wallets listed in the contract (whitelisting). Indeed, the micro-community coordinator, imagined by the writer in the figure of the condominium administrator, should have obtained from the condominiums, with the onboarding and whitelisting procedure, the authorization to sign a connected agreement that allows the distribution of the premiums. The energy profile is obtained and distributed equally among the subscribers' wallets. Therefore, in this scenario, it is planned to distribute, in a billing cycle to be defined, equally among all participants, an additional number of Energy Tokens equal to those obtained individually by the various members of the micro energy community identified in the wallets. Subscriber ID of the whitelisting agreement. In the Fig. 2, both the contract between the administrator of the micro community and the condominiums, and the contract signed between the administrator and the facilitator are present. At each billing cycle, the contract (Platform Agreement) will invoke the contract (whitelist) to obtain the ID of the wallets for the calculation of the rewards and the distribution of the additional bonus.

Based on the previous consideration, the following architecture (Fig. 3) to implement the Local Market Place for energy community services is proposed.

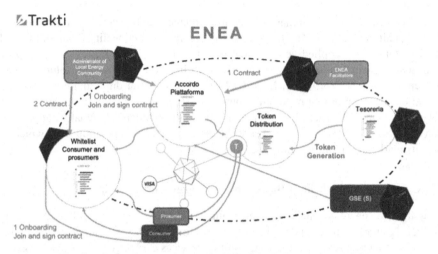

Fig. 2. The implemented scenario in Trakti-platform using real data.

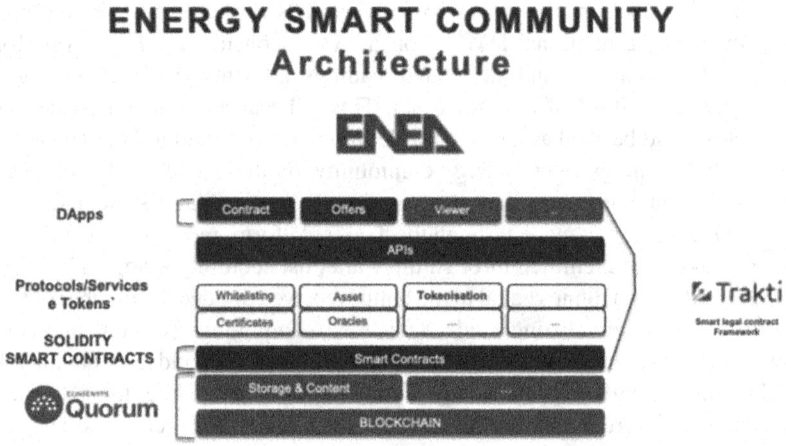

Fig. 3. The architecture layers of ENEA/Trakti platform.

The layer for the modelling and orchestration of contracts, as well as the definition of an initial prototype of a marketplace connected to it for the consumption of community services has been provided by Trakti. The Ethereum-blockchain with Solidity programme to develop the smart contracts has been used to deploy the layer (see the orange layer in Fig. 4) compatible with Quorum blockchain used in ENEA The Fig. 4 represents the framework used on the blockchain, the interfaces for users, contract management and marketplace.

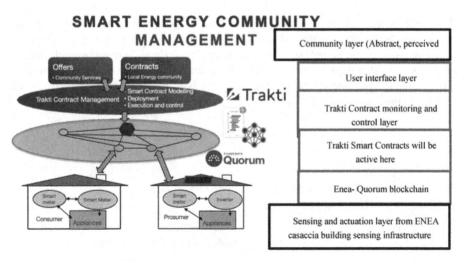

Fig. 4. Smart energy community management.

4   Technical Requirement and Results Discussion

This section provides a technical requirement on the smart contract before showing the achieved results.

4.1   Smart Communities: Reward Smart Contract with Trakti Platform

The smart contract is consisting of several modules: Campaign, Perk, Subscriber and Reward. In detail, in Trakti platform a user can define and use two different type of rewarding system using smart contract:

1. **Individual Reward Smart Contract:** A rewarding contract where each user earns rewards depends on their own activities.
2. **Community Reward Smart Contract:** A rewarding contract where each user earns rewards depends on any members of their group. All the rewards are distributed equally among each member of the group.

The first one works by distributing the rewards for the activities of each user. In Trakti, individual reward smart contract has three distinct phases: campaign creation, campaign subscription, reward negotiation and distribution. Meanwhile, in the Community Reward Smart Contract, there are mainly three parties involved. Community creator, subscriber and reward provider. In addition to that, there can be any number of other reward beneficiaries. For example, a condo manager can create a community and ask all the condo members to join in that community. He can then negotiate different reward rules with a service provider. Whenever a community member earns rewards from the service provider, it will be equally distributed according to the rules negotiated with the provider. Said that, in the platform there are two pathways to create a fully functional reward system. A campaign creator can first do negotiation with a reward provider.

This will generate a master contract in Trakti. Under that master contract, the campaign creators can then onboard subscribers to his campaign. The second way is campaign creator will first create an onboarding contract in Trakti. He will create two onboarding templates under that master contract. First onboarding template is to onboard subscriber to the campaign and second onboarding template is to negotiate and onboard reward provider to the campaign. The process works like below (Fig. 5):

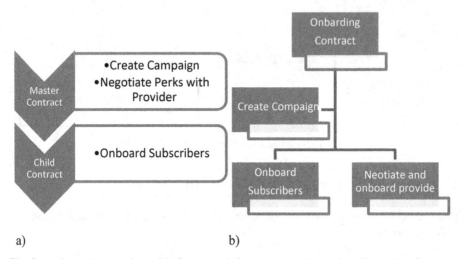

a)   b)

Fig. 5. a) Reward campaign with first negotiating rewards, then onboarding subscribers; b) Reward campaign with first onboarding subscribers, then negotiating rewards.

ENEA has a community reward system that follows the second workflow (onboarding subscribers and then negotiating rewards). The community manager is the condominium (building) administrator who creates an onboarding contract in Trakti. In the master template, he initiates the smart contract, which will enable him to add subscribers and negotiate rewards later in a separate child onboarding contract. After creating the onboarding contract, the condominium (building) administrator adds an onboarding template for all the condominium users to join the campaign. ENEA called it as whitelisting of users. When enough users get whitelisted, the condominium manager adds another onboarding template and negotiates rewards with a provider (in ENEA use case). All the rewards generated are then distributed equally among all whitelisted users. Detailed use case and step by step process of the workflow is given below. To create a community reward system, the condominium administrator first creates an onboarding contract in Trakti which launches a new campaign in the smart contract. There is a marketplace template to create a community reward campaign. In the following the steps:

1. **Step 1:** Go to add new contract model, select community reward campaign from the marketplace template
2. **Step 2:** The condominium administrator edits it accordingly and publish the template.
3. **Step 3:** After publishing the template, the condominium manager goes to his contract page and creates a new onboarding contract

4. **Step 4:** He then selects his newly published community reward campaign contract model as master agreement template. This allows him to do the configuration of his campaign like start and end date, maximum number of subscribers allowed etc.
5. **Step 5:** After submission, the admin waits for the blockchain transactions to be completed. It can take a couple of minutes to finish the transaction. The smart contract will be initialized according to the configuration and a decentralized application (dApp) interface will be loaded on his contract detail page.

After creating the campaign, the condominium (building) admin can add an onboarding template to start onboarding (whitelisting) members. There is a marketplace template to create a simple community reward subscription contract. After whitelisting is completed, the condominium (building) administrator adds another onboarding template to start negotiating terms of the rewards ENEA. There is a marketplace template which allows configuring up to two additional rewards.

4.2 Results

Based on the previous details about the smart contract creation for ENEA use case on Trakti platform, tokens assignment and the reward mechanism are presented in this section.

Token distribution contract, the control and monitoring dApps, and the tokens assigned contract under the defined scenario have been implemented on the Trakti platform (Fig. 6). The test with real data (Fig. 7) showed the tokens assignment on the active experimental campaign.

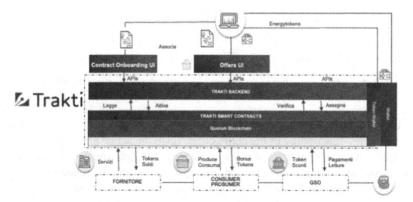

Fig. 6. Smart energy community flow.

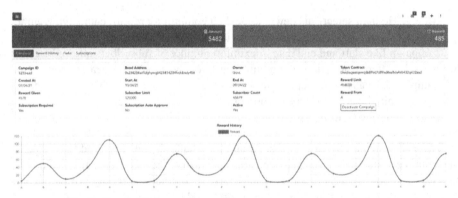

Fig. 7. Detail of token assignment in experimental contract campaign.

In the Fig. 8, several tokens are received in the system, and one pending is calculated based on the readings acquired by the Quorum blockchain and the due sums that need to be distributed. It is possible to notice as there could be a series of signed contract campaigns capable of generating a distribution of tokens over time.

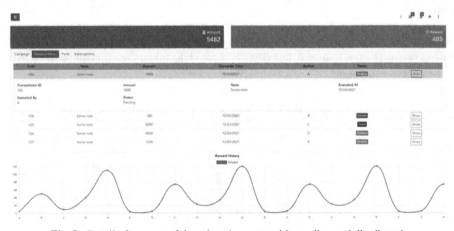

Fig. 8. Detail of amount of the tokens' system with pending and distributed.

In Fig. 9, details of bonus received are shown. Considering such results, it demonstrates the proper functioning of the entire chain, up to the actual generation of rewards and bonuses, thus validating as a proof of concept the opportunity of smart energy communities. Energy tokens can be hence defined to support the renumeration in the communities and lead also to a conversion of the energy into communities services.

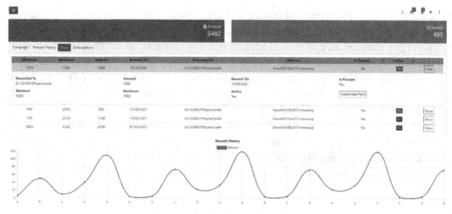

Fig. 9. Detail of bonus received.

In Fig. 10, the offers, dashboard and ENEA-Marketplace are presented.

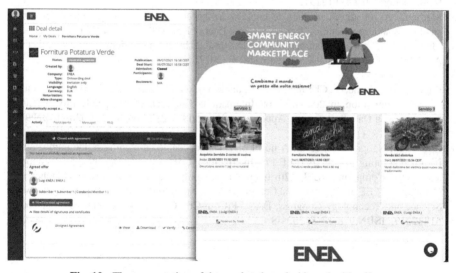

Fig. 10. The presentation of the marketplace dashboard with offers.

5   Conclusions and Future Works

To conclude, blockchain can benefit energy system operations, markets and consumers. They offer disintermediation, transparency and tamper-proof transactions. Still, most importantly, blockchains provide novel solutions for empowering consumers and small renewable generators to play a more active role in the energy market and monetise their assets. This paper shows, as in a peer to peer (P2P) way, a participatory logic aimed at reducing and self-consumption of energy and direct participation citizens to the electricity system, a proof of concept is created and tested using the Trakti blockchain platform (scalable) [5]; through an end-to-end approach, a new dynamic smart legal contract with real data for the local marketplace within a smart energy community is implemented. The results show that the new smart Legal Contract makes it possible to define an energy token, which remunerates the energy exchanges in communities between producers and consumers within a smart grid and converts the energy into community services. In this way, a blockchain-based system for the smart energy communities is possible and realise their potential. Blockchain represents, in the meantime, the challenges and opportunities to create a smart urban environment.

References

1. Energy Communities [online] Energy-European Commission. https://energy.ec.europa.eu/top ics/markets-and-consumers/energy-communities_en
2. Kounelis, I., et al.: Blockchain in Energy Communities, A Proof of Concept, EUR 29074 EN, Publications Office of the European Union, 2017, ISBN 978-92-79-77773-8, JRC110298. https://doi.org/10.2760/121912
3. Merlinda, A., et al.: Blockchain technology in the energy sector: a systematic review of challenges and opportunities. Renew. Sustain. Energy Rev. **100**, 143–174 (2019)
4. Mannaro, K., Pinna, A., Marchesi, M.: Crypto-trading: blockchain-oriented energy market. In: AEIT International Annual Conference. IEEE (2017)
5. www.trakti.com/
6. Rapuano, A., Iovane, G., Chinnici, M.: A scalable blockchain based system for super resolution images manipulation. In: 2020 IEEE 6th International Conference on Dependability in Sensor, Cloud and Big Data Systems and Application, DependSys 2020, pp. 8–15 (2020). ISBN:978-172817651-2
7. Iovane, G., Nappi, C.M., et al.: A novel blockchain scheme combining prime numbers and iris for encrypting coding. In: IEEE 17th International Conference on Dependable, Autonomic and Secure Computing, IEEE 17th International Conference on Pervasive Intelligence and Computing, IEEE 5th International Conference on Cloud and Big Data Computing, 4th Cyber Science and Technology Congress, DASC-PiCom-CBDCom-CyberSciTech 2019, pp. 609–618 (2019). ISBN:978-172813024-8

Acceptability and Usability of Location-Support Technologies for Cruise Ship Evacuations

Paul Liston[1]([⊠]) [iD], Alison Kay[1] [iD], Emma Delemere[1] [iD], Lazaros Karagiannidis[2] [iD], Margarita Kostovasili[2], Angelos Amditis[2] [iD], Dimitris Drakoulis[3] [iD], and Panagiotis Veltsistas[3] [iD]

[1] Centre for Innovative Human Systems, Trinity College Dublin, Dublin, Ireland
`pliston@tcd.ie`
[2] National Technical University of Athens, Athens, Greece
[3] Telesto Technologies Ltd., Athens, Greece

Abstract. Emergency evacuation information provided to cruise ship passengers is static and hard to access and understand by some passengers. The SafePASS project is working to provide technology solutions which provide passengers with dynamic, real-time information which they can understand and follow to aid their evacuation from cruise ships in event of an emergency. This paper reports on acceptability and usability analyses of a Passenger Mobile Application, a Smart Lifejacket and a Smart Wristband which were positively rated by passengers and crew in surveys and workshops. Passengers responded positively to the use of a Passenger Mobile Application for directions (suggesting a willingness to use smartphone technologies as support in emergencies), while they responded neutrally to wearable technologies (Smart Lifejacket, Smart Wristband). Crew responded positively to the use of smartphones and wearable technologies in emergency situations. This suggests high acceptability of smartphone-based technologies for use by crew in emergency situations. Workshops with industry experts and passengers highlighted the importance of data protection.

Keywords: Maritime safety · Acceptability · Usability · Location support · Human factors

1 Introduction

At present, the emergency evacuation information available to passengers onboard modern cruise ships is only offered on safety leaflets in cabins or at corridors. Some cruise line operators supplement this by making safety videos covering the evacuation procedures available on the in-cabin television system. Despite these recent efforts to increase passengers' engagement with audio-visuals on cabin-based entertainment systems or personalised applications,[1] the safety information is static and difficult to understand,

---

[1] https://www.royalcaribbean.com/blog/royal-caribbean-changes-the-game-with-muster-2-0/.

© Springer Nature Switzerland AG 2022
M. Rauterberg et al. (Eds.): HCII 2022, LNCS 13520, pp. 337–352, 2022.
https://doi.org/10.1007/978-3-031-18158-0_25

especially under stressful conditions, and in conditions of low visibility[2,3] (e.g. fire, or evacuation at night). These limitations are compounded by reduced user friendliness and the effects of language differences. Passengers receive a safety briefing and muster drill prior to departure. This is mandated by the International Convention for the Safety of Life at Sea (SOLAS) and is an emergency drill which consists of the sounding of the general emergency alarm, followed by safety announcements to passengers from the captain. Passengers head to their muster stations (assembly stations) and are instructed in the use of life vests, and what to do in an emergency.

In response to COVID-19, self-mustering of passengers has been introduced [1], in which passengers are provided their muster station upon boarding and must individually check in with staff at their muster station prior to departure. The use of technology to enhance self-mustering has also been noted, with Muster 2.0 as implemented by Royal Caribbean Group [2], allowing passengers to use their mobile device to complete the muster drill and navigate to their muster point. While these muster drills provide a valuable opportunity for passengers to increase their preparedness should an emergency scenario occur, as large passenger ships consist of complex infrastructures inclusive of several decks and public spaces, difficulties wayfinding in an emergency can emerge. Challenges are further compounded by the high volume of people on board, inclusive of both crew and passengers. Additionally, the ship's status during emergency evacuation situations is constantly changing with time and the present means do not account for such dynamic changes.

The SafePASS project is working to develop an integrated system to support the safe and timely mustering and abandonment of large passenger cruise ships during emergencies. This involves redefining the evacuation processes, and developing new technologies and equipment through real-time monitoring and location support for passengers (providing optimal evacuation routes) and enhanced life-saving appliances (life jackets and lifeboats). The SafePASS system for Dynamic Evacuation [3–6] can calculate where to send people. There are sensors on board, placed throughout the entire ship, and their status is constantly updated. This means that the system knows how many people are at each muster station, which muster stations are full or unavailable, and which is the nearest muster station for each passenger. The effect is that in the event of an emergency, all those people already at a muster station will be instructed to stay where they are (rather than making their way to a pre-assigned station which may be at the other end of the ship) and put on their lifejackets. Muster stations should never be overloaded because the system optimises where to send people and passengers are sent to their nearest available muster station.

---

[2] http://www.maritime-forum.jp/et/pdf/h29_Basic_Crowd_Management_Guidebook_en.pdf.

[3] International Aeronautical and Maritime Search and Rescue Manual, IMO, 2016 Edition.

The scope of the Location-Support Technologies developed during SafePASS was to design and develop components to address all these issues and offer passengers multiple powerful tools to assist them during ship evacuation. In particular, location-support technologies offer the capacity to locate passengers dynamically in the cruise ship wherever they might move to during the evacuation process. Building on this, the devices and applications implemented as part of the SafePASS system then provide personalised services and information to passengers for easy and safe evacuation based on their location at each moment. These SafePASS components, in addition to being fully personalised for passengers, are also easy to use and dynamic dependent on passengers' real-time status and position, and include:

1. Passenger Mobile Application: mobile app installed on mobile devices to provide dynamic and personalised navigation to the identified exits for each passenger based on his/her real-time location.
2. Smart Lifejacket enabled with audio and vibration-based navigation systems:
   Passenger Chatbot Application: dynamic audio instructions guiding passengers along the optimal evacuation route via an embedded earplug.
3. Haptic Navigation Module: vibration sensors guiding passengers via haptic feedback through intense vibrations on their shoulders in order to guide them to the correct path and safe exit.
4. Smart Wristband: wearable wristband uniquely identifying each passenger and measuring and tracking the passengers' biometric information and vital signals in order to calculate their stress levels.

All these components aim to provide personalised information to passengers and assist them to safely navigate along the ship along the designated evacuation routes and exits with the overall aim of reducing the time required for ship evacuation [7]. The involvement of user input is key to the meaningful deployment and successful implementation of the SafePASS solutions in the real word. To this end the research activities are supported by co-design activities involving both passengers and crew. Additional access requirements are key to these efforts and the SafePASS project runs a Community of Practice which is the mechanism to achieve a Social Licence to Operate (SLO) for the integrated SafePASS systems [8].

1.1 The SafePASS Project

The SafePASS project is an EU-funded Horizon 2020 research programme that aims to radically redefine the evacuation processes, evacuation systems/equipment and international regulations for passenger ships in all environments, hazards and weather conditions. The consortium consists of 15 partners including a shipyard, lifesaving appliance manufacturers, a cruise operator and academic institutions, and classification societies (http://www.safepass-project.eu/). The consortium contains all the stakeholders and expertise needed to develop an integrated system that can collectively monitor, process and inform both crew and passengers of the optimal evacuation routes during emergencies, coupled with advanced, intuitive and easy to use life-saving appliances, resulting in a significant reduction of the total time required for ship evacuation and increased safety. An important aspect of the SafePASS project is to design and develop personalized and location-based tools and applications, aiming to assist passengers during the evacuation process. Several location-support technologies have been developed and integrated into mobile devices and wearables, the most important ones being the Passenger Mobile Application and the Smart Wristband.

1.2 SafePASS Location-Support Technologies

Passenger Mobile Application

One of the main SafePASS applications, developed to provide location-based support during ship evacuation, is the Passenger Mobile Application. The main purpose of the application is to provide dynamic and personalized navigation to the identified safe exits, muster and abandonment stations for each passenger based on his/her real-time location. An indoor localization system, based on Bluetooth Low Energy (BLE) technology, has been implemented in order to track each passenger's location while onboard and it has been integrated with the mobile application. Moreover, the application facilitates the familiarization of passengers with the ship's areas and the safety instructions. The mobile app can also communicate with the SafePASS system and provide real-time passenger location information and biometric information when connected with the specially-designed Smart Wristband. Passengers can check their location onboard the ship at any time on the mobile app and use the map-based visual navigation in order to follow the appropriate evacuation route during an evacuation scenario. Additionally, a user-friendly interface is provided for text message chatting among groups of people (family members or companions travelling together) to enable instant communication even without 4G/5G cellular coverage. Furthermore, it offers passengers the opportunity to quickly, and easily, request assistance from the ship's crew via a "request for assistance" button- should someone become injured or distressed.

The Passenger Mobile Application can be installed on any mobile device carried by passengers, e.g. smartphone or tablet, who are requested to provide their active consent on location tracking, which is to be used only under emergency evacuation situations.

The following figures (Figs. 1, and 2), illustrate different screenshots of the Passenger Mobile Application, namely Home screen, Instructions screen, Personal Evacuation Navigation screen and Group Chatting interface, respectively.

Fig. 1. Home and instruction screen of mobile applications

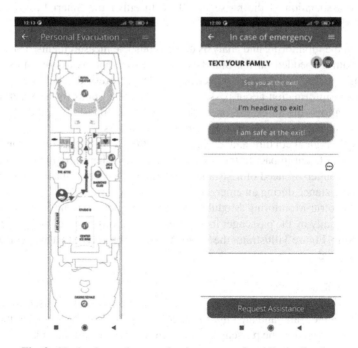

Fig. 2. Navigation and group chatting screen of mobile application

Smart Wristband. Another important SafePASS component is the Smart Wristband which is a wearable device that has been developed providing location support. The Smart Wristband integrates the Biometric Monitoring Module and its goal is threefold: (i) to uniquely identify each passenger or crew member, (ii) to enable physiological monitoring of passengers' vital signs, and (iii) to take it one step further, by providing a near-real time, reliable stress detection functionality upon ship evacuation, in case of an emergency. The Smart Wristband is intended to be handed out to each passenger at ship embarkation, containing a unique identifier associated with the specific passenger. Under emergency conditions, the Smart Wristband can be used for monitoring the passenger's biometric measurements (such as heartrate

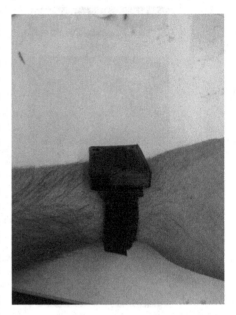

Fig. 3. Smart Wristband

and R-R interval (the time between beats of the heart), and oxygen saturation (SpO2)), and for the association of the passenger ID with either the Smart Lifejacket or the Passenger Mobile Application.

Through the monitoring and analysis of the biometric measurements, a stress detection algorithm embedded on the Smart Wristband runs and assess the stress level of the passenger. If and when the passenger is considered "stressed", the Smart Wristband sends relevant information about passenger ID and stress status to the SafePASS system and this allows the SafePASS operator can assess the physiological conditions and potential stress of passengers during an evacuation process.

The physiological condition, and in particular the stress, of passengers and crowds can have a significant impact in the evacuation process. Therefore, the timely identification of passengers in need of assistance and under stress can enhance crew response and timely assistance during an emergency.

The Biometric Monitoring Module is disabled in normal conditions, and can be activated manually by the passenger in emergency situations so as to initiate the physiological sensing. Figure 3 illustrates the Smart Wristband prototype that has been designed and implemented.

Smart Lifejacket

Lifejackets which are made up of buoyant or inflatable material are used to keep passengers safe in the water and are either handed out by the crew personnel at the muster stations or are located in the passenger cabins. In SafePASS, an inflatable lifejacket has been designed, to include novel technology and integrated into the lifejacket transforming it to a Smart Lifejacket. The Smart Lifejacket provides situational awareness, as well as on-demand navigation for the passengers. It incorporates an indoor localization system and complementary passenger navigation systems via audio instructions and haptics. The indoor localization system is based on Ultra-Wide Band (UWB) technology and provides real-time location tracking of passengers, while the navigation system guides them across the evacuation route towards the evacuation exits in case of an emergency. The navigation systems that have been implemented are based on haptic feedback in the form of vibration actuations on the lifejacket, and a chatbot in the form of audio instructions using earplugs.

The haptic navigation is perceived as vibration signals on the passenger's body towards a specific direction (front, left, right, back, up and down). The haptic navigation is easily activated by the passenger by pressing a button on the lifejacket.

Another essential feature of the SafePASS system is the automatic language identification of preferred languages. The Chatbot navigation is in the form of audio navigation instructions in the passenger's predefined language. The Chatbot is easily activated by the passenger by pressing the earplug's button, while automatic voice detection identifies the preferred language of the passenger.

The Smart Lifejacket is able to connect to both the Smart Wristband and the SafePASS backend system (which runs and supports the integrated SafePASS technologies) for receiving personalized evacuation routes and for sending the passenger location in real-time and in sub-meter level accuracy. Its main aim is

Fig. 4. Smart Lifejacket

to provide an alternative and complementary mean of personalized evacuation support to passengers, especially in low visibility scenarios and extreme emergency situations, as well as in cases where passengers are lost and no crew members are present for assistance.

1.3 Research Question

This manuscript seeks to explore the perspectives of passengers, crew and community of practice members on proposed Location Support Technologies within the SafePASS project. This is achieved through crew and passenger surveys and community of practice passenger workshops to examine the perceived usefulness of the proposed Location Support Technologies. From this, enhanced design of technologies will be achieved to support usability and acceptability for end-users.

2 Methods

To address the research question listed above, the present analysis consisted of 1) a passenger survey, 2) a crew survey, 3) a workshop with industry experts, and 4) a community of practice workshop.

2.1 Participant Recruitment

Survey: A sample of cruise passengers and ship crew were recruited to take part in the study between January and May of 2021. Eligibility criteria consisted of either 1) having been a passenger on a cruise previously or 2) having worked on board a cruise ship. Recruitment was conducted using a purposive snowballing strategy, with invitations to participate shared on social media and circulated by industry associations and representative bodies relevant to cruising. For crew, emails to current crew members were circulated by a cruise ship company to support recruitment.

Community of Practice Workshop: For the community of practice passenger workshop, participants were recruited directly from the SafePASS community of practice, which consists of representatives across stakeholder groups related to cruise ships, including those who work or stay on board. Any individual with interest in cruise ships can join the community of practice, with invitations to join shared frequently with stakeholder groups, at events and through social media. In addition, members of the public were also invited to attend through sharing of invitations to participate across SafePASS social media and with email contact lists.

Full ethical approval was obtained from the School of Psychology Ethics Committee (SPREC) at Trinity College Dublin (Ref: SPREC032021-09). Full informed consent was obtained from all survey participants through an online form and information sheet at the start of the survey. For those participating in workshops, information on the project objectives was provided during the workshop and informed consent was obtained earlier when the participants signed up to the SafePASS community of practice.

2.2 Survey

In order to determine crew and passenger perspectives on the usefulness of the proposed SafePASS technologies, two short surveys were developed. These surveys were developed in collaboration with technical partners and human factors specialists and sought to gather participant perspectives on the usefulness of location support technology in emergency situations on board cruise ships. Surveys were conducted online using Qualtrics.

Passenger Survey: The passenger survey consisted of 30 questions, and included sections exploring demographic variables, past cruise experience, experience with muster and abandonment and perspectives on the novel technologies. With regards to location support technologies, two questions were posed namely; 1) "How happy would you be to wear a wristband/other wearable tech that would allow crew to locate you in an emergency?" and 2) "How happy would you be to have your mobile device/tablet help crew in locating you in the event of an emergency?". Both of these were responded to using a five-point Likert-type scale from 1 (*completely unhappy*) to 5 (*completely happy*).

Crew Survey: The crew survey consisted of 26 questions exploring past experience onboard cruise ships, training for mustering and abandonment, perspectives on current Life Saving Appliances and Personal Survival Equipment, and perspectives on the novel technologies. Specifically crew were asked how strongly they agree or disagree with the following statements 1) I would like to have a smart phone application that would help me evacuate passengers and crew, 2) I would like to have additional information about the location of the passengers in case of an emergency; 3) I would use a smart phone application that would help me with the safety training, 4) It would be useful for me to have information about the vital signs of the passengers in case of an emergency, 5) It would be useful for me to have information about the vital signs of the crew in case of an emergency. Each of these statements were responded to using a 5-point Likert-type scale from 1 (*strongly disagree*) to 5 (*strongly agree*).

2.3 Workshop with Industry Experts

In June and July of 2021, workshops were carried out with members of the External Advisory Board of the SafePASS project. These members consisted of industry experts in data protection, maritime surveyance, the human element, maritime policy, coastguard and maritime safety assessment. The purpose of these workshops was to validate the socio-technical research approach and to ensure that it was comprehensive in nature, thus addressing concerns (from their respective expert fields) regarding data collection and the operational realities of implementing SafePASS technologies for human users. Feedback from the Advisory Board was invaluable and full detail of this is contained in the SafePASS project outputs [9]. In particular, feedback on data protection for both location and biometric data was useful. This features heavily in the human factors recommendations for implementation of SafePASS technologies and for future research to be carried out. These recommendations will inform SafePASS submissions to the International Maritime Organization (IMO).

2.4 Community of Practice Passenger Workshop

To add additional depth to the analysis, and to gather user input into the design of the SafePASS technologies, a community of practice workshop was hosted using Microsoft Teams with past cruise passengers on December 13th, 2021. The purpose of these workshops was to gather feedback from passengers on the SafePASS technologies and integrate input into the design of the technologies. Within this semi-structured workshop, a short emergency scenario was provided with participants asked how they would respond using current approaches. Following this a short overview of the SafePASS technologies was provided, the emergency scenario was re-presented, and attendees were asked to reflect on how they would respond with SafePASS technologies available. Open discussion followed, with questions posed determined in collaboration with the technology partners and sought to compare passenger perspectives on emergency procedures with and without the use of the proposed technologies. Broader insight into the use of smart-phones and wearable technologies within emergency procedures on cruise ships was also gathered.

2.5 Data Analysis

Survey data was analysed using Statistical Package for Social Sciences (SPSS), with basic descriptive analyses completed.

3 Results

Results obtained for the crew and passenger survey, and the community of practice workshop are presented in detail below.

3.1 Survey

Passenger Demographics: Passengers ($n = 215$) were primarily aged 65–74 (26%), from the United States (43%) or the United Kingdom (20%) and spoke English (85%). Additional detail on participant demographics is presented in Table 1 below. In terms of past cruise experience, 32% of respondents had been on more than 3 past cruises (so were experienced cruisers), 72% had travelled on their last cruise with family, while 35% of respondents were accompanied by children. Low volume of additional access requirements or individuals requiring further assistance were reported across passengers (3.26%) and their travel companions (5.9%), with the individuals with additional access requirements mostly aged over 65 (60%). Most passengers reported having had taken part in muster drills while on board (88%), and were confident in being able to find their muster station from their cabin (81.5%).

Table 1. Passenger demographics

		N	%
Passenger age	18–24	8	4%
	25–34	25	12%
	35–44	34	16%
	45–54	35	16%
	55–64	38	18%
	65–74	55	26%
	75+	20	9%
Nationality	United States	87	43%
	United Kingdom	41	20%
	Greece	18	9%

(continued)

Table 1. (*continued*)

		N	%
	Ireland	14	7%
	Italy	6	3%
	France	5	2%
	Other	23	24%
Languages spoken	English	209	85%
	French	27	15%
	Spanish	26	14%
	Greek	25	17%
	German	17	8%
	Italian	14	8%
	Other	26	13%

Passenger Perspectives on SafePASS Components: Passengers responded positively to the use of an official cruise app for directions ($M = 4.09$, $SD = .95$), suggesting a willingness to use smartphone technologies as support in emergency scenarios. With regards wearable technologies, passengers responded neutrally towards the use of a wristband or wearable technology ($M = 3.78$, $SD = 1.19$). It is of note that for the wearable technology, 16% of passengers reported that they would be unhappy to use this. This differs from the use of an official cruise app with only 3.5% unhappy to use. This highlights a need for exploration as to how use may be best supported for this group.

Crew Demographics: A total of 876 crew members responded to the survey, of whom 30.9% were marine officers, 30.4% were hotel crew, 24% were marine crew and 14.4% were hotel officers – 'marine' refers to those with responsibilities related to the sailing/maintenance of the ship, while 'hotel' refers to those with responsibilities related to serving passengers. Officers have a higher rank than crew. Few respondents were concessionaires (0.3%), though this is to be expected in the context of COVID-19, with cruise ships broadly not in service at the time of the survey, and as such staff more difficult to contact (concessionaires are independent staff working in gift shops, casinos, activities/entertainment and not directly employed by the cruise line). Broadly, crew felt that they had received sufficient training in mustering/evacuation ($M = 4.25$, $SD = 1.07$) and were able to complete their duties in an emergency ($M = 4.39$, $SD = 1.12$).

Crew Perspectives on SafePASS Components: Crew responded positively to the use of smartphones and wearable technologies in emergency situations as part of the SafePASS solutions. Crew agreed that they would like a smartphone app to aid crew and passenger evacuation ($M = 4.14$, $SD = .99$), more information on crew ($M = 4.49$ $SD = .85$), and passenger location ($M = 4.2$, $SD = .85$), and that they would use a smartphone app in safety training ($M = 4.09$, $SD = 1.04$). This suggests high acceptability of smartphone-based technologies for use in emergency scenarios. Additional detail is presented in Table 2 below.

Table 2. Crew perspectives on SafePASS components

		Marine Officer (N = 204)	Marine Crew (N = 117)	Hotel Officer (N = 91)	Hotel Crew (N = 129)	Total (N = 540)
Would like a smart phone application to aid the evacuation of passengers and crew	M	3.51	3.82	4.09	4.14	4.14
	SD	1.23	0.91	1.18	0.99	0.99
I would like to have additional information about the location of the passengers	M	4.15	4.16	4.41	4.18	4.2
	SD	0.89	0.77	0.89	0.79	0.85
I would like to have additional information about the location of the crew	M	4.2	4.15	4.49	4.24	4.49
	SD	0.89	0.78	0.85	0.83	0.85
I would use a smart phone application safety training	M	3.88	4.08	4.34	4.22	4.09
	SD	1.15	0.81	1.09	0.97	1.04

(continued)

Table 2. *(continued).*

		Marine Officer (N = 204)	Marine Crew (N = 117)	Hotel Officer (N = 91)	Hotel Crew (N = 129)	Total (N = 540)
It would be useful to me to have information about the vital signs of the passengers	M	3.87	3.99	4.19	4.23	4.04
	SD	0.96	0.86	0.99	0.85	0.93
It would be useful to me to have information about the vital signs of the crew	M	3.87	4	4.23	4.24	4.05
	SD	0.99	0.85	1.04	0.82	0.94

3.2 Community of Practice Workshop

A total of four community of practice members attended the workshop to explore their perspectives on location support technologies that are being developed as part of SafePASS. With regards to the as-is, or present-day scenario in the absence of SafePASS technologies, a reliance on smartphones during emergency situations was noted. Attendees reported that they would rely on their smartphones to remain in communication with their travel companions in an emergency, particularly if they are travelling with children. Phones would be used to ensure travel companions had successfully mustered, and to seek to reunite. With regards the use of smartphones more broadly, attendees were familiar with smartphone applications, and the use of smartphone-based navigation applications for location support. Concerns pertaining to smartphone use in emergencies included impact on battery, and requirements to have sufficient technology and internet access to allow for apps to be successfully downloaded and used. Concerns were raised regarding the acceptability of smartphone technology for senior citizens; however, it was felt that technological skill and comfort may have been positively impacted as a result of COVID-19. With regards to location tracking, an attendee noted that while they are familiar with these technologies, they would view them differently in the context of safety, and would be hesitant to have their location tracked at all times while onboard.

With regards to a wristband/smartwatch, attendees had no direct experience but were aware of these technologies. A preference for using mobile phones rather than wristbands/smartwatches was noted, due to the multifunctionality offered by a phone, comfort with use, and due to the potential for those who wear reading glasses not having them to hand during an emergency. For example, the legibility of text on a smart watch may be too small to read. Attendees' willingness to use a wristband for other activities on board (i.e. to pay for items or to open cabins), was mixed with some viewing it as a convenience, and others associating it with burden, as they would be required to keep track of an additional piece of technology.

4   Discussion and Conclusion

Emergency evacuation information provided to cruise ship passengers is static and may be reliant on understanding a foreign language, which includes all passengers who don't speak English or the language of the cruise ship company. The benefits of dynamically providing real-time information to passengers in emergency situations is easily understood by maritime safety specialists. From the analyses conducted as part of this piece of research it is clear that these benefits are understood also by passengers and crew. Existing and ongoing studies have contributed to the development of either smart life-jackets[4,5] or mobile apps[6,7] which provide passengers with situational awareness and basic evacuation instructions. Their goal is to digitize most of the emergency instructions, though major aspects of the evacuation process are not considered. The SafePASS integrated system on the other hand has included all the components required for end-to-end evacuation or mustering management, which can be viewed as a beyond state-of-the-art achievement. The SafePASS location-support technologies are viewed as being broadly acceptable and usable by both crew and passengers. Workshops highlighted the need to account for passenger demographics in terms of planning the implementation of the technologies, especially as it pertains to the elderly. Similarly, this will need to be taken into account for passengers with accessibility requirements. The present study is limited by the low number of passengers with access requirements who responded to the survey and participated in workshops, despite sustained efforts to disseminate the survey on social media posts of charities and accessibility associations in the EU. This will be remedied in further activities following engagement and liaison with the European Network for Accessible Tourism (ENAT).

In general, the results of the passenger and crew survey were very valuable and were taken into account during the development of the systems. The key points and insights that were extracted from the survey analysis provided an initial assessment of the under-development components and assisted the technical teams to focus on specific aspects that were considered as the most important and critical by the end users. In parallel, the outcomes of the Community of Practice workshop and the workshop with industry experts were used as a crucial starting point for the evaluation of SafePASS systems and were taken into account during their validation in a real ship environment. A pilot demonstration was conducted on a Royal Caribbean Group cruise ship that was in its final stage of construction at the Saint-Nazaire shipyard in France operated by Chantiers de l'Atlantique (SafePASS consortium member). During this pilot, several evacuation scenarios were performed (based on the format deployed in the workshops herein reported)

---

[4] https://cruising.org/~/media/Nawasena-Design-Report.

[5] https://iopscience.iop.org/article/10.1088/1742-5468/aaf10c.

[6] https://southpacificislands.travel/royal-caribbeans-safety-drill-goes-digital-with-new-app/.

[7] https://www.decurtis.com/suites/mobile-assembly-suite/.

and volunteers participated using real prototypes of the SafePASS systems mentioned above. After the completion of the demonstration, the participants provided their feedback through evaluation forms (using the same format as the surveys used in this piece of research), both from the operational point of view and the actual use of the systems. In general, the results extracted both by the survey and the workshop provided a detailed and accurate description of how the location-support should be conducted during an evacuation process and this analysis was borne out in the events experienced during the pilot demonstration. The results of this study were helpful in designing the pilot demonstration and the holistic approach to evaluation is driving the specification of an implementation roadmap using the results of the pilot demonstration evaluation.

For a technology to be effectively applied, it must meet the needs of those for whom it is intended. To ensure that SafePASS technologies are developed in a manner which addresses end-user needs, engagement with stakeholders across the development process was employed. Inclusion of stakeholders in the development of SafePASS technologies will ensure that end-user needs, preferences and barriers to use are reflected in the technologies developed, enhancing marketability in a competitive market space. It will also support the transferability of findings across projects and sectors, through establishing how user involvement in design may be effectively applied, and through identifying key factors of importance to stakeholders in this space.

A further survey on implementation is the final investigation in the SafePASS project. Once again, all stakeholders (both a wide range of passengers and all crew roles) in the Community of Practice will be invited to take part. This implementation survey will provide crucial feedback on how the implementation roadmap will be received by those who will use the SafePASS system and how the human factors recommendations on acceptability and usability may inform future IMO regulation and SOLAS. From sociotechnical analyses conducted in earlier in the project it is clear that there are practical barriers to implementation posed by the SafePASS technologies – primarily centered around impacts on existing processes and procedures, requirements for information campaigns targeting passengers, and needs for training and consultation with crew [9]. All these factors need to be included in an implementation roadmap to ensure that SafePASS realises its potential and achieves meaningful impact on operational settings.

Acknowledgements. The SafePASS project has received funding from the European Union's Horizon 2020 Research and Innovation programme under the Grant Agreement No. 815146. The opinions expressed herein are those of the authors and the European Commission is not responsible for any use that may be made of the information it contains. The authors thank those crew and passengers who gave their time.

References

1. Carnival Cruise Line. Safety Briefing - Muster Station Drill | Carnival Cruise Line (2021). https://help.carnival.com/app/answers/detail/a_id/1200/~/safety-briefing---muster-sta tion-drill. Accessed 08 Apr 2022
2. Future Cruise. Muster 2.0: a new kind of safety drill (2020). https://future-cruise.nridigital. com/future_cruise_nov20/safety_drill_cruise_ships. Accessed 08 Apr 2022

3. Drakoulis, D., et al.: The architecture of EVAGUIDE: a security management platform for enhanced situation awareness and real-time adaptive evacuation strategies for large venues. In: Akhgar, B., Kavallieros, D., Sdongos, E. (eds.) Technology Development for Security Practitioners. SILE, pp. 461–475. Springer, Cham (2021). https://doi.org/10.1007/978-3-030-69460-9_27

4. Bellomo, N., Clarke, D., Gibelli, L., Townsend, P., Vreugdenhil, B.J.: Human behaviours in evacuation crowd dynamics: from modelling to "big data" toward crisis management. Phys. Life Rev. **18**, 1–21 (2016)

5. Vreugdenhil, B.J., Bellomo, N., Townsend, P.S.: Using crowd modelling in evacuation decision making. In: Proceedings of the ISCRAM 2015 Conference - Kristiansand, Norway, 24–27 May 2015 (2015)

6. Townsend, P.S.: Crowd modelling for quasi-real-time feedback during evacuation in a situational awareness system. Transp. Res. Procedia **2**, 550–558 (2014)

7. Boulougouris, E., et al.: SafePASS - transforming marine accident response. In: Proceedings of 8th Transport Research Arena TRA 2020 (2020).https://traconference.eu/

8. Liston, P., Kay, A.M., Delemere, E.: Advancing a Social Licence to Operate for improved evacuation of cruise ships. In: Contemporary Ergonomics and Human Factors 2022. Proceedings of the Annual Conference of the Chartered Institute of Ergonomics and Human Factors (2022)

9. Kay, A., Liston, P., Delemere, E., Townsend, P., MacLean, I., Frænde, N.: D7.1 Sociotechnical Assessment of Evacuations: Current and Future, Project Deliverable to the European Commission, Submitted 31st August 2021 (2021)

The Environment and Its Implications in the Theory of Modern Science

Cristian Popescu[✉]

University of Bucharest, Bucharest, Romania
cristian.popescu@faa.unibuc.ro

Abstract. It has been written a lot about nature and the factors that influence and degrade the environment in recent years, in each represented domain, especially as a post facto reality. Through this paper it can be set out to investigate ancient writings that refer to the average factor and the causes of ecosystem imbalances in those periods and the correlation with modern events. It will be highlighting several objectives: to see if the environmental imbalances of modern times are related to modern events or not, or if the environmental imbalances based on past events have anything to do with those of today, and if yes what would be their cause? Among the ancient writings to which we will refer are the Bible, the testimonies of historians, recent writings representing modern assessments of past events, and so on.

Keywords: Environmental policy · Environmental crisis · Paradigm shift · Ecological footprint

1 Introduction

If the environmental factor at the beginning of the twentieth century was almost insignificant in research sciences, it began to capture the attention of the sciences during the twentieth century. In the twentieth century, research appeared in the field of scientific discovery focused on nature. This has had consequences in the humanities, such as theology, which raises the alarm about the vision of new researchers bent on modern heresies, such as anthroposophy, which develops concepts strictly related to the evolution of science, and removing God. Environmental exploitation is a phenomenon with long-term implications. And more recently, this overexploitation of the environment has led to its degradation with implications for human health. It is very clear that the approach to environmental impact has a multidisciplinary side, because the acquisition of bodily health is closely related to the health of the soul, which can be explained in mathematical terms with 2 seemingly unknown elements that depend on each other as a dichotomous system (soul-body) (Constantin 2021). Taking care of the soul, you will also take care of the environment because the environment-man relationship is in a

© Springer Nature Switzerland AG 2022
M. Rauterberg et al. (Eds.): HCII 2022, LNCS 13520, pp. 353–361, 2022.
https://doi.org/10.1007/978-3-031-18158-0_26

permanent harmony carefully described by the Holy Scriptures (Genesis, chapter 2–4). Thus, the elements that influence physical health (which in turn can influence mental health) can be numerous, these belonging to well-defined disciplines, such as medicine, psychology, chemistry and biochemistry, etc. in general the real sciences. Ecology could be said, at first glance, to be less important for human health, but correlated with other sciences and especially given the importance of the average factor in the current context of socio-economic development, we realize that the causal link between environment and health is increasingly direct.

2 Literature Research in the Field

The balance of nature through the two balance factors of flora and fauna is a hotly debated topic today, in line with the exact sciences, such as ecology, sustainable development or even economics, but it appears in an interesting context in the research of relative sciences, such as philosophy, psychology or theology in center being human. The link between these sciences is intrinsic, as we have a real problem facing today's society, namely the introduction of the average factor as a limiting factor on productivity in the global economic system due to pollution (OECD 2016). From the point of view of relative sciences, such as theology, the approach to assessing scientific progress has a broader view, on the present discovered, but also on the future that we are to discover ideas inspired and influenced by Greek philosophers (being in faith and prepared for the revelation of the divine revelation that is gradually revealed to us) (Lemeni 2013). The other approach, the exact sciences, considers only the present, and the aspect that science provides the answers to the existence of our lives, so that each stage of technological development is a new answer to human existence on earth (maximizing the results discovered by science until that moment) (Lemeni 2013). Looking at the economic development of the twentieth century and the emergence of the environmental factor in the equation of economic development by introducing the concept of sustainable development, we see that the impact of human environmental footprint has the effect of degrading life on earth with future effects. It is known that there are possibilities to predict some economic phenomena, only that the evolution of science is an unpredictable phenomenon, which will have effects on the predictions made.

People have become a major influencer, even indirectly, on the environment. That is why human footprints should be taken into account in environmental externalities, which can be quantified by the pollutants that influence human health. This idea is based on the assessment of the impact on the environment (by pollutants) and its effect on human health.

Why can we assess pollution (or economic impact on the environment) in terms of the effects of environmental exploitation on human health? Answer: Because at present there are more and more muted results through which the exploitation of the environment has the effect of making people sick, a phenomenon that happens in the long run. In other words, what was recorded as the cause by the exploitation of the environment at the beginning of the twentieth century, the indirect effects on human health manifest themselves after a number of years, in the middle or even at the end of the twentieth century. So, even if the time factor intervenes, the correlation between pollutant and health degradation is real and it can be quantified.

The direct correlation between cause and effect in economics regarding the impact of an environmental externality on an economic result can be written in the form of the utility function (Costel 2004):

$$U = f(x_{ij}),\ i, j \neq 0,\ i, j \in [1 \dots n]\ \text{natural numbers, where}\ U = \text{utility level;}$$

f = utility function as a function of variable j as an effect of the environmental externality generated by the agent and the polluter. In this case it is sought to see what is the level of influence of the polluting agent on the economic result, and as long as the effects of pollution are reversible and their costs cover the social benefit, then the polluting factor is accepted.

This means that the assessment of the exploitation of environmental resources is made taking into account:

1. Environmental resources, ie the degree of exploitation of the environment to allow the restoration of the environment following the use/pollution of the environment;
2. Economic and financial results (including operating costs), which strictly express the financial efficiency of the operation of a good (even environmental).

Statistics show that in the most exploited areas of the environment, in the countries with the highest GDPs, we also have a high level of pollution, and consequently there are serious health problems of the population.

For example, one of the indicators that shows the health status of the population related to pollution is HDI (Human Development Index) tells us that the most developed states are also the most polluted, and have the incidence of cancer among the highest values in the world. Below is a summary table with HDI - CO_2 and GDP emissions (Table 1).

Table 1. Statistical data of the quantitative and qualitative indices that show the dependence between wealth, and the rate indices that determine the diseases caused by the exploitation of the environment (pollution)

Country	GDP (nomial, 2017) mld USD	Cancer incidence (rate to 10,000 inhabitants, as average of the period 2003–2007)	HDI (Human Development Index very high)	CO_2 emissions/inhabitant (average 1995–2009)
United States of America	19.485,4	34.7525	0.914	16.9
Japan	4.872,4	21.805	0.89	9.2
Australia	1.323,4	32.585	0.933	18
Spain	1.314,3	26.125	0.869	6.3
Denmark	329,8	30.855	0.9	7.9
Slovakia	95,6	27.645	0.83	8.1

Source: authors calculations based on statistical data (from On the Economics of climate change and health: an overview, Popescu C. și Ion R., 2017).

This means that the incidence rate of cancer is correlated with CO2 emissions and HDI, and there is a link between the indicators.

The above table transposed into graphs gives us a better view of the proportionality between the variables taken into account (Fig. 1).

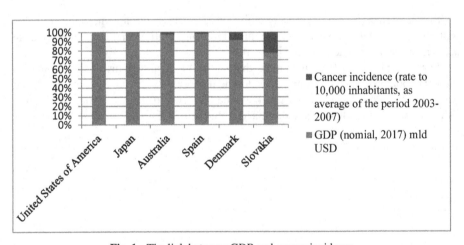

Fig. 1. The link between GDP and cancer incidence

Although developed countries pollute a lot, having the highest values for cancer incidences per 1000 inhabitants, when we relate these last values to GDP it is observed that the values are inversely proportional, which shows that wealth is not an encouraging factor to limit the effects of pollution, on the contrary, it could be said that richer countries have enough money to cover their losses caused by the exploitation of the environment through excessive pollution.

In other words, the wealth of highly industrialized states could be translated as a discouraging factor regarding the limitation of environmental exploitation, which in principle is already known, but which is now also proven by statistics.

However, if the incidence of "modern diseases" will increase, then in addition to any economic calculations there will be a strong social component that manifests itself in any kind of crisis. Thus, there can also be a manifestation of the environmental crisis which, if the excessive exploitation of the environment continues, then this will have as its starting point the impact of the environment on the degradation of human health (Fig. 2).

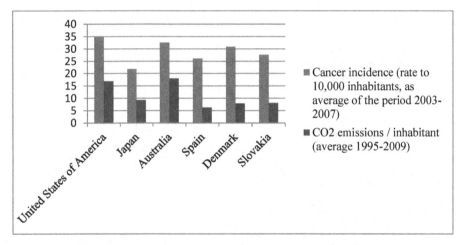

Fig. 2. Correlation of cancer incidence indices and CO2 emissions

From the graph above, we can see an almost perfect correlation of the two sets of data that show a close connection between the polluting factor and its effect on human health, i.e. cancer.

We agree that there could be a coincidence, but still there are many examples in specialized books that show this dependence between the cause-effect variables, that is, between the polluting factor and the degradation of health. The best example is the correlation between smoking and lung cancer. This correlation is presented in the graph below (Figs. 3 and 4).

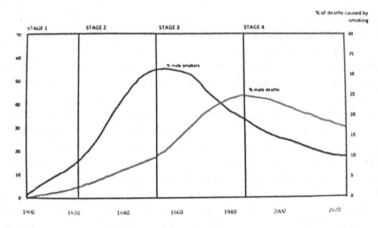

Source: Bernard W. Stewart, Christopher P. Wild, World Cancer Report 2014, p. 83

Fig. 3. Stages of tobacco epidemic in men in 20th century

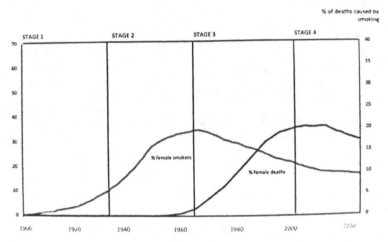

Source: Bernard W. Stewart, Christopher P. Wild, World Cancer Report 2014, p. 83

Fig. 4. Stages of tobacco epidemic in women in 20th century

From both graphs above, some ideas emerge that can be generalized regarding the cause-effect relationship in the case of exploitation-pollution-affecting the environment with an impact on people's health:

1. **Periods of 30–50 years represent very short periods of time (environment consideration)**: considering the reporting for a period of 20–30 years, we could say that the effect on the environment is long-term when there is pollution. It's just that, if we take into account that the pollution process is permanent and constant, and especially

that for thousands of years the environment has not undergone considerable changes due to human exploitation, the period of 30 years can be seen as a very short period of time. In other words, we pollute in 30 years what our ancestors did not do in thousands of years.

2. **The correlation between pollution effects on human health is very close.** Practically, for a person who starts smoking, according to statistics, after an average period of 30 years, he gets lung cancer. There are similar statistics on other polluting elements, especially regarding food pollution (Fig. 5).

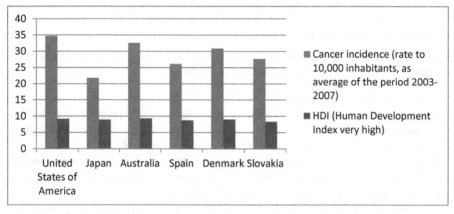

Fig. 5. Correlation of HDI (very high) with cancer incidence

This close link between an indicator that shows the standard of living Human Development Index and the increased rate of cancer in the respective countries shows once again that the rich, who pollute more, also have a very high rate of illness. Could we say that Nature takes revenge?

The concept of the ecological footprint, which connects nature with people's needs by quantifying natural resources for sustaining life on earth, is very current (Mathis 2019).

The evaluation of the ecological footprint at the planetary level is already carried out by having different environmental indicators to which the total population of the countries of the world is related (Fig. 6).

Source: https://data.footprintnetwork.org/#/

Fig. 6. The Ecological Footprint measures how much demand human consumption places on the biosphere. It is measured in standard units called global hectares.

From the data presented above, it can be seen that there is a quantitative evaluation of the human-environment link, so that it is possible to estimate the degree of occupation of a territory and the capacity of this territory to feed those people.

However, there is also an important qualitative component in the human-environment relationship, because, for example, in a certain region a much smaller population can pollute much more than a larger population in another region.

Therefore, as a stage conclusion, we consider that from this point of view, the change of the paradigm of evaluating the impact of environmental exploitation must move from the financial area to the social area where man is at the center, and the impact on the environment is evaluated as an effect on people's health, and which can have and an economic component. In other words, the social component being more important will be the focus of attention, and the economic component will derive from the results evaluated from a social point of view.

3 Reanalysis of Data from Anthroposophical Perspective

The above data tell us that the connection of the exploitation of the environment with the economic-financial effects should be made from an anthroposophical point of view as follows:

1. Man by his decisions is the main factor on which the exploitation of the environment depends, and the whole man is the one who can be held accountable by quantifying the effects of the exploitation of the environment by him.
2. The current system of assessing marginal utility and calculating direct effects in the form of environmental costs is no longer relevant because it is no longer motivational for the average individual because the (long-term) environmental effects do not motivate the average citizen who has a short-term perspective, to take a stand against the exploitation of the environment.

3. The system of values as a result of certain effects on the exploitation of the environment, taken into account by individuals in a society, must be changed according to the interests of those individuals, so that they have a positive, expected, immediate and much easier action. Communicated to people with tangible results.
4. There is a need for an immediate change in the paradigm of communication to society on the exploitation of the environment, in order to hold citizens accountable for the environmental impact on human health, more than does the current paradigm focused on economic and financial assessments of results with direct effects on environment.

4   Conclusions

Given the above, changing the paradigm of environmental effects on society and future generations, ie sustainable development, can only be achieved from an anthroposophical point of view, by quantifying the effects of environmental exploitation on human health.

The proposed model introduces the variable that will result in the effect of environmental exploitation on human health and not an economic outcome comparable to pollution costs and economic outcomes.

$$C = z(xij), i, \ ji, j \neq 0, \ i, j \in [1 \ldots n] \text{natural numbers}$$

where $C =$ the level of health costs; $z =$ function of health costs according to the variable j as an effect of the environmental externality generated by the agent and the polluter.

If in the case used so far we maximize the level of utility, in the second model we will minimize the function of health costs as an effect of environmental pollution to evolve the impact of environmental exploitation. This function can be applied for long periods of time, as the certain effects on human health as a result of the exploitation of the environment are measurable over such medium and long periods of time. The biggest advantage of this formula is that it allows science to respond to current communication needs to the population and to show in a scientific way what is the impact of environmental exploitation on the health of the population, a population that does not understand that environmental exploitation will have economic consequences. Diminish the ability of future generations to benefit from meeting their needs, just as current generations do.

References

Lemeni, A.: Apologetică Ortodoxă, vol. 1, vol. 2, Ed Basilica, București (2013)
Costel, N.: Bazele Economiei Mediului, Ed. Didactică și Pedagogică, București (2004)
World Cancer Report. WHO Press (2014)
Constanin, G., Cuvânt, Î.: la Meditație la Medicina Biblică, autori Pavel Chirilă și Mihai Valîcă, ed. Christiana, București (2021)
Mathis, W., David. L., Mikel, E., Laurel, H., Peter, R.: Defying the footprint oracle: implications of country resource trends, MDPI. https://www.mdpi.com/2071-1050/11/7/2164
OECD: The economic consequences of outdoor air pollution, OECD Publishing, Paris (2016) https://www.oecd.org/environment/indicators-modelling-outlooks/Policy-Highlights-Economic-consequences-of-outdoor-air-pollution-web.pdf
Cristian, P.G., Raluca, I.A. (2018). On the economics of climate change and health: an overview. In: Omran, A., Schwarz-Herion, O. (eds.) The Impact of Climate Change on Our Life. Springer, Singapore. https://doi.org/10.1007/978-981-10-7748-7_4
Other sites. https://data.footprintnetwork.org/#/

New Energy Hybrid Environment Power Management System: Design and Test Based on DSpace High-Fidelity Simulation

Yuyang Tian$^{(\boxtimes)}$, Han Ye, and Shaoyi (Stephen) Liao

City University of Hong Kong Shenzhen Research Institute, Shenzhen, Guangdong, China
yytian3-c@my.cityu.edu.hk

Abstract. Compared with batteries, supercapacitors have high density, and it can work in a wider range of climatic conditions. In addition, ultracapacitors have lower internal resistance and longer life span. Our study aims to design a new energy hybrid management system to solve the problem of the combination of batteries and supercapacitors in the most efficient way. Also, by using the real driving data, we can test how the system interact with the drivers on different roads. The efficient multi-energy power management system based on supercapacitors and batteries includes: bidirectional DC/DC (Direct Current to Direct Current) converters, battery modules and supercapacitor modules, ECUs (Electronic Control Units), motor controllers, motors, etc. We used models created in the existing DSpace-based simulation environment to detect and control the power flow in various driving scenarios. As a result, the hybrid energy vehicle effectively improves the steep acceleration, reduces the instantaneous high current output of lead-acid batteries, and effectively protects the power battery. We obtained a complete set of intelligent control strategies for energy management and verified the effectiveness of the designed optimal energy management control algorithm.

Keywords: New energy · Energy management systems · System design · Simulation

1 Background

The unparalleled profitability of the modern vehicle sector has accelerated the global economy's expansion. The global car population has surpassed 750 million, with an annual growth rate of over 10%. However, since air quality has deteriorated and petroleum resources have become increasingly scarce as a result of the emissions of many fuel cars, the energy-saving and environmental friendly have become increasingly important. In today's automobile business, developing new vehicles with low emissions and fuel consumption has become a priority. Electric vehicles (EV) and hybrid electric vehicles (HEV) can attain zero emissions, which is unquestionably the most effective solution to address the issue. With the rapid advancement of new energy vehicle technology in recent years, an increasing number of new energy cars have arrived on the

The original version of this chapter was revised: an acknowledgement has been added. The correction to this chapter is available at https://doi.org/10.1007/978-3-031-18158-0_39

© Springer Nature Switzerland AG 2022, corrected publication 2023
M. Rauterberg et al. (Eds.): HCII 2022, LNCS 13520, pp. 362–375, 2022.
https://doi.org/10.1007/978-3-031-18158-0_27

market. Common new energy vehicles include EV (pure electric vehicle), HEV (hybrid electric vehicle), PHEV (plug-in hybrid vehicle), etc.

Existing energy management systems for electric vehicles are constrained by two competing performance requirements, namely the balance between high energy demand and high power. Batteries are the most extensively utilized energy storage device. However, there are still various obstacles batteries: (1) The battery's power density must be sufficient to fulfill peak demand. Although high-capacity batteries are available, they are typically huge, heavy, and expensive; (2) frequent charging and discharging reduces battery life. Supercapacitors offer a higher power density than batteries, which can compensate for battery systems' low specific power. It also works in a broader range of weather situations. Supercapacitors also have a very low internal resistance and a million-hour life cycle. Supercapacitors are becoming increasingly popular as a result of their complementing performance to batteries.

The efficient multi-energy power management system based on supercapacitor and battery is a hybrid energy source that combines supercapacitor and battery modules to solve the present challenge of single energy source for new energy vehicles. By controlling bi-directional DC/DC for charging and discharging control, the energy system controller can fully utilize the advantages of the super capacitor and battery to improve the vehicle's power performance, extend the battery's service life, improve the vehicle's recovery efficiency, and extend the vehicle's range.

However, in order to maximize the benefits of hybrid energy, it must be used in conjunction with bi-directional DC/DC. The utilization of battery and supercapacitor is directly affected by bi-directional DC/DC for hybrid energy, which limits the application of hybrid energy. The accuracy of the bi-directional DC/DC influences the hybrid energy's performance and efficiency, impacting the vehicle's economy.

We propose an on-board bi-directional DC/DC converter for hybrid energy systems based on the aforementioned challenges. The system uses a bi-directional non-isolated BUCK/BOOST type to accomplish bi-mode bi-directional control of voltage and current, merging bi-directional DC/DC output control and high voltage management into one. Fast switching response is achieved using the new low-loss power technology GaN (gallium nitride) and a high anti-saturation inductor. Because the solution is totally digital, the optimal control may be chosen based on the current condition, and the control approach is more adaptable. Furthermore, this solution makes use of novel materials and magnetic integration technologies to improve efficiency and reduce size, resulting in a bidirectional DC/DC with improved dynamic response, higher efficiency, smaller size, and lighter weight. Finally, this solution is intended to develop a bi-directional DC/DC with precise voltage control that can endure high voltage and strong current, as well as humidity and high temperatures, while also providing a technical foundation for bi-directional DC/widespread DC's adoption.

2 Literature Review

Due to rising gasoline prices and environmental concerns, electric cars (EVs) are becoming more popular. Electric vehicles outperform gasoline-powered internal combustion engines (ICE) vehicles in terms of fuel economy and compliance with modern pollution regulations. EVs, in particular, are subjected to a variety of time-varying power needs, such as abrupt accelerations and decelerations (regeneration periods). This acceleration and regeneration time is analogous to a pulsed load change, in which the battery is forced to draw significant instantaneous charging currents that degrade battery performance.

Auxiliary energy storage technologies (supercapacitors) are sometimes employed to reduce the negative impact on batteries [1]. Different supercapacitor connection topologies can be used to reduce the effects of battery performance on abrupt charging and discharging. Because supercapacitors have a high power density, they can manage transient pulsed EV loads, reducing battery stress and increasing high-speed current requirements. We can meet short-term peak power demands with supercapacitors and long-term average power demands with batteries by combining batteries and supercapacitors [2, 3]. Supercapacitors have the advantage of being able to deliver and even absorb large transient pulses of power, ensuring that load needs are met during rapid acceleration and deceleration/regeneration of the drive.

Because the fundamental features of batteries and supercapacitors differ (for example, voltage levels or charging/discharging), a correct interface between the two sources is required. Because bidirectional DC-DC converters can achieve high utilization efficiency requirements, a real-time electric vehicle energy storage management approach (known as HESS) is necessary to better and more efficiently allocate the vehicle system's power demand among the energy storage devices [1, 6]. Between these devices, an improved hybrid energy storage system (HESS) will cut energy consumption and lengthen battery life [4].

Many HESS management schemes, such as fuzzy logic control schemes [9], rule-based control schemes [10], model predictive control schemes [11], and filtering-based schemes [12], etc., have been introduced over time. Hung et al. [13] proposed an optimization scheme involving hybrid source sizing and energy storage management strategies to achieve high performance and minimal operating costs for EVs. Since a single system contains different components, the constraints of electric vehicle size and power management must be controlled simultaneously, which can be integrated using rule-based HESS techniques [7, 14]. The integrated use of several energy storage systems in an electric vehicle enables the system to efficiently drive the system with different resources at different times [7, 15].

3 Method

3.1 Hybrid Energy Management System Structure

Bidirectional DC/DC (Direct Current to Direct Current) converters, battery modules and supercapacitor modules, ECUs (Electronic Control Units), motor controllers, motors are contained in the multi-energy power management system. The role of bidirectional DC/DC converter is to complete the voltage conversion and control between supercapacitor and battery. The role of battery and supercapacitor model system is to provide energy and recover energy. The two ends of the supercapacitor are connected to the bi-directional DC/DC. The bi-directional DC/DC tracks and monitors the terminal voltage of the supercapacitor in real time, and by controlling the operating state of the bidirectional DC/DC to orchestrate the matching work of the two energy sources.

3.2   Hybrid Energy Management System Control

Based on the relatively low operating voltage of the supercapacitor, a bidirectional DC/DC converter is used between the battery and the supercapacitor to control the power distribution and to limit the charging rate of the battery to the supercapacitor when driving at low power. Without the DC/DC converter, the battery and supercapacitor would have the same voltage value, resulting in the supercapacitor outputting and receiving power only when the battery voltage changes rapidly, weakening the load balancing effect of the supercapacitor. In the multi-energy power management system, the output power of the battery should be comparable to the average driving power demand of the vehicle, while the supercapacitor should output power higher than the average power demand and can absorb regenerative energy. When the actual driving power demand of the vehicle is higher than the maximum power of the supercapacitor, the excess is provided by the battery. The supercapacitor is charged by the regenerative energy and the remaining part is charged by the battery when driving at low power. When the supercapacitor is fully charged, regenerative braking energy recharges the battery. The hybrid energy system provides the drive energy for the vehicle and a place to store the recovered energy from the vehicle. The hybrid energy system is used in vehicles with the following three operating conditions where an efficient multi-energy power management system of supercapacitors and batteries achieves drive as well as storage of energy.

For normal driving conditions in Fig. 1, hybrid electric vehicles demand power usually $|P_{req}| \leq 50\%$Pmax, which is a high specific energy source, provides energy to the vehicle through bi-directional DC/DC. In order to have a high power output of the supercapacitor at all times, the battery is also charged to the supercapacitor under light load driving conditions.

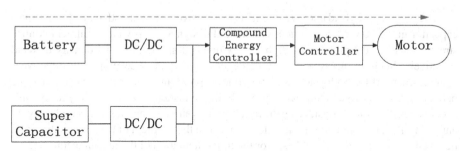

Fig. 1. Normal driving condition

When the vehicle accelerates or climbs a hill in Fig. 2, the demand power of the vehicle is usually at 50%Pmax $\leq$ Preq $\leq$ Pmax. The supercapacitor and the battery simultaneously provide energy for the vehicle to meet the power needs of the electric vehicle.

When the car is braking or driving downhill, the demand power of the vehicle is 50%Pmax $\leq$ $-$Preq $\leq$ Pmax. The motor is in engine mode in Fig. 3. The regenerative energy is charged for the super capacitor through the power converter. If the super capacitor cannot accept all the regenerative energy, the remaining part is absorbed by the battery.

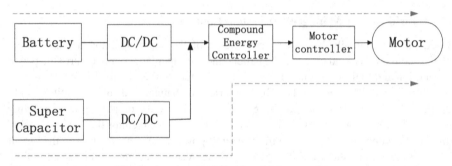

Fig. 2. Acceleration/climbing driving condition

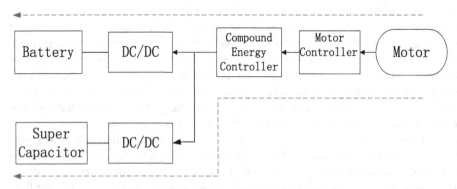

Fig. 3. Braking/downhill driving condition

The proposed "hybrid energy system" is to effectively embed both battery and super-capacitor in the power management system and design a precise and intelligent control strategy to solve the problem of high energy demand and high power density demand effectively. Such an effective energy management system is developed to effectively address the need for both micro and macro level problems. It is necessary to make the battery and the supercapacitor work properly in the instantaneous (possibly at the millisecond level) without considering the longitudinal vehicle dynamics, the vehicle driving and the traffic environment on micro-level, because the problem of proper collaboration between the two is a necessary basis for the implementation of the instantaneous energy control strategy. On the other hand, the vehicle driving dynamic mode is not described by the instantaneous traffic speed and acceleration, and the predicted energy demand of the EV is closely linked to the formal dynamic mode of the vehicle. Some other factors such as road surface inclination, road type, the driving conditions of adjacent vehicles may affect the energy demand of EVs. Therefore, the intelligent power system control strategy that only considers making the battery and supercapacitor work properly in transient time without paying attention to the overall traffic environment condition on the vehicle energy demand is not able to be applied in the actual traffic environment. This complexity in the design of energy control strategies due to traffic conditions and road conditions is called macroscopic complexity. So, we focus on the design of macroscopic control strategies that enable optimal control of the coordination between the battery and the supercapacitor in dynamic traffic systems.

3.3 Hybrid Energy Management Test Platform

The DSpace high-fidelity simulation environment is combined with a hybrid energy management testbed to build a simulation testbed for an entire vehicle energy control system as Fig. 4 shows. We use DSpace for modeling and algorithm implementation. DSpace provides a complete integrated development environment for embedded control software and supports a defined development process (especially for electronic control component development). This system supports modular control design and can be integrated with the MathWorks MATLAB/Simulink development environment. Because modular control design allows control engineers to focus only on functional development and to develop in an integrated software development environment, it is an efficient and cost-effective way to develop. This development process results in an optimized, validated system, and the probability that system components will not be optimally compatible with each other is very low. Due to its many advantages, it was chosen as the main development tool.

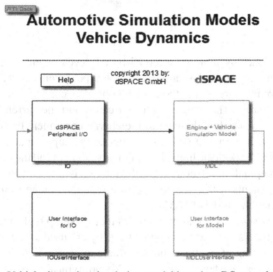

Fig. 4. Vehicle dynamics simulation model based on DSpace platform

The simulation test platform of the whole vehicle energy control system mainly includes DSpace whole vehicle simulation system, bi-direction DC/DC converter, battery and supercapacitor model system. The role of converter is to complete the voltage conversion and control between the supercapacitor and the battery, and the role of the battery and supercapacitor model system is to provide energy supply and recover braking energy for the whole vehicle. The two ends of the supercapacitor are connected to the bi-direction DC/DC, and the bi-direction DC/DC monitors the terminal voltage of the supercapacitor in real time, and allocates the matching work of the two energy sources by controlling the working state of the bi-direction DC/DC.

In Fig. 5, we use model created in the existing DSpace-based simulation real-time simulation environment to efficiently detect and control power flow in various driving scenarios. Driving simulators, acceleration and brake pedals, and driver steering wheels will be used to simulate driving behavior habits on specific roads as well as on unaware roads. In addition, the system provides a complete embedded control software and integrated development environment. With this new platform we are applying future speed prediction models, EV physical models, and supercapacitor/battery control strategies to the full vehicle simulation system in the lab to verify the feasibility and practicality of these models and strategies.

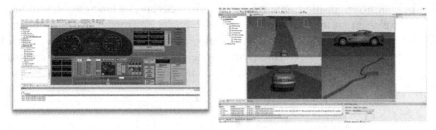

Fig. 5. Motion desk

We use the DSpace system and a model-based development approach for system level simulation and testing, and we also use a prototype system to evaluate our solution. The conceptual architecture is that the update controller connects the vehicle's engine to the rest of the system. The update controller can report the current state of whether charging is needed or the flow demand to the charge controller. The charge controller can then optimize the execution strategy to operate the supercapacitor and enable the battery system to handle both the high energy density demand and the high-power density demand. The conceptual architecture described above is implemented in DSpace, and the different components within the architecture will correspond to the corresponding Automotive Simulation Models (ASMs).

ASMs are open-source simulation modules that make up real-time simulation systems for cars and trucks and their components. They are used as device models for the development and testing of engine control, vehicle dynamics control, on-board power electronics, and driver assistance systems. ASMs are typically run in a DSpace simulation environment for the purpose of hardware loop testing of electronic control units (ECUs) or during the design phase of validating offline simulation control algorithms. More specifically, motor and update controllers, supercapacitors, battery systems and vehicle dynamics will be implemented by the corresponding ASMs. The charge controller just mentioned is an ECU that not only controls the supercapacitor and the battery system, but also receives signals from the regenerative controller of the electric motor. In addition, for data acquisition and system testing, we want to be able to let the user operate a virtual vehicle in DSpace like a driver with a series of real driving hardware. This requires a virtual electronic control unit to control a series of driving hardware. The vehicle simulation model can be used to combine with a real controller in a hardware-in-the-loop environment. This combination can be referred to as an online model. The vehicle simulation model can also be used in a model-in-the-loop mode, namely offline mode. We use this mode in situations when the transmission is not available. We use the online model in situations when the transmission must be used. We first collect three types of data: latitude, longitude, and altitude information of the road; real-time GPS data of the EV driving and its corresponding real-time power demand records; and a large amount of GPS data from any vehicle. Based on the above data, we then construct three mathematical models and one simulation model, which are: a future speed prediction model; a physical model for energy demand analysis; an optimal supercapacitor/battery control strategy generator; and a vehicle simulation model for the supercapacitor. The ultimate goal of being able to manage a hybrid energy vehicle is to control the flow of energy between the motor, the supercapacitor and the battery to achieve maximum efficiency. In order to achieve this goal, it is critical to accurately predict the upcoming power demand, and the predicted value of future speed is an important factor in the future energy or power demand model. With future speed as an input, we can then calculate the future power demand by using a power demand analysis model. Based on the prediction of the vehicle driving state, the vehicle power demand is built to meet its multiple objectives such as power and energy efficiency. Compared with the case of accurately obtaining the road slope in front of the vehicle, with error perturbation will lead to a strong randomness of the power demand of the power system, and this randomness will have a great impact on the reasonable power distribution of the battery and supercapacitor, so it is important to study the influence factors of error perturbation and its random distribution law, and determine the one-to-one correspondence between this distribution law and the power demand of the hybrid energy system to improve the hybrid, which is important to improve the energy management efficiency of the hybrid power system.

As shown in Fig. 6, the vehicle obtains the real-time latitude and longitude information through GPS, and the road slope information ahead of the vehicle can be obtained by querying the map information using the real-time latitude and longitude information. However, in practice, GPS/GIS will inevitably have errors, making the predicted slope ahead in error with the actual slope. The power demand forecasting algorithm will use the vehicle information as well as GPS information to analyze the influencing factors of the error perturbation of the vehicle and its random distribution law, so as to predict the current power demand of the vehicle and realize the reasonable utilization of the hybrid energy. An accurate physical model can effectively transform the driving data of a gasoline vehicle into the power demand data of a simulated electric vehicle. This transformed data will be used in the development of algorithms. The GPS data of the vehicle will be recorded and used as input to the physical model. The physical model will use the location and elevation information from these GPS traces to estimate the speed, acceleration, elevation, and eventual power demand at any point in its journey. Once the energy demand sequence for a particular route is calculated, we need a strategy to control the supercapacitor/battery for optimal energy efficiency and burst-assisted power performance. For example, when we predict an uphill climb ahead, we must ensure that the capacitor is charged to boost the upcoming acceleration. Conversely, if there is a downhill ahead, we can discharge the capacitor to collect as much energy as possible on the downhill. When designing the drivetrain of an electric vehicle, electrical energy storage is an important part of the system. One option is to use supercapacitors to store electrical energy. It is claimed that supercapacitors are more frequently used in the energy systems of electric vehicles than batteries, due to its high-power density advantage. When designing a new system, it is very necessary to create a simulation model for the system to test whether it will work properly in the future. The "ASM-Electric Components Model Package" provides a real-time simulation model of an auto-motive electric system. This package includes both an automotive electric system simulation component and a closed-loop simulation component. We develop a series of highly accurate models for electric vehicles, engines and engine con-trollers, battery and supercapacitor systems, and on-board charging and controllers. With these models, we also need to develop an algorithm that can predict future vehicle speed, energy demand, optimal energy output, etc. At the same time, we need to use a control principle to handle both power flows, such as the charging and discharging processes between the battery and the supercapacitor, and the energy transfer processes between the hybrid energy storage system and the electric motor as an energy consuming device. The control theory we adopt will be verified in a real-time simulation environment based on the DSpace real-time simulator to verify if this control theory operates and controls the power flow effectively through different driving states.

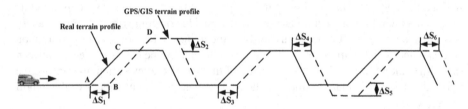

Fig. 6. Power demand forecasting method

4   Real-World Testing and Verification

After the motorcycle was successfully modified, the vehicle was safely started based on three typical road conditions: straight road conditions, slope road conditions, and steep intersections. Under different driving environments, the driving data of the modified hybrid energy motorcycle and the original lead-acid battery are filtered, compared and analyzed to optimize the modification strategy.

Based on the consideration of the cost budget, driving experience and power of the electric motorcycle. Focus on the cost, power and range of the electric motor-cycle to carry out a comparative analysis of three aspects. The current and voltage values of supercapacitor and battery are collected in real time during the driving process of the electric motorcycle, and the important parameters characterizing power such as 20 km/h, 40 km/h, 60 km/h acceleration time, slope acceleration, steep slope acceleration, peak speed, instantaneous peak power and range are calculated. The driving performance parameters of the motorcycle are com-pared and analyzed before and after modification, and effective solutions are proposed to optimize the performance indexes of the motorcycle.

4.1 Comparison of Electric Motorcycle Performance Test Under Direct Road Conditions

45Ah Electric Motorcycle Driving Test
Due to the dense collection of data points, the current data graph is not clear, and then the data is filtered and processed. Based on the real-time monitoring of current and voltage data, the output power of the electric motorcycle can be calculated and processed. From the comparison of Fig. 7 and Fig. 8, it can be seen that the acceleration performance of the electric motorcycle is up to 40% higher than that of the 45AH pure electric motorcycle during the acceleration process of 20 km/h, 40 km/h and 60 km/h, thus verifying that the power performance of the modified hybrid electric motorcycle has been greatly improved.

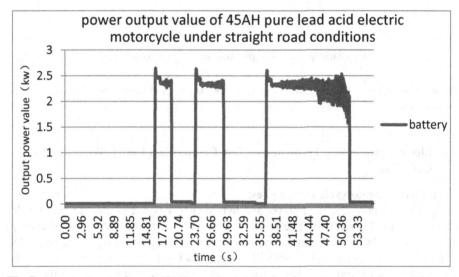

Fig. 7. Power output value of 45AH pure lead acid electric motorcycle under straight road conditions

32AH Hybrid Electric Motorcycle Driving Test
In the process of 0–20 km/h acceleration under direct road conditions, the percentage of 0–20 km/h acceleration of super capacitor and battery output can be seen in Figs. 5 and 6, which shows that the instantaneous power output of hybrid energy electric motorcycle battery accounts for 70% of the total output, and the remaining 30% is provided by super capacitor. In the process of 0–40 km/h acceleration, it can be seen from Fig. 8, 0–40 km/h acceleration supercapacitor and battery power output percentage that the instantaneous output power of hybrid energy motorcycle battery and supercapacitor each accounts for

about 50% of the total output. Effectively reduce the instantaneous high current output of lead-acid battery by 30%–50%, prevent the power battery from overcharging and over discharging, and effectively play a role in protecting the battery.

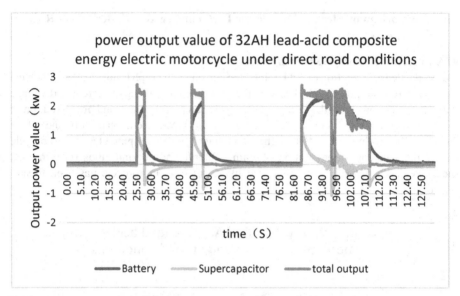

Fig. 8. Power output value of 32AH lead-acid composite energy electric motorcycle under direct road conditions

4.2 Electric Motorcycle Performance Test Comparison Under Slope Road Conditions

45Ah Electric Motorcycle Driving Test

Comparison of pure lead-acid power and hybrid energy power of electric motorcycle under slope road conditions. The recorded data shows that the 32AH hybrid energy motorcycle reaches a peak maximum speed of 59 km/h, with an arrival time of 22.9 s and an acceleration of $a = 0.72$ m/s^2. 45AH pure lead-acid battery motorcycle reaches a peak maximum speed of 57 km/h, with an arrival time of 25.9 s and an acceleration of $a = 0.61$ m/s^2. It is calculated that the acceleration of the slope of the hybrid energy motorcycle is effectively increased by 15%. And the maximum speed can still be reached and sustained under long slope conditions.

32AH Hybrid Electric Motorcycle Driving Test

In the slope road condition, from Fig. 9, the percentage of super capacitor and battery output of hybrid energy electric motorcycle, it can be seen that the instantaneous output power of 32AH hybrid energy electric motorcycle battery and super capacitor each account for about 50% of the total output, and the out-put power is slow and steady after reaching the peak of the slope, which effectively reduces the instantaneous high current output of lead-acid battery by about 50% during the starting process, and when the car reaches the top, the maximum speed reaches 59 km/h, the super capacitor still provides current output. It prevents the power battery from being overcharged and over discharged, and effectively plays the role of protecting the battery.

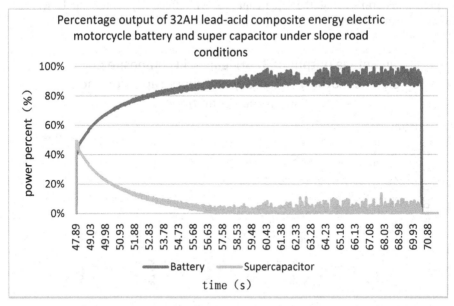

Fig. 9. Percentage output of 32AH lead-acid composite energy electric motorcycle battery and super capacitor under slope road conditions

4.3 Electric Motorcycle Performance Test Comparison Under Steep road Conditions

45Ah Electric Motorcycle Driving Test
Under the steep slope start, the instantaneous output current of the hybrid energy car accounts for 50% of the total output, and the remaining 50% is provided by the super capacitor, which effectively protects the instantaneous high current output of the lead-acid battery, and when the car reaches the top, the maximum speed is: 29 km/h, and the super capacitor still provides current output. The maximum speed of pure lead-acid electric is: 25 km/h. After calculation, the steep acceleration of the hybrid energy car is: $a = 1.21$ m/s^2, and the steep acceleration of the pure lead-acid power is: $a = 0.93$ m/s^2. As a result, the hybrid energy vehicle effectively im-proves the steep acceleration of electric motorcycle by 24%, reduces the instantaneous high current output of lead-acid battery by 50%, and effectively protects the power battery.

32AH Hybrid Electric Motorcycle Driving Test
In the steep slope road conditions, from Fig. 10, hybrid energy electric motorcycle super capacitor and battery power output percentage can be seen, 32AH hybrid energy electric motorcycle battery and super capacitor instantaneous out-put power each account for

about 50% of the total output, after reaching the peak of the steep slope output power slowly and smoothly, and when the car reaches the top, the maximum speed: 29 km/h, super capacitor still provides current output. It makes the battery output current rise smoothly, and effectively protects the battery instantaneous high current and high-power output. Long-term driving, the super capacitor will effectively protect the battery and extend the battery life.

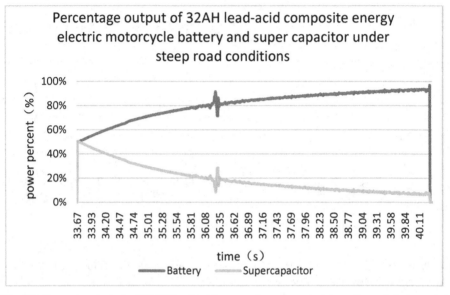

Fig. 10. Percentage output of 32AH lead-acid composite energy electric motorcycle battery and super capacitor under steep road conditions

5 Conclusion

This study proposes an EV/HEV energy management system and devotes research to hybrid energy management technology, based on the theoretical foundation of hybrid energy management system and practical application system, first by testing the dynamic characteristics of battery/supercapacitor single unit, module, and multi-module, using charge/discharge test equipment of low-current and low-voltage battery for battery/supercapacitor single unit, and high-current and high-voltage battery for battery/supercapacitor single unit The system creates a 16V/48V supercapacitor module and management system, as well as a bidirectional DC/DC controller for a hybrid energy system and a high-efficiency multi-energy power management system for supercapacitors and batteries.

The system can effectively tackle present technical obstacles including dynamic supercapacitor and battery energy matching and hybrid energy control strategy optimization. It can better control real-time battery/supercapacitor status, increase the safety and reliability of electric vehicles, and lower the battery replacement cost of electric vehicles by developing sophisticated energy management technology.

Acknowledgment. This work was supported in part by the development grants from Shenzhen Science, Technology and Innovation Commission (JSGG20170822145318071).

References

1. Fiori, C., Ahn, K., Rakha, H.A.: Power-based electric vehicle energy consumption model: model development and validation. Appl. Energy **168**, 257–268 (2016)
2. Kuperman, A., Aharon, I.: Battery–ultracapacitor hybrids for pulsed current loads: a review. Renew. Sustain. Energy Rev. **15**, 981–992 (2011)
3. Nikolaidis, P., Poullikkas, A.: A comparative review of electrical energy storage systems for better sustainability. J. Power Technol. **97**, 220–245 (2017)
4. Zimmermann, T., Keil, P., Hofmann, M., Horsche, M.F., Pichlmaier, S., Jossen, A.: Review of system topologies for hybrid electrical energy storage systems. J. Energy Storage **8**, 78–90 (2016)
5. Mishra, R., Saxena, R.: Comprehensive review of control schemes for battery and super-capacitor energy storage system. In: Proceedings of the 7th International Conference on Power Systems (ICPS), Pune, India, pp. 702–707, 21–23 December 2017
6. Deshpande, G., Kamalasadan, S.: An approach for micro grid management with hybrid energy storage system using batteries and ultra capacitors. In: Proceedings of the 2014 IEEE PES General Meeting Conference & Exposition, National, Harbor, MD, USA, 27–31 July 2014
7. Kachhwaha, A., Shah, V.A., Shimin, V.V.: Integration methodology of ultracapacitor-battery based hybrid energy storage system for electrical vehicle power management. In: Proceedings of the 2016 IEEE 7th Power India International Conference (PIICON), Bikaner, India, pp. 1–6, 25–27 November 2016
8. Li, J., Gee, A.M., Zhang, M., Yuan, W.: Analysis of battery lifetime extension in a SMES-battery hybrid energy storage system using a novel battery lifetime model. Energy **86**, 175–185 (2015)
9. Allegre, A.L., Bouscayrol, A., Trigui, R.: Influence of control strategies on battery/supercapacitor hybrid energy storage systems for traction applications. In: Proceedings of the IEEE Vehicle Power and Propulsion Conference, Dearborn, MI, USA, 7–10 September 2009.
10. Carter, R., Cruden, A., Hall, P.J.: Optimizing for efficiency or battery life in a battery/supercapacitor electric vehicle. IEEE Trans. Veh. Technol. **61**, 1526–1533 (2012)
11. Song, Z., Hofmann, H., Li, J., Hou, J., Han, X., Ouyang, M.: Energy management strategies comparison for electric vehicles with hybrid energy storage system. Appl. Energy **134**, 321–331 (2014)
12. Hadartz, M., Julander, M.: Battery-Supercapacitor Energy Storage. University of Chalmers, Gothenburg (2008)
13. Hung, Y.-H., Wu, C.-H.: An integrated optimization approach for a hybrid energy system in electric vehicles. Appl. Energy **98**, 479–490 (2012)
14. Song, Z., Hofmann, H., Li, J., Han, X., Ouyang, M.: Optimization for a hybrid energy storage system in electric vehicles using dynamic programing approach. Appl. Energy **139**, 151–162 (2015)
15. Khalid, M.: A review on the selected applications of battery-supercapacitor hybrid energy storage systems for microgrids. Energies **12**, 4559 (2019)
16. Roche, M., Sabrià, D., Mammetti, M.: An accessible predesign calculation tool to support the definition of EV components. World Electr. Veh. J. **7**, 101–113 (2015)
17. Xu, W., Hussien, M.G., Liu, Y., Allam, S.M.: Sensorless control of ship shaft stand-alone BDFIGs based on reactive-power MRAS observer. IEEE J. Emerg. Sel. Top. Power Electron. **9**, 1518–1531 (2019)

Widespread of Stray Animals: Design a Technological Solution to Help Build a Rescue System for Stray Animals

Lianfan Wu[1], Minghui Shao[2], Shuqi Wei[2], Rouxuan Lu[3], and Bingdie Huang[2]([✉])

[1] Wenzhou Polytechnic, Wenzhou, China
[2] Wenzhou Business College, Wenzhou, China
bingdiehuang@gmail.com
[3] Zhejiang University of Technology, Hangzhou, China

Abstract. The issue of stray animals in cities has received continuous attention from government agencies and animal organisation around the world. However, the lack of relevant laws and regulations, as well as the lack of public service resources (e.g. funding, space and labour), poses a considerable challenge to the survival and rescue of stray animals. To address this challenge, this study attempts to optimize the current social rescue system for stray animals through a technological design solution. This study investigates and develops a rescue system of stray animal through Human-Centred Design. This research has mainly discussed around the current situation of stray animals, their causes, hazards and rescue issues. The results of this research indicate that (1) the main causes of having stray animals in cities are lost, abandoned and disorderly breeding, as well as lack of regulations. Additionally, stray animals live in poor conditions with health many problems; (2) stray animals pose a serious threat to the development of cities. There is an urgent need to optimise the stray animal rescue system at the levels of individuals, shelters and social system; (3) a technological public welfare platform would be a reliable solution to effectively improve the situation of stray animals. As a result of the research, this study designed a stray animal public welfare platform APP, which has applied big data, AI and other relevant intelligent technologies. Additionally, it solves the pain points of current public welfare rescue platforms and optimises the existing stray animal rescue process and experience, as well as make an important reference for developing the construction of a technological stray animal rescue system.

Keywords: Stray animals · Rescue system · Human-centred Design · Mobile application Design · Grounded Theory

1 Introduction

Stray animals are unowned animals that are not appropriate for living in open air and have been meandering around urban open-air spaces such as parks, campuses and residence area for a long time [1]. Stray animals have long been regarded as a destabilising factor

© Springer Nature Switzerland AG 2022
M. Rauterberg et al. (Eds.): HCII 2022, LNCS 13520, pp. 376–396, 2022.
https://doi.org/10.1007/978-3-031-18158-0_28

in cities, easily endangering people's physical and mental health, urban public safety and the ecological environment. Traditionally, most countries have adopted euthanasia as the main approach to the management of stray animals [2]. However, euthanasia alone has proven to be ineffective in tackling the increasing of stray animal and alleviating the suffering of stray animals and their caregivers [3].

Studies have shown that a comprehensive rescue system of stray animal would be more effective in addressing the problem of urban stray animal proliferation than brutal euthanasia [4]. In the past three to four decades, countries such as Australia, Germany and the United States have built up their stray animal rescue systems, cooperating with Non-Governmental Organisations (NGOs) to increase the provision of shelter, rescue, adoption, education and other related services to slow down the proliferation of stray animals [5]. Currently, this has been effective in reducing the number of stray animals, but in general, it finds difficult for urban governance to build a better stray animal rescue system. Similar to certain developed countries, many cities in China have also faced an increasing of stray animal in recent years. According to data in authoritative media, the number of stray dogs in China has exceeded 40 million by 2019. Therefore, it is a worthy of in-depth study in China and worldwide about how to give stray animals more survival benefits and to optimise the existing stray animal rescue system based on the integration of existing social resources.

As a potential productive force, a wave of technology, with information technology such as big data, artificial intelligence and blockchain, is driving the sustainable development and transformation of society and production methods and has played a huge role in the stray animal rescue system. Previously, most of the research on stray animal rescue systems has favoured the exploration and application of the technical aspects. For example, Huang et al. developed an intelligent audit system based on deep learning and a majority voting to assist animal care organisations in Taiwan to automatically identify and audit the regulation of stray animal de-sexing photos [6]. Wang and Liu designed a low-cost animal detection system based on infrared thermal imaging technology) to help animal protection organisations to achieve systematic search and rescue and real-time monitoring of stray animals in cities [7]. It is easy to see that these studies have combined information technology with local application scenarios to optimise the stray animal rescue system. However, there are limitations in these studies. On the one hand, they do not take a comprehensive view of the stray animal rescue process from the user's perspective, on another hand, their practical usefulness for the overall optimisation of the existing rescue system is still open to question.

In a conclusion, this study strengthens the whole process of thinking about stray animal rescue systems in a holistic manner from the perspective of Human-Centred Design. Through the Empathize, Define, Ideate, Prototype and Test, the research will explore the shortcomings and user requirements of the system, optimise the current rescue process, and build a technological stray animal rescue system to provide design support for solving the population problem of stray animals.

2 Literature Reviews

2.1 Research Related to Stray Animal Rescue

Due to the multiplication of stray animals, governments have adopted a number of measures to combat the problem. This study summarises the common measures on the market, which includes Trap-Neuter-Release (TNR), adoption and other related regulations.

Promoting Regulations. With the impetus of animal protectors and related organisations, hundreds of countries and regions around the world have enacted numerous regulations related to stray animals, which have profoundly influenced the process of protecting and rescuing stray animals worldwide. It has been stated by Animal Welfare Act in the United States that local government shelters will be responsible for the re-homing of stray animals, including temporary re-homing, daily management and registration, and finding new owners [8]. In Japan's Animal Care and Control Law, intentionally abandoning pets has been regarded as a criminal offence and will result in a conviction for abuse or intentional injury depending on the actual situation [9].

Trap-Neuter-Release (TNR). Although there is an ongoing debate on whether the TNR comes with humanism, it is still an effective way to address the problem of urban stray animals [10]. This method is usually led by government agencies, animal protection groups, and other organizations to capture and neuter stray animals and then release them back to the original captured area after recovery, thereby which can help to reduce the natural breeding population of stray animals [11]. TNR has been widely used in management of stray animal globally, and the measure are localized in different places according to the actual situation. For example, in Taiwan and the Florida Keys, vaccination has been added as a step to strength the protection of urban residents in response to the vulnerability of stray animals to carry infectious disease and viruses [12, 13].

Encouraging Adoption. Studies have shown that encouraging adoption is an important measure to control the number of stray animals [14]. Petfinder, a stray adoption platform, collects and publishes photos and descriptions of stray animals from across North America in order to increase the willingness of adoption [15]. The American Society for the Prevention of Cruelty to Animals (ASPCA) reduces the chance of returning stray dogs after adoption by implementing the Meet Your Match Canine-ality Adoption Program [16]; In Taiwan, a group of local cat adoption have used Facebook for posting adoption message to help stray cats find In Taiwan, the local cat adoption society uses Facebook to help stray cats find suitable adopters [17].

2.2 Current Research Related to Human-Centred Design

Explanation of the Meaning of Human-Centred Design. In 1986, the concept of Human-Centred Design is originated from User-Centred Design introduced by Donald·A·Norman [18]. In 2019, according to a broad consensus among designers and scholars, the International Organization for Standardization (ISO) extended the design object of "User-Centred design" from end-users to stakeholders in its latest standard ISO 9241-210, and renamed this design approach as Human-Centred design (HCD) [19]. Therefore, it can be said that HCD is a design process and method based on deep insight into people, their needs, perspectives and experiences for design and evaluation [20]. Currently, many designers and scholars have started to explore how to involve various stakeholders in the design process through various methods and techniques. The research and practice of HCD can be divided into five phases: empathise, define ideate, prototype and test [21], see Table 1..

Table 1. Five phases of HCD.

Stage	Aims
Empathise	To understand a user's motivations and pain points about a particular product, service, experience, or area of need
Define	To define core problems and form a clear and actionable problem statement, based on research in Empathy
Ideate	To explore the solution space broadly and to generate that extend beyond current constraints
Prototype	To translate an abstract concept into a tangible asset that can be interacted in reality
Test	To iteratively refine the concept capturing the feedback from the users and ensure that their needs are being met

3   Methodology

3.1   Research Framework of Human-Centred Design

Based on the concept of Human-Centred Design, this study investigates the issue of intelligent stray animal rescue system construction and design practice through five stages: Empathise, Define, Ideate, Prototype and Test. This study focuses on the first four design stages. The stage of Empathise consists of semi-structured interviews and grounded theory analysis. The stage of Define consists of user persona construction and key problem statements. The stage of Ideate involves brainstorming and identifying preliminary solutions. The stage of prototype involves the refinement of the solution and the development of a final solution. The stage of test is beyond the scope of this study due to the detailed prototyping and a need for additional testing.

3.2 Empathise

Semi-structured Interviews. In the semi-structured interviews, the study developed outlines of semi-structured interview for stray animal carers and related practitioners. Before the formal interviews, the researcher invited two experts who were familiar with the situation of stray animal rescue and interview methods to conduct pre-interviews, then revised and refined the specific questions for formal interviews based on the questions and feedback that emerged during the pre-interviews. The main questions included the following 5 main questions: (1) What would describe the current situation of the survival of stray animals? (2) What impacts do you think stray animals would pose? (3) What would be the basic reason for the presence of stray animals? (4) What do you think are the problems in the rescue process of stray animals? All interviews were conducted between April 2022 and May 2022.

In this study, respondents were recruited using purposeful sampling. According to the principles of qualitative research target selection, all respondents are invited to meet the following criteria: (1) respondents had to have relevant experience in stray animal management, rescue, adoption or donation; (2) at least 1/4 of the participants have actually worked in a stray animal shelter. The contact details of the respondents were mainly obtained via internet and friends. After informed consents, research had formal interviews with respondents.

Content Analysis. The research is based on Grounded Theory's three levels of coding (open coding, axial coding and selective coding) and theoretical saturation tests to parse and decode the interview data, drawing on inductive reasoning to gain insights into the current situation, challenges and user needs of stray animal rescue. The coding data was derived from the converted text data of the interview recordings, which consisted of words, lines and paragraphs of relevant text. Three researchers were involved in the entire interview analysis process. Before conversion, the interview recordings were pre-processed using Xunfei's speech conversion software and manually verified by two researchers. In the analysis, the coding and checking of the rooted theory will be carried out independently by the two researchers. In case of disagreement, the third researcher within the working group will discuss with them and eventually reach an agreement.

3.3 Define

Persona. Persona is a tangible representation of the target user, with real characteristics, and can basically reflect the design requirements of target users. Based on the interview analysis data, the researchers apply personal knowledge and experience to extract the group types and characteristic labels of the target users, and clusters the user labels. In the whole constructing process, three researchers are involved in every discussion and then formed personas of this study.

Problem Statement. In the problem statement, the study presents the problem of stray animal rescue in the form of a 'how might we' statement which is a typical Human-Centred Design approach in the definition phase. In addition, it helps to reinforce the designers to think from the perspective of Human-Centred Design and avoiding a shift towards object-oriented solutions. From the interview analysis the researcher will gain insight into the current problems and develop a problem statement that is relevant to the characteristics of each persona.

3.4 Ideate

Brainstorming. Holding two brainstorming sessions is aim to discuss the problems that described in the problem-solving statement and to produce a concrete design concept, both involving six designers from different professional backgrounds, two of whom have some experience with stray animals. The brainstorming sessions will be based on the thinking of Human-Centred Design, which encourages incredible and seemingly impossible ideas and developed them into potential design solutions.

3.5 Prototype

Prototype in Figma. The research has deepened the design details based on the initial solution, integrated and extended the corresponding functions to develop an app design for stray animal rescue. The design has been further visualised using Figma to create a high-fidelity prototype of the stray animal rescue with a realistic experience.

4 Results

4.1 Empathize

Participants. After repeated communication and screening, fourteen respondents from the three major cities of Wenzhou, Hangzhou and Ningbo in China participated in this study. All respondents were from 18 to 33 years old, including ten females and four males. Eight of them were university students, two were university teachers, and four were stray animal rescue related practitioners (see Table 2.).

Table 2. Basic information of participants.

Item	Information	Numbers of people
Gender	Male	4
	Female	10
Age	18–22	7
	23–28	4

(continued)

Table 2. (*continued*)

Item	Information		Numbers of people
	≥29		3
Occupation	Animal protector	University student	8
		University Lecturer	2
	Stray animal related practitioners		4
Rescue experience	<2		9
	≥2		5

Content Analysis. The study carefully sorted through the fourteen interview data, using open coding, axial coding, selective coding and theoretical saturation tests to gain insight into the current situation and problems of the stray animal rescue system. During the coding process, it was found that no new concepts or categories had emerged since the 13th interview data. According to the criteria of theoretical saturation, theoretical saturation state is considered to be reached when new data no longer produces new concepts or categories.

After refining and summarising the interview content, the researchers further listed the frequency of coding and interview statements. In total, the study obtained 217 codes, through separating coding by the researchers and co-ordinated analysing by the leader. The study collated and summarised the codes, then analyse the internal links between each code, which in turn led to fifty-three initial concepts and nineteen categories, and ultimately to four themes (see Table 3.).

Table 3. Themes based on the content analysis.

Serial	Theme	Quote	Expression
1	Survival status	2	The survival status of stray animals, especially the external environment and their own conditions
2	Cause	4	Reasons for the flooding of stray animals
3	Hazard	4	The impact of the flooding of stray animals on cities and citizens
4	Rescue problem	9	Adverse factors in the implementation of stray animal rescue

Analysis of the Survival of Stray Animals. Based on the analysis of the codes for the survival of stray animals, this theme was counted to a total of 29 codes, mainly covering two main areas of poor survival environment (48.62%) and the health problems (41.38%), as shown in Table 4.. According to the proportion shown in Table 3., the difference between the two was not obvious. Considering poor survival environment, participants generally regarded the lack of stable food, overpopulation and poor living conditions as the key challenges faced by stray animals, while in terms of health problems, suffering from various diseases was identified as the core reason for the plight of stray animals.

Table 4. Current status of stray animals codes, frequencies and original expression of interviewees.

Serial	Category (Quote)	Cluster (Quote)	Original expression
1	Poor survival environment	Overpopulation (4)	Even in the face of harsh living conditions, the number of stray animals is increasing
		Poor living conditions (4)	The living environment is mostly poor for stray animals
		Being abused (2)	Stray cats are also abused and killed humans
		No consistent food supply (7)	As stray cats live in groups for a long time in poor living conditions, they are in hunger for the shortage of healthy food and drinking water
2	Health problems	Carrying various diseases (8)	Stray animals carry various types of diseases
		Suffering from psychological trauma (4)	Along with the fear and fright brought by humans, most stray cats have a very short span on average

Analysis of the Causes of Stray Animals. According to the participants, the reasons for the generation of stray animals could be categorized into four categories: lost pets (about 17.24%), human abandonment (50%), disorderly breeding (about 24.14%) and lack of restraint of relevant regulations (about 8.62%), which generated a total of 58 codes, as shown in Table 5.. Among these reasons, the most frequently mentioned by participants was human abandonment. Participants generally believed that many people didn't not mentally prepare for having their pets, which indicated that they were more likely to abandon their pets when their enthusiasm faded or they felt it took unaffordable time and effort to be involved in keeping them. In the coding analysis, the study also identified the category of lack of regulations. The study found that there has been no entry threshold for pet ownership in China and no regulations in place to protect stray animals, which led to many pet abandoners and in turn exacerbates some of these abandonment behaviours.

Table 5. The causes of stray animals codes, frequencies and original expression of interviewees.

Serial	Category (Quote)	Cluster (Quote)	Original expression
1	Pet loss (10)	Negligent management (2)	It is mainly negligence of breeders that leads to lost animals
		Animal trapping (4)	If a dog is stared at by bad guy and has not been trained to refuse food, it can easily be tricked away
		Poor road recognition (4)	Some dogs and cats are inherently spoilt and will only get anxious if they get lost and don't know how to recognize the way back
2	Abandonment (29)	Over fertility (4)	Pets breeds many pups causing some people to give up breeding
		Pet aging (4)	Some breeders abandon their pets because they are aging
		Disease (4)	A part of the pet will be abandoned by the owner after the disease
		Unable to afford breeding expenses (3)	The high cost of keeping pets has led some people to give up keeping them
		Lack of breeding experience (3)	Some people have no experience in keeping animals and abandon them once they are not well kept
		Loss of interest in breeding (4)	As time goes on, owners tend to lose or shift their interest in their animals and abandon them for various reasons such as moving house or getting married
		Lack of responsibility (4)	Some owners are more irresponsible and abandon their pets

(continued)

Table 5. (*continued*)

Serial	Category (Quote)	Cluster (Quote)	Original expression
3	Disorderly breeding (14)	High fecundity (5)	Stray animals themselves breed quickly, with some figures showing that 12 cats can become 10 million in nine years if left uninterred untouched
		Lack of natural predators (2)	Many stray animals have no natural predators of their own and it is difficult for anything other than disease factors to pose a threat to the colony
		Delayed sterilization (5)	Many people do not spay or neuter their pets in time, resulting in pets that are still very capable of breeding after becoming strays
		Adequate food (2)	Some people are reluctant to adopt but are quite willing to feed, which may also be a cause of the overflow of stray dogs and cats in urban downtown
4	Lack of relevant regulations (5)	Lack of family pet ownership access threshold (2)	The threshold for raising pets in China is extremely low, without any conditions can be raised
		Lack of relevant laws and regulations for abandoned animals (3)	Abandonment is not legally responsible, resulting in many pet owners being emboldened to abandon their pets

Analysis of Hazards of Stray Animals. Respondents thought the hazards of stray animals, as shown in Table 6.. Stray animals pose a serious impact on public security, which is considered to be the primary hazard to the city, accounting for up to 61.29%. Respondents reckon that stray animals (especially stray cats and dogs) are highly aggressive and often carry various pathogens, which threatens citizens' health and additionally makes urban traffic vulnerable. Besides, other hazards mentioned by them included affecting city outlook (about 19.35%), damaging the urban ecological environment (about

6.45%) and disrupting order of people's daily life (about 12.9%). They thought the hazards were the underlying causes of the escalating conflicts between stray animals and human beings. In a result, the hazard caused by stray animals has fully pervaded the urban life. At present, measures to control the stray animal population and reduce the harmful effects of stray animals on the city are pressing issues.

Table 6. Hazards of stray animals codes, frequencies and original expression of interviewees.

Serial	Category (Quote)	Cluster (Quote)	Original expression
1	Affecting city outlook (6)	Remaining livestock excreta (4)	It is mainly negligence of breeders that leads to lost animals
		Causing the dustbin around in a mess (2)	Stray animals also affect the appearance of the city by urinating and defecating in public
2	Damaging the urban ecological environment (2)	Damaging the urban ecological environment (2)	Stray animals have become a serious ecological hazard and there is an urgent need to find a solution
3	Affecting public security (29)	Causing traffic accidents (6)	Pets breeds many pups causing some people to give up breeding
		Being aggressive (8)	Many stray cats and dogs are aggressive
		Being prone to spread disease (5)	They can even spread disease and pose a risk to personal safety
4	Disrupting order of people's daily life (4)	Disturbing the teaching order (1)	The invasion of stray animals affects the orderly appearance of schools and communities as well as posing a public health safety hazard
		Disrupting residents' work and rest (3)	The sound of animals calling in the midnight affects residents' rest and ultimately leads to escalating conflicts between stray animals and people

Analysis of Problems in Stray Animal Rescue. According to the coding analysis, a total of 99 questions were generated in the process of implementing stray animal rescue, as shown in Table 7.. These problems cover a wide range of areas, involving three major levels: individual, animal shelter and social system. The problems at the individual level accounted for about 30.3%, including the lack of adoption conditions (about 9.09%), the lack of intention to adopt (about 8.08%) and the high difficulty in getting involved in rescue (about 14.14%). The problems at the shelter level accounted for about 54.55%, including the lack of human support for rescue (about 16.16%), the lack of material support for rescue (about 13.13%), poor management of stray animals (about 14.14%), ineffective online publicity (about 11.11%) and poor rescue channels (about 5.05%). The problems at the social level refer to the inadequate construction of the social rescue system for stray animals, accounting for about 10.1%. In terms of the percentage of the three main levels, participants believe far more problems with shelters than other two. From another perspective, shelters, mainly formed by private initiative, actively perform the function of sheltering and adopting stray animals, but they suffer from the lack of government and public support. Additionally, their work is carried out in a relatively sloppy manner. Therefore, shelters should be made more efforts to improve daily management.

Table 7. Problems in stray animal rescue codes, frequencies and original expression of interviewees.

Serial	Category (Quote)	Cluster (Quote)	Original expression
1	Lack of adoption conditions (9)	Lack of rearing energy (5)	Adopting stray animals consumes energy, thus making most people only willing to feed stray animals
		Lack of rearing time (2)	Busy work schedules make it harder to find time to take care of pets
		Lack of space for rearing (2)	There's not enough space in the house for pets to move around
2	Lack of intention to adopt (8)	Lack of love (2)	Stray animals have affected the survival of urban animals and as a result people are number to the problem of stray pets

(*continued*)

Table 7. (*continued*)

Serial	Category (Quote)	Cluster (Quote)	Original expression
		Have already haven pets (2)	Some people have already adopted animals, so they don't want to adopt again even if they are paid, because they have reached the upper limit of their feeding capacity
		Higher risk of disease (2)	Adopting a stray animal is more difficult than owning a pet, because stray animals may carry some diseases
		Lack of adoption consensus among family members (2)	Family members do not have same view on adoption, such as parents not allowing the adoption of stray animals
3	High difficulty in getting involved in rescue (13)	Lack of diverse forms of participation in rescue (5)	Nowadays, the only way to participate is to adopt, volunteer or donate supplies, but some people are willing to participate but do not have the time and money to do so
		Waste time in familiarizing volunteers work (5)	Those involved in stray animal rescue work are mostly volunteers and need some time to learn
		The difficulty of catching stray animals (3)	Stray animals are naturally active and not easy to catch and control
4	Lack of human support for rescue (16)	Low number of resident volunteers (5)	The threshold for raising pets in China is extremely low, without any conditions can be raised
		Low number of shelter managers (4)	The work at the shelter is very busy. There are only two people here, but they have to feed hundreds of stray dogs and cats

(*continued*)

Table 7. (*continued*)

Serial	Category (Quote)	Cluster (Quote)	Original expression
		Insufficient professionalism of staff (7)	There is a shortage of skilled veterinarians and staff who can run the network
5	Lack of material support for rescue (13)	Shortage of shelter materials (4)	In the traditional environment, shelters have little influence and are often plagued by shortages of supplies
		Lack of funding for shelters (9)	Most animal shelters are funded by private individuals and are inherently poorly funded
6	Poor management of stray animals (14)	Poor environment (5)	Dogs and cats can be heard barking before they even see the shelter, and the shelter is next to a cattle farm, making the sanitary conditions very poor
		Inappropriate arrangement of shelter (2)	The cramped space and poor environment in the shelter make it easy for animals to cluster and become infected
		Lack of management of categorisation (2)	On the one hand, the living conditions of stray animals are in urgent need of improvement, On the other hand, different animals are not managed separately, so there is a mess
		Lack of cooperation among rescue agencies (4)	The public shelters also do not cooperate effectively with animal protection organizations, and the form is more important than the content

(*continued*)

Table 7. (*continued*)

Serial	Category (Quote)	Cluster (Quote)	Original expression
		Poor transport arrangements (1)	In the process of transferring, too many animals in transport often cause animals to crush each other and the environment is stuffy, which eventually causes animal death
7	Ineffective online publicity (11)	Lack of diversity in online channels (4)	Most online promotions only publish on official WeChat account and should be extended to more platforms
		Inadequate online promotional and operational capabilities (7)	People may unfollow a public number at any time, so it is difficult to keep people's ongoing attention and willingness to communicate
8	Poor rescue channels (5)	Lack of effective contact with shelters (4)	Many people who want to help out with stray animals do not know how they can contact the rescue stations
		Remote location of shelters (1)	Some rescue stations are rather rudimentary and geographically isolated, which can affect the motivation to volunteer
9	Inadequate social rescue system construction (10)	Inadequate rescue system for stray animals (2)	In terms of improving the welfare of stray animals and solving the problem of stray animals in society, China has not yet developed a systematic and effective system and programme
		Limitations of stray animal management methods (2)	There are limitations in the way local governments and relevant departments are managed and organised

(*continued*)

Table 7. (*continued*)

Serial	Category (Quote)	Cluster (Quote)	Original expression
		Lack of unified official platform (2)	Nowadays, there are actually online adoption platforms, but the visibility is low, and the regularity is not guaranteed
		Now there are actually online adoption platforms, but the visibility is low, and the regularity is not guaranteed (4)	China still lacks the relevant laws and regulations to protect stray pets, many people believe that legislation should be enacted to protect them and safeguard their right to survival

4.2 Define

Persona. In the stage of Define, the study combined information on the social characteristics, cognitive state and user needs of the target users, further sorted and summarised the coded data, and constructed three target user personas of warm-hearted citizen, stray animal volunteer and shelter manager respectively (see Fig. 1).

Fig. 1. Personas of warm-hearted citizen, stray animal volunteer and shelter manager.

Problem Statement. According to the concept of Human-Centred Design, this research has applied the approach of How Might to extract and transform the problems that are found during the rescue process. It can help to obtain a problem statement that is used for guiding the development of the design prototype, as shown in Table 8.. In the problem statement, we were able to visualise the thoughts and needs of the target users and aim to define the problem of stray animal rescue in a comprehensive and systematic way.

Table 8. How might we.

Persona	Need
Warm-hearted citizen	How might we use smart apps to help more people get involved in stray animal rescue?
Volunteer	How might we use smart apps to help volunteers develop their strengths and manage to tackle issues of stray animal rescue?
Manager	How might we can use smart apps to help managers run shelters better and drive change at a social system level?

4.3 Ideate

Brainstorming. Based on the problem statement presented in the previous phase, the research used brainstorming to inspire and develop design concepts. With the efforts of the team members, the study generated 3 initial design concepts. After further consultation with users and a week of development and refinement, the study resulted in an intelligent stray animal rescue App based design as the final solution for this study.

4.4 Prototype

Prototype. Finally, the research develops the function and interface design of the stray animal rescue app, called 'Pet Home', in a design platform, Figma. The solution attempts to improve the current stray animal rescue system through six modules: Shelter, Donation, Volunteer, Pet hospital, Petfinder and Adoption (see Fig. 2). This app is aim to inspire more users to participate in the stray animal rescue.

Functions of six modules are described respectively below:

- **Shelter,** which is used to showcase the daily life of the shelter, with main features such as AR Live View and Live Rescue Push: 1) AR Live View, the platform will use the cameras in the shelter to help generate AR Live View of the shelter, allowing users to view and understand the daily situation of the shelter and stray animals online in real time; 2) Rescue Live Streaming, This feature allows shelters to attract and operate fans by opening live streams of stray animal rescue affairs. This feature allows users to comment, like, reward and share on the rescue live streams to enhance interaction with the shelter.

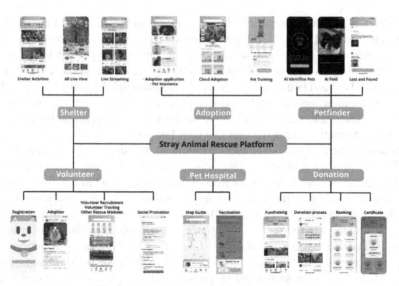

Fig. 2. App interfaces of six main modules.

- **Adoption,** which can offer an online service for adopting and open up adoption channels for both supply and demand. The module includes four sections: adoption application, cloud adoption, adoption assistance and pet insurance: 1) Adoption Application, this section is used to display adoption information (e.g. photos, basic information, physical condition, etc.) of stray animals posted by shelters and individuals. Users who are interested in adopting can communicate with the publisher online and make a comprehensive decision on whether to adopt. This section provides a safe and convenient adoption channel for those who want to adopt a stray animal; 2) Cloud Adoption, this section is for those who are hesitant to adopt, and offers cloud adoption as a pre-adoption method. After adopting a pet in the cloud, users can interact with the adopted pet remotely (e.g. watch updates, reminders to feed, donate supplies, etc.). The purpose of this section is to foster responsibility and familiarity with the pet, which in turn motivates the user to trigger an adoption; 3) Pet Training: this section contains functions of adopter training, pre-adoption checks and post-adoption tracking respectively. In the training section, users can learn about the habits of stray animals and scientific feeding strategies in advance through video teaching and expert advice, allowing users to prepare their feeding knowledge in advance. In the pre-adoption inspection section, the platform will assist shelters to verify the physical condition and vaccination status of stray animals to reduce users' worries about adoption. In the post-adoption tracking section, the platform will work with the shelter to keep an eye on the pet's adaptation and integration with the owner through online visits, and urge adopters to raise their own awareness of responsibility; 4) Pet Insurance, the pet insurance section covers pet-related insurance, including medical insurance, liability insurance, and consignment insurance. Users can choose pet insurance for their pets according to their own situation to minimize the risk of pet ownership.

- **Petfinder,** which helps users to find their lost pets, and includes the functions of AI Find and Lost and Found. 1) AI Find, it allows users to upload a photo of their pet and use the platform's AI recognition technology to automatically match the photo data of existing stray animals in the database and notify the owner immediately if there is a match; 2) Lost and Found, this function allows you to upload your pet's photo, basic features, location and other information, and set a reward amount. The platform will push pet search information to users within a 5 km radius based on the publisher's location information to help owners find their lost pets.

- **Volunteer,** which provides volunteer recruitment, training and promotion of social welfare services for stray animals, including volunteer recruitment, volunteer training and social promotion: 1) Volunteer Recruitment, Shelters can post volunteer recruitment information on the platform according to their own needs (e.g. recruitment needs, job positions, number of recruits, etc.), while shelters will also work together with the platform to provide users with simple insurance, volunteer hours certificates and other related services to ensure the common rights of both parties; 2) Volunteer Training: volunteers will be familiar with the daily affairs of the shelter in advance through online teaching courses such as videos, pictures and texts. At the same time, the beginner training will also provide much-needed theoretical training for shelters (e.g. pet first aid, online operation, etc.), so that volunteers and shelter managers can browse through the relevant courses to improve their rescue skills and experience; 3) Social Promotion, in this section, users can use the platform's social activities and discussion forums to promote the development of rescue systems of urban stray animals. Users can participate in social projects of interest and work together to improve the social welfare of stray animals by planning rescue skills training, promoting legislation and other activities.

- **Pet Hospitals,** which provides medical support services for pets, including pet visits and vaccinations: 1) Map Guide, shelters or individuals can search for nearby pet hospitals, search for information, book appointments in advance and be guided by directions in this function. In addition, the platform will also guide pet hospitals to participate in public service medical for stray animals by giving them a public service logo and increasing their exposure; 2) Vaccination, this function allows users to check the availability of vaccination points and the stock of free vaccines, and to select the appropriate vaccine for appointment according to their pet's condition. This function will also work with the user's appointment status and provide reminders via SMS and ringing to ensure a smooth vaccination process.

- **Donation,** which can be used to gather various activities of public service funding posted by the shelter. It is divided into the Fundraising and Ranking: 1) Fundraising, users can participate in donations for stray animals in a variety of ways including designated donations, crowdfunding donations and automatic monthly donations. The raised funds will be used to purchase food and supplies for the animals in the shelter, pay for neutering and other medical expenses, etc.; 2) Ranking, for those who donate, the shelter and the platform will award them with a badge of honour to motivate them to continue to participate in the rescue of stray animals.

5   Conclusion

Thanks to the challenges of stray animals, this research aims to apply emerging technologies to drive changes in rescue system of stray animals in China. Based on the concept of Human-Centred Design, this research systematically investigates the social rescue system for stray animals through four stages: Empathise, Define, Ideate and Prototype. Furthermore, a technological public welfare platform, named as Stray Animals Rescue App, has been designed for reducing the population of stray animals in the city. The App has demonstrated a potential to help rescue stray animals. Due to the constraints of time and conditions, this study did not test the App, however, the results of this study need to be tested in a real environment in the future to prove the effectiveness of the results in optimising the rescue system of stray animals.

Acknowledgements. This work was made possible with the support of the Wenzhou Business College which provided financial support for the subject study (XSKY20210025).

References

1. Kruk, E.: Polskie i estońskie uregulowania prawne dotyczące zwierząt bezdomnych (bezpańskich). Studia Iuridica Lublinensia. **30**, 145 (2021)
2. Zawistowski, S., Morris, J., Salman, M., Ruch-Gallie, R.: Population dynamics, overpopulation, and the welfare of companion animals: new insights on old and new data. J. Appl. Anim. Welfare Sci. **1**, 193–206 (1998)
3. Reese, L.: The dog days of detroit: urban stray and feral animals. City Community **14**, 167–182 (2015)
4. Li, X., Dai, J.: Service design of stray cat feeding based on the theory of sustainable development. In: Stephanidis, C., Antona, M., Ntoa, S. (eds.) HCII 2021. CCIS, vol. 1419, pp. 351–357. Springer, Cham (2021). https://doi.org/10.1007/978-3-030-78635-9_46
5. Liu, S., Chen, H.: Solving stray-animal problems by economic policies. Taipei Econ. Inquiry **54**, 1–27 (2018)
6. Huang, Y., Chuang, T., Lai, Y.: Classification of the trap-neuter-return surgery images of stray animals using Yolo-based deep learning integrated with a majority voting system. Appl. Sci. **11**, 8578 (2021)
7. Wang, Z., Liu, X.: Design of animal detector based on thermal imaging sensor. J. Phys: Conf. Ser. **1550**, 042066 (2020)
8. USDA APHIS | Animal Welfare Act, https://www.aphis.usda.gov/aphis/ourfocus/animalwelfare/sa_awa
9. Act on Welfare and Management of Animals. https://www.env.go.jp/nature/dobutsu/aigo/1_law/index.html
10. Zito, S., Aguilar, G., Vigeant, S., Dale, A.: Assessment of a targeted trap-neuter-return pilot study in Auckland. New Zealand Anim. **8**, 73 (2018)
11. Boone, J.: Better trap–neuter–return for free-roaming cats. J. Feline Med. Surg. **17**, 800–807 (2015)
12. Wang, X.: TNVR, Let they live (讓牠活下去). https://www.lca.org.tw/column/node/4612
13. Kreisler, R., Cornell, H., Levy, J.: Decrease in population and increase in welfare of community cats in a twenty-three year trap-neuter-return program in Key Largo, FL: the ORCAT program. Front. Vet. Sci. **6**, 7 (2019)

14. Bir, C., Widmar, N., Croney, C.: Stated preferences for dog characteristics and sources of acquisition. Animals **7**, 59 (2017)
15. Marder, A., Duxbury, M.: Obtaining a pet: realistic expectations. Vet. Clinics N. Am. Small Anim. Pract. **38**, 1145–1162 (2008)
16. Reese, L.: Make me a match: prevalence and outcomes associated with matching programs in dog adoptions. J. Appl. Anim. Welfare Sci. **24**, 16–28 (2020)
17. I would like to have a cat (我要領養貓). https://www.facebook.com/groups/979903922059 977/
18. Norman, D.: User Centered System Design. Erlbaum, Hillsdale (1986)
19. ISO 9241-210:2019. https://www.iso.org/standard/77520.html
20. Carayon, P., et al.: Human-centered design of team health IT for pediatric trauma care transitions. Int. J. Med. Informatics **162**, 104727 (2022)
21. Termglinchan, V., Daswani, S., Duangtaweesub, P., Assavapokee, T., Milstein, A., Schulman, K.: Identifying solutions to meet unmet needs of family caregivers using human-centered design. BMC Geriatrics. **22**, 94 (2022)

Research on Healthy City Construction from the Perspective of City Brand: Focus on Case of Seoul

Xu Yang[1], Xin Sun[2], Le Wang[3,4], and Kevin C. Tseng[4,5(✉)]

[1] School of Design Art and Media, Nanjing University of Science and Technology, Nanjing, China
[2] Nanjing Bushu Culture Communication Co., Ltd., Nanjing, China
[3] Department of Design, National Taiwan Normal University, Taipei, Taiwan
[4] Product Design and Development Laboratory, Taoyuan, Taiwan
ktseng@pddlab.org
[5] Department of Industrial Design, National Taipei University of Technology, Taipei, Taiwan

Abstract. In the post-epidemic era, health has become people's major concern. An increasing number of people have shown their interest in the planning and construction of healthy cities, which are related to the quality of life and the choice of the city to live in. The concept of a healthy city has received extensive attention since it was first proposed in the 1980s. To construct healthy cities is conducive to addressing health-related problems in the city, while also driving sustainable development for the city in the long run. With the continuous practice and development of healthy cities in recent years, healthy cities have been more closely linked to all aspects of urban development on the premise that the aim of healthy city construction is to improve the health of the residents and promote sustainable development. Based on the literature and case studies of Seoul, this study discusses the beneficial experience of building a healthy city from the perspective of brand construction, and puts forward the connotation of multi-disciplinary cooperative healthy city brand construction.

Keywords: City brand · Healthy city · Seoul city

1 Research Background

The sudden outbreak of the epidemic in late 2019 brought the world's attention to the field of health and health has become people's major concern and focused topic.Residents are paying an increasing attention to the quality of life from another level, which drives the cities to make improvementin terms of soft facilities. In order to create a livable image, cities have made a lot of efforts from the perspectives of culture, politics and economy. On top of what these cities have achieved, the topic of urban health has gained new attention. Citizens living in cities long for a more beautiful environment, clean air, high-quality medical care, convenient elderly security, and fast transportation. These issues are all related to the concept of urban health. The World Health Organization has

© Springer Nature Switzerland AG 2022
M. Rauterberg et al. (Eds.): HCII 2022, LNCS 13520, pp. 397–414, 2022.
https://doi.org/10.1007/978-3-031-18158-0_29

put forward the concept of "healthy city" in 1994, holding that "a healthy city should be a city that continuously develops, develops the natural and social environment, and continuously expands social resources so that people can support each other in enjoying life and realizing their full potential [1]." The development concept of healthy city is similar to that of cultural city [2], creative city [3]and historical city [4]. They all aim to promote the sustainable development of a city from the perspective of urban construction.

Looking back at the history of urban development, with residents in the city being the center, the optimization and exploration of healthy living in urban space has never stopped Urban managers have made efforts in promoting the extension of people's survival from the initial development and construction of reasonable and convenient living space in the city. With the acceleration of urbanization, an increasing number people tend to live in cities [5], thus cities become more closely related to people's lives. Urbanization has brought about population growth and the development of traditional industries, and promoted the progress of cities. However, on the other hand, it has caused problems such as environmental pollution, traffic jams, gaps between the rich and the poor, and new diseases, which makes people attach more importance to urban living spaces. Therefore, there are various attempts at urban construction and development such as urban regeneration [6], green city [7], etc. Based on a series of urban construction practices that solve specific problems for the purpose of promoting urban health and improving the quality of life of citizens, researchers have conducted various studies in the fields of urban construction, urban health or health sciences. The purpose of urban construction is to build a livable city for its residents to have a higher quality of life.

In addition to urban renewal with the improvement of urban infrastructure being the main form, more cities have begun to improve the overall appearance of the city by creating their own intangible values (such as cultural influence, urban image, etc.), thus people living in the city can be the main body, and creative culture is developed to create an urban humanistic environment with a sense of satisfaction and happiness. The resulting concept of "city brand"can promote the recombination of the city's internal resources, improve the city's image and create new development opportunities for the city.

The city brand here covers all aspects of the city, reflecting the different characteristics of the city itself from other cities. The author has conducted research on the relationship between creative city brand identification strategy and city image, and the obtained creative city product identification strategy model includes subdivision factors related to urban health. Health is one of the important factors in city brand model [8]. This research starts from the health factors of urban development, takes "healthy city" as the core topic of the research, explores the elements of building "healthy city" from the perspective of urban brand and clarifies the content of "healthy city" in the construction of urban brand.

This study takes the city of Seoul as an example to analyze its practical experience in the construction of healthy city from the perspective of city brand. Through this study, the construction connotation of "healthy city" is further clarified, and the composition of health factors in urban brand building is further improved, hence the results of this research can serve as a useful reference for healthy city building.

In summary, this research aims to: 1) further clarify the subdivision elements related to healthy city construction in the city brand strategy through theoretical research; 2) organize and analyze the healthy city policies and practices involved in the city brand building of Seoul, and to further clarify the practical connotation of healthy city construction.

2 Theoretical Background

2.1 City Brand

The etymology of "Brand" comes from the Norwegian "Brander", which means "To Burn". It is later derived to have the meaning of "Ownership".For example, it is used to indicate ownership of an item or to distinguish it from other products to emphasize "Made by Me", etc. People distinguish their own products from others' through the form of such a mark, thus the brand is endowed with three functions of ownership, origin, and identity in the early stage [9]. With the mass production of the industrial revolution, brands have been used to distinguish different products, and even through a series of brand marketing activities, products can gain an advantage in market competition [10]. As a result, the concept of brand has been continuously expanded, and its importance has also received widespread attention. The concept of branding is given by the American Marketing Association as "a name, symbol, term, design, symbol or combination thereof used to distinguish a seller or seller of goods, services, products and products of another competitor" [9]. The concept of brand has the following characteristics.First of all, it emphasizes the difference, which means the significant distinction amongvarious products. The second is message delivery, which is the intentional delivery of the message or content the brand wants to convey. The third is dynamic communication, which means to communicate with consumers in a certain way. Therefore, a brand is usually composed of conceptual elements, linguistic elements, visual elements, and expansion elements. Conceptual elements refer to the unique content of the brand itself, namely the element content that differentiates the brand itself from other brands, and certain target information that it conveys to consumers. Linguistic elements refer to those content that can be expressed through language, such as brand names, brand slogans, etc. The visual element is to convey the information of the brand through the formation of marks or images, and it is a means of conveying the brand information in a perceptual way. Expansion elements refer to other means of communication used by brands in order to further promote information transmission and establish closer links with consumers in addition to the above elements, such as designing corresponding packaging for products or advertisements, etc. [11] (Table 1).

The scope of the brand continues to expand. Due to its significant role in promoting the establishment of a product's identity in the minds of consumers, the concept of the brand has gradually extended from the product to other fields, for example, national brands under the category of countries, regional brands divided by regions, venue brands with specific venues being the core elements, and some local self-government-based brands of local self-governing groups, etc. (Table 2) The emergence of urban brands is considered to regard the city as a product. Through a series of marketing activities for consumers, a city aims to build a new image, especially to establish a unique and

Table 1. Definition of brand

Researcher	Definition
Kotler (1991)	Differentiate from competitors (products, services) by name, signal, logo, design, or any combination of them, to make the seller's service and product specific
Aaker (1991)	Similar concepts such as trademarks, symbols or slogans associated with a brand name
Keller (1993)	Brands bring different effects in marketing activities. Brands are not a tool used to identify the company's products and other companies' products, but a representative symbolic tool for specific products such as quality assurance and identity display
Son, I.K (2003)	A word, text, batch of text, design, or combination thereof used to distinguish the products and services of a particular seller or sales group from other competitors
Korea Brand Management Association	The manufacturer or seller's sense of identity in their own products or services, and the differences between competing products or services and the owners. A combination of terms, names, numbers, symbols, slogans, characters, designs, packaging, etc., which customers can be used to differentiate

differentiated image in urban competition to make people willing to come to this city to live, and prompt investors to invest in this city to achieve the purpose of bringing new impetus to urban development. A city brand is defined as "a series of strategies that treat a city as a commodity and establish a unique image to distinguish it from other cities, and the city's inherent natural resources, cultural resources, historical resources, etc. will be utilized to form a city name, a symbol system, etc. that distinguish it from other cities [12]." The city brand is built based on the unique resources of the city. The inherent resources of a city include elements such as nature, history, culture, environment, policies, services, personnel, etc., which are the basis for distinguishing among cities. In this way, through the integration of these elements, the concept of urban differentiation is conveyed to the residents, visitors and investors of the city, usually through the use of symbolic systems such as names, city symbols, slogans, etc., and finally through the city brand identification. The system transmits the information the city intends to convey, and presents a positive image of the city to the residents.

Table 2. Aconcept similar to the city brand

Concept	Content	Example
National Brand	The national brand takes countries as the category, conveys the country's advantageous image to citizens or foreigners through a series of symbol systems, and enhances the country's image through more abundant strategies.	Ukrainian national brand logo
Regional Brand	Regional brand is smaller in scope than the national brand. A region here is a "Region" of geographic space, such as a place, area, courtyard, etc.	Jeju Special Self-Governing Province
Place Brand	The scope of place brand is narrower, usually targeting a specific place, and the purpose is also to enhance the awareness and image of that particular place.	Namsangol Hanok Village
Local Self-governing Group Brand	Local self-governing groups are the main body of self-governing administration, and are public body that have been given partial administrative power by the state. It is interlinked with urban activities.	Seoul Design Foundation

2.2 Healthy Cities

The problems encountered in the current urban development have brought a lot of changes. For example, as the population has tended to choose cities, enterprises have followed the trend of the population. The major factor that influences people's choice of cities is whether the city can provide a life with high level of quality. Especially in the post-epidemic era, the public's attention to health is constantly increasing. People's living environment, medical conditions, and response to emergencies have become important concerns for the public when they evaluate a city.

Health is a more complex concept. The public's perception of health often lies in the absence of diseases, while actually people's physical and mental health is equally important. WHO defines health as follows, "health is a state of complete physical, mental and social well-being and not merely the absence of disease or infirmity", which emphasizes that the state of health is physical, psychological, and social. Among them, the social category means that people are living in a certain social environment, which is closely related to the city. In 1986, Ottawa Charter for Health Promotion mentioned that "health should be regarded as a resource of daily life, not as a goal of life. Health is a positive concept, which is not only a manifestation of personal qualities, but also a social and personal resource [13]." In 2003, the Mississippi State and UTM working group proposed that "health should include four aspects: individual health and tranquility, community integration, healthy ecology, and efficient social system", which shows the important relationship between space and health [14].

This conceptwas introduced into the category of urban space. In order to create a livable urban space, similar concepts such as environment-friendly city, ecological city, green city, etc. have been proposed. The concept of a healthy city first appeared in the "Healthy Toronto 2020" workshop held in 1984, after which WHO attempted to build healthy cities in 1986, and then launched a healthy cities project in some cities in Europe. According to WHO, "a Healthy City is one that is continually creating and improving those physical and social environments and expanding those community resources which enable people to mutually support each other in performing all the functions of life and in developing to their maximum potential [1]." In other words, under the goal of realizing the health of all members of the urban society, a city should have a system for realizing health as well as a communication channel for the health and tranquility of the citizens, and it should pay attention to the dynamic process of improving the quality of life. In the ever-developing concept of healthy city, two tendencies have been gradually formed. One is that a healthy city combines human beings with the environment and society,thus cities can support each other to maximize their potential. The other is to emphasize that a healthy city should have a clean and beautiful environment as well as a sustainable ecosystem that can provide the necessary conditions for people's healthy life [14].

2.3   Healthy City Practice

The specific connotation of healthy city is more reflected in the construction practice of many cities. The Healthy Cities Project initiated by WHO has transformed people's concern about health problems from a purely medical model to a social model [15]. Fields other than the medical field also have an impact on health, and factors such as society, nature, population, economy, politics, etc. contained in urban space also play a certain role in health promotion.

WHO first established the Healthy Cities Project in 1986 under the principle of "Health for All", focusing on health disparities similar to urban poverty, the needs of vulnerable groups, public participation and other social factors that affect health [16]. The purpose of this project is health promotion. Building a healthy city is to promote the city to attach importance to the factors that affect health in the process of development, for example, to promote health by raising the awareness of residents or using the government's administrative services. The establishment of WHO's Healthy Cities Project has provided reference for a number of international cities and regions in their construction of healthy cities.

In 1987, WHO's Healthy Cities Project began to be promoted in Europe, and corresponding organizations, Network of Healthy Cities in Europe and a specific 5-year action plan were established. Network of Healthy Cities in Europe put forward a specific action plan based on the principles of health equity, community participation, health promotion, cross-departmental cooperation, primary care and international cooperation. Moreover, a corresponding action plan was designed in a 5-year period. In the first phase (1987–1992), preparations were made and foundations were laid for the creation of healthy cities. The second phase (1993–1997) was more oriented, which further organically combined urban development with health and put forward a series of specific policy plans for building healthy cities. In the third phase (1998–2002), a comprehensive healthy urban development plan was formulated based on equity and sustainable development [14]. In the fourth phase (2003–2008), activities with the theme of Healthy Urban Planning and Health Impact Assessment, Healthy aging, etc. were carried out. The fifth phase (2009–2013) focused on protecting the environment, healthy living, and healthy urban design. In the sixth phase (2014–2018), the Health Improvement for All and Reducing Health Inequalities, Health Leadership and Improving Health Governance [17] were emphasized. At the beginning of the project, more than 30 European cities participated. Since then, an increasing number of European cities have joined the Healthy Cities Project.

The concept of healthy city has been introduced to Korean academic circles in 1986, and the related demonstration projects were started in Gwacheon in 1996 [18], and in 2004, Seoul, Busan, Wonju, Gangwon, and Changwon, Gyeongsangnam-do started building healthy cities as founding members of The Alliance For Healthy Cities (AFHC). Since then,a number of autonomous groups have joined AFHC. The construction of healthy cities in South Korea can be divided into the introduction period (~2003), the investment period (2004–2006), the expansion period (2006–2009), and the mature period (2010–2012) [17].

Table 3. International practice of healthy cities

Institution/Region	Time	Main content
WHO	1986~	Expanding the concept of health and establishing the Healthy Cities Project
European Healthy Cities Movement	1987–1992	Preparation and foundation for building a healthy city
	1993–1997	Healthy Cities Policy Planning
	1998–2002	A comprehensive healthy urban development plan has been formulated based on sustainable development
	2003–2008	Healthy Urban Planning, Health Impact Assessment, Healthy Aging
	2009–2013	Environmental Protection, Healthy Life, Healthy Urban Design
	2014–2018	Health Improvement for All, Reducing Health Inequalities, Health Leadership and Improving Health Governance
Korea Health City	1996~	Started in Gwacheon in 1996; Health Policy Division under the Ministry of Health and Welfare, Korea Healthy Cities Partnership (KHCP) and Alliance for Health Cities (AFHC)

Source: Yoo, S.H, Health Promotion Approaches and Directions for Urban Health: A Qualitative study on research trends and Healthy Cities cases in Seoul[J], Health and Social Science, 2015,Vol.22, No.4, p36, reorganized and modified.

The construction of healthy cities in South Korea is at the government level. The Health Policy Division under the Ministry of Health and Welfare is responsible for the development and support of related projects nationwide, including the development of related project planning guidelines, the investment in healthy city certification system, health impact assessment, etc. In addition, the Korea Healthy Cities Partnership (KHCP) and the Alliance for Health Cities (AFHC) are the representative self-governing groups related to the promotion of healthy cities. Korea Healthy Cities Partnership (KHCP), established in 2006, is an organization that aims to improve the quality of life of citizens, achieve a high level of health and healthy balance, and share local government and public policy information.It strives for the sustainable development of urban science. Alliance for Health Cities (AFHC) is a healthy city alliance mainly established by the autonomous groups of the Western Pacific region [19] (Table 3).

3   Guideline for the Analysis of Healthy City Construction from the Perspective of City Brand

3.1   City Brand Model

In terms of city brand, the city is regarded as a commodity, and the tangible and intangible elements related to the city are the basis for building a city brand. In addition, the city brand is composed of the core elements, basic elements and expansion elements of the brand like general commodity brands. Anholt-GMI (2006) proposed the City Brand Index model of world cities as the main object, which includes 6 levels: presence, place, potential, pulse, people, and prerequisites. With the theme of "place marketing strategy", Lee, M.Y (2005) proposed that a successful place marketing strategy needs to satisfy political factors (sustainability), cultural factors (sincerity), social factors (comprehensiveness), organizational and spatial factors (connectivity), as well as economic factors (economy). An, S.H (2008) took the relationship between urban brand personality level elements and loyalty as the research object, and proposed that the urban brand model should include six elements of urban environment, resources and infrastructure, which are natural elements, urban basic elements, economic elements, cultural elements, human elements, and social elements. Koo, J.R (2015) divided the city brand model into 7 parts including the core identity symbol of city brand, the subjects of city brand, target group, hard branding, support, services, and communication.Kwon, J.H and Park, S.H (2018) proposed in the study that the factors of urban brand formation include 1) landscape factors, 2) administrative factors, 3) historical and cultural factors, 4) cognitive factors, and 5) empirical factors. The researchers classified landscape factors and administrative factors as intentional factors, historical and cultural factors and cognitive factors as composite factors. Lim, H.W (2021) proposed the ingredients for great city branding model with City Brand Policy as the research object, including: 1.Embodying a clear, distinctive, ambitious yet realistic brand position and persona; 2. Positioning the brand on the population's values, attitudes, behaviors, and characteristics; 3.Reflecting a clear city strategy and its emphasis on skills, resources, and capabilities; 4. Adapting effectively to deliver benefits to target groups; 5. Communicating successfully to internal key influences; 6. Integrating efficiently across various marketing communications media 7. Consistent over time [19] (Table 4).

Table 4. City brand model

Project		Content	Source
Core Factors	Tangible factors	Physical composition of the city, place of existence, nature, infrastructure	Anholt-GMI Lee, M.Y Koo, J.R
	Intangible factors	Culture, history, folklore, experience, accumulated fame or image	
	Position	A clear and unique brand position, core connotation or competitiveness	
Basic Factors	Linguistic factors	Name, slogan	Lee, M.Y Koo, J.R Lim, H.W
	Visual factors	Logos, designs, characters, fonts, colors, etc.	
	Action factors	Marketing strategies, campaigns, advertisements, etc.	
Expansion Factors	Communication	Timely feedback of information	Kwon, J.H & Park, S.H Lim, H.W
	experience	The formation of lasting intangible experiences	

First of all, in terms of core factors, the physical composition of the city itself, such as representative places, natural environment, basic facilities, etc. are the basic factors of a city brand, which means that a city brand is often built on the unique factors of the city itself.In addition to the physical composition of the city, the intangible factors are also of importance, such as the city's representative culture, history, folklore, as well as accumulated reputation and image. Despite that these specific factors cannot be measured in real terms, they exist in the public's perception and are also an important foundation for a city's brand. Moreover, the clear and unique brand position, core connotation or competitiveness related to the city brand also fall into the category of core factors. The second is the basic factors that constitute the city brand [19, 21], including linguistic factors, visual factors and action factors. Linguistic elements generally refer to the content that is communicated through language, such as city names, slogans, etc. Visual factors are an important part of the city brand, usually conveying brand information through signs or images in a perceptual way. Action factors include behavioral factors in city branding, such as brand marketing activities. Finally, the expansion factors of the city brand refer to other means of communication adopted by consumers to establish closer links.

3.2 Indicators Related to Healthy Cities

WHO put forward that in the early stage of healthy city construction, a healthy city should have the following characteristics: 1) a clean and safe physical environment of high quality (including housing quality); 2) an ecosystem that is stable now and sustainable in the long term; 3) a strong, mutually supportive and non-exploitative community; 4) a high degree of participation and control of the citizens over the decisions affecting their lives, health and well-being; 5)the meeting of basic needs (food, water, shelter, income, safety and work) for all the people in the city; 6) access to a wide variety of experiences and resources, with the chance for various ways of contact, interaction and communication; 7) a diverse, vital and innovative economy; 8) connectedness with the past, with the cultural and biological heritage of city dwellers and with other groups and individuals;9) a form that is compatible with and enhances the preceding characteristics; 10) an optimum level of appropriate public health and sickness care services, accessible to all; and 11) a high status of health (high levels of positive health and low levels of disease) [22]. The above 11 characteristics can be divided into the following three types. First, a healthy city should have a favorable physical environment to meet the life of all residents. Second, a healthy city should have a management system and a communication channel that can improve people's health. Third, a healthy city values the human experience, emphasizing that everyone can benefit from the city. Fourth, a healthy city focuses on innovation, and encourages and supports a high degree of residents' participation in the city construction.

The construction of healthy cities also follows a series of basic principles, including: 1) Equalityprinciple, which means that everyone has the right and possibility to realize their full potential. Political, economic and social inequalities in urban populations clearly affect their health status. 2) Sustainability principle, which is the core principle of the healthy city construction process, and the health and well-being of urban people is an important indicator of the success of sustainable development strategies. 3) Cross-sectoral collaboration, which means that cross-sectoral collaboration is required in the social model of health promotion to reduce duplication and conflict, and maximize health benefits with limited resources. 4) Community participation, which indicatesan active and engaged community with first-hand information is an indispensable partner in determining the order of problem solving, as well as making and revising decisions. 5) International action and solidarity, which emphasizes thatthe Healthy Cities Project is based on true collaboration, not only among multi-sectoral collaborations, but also among cities and countries, such as the WHO Healthy Cities Project Network [15]. From the above principles, it can be found that in the construction of a healthy city, the participation and responsibility of residents are valued, and residents have close exchanges with each other.

Kim, M.H (2006) proposed a checklist related to the elements of urban health in urban planning based on the urban construction of London, specifically including 1) Healthy Lifestyles, which includes the provision of facilities or policies that can promote health, the provision of healthy public spaces, and the improvement of park environments, etc. 2) Housing Quality, which includes programs and policies to enhance and improve the living environment, high-efficiency energy plans, and the use of clean materials. 3) Access to Work, which includes the provision of vocational education opportunities and programs, and considers the actual employment of residents to create or provide corresponding opportunities. 4) Accessibility, whichspecifically includes convenient transportation policies and programs, advocates the use of public transportation, and promotes environmentally friendly travel methods. 5) Crime Reduction and Community Safety, which includes crime prevention and related safety policies, efficient management, etc. 6) Air Quality and Neighborhood Amenity, which includes plans to improve the environment, high-quality urban design, and reduce air pollution. 7) Resource Minimization,which includes reducing waste discharge, promoting reuse of resources, and reducing soil pollution. 8) Climate Change, which includes countermeasures against climate change, reducing energy waste in buildings and vehicles, etc.

Xu, C.B.; Zhong, D.K; Li, N (2005) put forward the basic framework of healthy city construction from the perspective of urban planning. 1) To define the corresponding healthy city implementation system and coordinate and mobilize the positive factors of all parties; 2) To emphasize policy orientation, establish a responsibility mechanism for only departments and multiple parties, and supervise each other; 3) To participate in planning and design, collaborate with each other, and revise or compile based on health promotion guidelines; 4) To lay out the urban functional structure on the basis of detailed research; 5) To strengthen the transportation network that provides efficient borders; 6) To follow the principles of healthy city, attach importance to physical, mental and social health, focus on cross-departmental cooperation and promotes diverse participation.

3.3   Checklist of Healthy City Construction from a Brand Perspective

In order to analyze the practical connotation of healthy city construction from the perspective of brand, this study takes Seoul as an example to investigate and analyze the content related to healthy city in the brand construction of existing cities. In order to obtain the checklist of case studies, the following research analytical tools are designed with reference to the relevant theoretical background in the previous articles. The analytical model consists of three parts, the first of which is the core factors of the city brand, including research and analysis on the status quo of the city, urban transportation, medical care, natural resources, and whether the concept of a healthy city is included in the city brand positioning. The second part is the basic factors of the city brand, which includes the content of whether the principles and characteristics of a healthy city are reflected in the language factors, visual factors, and action factors of the city brand. The last is the expansion factors in the city brand, focusing on further exchanges and experiences, such as whether a series of city brand projects show diversification or cross-departmental cooperation, and whether the projects encourage innovation and adapt to local conditions, improve the living standards of residents and promote sustainable development of the city (Table 5).

Table 5. Checklist of healthy city construction from the perspective of brand

Project		Content
Core Factors	Physical Environment	1. High-quality physical environment (residential and public spaces) 2. Transportation 3. Medical resources
	Natural Resources	1. Basic ecosystem 2. Green space, parks 3. Environmental protection, climate change
	Position	Whether the city brand position includes the concept of a healthy city
Basic Factors	Linguistic Factor	Slogans
	Visual Factors	Visual symbols and advertising
	Action Factors	Activities, education, publicity, concept guidance
Expansion Factors	Communication	Cross-departmental cooperation
	Experience	Policy update

4 Seoul City Case Study

4.1 Overview of Seoul City

Seoul Special City (hereinafter referred to as: Seoul) is located in the northwest of the central part of the Korean Peninsula and is the capital of the Republic of Korea. Seoul is the center of culture, politics, economy, trade, technology and education of Korea. With a total area of 605.2 square kilometers, Seoul has 25 jurisdictions and a population of 9.5 million. The Han River loops through Seoul, naturally dividing the city into two areas, North and South.

Seoul experienced a rapid economic development and urbanization in the 1970s and 1980s, thus in order to attract more development opportunities and attention, the government began to invest in tourism marketing strategies, and attach importance to the city's external publicity to strengthen its major characteristics. During this period, some local self-governing groups carried out a branding practice similar to "enhancing urban characteristics", thus urban symbols such as Urban Symbolic Elements (1971) initially appeared. Afterwards, planning began in 1995, and in the next year, the city emblem representing the history, nature, and vitality of Seoul was voted by citizens and has been applied since then. The emblem is composed of patterns of the sun, mountains and rivers, symbolizing that Seoul is a city full of history and vitality with a humanistic atmosphere. In order to cope with the rapid changes of the times and further publicize the city, a new city brand Hi Seoul was developed in 2002. In 2009, the Haechi symbol was designed and developed for the purpose of enhancing the urban competitiveness and brand value of Seoul, enriching the connotation of the city brand, conveying the tradition and modernity of Seoul, and bringing hope to the citizens with the core theme of the city. In the same year, the development of the character image of Haechi symbolized by the traditional Korean beast was completed, and the original image was further developed and expressed in a more cute and anthropomorphic form.In 2011, the city brand slogan of Seoul was voted by the citizens and changed to "Seoul, Together We Stand" in 2014. The city brand was updated in 2015, and the new Seoul city brand "I.Seoul.U" was voted on the basis of a thorough research on citizens. Its core connotation is that "Seoul links you and me" [23] (Fig. 1).

Fig. 1. Seoul city's urban brand-related designs in various periods

Aiming to enable all citizens to live a healthy life, Seoul formulated policies to create a "healthy and safe city", and has been striving to improve urban health and the life quality of all citizens. The background of promoting this project is the overall trend of the world's population gathering in cities and the situation of Seoul, which has prepared for the arrival of a super city with a population of 10 million. There is an urgent need to formulate a healthy city policy in accordance with the WHO "Healthy City Plan",thus the hazards to the living environment of the city can be managed and the related problems can be solved.It is of significance to encourage the active participation of local self-governing groups, relevant institutions, experts and citizens to establish a system platform for cooperation among all parties. The project construction was carried out mainly through the promulgation of the Health City Project Promotion Plan (Mayor's Policy No. 646) in 2003. In October 2003, it participated in the WHO Western Pacific Region Healthy City Council, and in January 2004, Seoul National University Health Care Graduate School signed a research cooperation agreement with the WHO Kobe Health Development Center In June of the same year, Seoul joined the Healthy Cities Alliance in the West Pacific Region. In June 2005, the Seoul City Healthy City Committee was established and the operating regulations were formulated. In 2006, it joined Korea Healthy City Council (KFHC). In 2007, a healthy city indicator and management system was formulated to provide support for the autonomous regions' healthy city project (14 districts), which was further expanded (22 districts) in 2010, and the Seoul Metropolitan Government's Sustainable and Environmentally Friendly Mass Transportation Policy was announced. In 2015, the demonstration and promotion of the basic supportive project for the establishment of a healthy ecosystem of small living circles was carried out [24].

4.2 Healthy City Construction from a Brand Perspective

Taking the city brand construction of Seoul as an example, this study focuses on the analysis of the urban brand planning projects and practices related to healthy cities in relevant projects. The scope of the case is limited to the related projects that have been involved since the renewal of the new city brand "I.Seoul.U" in 2015, the reasons for whichinclude: 1) With the continuous advancement of urban branding and healthy city projects, related subdivision projects have become more diverse and complete, and the types of projects available for investigation and research are diverse. 2) In recent years, the relevant projects have been aimed at the urgent problems that need to be solved or the countermeasures made in response to the current trends of urban development, thus they are of more reference value. 3) The overall goal of urban construction has become more prominent. Whether it is urban brand building or healthy city construction, the ultimate goal is to improve the life quality of urban residents and promote sustainable urban development. Therefore, more relevant practical experience can be explored to clarify the practical connotation of healthy city construction.

First of all, in terms of core factors related to the improvement of the high-quality physical environment (houses and buildings) of the city, Seoul City issued the "Seoul Urban Planning Charter" based on a thorough survey of urban residents in 2015. The charter stipulates the direction and goals of future construction of Seoul for a century. The task of Seoul's urban planning is to fully protect the natural environment and the city's history and culture, continue to improve the life quality of residents, innovate urban functions, and enhance Seoul's urban reputation. Specific requirements include: 1) Complete protection of the natural environment; 2) Preserving and inheriting the historical literature and tigers, and contributing to the revitalization of the city; 3) Improving the urban structure and building a convenient city; 4) Constructing convenient, safe and green urban transportation, reducing pollution and traffic jams, and promoting green travel; 5) Utilizing urban space resources to create a safe city; 6) Environmental protection and energy saving, and reducing waste with the application of new energy; 7) Building a harmonious urban landscape; 8) Creating a place-based city with a shared memory; 9) Expanding the communication channels of residents and building a city that can participate in communication; 10) Creating a city that values the coexistence of caring and multiple cultures. In 2018, the "2025 Seoul Urban Regeneration Strategic Plan" was formulated, stating that the goal and vision of urban regeneration is to redevelop the city with sustainable power to create a livable and vibrant city for residents through the following means: 1) Creating a global economic base throughinternational cooperation; 2) Ensuring the growth of the employment ecosystem and securing the driving force of future growth; 3) Creating a safe living environment and providing diversified housing regeneration support; 4) Building a public cooperation system led by the people for sustainable development. In the practice related to the construction of green transportation, the vision of Seoul Metropolitan Transportation is to create transportation that can improve the life quality of citizens and the level of the city, and the goal is to create a safe future-oriented transportation environment, the details of which include: 1) Building a safe and convenient mass transportation system; 2) Expanding sustainable green transportation; 3) Officially promoting a pedestrian-friendly city; 4) Building a transportation system in the post-epidemic era. In the field of urban medical care, there are a number of issues involved in building a healthy city, including: 1) Disease prevention; 2) Strengthening public health care; 3) Creating a healthy living environment; 4) Creating a safe eating environment; 5) Running a series of public utilities that promote health (for example, healthy classrooms, disease prevention activities, etc.).

Secondly, the relevant practices related to urban natural resources in terms core factors specifically include: 1) Improving the problem of haze weather; 2) Carbon neutral; 3) Building a sustainable resource recycling city; 4) Improvingthe effects of policies by implementing environmental policies in various fields and systems; 5) Strengthening cooperation between domestic and foreign cities to create synergies; 6) Creating green, safe, and close-up enjoyment of forests and courtyards; 7) Planting trees. 8) Park development and renovation, etc.

Thirdly, in the design of city brand positioning in the core factors, the identity of the Seoul city brand is set with "Harmonious Seoul", "Passionate Seoul" and "Leisure Seoul" as the core keywords. "Harmonious" here refers to a city where the urban environment, man and nature, past and present can coexist in harmony, "Passionate" refers to a city full of passion for creating a better life in the future, and "Leisure" is the main theme of life value, which means the city emphasizes mutual respect and mutual care.

In the practice related to the basic factors of the city brand, such as language, vision, action, etc., the "I.Seoul.U" city brand developed in 2015 is a variable visual system, which can change the factors in accordance with the scene. Therefore, in practice, the factors of brand identification can vary with usage scenarios. For example, factors related to nature can be used in activities related to environmental protection to express a healthy and green image of the city. In addition, a series of publicity, activities, education, concept guidance and other practices and the relevant factors of the city brand can be utilized to carry out health promotion. In the practice related to the factors of urban brand expansion, the city of Seoul attaches great importance to exchanges and cooperation with international groups, research institutions and scholars, which include: 1) Research on relevant policies and evaluation systems; 2) Holding international forums; 3) Involving residents in policy making; 4) Cooperation between departments; 5) Information disclosure and investigation of the situation, etc.

4.3 Summary

Numerous specific actions related to building a healthy city can be found in the practice of city (brand) construction, and these practices also promote the construction of a healthy city in various ways.For example, in the project practice related to improving the physical environment of the city in terms of the core factors, a number of plans have been formulated to continuously improve the urban physical space and develop public services to meet the needs of promoting residents' health. These detailed construction practices reflect the concept of "health for all" in the process of building healthy cities. The diversified and constantly updated policy guidance for solving new problems is also continuously improving the implementation plan of building healthy cities, which plays a positive role in promoting healthy cities in an orderly manner (Fig. 2).

Fig. 2. Healthpromotion using city brand visual system

5   Conclusion

Urban construction, urban brand development and healthy city development overlap in a number of aspects. Urban construction has a common goal, which includes sustainable development of the city, improved living standards of the residents, and expanded international influence. In the context of the post-epidemic era, urban development has entered a more health-conscious phase. The construction of a healthy city is not just a matter of independent public health services, but diversified and cross-disciplinary cooperation to integrate urban health concepts into urban construction practices.

Firstly, health and urban development have mutually promoted and influenced each other, and health promotion has become a trend in urban development. Public policies in related to "health promotion" can be seen in various urban development frameworks and characteristic urban development plans formulated by urban managers, which exert influence on the city's development toward sustainability, residentially and high quality of life. The importance of urban health issues should be emphasized in various urban development plans, and health related concepts should be incorporated into urban construction frameworks, systems, services and policies.

Secondly, the basic principles of healthy urban construction include inter-departmental collaboration, which is reflected in a variety of urban cases. Urban construction is an organic system that can be promoted effectively only through the multi-sector and multi-disciplinary collaboration. In the case of Seoul, building a healthy city is not an independent act, and health-related ideologies are reflected in the city's numerous frameworks. The Seoul municipal government adopted the concept of harmonious "coexistence" of people and the city as an urban brand in the process of implementing urban brand construction. The core identification is the health concept of harmonious coexistence between man and the city, which is integrated into the city brand construction. Therefore, the cooperation is still one of the important principles of constructing a healthy city. Furthermore, with the continuous development of science and technology, cross-border cooperation between science and technology and healthy city construction should be emphasized. Some of the problems that arise in cities can be solved with technological means in the process of the construction and management of healthy cities.

Thirdly, the participation of citizens should be emphasized in building a healthy city. The Seoul municipal government has changed from top-down policy promotion to citizen participation policy formulating in the process of building a city brand and a healthy city.

At present, a lot of cities are accelerating the construction of "healthy city", thus we will interpret the meaning of healthy city practices from an urban brand perspective. The case study on the city of Seoul will provide useful references for other cities.

References

1. WHO: Building A Healthy City: A Practitioners Guide (1995)
2. Jeon, G.J.: City and culture, cultural city and urban culture: based on cultural studies' interpretation and analysis of the dictionary definitions of South Korean, Chinese, Japanese, Vietnamese, and English. Soc. Chin. Hum. Korea **76**, 453–477 (2020)
3. Nahm, K.B.: Recent agenda of UNESCO creative cities network (UCCN) and alternative urban cultural policy discourse. J. Cult. Contents **21**, 7–39 (2021)
4. Kim, S.M.: An integrated conservation of historic city and analysis of its impact on local land price: focusing on historic landscape improving project in buye. 지역과 문화 7(4), 21–48 (2020)
5. U. N. H. S. Programme: World Cities Report 2016 (2016)
6. Park, H.S., Kim, J.Y.: A study on the classification analysis of urban regeneration projects by analyzing urban regeneration plans - focus on general neighborhood urban regeneration projects in Seoul. J. Korea Inst. Spat. Des. **16**(1), 223–232 (2021)
7. Choi, B.D., Shin, H.R.: Green urbanism as a strategy for carbon control: a reflexive reconsideration. Space Environ. **23**(2), 40–85 (2013)
8. Yang, X.: A Study on Brand Identity Strategy and Brand Image for Creative Cities: Cases of Creative Cities in Korea and China. SungKyunkwan University, Seoul (2019)
9. Kim, D.Y.: Brand. Y-Books, Seoul (2017)
10. Son, I.K.: Brand Identity. Management Spirit, Seoul (2003)
11. Seoul Metropolitan city: It's easy: Seoul's policy brand, Seoul (2018)
12. Zhang, X.R.: A Study on the Impact of Image Recognition on Brand Value of City Brands. Graduate School, Daegu University, Gyeongsan (2021)
13. Chen, L.Q.: Healthy city construction and its development trends. China Mark. **33**, 50–63 (2010)
14. Zhou, X.H.: Experience and practices around europe: briefly on the development threads of healthy city project and its basic rules. Urban Plan. Int. **04**, 65–70 (2007)
15. Xu, C.B., Zhong, D., Li, N.: Basic theories of international healthy city movement. City Plan. Rev. **10**, 52–59 (2005)
16. Wu, Z.Y., Shan, J.J.: International practice and trend of healthy city. Urban Insight (06), 138–148 (2017)
17. Yoo, S.H.: Health promotion approaches and directions for urban health: a qualitative study on research trends and healthy cities cases in Seoul. Health Soc. Sci. **40**, 29–55 (2015)
18. H. C. R. Center.: Yonsei University, Analyzing the Healthy Cities Types and Policy Development for the Korean Healthy Cities (2009)
19. Lim, H.W.: A study on strategic city brand policy: based on the comparative analysis of city brand slogans in Seoul and overseas case studies. J. Digit. Converg. **19**(7), 41–50 (2021)

20. Koo, J.Y.: Strategic management of public brand, Hankyungsa, pp. 184–185 (2015)
21. Lee, M.Y.: The Place Marketing Strategy and the Cultural Politics of Space. The Institute for Korean Regional Studies, Seoul National University, Seoul (2003)
22. 01-28 2022. https://www.euro.who.int/en/health-topics/environment-and-health/urban-hea lth/who-european-healthy-cities-network/what-is-a-healthy-city/healthy-city-checklist
23. Kim, H.Y., Hyun, E.R.: The influence in negative media evaluation of Seoul metropolis brand symbol upon consumers' perception and attitude. J. Korea Des. Forum **23**(2), 129–140 (2018)
24. 01-29 2022. https://news.seoul.go.kr/welfare/archives/201134

Effect of Street Canyon in Urban Soundscape by the Discussion of Computer Simulation

Hui-Zhong Zhang[1] and Wei Lin[2(✉)]

[1] Infrastructure Planning and Engineering, Feng Chia University, Taichung, Taiwan
hz@mail.fcu.edu.tw
[2] School of Architecture, Feng Chia University, Taichung, Taiwan
wlin@fcu.edu.tw

Abstract. As an invisible physical element in space, sound is an important perceptual factor for people to perceive space. In the quantitative study of soundscape visualization, sound field simulation was used to rebuild the construction system of historical blocks. For example, due to the limitation of computer technology development in the 1960s, researchers recorded by hand drawing. With the development of sound field simulation technology, sound energy is displayed by visual color images. The software can not only simulate the space field but also predict the sound field in different spaces. Shilin is the most representative commercial block in Taiwan, and it has a unique night market trading mode. The local arcade space is part of the urban public pedestrian space, which enables people to perceive a more complex sound field environment in their walking experience. This study wants to analyze people's perception of the basic spatial unit of the street canyon and combined it with the analysis of the influence factor of the acoustic field, such as building height, the presence of buildings, shutter height, and building density. This research simulates and analyzes the basic scale street canyon space of urban streets and explores the systematic method of reconstruction of Shilin Historic District in Taipei.

Keywords: Urban soundscape · Soundwalk · Street canyon · Shilin night market · CadnaA

1 Introduction

Soundscape, derived from Landscape, attempts to understand sound waves in the environment [5]. The acoustic environment that people perceive, understand and experience, is soundscape reconstructed by the sound from all sound sources in all directions [6]. Although the concept of soundscape has been put forward for several decades, there is no fixed theory on the understanding angle and research scope of soundscape. In other hand, soundscape studies the relationship among people, sound, and environment. Sound types are believed to affect the perception of soundscape, for example, natural sound is believed to affect the sense of pleasure [7, 8], based on the existing research, it is known that soundscape can affect human perception. In the existing studies, soundscape

© Springer Nature Switzerland AG 2022
M. Rauterberg et al. (Eds.): HCII 2022, LNCS 13520, pp. 415–425, 2022.
https://doi.org/10.1007/978-3-031-18158-0_30

is regarded as a topic in the comprehensive field, the research on soundscape explores the relationship between sound and environment, and the existing research directions include health restoration, landscape construction, cultural conservation, environmental awareness, and urban renewal. Most scholars believe that soundscape was proposed by Canadian composer and Naturalist, R. Murray Schafer in the 1970s. But in an interview [14] with Carlotta Daro in 2013, Schafer himself attributed the term to the master's thesis [15] of Michael Southworth, an urban planner who was a student of Kevin Lynch in MIT. In other words, soundscapes were originally created by Michael Southworth and popularized by R. Murray Schafer. Lynch says that all the "image elements", such as paths, nodes, areas, edges, and landmarks, can be identified from the highway, remembering, and providing direction and familiarity. Using two-dimensional images to show urban forms is limited, and it changes the relationship between form and space. Paths are organizations and activities in space. Edges are real and perceptible, such as borders, walls, buildings, and streets. An area is a plane that people can pass through and have common features that can be identified. Nodes are the focal points of the entry zone, and they can represent the characteristics of the surrounding environment and have special core elements to provide. Landmarks can be buildings or natural landscapes, etc., which are unique and memorable in the environment [9]. In addition to the five rational and concrete elements of Kevin Lynch, the city has more emotional expressions. People's perceptual state in the city also affects people's emotions [1]. The "View from the Road" [16] study repeatedly borrows and uses Kevin Lynch's conceptual elements of spatial cognition from his 1960s book "The Image of the City", based on his research. "The View from The Road" argues that highways can provide a means of reestablishing coherence and order on a metropolitan scale and address the formless problem of urban vision by providing visual sequences to observers in motion. Based on the background of the complex and diverse information environment in the city, the physical characteristics of urban sound do not represent the perception state in the city. The perception of sound will change with people's behavior, psychological state and special time and place, for example, in a busy business district, people do not hate the noise, and in a quiet park, people may also feel sad. Visual recording of sound field changes can be simulated by software to distinguish sound pressure levels with different colors, in this way, spatial characteristics can be clearly judged and analyzed. From the urban fabric, we can see that different cities develop into different urban appearances and forms. From large to small scale, the universal city corresponds to neighborhood districts and blocks, and it turns to surface sound sources, line source, and point source. The city contains different spaces in the form of points, strips, and planes. Under the coverage of urban traffic noise and natural sound, strip spatial structure is an important interface element of urban development, and its sound field distribution can reflect the characteristics of the connection between different areas in urban space. The urban street canyon, as slices of strip blocks, is the basic unit of space that someone can perceive, when the roads in the city expand, the urban space connected by the roads will become complicated, and the adjacent buildings and roads will form street canyons. Therefore, the basic urban unit, Street Canyon, is taken as the scale of the research object [13], and the urban soundscape is studied with the scale of urban space that people can perceive. In urban studies, the discussion of the urban street sound environment is lacking because the traffic has the characteristics of continuity and dispersion. In urban road traffic, continuous traffic noise and discrete traffic noise have periodic and continuous influence on the sound field of urban street canyon. In this study, road vehicle noise is taken as the source of line sound, and the factors that affect the sound environment of street canyon include road surface material, building height on both sides, walking space scale, buffer space form, vehicle flow, and proportion of heavy vehicles, use form of building space and other factors.

2 Research Object

This study selects the Taipei urban planning zoning of the site as shown in Fig. 1, with the landmark Taipei Performing Arts Center (TPAC) as the center and a 10-min walking distance as the boundary. Figure 1 shows the relationship between spatial use zoning and urban texture. Jihe Road is the branch of the former Keelung River, the urban form of this area is an organic model, which is mainly divided into three parts, including Hougang community area, river reconstruction area and Shilin Night Market area. Shilin is the birthplace of Taipei culture, it was an important place for early traders to trade agricultural products. Since 1909, Shilin Market has developed into a famous night market in the business circle of Taipei city from the square trading style in front of a temple. Wenlin Road, as the main road in this area, connects the night market business district with the traffic hub, and it is also the only road for recreation and sightseeing. The research object is Wenlin Road, which is about 500 m long and connects six intersections around Shilin Night Market, with rich sound field environment.

Fig. 1. Figure of partial urban planning zoning map of Shilin district in Taipei

3   Research Methods and Process

Based on the existing soundscape research that already exists, this study explores the spatial scale characteristics of urban soundscape and finds the relationship between soundscape, city, and street canyon through literature. This study, which is in Taipei commercial recreation district, uses urban canyon unit space for summarizing analysis and its sound energy distribution. The sound field environment uses CadnaA software simulation to predict urban road maps with visual analysis. Shilin night market Wen Lin Road was selected as the research object, which includes pedestrian space, arcade corridor space, pavement parking space, and vehicle space. Finally, discuss the acoustic energy distribution in Shilin night market area and the acoustic environment characteristics of urban canyon under different spatial scales.

The influencing factors of sound environment include sound source, propagation environment and human perception. The sound source in the urban scale can be divided into point sound source, line sound source and surface sound source. Nodes and landmarks can be regarded as point sound sources, paths and edges can be regarded as line sound sources, and regions can be regarded as plane sound sources. The urban morphology hierarchy include building pattern, plot pattern and street pattern. From the perspective of human perception, the urban boundary is perceived from the perspective of vision. The urban canopy is the space used by human at the urban scale, and the physical environment of the city can be perceived at the scale of urban street canyon. As the basic enclosed public space form in urban space, the main index to describe urban street pattern is height to width ratio (H/W). As shown in Fig. 2, the proposed building height is 10 m, and the corresponding proportions of urban canyon morphology with different aspect ratios can be divided into three categories: H/W = 1 for regular level, H/W < 0.5 for avenue level, and H/W > 2 for deep level [13]. Temporary marquee is attached to buildings in urban streets in Taiwan, which exist in the form of shutters in space and affect the sound field of street canyon. Therefore, the factors that change the sound pressure level of street canyon include the following conditions:

(1)   Building height

In this study, road parameters were set unchanged and different building heights were H, 1/2H and 2H respectively. The sound spillover and dispersion patterns are shown in Fig. 2-A.2–B.2-C. As shown in Fig. 2-A, when the aspect ratio of street canyon is 1, the sound pressure level (LAeq) above the building is about 75–80 (dB). As shown in Fig. 2-B, when the aspect ratio of street canyon is less than 0.5, the sound pressure level (LAeq) above the building is about 80 (dB). As shown in Fig. 2-C When the aspect ratio of street canyon is greater than 2, the sound pressure level (LAeq) above the building is about 70–75 (dB).

(2)   Shutter structure

The research follows the results of the previous software simulation of street canyon and explores the acoustic field optimization prototype of street canyon. Shutter change length, as shown in Fig. 2-D.2–E.2-F. to join under different shutter module, shutter length L to H are planned to be H, 1/2H, and 1/2H under different palette modes. Figure A is the prototype with additional shutter simulation discussed. As shown in Fig. 2-D, when the height-width ratio of the shutter is 1, the sound pressure

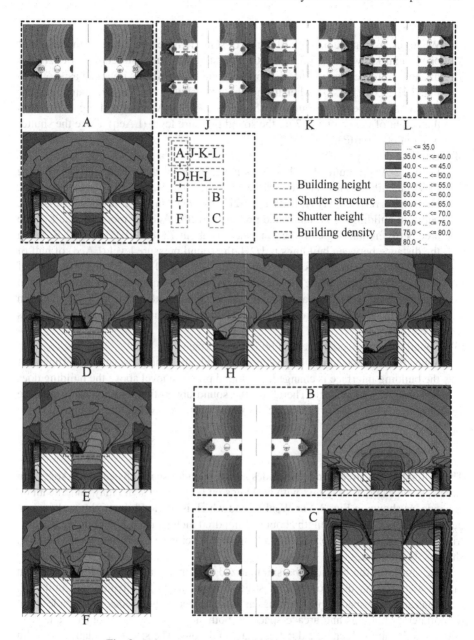

Fig. 2. Urban canyon sound field simulation in CadnaA

level (LAeq) above the shutter is about 59 (dB). As shown in Fig. 2-E, when the aspect ratio of the shutter is 2, the sound pressure level (LAeq) above the shutter is about 62 (dB). As shown in Fig. 2-F, when the height-width ratio of the shutter is 3, the sound pressure level (LAeq) above the shutter is about 66 (dB).

(3) Shutter height

When discussing the height difference of shutters based on Fig. 2-E, the height of one level is known to be 3.5 m, and the height of the shutter structure is set to be 3.5 m and 7 m respectively. The distribution state of the SPL is obtained as shown in Fig. 2-H.2-L. In Fig. 2-I, when the height of the shutter is 3.5 m, the sound pressure level (LAeq) above the shutter is about 70–80 (dB). As shown in Fig. 2-H, when the height of the shutter is 7 m, the sound pressure level (LAeq) above the shutter is about 60–80 (dB).

(4) Building density

In Fig. 2-A, the number of buildings is increased or decreased, and the spacing between buildings is changed as shown in Fig. 2-J.2-K.2-L. The distance between buildings is respectively H, 1/2H and 1/2H. As shown in Fig. 2-J, when the distance between buildings is H, the sound pressure level (LAeq) of more than half of the area between buildings, on the same side, is about 75–80 (dB). In Fig. 2-K, when the distance between buildings is 1/2H, the sound pressure level (LAeq) of half of the area between buildings, on the same side, is about 70–75 (dB), and the other half is about 75–80 (dB), while the sound energy distribution of the area, with the sound pressure level (LAeq) greater than 80 dB, is significantly reduced. 7. As shown in figure L, the sound pressure level (LAeq) between buildings, one-third H, decreases to 65 (dB).

(5) Sound absorption coefficient of building interface

When Fig. 2-A is taken as the prototype and only the sound absorption coefficient of the building interface is changed, the sound pressure level above the building does not change significantly. Therefore, the sound absorption coefficient of building interface is not a factor to change the sound pressure level of street canyon.

Site Description

The spatial form of street canyon includes arcade corridor space on pedestrian street. On streets, some canyons may mix with buildings on both sides, some may underneath on one side, as shown in Fig. 3. For Wenlin road which is in the Shilin night market main pedestrian street, the road length about five hundred meters, including buildings, pedestrian streets, arcade corridor space, parking space, vehicles roads, temporary building shutters distribution.

The space on the base can be summarized into five spatial prototypes, as shown in Fig. 4. Based on the prototype of street canyon, it can be divided into unilateral buildings and open space, with buildings and open space on both sides, and arcade space on unilateral buildings and arcade space on both sides. Space usage objects and road widths on the site will change due to actual conditions. The streets and lanes of Shilin night market are mostly used for walking, so the use of roads in the night market and the road facing the street is different. Figure 3 shows the intersection of Wenlin Road and Dabei Road, where the flow of people and vehicles is large. The arcade space of the beverage shop is located at the place with the screen, which is connected with the walking road to provide tourists with waiting space.

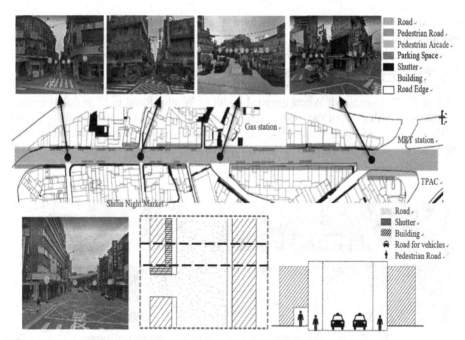

Fig. 3. Street characteristic of spatial form of street canyon includes arcade corridor space on pedestrian street.

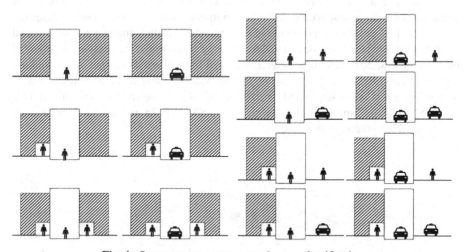

Fig. 4. Street canyon prototype and usage classification

4   Visualization of Sound Distribution

In this study, acoustic software CadnaA was used for sound field analysis to simulate the distribution characteristics of sound pressure level of urban recreation space and to collect sound pressure level by noise meter. The software simulation parameters are selected from Wenlin Road of Taipei city traffic flow survey data in 2019. During the morning peak hours (07:15–08:15), the equivalent number of passenger cars per hour is 1524, and that of heavy vehicles is 5%. In the evening peak period (17:30–18:30), the equivalent number of passenger cars per hour is 1554, and that of heavy vehicles is 4% [4]. As shown in Fig. 5, CadnaA simulation diagram of sound pressure level of Wenlin Road is obtained. When the road width of Wenlin Road is 17 m and there are buildings on both sides of the road, LAeq of building volume evaluation is about 75–80 (dB). When the width of Wenlin Road is 17 m and there are buildings on one side of the road, the sound pressure level (LAeq) of buildings far away from the road is about 70–75 (dB).

Fig. 5. CadnaA sound pressure level analysis simulation diagram

Open space area sound pressure level (LAeq) is about 60–75 (dB) when the width of Wenlin Road is 25 m and Wenlin Road has an intersection with other roads. Therefore, when there is open space on one side of the road, the overflow and dispersion of sound field are more obvious. The measured data of the second stage of the study were collected on December 8, 2019. The noise meter was used to measure the points of the walking road on Wenlin Road, as shown in Fig. 6. The walking route was 520 m long, and 28 measuring points were distributed on average (S0–S27). The road width of measuring points S6–S27 is 17 m, that of measuring points S3–S5 is 25 m, and that of measuring points S0–S2 is greater than 25 m.

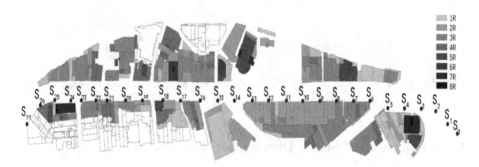

Fig. 6. Measuring point map

Table 1. List of general conditions of the on-site measurement.

Measuring point	Measure Sound Pressure Level LAeq(dB)	CadnaA Sound Pressure Level LAeq(dB)	Deviation
S0	74.6	62	12.6
S1	78.1	64	14.1
S2	81.2	68	13.2
S3	81.3	72	9.3
S4	81.7	73	8.7
S5	78.3	74	4.3
S6	79.5	79	0.5
S7	79.5	77	2.5
S8	75.4	76	0.6
S9	79.5	79	0.5
S10	76.5	76	0.5
S11	78.9	78	0.9
S12	80	79	1
S13	86.6	77	9.6
S14	80.1	74	6.1
S15	80.9	75	5.9
S16	83.6	71	12.6
S17	79.3	77	2.3
S18	75.7	78	2.3
S19	75.4	79	3.6
S20	80.2	80	0.2
S21	78.4	79	0.6
S22	77.1	79	1.9
S23	80.5	73	7.5
S24	79.1	75	4.1
S25	77	77	0
S26	79.2	77	2.2
S27	76.2	75	1.2

The measured sound pressure value and CadnaA simulated sound pressure value are sorted out as shown in Table 1. The measurement points can be divided into two groups according to the current situation of the base by observation. The first group is measuring points S0–S5, with a total of six measure points. The road width is more than or equal to 25 m. The second group is S6–S27, with a total of 22 measure points and a road width of 17 m. Its spatial form is similar to the prototype of street canyon space and the difference between measured and simulated sound pressure values. In measure points S6–S27, the public space of streets and lanes in Shilin Night market is crowded due to the connection of Wenlin Road and Lane 101 of Wenlin Road, Anping Street, Da Nan Road and Da Bei Road. It can be seen from the Table 1 above that measure points S13–S16, S18–S19 and S23–24 near the intersection of streets, and lanes show a large difference between measured sound pressure values and simulated sound pressure values. The SPL difference of other measuring points is small. As shown the actual measured SPL value is similar to the simulated SPL value, and the similar measurement points are S6–S12, S17, S20–S22 and S25–S27.SPSS was used to conduct consistency test between measured sound pressure value and CadnaA simulated sound pressure value. The value of significance test was 0.060, so there was no consistency between measured sound pressure value LAeq (dB) and CadnaA simulated sound pressure value LAeq (dB), with internal variability.

5   Discussion

In this study, the prototype space of urban street canyon was summarized, and the longitudinal interface space and sound pressure level distribution of different spatial forms were analyzed. Taking Shilin commercial and recreational district in Taipei as an example, CadnaA software was used to simulate and predict the sound pressure level of urban road. Wenlin Road in Shilin night market was selected as the research object, and the sound pressure level was measured on the spot. Conclusions and suggestions can be drawn from the above:

(1) Taipei urban commercial and recreational streets can be summarized into five types of spatial prototypes: building on one side and open space on the other; arcade space on one side and open space on the other; buildings on both sides, building on one side and arcade space on the other; arcade space on both sides.
(2) Using street canyon scale to analyze urban road as the research object for urban soundscape discussion, the various factors of urban street canyon include building height, with or without building shade, shade height and building spacing.
(3) At the street canyon ratio, when the road width is unchanged, the higher the building is, the greater the diffusion degree of SPL value inside the building is. The sound energy attenuation will be affected by the shading structure of buildings. The longer the building shutter is, the greater the influence of diffusion degree of sound pressure level is. The sound pressure above the shutter (LAeq) can decrease from 75–80 (dB) to 59 dB at most. The lower the height of the shutter, the greater the impact on the high sound pressure level, and the value can reach 80 dB. The greater the distance between buildings, the more obvious the attenuation of sound pressure level. When the distance between buildings is ?H, the sound pressure level (LAeq) between buildings on the same side is attenuated to 65 dB.
(4) Sound pressure level simulated by software and measured sound pressure level; some streets are greatly affected by the actual situation of the site. This study only takes Wenlin Road as an example for sound energy distribution simulation, without

considering the space where Wenlin Road intersects with other vehicles. Therefore, the measured value of sound pressure at S0–S5 measurement point is far higher than the simulated value at the open space with road width greater than 17 m.

(5) The consistency test of measured sound pressure value and CadnaA simulated sound pressure value shows that the p-value of significance test is 0.060, so there is no consistency between measured sound pressure value LAeq (dB) and CadnaA simulated sound pressure value LAeq (dB), with internal variability.

References

1. Wang, J.: The beginning of environmental sociology: making Feng Shui in the hometown look good. Gwan, Taipei (1994)
2. Weng, J.: Study on urban design planning outline of Tainan City; 3. Construction of urban texture and form, Tainan. Cheng Da Architectural Culture and Education Foundation (2001)
3. Wang, J.: Urban expression of soundscapes: A Tale of Two Cities in the environmental socio-logical imagination. Natl. Taiwan Univ. J. Archit. Urban Rural Stud. **10**(2001/12/01), 89–98 (2001)
4. A survey of traffic flow and characteristics in Taipei CITY N014 (2019)
5. Schafer, M.: Raymond. The Tunning of the World. Ed. A. (1977)
6. ISO: ISO12913-1Acoustics–Soundscape–Part 1: Definition and Conceptual Framework (2014)
7. Brambilla, G., et al.: The perceived quality of soundscape in three urban parks in Rome. J. Acoust. Soc. Am. **134**(1), 832–839 (2013)
8. Axelsson, Ö., Nilsson, M.E., Berglund, B.: A principal components model of soundscape perception. J. Acoust. Soc. Am. **128**(5), 2836–2846 (2010)
9. Lynch, K.: The Image of the City. The MIT Press, Cambridge (1960)
10. Bell, M.M.: An Introduction to Environmental Sociology. Sage Publication, New York (1998)
11. Schafer, R.M.: Five Village Soundscape, No. 4, Music of the Environment Series, WPS, Vancouver: ARC Publications (Co-author with B. Truax and B. Davis) (1977)
12. Alves, S., Estévez-Mauriz, L., Aletta, F., Echevarria-Sanchez, G.M., Romero, V.P.: Towards the integration of urban sound planning in urban development processes: the study of four test sites within the SONORUS project: noise mapping, vol. 2, no. 1 (2015)
13. Oke, T.R.: Boundary Layer Climates (1988)
14. Darò, C.: Avant-gardes sonores en architecture (2013)
15. Southworth, M.: The Sonic Environment of Cities (1969)
16. Appleyard, D., et al.: The View From the Road (1965)

Interaction in Automated Vehicles and Mobility

Purchase Intention Towards Electric Vehicles in India: A Theory of Planned Behavior Perspective

Jitender Kumar Atri[✉], Woon Kian Chong, and Muniza Askari

S P Jain School of Global Management, Singapore 119579, Singapore
{Jitenderkumar.db1804007,tristan.chong,Muniza.askari}@spjain.org

Abstract. The growth of India's electric vehicle (EV) market has been exponential. This research investigates the factors influencing purchase intention (PI) of EV customers drawing upon the extended theory of planned behavior (TPB). We employ a qualitative study involving ten semi-structured interviews of highly experienced professionals in India across various automobile companies (passenger cars, commercial vehicles, and 2-wheeler). The factors that were revalidated by this study include price value, range confidence and infrastructure readiness, attitude, subjective norm, and perceived behavioral control. However, there were mixed opinions about environmental concerns and emotional value. The result has further identified four new factors: competition, new technology, previous experience, and safety that align with the proposed model's exploratory nature while adhering to TPB's nomology. Our results suggest a mix of push (government policies, technology improvement, infrastructure, etc.) and pull (customers purchase intention) strategies to accelerate the EV market growth.

Keywords: Electric vehicles · Qualitative research · Purchase intention · Theory of planned behavior

1 Introduction

The transport sector is amongst the largest energy-consuming sectors. It is globally overly dependent on hydrocarbon-based fossil fuels. The sector is also a major source of Green House Gas (GHG) emissions and accounts for 24% of total global energy-related carbon dioxide (CO2) emissions [1]. To reduce vehicle emissions, the global automotive industry is in a phase of a change to find alternatives to internal combustion engines (ICE). Electrification is one of the solutions to address the increasing levels of vehicle pollution [2]. Additionally, electric mobility is multiplying by technological advancements supported by government incentives, policies, and regulations. The global EV fleet going past 5.1 million in 2018, up by 2 million since 2017 [3]. The transport sector of India is the third most GHG emitting industry, of which the road transport sector is the major contributor. Out of the total CO_2 emissions in India, it was reported that 13% come from the transport sector [4].

© Springer Nature Switzerland AG 2022
M. Rauterberg et al. (Eds.): HCII 2022, LNCS 13520, pp. 429–439, 2022.
https://doi.org/10.1007/978-3-031-18158-0_31

To create momentum for the adoption of EVs in India, the government is working towards providing tax incentives, stringent targets for carbon emissions via Corporate Average Fuel Consumption (CAFC), and Faster Adoption and Manufacturing of Electric Vehicles (FAME) in order to enhance fundamental infrastructure, and supporting Research & Development (R&D) for technological advancement [5]. These steps and policies will create a push towards creating an environment that is more acceptable towards EVs. In conjunction with improved technology, a pull by the customers will be created with improved infrastructure, range and price reduction. Marketing also has to be aligned to make a positive attitude of customers for EV by improving perceived value, creating an emotional connection, and environmentally conscious customers.

2 Literature Review

2.1 Theory of Planned Behavior (TPB)

The Theory of Planned Behavior (TPB) has been an adequate and influential model in explaining or predicting behavior [6–11]. Moreover, it has successfully attracted wide application and empirical support to several pro-environmental behaviors as illustrated below:

- **Attitude** refers to individuals' positive or negative evaluation of performing a behavior. Attitude results from behavioral beliefs and outcome evaluations. Behavioral belief refers to the unique idea about the consequences of engaging in a particular behavior. In contrast, outcome evaluation refers to the corresponding favorable or unfavorable judgment about the possible consequences of the behavior [11].
- **Subjective norms** represent the social pressure from the members of a reference group to act out a given behavior. It is defined as social pressure exerted on individuals to engage in a particular behavior. Subjective norm is an outcome of normative belief and motivation to comply. Normative belief refers to an individual perception about how others (those who are significant to the individual) would like one to behave in a certain situation, whereas motivation to comply refers to the individual desire to adhere to the opinion of significant others [11].
- **Perceived behavioral control (PBC)** concerns the perceived ease or difficulty of performing a behavior. PBC is an outcome of control beliefs and perceived power. Control belief can be defined as the belief of the individual towards the presence of certain factors that may facilitate or impede the performance of a particular behavior (e.g., time, money & opportunity). In contrast, perceived power refers to personal evaluation of the impact of these factors in facilitating or impeding the particular behavior [11].
- **Behavioral Intention**: It is an indication of an individual's readiness to perform a given behavior. It is assumed to be an immediate antecedent of behavior [12]. The more favorable the attitude towards behavior, the more favorable the subjective norm, and the greater the perceived behavioral control, the stronger will be the individual's intention to perform the behavior.

2.2 Extended Theory of Planned Behavior

"The theory of planned behavior is, in principle, open to the inclusion of additional predictors if it can be shown that they capture a significant proportion of the variance in intention or behavior after the theory's current variables have been taken into account." [11]. Although it is well known that TPB assumes that intention to perform the behavior is derived from attitude, subjective norm, and PBC, however, researchers in the past advocate for domain-specific factors which are not included in this model. Perceived value and willingness to pay a premium (WPP) were added along with Attitude, Subjective Norm and Perceived Behavioral Control for measuring consumers' green purchase intention [8]. Researchers have also considered price and emotional value, as it plays a vital role in green purchase decisions as consumers will not compromise on the functional benefit of the product just for the sake of the environment. Therefore, understanding consumers' value of green products is crucial. Further, willingness to pay a premium was considered as the high price of eco-friendly products is still an issue for price-sensitive Indian consumers [8]. Based on the above, we anticipated that the following factors are important as illustrated in the following figure:

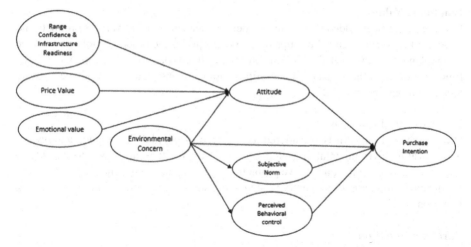

Fig. 1. Conceptual framework

Range Confidence and Infrastructure Readiness

The driving range of EVs has long been considered a significant barrier to the acceptance of electric mobility. Due to the limited range of battery EVs (BEV), drivers feel stressed about becoming stranded if the battery charge is depleted, which is known as range stress. Higher levels of trust in range estimates lead to lower range stress and higher acceptance of BEVs [13]. Effects of range anxiety can be significant but are reduced with access to additional charging infrastructure [14].

High acquisition costs and short driving ranges are the main factors that impede the diffusion of EVs [15]. EVs suffer from a short travel distance on a battery charge, a lack of charging infrastructure, and long charging times collectively called charging risk, which are primary reasons consumers are reluctant to adopt them [16]. Fast-charging infrastructure will benefit and facilitate long-range drives for EVs, and this may be crucial to push the market penetration of EVs. Thus, Infrastructure readiness plays an important role in increasing market penetration and public acceptance [5, 17].

Price Value
Price value can be defined as consumers' mental tradeoff between the perceived benefits of the action and the cost of using them [18]. The price value is positive when the advantages of using technology are perceived to be greater than the cost.

Price value predicts behavioral intention to use technology [19]. The price value is a crucial determinant of the purchase intention of alternative fuel vehicles [20]. EVs lack economies of scale and so they are relatively expensive. The cost of replacing batteries in EVs is also a burden that ICE vehicles do not impose. Therefore, price and battery cost negatively affect the perceived value of EVs [16]. Willingness to pay premium (WPP) was not found to have a significant influence on green purchase intention, implying that the consumers in India are more sensitive towards price value [8].

Emotional Value
Emotions have been added to decision models such as the TPB for various products and issues and have been proved to improve predictability of the model. Emotions enhance the explanatory power of the TPB in predicting intentions to cornea donations [21]. Emotions towards the EVs and thoughtful emotions towards car driving, have a strong effect on usage intention [22].

Environmental Concern
"Environmental concern is considered as a degree of people's knowledge and awareness towards environmental consciousness and support they are ready to provide to preserve the environment and solve problems regarding the environment." [5]. Concern for the environment is significantly related to consumer behavior, including purchasing intentions [23].

Purchase Intention
Intention is defined as an indication "of how hard people are willing to try, of how much of an effort they are planning to exert, in order to perform the behavior." [15] Purchase Intention of environmentally friendly products can be defined as "the likelihood that a consumer would buy a particular product resulting from his or her environmental needs" [24].

In the context of this study, the behavior is the actual purchase of EVs. According to the theory of reasoned action [25], which is a predecessor of TPB, the most immediate antecedent of intention is attitude, which is "determined by salient beliefs regarding the consequences of performing the behavior" [26].

3   Methodology

We adopt qualitative research methodology to explore the various factors that influence purchase intentions of BEVs in India. Semi-structured interviews were conducted with key professionals from Original Equipment Manufacturers (OEMs) who have extensive experience and knowledge of the Indian automotive market, across passenger cars, commercial vehicles as well as 2-wheelers. One expert from battery manufacturing was also interviewed. The selection of the interviewees was based on purposive sampling (a non-probability sampling method).

Based on the literature study and extended TPB, an initial framework (Fig. 1) was generated. The qualitative research was planned to discuss and reconfirm the variables that are important towards the PI of EVs in India.

We encouraged the respondents to share their detailed views. Notably, each question was followed with 1–3 probing questions. After covering all the questions, we asked the interviewees to add any thoughts that they wanted to bring forth that were not included in the earlier questions. Essentially, we encouraged the participants to speak their minds and opinions openly.

The interviewees were informed about the objective of the interview, and interview protocol was shared with them. All ten Interviews were conducted between September-December 2021, telephonically with an average duration of 30 min for each interview. The interviews were transcribed in MS Word and imported into NVIVO for analysis.

To analyze the data, coding was done in NVIVO to capture the information into codes and cases. In qualitative research, code could be a word or phrase that describes the essence or theme for a portion of input data. Coding is the process of categorizing data into these codes and cases. Cases are the individuals who have provided the qualitative data (Table 1).

Table 1. Example quotes for various codes

Code	Example quote
Attitude	Attitude towards EVs is more as "Dominance/Status seeker"; "Misconceptions on safety to be removed by forming Consortiums"; "Lack of awareness of EVs, never experienced drivability, people ask does it really run-on battery"
Competition	"Govt to create environment that allows for a high level of innovation and healthy competition in the EV space"; "not many players for choice"
Environment concern	Customers in India are "Pretentious green only"; EV is "only a style statement"; "Environment is every one's responsibility"; "Government is also pushing - focus on EVS, renewable energy"
New technology	"Battery cost & Life is uncertain in the mind of customer"; "Reliability still uncertain"; "Battery technology is very new, current tech may become obsolete and the new battery may not be compatible with old car architecture"; "Flooded roads - What will happen, Battery range/life - What after battery life - Technology to evolve to address these concerns"
PBC	"Yes, would buy EV - if Price parity is maintained with ICE vehicles, even with a budget stretch customer will buy"
Emotional value	"Cleaner world - children, environmentally friendly, design differentiation/ tech advancement/ green imagery"; "Like any other car, for mass market nothing unique for EVs, total cost, maintenance, less pollution – Economical reasons drives the emotional decision"
Infrastructure	"Charging points - house and office is enough"; "Infrastructure is more important than range"; "Outside of city - fast chargers are needed"; "Highways - 0–80%: 20–30 min is acceptable", "30 min–250 kms range, under 30 min for 50%"
Price value	"Smart value of money- Total cost of ownership 3–5 years"; "Maintenance/Servicing cost is negligible, very fewer moving parts"; "Fuel prices - Psychological barrier, increased price of fossil fuel"
Range	"Driving range is not so important if say 500 kms range is achievable"; "Driving Range should be more like fuel range"; "Range anxiety for 300 kms range is not much"; "200 kms is minimum Range expected"; " Mostly players are with 200–250 kms - 20–25 KwH, with battery cost as the driving factor", "Real Range of 250–300 Kms"
Safety	"Fear of battery catching fire"; "Safety of EVs - fire incidents"

(continued)

Table 1. (*continued*)

Code	Example quote
Subjective norm	"Yes - are influenced by social media, with customers being accessible to all media"
Willingness to pay	"very less people willing to pay price premium for Evs"; "no willingness to pay premium"; "Premium only if customers are TCO (Total Cost of Ownership) educated"

4 Findings

The coding identified the number of times a particular code was referenced by each of the interviewees. Table 2 summarizes the same. We see that infrastructure and price value are the most referenced codes suggesting the two codes to be the most important factors of PI.

Table 2. Number of references for various codes

Code	Cases – Ten interviews									
	1	2	3	4	5	6	7	8	9	10
Attitude	1	1	1	0	1	0	1	1	1	1
Competition	2	1	0	0	0	0	3	0	1	0
Environment concern	3	1	1	1	2	0	1	0	1	1
New technology	0	3	0	0	2	1	0	1	1	2
PBC	1	1	1	1	1	0	1	1	1	1
Emotional value	2	1	1	1	1	1	1	1	1	1
Infrastructure	4	2	2	5	2	1	3	1	3	2
Price value	4	4	4	5	2	1	3	3	2	4
Range	2	1	2	1	1	0	2	1	2	1
Previous experience	0	0	2	0	1	0	0	0	0	1
Safety	2	0	0	0	0	1	0	0	0	0
Subjective norm	1	1	1	1	1	0	1	1	2	1
Willingness to pay	1	1	1	1	1	0	0	1	1	0

Based on the inputs by the participants, in addition to the 8 variables (codes) as identified in the literature review, there were a few more variables that were proposed viz.

(i)   Competition
(ii)   New Technology
(iii) Safety
(iv)   Previous experience
(v)   As a further subdivision of the price value variable, sub variables like cost of
       ownership, fuel prices, government subsidies, regulation got generated

Coding in NVIVO, was done to not only capture the codes (variables like Attitude, Competition etc.) and cases (Interviewees), but also the sentiments against these variables. The below table summarizes the sentiment against each code (Table 3).

Table 3. Sentiment for various codes

Code	Very positive	Positive	Moderately positive	Negative	Moderately negative	Very negative
Attitude	0	9	1	1	0	0
Competition	0	7	0	0	0	0
Environment concern	1	6	0	7	3	0
New technology	0	7	0	3	3	0
PBC	3	10	0	0	0	0
Emotional value	0	7	2	4	1	0
Infrastructure	0	17	1	0	0	0
Price value	3	33	0	0	0	0
Range	0	12	3	1	0	0
Previous experience	0	5	0	0	0	0
Safety	0	3	0	1	0	0
Subjective norm	0	10	0	1	1	0
Willingness to pay	0	2	0	6	3	0

5   Discussion

5.1   Theoretical Contribution

This study explores the factors that influence the PI of BEV in India. This study captures inputs by interviewing highly experienced relevant OEM professionals across many companies. Developing on extended TPB, in addition to Attitude, Subjective Norm, and PBC, the framework was expanded to other factors such as range confidence, price value, emotional value and environmental concern. Additionally, price value-related sub-themes were also generated, including government subsidies, regulations, cost of ownership, and willingness to pay the premium. From the exploratory study and the above considerations, the other factors that emerged as significant include competition, new technology, previous experience, and safety.

5.2 Practical Implications

The government of India has initiated many reforms, subsidies, and regulations to promote nationwide BEV volumes [2]. Additionally, to bring more competition to the market. Production Linked Incentive (PLI) schemes have already been rolled out by the government in 2022. There have been more than 100 companies that have opted for the PLI scheme. The scheme will also facilitate OEMs to invest in R&D as well. The technological advancement and subsidies will help address the most critical factor of price value (cost of acquisition, cost of ownership) and range improvement. With infrastructure being identified as another critical factor, the collaboration between charger manufacturers, OEMs and the government is needed to build the necessary infrastructure. Further, there can be a collaborative initiative between the government and manufacturers to start manufacturing Lithium-Ion batteries in India and manage the complete lifecycle of BEV batteries. As an extension to this study, a quantitative study is needed to understand the customer mindset around reasons that they would buy BEVs. The outcome from the study will help focus on the critical factors. This will also help to plan the necessary marketing communication across various channels and focused groups that will be identified from the study.

5.3 Conclusion

India has been witnessing exponential growth in BEV during the last two years. It is evident that the Indian market is moving towards BEV. However, work needs to be done at multiple levels for this change to be smooth and faster. With price value as the most critical factor for success, technological innovation is very important to reduce not only the cost of acquisition but the overall cost of ownership. To further improve the buying proposition of BEVs, government subsidies towards BEVs and stringent regulations towards ICE vehicles need to continue. A consistent, reliable actual driving range of at least 250 Kms in a full charge is very important. A charging facility at home or at workplace is expected by the BEV customer. For intercity commutes, fast charging at distances of 200 Kms from major cities is important that can charge up to 80% in 30–45 min. All this can be successful only if the abundant green source of electricity is available across the country. To help increase competition and provide options to potential customers, government initiatives like the PLI will significantly boost OEMs to invest in BEVs. Standardization of chargers across different vehicles will help the utility of any charging facility. An industrywide collaboration will help to standardize charging facilities across manufacturers. To educate customers towards BEV benefits, environmental benefits need to be communicated widely via all communication channels, including the internet and social media. First-mover anxiety can be reduced as more and more players will come and people start experiencing BEVs. Improved battery technology will not only improve reliability, range confidence but also drive away the fear of safety. Experience will help people overcome range anxiety, and a further improvement in battery technology and improved infrastructure will help strengthen the BEV market.

The study results show different inspirations why different people would purchase BEVs, where for many customers price value and Infrastructure are most important, whereas for some Environment concern, enhancement of their positive self-image, and desire to try something new is important. There is a lack of communication for the awareness of BEV, and that's why the attitude towards EVs hasn't yet improved. Appropriate communication and battery environment need to be created around the motivating factors. There is a lack of visibility of BEVs on the road, and with limited options and anxiety of new technology, the BEV market in India is yet to catch the pace. Government policies to encourage BEV and regulate ICE vehicles along with subsidies needs to continue to make BEVs lucrative both for manufacturers and customers.

References

1. IEA: Tracking Transport 2020, IEA, Paris (2020). https://www.iea.org/reports/tracking-tra nsport-2020
2. Dhawan, R., Gupta, S., Hensley, R., Huddar, N., Iyer, B., Mangaleswaran, R.: The future of mobility in India: challenges & opportunities for the auto component industry. In: Automotive Component Manufacturers Association of India annual conference, no. 3, pp. 1–36, September 2017
3. Global EV Outlook (2019). www.iea.org/publications/reports/globalevoutlook2019/
4. Ministry of Environment & Forests Government of India (2010). INCCA: Indian Network for Climate Change Assessment. http://www.indiaenvironmentportal.org.in/files/fin-rpt-incca.pdf
5. Mishra, S., Malhotra, G.: Is India ready for e-mobility? An exploratory study to understand e-vehicles purchase intention. Theor. Econ. Lett. **9**(2), 376–391 (2019)
6. Arli, D., Tan, L.P., Tjiptono, F., Yang, L.: Exploring consumers' purchase intention towards green products in an emerging market: the role of consumers' perceived readiness. Int. J. Consum. Stud. **42**(4), 389–401 (2018)
7. Bhutto, M.Y., Zeng, F., Soomro, Y.A., Khan, M.A.: Young Chinese consumer decision making in buying green products: an application of theory of planned behavior with gender and price transparency. Pak. J. Commer. Soc. Sci. (PJCSS) **13**(3), 599–619 (2019)
8. Yadav, R., Pathak, G.S.: Determinants of consumers' green purchase behavior in a developing nation: applying and extending the theory of planned behavior. Ecol. Econ. **134**, 114–122 (2017)
9. Shankar, A., Kumari, P.: Exploring the enablers and inhibitors of electric vehicle adoption intention from sellers' perspective in India: a view of the dual-factor model. Int. J. Nonprofit Volunt. Sect. Mark. **24**(4), N.PAG (2019)
10. Kumar, A.: A study of mobile app based household purchasing by working women in a developing country: an empirical validation of theory of planned behaviour. Optim. J. Res. Manag. **11**(2), 37–45 (2019)
11. Ajzen, I.: The theory of planned behavior. Organ. Behav. Hum. Decis. Process. **50**(2), 179–211 (1991)

12. Ajzen, I.: Perceived behavioral control, self-efficacy, locus of control, and the theory of planned behavior 1. J. Appl. Soc. Psychol. **32**(4), 665–683 (2002)
13. Nastjuk, I., Werner, J., Marrone, M., Kolbe, L.M.: Inaccuracy versus volatility–which is the lesser evil in battery electric vehicles? Transport. Res. F Traffic Psychol. Behav. **58**, 855–870 (2018)
14. Neubauer, J., Wood, E.: The impact of range anxiety and home, workplace, and public charging infrastructure on simulated battery electric vehicle lifetime utility. J. Power Sour. **257**, 12–20 (2014)
15. Degirmenci, K., Breitner, M.H.: Consumer purchase intentions for electric vehicles: is green more important than price and range? Transp. Res. Part D Transp. Environ. **51**, 250–260 (2017)
16. Kim, M.K., Oh, J., Park, J.H., Joo, C.: Perceived value and adoption intention for electric vehicles in Korea: moderating effects of environmental traits and government supports. Energy **159**, 799–809 (2018)
17. Sang, Y.N., Bekhet, H.A.: Exploring factors influencing electric vehicle usage intention: an empirical study in Malaysia. Int. J. Bus. Soc. **16**(1) (2015)
18. Dodds, W.B., Monroe, K.B., Grewal, D.: Effects of price, brand, and store information on buyers' product evaluations. J. Mark. Res. **28**(3), 307–319 (1991)
19. Venkatesh, V., Thong, J.Y., Xu, X.: Consumer acceptance and use of information technology: extending the unified theory of acceptance and use of technology. MIS Q., 157–178 (2012)
20. Karunanayake, T., Samarasinghe, D.: The effect of perceived risk on the purchase intention of alternative fuel vehicles. Sri Lankan J. Manag. **23**(2), 67–98 (2018)
21. Bae, H.S.: Entertainment-education and recruitment of cornea donors: the role of emotion and issue involvement. J. Health Commun. **13**(1), 20–36 (2008)
22. Moons, I., De Pelsmacker, P.: An extended decomposed theory of planned behavior to predict the usage intention of the electric vehicle: a multi-group comparison. Sustainability **7**(5), 6212–6245 (2015)
23. Lai, I.K., Liu, Y., Sun, X., Zhang, H., Xu, W.: Factors influencing the behavioural intention towards full electric vehicles: an empirical study in Macau. Sustainability **7**(9), 12564–12585 (2015)
24. Chen, Y.S., Chang, C.H.: Enhance green purchase intentions: the roles of green perceived value, green perceived risk, and green trust. Manag. Decis. (2012)
25. Fishbein, M., Ajzen, I.: Belief, attitude, intention, and behavior: an introduction to theory and research (1977)
26. Ajzen, I., Fishbein, M.: Scaling and testing multiplicative combinations in the expectancy–value model of attitudes. J. Appl. Soc. Psychol. **38**(9), 2222–2247 (2008)

Participatory Design Fictions with Mixed Reality: A User Study Framework for Future Smart Cockpit

Cheng Chi, Yiwen Zhang, Yate Ge, Wenjia Wang, Jianuo Li, and Xiaohua Sun[✉]

College of Design and Innovation, Tongji University, Shanghai, China
{1933633,zhangyw,xsun}@tongji.edu.cn

Abstract. Before widely adopting in the real life, Emerging technologies and design concepts require appropriate user studies to explore demands from users. Smart cockpit is a typical fields driven by cutting-edge technologies, and vehicles are becoming more intelligent touchpoints empowered by V2X technologies. A repeated, correlative and continuous framework was employed for future-oriented user study such as smart cockpit's connectivity capability in the context of V2X, by presenting the Participatory Design Fictions with Mixed Reality, which aims for stimulating imagination of the participants to gather their views and discussions about the future. Thematic analysis, discourse analysis and creative analysis were adopted to evaluate this framework and method. Results indicated that Participatory Design Fictions with Mixed Reality provided researchers with more in-depth insights about the preferable futures articulated by different groups when conducting future-oriented, demand mining-oriented user study as a effective tool and method.

Keywords: Design Fiction · User study · Participatory design · Mixed reality · Smart cockpit

1 Introduction

Currently we are living in a time when science and technology are developing at one of the fastest rates in the history, with numerous innovative ideas in laboratories around the world that have already changed, or could be profoundly change all aspects of our daily lives in the future. So it is necessary to find out how users want these things to be before they actually come to life. Researchers need to find a creative form to present future technology and design in advance, which can stimulate the imagination and thinking of users, in a way that invites them to create a better vision of future life.

Among these future topics, Vehicle to Everything (V2X) has received a lot of attention and discussion. It takes the moving vehicle as the information sensing object and realizes the interconnection between the vehicles and other ones, people, roads, service platforms, and urban facilities with the help of information

© Springer Nature Switzerland AG 2022
M. Rauterberg et al. (Eds.): HCII 2022, LNCS 13520, pp. 440–459, 2022.
https://doi.org/10.1007/978-3-031-18158-0_32

and communication technology [23]. In the context of V2X, the smart cockpit will not only be a daily travel tool, but also a comprehensive and integrated mobile terminal in the future life, and a mobile touchpoint in the future smart city [22]. As an important part of V2X, the connectivity ability of the smart cockpit will bring many new service scenarios that can profoundly affect the travel experience, and life style. Therefore, this paper attempts to use this topic as an example to explore methods for conducting future-oriented and requirements-mining-oriented user study.

2   Related Work

2.1   Science Fictions

Definition. Many future technologies and conceptual designs are often found in Science Fictions (Sci Fi), and the public is becoming familiar with regarding Sci Fi as a channel to learn about future visions. Sci Fi is a genre of speculative fiction that typically deals with imaginative and futuristic concepts such as advanced science and technology to explores the potential consequences of these innovations. [11] Sci Fi is often referred to as "literature of ideas" because of the depth of thought and the quality of the work itself [3], which can inspire the audience to think and discuss accordingly. So Sci Fi, in addition to providing entertainment, can often serve as a starting point for criticism and reflection on today's society [1]. Rising rapidly in popularity during the first half of the 20th century, Sci Fi was closely tied to the popular respect paid to science at that time, as well as the rapid pace of technological innovation and new inventions [4]. In fact, the relationship between Sci Fi and future technology is much closer than one might think, and the history of science has demonstrated that the dividing line between science fiction and scientific fact is often overlapping [24], with some of the imagery that appeared in completely unrealistic Sci Fi works at one time may become scientifically possible even guide the development of science within a few decades. [5,14]

Features. From books and drawings to the powerful visuals of today's film industry, Sci Fi can provide a "sense of wonder". [20] More importantly, Sci Fi criticize present-day society and explore alternatives, provide the audience with the inspiration to think and reflect on its subject matter. The thought-provoking nature of Sci Fi makes it an infectious medium, with George Slusser (2019) commenting that Sci Fi "is the one real international literary form we have today, and as such has branched out to visual media, interactive media and on to whatever new media the world will invent in the 21st century.". And based on the qualities that Sci Fi possesses to depict the future, the more better the visual and interactive experience in these media forms, the more profound the impact of Sci Fi on the audience.

For Design Research. Design researchers have also discovered the value of Sci Fi and have used Design Fictions (DFs) as a research tool for the recently emerging design practice and design research [15], or rather, DFs are design practices that aim to explore and critique possible futures. DFs draw on both science fiction's ability to depict imagined design objects within a diegesis and its critical potential in exposing the use of technologies within possible worlds with using Design Thinking to integrate design solutions into future scenarios [24].

Brief Summary

- Sci Fi is a genre of speculative fiction, with a "sense of wonder" and "critical-ity" that often provokes the viewers to explore and think about the future;
- Sci Fi has a profound impression on the viewer and is an infectious medium that takes many forms, and the better the sensory effect and interactive experience, the more profound the impact created;
- Sci Fi is recognised as a research method and tool in the form of DFs in the field of design research.

2.2   Participatory Design Fiction

Speculative Design and Design Fictions. DFs' criticality comes from Speculative Design thinking. In fact, Speculative Design is a subsidiary of critical design extracted by Dunne and Raby [7], which does not aim to propose commercial or solution-driven design solutions, but rather to design proposals that identify and discuss key issues that may occur in the future. This anti-solutionist tendency is a good example of the critical nature of Speculative Design, and as such, Speculative Design is used to challenge preconceptions, raise questions and to provoke debate [6].

Speculative Design is an approach enabling us to think about the future prospectively and critically [12], and one of its main manifestations is through the negation of the status quo and the initiation of discussion of possible future scenarios through a confrontation with a tangible object or process, the so called DFs [24]. However, DFs are not always tangible, prototyping is only intended for more arguments [10], and DFs can be created in a variety of mediums to inspire viewers and get them started on exploring the future. In addition, DFs are defined as design practices that explore and critique possible futures by creating speculative, provocative scenarios through design artifacts, which is a way to facilitate and foster debates [7]. The important characteristics of DFs are mentioned here: future scenarios, criticality, and encouraging debate. With DFs, prototypes and stories remove the obstacles of understanding, creating spaces where the audience holds an openness to change [17]. Thus, DFs serve both to give account and intervene [24]. DFs make the future understandable, the diegetic prototype is a form of explaining future technological needs and feasibility to the viewers [13]; the intervention role stimulates discussion and finds insights, DFs do not claim to predict the future, they act as aids to enable their audiences to act as interlocutors.

Participatory Design Fictions in Design Research. One of the challenges and issues of DFs is that they are typically designed and developed by individuals with a certain educational background and skillsets [2]. The individual perceptions and opinions of designers or researchers have a great impact on users and their lives, which is the "Butterfly Effect of Design"[?]. Future-oriented user study needs to focus on the perceptions of people and the daily lives they represent, which means bottom-up innovation and continuous discussion. The characteristics of DFs, which are creative provocation, questioning, innovation and exploration have been seen as highly suitable for participatory activities [18]. Lyckvi explores the possibility of integrating DFs with participatory design processes and suggests that Participatory Design Fiction (PDF) is a critical approach that means re-imagining, a participatory approach that means co-speculating, a interventionist approach that means rehearsing, and a discursive approach that means debating. PDF can take into account the perspectives of people who are marginalized in society, as Nägele focused on vulnerable's perspectives, which were collected in healthcare-related DFs to allow the public to hear their voices and reflect on their situation and imagine a more reasonable future together [19]. It is the vision and responsibility of designers and researchers to build confidence and good experience for more users to face the unknowable future problems and life. We are also concerned that DFs with more interactive effects and better sensory effects will get more attention and collect more discussions.

Brief Summary

- DFs are an approach that allow us to think critically about the future, it serve both to give account and intervene;
- PDF has the potential to bring social groups together to provoke, innovate and explore the future;
- With better presentation and interaction, as well as repeated and continuous discussions, PDF can create a more profound impact among the viewers.

2.3   Virtual Simulation

Scenario Simulation. Scenario building means that empathy can be shared more efficiently, and scenarios that correspond to the research topic can enhance the understanding of the user's context and thus facilitate the achievement of the research objectives [25]. Thomas Kohler investigated that participants' willingness to participate and express, effectiveness of expression, and creativity and imagination were all enhanced when a consistent and enjoyable experience was created for them in a simulated scenario [16]. Aceituno compared the feedback given by participants on driving related research in the driving simulation scenario and ordinary interview scene. Aceituno defined several dimensions and made quantitative and qualitative analysis on the user feedback content under these dimensions, The results showed that user interviews in driving simulation scenario can obtain more effective feedback [9].

AR/VR/MR Based Simulation. AR/VR/MR based simulation is called Virtual Simulation technology which has a powerful ability to create scenarios. Current researchers have begun to explore the use of Virtual Simulation in design research. El-Jarn explored the possibility of using XR technology for co-creation in the initial stages of the design process, examining emerging tools and checking whether they offered the potential to improve the design process [8]. The technical features of Virtual Simulation technology are well suited to help in the field of design research that relies on future service scenarios such as robotics and automobiles, Rosa explored the construction of robot models in MR environments and assisted researchers in presenting diverse design solutions and inviting users to participate in tests to gather the extent and dimensionality of the robot's appearance on the user's interaction with the robot [21].

Brief Summary

- Scenario research is a key step in understanding users' pain points, motivations and needs, requiring a way of depicting scenarios that can build consensus between researchers and participants;
- Virtual Simulation has a powerful ability to create immersive, interactive, illusory, and vivid scenarios, and has a wide range of applications in all phases of design research.

3   Method

3.1   User Study Framework

Three Main Phases. The entire user study practice is divided into three phases: 1) expert workshop, 2) PDF, and 3) MR simulation. we hope to stimulate participants' imagination, expression and discussion repeatedly, correlatively and continuously, and to explore future users' needs in these talks to support the exploration of more design opportunities (see Fig. 1).

- In the first step we conducted an expert workshop based desktop research and literature review on the topic to think of possible scenarios and plots for PDF as stimulus to help facilitate the understanding and imagination for the participants in the subsequent session;
- The methodology of PDF was used in the co-creation phase, where participants imagined and created DFs, and scenarioized and storytold them. The DFs created will be used as stimulus tools for more discussion in the final session;
- The final interviews will be conducted in the MR environment, which simulate the DFs created at previous phase. We re-invited the participants and some creative professionals for interviews and discussions after experiencing DFs in MR to explore their thoughts and suggestions on the relevant plots in DFs.

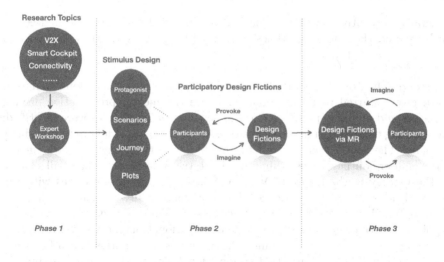

Fig. 1. The user study framework.

Ethical Considerations. The user study focused on the participants' reactions, imaginations, and discussions of future scenarios. The co-creation study was ethical in nature, but it also included the participants' own information and past experiences to support their imaginations and expressions, as well as their physiological acceptance of MR.

- Throughout the user study, we provided each participant with a personal information sheet before participating in the formal user study, asking whether they would consent to audio and video recording during the study while maintaining privacy protection, and allowing sufficient time for each participant to ask questions and make decisions;
- Each participant was asked about their physiological acceptance of extended reality (i.e., VR/AR/MR) in first-person perspective and any previous relevant experiences. Advice and assistance was provided in the event of any discomfort for the participant during the study;
- Most importantly, given the subject matter, they will need to have a driver's license.

3.2 Phase 1: Expert Workshop

Workshop Design The workshop was held in Shanghai and featured eight experts in automotive HMI and eight automotive consumers.

Participants. The experts include university professors, university PhDs, and automotive industry research experts. The experts will be divided into 4 groups with 8 consumers to discuss relevant topics and prepare debriefings. The 8 typical consumers are divided according to car grading criteria (A/B/C/D) and their general family situation, one single and one married consumer are invited for each car tier. (Females = 4, Males = 4; Aged form 23 to 34, M = 28 years old, SD = 3.74 years old).

Procedure. The workshop started with a discussion on the main driving scenarios. Each group started to think about what are the most representative driving scenarios and prepared presentation. Finally, four main scenarios were identified: Commuting to work, Go to a party with friends, Road trip, and Go to a business meeting. The group then started to enrich the story of each scenario in the form of user journey maps, thinking about two questions: What will change in the journey in the future of V2X, and what features and services will help us get a better driving experience? The workshop finally determined that five types of functions and services would be the key research directions: Third-party Application Ecology, LBS Services, Face Recognition, Context Awareness, Active Learning, and Intelligent Assistant. These 4 types of scenarios and 5 functions and services will be the important support for designing the stimuli used in the next phase of PDF.

The Stimulus for Participatory Design Fiction (PDF). Based on the results of the expert workshop, we designed a stimulus toolkit for PDF (see Fig. 2).

Scenario Cards. Four main scenarios and others mentioned in the discussion. Participants can choose and add to them.

Protagonist Cards. In which each group creates a character to be the protagonist of the DF according to the content of the information on the cards and considers the impact of these information on the DFs.

Scenario Journey Cards. Where each group of participants portrayed the entire journey according to the chosen scenario, including the protagonist's goals, the plot story at each point and the corresponding touchpoints, needs, helps and hindrances.

Function Depiction Cards. From the 5 categories of functions and services, which included an image and a fictional passage depicting a specific function, and formatting annotations to help each group of participants to imagine and edit.

3.3 Phase 2: Participatory Design Fiction (PDF)

The phase 2 included 14 workshops in 7 key cities in China (Shanghai, Beijing, Hangzhou, Xi'an, Chengdu, Zhengzhou, Guangzhou), and each workshop invited 6–8 participants and divided into two groups according to car classification criteria, gender and family status. 96 participants were invited to the workshop, 52 males and 44 females, with an age distribution of 24–35 years (M = 28.61; SD = 3.37).

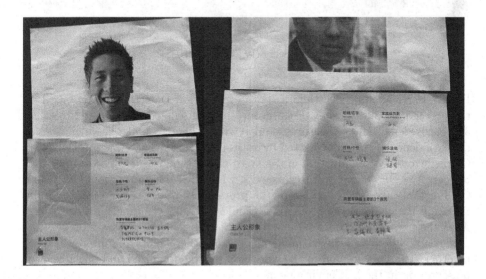

Fig. 2. Stimulus for participatory design fiction (PDF).

Protagonist. Creating the protagonist is also seen as an icebreaker. After completing the grouping, each participant is asked to briefly introduce themselves, and the facilitator will remind the other group members to focus on the similarities to themselves. The group's protagonist is then created by following the format of the content of the Protagonist Card. The information includes a portrait image, nickname, number of family members, personality, recreational activities, and the most important reason for acquiring the vehicle. During the creation process, participants instinctively brought their own situation and ideal situation into the protagonist, which helped the transition from realistic to imagined perspective (see Fig. 3).

Fig. 3. Sample outputs of protagonist cards.

Journey. After the discussion and addition of scenarios, each group freely decided to choose 2 Scenario Cards. (see Fig. 4) Firstly, the group members discussed the goals and expectations of the protagonist from both the driver and passenger aspects. Because the protagonist persona draws on the commonalities among the group members, which helps to reflect the real situations. Secondly, group members collaborated to write down what the protagonist might do and the events that would be encountered by sticky notes, and then which touchpoints are involved, which things will help protagonist accomplish the goals, and which things will prevent the protagonist from accomplishing goals. After the journey is completed the group members rearranged the order of the sticky notes for a complete and smooth story, which contains the real needs and pain points of the users. Finally, intergroup debriefing allowed two groups to learn about each other's stories and vote for the representative plots. The voting rules included which ones were the most helpful and the most depressing according to the protagonist's goals and experience, which led to a shift in the participants' perspective towards seeking help from future functions.

Fig. 4. Scenario journey cards.

Plots. Participants chose from a series of Function Depiction Cards based on the protagonist and journey. Each group freely discussed and decided to select 3–4 cards depicting the features, and rewrote them to make them better for the experience of the plots elected by votes (see Fig. 5). The Function Depiction Cards introduced the function in a easy-to-understand format. The group members created DFs based on three aspects: what the protagonist would do before the function takes effect, the steps the protagonist would take to use the function, and the changes the protagonist would feel after the function takes effect. After the creation of the DFs, there was also a debriefing and discussion between the groups, where they gave comments on each other's plots and improved them together. The DFs created in the workshop will be organized and optimized for presentation in the MR environment.

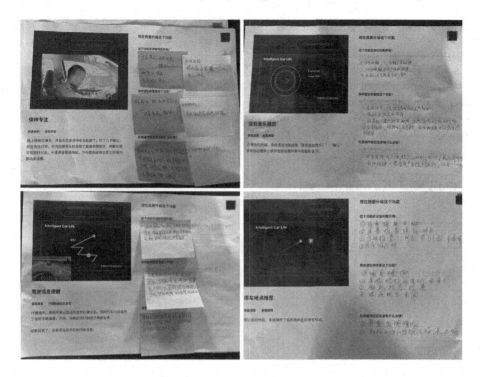

Fig. 5. Function depiction cards.

Summary. Obviously, it is unrealistic to make participants think and discuss a series of incomprehensible future technologies and conceptual designs at the beginning. The workshop divided the co-creation of DFs into three phases: protagonist, journey, and plots, aiming at gradually shifting the participants from a realistic to an imaginative perspective. In terms of scenarios, the most frequently selected ones in the 14 workshops were Commuting to work, Go to a party with friends, Road trip, and Go to a business meeting. This is consistent with the results of the preliminary expert workshop, which validates the representativeness of these four typical scenarios in daily life. In terms of functions, participants' interests in the 14 workshops were ranked in the order of Intelligent Assistant, Context Awareness, Third-party Application Ecology, and Face Recognition. It was worth noting that in the DFs, participants consistently showed a preference for quick, accurate and efficient voice interaction. Overall, the DFs from the 14 workshops will be thematically categorized together, optimized with current forms of travel and lifestyles, and ultimately presented in MR.

3.4   Phase 3: MR Simulation

Implementation. MR's powerful ability to simulate scenarios allows presenting visual experiences with a sense of reality and immersion, which is the advantage of MR as a design research tool, and a more inspiring and provocative way to present DFs. Since the subject of this user study is related to driving, the development of the MR also requires the realization of the cockpit experience in reality, in line with the virtual scenario (see Figs. 6 and 7).

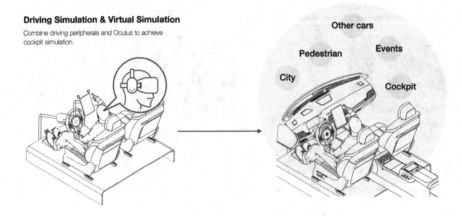

Fig. 6. The technical architecture of DFs via MR.

The driving simulation is achieved through a series of hardware devices, including the seat, steering wheel, throttle, and brake. These devices are programmed by Unity to ensure that when the participant turns the steering wheel in reality, the corresponding perspective reversal occurs in the virtual context, e.g. At the same time, the human- machine scale of the devices is aligned with the virtual context, which ensures a consistent experience and focuses the participant's attention on the storyline of the driving journey.

The virtual scenario is realized using the Oculus rift. Participants wearing the Oculus find themselves in a car parked on a city road. The virtual scenario includes city buildings and roads, pedestrians, other vehicles, cockpit models, HMI design and pre-defined events, which make up the complete content of the DFs.

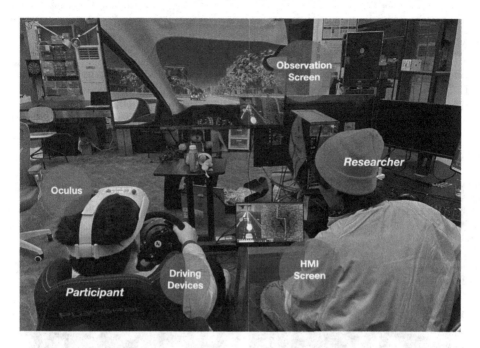

Fig. 7. Apparatus supporting participants to experience DFs via MR.

The participant can receives and interacts with the HMI content on the center screen of the smart cockpit in the virtual scenario. This behavior needs to be consistent with the reality. A touch-screen and voice-enabled computer is configured to display the HMI content in reality, and the display is linked to the HMI content in the virtual scenario. At the same time, the click position and the actual scale in the reality were also aligned with the virtual.

A display was set up to show the first-person view of participants wearing the Oculus, allowing researchers to observe the participants' vision and related behaviors, as well as to provide assistance and advice in the event of special circumstances.

Stimulus Design. A specific plot in the DFs, i.e., an event, is treated as a stimulus. An event includes the triggering conditions, the occurrence and the feedback, these three phases also correspond to the three content formats of the Function Depiction Cards. Events are portrayed in a version that is close to everyday life. The many coherent events form a complete DFs and a complete experience script. Although the final DFs presented was optimized and not exactly the version co-created by the participants in the workshop, the discussion and imagination of the participants in the workshop were retained as much as possible. This means that the DFs have undergone an iterative design process, and after inviting participants to experience it, it will be subject to their thoughts and modifications again, which satisfies the purpose of continuously prototyping arguemets. A sample design fiction, the "Commuting to work", in MR environment was presented as follows.

Scenario. Scenario "Commuting to work" is set on a city road, where the participants will drive a car from the starting point and drive a distance to the designated location. During the process, the participants will see the relevant city facilities, buildings, pedestrians and other vehicles (see Fig. 8).

Fig. 8. A sample scenario "commuting to work".

Events and HMI. The DF "Commuting to work" includes 5 important plots: 1) Boarding And Face Recognition, 2) Navigation And Route Selection, 3) Intelligent Music Recommendation, 4) Intelligent Route Switching, 5) Breakfast reservation, and 6) Parking.

- *Boarding and Face Recognition. Yuki (the protagonist) enters the vehicle, the intelligent assistant performs face recognition and greets, then adjusts the settings according to Yuki's habits, gets Yuki's schedule and proactively asks for destination. Yuki can see how other smart devices are connected to the car, including smart phones and furnitures.*
- *Navigation and Route Selection. Based on the schedule and Yuki's driving habits, the intelligent assistant recommends two routes and displays specific information, and after selection the vehicle switches on driving mode.*
- *Intelligent Music Recommendation. When driving near the traffic lights and waiting, the intelligent assistant can sense the situation, actively ask whether to play music, and recommend different types of music according to Yuki's habits and emotional state at that time. Yuki can view the song list in the music application, switch music, or operate on phone. The music volume will automatically decrease during voice interaction.*

- *Intelligent Route Switching. Yuki can switch routes ahead of time to avoid congestion by using the intelligent assistant that detects congestion ahead of the route and proactively explains the situation and recommends a new navigation route.*
- *Breakfast reservation. When approaching the restaurant where Yuki is accustomed to, the intelligent assistant will actively recommend according to Yuki's habits, Yuki can adjust the products and quantity, and choose the pickup method.*
- *Parking. When approaching the destination, the intelligent assistant will analyze road information to proactively recommend places to park. After Yuki finishes parking, it will remind Yuki of next travel schedule.*

Execution

Participants. Ten of the participants (Females = 5, Males = 5; Aged from 25 to 31, M = 28 years old, SD=1.79 years old) were members of the previous workshop and were re-invited to experience DF in MR and describe the difference of imagining and modifying DFs between two occasions. The other 45 (Females = 21, Males = 24; Aged from 22 to 28, M = 25.11 years old, SD = 2.08 years old) participants included typical consumers as well as some creative practitioners and automotive industry personnel. Fifteen of the participants read the printed sheet version of the DF, another 15 watched a video of the first-person perspective experience of the DF, and the final 15 experienced it in an MR and then discussed and imagined it.

Procedure. DFs in MR subtly curates illuminating details for the participants' experience. For example, the voice mood of the intelligent assistant changes each time a different event occurs: it is upbeat when actively recommending music and gentle when booking breakfast. These details can stimulate the participants' interest and open their imagination to reinforce the stimuli.

During the experience, participants are not limited in their responses to events, or they can respond in any way they want. This is completely different from the logic of the usability test, for example, participants can choose to control the screen by tapping on it or by voice interaction, and these reactions and behaviors are all considered correct and recorded as a topic of discussion after the experience. At the end of the experience, participants will go back the DF with the researchers and discuss how they reacted, tell their attitudes and feelings, and imagine a more ideal form.

4   Evaluation and Discussion

4.1   Analysis and Results

Thematic Analysis. The first step was to thematically categorize participants' discussions and imaginations of the DF, and to explore the characteristics of narrative data that emerged from this user study. This included 10 participants who had previously participated in the PDF workshop, and these characteristics were more distinct with their talk about the experience of imagining and modifying the DFs. The analysis of the collected texts and recordings revealed four themes, which are described in more detail below.

Understanding and Acceptance of Future. The value and potential of DFs to increase participants' understanding and acceptance of future technologies and conceptual designs was one of the key themes in the analysis of the interview data, and the DFs presented in MR will be even more characteristic of this. It is difficult for participants to start discussions when faced with these technologies and designs that are not yet available. With the help of DFs, which presents future technologies and conceptual designs in a form that is close to everyday representations, they quickly and well understood these features, built consensus among the group, and started to share their ideas.

"Some of these features I once seemed to have read somewhere that probably meant the same thing. I can't remember exactly what it was, because that article was written so professionally but I just wanted to read it briefly."

For participants who had attended the PDF workshop before, the immersive experience of DF in MR environment was more realistic and immersive.

"When I wrote it on paper before, I was understanding it more in the context of my own experience based on the pictures and the introduction, and I tried to put myself in that situation. But everything changed when I put on the glasses, and being there and experiencing the story was impressive."

Imagination and Contextualization of Future. The fact that DFs served as a stimulus to open the participants' imagination and consistently stimulate their thinking and expression was certainly a surprise to the researchers.

"Sitting inside this car, what had just happened seemed to exist in my mind as if it were a true memory of reality, and I could base my thinking on first reaction at the time as well as my imagination to help me think."

The participants who attended the PDF workshop said that the inspirational nature of the DF presented in MR made them start thinking about issues and scenarios they had not thought about before.

"When I was imagining how to use this feature, I closed my eyes and imagined myself sitting in the car in the picture. And now that I have glasses on, I can imagine more things, the range becomes broader, and I start to imagine what to do if there is a change in the external environment like being distracted while operating music and getting into a dangerous situation."

"Is it possible that the interior of the cockpit is a very different design from what it is now? Maybe I don't need a steering wheel, the screen will be bigger and I want the content to be displayed on it..."

Interests and Expectations for Future. Participants reported that they were interested in reading, thinking, and writing DFs, and were willing to share and listen to others' passages. Repeated, correlative and continuous DFs study have the advantage of maintaining participants' interest and attracting their continued participation and active contributions.

"I feel that in either form, sheet or just in MR, this is more interesting than a bland and emotionless description of a feature. I'm eager to continue to learn more, and I keep looking forward to the later parts."

In addition to showing their interest in the future of technology and conceptual design in daily lives, the participants were excited about the features included in the DFs after experiencing it in MR.

"When I wrote on the printed DF, I was just describing an ideal situation and not fully thinking about whether it was possible. But after I just experienced MR, I think these things are achievable, I'll believe in it, and I'll pay for it."

Requirements Extraction. DFs can help researchers observe participants' reactions and collect their discussions and statements to identify future design needs, opportunities, and challenges, and it acts as a stimulus to help researchers capture these perceptions of the future.

"The intelligent assistant has a pretty interesting voice, and I was wondering if I could go to a nickname for it or configure some of its features to my liking."

"While the music is playing, is it possible to transfer the navigation information to be displayed on the HUD instead of continuing by voice?"

While experiencing DF in MR, the immersive experience allows participants to put themselves more into the scenario and think about the issues more comprehensively and rationally.

"When I was participating in the workshop before, I thought I could pick up my breakfast after booking it directly after passing through the restaurant. But after the MR experience, I considered the fact that parking is not always available on the side of the road, perhaps setting up take-out delivery and controlling the timing of the order would be a better way to go."

Discourse Analysis. A control experiment was set up between other 45 participants with different forms of DF. The objective metrics adopted for this analysis are the number of words spoken, the variety of words (number of unique words occurring in the expression), and the length of time it takes to complete the expression, for the discussion after the DF experience (see Fig. 9).

For the number of words in the expression, participants who experienced MR gave the longest answers, exceeding both printed sheet and video forms (MR: Printed, $p < .001$; MR:Video, $p < .001$; see Fig. 9(a)). Regarding the variety of vocabulary used, participants who experienced MR narrated more diverse expression, exceeding printed sheet ($p = .004$). However, no significant difference were found between MR and video groups (see Fig. 9(b)). For interview duration, participants who experienced MR maintained sustained expression for a longer period of time than using printed sheet and video (MR: Printed, $p < .001$; MR: Video, $p < .001$; see Fig. 9(c)).

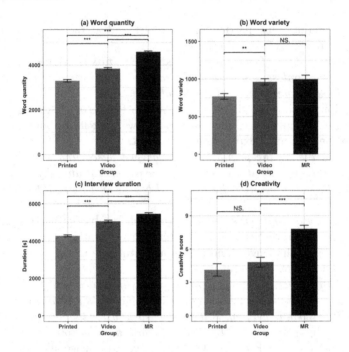

Fig. 9. Results of discourse analysis and creative analysis.

Creative Analysis. The Consensual Assessment Technique was used to estimate the degree of creativity of the interview contents which relies on the judgement of a panel of experts for the evaluation of creative achievement. The panel of experts re-invited the eight experts who had initially participated in the workshop in Shanghai to assess the imagination and rewriting of DF in different forms by three groups of participants. Each of the eight professional experts was first asked to articulate his or her own personal definition of creativity and to define the criteria for measuring it in a series of statements. The declared self-selected criteria of creativity included the concepts of positive thinking, elaboration, surprise, originality, abstractness and novelty. Each expert read the 45 scattered statements and scored according to their own creativity criteria (from 0–10). Then, the average score given by the entire panel of experts was calculated as the score for that statement. Finally, a comparison of the scores within the 3 groups was performed. Participants who experienced MR made more creative expressions when they engaged in subsequent reflection and imagination (MR: Printed, $p < .001$; MR: Video, $p < .001$; see Fig. 9(d)).

4.2   Discussion

The results of the user study and data analysis reflect several findings, which are discussed in this section.

The Use of PDF as a User Research Method. DFs integrates future ideas into everyday life scenarios, providing a starting point for participants' imagination and speculation. The imagination of the participants in the PDF was subtle, profound, and constructive, the results showed that the participants had many creative and reasonable insights in imagining the smart cockpit's connectivity capabilities. The inspirational nature of DFs, as well as the authenticity and immersion, make them a tool in participatory design that provoke participants into delving more in-depth and offering valuable insights.

Immersive Imagination: Presenting DFs in MR. The contextual depiction of the future in DFs is what makes them so important for participants to be able to understand and be motivated quickly. The presentation of DFs in MR further expands the sense of authenticity, immersion and inspiration. On the one hand, for the participants, the immersive experience of DFs in MR was more attractive, and to a certain extent, deepened their understanding and expectations of the technology. On the other hand, for the researchers, the DFs in MR increased participants' willingness to participate and contribute to the study, and the length, richness, creativity, and validity of the expressions were significantly improved.

Future Oriented User Study Needs to Prototype Arguments Repeatedly, Correlatively and Continuously. DFs are meant to stimulate more perspectives and discussions, which can help user study, not as an iteration-oriented usability test, but as a way to create future life scenarios with the wisdom of the group, and then put the group in the scenarios for reflection and discussion. Participants in both the PDF workshop and the MR experience showed enthusiasm for repeated participation, as well as a more in-depth and more detailed imagination.

5   Conclusion

The future life scenarios depicted in DFs can stimulate the viewer's speculations and are particularly relevant to the exploration of innovations affecting interaction design, especially human-computer interaction. Further more, DFs' conjunction with participatory design is considered an effective method for design research. The technical characteristics of MR have driven it to become a key direction for interaction design research and a tool to support design research. MR provides participants with an immersive experience of the future scenarios, allowing researchers to represent concepts that would be difficult to prototype in reality.

For the trend of smart cockpit's connectivity capabilities in the contxet of V2X, this study explored a repeated, correlative, and continuous user study framework, presenting the DFs co-created using MR and maintain the space for the imagination of the participants to gather their views and discussions about the future.

After compiling the interview data, four themes were identified for PDF with MR. First, the value and potential to increase participants' understanding and acceptance of future technology and conceptual design; second, it facilitated participants' imaginations, encouraged expressing, sharing, and discussing in-car features and scenarios; third, it increased participants' interests and expectations, and strengthened their support for future technology and conceptual design; fourth, it captured participants' real perceptions into future technology needs and design opportunities, supporting the conception of new in-vehicle features and services. In addition, MR enhances participants' contributions to the study compared to other forms of DFs to help researchers better understand, more effectively analyze the desirable futures proposed by different groups.

Finally, this study provides a basis for exploring the application of PDF and MR technology, and the integration of the two as a method for future-oriented user study, the opportunity and value of which suggests that this area merits further research explorations.

References

1. Asimov, I.: How easy to see the future. Nat. Hist. **84**(4), 92 (1975)
2. Auger, J.: Speculative design: crafting the speculation. Digital Creativity **24**(1), 11–35 (2013)
3. Barthell, R.J.: Science fiction: a literature of ideas. Extrapolation **13**(2), 56 (1971)
4. Cheng, J.: Astounding wonder: Imagining science and science fiction in interwar America. University of Pennsylvania Press (2012)
5. Dourish, P., Bell, G.: "Resistance is futile": reading science fiction alongside ubiquitous computing. Personal Ubiquit. Comput. **18**(4), 769–778 (2014)
6. Dunne, A.: Hertzian tales: Electronic products, aesthetic experience, and critical design. MIT press (2008)
7. Dunne, A., Raby, F.: Speculative everything: design, fiction, and social dreaming. MIT press (2013)
8. El-Jarn, H., Southern, G.: Can co-creation in extended reality technologies facilitate the design process? J. Work-Appli. Manag. **17**, 1254–1269 (2020)
9. de la Flor Aceituno, D., Giacomin, J., Malizia, A., Skrypchuk, L.: Virtual workshops on the road: co-designing with drivers, within context in real-time. In: Ahram, T., Taiar, R., Colson, S., Choplin, A. (eds.) IHIET 2019. AISC, vol. 1018, pp. 35–41. Springer, Cham (2020). https://doi.org/10.1007/978-3-030-25629-6_6
10. Forlano, L., Mathew, A.: From design fiction to design friction: Speculative and participatory design of values-embedded urban technology. J. Urban Technol. **21**(4), 7–24 (2014)
11. Gilks, M., Fleming, P., Allen, M.: Science fiction: The literature of ideas. Writingworld.com (2003)
12. Hales, D.: Design fictions an introduction and provisional taxonomy. Digital Creativity **24**(1), 1–10 (2013)
13. Kirby, D.: The future is now: diegetic prototypes and the role of popular films in generating real-world technological development. Soc. Stud. Sci. **40**(1), 41–70 (2010)
14. Kirkpatrick, C.J., Fuchs, S., Peters, K., Brochhausen, C., Hermanns, M.I., Unger, R.E.: Visions for regenerative medicine: interface between scientific fact and science fiction. Artif. Organs **30**(10), 822–827 (2006)

15. Knutz, E., Markussen, T.: The role of fiction in experiments within design, art & architecture-towards a new typology of design fiction. Artifact J. Des. Pract. **3**(2), 1–8 (2014)

16. Kohler, T., Fueller, J., Stieger, D., Matzler, K.: Avatar-based innovation: Consequences of the virtual co-creation experience. Comput. Hum. Behav. **27**(1), 160–168 (2011)

17. Lindley, J., Coulton, P.: Back to the future: 10 years of design fiction, pp. 210–211 (2015)

18. Lyckvi, S., Roto, V., Buie, E., Wu, Y.: The role of design fiction in participatory design processes. In: Proceedings of the 10th Nordic Conference on Human-Computer Interaction, pp. 976–979 (2018)

19. Nägele, L.V., Ryöppy, M., Wilde, D.: Pdfi: participatory design fiction with vulnerable users. In: Proceedings of the 10th Nordic Conference on Human-Computer Interaction, pp. 819–831 (2018)

20. Prucher, J.: Brave New Words: The Oxford Dictionary of Science Fiction. Oxford University Press (2007)

21. de la Rosa, S., et al.: Visual appearance modulates motor control in social interactions. Acta Physiol. (Oxf) **210**, 103168 (2020)

22. Sharma, S., Kaushik, B.: A survey on internet of vehicles: applications, security issues & solutions. Veh. Commun. **20**, 100182 (2019)

23. Shen, X., Fantacci, R., Chen, S.: Internet of vehicles [scanning the issue]. Proc. IEEE **108**(1), 242–245 (2020)

24. Tsekleves, E., Darby, A., Whicher, A., Swiatek, P.: Co-designing design fictions: a new approach for debating and priming future healthcare technologies and services. Archives Des. Res. **30**(2), 5–21 (2017)

25. Wang, P., et al.: A comprehensive survey of AR/MR-based co-design in manufacturing. Eng. Comput. **36**(4), 1715–1738 (2020)

Do Additional Auditory Instructions in Smartphone Navigation Con-Tribute to the Road Safety of Cyclists? A Field Study Evaluating the Gaze Behavior of Cyclists

Yasmin Dufner[1], Mathias Trefzger[2(✉)], Naemi Gerst[2], and Thomas Schlegel[2]

[1] Karlsruhe University of Applied Sciences, Moltkestr. 30, 76133 Karlsruhe, Germany
duya1014@h-ka.de
[2] Institute of Ubiquitious Mobility Systems, Karlsruhe University of Applied Sciences, Moltkestr. 30, 76133 Karlsruhe, Germany
iums@h-ka.de

Abstract. In this paper, we present an eye tracking study evaluating the effects of visual versus visual and auditory navigation instructions on the gaze behavior of cyclists. One group received purely visual navigation instructions via a smartphone on the handlebars to complete the route, while the other group additionally received auditory navigation instructions via headphones. We found that the distribution of attention depends strongly on the traffic situation. Comparing the attention distribution of the two groups over the five situations evaluated, we see that the purely visual group paid 31% less attention to the surroundings. In the complex situation, it turned out that purely visual navigation is preferable, since fewer glances are directed at the smartphone and thus greater attention can be paid to the surroundings. On the other hand, additional auditory instructions in less complex situations enable the cyclists to focus more on the surroundings.

Keywords: Eye tracking · Cyclists · Real-world environment · Visual and auditory navigation

1 Introduction

Cyclists are engaged in actual riding as well as wayfinding at all times. Navigation systems can support the cyclists in their navigational tasks, but attract attention, which means that other elements in the environment can be overlooked more often. Therefore, we want to investigate whether additional auditory instructions help cyclists to focus their attention more on the surroundings as this could have a positive effect on traffic safety.

© Springer Nature Switzerland AG 2022
M. Rauterberg et al. (Eds.): HCII 2022, LNCS 13520, pp. 460–470, 2022.
https://doi.org/10.1007/978-3-031-18158-0_33

The implementation of eye tracking solutions for the analysis of gaze behavior began in laboratories, in which the desired traffic environment could be simulated [1, 3]. This method had the disadvantage that the real traffic behavior of the participants could not be recorded. Therefore, experiments are nowadays widely conducted in the real traffic environment [7, 9].

Various eye tracking studies have already investigated the gaze behavior of cyclists. For example, Mantuano et al. [5] used an eye tracking study to investigate the gaze behavior of cyclists due to the accumulation of accidents involving cyclists. In a study by Trefzger et al. [8], the gaze behavior of pedestrians and cyclists was compared. Research on the effects of auditory navigation in road traffic can already be found with respect to the gaze behavior of car drivers [4]. In contrast, cyclists and their gaze behavior with auditory navigation and navigation using smartphones seem to be quite unexplored. In this paper, we consider the gaze behavior of cyclists with visual navigation instructions via smartphone and additionally auditory instructions via headphones in a real-world eye tracking experiment. At the beginning of this paper, we present the study design with the research questions posed and the experimental procedure. Then we present the obtained results of the fixation metrics. In addition, the main results from the questionnaires asked are presented and in the discussion section we answer our research questions. Finally, there is a Conclusion about the obtained findings and an outlook on future works.

2 Study Design

In the following, we present an eye tracking experiment and its scope and procedure. In this eye tracking experiment, cyclists received navigation instructions via a smartphone app, partly by way of visual and partly by way of combined auditory and visual output.

2.1 Experimental Design and Research Questions

To investigate effects on the gaze behavior, both groups completed the same predefined route. In our paper, we want to evaluate following questions:

- What is the impact of the additional use of auditory navigation instructions compared to purely visual navigation?
- Does visual navigation via smartphone have negative effects on the perceived safety?
- How does the distribution of attention change from auditory and visual navigation to purely visual navigation?

In this work, we analyze different sections within the traveled distance. Five situations were considered, which had different characteristics (see Fig. 1). We classify one situation as complex and the other four as simple situations. The classification is based on potential encounter cases as well as the road cross-section.

Fig. 1. Evaluated situations (Left: complex situation (1): cyclists had to cross the street to turn left at the traffic lights; Right: example for simple situation (2–5): cyclists had to turn into road)

2.2 Participants

The eye tracking experiment was conducted with 20 volunteers. Due to technical problems, 17 of the eye tracking recordings were usable. The volunteers were divided into two groups. The group with purely visual instructions consisted of one female and eight male volunteers at an age of 20 to 31 years (Ø 23,67 ± 2,87). The group with auditory and visual instructions consisted of three female and five male volunteers at an age of 20 to 28 years (Ø 23,88 ± 2,20). The participants indicated frequent bicycle use in everyday life (ten volunteers daily, seven volunteers at least once a week). In addition, it was determined that eleven of the volunteers already had experience with navigation via smartphone.

2.3 Experimental Procedure

We asked the participants to cycle the predefined route (see Fig. 2). At the beginning of each trial, the participants had to sign a consent form and fill out a demographic questionnaire. We used the Tobii Pro Glasses 2 to record the data. If needed we adjusted the lenses for the participants with impaired eyesight.

To ensure that the participants were able to complete the route, each one received a short introduction to the navigation interface of the smartphone app 'bikemap'. The only instruction given to the participants was to follow the app's directions. One group only received purely visual instructions via the smartphone display, whereas the other group additionally received auditory instructions via a single in-ear headphone.

After the participants had returned, they completed another questionnaire to obtain answers about their experience with the navigation app and its influence on their feeling of road safety.

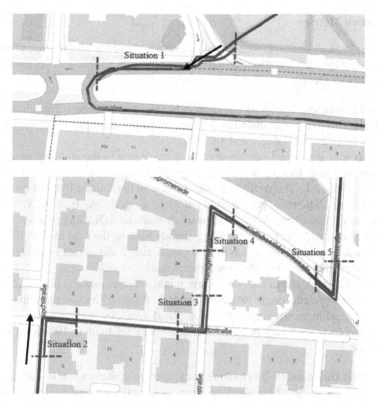

Fig. 2. Areas of the mapped situations a) situation 1 crossing the lanes to the left turn lane b) situations 2 to 5 left or right turn event. Map legend: course of the route (blue line); direction of travel (black arrow) (Color figure online)

2.4 Data Analysis

We analyzed the recordings obtained from the study using Tobii Pro Lab. We mapped each situation onto separate abstract reference pictures. For situation 1, we mapped the gaze points while crossing the lanes to the left turn lane. Situations 2 to 5 contained either a left or right turn event. To use the data for analysis, the gaze points were assigned to the reference pictures frame by frame in the Tobii Pro Lab analysis software.

3 Results

In the following sections, we will present our results to be able to answer the questions from Sect. 2.1. In addition, we present the most important results from the questionnaires as well as the assessments of the participants.

3.1 Fixation Metrics

Using Tobii Pro Lab software, we analyzed the standard eye tracking metrics (Total Visit Duration, Average Visit Duration, Visit Count) to obtain the differences in gaze behavior between the two groups.

Total Visit Duration. Total Visit duration indicates how much time participants spent on the AOIs. This can be calculated as the share of total time in percent or the total visit duration in seconds (see Table 1 and Table 2).

If we look at situation 1, we see that the participants in the auditory group spend 25% of the total time looking at the "Smartphone" compared to the participants in the other group with 12%. The AOI "Road far" is viewed the longest by both groups with about 45% of the total time. And with about 24%, the participants of the visual group also spent more time on the AOI "Road near" than on the AOI "Smartphone".

In situations 2 to 5, the participants had already been on the road for 8 to 10 min and were thus able to get used to the navigation app. Figure 3 shows that the smartphone is viewed less and that there is a shift towards the road.

In a direct comparison of the two groups, it is also noticeable that the participants of the auditory group spend longer looking at the AOI "Road far" and the participants of the visual group tend more strongly to the AOI "Road near". Furthermore, the percentage of viewpoints on other things in traffic increases from 3% to up to 10% from situation 2 to situation 5.

Average Visit Duration. When looking at the average visit duration, it is again noticeable that the participants of the auditory group looks at the smartphone longer. Overall, the AOIs "Smartphone", "Road far" and "Road near" are viewed the longest. The duration of gaze on parked cars and other objects in traffic remain constant for the most part.

About the AOIs of the "Parked cars left" and "Parked cars right", it is noticeable that the participants also tend to look more at the respective parked cars on the right or left, depending on the turning process (see Table 3).

Visit Count. The visit count shows the number of visual visits of the participants made to each AOI. Table 1 and 4 represent the average visit count of the most important AOIs.

In situation 1, we can see that the participants of the visual group look more often at the AOI "Road far" as well as at the AOI "Road near" than the participants of the other group. On the other hand, the participants of the auditory group look more often and longer (see Sect. 3.1) at the AOI "Smartphone".

The results obtained from situations 2 to 5 (see Table 4) show that the participants of the auditory group look at the smartphone less often compared to the other group, but somewhat longer (see Sect. 3.1). For the AOI "Road near" and "Smartphone", a correlation can be found for the visual group. As soon as the smartphone is looked at more often, the number of visits to the AOI "Road near" also increases. This correlation cannot be proven for the auditory group. This could have implications for road safety.

Table 1. Total Visit Duration (incl 0) in seconds; Average Visit Duration in seconds; Visit Count (incl 0) for situation 1

AOI	Navigation instructions	Total visit duration	Avg. visit duration	Visit count
		Situation 1	Situation 1	Situation 1
Smartphone	v	2,07 ± 1,48	0,74 ± 0,33	2,67 ± 1,22
	a + v	4,67 ± 3,23	1,25 ± 0,94	4,17 ± 2,04
Shoulder check	v	1,97 ± 2,50	0,46 ± 0,47	3,22 ± 1,92
	a + v	1,91 ± 2,07	0,47 ± 0,40	3,50 ± 0,84
Road far	v	7,21 ± 3,95	0,74 ± 0,27	9,78 ± 4,24
	a + v	8,37 ± 3,29	1,04 ± 0,29	8,17 ± 2,32
Road near	v	3,82 ± 2,59	0,57 ± 0,18	6,33 ± 3,20
	a + v	2,16 ± 2,36	0,28 ± 0,13	6,17 ± 4,67

Table 2. Total Visit Duration (incl 0) in seconds for situation 2 to 5

AOI	N I	Situations			
		Situation 2	Situation 3	Situation 4	Situation 5
Smartphone	v	1,21 ± 0,95	0,95 ± 0,66	0,28 ± 0,56	1,14 ± 1,34
	a + v	1,43 ± 1,93	0,34 ± 0,64	0,17 ± 0,40	0,54 ± 0,74
Road far	v	1,58 ± 1,17	2,34 ± 1,78	1,43 ± 1,05	2,25 ± 1,34
	a + v	1,22 ± 1,31	2,30 ± 2,28	1,92 ± 0,88	2,55 ± 1,73
Road near	v	0,99 ± 0,74	1,01 ± 0,92	1,07 ± 0,75	1,98 ± 1,44
	a + v	0,78 ± 0,81	0,67 ± 0,92	0,94 ± 0,96	1,28 ± 1,17
External	v	2,00 ± 0,82	1,24 ± 0,96	1,82 ± 0,94	1,46 ± 1,13
	a + v	1,59 ± 1,16	1,14 ± 0,90	0,91 ± 0,65	1,61 ± 1,16
Street sign	v	0,11 ± 0,18	0,00 ± 0,00	0,01 ± 0,04	0,00 ± 0,00
	a + v	0,20 ± 0,40	0,02 ± 0,05	0,00 ± 0,00	0,00 ± 0,00

Table 3. Average visit duration in seconds for situation 2 to 5

AOI	N I	Situations			
		Situation 2	Situation 3	Situation 4	Situation 5
Smartphone	v	0,75 ± 0,16	0,69 ± 0,55	0,56 ± 0,26	1,04 ± 0,58
	a + v	1,45 ± 0,88	0,50 ± 0,34	0,59 ± 0,69	0,96 ± 0,34
Road far	v	0,54 ± 0,38	0,69 ± 0,55	0,49 ± 0,23	0,91 ± 0,76
	a + v	0,35 ± 0,26	0,76 ± 0,73	0,52 ± 0,31	0,77 ± 0,48
Road near	v	0,33 ± 0,13	0,32 ± 0,14	0,42 ± 0,27	0,59 ± 0,42
	a + v	0,58 ± 0,28	0,32 ± 0,21	0,34 ± 0,17	0,58 ± 0,58
External	v	0,84 ± 0,42	0,62 ± 0,39	0,86 ± 0,42	0,73 ± 0,48
	a + v	0,61 ± 0,42	0,61 ± 0,46	0,52 ± 0,32	0,79 ± 0,57
Street sign	v	0,24 ± 0,21	0,00 ± 0,00	0,12 ± 0,00	0,00 ± 0,00
	a + v	0,69 ± 0,55	0,14 ± 0,00	0,00 ± 0,00	0,00 ± 0,00

Table 4. Visit Count (incl 0) for situation 2 to 5

AOI	N I	Situations			
		Situation 2	Situation 3	Situation 4	Situation 5
Smartphone	v	1,56 ± 1,01	1,33 ± 0,87	0,44 ± 0,73	0,89 ± 1,27
	a + v	0,86 ± 0,69	0,57 ± 0,79	0,29 ± 0,49	0,57 ± 0,79
Road far	v	2,78 ± 1,72	3,44 ± 1,42	2,89 ± 1,27	3,22 ± 1,56
	a + v	3,29 ± 1,60	2,86 ± 0,69	4,00 ± 1,15	3,29 ± 1,60
Road near	v	2,78 ± 1,56	2,89 ± 1,96	2,89 ± 1,27	3,44 ± 1,67
	a + v	1,57 ± 1,81	1,86 ± 1,68	2,29 ± 1,80	2,71 ± 2,36
External	v	4,78 ± 2,57	3,67 ± 2,21	3,78 ± 1,13	3,11 ± 1,73
	a + v	3,75 ± 2,28	3,38 ± 1,93	2,88 ± 1,96	3,63 ± 2,00
Street sign	v	0,44 ± 0,53	0,00 ± 0,00	0,11 ± 0,33	0,00 ± 0,00
	a + v	0,29 ± 0,49	0,14 ± 0,38	0,00 ± 0,00	0,00 ± 0,00

3.2 Evaluation of the Questionnaires

To record the participants' impressions and experiences after the rides, we created a questionnaire according to ISONORM 9241/110 [2] to evaluate certain dialog principles [6].

In the visual group (see Table 5), seven of the ten participants did not feel noticeably restricted by the visual instructions either in their sense of safety or in their perception of their surroundings. However, there were three participants who felt slightly to moderately restricted both in their sense of safety and in their perception of their surroundings.

The participants in the auditory group (Table 6) rated the number of necessary eye contacts with the smartphone even more positively than the participants in the visual group did. When asked about the number of auditory instructions that occurred, only one participant stated that he felt restricted by the auditory instructions. The distribution of answers was also positive for the perception of the surroundings.

In a direct comparison of the two groups, the participants in the auditory group felt less restricted than the participants in the visual group.

Table 5. Response distribution of the visual group

	Response options						
	−	− −	− +	+ +	+ + +		
The navigation app required a lot of eye contact, which made me feel unsafe	1	2	2	5			The navigation app required little eye contact, which still made me feel safe
I felt limited in my awareness of my surroundings due to the visual instructions	1	2	1	4	2		I did not feel limited in my awareness of my surroundings due to the visual instructions

Table 6. Response distribution of the auditory group

	Response options						
	−	− −	− +	+ +	+ + +		
The navigation app required a lot of eye contact, which made me feel unsafe	1	1	3	1	4		The navigation app required little eye contact, which still made me feel safe
The navigation app provided too many auditory navigation instructions, which made me feel unsafe	1		1	3	5		The number of auditory navigation instructions did not affect my sense of safety
I felt limited in my awareness of my surroundings due to the auditory instructions	1	1	3	3	2		I did not feel limited in my awareness of my surround-ings due to the auditory instructions

4 Discussion

In this section, we will discuss the results, as well as the observations already described and answer the research questions posed (see Sect. 2.1).

The first research question was: What is the impact of the additional use of auditory navigation instructions compared to purely visual navigation? One advantage of auditory navigation expected at the beginning of this work was that less attention on the smartphone is necessary, allowing the participants to better concentrate on the traffic situation at hand. To answer this assumption, we count all set-up AOIs with the exception of the "Smartphone" AOI to the cyclist's environment. Thus, only the differences of the attention distribution of the AOIs "Smartphone" of the two groups can be considered.

To obtain an accurate value for the existing difference of the two groups we calculated the relative deviation of the attention distribution of the AOIs "Smartphone" from group visual to group auditory. For situation 1, this resulted in a relative deviation of −52%. The participants of the visual group thus looked 52% less at the smartphone in situation 1 than the participants of the auditory group. In situation 2, the relative deviation is −23%. Again, the participants of the visual group looked less at the smartphone than the participants of the other group. In comparison, we were able to determine a clear difference in situations 3 to 5. The relative deviations here were 87.5% (situation 3), 66.66% (situation 4) and 77.77% (situation 5).

This suggests that a complex situation can be mastered with less fixations at the smartphone in the case of purely visual navigation. On the other hand less complex situations without auditory support lead to more fixations on the smartphone. In less complex situations, the number of visits of the auditory group drops significantly compared to the participants in the purely visual group (see Table 4). Here, the auditory instructions seem to support the participants. The results showed, that the participants of the auditory group in the complex traffic situation 1 checked the auditory instructions by looking at the smartphone more often and for longer periods of time. Therefore, we can state that this tends to be a disadvantage of auditory navigation. If the auditory instructions are not passed on to the cyclist correctly or appropriately for the situation, the cyclist will inevitably have to inform himself visually about the upcoming action.

The average of all relative deviations is 31.36%, which means that the participants of the visual group paid 31% less attention to their surroundings compared to the auditory group. However, the individually presented values should make clear that the result depends strongly on the considered traffic situation.

To answer the second research question: Does visual navigation via smartphone have negative effects on the perceived and measurable safety? We looked at the results from the questionnaires. For seven out of ten participants in the visual group, there was no negative feedback on the feeling of safety or the perception of the surroundings due to the visual navigation instructions. The participants did not seem to feel restricted in their sense of safety by the smartphone.

The participants of the auditory group rated the visual instructions more positive. The participants in the auditory group were also able to navigate visually via the smartphone display. Thus, the results indicate that the use of a smartphone by cyclists in road traffic has a negative effect on the feeling of safety in 30% of the cases, but in 70% of the cases there are no noticeable restrictions.

To study the traffic safety, we evaluated how the attention distribution changes to different objects in road traffic due to the smartphone-app. For complex traffic situations like in situation 1, we were able to determine an attention distribution of up to 25% of the total time on the smartphone. Other objects in traffic, such as signs, were only observed with up to 8% of the total time. In addition, the direct comparison of the two groups showed that the participants in the auditory group looked at the smartphone for a non-negligible proportion of the total time, up to 25% of the total time compared to 12% for the other group. This could have consequences for traffic safety.

In the other less complex situations like situations 2 to 5, in which the participants were supposed to turn either left or right, there was no such clear distribution of attention on the smartphone. Also, there weren't noticeable differences between the two groups.

The third research question was: How does the distribution of attention change from auditory and visual navigation to purely visual navigation? The attention distribution of both groups shows a larger proportion for the AOI "Smartphone" for the auditory group than for the visual group. In all situations considered, a tendency of the visual group towards the AOI "Road near" can be observed, while the participants of the auditory group tend towards the AOI "Road far". Contrary to expectations, there are no significantly higher values on AOIs of other objects in road traffic among the participants of the auditory group. Here, we had assumed at the beginning that these participants would have to pay less attention to the smartphone due to the auditory instructions and therefore would increasingly look at their surroundings. However, it seems that the participants in the auditory group look more at the smartphone to make sure that the instructions they have just received are correct.

5 Conclusion

In this paper, we evaluated the effects of visual versus visual and auditory navigation instructions on the gaze behavior of cyclists. We compared the attention distribution of the two groups. We found that the distribution of attention depends strongly on the traffic situation. Comparing the attention distribution of the two groups over the five situations studied, we see that the purely visual group paid 31% less attention to the surroundings. In the complex situation, it turned out that purely visual navigation is preferable, since fewer glances are directed at the smartphone and thus greater attention can be paid to the surroundings. On the other hand, additional auditory instructions in simple situations enable cyclists to focus more on the surroundings.

We cannot yet conclusively assess the original question of whether additional auditory instructions have a positive effect. However, due to the fact that in complex situations the user has to look more at the smartphone when receiving auditory instructions, we assume that this has a negative rather than a positive effect. We hold this opinion because in complex situations in particular, glances at the surroundings are more important than in less complex situations due to more potential encounters with other road users.

In the future we want to expand the study with a auditory only group to assess the impact of visual navigation via smartphone on cyclists.

References

1. Bock, O., Brustio, P.R., Borisova, S.: Age-related differences of the gaze pattern in a realistic pedestrian traffic task (2015)
2. DIN Deutsches Institut für Normung e.V. Ergonomie der Mensch-System-Interaktion - Teil 110: Grundsätze der Dialoggestaltung DIN EN ISO 9241-110:2008-09 DIN EN ISO 9241-110:2008-09
3. Jäger, M., Nyffeler, T., Müri, R., Mosimann, U.P., Nef, T.: Adapting a driving simulator to study pedestrians' street-crossing decisions: a feasibility study. Assist. Technol. **27**(1), 1–8 (2015)
4. Jakus, G., Dicke, C., Sodnik, J.: A user study of auditory, head-up and multi-modal displays in vehicles. Appl. Ergon. **46**, 184–192 (2015)
5. Mantuano, A., Bernardi, S., Rupi, F.: Cyclist gaze behavior in urban space: an eye-tracking experiment on the bicycle network of Bologna. Case Stud. Transp. Policy **5**(2), 408–416 (2017)
6. Prümper, J.: Beurteilung von Software auf Grundlage der Internationalen Ergonomie-Norm DIN EN ISO 9241-110 (2008)
7. Schmidt, S., von Stülpnagel, R.: Risk perception and gaze behavior during urban cycling – a field study (2018)
8. Trefzger, M., Blascheck, T., Raschke, M., Hausmann, S., Schlegel, T.: A visual comparison of gaze behavior from pedestrians and cyclists. In: ETRA 2018, pp. 1–5 (2018)
9. Vansteenkiste, P., Zeuwts, L., Cardon, G., Philippaerts, R., Lenoir, M.: The implications of low quality bicycle paths on gaze behavior of cyclists: a field test. Transp. Res. F Traffic Psychol. Behav. **23**, 81–87 (2018)

Comparative Study on Sentiments of New Energy Vehicle Owners Based on Opinion Mining

Deke Li[(✉)] and Hong Chen

East China University of Science and Technology, Shanghai, China
engoy2008@163.com

Abstract. In recent years, under the joint action of policy support, technological progress, economic development and other factors, the new energy vehicle market has become an important engine for the continuous growth of China's auto market. Extended Range Electric Vehicle (EREV), Battery Electric Vehicle (BEV) and Plug-in Hybrid Electric Vehicle (PHEV) are three types of new energy vehicles, which are favored by different vehicle owners. In order to fully perceive vehicle owners' emotional preferences for three new energy vehicles, by constructing a SnowNLP-based sentiment analysis model and a semantic network model, this paper proposes an opinion mining model based on the method of opinion mining, realizes the collection of user comments on different dimensions of three new energy vehicles from the Autohome website (the largest automobile website in China), and uses Python to perform data preprocessing, comment segmentation, word frequency statistics, sentiment analysis and semantic network analysis, so as to gain insight into the emotional differences of vehicle owners of three new energy vehicles, provide suggestions for enterprises, and then improve the car-machine interaction experience of vehicle owners.

Keywords: New energy vehicles · Python · Sentiment analysis · Semantic network

1 Research Background

From 2015 to 2020, after about five years of market cultivation, China's new energy vehicle market has ushered in more rapid development in 2021, and the penetration rate of new energy vehicles jumped from 5.3% in 2020 to 13.4% in 2021. According to data from the China Automobile Association, the overall sales volume of Chinese self-owned brand passenger vehicles in January 2022 was 1.004 million, among which 321,000 were new energy passenger vehicles, accounting for more than 30% for the first time [1], setting a new record, and the development momentum of new energy vehicles in the Chinese market is evident. Therefore, in-depth research on the emotional preferences and user experience of new energy vehicle owners will help inspire the design, research and development and manufacturing of new energy vehicles, improve

© Springer Nature Switzerland AG 2022
M. Rauterberg et al. (Eds.): HCII 2022, LNCS 13520, pp. 471–486, 2022.
https://doi.org/10.1007/978-3-031-18158-0_34

product competitiveness, and promote the continuous and healthy development of the new energy vehicle industry.

Opinion mining, also known as text sentiment analysis, refers to the whole process of analyzing, processing, inducing and reasoning subjective texts with emotional color, so as to analyze the opinions, emotions, evaluations, attitudes and sentiments expressed by users about entities and their attributes, and then dig out useful information and knowledge [2]. In terms of literature research, Cai Yushu et al. [3] combined the two sub-tasks of opinion word extraction and category classification in aspect-level sentiment analysis, and proposed a BERT-based end-to-end opinion mining method for travel reviews. Jiang Fan et al. [4] used the attention convolutional neural network to analyze the user comments sentiment of life APP, and combined the analysis results to build a gray satisfaction prediction model. Li Lanyou et al. [5] provided a data mining method based on the LDA topic model. Through the steps of emotional information extraction, classification and sentiment analysis, they conducted tendency judgment and hidden information mining on the massive review texts of the appearance of SUV models, obtained the analysis results of user sentiment tendency of SUV models, and excavated the advantages and disadvantages of the appearance of specific SUV models; Yu Fan [6] took the online comments of new energy vehicle users as the research object, combined the sentiment dictionary to analyze the comments, and excavated the emotional tendencies of new energy vehicle users; Cheng Ran [7] solved the problem of recognition of review attributes in vehicle review texts and the problem of sentiment analysis of specific attributes by using natural language processing technology, and proposed an attribute recognition model based on multi-label classification and an attribute sentiment analysis model based on the attention mechanism.

In the existing literature on the research on review texts, scholars mostly use the method based on sentiment dictionary, which relies on the quality of sentiment dictionary and judgment rules, and its pros and cons largely depend on manual design and priori knowledge. Besides, it does not have a good effect on the recognition of many new words such as proverbs, idioms or network special terms, and it is easy to ignore the contextual connection. In the existing literature on the research on the user sentiment of automobiles, scholars mostly focus on a certain category, such as new energy vehicles and traditional vehicles, SUVs and sedans, etc., but there are few comparative studies focusing on specific categories and subdivisions, lacking certain target pertinence and opinion orientation. In order to better understand the sentiment of vehicle owners in China's new energy vehicle market, this paper selected sales representatives of three different price points under three new energy vehicles, EREV, BEV, and PHEV, and on the basis of training a large number of vehicle comment corpus using SnowNLP library of Python, a comparative study on sentiments of new energy vehicles owners based on opinion mining was carried out, which improved the accuracy of sentiment analysis of vehicle owners' comment texts.

2 Opinion Mining Model

2.1 Sentiment Analysis Model Based on SnowNLP

Since most of the natural language processing libraries are for English text, SnowNLP came into being in order to better process Chinese text. SnowNLP is a class library inspired by TextBlob and written in Python, which can easily process Chinese text content. Unlike TextBlob, it does not use NLTK (Natural Language Toolkit), but implements all algorithms by itself, and comes with some dictionaries that have been trained. With SnowNLP, a series of Chinese text content operations such as Chinese word separation, lexical annotation, sentiment analysis, text classification, etc. can be completed. Among them, the core of the sentiment analysis module is sentiment classification, and the basic model of sentiment classification is the Bayesian model. For the Bayesian model, it mainly involves the naive Bayes principle, that is, for a classification problem with two categories c_1 and c_2, the features are $w_1, \ldots, w_n$ and the features are independent of each other [8]. Among them, the basic process of the Bayesian model belonging to category c_1 can be expressed as:

$$P(c_1|w_1, \ldots, w_n) = \frac{P(w_1, \ldots, w_n|c_1) \cdot P(c_1)}{P(w_1, \ldots, w_n)} \tag{1}$$

$$P(w_1, \ldots, w_n) = P(w_1, \ldots, w_n|c_1) \cdot P(c_1) + P(w_1, \ldots, w_n|c_2) \cdot P(c_2) \tag{2}$$

The existing model of the sentiment analysis module in the SnowNLP library is trained based on the review data of the product, so in the actual use process, the existing model needs to be retrained according to the object of sentiment analysis. The usual practice is to first prepare the positive and negative corpus and save them separately, for example, save the positive corpus to pos.txt, and save the negative corpus to neg.txt; secondly, use SnowNLP to train a new model; finally, save the new model file and perform file replacement. Accordingly, this paper completes the construction of a sentiment analysis model based on SnowNLP by preparing a positive and negative corpus dataset of user opinions in the automotive industry for sentiment model training, replacing the trained model files with the existing files, and achieving a good match between the sentiment analysis module and the comment data in the automobile industry.

2.2 Semantic Network Model

Semantic network model is a knowledge expression method proposed by J.R. Quillian, which first appeared in the 1970s and is widely used in the field of natural language processing to express complex concepts and their relationships. The components of the semantic network model are the nodes, and the arcs connecting the nodes. Each node corresponds to a different concept word, and each arc represents the correlation between the nodes. Semantic network graph is a specific form of semantic network model, which can qualitatively mine text information, explore the position of different nodes in the network graph, and understand the relationship between nodes. A large number of arcs connecting a node in a semantic network graph indicates that the node is a key node in the semantic network graph [9]. A is a key node in the semantic network graph (Fig. 1).

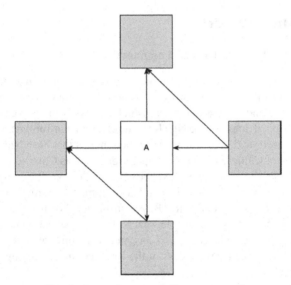

Fig. 1. Semantic network diagram example.

In the process of sentiment analysis of the overall structure of the Chinese comment text, the semantic network model can be used to re-integrate the messy content relationship after the text segmentation, and then clearly restore the semantic content contained in the original comment text. Accordingly, this paper extracts the review data into positive and negative aspects after data preprocessing, comment segmentation, word frequency statistics and sentiment analysis in Python, reconstructs the semantic network of the positive and negative data groups, and conducts interactive diagnosis, in order to complete the judgment of the advantages and disadvantages of the corresponding vehicle models and the insight into the consumers' concerns with the help of the reconstructed semantic network graph.

2.3 Analysis Methods and Processes

The sentiment analysis model based on SnowNLP and the semantic network model jointly build an opinion mining model. The main steps are as follows (Fig. 2):

1. Collect the opinion corpus of users in the automotive industry and use Python's SnowNLP library for emotional model training.
2. Use Python to collect comment data on the pre-selected vehicle models of the Autohome website.
3. Use Python's Pandas library and regular expressions to deduplicate data and delete irrelevant emoticons, symbols, and text information in comments, as well as to complete the pre-processing of the comment data with manual spot-checking.
4. Use Python's open source Chinese word segmentation tool jieba's precise mode and HMM to segment the obtained comment data set and perform word frequency statistics to understand the main concerns of vehicle owners.

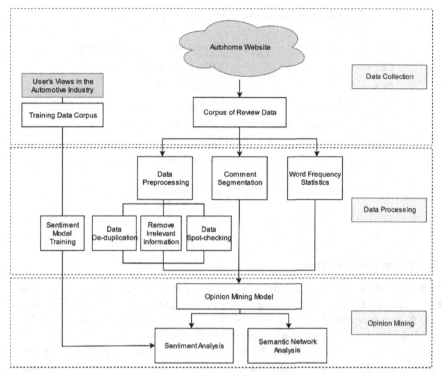

Fig. 2. Analysis process of opinion mining model.

5. Analyze the comment data in various aspects by opinion mining model.
6. Obtain the analysis results of users' emotional tendencies, excavate the advantages and disadvantages of the three vehicle models, and draw relevant conclusions and suggestions to help improve the car-machine interaction experience of vehicle owners.

3   Research Process

3.1   Operating Environment

The operating PC platform processor is AMD Ryzen 7 4800H with Radeon Graphics 2.90 GHz; the memory is 16G; the system is Windows 10 Home Edition; the Python version used is 3.8.5, the Python IDE is PyCharm Community Edition 2022.1, and all open sources libraries are latest and have passed compatibility tests (Table 1).

Table 1. Table of operating environments for development.

	Instructions for use	Name and version information
1	Client operating system	Windows 10 Home Edition
2	Python	Python 3.8.5
3	Python IDE	PyCharm Community Edition 2022.1
4	Semantic web analysis tools	ROSTCM6(5.8.0.603)
5	Major Python packages	pandas 1.4.2 snownlp 0.12.3 requests 2.27.1 jieba 0.42.1 fonttools 4.33.2 bs4 0.0.1

3.2   Training Data Corpus

The training data is from the GitHub project, which is a dataset comment segmentation program project for the 2018 CCF Big Data and Computational Intelligence Competition in the Automotive Industry among the User Opinion and Sentiment Recognition Theme [10]. This paper selects the training set files of this project as the positive and negative corpus of training data, with a total of 9,947 comment texts. The themes of the data in this training set are divided into 10 categories, including: power, price, interior, configuration, safety, appearance, control, fuel consumption, space and comfort; the sentiment was divided into 3 categories, with the numbers 0, 1 and −1 indicating neutral, positive and negative respectively.

3.3   Comment Data Corpus

The review data comes from the Autohome website, which is the largest vehicle website in China and is committed to providing consumers with one-stop vehicle viewing, vehicle buying, and vehicle use services. The Autohome website has a multidimensional and large amount of vehicle review data in high quality. In this paper, 36,132 reviews of relevant models were obtained, covering eight dimensions: space, power, control, energy consumption, comfort, appearance, interior and cost performance. In order to make the study more representative and informative, three price ranges were selected, covering mainstream new energy vehicles in China, which respectively are RMB 100,000–200,000, RMB 200,000–300,000 and RMB 300,000–500,000. The best-selling vehicle models of EREV, BEV and PHEV in the Chinese auto market in the past year were selected in the corresponding price ranges. This ensures that the comparison is consistent, representative and informative.

Among them, EREVs include FENGON E3 in the price range of RMB 100,000–200,000, SERES SF5 in the price range of RMB 200,000–300,000, and LI One, VOYAH FREE and AITO M5 in the price range of RMB 300,000–500,000, for a total of five vehicle models; BEVs include AION S and WM EX5 in the price range of RMB 100,000–200,000, XPENG P7 and Model 3 in the price range of RMB 200,000–300,000, and

Model Y and NIO ES6 in the price range of RMB 300,000–500,000, for a total of six vehicle models. PHEVs include Song DM-i and ROEWE RX5 in the price range of RMB 100,000–200,000, Han DM-i and Passat PHEV in the price range of RMB 200,000–300,000, and LYNK&CO 09 PHEV and BMW 5 Series PHEV in the price range of RMB 300,000–500,000, for a total of six vehicle models. During the data acquisition process, it was found that among the three new energy vehicle types, the corresponding models of EREV are less than that of BEV and PHEV, mainly covering the price range of more than RMB 200,000 yuan, and the review data is relatively small, which correlates with the fact that there are fewer vehicle models of EREVs in the Chinese new energy vehicle market and the overall sales are relatively low.

3.4 Data Preprocessing

The textual information in the comment corpus comes from the comment data obtained from web pages. Due to its irregular format, the text is usually colloquial, so there may be redundant comment information of low value that is not relevant to the requirements such as spaces, blank lines, network terms, special symbols and abbreviated expressions [11]. This information can interfere with sentiment analysis, so the Python Pandas library and regular expressions are used to automatically clean the comments, including de-duplicating the data and removing irrelevant emoticons, symbols and text information from the comments. At the same time, with manual random checks, a total of 35,567 comments were obtained and subdivided according to the three types of new energy vehicles and the corresponding comment dimensions (Table 2).

Table 2. Statistics of EREV, BEV and PHEV reviews after data cleaning.

Comment category	Amount	Comment category	Amount	Comment category	Amount	Total
EREV	4321	BEV	16422	PHEV	14824	35567
Space	541	Space	2054	Space	1852	4447
Power	541	Power	2053	Power	1853	4447
Control	541	Control	2054	Control	1856	4451
Energy consumption	543	Energy consumption	2055	Energy consumption	1855	4453
Comfort	538	Comfort	2050	Comfort	1852	4440
Appearance	540	Appearance	2055	Appearance	1850	4445
Interior	539	Interior	2052	Interior	1852	4443
Cost performance	538	Cost performance	2049	Cost performance	1854	4441

Data Deduplication. Sometimes there are repeated text information in the obtained car review data. This is usually due to the laziness of some users and they have copied and pasted other users' comments, which is not valuable for opinion mining and can cause errors in word frequency statistics, so data deduplication is necessary. Using the dropna function in Python's third-party Pandas library, missing data can be removed; using the unique function, duplicate text and blank lines can be removed by comparing the text content.

Removing Irrelevant Information. The acquired vehicle review data usually contains irrelevant content such as emoticons, symbols and text information, which can cause some interference to the subsequent sentiment analysis task and affect the effectiveness of sentiment analysis. Therefore, it is necessary to use regular expressions for content matching to remove information that is irrelevant to the task of opinion mining, including non-text, labels, and special symbols.

Manual Spot Checks. After using Python to remove duplicate information and irrelevant information, there is still a certain probability that there is a small amount of unrecognizable and useless information in the comment data. At this time, it is necessary to carry out a random check of the effect of data preprocessing in a manual way in order to eliminate useless information such as emoticons and symbols that can easily be missed.

3.5 Comment Segmentation

Comment segmentation plays an important role in opinion mining tasks, because words are the smallest meaningful language components that can act independently in natural language understanding, so identifying words in natural language facilitates content segmentation, concept extraction and topic analysis, leading to a better understanding of natural language and the emotions expressed. Generally speaking, the separation process that the words of the sentence are automatically recognized by the computer and boundary markers are added between the words to separate each vocabulary, is Chinese word segmentation. In this paper, the precise mode of the Python open source Chinese word segmentation tool jieba and HMM (Hidden Markov Model) are used to segment the obtained comment data corpus, and the "Chinese Stopwords" stop word library is used to remove stop words in the comments.

The jieba library is an excellent third-party Chinese word segmentation library for Python, supporting three kinds of word segmentation modes: precise mode, full mode and search engine mode. It combines both rule-based and statistical-based approaches, with rich functions, easy to use, and is constantly being updated. For example, jieba provides functions such as word segmentation, lexical annotation, unregistered word recognition, user dictionary, deactivated word filtering and so on. HMM is a statistical model that describes a Markov process with implicitly unknown parameters and it is often used in scenarios such as speech recognition and Chinese word segmentation by observing the sequence of another set of states to obtain relevant information. Therefore, for the segmentation of unregistered words, the jieba word segmentation tool adopts the HMM based on the ability of Chinese characters to form words, and uses the Viterbi algorithm to solve the problem, which has a good word segmentation effect.

3.6 Word Frequency Statistics

After completing the comment segmentation, word frequency statistics are performed on all the segmented words. In the process of word frequency statistics, lexical analysis is performed on the word or phrase to identify whether the current object's attribute is an adjective, verb or noun, etc. By extracting the high frequency nouns related to the attributes of the three vehicle models, the final Top15 high frequency nouns for the reviews of the three models were obtained (Fig. 3, 4 and 5).

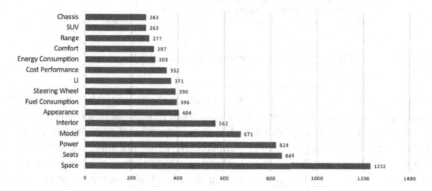

Fig. 3. Top 15 high frequency nouns for EREV reviews.

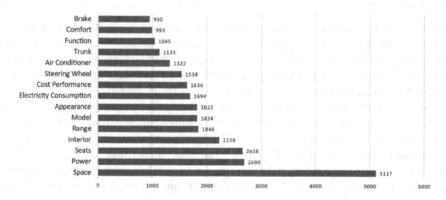

Fig. 4. Top 15 high-frequency nouns for BEV reviews.

The statistics show that owners of all three models are highly concerned about nouns "space", "seats", "power", "interior", "energy consumption", etc. "space", "seats" and "power" are the most important attributes for all vehicle owners. In addition, EREV owners also focus on "SUV" and "chassis", which correlates with the fact that EREVs in the Chinese market are mainly SUVs; BEV owners also focus on "range" and "brakes", which is consistent with the fact that the range and braking effect of BEVs are highly discussed in the Chinese market; PHEV owners also focus on "engine", which is related

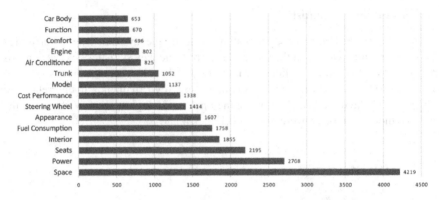

Fig. 5. Top 15 high-frequency nouns for PHEV reviews.

to the fact that PHEVs have two powertrains and are characterized by interoperability. According to the frequency of words in the reviews of three models, it can be found that because the models are mainly SUVs, EREV owners pay a lot of attention to the comfort of the chassis; due to the pure electric property, BEVs do not solve the user's "range anxiety" like EREV and PHEV, and owners pay a high degree of attention to range; with two powertrains, PHEV owners have a high level of concern about the engine intervention rules.

3.7 Sentiment Analysis

Referring to the construction process of the sentiment analysis model based on SnowNLP mentioned above, for a corpus of 9,947 positive, negative and neutral sentiment data that have been prepared, use SnowNLP, a class library focused on Chinese text processing, to perform corpus data set training, combine the trained sentiment analysis model with the general model that comes with SnowNLP, and perform file replacement.

Sentiment analysis is performed on the comment data corpus using SnowNLP's sentiment analysis module, with the results taking values between 0 and 1, with closer to 1 indicating positive sentiment and closer to 0 indicating negative sentiment. Specifically, when scoring the above review dataset for sentiment, greater than 0.6 is positive, less than 0.4 is negative, and between 0.4 and 0.6 is neutral. This paper conducts sentiment analysis on the reviews of EREV, BEV, and PHEV, and expresses it in the form of the percentage of each dimension (Fig. 6).

The distribution of the sentiment ratings shows that the sentiment preferences of the three vehicle types are relatively similar, with more positive sentiment towards the appearance and power of the vehicle and more negative sentiment towards energy consumption and comfort, which is consistent with the good dynamic characteristics of new energy vehicles and the status quo that the energy consumption scheme needs to be optimized. The majority of owners believe that new energy vehicles have plenty of power and avant-garde styling, but that the overall ride comfort and energy consumption plan need to be improved. In particular, the energy consumption of new energy vehicles can sometimes be a source of concern, creating "range anxiety" or increasing

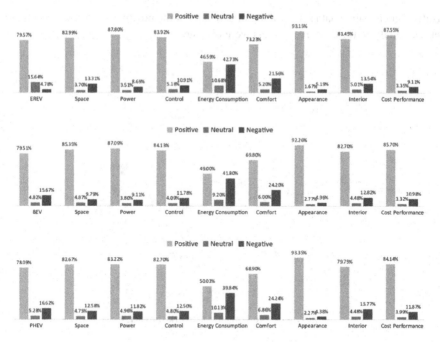

Fig. 6. Sentiment analysis results of EREV, BEV, and PHEV owners.

the "cognitive cost" of the powertrain. In addition, the performance of the three models varies in different dimensions due to differences in power schemes, design styles, etc. For example, EREVs and PHEVs use extended-range hybrid and plug-in hybrid solutions respectively, so they have a more balanced performance in terms of power, cost performance and energy consumption, which can take into account the characteristics of new energy vehicles with abundant power, but also can meet the public's demand for long-distance travel range and energy consumption, with a higher cost performance. BEVs use pure electric power solutions, and since most of these vehicle companies are new vehicle companies, they have more space to play with, more intelligent and experiential elements in the design of space and interiors, and more advantages in terms of control. Therefore, a comparison of the three models shows that EREV has a better performance in terms of power, comfort and cost performance; BEV is better in terms of space, control and interior; and PHEV is better in terms of energy consumption and appearance (Fig. 6).

3.8 Semantic Network Analysis

The semantic network analysis of the positive and negative reviews of the three models of EREV, BEV and PHEV was carried out separately using the semantic network model, which is conducive to mining the positive and negative affective influences of users. The review data were extracted into 2 aspects of positive and negative, and the text mining tool ROSTCM6 was used to reconstruct and visualize the semantic network for both positive and negative data sets, and the final results of the positive and negative semantic network analysis for the three models were obtained.

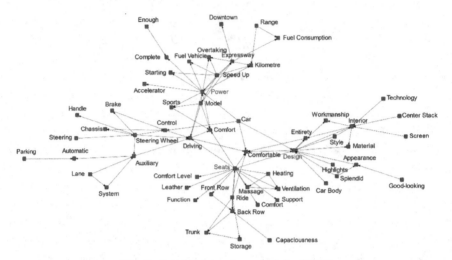

Fig. 7. Positive semantic network for EREV.

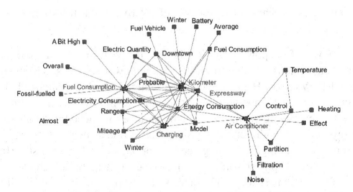

Fig. 8. Negative semantic network for EREV.

EREVs have positive ratings in terms of power, seats and design, as they are mostly SUVs and have an extended hybrid system, which not only provides enough space inside the vehicle, but also can combine strong power to meet owners' needs for short and long distance driving. At the same time, due to the nature of the EREV hybrid system, its battery capacity is lower than that of a pure electric vehicle. When driving long distances, the vehicle tends to go into a state of power deficit, which can easily lead to higher fuel consumption and increased noise, affecting the owner's driving experience (Fig. 7 and 8).

BEVs have a positive evaluation in terms of interior, design, control and power, as they adopt a pure electric power solution and such car companies pay more attention to the intelligence and user experience of the vehicle, with more possibilities to design in

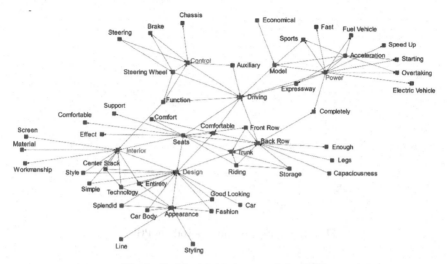

Fig. 9. Positive semantic network for BEV.

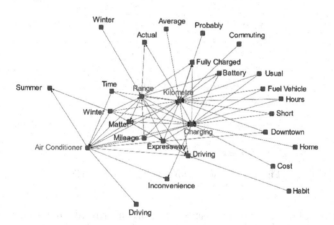

Fig. 10. Negative semantic network for BEV.

space and interior, more intelligence and experience elements, and more advantages in terms of control. However, the BEV does not solve the "range anxiety" of users, who still have many concerns about charging and range, and may even reduce the use of air conditioning in the heat and cold due to the power issue, so the BEV has a negative rating in terms of charging, kilometers, range, air conditioning, etc. (Fig. 9 and 10).

PHEV is similar to EREV in that it has a more balanced performance in terms of power and cost performance. It is able to combine the characteristics of a new energy vehicle with plenty of power while meeting the public's demand for range and energy consumption for long-distance travel, so it has a positive rating in terms of power, appearance and fuel consumption. However, due to the two powertrains, the PHEV makes some sacrifices in terms of space, and the engine makes some noise when it is

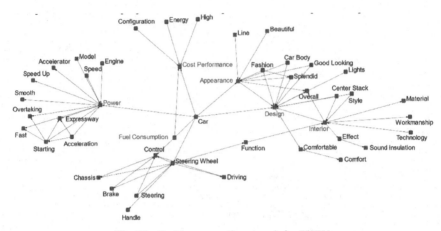

Fig. 11. Positive semantic network for PHEV.

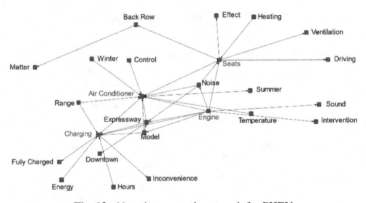

Fig. 12. Negative semantic network for PHEV.

running at a loss of power, so it has a negative rating in terms of engine and seats (Fig. 11 and 12).

4 Research Results

By constructing an opinion mining model, this paper has carried out sentiment analysis on users of three new energy vehicle models, EREV, BEV and PHEV, and conducted a semantic network analysis on the review data. Final conclusions and recommendations are below.

1. Space, energy consumption and interior are the most direct factors influencing user sentiment, especially energy consumption and interior. Owners of all three vehicle models have more positive emotions towards appearance and power, and the most negative emotions towards energy consumption and comfort. The disadvantages that car manufacturers need to improve are charging, range, seats and rear space, and the

advantages that car manufacturers need to maintain are splendid appearance and strong power.

2. EREV maintains advantages of comfort and cost performance, while reducing the disadvantages of high fuel consumption and poor driving experience in power deficit condition.

3. BEV continues to focus on intelligence and user experience, as well as its strengths in control, interior and power. Moreover, optimize the three-electricity system and the charging process to ensure range and eliminate users' 'range anxiety'.

4. PHEV continues to maintain the advantages of energy consumption and appearance. Moreover, optimize the design of the car's interior space and solve the problem of the engine generating a certain amount of noise in the condition of a power shortage.

5 Conclusion

In the era of digital transformation, China's new energy vehicle industry is booming. Functionalization, intelligence, and humanization run through the design, R&D, and manufacturing of new energy vehicles, and are an inevitable choice to solve transportation, energy, and environmental problems [12]. In order to continuously improve the car-machine interaction experience of new energy vehicle owners, enhance product competitiveness and promote the healthy development of the new energy vehicle industry, this paper proposes an opinion mining model based on the opinion mining method, and completes a study on the emotional differences between users of three new energy vehicle models, EREV, BEV and PHEV, by constructing a sentiment analysis model based on SnowNLP and a semantic network model. Some suggestions are provided for enterprises to promote their strengths and avoid their weaknesses.

In the existing research on vehicle owner sentiment, most of the studies focus on a particular category, such as new energy vehicles vs. traditional vehicles, SUV vs. sedan, etc. There are few comparative studies focusing on specific categories and subdivisions, lacking certain targeting and opinion directivity. The opinion mining model proposed in this paper conducts sentiment analysis and semantic network analysis for three different price points of sales representatives of EREV, BEV and PHEV new energy vehicle models, which can provide a new way of thinking for research in this field.

References

1. Zheng, X.: Analysis of new energy vehicle market in January 2022. Auto Rev., 112–117 (2022)
2. Cui, B.: Design and implementation of emotion analysis subsystem of user portrait platform for autohome. School of Artificial Intelligence, University of Chinese Academy of Sciences (2020)
3. Cai, Y., Cao, Y., Jiang, W., Zhan, J., Li, X., Yang, R.: End to end opinion mining method based on Bert for tourism comments. Comput. Technol. Dev. **31**, 118–123 (2021)
4. Jiang, F., Xing, W., Wang, J., Zhang, B.: User satisfaction prediction model of life app based on user comment sentiment analysis. Tech. Autom. Appl. **41**, 104–107 (2022)
5. Li, L., Lu, J., Zhang, J.: Sentiment analysis based on the texts of SUV Model appearance reviews. Chin. J. Automot. Eng. **11**, 93–101 (2021)

6. Yu, F.: Sentiment analysis of new energy car users based on text mining. Logist. Eng. Manag. **44**, 137–140 (2022)
7. Cheng, R.: Sentiment analysis of car review text based on multi-label classification. Donghua University (2021)
8. Sentiment Analysis: In-depth study of SnowNLP principles and practices. https://blog.csdn.net/google19890102/article/details/80091502
9. Liu, J.: Research on express service defects based on semantic network model and SERVQUAL evaluation model. Jilin University (2021)
10. CCF Bigdata. https://github.com/shawnco411/ccf_bigdata
11. Fei, Y.: Research on sentiment analysis of review texts in the automotive field. Jilin University (2021)
12. Hao, H., Cai, R., Tao, S.: Research on the intelligent development of new energy vehicles in the era of digital transformation. Auto Time, 118–120 (2022)

Situating Audio Zone: In-Vehicle Personal Audio Zone Use in Context

Jun Ma, Qianwen Zhang[✉], Zhipeng Hu, and Dachuan Liu

Tongji University, Shanghai, China
zhangqianwen@tongji.edu.cn

Abstract. Personal audio zones can transmit sound to a specific area, making people outside cannot hear the sound clearly. The in-vehicle infotainment system is also a good platform for using this technology, which is conducive to reducing the interference between drivers and passengers and protecting the privacy of drivers. At present, there is still a lack of systematic context discussion on the personal audio zone. Therefore, it is an interesting topic to study whether and how context affects people's tendency to use personal audio zones, which can help to define the adaptive rules of speaker selection in a cabin. This research was conducted in two parts. The first part conducted a 1-on-1 survey to explore user attitudes towards using personal sound zones in different activity contexts. In the second part, a real car experience and after-experience questionnaire were conducted to obtain more realistic feedback. This paper proves that the personal audio zone is a context-sensitive function, and summarizes the key contextual influencing factors in 4 categories and 7 sub-categories. Finally, the suggestions on the initiation strategy of the personal vocal area and the direction of subsequent optimization are expounded.

Keywords: Personal sound zone · Adaptive system · User research

1 Introduction

1.1 In-Vehicle Personal Audio Zones

Personal audio zones can transmit sound to a specific area, making people outside cannot hear the sound clearly. It had applied in many places like the waiting area in the hospital, and amusement facilities in the playground. The in-vehicle infotainment system is also a good platform for using this technology, which is conducive to reducing the interference between drivers and passengers and protecting the privacy of drivers.

Research on the in-vehicle personal audio zones has mostly focused on the acoustic effect. V. Molés-Cases et al. [1] optimized personal sound zones via subband filtering and time domain. G. Pepe et al. [2] described an approach to achieve Individual Listening Zones by exploiting general-purpose car loudspeakers and processing the signal through carefully designed Finite Impulse Response (FIR) filters, which used a deep neural network.

© Springer Nature Switzerland AG 2022
M. Rauterberg et al. (Eds.): HCII 2022, LNCS 13520, pp. 487–498, 2022.
https://doi.org/10.1007/978-3-031-18158-0_35

Usually achieved by speaker arrays, the design of the loudspeaker layout for personal sound zones has also been paid attention to by researchers. Liao et al. proposed a loudspeaker array mounted on the ceiling of a car cabin to provide acceptable control over a larger audio bandwidth [3]. S. Goose et al. constructed a system that enables the configuration of in-vehicle personalized audio zones (PAZs) that don't require earphones [4]. The PAZ system comprises a novel user interface, custom-designed headrests, and an infotainment noise-control subsystem. Stephen J. Elliott et al. improved the effectiveness of active headrests in aircraft seats [5].

1.2 The Context in Adaptive Interactive System

In the past 20 years, the context-aware interactive system has attracted great interest in various disciplines. The advancement of technologies such as the internet of things, mobile internet, and big data enables the system to recommend products or services based on a large number of customer behavior data and using context.

Context is an important factor affecting user demand and behavior. Daniela Stier [6] found that language use varies greatly in different driving contexts, which should be taken into account in the generation of voice output. J. Holzinger's research [7] has proved that whether on-board ADAS can make driving more comfortable or fuel-efficient also depends on the context, and the control parameters should be adjusted according to the situation. Therefore, the adaptive rules of intelligent systems must consider contexts.

Many intelligent systems have taken context as one of the important influencing factors of decision-making. Fernandez-Rojas published a survey of contextual awareness in Human-Advanced-Vehicle Systems [8], which summarized various types of context-aware systems. Campigotto developed a personalized and situation-aware approach for multimodal route recommendations [9]. Bader developed a context-aware approach for POI recommendations in an automotive scenario [10].

Contexts are not only important in the development of adaptive interactive systems but also need to be taken into account during usability testing. Research [11]shows that it is evident that defining usability depends on the context of the use of the device in question. The aim of this review, therefore, is to define usability for in-vehicle devices by selecting a set of criteria to describe the various factors which contribute to usability in this specific context of use.

1.3 Objectives of the Current Study

Whether users tend to use personal sound zones depends on the context. For example, the driver may prefer to have a private sound zone or an earphone when making a phone call, and someone is nearby. But when traveling with family and playing music, drivers may want to share it with passengers.

At present, there is still a lack of systematic context discussion on the personal audio zone. Therefore, it is an interesting topic to study whether and how context affects people's tendency to use personal audio zones, which can help to define the adaptive rules of speaker selection in a cabin. The goal of this study is to answer the following questions:

- (RQ1) Whether the personal audio zone is a context-sensitive function in the vehicle
- (RQ2) If yes, what are the contextual factors that affect users' use of personal audio zones? How does it affect users?
- (RQ3) What are the design recommendations for in-vehicle speaker selection? (Personal audio zones vs normal audio speaker)

The results of the study can provide a basis for the selection and design of the sound channel in the car, and provide our opinions according to the existing situation. Quantitative and qualitative analysis will be used together in the research.

2 Procedure and Method

This research was conducted in two parts. The first part conducted a 1-on-1 survey to explore user attitudes towards using personal sound zones in different activity contexts. In the second part, a real car experience and after-experience questionnaire were conducted to obtain more realistic feedback. Participants were asked to describe in detail the scenarios and reasons for their willingness to use personal sound zones or not to obtain more comprehensive context variables.

2.1 Sample

In sum, N = 80 car owners from Shanghai, China participated in this study. Among them, 60 participated in the survey of **Study 1**, and 20 participated in the real car experience and interview of **Study 2**.

The participant's age range is between 20 and 35, with a mean age of M = 30.10 years (SD = 4.27). The gender composition of the participants was 31 women and 49 men. The backgrounds of the participants come from a variety of fields such as the construction industry, engineering, and finance. Everyone has a driver's license for more than one year and has experience in using in-vehicle infotainment systems.

In conducting our research, the participants provided their written informed consent to participate in this study. Ethical review and approval were not required for the study by the local legislation and institutional requirements.

2.2 Materials and Procedures

The research is divided into questionnaires, real car experience, and post-experience interviews. The questionnaire survey mainly collects users' attitudes towards directional sound transmission technology, using the Richter 7-point scale, which is considered to be an effective method to obtain users' subjective attitudes.

Study 1. To explore user attitudes towards using personal sound zones in different activity contexts, a survey was carried out on users' willingness to use personal sound zones. 60 users were invited over for a 1-on-1 survey. First, the researchers introduced the purpose of the study and the concept of personal sound zones to the participants, to let the participants understand this technology. Within the scope of our investigation, personal sound zones technology is not used in any production model, so it is very necessary to do so. Afterward, to understand the use of personal sound zones in the participants' daily travel, the participants were asked about the frequency of sound-related pain points. Finally, for the five commonly used contexts in the car, as shown in Table 1, the participants scored their willingness to use each activity context.

Study 2. To give participants a more realistic experience of personal audio zones, we installed two-directional audio transmission devices in the rear of a BMW 7 series. The device is Focusound Screen®, a screen solution for directional sound transmission, from audfly, shown in Pic. 1. One participant and one researcher sat in the rear together and tried the effects of the inside and outside of the sound zone, as well as the normal speaker in the car. A driver was driving the car throughout the whole process to provide the most realistic experience.

Five common in-vehicle activity contexts are also arranged in this study, as shown in Table 1. We prepared the corresponding audio material and had a staff member call the customer off-site. In each context, the sound was played three times, respectively: a. Participant's seat (back right) b. Interviewer's seat (back left), as shown in Pic. 2, and c. Normal speaker in the car.

After each experience, the participants were asked to talk about their needs for using personal audio zones in this scenario, possible application contexts, and usage feelings. We made recordings with the user's permit, and this part of the corpus is an important material for mining and sorting out key contextual factors that affect personal audio zone usage strategies.

Table 1. In-vehicle activity contexts in research and corresponding common pain points

Activity	Common pain points
Personal call	Privacy issues
Music	Interference; music preference conflict
Video	Driving distraction; interference
Navigation	Disturbing passengers
Game	Driving distraction; interference

Pic. 1. Focusound screen (device for personal audio zone)

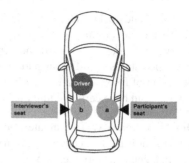

Pic. 2. Seats of real car experience

2.3 Data Processing and Analysis

The dataset includes the questionnaire data and audio records. Excluding the data of one participant, a total of 60 questionnaires and 19 post-experience interview data were used for subsequent analysis.

We conducted quantitative and qualitative analyses on the collected data. Firstly, we made descriptive statistics on the questionnaire data of the participants. To explore whether there are significant differences in users' attitudes towards personal audio zones in different contexts, a one-way ANOVA was conducted. Secondly, we used the grounded theory method to summarize the context factors that influence users' tendency to use personal audio zones. The user's context description slices were extracted and the content is encoded. The code contains 4 important context labels and 7 sub-context labels, as shown in Table 5. 108 context description slices of 19 users were extracted, and each user provided an average of 5.68 context descriptions that tended to use personal audio zones.

3 Results

To answer the question of whether the personal audio zone is context-sensitive, the survey results of 60 participants were quantitatively analyzed. Descriptive statistics and one-way ANOVA were used. In addition, a summary of context factors affecting personal audio zone usage based on 108 interview slices of 19 participants is described, and relevant frequency statistics are performed.

3.1 Participant's Attitudes Toward Personal Audio Zones in the Context

Descriptive Statistics. After learning the concept of the personal audio zone, 60 participants scored the usefulness of this function in each activity context. The results are shown in Fig. 1. In the context of *Personal calls*, the usefulness of the personal audio zone is considered to be the highest, with avg = 6.08. This is followed by the *Music* (avg = 5.58) and the *Navigation* (avg = 4.93). The usefulness of users of *Video* and *Game* has dropped significantly, avg (Video) = 4.52 and avg (Game) = 3.32, respectively.

The Standard Deviation (Std. Deviation) can reflect the difference in the attitudes among participants in this context. The largest Std. Deviation is *Game* (sd = 1.88), followed by *Video* (sd = 1.76) and *Navigation* (sd = 1.76). In these contexts, the needs and expectations of different participants are quite different. In comparison, the Std. Deviation of *Personal calls* and *Music* is small, proving the user's needs are not much different and have certain commonalities in these contexts.

One-Way ANOVA. To evaluate whether there are significant differences in users' attitudes towards personal audio zones in each context, a one-way ANOVA was performed. The independent variable is Activity, and the dependent variable is the participant's attitude toward Usefulness. The analysis results are shown in Tables 2-1 and 2-2.

The results show that P(Sig.) < 0.001 between different activity groups, which proves that the participants' attitudes toward personal audio zone usefulness are significantly different. To further verify the difference between the groups, we also performed a post-hoc test LSD. The results show in Table 3. There are 10 pairs of combinations in the 5 activities under investigation. The results show that among these 10 pairs of combinations, 7 pairs have obvious differences and 3 pairs have little difference, respectively Personal-call & Music, Music & Navigation, and Video & Navigation.

Between-group ANOVA uses statistics data, ignoring individual user selections. Therefore, paired T-test analysis was performed for the three combinations with no significant differences. The result shows in Table 4, that among the three combinations, two had significant differences of P < 0.05, and only one group (Video & Navigation) had lower differences.

To sum up, we believe that users' attitudes towards the usefulness of personal audio zone technology in different contexts are significantly different. Furthermore, the personal sound zone function is a context-sensitive feature.

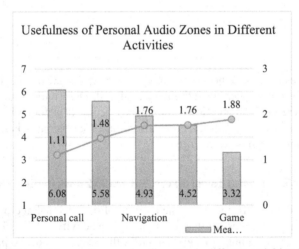

Fig. 1. The usefulness of personal audio zones in different activities. N = 60

Table 2-1. Tests of homogeneity of variances

		Levene statistic	df1	df2	Sig.
Activity	Based on mean	6.213	4	295	<.001
	Based on median	5.500	4	295	<.001
	Based on median and with adjusted df	5.500	4	270.538	<.001
	Based on trimmed mean	6.007	4	295	<.001

Table 2-2. Result of one-way ANOVA usefulness

	Sum of squares	df	Mean square	F	Sig.
Between groups	271.280	4	67.820	25.820	<.001
Within groups	774.867	295	2.627		
Total	1046.147	299			

Table 3. Result of post hoc test (LSD)

Dependent variable: activity

(I) Activity	(J) Usefulness	Mean difference (I-J)	Std. error	Sig.	95% confidence interval	
					Lower bound	Upper bound
Personal call	Music	.500	.296	.092	−.08	1.08
	Video	1.567*	.296	<.001	.98	2.15
	Game	2.767*	.296	<.001	2.18	3.35
	Navigation	1.150*	.296	<.001	.57	1.73
Music	Personal call	−.500	.296	.092	−1.08	.08
	Video	1.067*	.296	<.001	.48	1.65
	Game	2.267*	.296	<.001	1.68	2.85
	Navigation	.650*	.296	.029	.07	1.23
Video	Personal call	−1.567*	.296	<.001	−2.15	−.98
	Music	−1.067*	.296	<.001	−1.65	−.48
	Game	1.200*	.296	<.001	.62	1.78

(*continued*)

Table 3. (*continued*)

Dependent variable: activity

(I) Activity	(J) Usefulness	Mean difference (I-J)	Std. error	Sig.	95% confidence interval	
					Lower bound	Upper bound
Game	Navigation	−.417	.296	.160	−1.00	.17
	Personal call	−2.767*	.296	<.001	−3.35	−2.18
	Music	−2.267*	.296	<.001	−2.85	−1.68
	Video	−1.200*	.296	<.001	−1.78	−.62
Navigation	Navigation	−1.617*	.296	<.001	−2.20	−1.03
	Personal call	−1.150*	.296	<.001	−1.73	−.57
	Music	−.650*	.296	.029	−1.23	−.07
	Video	.417	.296	.160	−.17	1.00
	Game	1.617*	.296	<.001	1.03	2.20

* The mean difference is significant at the 0.05 level.

Table 4. Result of paired samples test

		Mean	t	df	Significance	
					One-sided p	Two-sided p
Pair 1	Personal call –music	.50000	2.088	59	.021	.041
Pair 2	Music - navigation	.65000	2.105	59	.020	.040
Pair 3	Video - navigation	−.41667	−1.335	59	.093	.187

3.2 Key Context Factors for Personal Audio Zones Usage

Through dialogue analysis with participants in real car experience and interviews, 108 context description slices were identified, including scene elements that participants are willing to use in personal audio zones. After the researchers' summary and discussion, a scene affecting the personal audio area was concluded. The list of elements is shown in Table 5.

Personal Behavior. Personal behavior refers to the behavior of passengers and drivers in the vehicle, including the use of the infotainment system and other related behaviors. Interference between individual behaviors is an important reason for users' demand for personal audio zones.

Infotainment activities refer to the infotainment activities related to sound in the car, such as phone calls, navigation, music, video, and games. Since these activities are often the source of sound in the car, the application of a personal audio zone is very relevant to these activities. In navigation scenarios, drivers who are accustomed to listening to navigation sounds rely heavily on this information, but navigation sounds are invalid information for passengers and will disturb passengers, especially when they are sleeping. The music scene is special, most of the time people are willing to share music, and the sound effect of the normal speaker is better. But again, if other people are sleeping or listening to their music instead of the driver's, it can be disruptive to passengers. The pain point of the personal call is the most obvious. The driver can't pick up the phone to answer while driving. If there are other people in the car at this time, there is a risk of leaking privacy, making the driver feel very embarrassed. Videos and games are often played by passengers, making sounds that distract and interfere with drivers. Especially the loud gun battle games will make the driver very irritable. Videos can also attract the driver's attention and cause driving distractions.

Table 5. Context labels for personal audio zones usage

Context label	Sub context label	Options
Personal behavior	Infotainment activities with sound	Personal call; music; video; game; navigation …
	Other behavior	Sleep; working meeting…
Social context	Passenger - driver relationship distance	Close (family, good friends); far (colleagues, leaders, strangers)
	Number of passengers	0;1; 2;3…
Preferences and personality	Preferences	Music preference; other audio content preference…
	Mood	Happy; fretful…
Environment	Environment noise	Wind noise; tire noise…

Other related behaviors were driver or passenger behaviors related to personal audio zones use, with sleep being the most common one found in the study. Passengers often do not want to be disturbed by sound when they are sleeping, and drivers often need sounds such as navigation and music to keep themselves driving smoothly. The same goes for work meetings, where some drivers listen to meetings while driving, which is useless information and a distraction to passengers.

Social context refers to the social context of the driver in the vehicle. Including how many passengers are present, and the relationship between the passenger and the driver can affect the need for a personal audio zone.

Driver-Passenger Relationship Distance. When the relationship is far away, the driver pays more attention to privacy and cares about each other's preferences and whether they will disturb others. Therefore, the willingness to use personal audio zones will be higher. When the relationship is close, preferences and privacy have less influence.

Number of Passengers. Having a passenger is a necessary condition for the value of personal audio zones. If there is only the driver in the car, the personal audio zone loses its most important value. When the number of passengers is large, if everyone is doing activities with sound, the interference with each other will be great, and it will also affect the driver's driving. Therefore, it is necessary to divide the sound of each person at this time.

Preferences and Personality

Preference refers to the driver's or passenger's preference for various types of activity audio. For example, music preference, content preference, etc. Such preferences affect whether drivers and passengers can share audio, mainly music. This phenomenon is especially obvious when the driver passenger relationship is far away. Some participants believe that music represents their taste. If they play the music that their colleagues or leaders don't like, or think that the music has bad taste, it will affect their image.

Mood. Some participants mentioned that whether they mind other sounds is also related to their mood. When they are upset, they will be impatient with the noise made by passengers. And when they are happy, they may be more tolerant.

Environment. Environment refers to the sound environment inside and outside the vehicle. For example, whether there is wind noise or tire noise. The environment will affect the selection of the speaker. The original loudspeaker on the vehicle may have an active noise reduction function. Therefore, participants should consider the actual sound effect.

4   Discussion

4.1   Suggestions on the Selection Strategy of Scene-Based Speakers

Whether the personal audio zone is desired by the user is determined by context. First, the social environment was the primary influencing factor for the use of personal audio zones. If there are no passengers, there is no need to use it. Second, from a behavioral point of view, the functions that drivers need to use personal audio zones the most are phone calls and navigation. For passengers, it is best to use the personal audio zone when the volume of their videos and games in the car is very high, so as not to interfere with driving or disturb others. Also, if someone is sleeping in the car, the other person's sound zone should be enabled. Third, for personal preference and mood, since data is difficult to obtain, it is recommended to enable the personal audio zone by default, and control it through appropriate interaction if necessary. Finally, for environmental factors, it's not the difference between personal audio zones and public speakers. It is recommended to turn on the active noise reduction system separately when there is noise.

4.2 Directional Sound Transmission System Optimization Direction

Human Body Tracking: The personal audio zone is to spread the sound to a certain area, and when the user is sitting in the car, the head inevitably moves left and right. If the user's head deviates from the sound zone, it can cause inaudibility. Therefore, it is necessary to develop functions that can track the position of the human body in the future.

Sound Effect and Volume. Different technologies have different sound effects. The current technology has low sound and thin sound effects, which cannot well reflect the atmosphere of music. The development of this aspect can also continue to improve.

Control Interaction Design. Even with in-depth research on the context, it is often difficult for the system to understand user needs 100% accurately. Therefore, it is necessary to leave a control interface for the user. The driver must have simple control and status visibility. When the personal audio zone is enabled, the user has no way of knowing if other people really can't hear the sound, so visual visibility is necessary.

5 Conclusion

This paper explored the question of whether the personal audio zone is a context-sensitive function. Through surveys, interviews, and real car experiences of 80 participants, the study proves that the personal audio zone is a context-sensitive function, and summarizes the key contextual influencing factors in 4 categories and 7 sub-categories. Finally, the suggestions on the initiation strategy of the personal vocal area and the direction of subsequent optimization are expounded.

Acknowledgments. Supported by the Shanghai Municipal Science and Technology Major Project (2021SHZDZX0100) and the Fundamental Research Funds for the Central Universities.

References

1. Moles-Cases, V., Pinero, G., De Diego, M., Gonzalez, A.: Personal sound zones by subband filtering and time domain optimization. IEEE/ACM Trans. Audio Speech Lang. Process. **28**, 2684–2696 (2020). https://doi.org/10.1109/TASLP.2020.3023628
2. Pepe, G., Gabrielli, L., Squartini, S., Cattani, L., Tripodi, C.: Deep learning for individual listening zone. In: IEEE 22nd International Workshop on Multimedia Signal Processing, MMSP 2020 (2020). https://doi.org/10.1109/MMSP48831.2020.9287161
3. Liao, X., Cheer, J., Elliott, S.J., Zheng, S.: Design of a loudspeaker array for personal audio in a car cabin. AES J. Audio Eng. Soc. **65**, 226–238 (2017). https://doi.org/10.17743/JAES.2016.0065
4. Goose, S., Riddle, L., Fuller, C., Gupta, T., Marcus, A.: PAZ: in-vehicle personalized audio zones. IEEE Multimedia **23**, 32–41 (2016). https://doi.org/10.1109/MMUL.2015.94
5. Elliott, S.J., Jones, M.: An active headrest for personal audio. J. Acoust. Soc. Am. **119**, 2702 (2006). https://doi.org/10.1121/1.2188814

6. Stier, D., Munro, K., Heid, U., Minker, W.: Towards situation-adaptive in-vehicle voice output. In: ACM International Conference Proceeding Series (2020). https://doi.org/10.1145/3405755.3406127
7. Holzinger, J., Tkachenko, P., Obereigner, G., Del Re, L.: Context aware control of ADAS. In: Proceedings of American Control Conference 2020, pp. 2288–2293, July 2020. https://doi.org/10.23919/ACC45564.2020.9147710
8. Fernandez-Rojas, R., et al.: Contextual awareness in human-advanced-vehicle systems: a survey. IEEE Access 7, 33304–33328 (2019). https://doi.org/10.1109/ACCESS.2019.2902812
9. Campigotto, P., Rudloff, C., Leodolter, M., Bauer, D.: Personalized and situation-aware multimodal route recommendations: the FAVOUR algorithm. IEEE Trans. Intell. Transp. Syst. 18, 92–102 (2017). https://doi.org/10.1109/TITS.2016.2565643
10. Bader, R., Neufeld, E., Woerndl, W., Prinz, V.: Context-aware POI recommendations in an automotive scenario using multi-criteria decision making methods. In: ACM International Conference Proceeding Series, pp. 23–30 (2011). https://doi.org/10.1145/1961634.1961640
11. Harvey, C., Stanton, N.A., Pickering, C.A., McDonald, M., Zheng, P.: Context of use as a factor in determining the usability of in-vehicle devices 12, 318–338 (2010). https://doi.org/10.1080/14639221003717024

Traffic and Transport Ergonomics on Long Term Multi-Agent Social Interactions: A Road User's Tale

Naomi Y. Mbelekani[✉] and Klaus Bengler

Chair of Ergonomics, Technical University of Munich, Boltzmannstr. 15,
85748 Garching b. Munich, Germany
ny.mbelekani@tum.de

Abstract. There are public debates concerning the meaning highly automated vehicles (HAVs) will possess in society and on road social interactions, with the topic of autonomy being frequently stressed. The de-contextualised and abstract discussion has influenced the development of the on-road Multi-Agent Social Interaction (MASI) concept. By addressing socially sensitive road users' co-experiences with HAVs, a range of social situations, and how the social dimensions comes to play in different future scenarios may aid scholars and manufacturers gain insights as well as challenge perceived assumptions. For prolific future mobility research and development, we need to consider long-term automation effects to on-road social interactive behaviours – an under-addressed and often overlooked issue. Thus, we revised ideas that infer social interaction patterns, in hopes to try to interrogate and situate these patterns within the context of MASI. These viewpoints are compared and integrated to formulate a structured and explorative framework, describing MASI in the context of space sharing, as this is important to consider in the early stage of HAV development. This paper aims to situate the experiences of road users within an illustrative urban context, as real-world commuting experiences may include multiple people interacting with HAVs at the same time. Further offers significant contributions, which is a description of "MASI": in short, as on-road social interaction consisting of different road users (humans and automated vehicles), as agents that socially interact with and react to each other, simultaneously. In essence, a classification of co-experiences that users' may exhibit in in-group social interactions with HAV and interaction dynamics with automation tailored for different road-user types, and further supports several multimodalities. This framework is helpful in envisioning better-equipped systems, models, theories, human factors requirements for interaction designed strategies, and in-group-out-group humans-automation collaborative research.

Keywords: Automated vehicles · Human factors · Traffic and transport ergonomics · MASI · Long-term automation effects · User experiences

1 Introduction

Rapid advancements in science and technology have become a driving force for vehicle automation developments for future urban societies, a future like none other. For

© Springer Nature Switzerland AG 2022
M. Rauterberg et al. (Eds.): HCII 2022, LNCS 13520, pp. 499–518, 2022.
https://doi.org/10.1007/978-3-031-18158-0_36

example, advanced driver assistance systems (ADAS) have benefited "drivers and other road users by providing relief from tedious control tasks, alerting drivers about dangerous conditions, and intervening on drivers' behalf when physical limitations preclude an effective driver response" [51]. Due to the benefits that automation provides, automated driving systems (ADS) are progressing into highly automated vehicles (HAV) and will gradually infiltrate traffic and transport environments over the next decades, with 20–30% HAV predicted to emerge in 2030 [21]. HAV are anticipated to become an influential part of human life and the transport industry. These are classified as level 4–5 for taxonomy and definitions terms related to automation systems for on-road vehicles [41]. We perceive a move towards a world where HAV are the future of mobility, thus *a new normal, a new way of life, an innovative way of travelling* and *being in traffic*. For example, Mercedes-Benz Vision AVTR and Mercedes-Benz F 015, Volvo Concept 26 and Volvo Cars 360c, Volkswagen Group Concept Sedric, and the Apple car (code-named "Project Titan") are all possibilities. Therefore, autonomous Car-as-a-Product (CaaP: ownership model for private purchase, with the option to drive yourself or switch to full or other automation modes) and Car-as-a-Service (CaaS: service model for on-demand taxis, car/ride sharing service, the only option is autonomous mode) may represent up to 42% of the mobility portfolio in the U.S. and 39% in Germany, thus attractive and dominant future transport modes [24]. As a result, when considering at the overall mobility structure, vehicles as we know them will move into new directions, with the *virtual urbanite* and *proud achiever* as the most tech receptive consumer segments [24].

1.1 Unfolding Multi-Agent Social Interaction (MASI)

This framework aims to conceptually explore the neglected topic of multi-agent interaction between different road users and how they may play out in the future. Importantly, the topic of what social autonomy means in future mobility, and whether we can learn anything by assessing our own social or human autonomy. Reference [49] partially flesh out which agents and intelligences are present in the system in order to try to understand which parties need to be social with each other, and thus understand whom to apply the metaphor 'social' to. Some of the issues highlighted are: is the human interacting with an intelligent vehicle or interacting with an intelligent agent controlling a normal vehicle, or even an intelligent agent controlling a HAV? These questions have one thing in common, which is unfolding on-road social interactions, and in the simplest sense, to inquire whether humans want to be social with a machine at all or whether it is useful to consider the HAV to be a social agent rather than just an advanced piece of machinery [49]. The de-contextualised and abstract discussion has influenced the development of the Multi-Agent Social Interaction (MASI) concept. In its simplest form, this is the process of reciprocal influence exercised by humans and AVs over one another during on road social encounters. MASI consist as a fundamental unit of analysis within human factors research, and describes any voluntary and involuntary as well as verbal and nonverbal interactive relationship between more than one human and AV agents within and/or between groups (*in-group* and *out-group*). In this MASI context, we explore the interaction with prefixes such as *out-group* referring to existing between agents (infer those outside the AV), and *in-group* referring to within the HAV. *Primary user* internally interact with automation when driving, and are set to partially or impartially occupy the position of the *driver* in case of system error, and *secondary users* are rather seen as *passengers*, and subdivided into social network groups such as clients/co-workers, family and friends. There is a neglect in research covering all those inside the vehicles, such as passengers [37], however, [49] argues that family settings for commutes set demands on social interactions and the co-experience of technology use inside the vehicle. Vulnerable road users (*VRUs*) are those who come into contact or exposure with automation as they commute on public roads and space sharing, such as *pedestrians, cyclists* and *vehicles*.

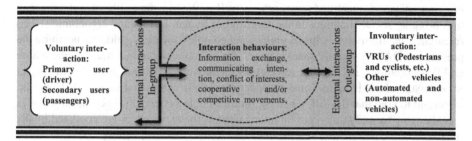

Fig. 1. In-group-out-group road user interaction factors

This space sharing may encompass different forms of interactive factors (see Fig. 1), as humans and AVs negotiate their on-road interactions. The social road is full of complex interactions and intricate on road effects. Although, there are not many studies that infiltrate this space to envision how automation may influence this space long-term, it is important that we try to infer what it means to be social on the road. Multi-agent models for AVs have focused on systems that determine features of different drivers, and also considers the effects that drivers' movements have on other road users. Important to consider is that AV users do not operate in isolation, for instance, a HAV's actions or behaviour has effects on what others occupying the same space will do [11], other drivers, vulnerable road users (VRUs), AVs, among others. We thus attempt to add to this discussion in this paper, by scrutinising on road MASI as inherently social, logistical, complex, and as a transaction of meanings and intentions. As a result, consider how different road users make sense of and make use of others behaviours. Moreover, this shared space infers social complexity(ies), for example, cooperative interactions between road users (e.g. giving right of way, etc.) as well as also competitive and conflictual (e.g. forceful and aggressive driving or movements, etc.). Author [70] quotes a driver who explains that they never indicated when driving in LA, as that would just be 'giving information away to the enemy'. As a result, human-automation transparency becomes an interesting topic to consider, as transparent road user intentions on congested roads might at times be hard to comprehend. Hence transparency and social may be parallel. Thus, this opens up discussions surrounding how transparent HAV might end up being exploited on the road by other road users, because humans may assume that the HAV will always stop for them to avoid collision, for example. This can be typical to the three laws of robotics by Isaac Asimov. Thus, 'risk compensation' [71] or the risk homeostasis theory is essential to consider in order to understand long-term MASI, as risk compensation may be a factor for both internal (in-group) as well as other external (out-group) road users who might take advantage of the cautiousness of the HAV. It is imperative to investigate automation effects (desirable and undesirable effects) and how they may influence and relate to psychological safety and inclusion.

By addressing socially sensitive road users' co-experiences with HAV, a range of social situations, and how the social dimensions comes to play in different future *contexts of use* (by in-groups) and *context of exposure* (to out-groups) scenarios, may aid manufacturers gain new insights as well as challenge perceived assumptions. This can be connected to HAVs broad point of entry into the real world, by digging deep into the topic of communicating intent and awareness as well as the transferability of solutions, and thus bringing social situations in the forefront of human factors and ergonomic (HFE) research. This discussion helps us understand complex social situations concerning the presence of HAV in socially shared spaces, for example human-automation interaction (HAI) negotiations and conflict resolutions or intentions. Thus, it becomes important to understand how humans come to understand their automated cars [14]. However, important to note that the differences in future vehicle systems in space sharing makes it challenging to study this types on interactions as the experiences are conflated by the reliability of the automation and the unpredictability of human factors.

Author [11] explored social interaction on the road, and based on how humans communicate through and interpret the movement of vehicles on public roads. For the entirety of this paper, we will build our framework based on an envisioned future scenario:

On a busy Saturday afternoon in a city, a family of four and their dog have just finished their dining at a restaurant. They start to walk towards the crosswalk of a four-way intersection on the main street. A HAV starts to inch forward and in the HAV is a couple of friends sitting in a conversation position with the front seats rotated inboard (communicating with a friend already at the airport via video conferencing). The family mother grabs his young child who is about to run after his dog when the positioned driver applies the brake as the system had experienced an error in quickly sensing the child and his dog, and the passenger waves the family on. As they cross, the cyclists raises their hands to indicate that they are turning and the family waves to thank those inside the HAV.

The assessment approach is that of a MASI scenario-centred approach. Scenarios like this one exemplify the significance of HFE research in analysing the intricacies of the future and understanding how to better prepare for it. We thus consider potential shortcomings and the neglected social aspect of shared experiences by overlooking a significant aspect of being human and what humans do when they are together and towards automation. Moreover, to overlook significant human related factors of social interactions in space sharing would be to overlook multi-dimensional interactions in complex traffic. Thus, we believe manufacturers in collaboration with HFE researchers must strive to decrease levels of uncertainty in traffic situations, if the aim is towards increasing trustability, acceptability, maintaining safety and efficiency in negotiated complex multimodal and multiparty road environment. A simultaneous understanding of future interaction patterns between internal in-group users (influenced by HAV interior) and external out-group VRUs (influenced by HAV exterior) will help guide interaction design strategies (IxDS) for efficient MASI well suited for future cities, and thus foster durability and long-term satisfactoriness.

2 The Interaction: A Context of Use and Context of Exposure

With more AVs entering human lives and the roads that humans move/commute, many interactions will include multiple humans interacting with the same automation. These group interactions may pose unique dynamics, challenges, and outcomes compared to one-on-one human interactions with automation. To design efficient HAVs and generate positive MASIs, it is critical to account for the conditions in which different road users will simultaneously (internally and externally) interact with the dynamic nature of the HAV when compared to one-on-one interactions. Therefore, we have concluded that interaction studies on one hand, have to some degree focused on the AVs' outside inter- action with road traffic and VRUs [32], and the other hand, focused on the AVs' inside interaction with the driver/passengers [4], separately. However, what is usually neglected is the intersection of these two worlds. Author [32] proposed useful definitions of *inter- action* as "a situation where the behaviour of at least two road users can be interpreted as being influenced by a space-sharing conflict between the road users." They further expanded on the definition, as "a situation where the behaviour of at least two road users can be interpreted as being influenced by the possibility that they are both intending to occupy the same region of space at the same time in the near future" [32]. We can argue that social interaction in its complexity is an ambiguous term or phenomenon, a con- cept that is surrounded by different variables and rhetoric that is continuously changing to meet the needs and nature of the on-road situation, road user types/characteristics, and automation maturity level. Additionally, we believe in a philosophical perspective that when something has reached a point at which it is unreservedly definable and only occupies a single meaning, then progress has stopped because the world is always in constant change. Such is the view we hold with respect to the concept [*interaction*] as it is exposed to new ways of life, social aspects and social dynamics of influence. Equally as precarious, are the ways AVs as their technology matures by becoming increasingly intelligent social partners.

To fully understand MASI with automated systems, we extrapolated different knowl- edge dispositions, from both human-robot interactions (HRI) and human-AV interactions (HAVI) fields. We believe these extractions are important to consider when aiming to employ IxDS that include multiple agents through space sharing, as focus has been placed on "dyadic interaction (i.e., one human and one robot) in controlled environ- ments that do not represent real-world conditions" [64]. Significant research efforts within HRI have been recently motivated by the idea that robots will interact around and with human groups [61]. HRI has often been considered within the CASA (computers as social actors) framework, which notes that "people perceive and react to computational artefacts in similar ways as they react to other humans" [59]. For instance, as robots become part of human teams, [56] feels it is important to consider how the actions of the robot may influence the team's social dynamics and interactions. This is because, autonomous robots are increasingly being "placed in contexts that require them to inter- act with groups of people rather than just a single individual", and as further argued by

[57], "interactions with groups of people introduce nuanced challenges for robots, since robots' actions influence both individual group members and complex group dynamics". Thus, [58] recognises inclusion as a crucial factor to successful and productive groups/teams, as [60] express these agents are gradually becoming prevalent behind the scenes and also as members of human teams. Because humans and robots have different skillsets, thus such teaming may be critical for advancing society, as they complement each other's expertise to enhance team outcomes [60]. As a result, "appropriate robot behaviour in public, open spaces cannot occur without the ability to automatically detect conversational groups of free-standing people" [62]. Author [63] argues that, it is important that robots understand human social interaction as they enter human spaces and begin to work proximately with people. Thus, these automated systems "must be able to perceive human social signals and understand how to adapt to groups" [63]. This is because in human environments, "robots are often tasked with interacting with groups of people", it is thus vital that they have efficient understanding of social groups [63].

Furthermore, within human-automated vehicle interaction (HAVI), the role of humans in the next generation of intelligent vehicles is important to consider, with focus on understanding, modelling, and predicting human agents in three domains where humans and HAV interact: inside the vehicle, around the vehicle, and inside surrounding vehicles [65]. In the past years, HAV have become among the most actively discussed researched topics, and by all definitions, [66] argues that "these systems, as a third robotic revolution, belong to the robotics field, despite the fact that people generally assign them to a specific domain of the automotive industry". There are countless engineering challenges based on replicating the complex task of human driving by automation, including environment perception, decision making, and control [66]. AV have the potential to cause profound shifts across a wide range of areas of human life, including economic structures, land use, lifestyles and personal well-being, thus "failing to anticipate a wider range of profound social implications may have serious negative consequences" [67]. As interaction between traffic participants is one underlying necessary condition of safe and efficient traffic, thus even through, it is not yet foreseeable when HAV will be on the market, "measures must be taken at an early stage to ensure a smooth mixed traffic" [68]. Author [68] stipulates that, it is essential to solve technical issues and also to ensure the social acceptance of AV [68].

In terms of VRUs, [55] found that moving behaviour of pedestrians is not only dependent on their own paths from the past, but also driven by social interactions with others nearby. Author [27] explored group effects on pedestrians in interaction with vehicles, and they found that most of pedestrians' have a tendency to look up and down the street to check for oncoming traffic while they approach the street curb. Given that HAV are expected to become an integral part of the everyday life, thus, understanding how humans are to socially interact with them is quite important for their future use and exposure, and the competent rule of conduct. Author [49] reasoned that, "in order for autonomous vehicles to become successfully integrated, the social interactions surrounding them need to be purposefully designed." In essence, the social aspects of HAV in strategic areas, for example, the vehicle as a social entity in traffic, co-experience within and outside the vehicle, and the human(s)-HAV relationship need to be addressed. Accordingly, context is descried as "any information that characterizes the situation of an entity" [21].

Thus, we need to pay attention to challenges in terms of *"interactors as context"* and targeting the design to ideal types of interactors and positions, thus fostering long-term IxDS. We should consider describing the *context of automation use* (inside-vehicle or in-groups) and *context of automation exposure* (outside-vehicle or out-groups) based on all *road users (interactors) as context* (simultaneously), the specification of different requirements, and the developments of design solutions suited for MASI.

2.1 Human-Machine Interface (HMI) and IxDS

During the early stage of HAV development, it is crucial to consider future interaction scenarios and challenges concerning the usability of systems that "exploit new forms of interfacing with the product" [47] towards goals, tasks, equipment, and environment [7]. In order to generate understanding of future HAI, we consider the evolution of automation in urban cities, and as a balancing phenomenon, situate the interaction to different social agents. Thus, behavioural changes, safety and risks issues need to be considered as these systems are integrated into driving routines [51]. Thus, understanding user needs and behaviour is essential for future in-vehicle interface and service design [16] as well as external-vehicle interface and design. Author [4] considers factors that influence interaction from an AV HMI's internal and external point of view. Thus, additional research on the interactors' interactive attributes within the baseline of design and function (of the internal interior and external exterior dHMI – dynamic HMI) may help pinpoint aspects that may be affected and better quantify the likely magnitude. As HMIs will most likely be designed with an artificial intelligence (AI) and augmented-reality (AR) dashboard in mind, the ultimate head-up display, especially like Apple car's approach to ambient cabin lighting, and an interior with "creviceless" surfaces, thus, interactors will be sharing HAV experiences with each other. An experience known as a merger of visual design DNA (Deoxyribonucleic acid). We thus use the term "HMI" loosely and in a broad sense due to the engineering investment that many developers have in mind, thus encompassing a variety of categorical experiences as well as imbedded interaction between different interactors (as co-experience) and the HAV might prove useful. In most cases, other humans indirectly become interactors, making the interaction complex and multifaceted with various interactive degrees and aspects, and further influenced by the possibilities of environment factors.

Based on envisioned IxDS, there is a presumed challenge for manufacturers to ensure that the basic design principles are achievable. This is because during group interactions with HAV, social aspects usually take a stance. A key challenge would be HAVs' ineffective interaction with other road users as the "demands of city driving require this; urban contexts are interaction rich" [52]. The goal is to ensure socially acceptable highly automated driving, and this means driving in which AVs (1) operate smoothly and in a manner appropriate to the specific interactional context when interacting with other road users, (2) behave neither too aggressively nor yield incessantly to other road users, neither impede the normal flow of traffic nor cause undue notice, (3) smoothly integrate into the flow of traffic and handle roadway interactions without disrupting other road users [52]. However, it should be noted that socially acceptable interactions would include other social aspects and factors due to the complexity of human nature. This is because of the increasing number of humans' inside-outside the vehicle, magnitude and variety by which they may interact with the system. Thus, the aim is that those individuals are conditionally aware of how the system works, and are not necessarily distracted, information overloaded or operationally confused by the system. Many studies have proposed that if a system is not designed to suit potential road users' expectations and diversified to embrace different user types, it may be regarded as annoying. Moreover, emphasis should be placed on the modality for system communication and position for messages.

As technical realisation of HAV draws closer, attention is being shifted from sheer feasibility to questions on how an acceptable interior configurations, driving style and comfort can be implemented due to the nature of future social seating arrangements. With future vehicles (e.g. Mercedes- Benz F 015, Volvo Cars 360c, Apple car codenamed "Project Titan", etc.), the seating positions will change, so how these changes will influence social interaction, comfort and experience is still unknown. There has been quite an interest in shuffles [29] as well as non-driving related activities (NDRAs) [23]. In order to lay a basis on how HAV should interact to ensure comfort and satisfaction. Thus, different people in the space sharing scene should be explored based on different variations of the context in order to identify comfortable social IxDS, behaviour traits, driving style and preferences of automated manoeuvres. As the slightest effect of lane changes, accelerations, motion, and user interfaces are advisable to be influential factors in comfort and social interaction syntheses for different users' experiences. The concept of offering car seats as a service instead of a product may become imperative [43]. Furthermore, examining the different users' experiences when it comes to comfortability, as it relates to comfort boundaries and comfort zones on motion, interaction or communication comfort with HMIs and their positioning, and seating positions [26, 34]. As well as satisfaction, acceptability, trustworthiness.

There is high anticipation for HAV to express social cues and rule competencies such as being able to communicate intentions and flexibly [40]. This is because there are social dynamics attached to vehicle use, however, the social relationship will mature once the vehicle gains increasing agency through automation – as HAV [49]. Author [40] regards movement patterns are a central method of communication within the context of road geometry, road activity, and culture. Their meaning communicates the intention of the HAV (jerky vehicle movements to communicate uncertainty) and humans (the use of gesture as movement to communicate intention to other road users), which influences traffic social interactions and scalable in MASI. A social relationship needs to be established and supported by communicating intentions in order to share collaborative interactions within road traffic [19]. To support smooth streams of traffic flow, current drivers explicitly have to communicate with other road users by multiple means: movement (gestures, posture, waving), eye contact, and by using the vehicle itself (slowing down, flashing the headlights, etc.) [39, 40]. Likewise, other road users interpret these signs or signals as aspects of the human drivers' intentions, cognizance and awareness, such as the eye contact established when crossing the road between driver and pedestrians or cyclists [40, 50]. However, "with the increasing level of automation in vehicles, drivers will no longer be able to represent the vehicle's actions, and will instead be engaging in tasks such as reading, socialising or sleeping", thus the HAV needs to cooperate with others, and act as a social entity in traffic without relying on human driver-centric communication cues [49]. It is important that the vehicle clearly conveys its awareness and intentions through efficient negotiation practises and cues [52]. The absence of clear indications of the vehicle's intent and lacking ability to interpret and react to social norms in traffic may be met with mistrust and frustration [11].

Although there is a celebrated shrift towards an autonomously motorised world, there exists a neglected focus in exploring the learning patterns in the MASI process. The human experiences and learning patterns are considered important when designing for interaction success, thus we pursue and extend focus on learning to go beyond the one-on-one perspective, but to also take account of MASI perspectives, and as a result, how people learn in groups. This begs us to question who are we designing these HAV for, and do we even know their social dynamic way of mobilised life and interactive routines when it comes to travelling. In doing so, offers an important question – how to educate manufacturers to make fruitful decisions, which are fittingly and inclusive imperative decisions for user satisfaction. Thus, focus on interactions with primarily the driver as opposed to all passengers has to be questioned [37], shared services for HAV as they emerge and evolve as a prospect or opportunity [18], and the co-experience as it becomes a significant aspect of vehicle use [3]. Most studies tend to neglect the social learning aspects, as well as exploring the vehicle as a social entity that continuously learns, and thus how this influences the whole on-road interaction process in shared spaces. For example, the influence of cultures [52], lack of inclusivity – in terms of personalities, emotions, intelligence, age, gender which are based on different user/passenger types, or long-term automation effects.

2.2 From Mental Model to Mental Models

The evolution of mental models in relation to initial information during automated driving has become a trendy topic in HAI [9] and in Human-Computer Interaction [6]. In the context of system design and usability, Norman [20] refer to mental models as: "In interacting with the environment, with others, and with the artefacts of technology, people form internal, mental models of themselves and of the things with which they are interacting. These models provide predictive and explanatory power for understanding the interaction." We presume that these formulated mental models may be different, as different people experiences the same things differently. The system's usability seems to be highly linked to the "quality of the matching of the user's mental model of a system and the system functionality" [20]. In Human-Human Interactions, each individual has a mental model of the other person or persons, whose neurological representation is, for example, described in the compelling concept of mirror cells. Applying this thought process to MASI space sharing; each human road user within the interaction loop or space builds up a mental model, which is continuously changing based on various factors, e.g. emotions, personality, their psychology at a particular moment, and environment factors (Fig. 2).

However, it is important to consider whether the HAV has a constructed mental model of the interaction with multiple people, both internally and externally. Author [20] explains that "this information can be made available in an explicit way for example by user profiles or in an implicit way by the computer itself, analysing the users past behaviour." For example, through the use of social learning and machine learning. Though we should note that to build up a "mental" model of both internal and externals

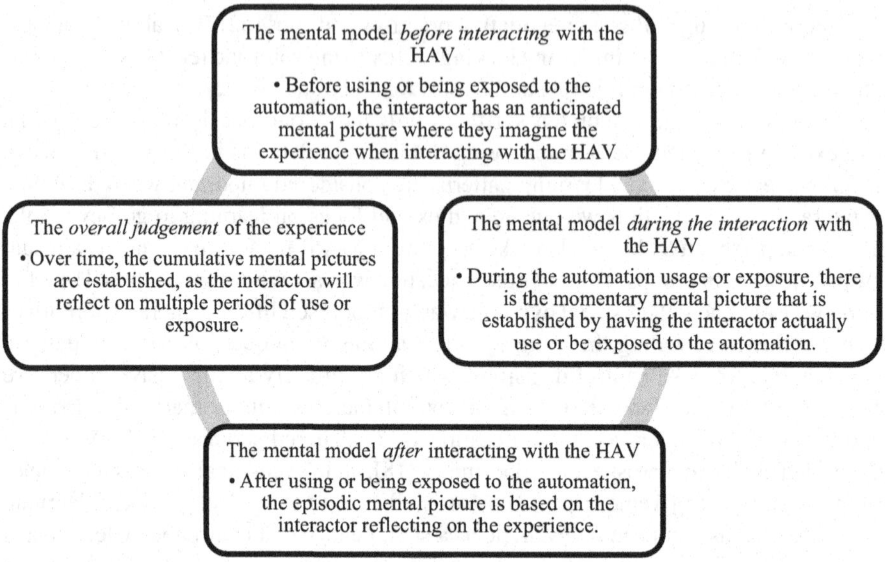

Fig. 2. Models of automation *use* and *exposure*

might be quite difficult as humans are complex beings and the social nature of their interactions changes based on a variety of factors. Humans in their complexity, especially regarding emergent effects that are much more difficult to model than deterministic effects may influence the interaction process.

A key challenge here is to develop, refine and communicate a common and clear "picture", a shared mental model of MASI early enough in the interaction design process. Norman [20] defines the terms "Gulf of Execution" and "Gulf of Evaluation" and illustrates that the "fitting of the mental representation of the user and the physical components and functionality of a system is essential for good usability." In addition, the term "Gulf of Execution" refers to how well a "system provides actions that correspond with the intention of a person", whereas the term "Gulf of Evaluation" emphases on feedback issues) [20]. Author [20] claimed that, "in order to gain and maintain situation awareness, there has to be a sufficient representation, a mental model of the automation inside the operator", thus emphasis is on human experience with the system [54], their level of trust, expectations and mental model of system capabilities [45]. An important mediator shaping the trust/acceptance/mental models etc. of road users is the nature of the dHMI, the timing and type of information it provides, transparency and reliability, accuracy and value of the messages. Automation also contributes to a lack of, or incorrect, mental representation of the automated system's capabilities for humans [42], which may lead to human exploitation [35]. If designed well, and with the different types of road users in mind, the dHMIs should mitigate some of the negative effects, ensuring mutual comprehension between HAV and different road users. As [51] notes that humans will act based on their mental model of system performance, their trust that the system will behave reliably, and their sureness that their understanding and situation awareness is accurate. Gugerty [51] concisely defines situation awareness (SA) in the context of experience as "the updated, meaningful knowledge of an unpredictably-changing, multi-faceted situation that operators use to guide choice and action when engaged in real-time multitasking." Author [17] distinguished three levels of SA: perception of elements in the environment (1), comprehension of the current situation (2), and projection of future status (3). SA means "knowing what is going on around you" [51]. The idea to externally represent the vehicle's SA by mirroring its knowledge and thereby instilling a sense of safety to the surrounding road users is important [49].

When it comes to road users, we can argue that people learn by observing others and through their thought process of those observations, with the environment, experience, and cognition acting as key factors that influence behaviour and attitude changes in a reciprocal triadic relationship. We believe that each use and exposure behaviour that is observed has the potential of changing a road user's way of thinking (mental model), as they repeatedly use or are exposed to automation. Thus, it slowly becomes their routine co-experience, and part of their daily life, which then influences how they cognitively see and experience it through prolonged interaction. For example, secondary users may mirror either primary users or the other way around; and external road users may mirror each other's behaviours. When designing experiences with a HAV for primary users, you would thus also like to reach out to the needs of their social networks, as the experience will need to suit the needs of many. Thus, keeping these priorities in mind: functionality, transparency, safety, comfortability, learnability and usability. Human factors experts may also need to keep in mind the needs and requirements of different internals, balancing them with the needs of externals. Also consider the likely occurrence of impending conditions, where an automation reaches the limits of its Operational Design Domain (ODD) [28].

2.3 Negotiating the Co-experience in Contextualised Interactions

How AVs come to be socially experienced is not reducible to the material design [8] alone, but encompasses a variety of factors. Understanding the embodied experiences of HAVs in real world context is vital for the development of impactful machines, and acceptance of AVs may likely be contingent on the systems being able to offer a great user experience. Author [46] highlights traveling's affective and emotional dimensions in generating attachments and meanings, as manufacturers may need to engineer human experiences into the vehicle's design [38]. The attitude toward technology (ATT) use, and affective satisfaction (AS) which indicates "the extent of emotional/sentimental experience that an individual perceives while using a technology" are noted [15]. Usually what motivates humans to start an action might change while they are performing that action, as human motivation is inherently dynamic [1], therefore, humans' long-term interactions with automation gives rise to more transitional experiential textures, for example, exploration of repetitious social factors. The social experience can be described as dynamic, time dependant, and beyond the instrumental. The aim is to understand "the role of affect as an antecedent, a consequence and a mediator of technology" [5], thus explore the effects of HAV driving [52] with focus placed on the experiential and existential dimensions. Dynamics of future experiences based on author's [8] emphasis on the effect of transforming experiences informs us about strategic travel planning and scheduling change in a world of HAVs, time spent in complex traffic, the sensory/physical dimensions of being on the move, novel digital communications, and the experience of co-presence while on the move. HAVs might be seen as a mode of private or professional 'dwelling space' and thus domesticated, as manufactures aim to transform vehicles into mobile entertainment/communication pods, such as infer social interaction possibilities, as interior is reconfigured to increase flexibility for leisure, work, and related social activities.

As user experience focuses on positive emotions and emotional outcomes such as joy, fun and pride [5], the existing proposals of 'hybrid spaces' and work on 'connected presence' urges us to consider HAVs as a kind of multifaceted mobile system that encompasses communication modalities in and of themselves. The concept of 'miniaturised mobilities' [72] refers to how communications technologies used while driving can construct novel relations, comprising multiple coordination processes, (re)negotiation and synchronisation with others. This influences a transition from prompt experience to negotiated experience. Thus, experience has been perceived as the "next new business in addition to selling products and services" [2]. Experts have expressed different interpretations and perspectives of what the user experience truly is [30] through dedicated time and effort in describing and defining experience and the elements that influence that experience [3]. Author [30] propositioned that user experience "focuses on interaction between a person and something that has a user interface". The ISO 9241–11:2018 defined it as "a user's perceptions and responses that result from the use and/or anticipated use of a system product or service". The main concentration is on how the persons using the system evaluates it [21]. However way is it defined, we can all agree that *experiences can be different, personal and subjective*, and what remain to be designed are the "contexts for experience" based on the different road users involved. As much as experiences are subjective, we do believe that some experiences come to life in shared spaces. Author [2] mentioned that "the concept of user experience needs to be expanded to encompass not only the individual side of experience, but also to take into account the *social side.*"

Different road users may express different expectations based on their positions on the interaction spectrum or axis, thus HAVs must be able to assess and understand both the internal situation inside and external environment outside, as a result have a well-educated automation software and be quite intuitive in their social interactive manners, including the intricacies of in-group interactions. Author [44] notes that group life provides a basis by which individuals fit into society and through which social structures shape them, and that the group establishes and validates meanings that constitute the propriety of action within the wider social system. Therefore, consideration has been placed on complex patterns of social interaction, not because humans share any vague values regarding the broad organization of society, but due to idea that "their relations are pervaded by less ethereal feelings like trust," and that they get something out of the interactions [44]. Experiencing is regarded as a constructive activity, and thus co-experience is the experience, which is "created in social interaction, and is the seamless blend of user experience of products and social interaction" and further, the experience, "while essentially created by the users, would not be the same or even possible without the presence of the product and the possibilities for experience that it provides" [2].

Essentially, co-experience is seen within the relationship context of multi-agent interactions, constructed based on a basis of space sharing. While user experiences concerns a singular human, multi-agent co-experience are a combination of multiple road users. The diagram (Fig. 3) helps us understand human life(s) with automation and illustrates the interactive faculties of shared experiences: the positioned driver experiences, passengers' experiences, and vulnerable road users' experiences with HAV. This fosters consideration on what people do in shared spaces with each other and why, in comparison to what they do when they use things alone. Neglecting the social aspect of group experiences with HAV would be to overlook an important facet of being human, and what humans do when they are space sharing.

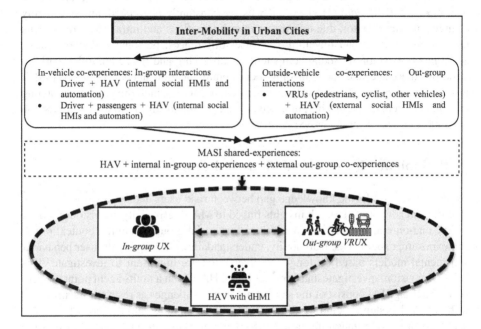

Fig. 3. Inter-mobility and intersection of in-group co-experiences

2.4 'More than One – Less than Many'

Due to technological advancements, more aspects of human life can be assisted or automated by technical artefacts [20], thus introducing unique demands on IxDS for the road ahead [36]. AVs are generally used to provide mobility, monitoring and maintaining safety. Although, AVs are presented to cater for safety and counter human error when driving, they have also been identified to cater for leisure and social activities. Thus, a single AV can cater for many use cases under the classification of an automated machine. This considers what HAV mean to people and how that meaning may evolve longitudinally. For example, a HAV with different automated systems working to maintain different means, for instance: automated driving (for systems such as vehicle safety control), automated comfort (for systems equipped for comfortable seating positions), automated pleasure (for systems such as in-vehicle infotainments), etc. HAVs acting as a conduit for socialising, supporting social networks to interact with others remotely (through video conference while on the move) or adjacent communication in the vehicle. HAV presenting itself as a social entity, providing entertainment scenarios that reduce the effect of fatigue or provide companionship to reduce boredom. This means they have a multidimensional construct, as an HAV introduced in one scenery as aiming to deliver a service may also be introduced in another context as delivering a personal need, therefore making them *'multi-stable'* artefacts that are capable of producing multifaceted experiences. Thus, philosophically speaking, a HAV can be one and many things, as well as humans can be one and many interactors as either internals or externals – *more than one, less than many*. HAI experiences are constantly negotiated, and not merely a single and static factor, due to cross or inter-interactions and intra-interactions. This requires recognising and unveiling road user differences, personalising experiences, acquiring and exhibiting social competencies, observing and interpreting the world in terms of experience, and understanding social communication and norms models [48]. It is important to consider socially dynamic in-group contexts, including dynamics among the human agents, among the automated systems, among the HIMs, and interaction dynamics, through framing MASI *co-experiences*.

3 Preliminary Recommendations and Conclusion

This discussion refills the knowledge gap between road users and automations in space sharing, and addresses research insights linked to MASI, especially as this differs from dyadic one-on-one interactions. We assume that social group dynamics, context of use and exposure, experiences, learnability, understandability, transparency, user behaviour and mental models based on long-term interaction are important to investigate. This helps to envision, investigate and consider future HAV from a multi-agent point of view. As researching HAI consist of the same if not more challenges as researching any novel technological system, including the difficulties of imagining simultaneous future use and exposure, while imagining how the automation should fit into an already existing and highly interactive stream of traffic where safety is imperative. This is because, as automation matures, the relationship between the vehicle, humans inside and those outside radically changes. Thus, we believe employing human factors research approaches to light at early stages of HAV development may be influential, as descriptions of potential future social interactions may bring the discussion of what a HAV really is or ought to be in terms of social interaction by placing the HAV's new agency into focus. In addition, highlight assumptions concerning what it is that humans are interacting with when the intelligence of the HAV matures, the HAV itself as a social entity rather than a piece of machinery, whether an intelligent computer is driving the HAV (computerised vehicle), or a number of computers controlling different parts of the HAV. Grounded on reflections, research methods should provide the ability to experience possible futures states with both analysis and synthesis elements. Thus proposing methods to a varying degree able to explore possible futures, and bring future situations to life in the exploration and reflection of MASI. For example, using Wizard of OZ (WoOz) and mixed reality may possibly manage to put participants in the state of future users by their role as road users. In essence, AR [22] and mixed reality [31] research approaches may be able to surface underlying assumptions and alternative interpretations by providing insight into what a potential future could be and bring varied perspectives to the forefront. Participants may acquire an understanding for the social interplay and negotiation of situations, and thus mapping out the different perspectives, as found in previous research [10]. Dimensions of how the physical environment would affect the social situation may become evident as well as engaging in making the problems tangible in representations. Human factors approaches that play an important role for bringing concreteness into the exploration and capturing the dynamics and the tacit aspects of the IxDS as well as provide a space for researchers to improvise and create a common focus on the future are important. This is because one crucial feature that is present is contextualisation, signifying the importance of constructing immersed experiences on MASI in order to be able to design the interactions with it, i.e. simulating situations that can probe into the future. Further approaches that include physical artefacts that may be used to help participants enter different roles and to concretise their MASI experiences. The use of physical objects to relate to and to modify has been exemplified in foremost participatory approaches as useful for understanding use and users [10]. Contextualisation may trigger a higher degree of emotional awareness and presence [13]. However, the experience of both user groups might be hampered by how the approach's "HAV" communicates and gives feedback through its channels, as seemingly unreal.

HAVs may have to negotiate their presence and fit a world designed for human beings by human beings, thus surpass stereotypical role behaviours and dynamically deliver roles that suit the humans' environments in order to not risk the possibility of becoming objects decorated on shelves, without use tenets. Thus, HAVs have to be "designed to fit into an existing social context, at the same time as they will trigger shifts and new social aspects that are relevant to design for will emerge" [49]. A general understanding of how humans interact and communicate with each other [32] is significant. As, facilitated by the evolution of science, technology and society, and pulled by human phenomenological demands, when dealing with experiences, it is important to not only address the usefulness and ease of use, but also to interrogate the interaction in terms of the interpersonal or sociality of the HAV. This is because humans may authenticate interaction that is more relaxed, social and conversational by being more expressive [49]. We argue that the vehicle that humans once knew takes a new identity and a new shape, it becomes an "anthropoid machine", which means that the HAV elicits the same level (if not more) of human reasoning and intelligence during social interaction. Thus, we need to infer appropriate metaphors for road users' social contract with technology, as this has the potential for enormous payoff in terms of establishing cooperative user-friendly systems [12]. We need to keenly explore and probe the future directions of socialising systems and MASI co-experience.

Scalability is a critical factor; while identifying and displaying a handful of traffic flow within the limited display space is possible, unambiguous communication of a multitude of VRUs within the HAV's viewing trajectory may pose interesting challenge [49]. Author [51] noted that "it is fair to say that the theoretical landscape is replete with concepts and ideas, but tying so many pieces together into a coherent picture has become a considerable challenge." As [49] puts it, we need approaches that facilitate "flexible idea exploration, but in a contextualised and concrete manner through tangible objects and enactment to stage future use situations." As a result, we highly believe that long-term assessment can prove useful. Scholars are encouraged to envision and visualise new futures and new normalities, and thus scrutinise issues that do not yet exist. We need approaches that explore the imaginable future between road users and HAVs. In conclusion, we provided strong arguments in support of this kind of research and a discussion surrounding interactions with HAV from inside the vehicle cabin, around the vehicle, and in surrounding vehicles.

References

1. Alam, M.D., Porras, J.: Architecting and designing sustainable smart city services in a living lab environment. Technologies **2018**(6), 99 (2018). https://doi.org/10.3390/technologies6040099
2. Battarbee, K.: Defining co-experience. In: Proceedings of DPPI 2003. ACM, New York (2003). https://doi.org/10.1145/782896.782923
3. Battarbee, K., Koskinen, I.: Co-experience: user experience as interaction. CoDesign **1**(1), 5–18 (2005). https://doi.org/10.1080/15710880412331289917
4. Bengler, K., Rettenmaier, M., Fritz, N., Feierle, A.: From HMI to HMIs: towards an HMI framework for automated driving. Information **11**, 61 (2020)
5. Bernhaupt, R., Manciet, F., Pirker, M.: User experience as a parameter to enhance automation acceptance: lessons from automating articulatory tasks. In: 5th International Conference on Application and Theory of Automation in Command and Control Systems (ATACCS 2015) (2015). https://doi.org/10.1145/2899361.2899376
6. Bernsen, N.O.: Mental models in human-computer interaction (2010). https://doi.org/10.17226/790
7. Bevan, N., Carter, J., Earthy, J., Geis, T., Harker, S.: New ISO standards for usability, usability reports and usability measures. In: Kurosu, M. (ed.) HCI 2016. LNCS, vol. 9731, pp. 268–278. Springer, Cham (2016). https://doi.org/10.1007/978-3-319-39510-4_25
8. Bissell, D., Birtchnell, T., Elliott, A., Hsu, E.L.: Autonomous automobilities: the social impacts of driverless vehicles. Curr. Sociol. **68**(1), 116–134 (2020). https://doi.org/10.1177/0011392118816743
9. Blömacher, K., Nöcker, G., Huff, M.: The evolution of mental models in relation to initial information while driving automated. Transp. Res. F Traffic Psychol. Behav. **68**, 198–217 (2020)
10. Broberg, O., Andersen, V., Seim, R.: Participatory ergonomics in design processes: the role of boundary objects. Appl. Ergon. **42**(3), 464–472 (2011). https://doi.org/10.1016/j.apergo.2010.09.006
11. Brown, B., Laurier, E.: The trouble with autopilots: assisted and autonomous driving on the social road. In: Proceedings of the 2017 CHI Conference on Human Factors in Computing Systems, pp. 416–429. ACM (2017). https://doi.org/10.1145/3025453.3025462
12. Bruemmer, D.J., Gertman, D.I., Nielsen, C.W.: Metaphors to drive by: exploring new ways to guide human-robot interaction. Open Cybern. Syst. J. **1**, 5–12 (2007). https://benthamopen.com/contents/pdf/TOCSJ/TOCSJ-1-5.pdf
13. Buchenau, M., Fulton-Suri, J.: Experience prototyping. In: Proceedings of the 3rd Conference on Designing Interactive Systems: Processes, Practices, Methods, and Techniques, pp. 424–433. ACM (2000)

14. Carsten, O., Martens, M.H.: How can humans understand their automated cars? HMI principles, problems and solutions. Cogn. Technol. Work **21**(1), 3–20 (2018). https://doi.org/10.1007/s10111-018-0484-0

15. Cho, Y., Park, J., Park, S., Jung, E.S.: Technology acceptance modeling based on user experience for autonomous vehicles. J. Ergon. Soc. Korea **36**(2), 87–108 (2017). https://doi.org/10.5143/JESK.2017.36.2.87

16. Detjen, H., Pfleging, B., Schneegass, S.: A wizard of Oz field study to understand non-driving-related activities, trust, and acceptance of automated vehicles. In: 12th International Conference on Automotive User Interfaces and Interactive Vehicular Applications (AutomotiveUI 2020). ACM (2020). https://doi.org/10.1145/3409120.3410662

17. Endsley, M.R.: Toward a theory of situation awareness in dynamic systems. Hum. Factors J. Hum. Factors Ergon. Soc. **37**(1), 32–64 (1995). https://doi.org/10.1518/001872095779049543

18. Fagnant, D.J., Kockelman, K.M.: The travel and environmental implications of shared autonomous vehicles, using agent-based model scenarios. Transp. Res. Part C Emerg. Technol. **40**, 1–13 (2014). https://doi.org/10.1016/j.trc.2013.12.001

19. Flemisch, F., Heesen, M., Hesse, T., Kelsch, J., Schieben, A., Beller, J.: Towards a dynamic balance between humans and automation: authority, ability, responsibility and control in shared and cooperative control situations. Cogn. Technol. Work **14**(1), 3–18 (2012). https://doi.org/10.1007/s10111-011-0191-6. https://link.springer.com/content/pdf/10.1007/s10111-011-0191-6.pdf

20. Flemisch, F., Kelsch, J., Löper, C., Schieben, A., Schindler, J., Heesen, M.: Cooperative Control and Active Interfaces for Vehicle Assistance and Automation (2008). https://elib.dlr.de/57618/1/FISITA2008_DLR_FlemischEtAl_CooperativeControl.pdf

21. Frison, A.-K., Wintersberger, P., Liu, T., Riener, A.: Why do you like to drive automated?: a context-dependent analysis of highly automated driving to elaborate requirements for intelligent user interfaces. In: 24th International Conference on Intelligent User Interfaces (IUI 2019) (2019). https://doi.org/10.1145/3301275.3302331

22. Hartmann, M., Viehweger, M., Stolz, M., Watzenig, D., Spitzer, M., Desmet, W.: "Pedestrian in the Loop": an approach using augmented reality (No. 2018-01-1053). SAE Technical Paper (2018)

23. Hecht, T., Sievers, M., Bengler, K.: Investigating user needs for trip planning with limited availability of automated driving functions. In: Stephanidis, C., Antona, M. (eds.) HCII 2020. CCIS, vol. 1226, pp. 359–366. Springer, Cham (2020). https://doi.org/10.1007/978-3-030-50732-9_48

24. HERE: Consumer Acceptance of Autonomous Vehicles: 3 Key Insights for the Automotive Industry (2017). © 2017 HERE | here.com

25. ISO 9241-11:2018. Ergonomics of human-system interaction — Part 11: Usability: Definitions and concepts. International Organization for Standardization

26. Jorlöv, S., Bohman, K., Larsson, A.: seating positions and activities in highly automated cars – a qualitative study of future automated driving scenarios. In: IRCOBI Conference 2017 (2017). http://www.ircobi.org/wordpress/downloads/irc17/pdf-files/11.pdf

27. Kalb, L., Bengler, K.: The importance of the approach towards the curb before pedestrians cross streets. In: Black, N.L., Neumann, W.P., Noy, I. (eds.) IEA 2021. LNNS, vol. 221, pp. 674–681. Springer, Cham (2021). https://doi.org/10.1007/978-3-030-74608-7_82

28. Koopman, P., Fratrik, F.: How many operational design domains, objects, and events? In: SafeAI@ AAAI, 4 (2019)

29. Köhler, A.L., et al.: How will we travel autonomously? User needs for interior concepts and requirements towards occupant safety. In: 28th Aachen Colloquium Automobile and Engine Technology (2019). www.aachener-kolloquium.de/en

30. Law, E.L.-C., Roto, V., Hassenzahl, M., et al.: Understanding, scoping and defining user experience: a survey approach. In: Proceedings of CHI 2009. ACM, New York (2009)
31. Mann, S., Furness, T., Yuan, Y., Iorio, J., Wang, Z.: All reality: Virtual, augmented, mixed (x), mediated (x, y), and multimediated reality. arXiv preprint arXiv:1804.08386 (2018)
32. Markkula, G., et al.: Defining interactions: a conceptual framework for understanding interactive behaviour in human and automated road traffic. Theor. Issues Ergon. Sci. (TTIE) (2020). https://doi.org/10.1080/1463922X.2020.1736686
33. Milgram, P., Colquhoun, H.: A taxonomy of real and virtual world display integration. In: Mixed Reality: Merging Real and Virtual Worlds, vol. 1, pp. 1–26 (1999)
34. Östling, M., Larsson, A.: Occupant activities and sitting positions in automated vehicles in China and Sweden. In: Proceedings of 26th International Technical Conference on the Enhanced Safety of Vehicles (ESV), Eindhoven, Netherlands. Paper Number 19-0083 (2019). https://www-esv.nhtsa.dot.gov/Proceedings/26/26ESV-000083.pdf
35. Parasuraman, R., Riley, V.: Humans and automation: use, misuse, disuse, abuse. Hum. Factors 39(2), 230–253 (1997). https://doi.org/10.1518/001872097778543886
36. Pettersson, I., Ju, W.: Design techniques for exploring automotive interaction in the drive towards automation. In: Proceedings of the 2017 Conference on Designing Interactive Systems, pp. 147–160. ACM (2017). https://doi.org/10.1145/3064663.3064666
37. Pettersson, I., Karlsson, M.: Setting the stage for self-driving cars: exploration of future autonomous driving experiences. IET Intell. Transp. Syst. J. 9(7), 694–701 (2015)
38. Thrift, N.: Driving in the city. Theory Cult. Soc. 21(4–5), 41–59 (2004)
39. Rakotonirainy, A., Schroeter, R., Soro, A.: Three social car visions to improve driver behaviour. Pervasive Mob. Comput. 14, 147–160 (2014). https://doi.org/10.1016/j.pmcj.2014.06.004
40. Risto, M., Emmenegger, C., Vinkhuyzen, E., Cefkin, M., Hollan, J.: Human-vehicle interfaces: the power of vehicle movement gestures in human road user coordination. In: Proceedings of the Ninth International Driving Symposium on Human Factors in Driver Assessment, Training and Vehicle Design, Manchester Village, Vermont. Iowa City, 26–29 June 2017, pp. 186–192 (2017). https://doi.org/10.17077/drivingassessment.1633
41. SAE International: J3016_202104 Taxonomy and Definitions for Terms Related to Driving Automation Systems for On-Road Motor Vehicles; J3016; SAE Standard J3016_202104, pp. 1–41. SAE International, USA (2021)
42. Saffarian, M., de Winter, J.C.F., Happee, R.: Automated driving: human-factors issues and design solutions. Proc. Hum. Factors Ergon. Soc. Annu. Meet. 56(1), 2296–2300 (2012). https://doi.org/10.1177/1071181312561483
43. Schoenberger, R.: Automotive companies look to the skies for clues on autonomous designs. Today's Motor Vehicles (2018). https://www.todaysmotorvehicles.com/article/best-of-2018-autonomous-designs-aerospace-122618/
44. Serpa, S., Ferreira, C.M.: Micro, meso and macro levels of social analysis. Int. J. Soc. Sci. Stud. 7(3) (2019). https://doi.org/10.11114/ijsss.v7i3.4223
45. Seppelt, B., Victor, T.: Driver's mental model of vehicle automation. In: Handbook of Human Factors for Automated, Connected, and Intelligent Vehicles, pp. 55–66 (2020)
46. Sheller, M.: Automotive emotions: feeling the car. Theory Cult. Soc. 21(4–5), 221–242 (2004)
47. Simões-Marques, M., Nunes, I.L.: Usability of Interfaces. Ergonomics – A Systems Approach. Source: InTech (2012)
48. Steinfeld, A., et al.: Common metrics for human-robot interaction. In: HRI 2006, Salt Lake City, Utah, USA. Association for Computing Machinery (2006)
49. Strömberg, H., et al.: Designing for social experiences with and within autonomous vehicles – exploring methodological directions. Des. Sci. 4, E13 (2018). https://doi.org/10.1017/dsj.2018.9

50. Sucha, M.: Road users strategies and communication: driver-pedestrian interaction. In: Transport Research Arena 2014 Proceedings. Elsevier Transportation Research Procedia (2014). https://www.ictct.net/wp-content/uploads/26-Maribor-2013/26-Sucha-Full-paper-2.pdf

51. Sullivan, J.M., Flannagan, M.J., Pradhan, A.K., Bao, S.: Literature review of behavioral adaptation to advanced driver assistance systems. In: AAA Foundation for Traffic Safety (2016)

52. Vinkhuyzen, E., Cefkin, M.: Developing socially acceptable autonomous vehicles. In: Ethnographic Praxis in Industry Conference Proceedings, vol. 2016, no. 1, pp. 522–534 (2016). https://anthrosource.onlinelibrary.wiley.com/doi/pdf/10.1111/1559-8918.2016.01108

53. Winner, H., Wachenfeld, W.: Effects of autonomous driving on the vehicle concept. In: Maurer, M., Gerdes, J.C., Lenz, B., Winner, H. (eds.) Autonomous Driving, pp. 255–275. Springer, Heidelberg (2016). https://doi.org/10.1007/978-3-662-48847-8_13

54. Yang, X.J., Unhelkar, V.V., Li, K., Shah, J.A.: Evaluating effects of user experience and system transparency on trust in automation. In: 2017 12th ACM/IEEE International Conference on Human-Robot Interaction (HRI), pp. 408–416. IEEE (2017)

55. Zhang, C., Berger, C., Dozza, M.: Social-IWSTCNN: a social interaction-weighted spatio-temporal convolutional neural network for pedestrian trajectory prediction in urban traffic scenarios (2021). https://arxiv.org/abs/2105.12436

56. Sebo, S., Dong, L.L., Chang, N., Lewkowicz, M., Schutzman, M., Scassellati, B.: The influence of robot verbal support on human team members: encouraging outgroup contributions and suppressing ingroup supportive behavior. Front. Psychol. **11**, 3584 (2020)

57. Sebo, S., Stoll, B., Scassellati, B., Jung, M.F.: Robots in groups and teams: a literature review. In: Proceedings of the ACM on Human-Computer Interaction, vol. 4, no. CSCW2, pp. 1–36 (2020)

58. Strohkorb Sebo, S., Dong, L.L., Chang, N., Scassellati, B.: Strategies for the inclusion of human members within human-robot teams. In: Proceedings of the 2020 ACM/IEEE International Conference on Human-Robot Interaction, pp. 309–317 (2020)

59. Smith, E.R., Šabanović, S., Fraune, M.R.: Human-robot Interaction Through the Lens of Social Psychological Theories of Intergroup Behavior. V1 (2) (2021). https://doi.org/10.1037/tmb0000002

60. Fraune, M.R.: Our robots, our team: robot anthropomorphism moderates group effects in human–robot teams. Front. Psychol. **11** (2020)

61. Vázquez, M., Carter, E.J., McDorman, B., Forlizzi, J., Steinfeld, A., Hudson, S.E.: Towards robot autonomy in group conversations: understanding the effects of body orientation and gaze. In: 2017 12th ACM/IEEE International Conference on Human-Robot Interaction, pp. 42–52. IEEE (2017)

62. Vázquez, M., Steinfeld, A., Hudson, S.E.: Parallel detection of conversational groups of free-standing people and tracking of their lower-body orientation. In: 2015 IEEE/RSJ International Conference on Intelligent Robots and Systems (IROS), pp. 3010–3017 (2015)

63. Taylor, A., Riek, L.D.: Robot perception of human groups in the real world: state of the art. In: 2016 AAAI Fall Symposium Series. 2016. The 2016 AAAI Fall Symposium Series: Artificial Intelligence for Human-Robot Interaction Technical Report FS-16-01 (2016)

64. Taylor, A., Chan, D.M., Riek, L.D.: Robot-centric perception of human groups. Trans. Hum. Robot Interact. **9**(3) (2020). https://doi.org/10.1145/3375798

65. Ohn-Bar, E., Trivedi, M.M.: Looking at humans in the age of self-driving and highly automated vehicles. IEEE Trans. Intell. Veh. **1**(1), 90–104 (2016). https://doi.org/10.1109/TIV.2016.2571067

66. Takács, Á., Rudas, I., Bösl, D., Haidegger, T.: Highly automated vehicles and self-driving cars [industry tutorial]. IEEE Robot. Autom. Mag. **25**(4), 106–112 (2018). https://doi.org/10.1109/MRA.2018.2874301

67. Cohen, T., et al.: A constructive role for social science in the development of automated vehicles. Transp. Res. Interdisc. Perspect. **6**, 100133 (2020)

68. Fuest, T., Sorokin, L., Bellem, H., Bengler, K.: Taxonomy of traffic situations for the interaction between automated vehicles and human road users. In: Stanton, N.A. (ed.) AHFE 2017. AISC, vol. 597, pp. 708–719. Springer, Cham (2018). https://doi.org/10.1007/978-3-319-60441-1_68

69. Dourish, P.: Accounting for system behavior: representation, reflection, and resourceful. In: Computers and Design in Context, Cambridge, MA, USA, pp. 145–170 (1997)

70. Katz, J.: How Emotions Work. University of Chicago Press, Chicago (1999)

71. Evans, W.N., Graham, J.D.: Risk reduction or risk compensation? The case of mandatory safety-belt use laws. J. Risk Uncertain. **4**(1), 61–73 (1991)

72. Elliott, A., Urry, J.: Mobile Lives. Routledge, London (2010)

Investigating End-User Acceptance of Last-Mile Delivery by Autonomous Vehicles in the United States

Antonios Saravanos[(✉)] [iD], Olivia Verni, Ian Moore, Aboubacar Sall, Jen Arriaza, Sabrina Jivani, Audrey Bennett, Siqi Li, Dongnanzi Zheng, and Stavros Zervoudakis

New York University, New York, NY, USA

{saravanos,orv209,inm220,as15872,jen.arriaza,sj2903,aab883,
s17137,dz40,zervoudakis}@nyu.edu

Abstract. This paper investigates the end-user acceptance of last-mile delivery carried out by autonomous vehicles within the United States. A total of 296 participants were presented with information on this technology and then asked to complete a questionnaire on their perceptions to gauge their behavioral intention concerning acceptance. Structural equation modeling of the partial least squares flavor (PLS-SEM) was employed to analyze the collected data. The results indicated that the perceived usefulness of the technology played the greatest role in end-user acceptance decisions, followed by the influence of others, and then the enjoyment received by interacting with the technology. Furthermore, the perception of risk associated with using autonomous delivery vehicles for last-mile delivery led to a decrease in acceptance. However, most participants did not perceive the use of this technology to be risky. The paper concludes by summarizing the implications our findings have on the respective stakeholders, and proposing the next steps in this area of research.

Keywords: Technology adoption · End-user acceptance · Last-mile delivery · Autonomous delivery vehicles · Autonomous delivery robots

1 Introduction

In this work, we investigate the end-user acceptance of last-mile delivery carried out by autonomous delivery vehicles (ADVs), also known as autonomous delivery robots (ADRs), within the United States. It has been noted that "the rapid growth of e-commerce and package deliveries across the globe is demanding new solutions to meet customers' desire for more and faster deliveries" [8]. Accordingly, "with the significant rise in demand for same-day instant deliveries, several courier services are exploring alternatives to transport packages in a cost- and time-effective, as well as, sustainable manner" [23]. Thus, an understanding of the determinants leading to the acceptance of this technology by end-users is of value to stakeholders. The first study to examine such acceptance was carried out by Kapser and Abdelrahman [15], who focused exclusively on the German market. However, considerable evidence demonstrates that consumer

© The Author(s) 2022
M. Rauterberg et al. (Eds.): HCII 2022, LNCS 13520, pp. 519–532, 2022.
https://doi.org/10.1007/978-3-031-18158-0_37

behavior concerning the adoption of technology varies by culture [2, 3, 7, 13, 25, 27]. Consequently, there is value in expanding that work to investigate the United States consumer context.

2   Materials and Method

For our work, we rely on Kapser and Abdelrahman's [15] technology adoption model – an extension of the Unified Theory of Acceptance and Use of Technology (hereafter UTATU2) model, which has incorporated consumer risk perception. The model contains a total of eight constructs with respect to the 'Behavioral Intention' (BI) factor: 'Effort Expectancy' (EE), 'Facilitating Conditions' (FC), 'Hedonic Motivation' (HM), 'Performance Expectancy' (PE), 'Perceived Risk' (PR), 'Price Sensitivity' (PS), 'Social Influence' (SI), and 'Trust in Technology' (TT). It also contains six control variables: 'Age' (AGE), 'Education' (EDU), 'Employment' (EMP), 'Gender' (GEN), 'Heard Before' (HEB), this factor reflecting whether an individual has previously heard of the autonomous delivery vehicle technology, and 'Income' (INC). For conciseness, we refer the reader to Kapser and Abdelrahman's [15] paper for a more complete definition of each of these constructs.

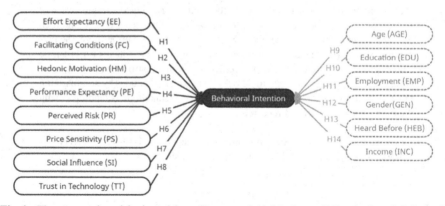

Fig. 1. The proposed model adapted from Kapser and Abdelrahman [15], who based their work on Venkatesh et al.'s [13] UTAUT2 framework.

We supplement this model by incorporating a factor to reflect consumer trust in the technology, appropriately titled 'Trust in Technology' (TT), adapting the construct from the research of Kim et al. [16]. This inclusion is supported by the work of Panagiotopoulos and Dimitrakopoulos [20], who write [9] that "few adaptations of the technology acceptance model have considered trust as a determinant of acceptance; however, those who have done so have found trust to be a determinant of intention to use, i.e. in the context of e-services and e-government applications", pointing to the publications of Mou et al. [19] and Gupta et al. [9]. Furthermore, in a later study by Kapser et al. [14], also investigating autonomous delivery vehicles, the authors incorporate such a construct. Lastly, it should be noted that the practice of adapting the UTAUT2 model for a specific technology is quite common, and Hino [11] describes the (UTAUT) model as "flexible enough to be modified by incorporating additional variables into the original model". The author goes on to point to the work of Yu [26], who justifies this practice by writing that the model is "thus better explaining the acceptance of innovative technology". The final model can be seen illustrated in Fig. 1, and the corresponding hypotheses are outlined in Table 1.

Table 1. List of hypotheses with respective relationships.

Hypothesis	Relationship
H1	Effort Expectancy (EE) → Behavioral Intention (BI)
H2	Facilitating Conditions (FC) → Behavioral Intention (BI)
H3	Hedonic Motivation (HM) → Behavioral Intention (BI)
H4	Performance Expectancy (PE) → Behavioral Intention (BI)
H5	Perceived Risk (PR) → Behavioral Intention (BI)
H6	Price Sensitivity (PS) → Behavioral Intention (BI)
H7	Social Influence (SI) → Behavioral Intention (BI)
H8	Trust in Technology (TT) → Behavioral Intention (BI)
H9	Age (AGE) → Behavioral Intention (BI)
H10	Education (EDU) → Behavioral Intention (BI)
H11	Employment (EMP) → Behavioral Intention (BI)
H12	Gender (GEN) → Behavioral Intention (BI)
H13	Heard Before (HEB) → Behavioral Intention (BI)
H14	Income (INC) → Behavioral Intention (BI)

An experimental approach was taken to evaluate the aforementioned model (see Fig. 1), following the specifications also set by Kasper and Abdelrahman [15] for their study, namely: an information sheet to expose participants to the autonomous delivery vehicle technology; subsequently an instrument (i.e., questionnaire) designed to capture participant demographics and participants' perception of the technology. The questionnaire was slightly adapted for the United States context with regard to language and units of measurement. We would note that the questions for the construct of 'Trust in Technology' were derived from the work of Kim et al. [16]. All questions for the constructs were measured using a 7-point Likert scale (strongly disagree; moderately disagree; somewhat disagree; neutral, neither agree nor disagree; somewhat agree; moderately agree; and strongly agree).

2.1 Sample and Data Collection

A series of web-based experiments were performed where participants were solicited using the Amazon Mechanical Turk crowdsourcing platform, which has been demonstrated to be an effective tool [22] to solicit participants but requires care [24] with respect to participant inattention. Following the obtainment of informed consent, participants were asked to read through the aforementioned 'informational sheet' on autonomous delivery vehicles, and then complete the questionnaire. A total of 296 participations were collected. Specifically, participants were asked to 'take part in a research study soliciting perceptions on autonomous delivery vehicles' and were also presented with two keywords: 'experiment' and 'user perceptions'. The selected qualification requirements for all requesters on the portal were: (1) a HIT Approval Rate greater than 98; (2) that they are located in the United States; (3) a Number of HITs Approved greater than 5000. The survey included two attention check questions adopted from Abbey and Meloy [1]. The first was 'I would rather eat a piece of paper than a piece of fruit', and the second 'At some point in my life, I have had to consume water in some form'. Participants were asked to answer these questions through a 7-point Likert scale (again ranging from 'strongly disagree' to 'strongly agree'). Accordingly, participants who did not answer the first question with 'strongly disagree' and the second with 'strongly agree' were removed from the sample as they were undoubtedly not paying attention. This resulted in a total of 34 participants who failed these attention checks being removed, leaving 262 participants. The sample characteristics can be seen in more detail in Table 2.

Table 2. Participant demographics.

Characteristic	Category	N	Percentage
Age	18–25	1	0.38%
	26–30	1	0.38%
	31–35	24	9.16%
	36–45	52	19.85%
	46–55	95	36.26%
	56 or older	43	16.41%
	Prefer not to answer	46	17.55%
Gender	Female	105	40.08%
	Male	157	59.92%
Income	Less than $10,000	4	1.53%
	$10,000–$19,999	8	3.05%
	$20,000–$29,999	12	4.58%
	$30,000–$39,999	24	9.16%
	$40,000–$49,999	30	11.45%
	$50,000–$59,999	36	13.74%
	$60,000–$69,999	22	8.40%
	$70,000–$79,999	22	8.40%

(continued)

Table 2. (*continued*)

Characteristic	Category	N	Percentage
	$80,000–$89,999	21	8.02%
	$90,000–$99,999	18	6.87%
	$100,000–$149,999	15	5.73%
	$150,000 or more	34	12.98%
	Prefer not to answer	16	6.11%
Schooling	High school graduate (high school diploma or equivalent including GED)	1	0.38%
	Some college but no degree	32	12.21%
	Associate degree in college (2-year)	42	16.03%
	Bachelor's degree in college (4-year)	37	14.12%
	Master's degree (e.g., MA, MS)	115	43.89%
	Professional degree (e.g., MBA, MFA, JD, MD)	28	10.69%
	Doctoral degree (e.g., PhD, EdD, DBA)	4	1.53%
	Prefer not to answer	3	1.15%

3 Analysis and Results

The proposed model is validated using the partial least squares-structural equation modeling (PLS-SEM) approach. PLS-SEM can be described as "a causal modeling approach aimed at maximizing the explained variance of the dependent latent constructs" [10]. Hair et al. [10] explain that "a structural equation model with latent constructs has two components" and further elaborate, "the first component is the structural model—typically referred to as the inner model in the PLS-SEM context—which shows the relationships (paths) between the latent constructs". They also state that "the second component of the structural equation model comprises the measurement models, also referred to as outer models in the PLS-SEM context" [10].

With respect to the measurement model, we assessed convergent validity, construct reliability, and discriminant validity. For the first, convergent validity, we looked at the factor loadings, removing those manifest variables that had values that were lower than 0.7 (see Chin [5]). This saw us remove PS3 (0.552) and TT4 (0.698), with the remaining items being statistically significant (see Table 3). Secondly, with regard to construct reliability, we relied on composite reliability (CR) and Cronbach's Alpha, where, given that all statistics were above the 0.7 recommended threshold, we concluded that construct reliability was satisfactory (see Table 4). Next, discriminant validity was tested using the Fornell-Larcker criterion (see Table 5) and cross-loadings. All values were within the recommended guidelines; therefore, we assumed that the discriminant validity of our measurement model was satisfactory. Thus, in short, our model was found to have suitable convergent validity, construct reliability, and discriminant validity.

Table 3. Summary of convergent validity testing.

Factor	Item	Loading	t-Statistic	AVE
BI	BI1	0.955	141.305**	0.912
	BI2	0.955	132.313**	
EE	EE2	0.945	99.233**	0.894
	EE4	0.947	106.845**	
FC	FC1	0.813	21.599**	0.645
	FC2	0.816	25.245**	
	FC3	0.821	23.734**	
	FC4	0.760	16.380**	
HM	HM2	0.965	231.385**	0.914
	HM3	0.947	90.150**	
PE	PE1	0.929	74.056**	0.886
	PE3	0.947	127.476**	
	PE4	0.947	105.055**	
PR	PR2	0.950	101.295**	0.901
	PR3	0.948	95.600**	
PS	PS1	0.903	54.842**	0.796
	PS2	0.919	62.701**	
	PS4	0.905	51.163**	
	PS5	0.841	27.826**	
TT	TT1	0.958	146.783**	0.911
	TT2	0.951	120.325**	

* p < 0.05; ** p < 0.01

Regarding the structural model, we first appraised the level of collinearity of our latent variables by looking at the variance inflation factor, also known as the VIF (see Table 6). We removed all values that were above the recommended threshold of 5 (see Hair et al. [10]) to resolve any issues regarding collinearity. These were: SI1 (12.850), TT3 (11.117), PE2 (7.608), SI2 (7.233), BI3 (7.164), EE1 (6.208), HM1 (6.105), PR1 (6.074), and EE3 (5.802). With respect to the variance explained by our model, BI had an R^2 of 0.696 which, according to Chin [5], can be described as substantial, given that it is above 0.67. With respect to the individual factors (see Table 7), PE played the greatest role, where an increase of 1 unit in PE ($\beta = 0.388$; p < 0.01) resulted in an increase of 0.388 units in BI; thus, hypothesis 4 was supported. Following PE, we observe SI ($\beta = 0.179$; p < 0.01) playing the second most prominent role, where an increase in 1 unit in SI leads to an increase of 0.179 units in BI; thereby supporting hypothesis 7. Next was HM ($\beta = 0.162$; p < 0.05), where an increase of 1 unit in HM induces an increase of 0.162 units in BI, allowing us to accept hypothesis 3. Subsequently, the fourth greatest role was played by GEN ($\beta = 0.099$; $p < 0.01$), where identifying as male led to a 0.099 increase in BI, consistent with hypothesis 12. Lastly, PR ($\beta = -0.121$; $p < 0.05$) exhibited a negative effect. Accordingly, an increase of 1 unit in PR leads to a decrease of 0.121 in BI; therefore, the result was consistent with hypothesis 5. The results from the hypotheses testing are summarized in Table 8.

Table 4. Summary of reliability testing.

Construct	Number of items	Cronbach's Alpha	CR
BI	2	0.904	0.954
EE	2	0.882	0.944
FC	4	0.816	0.879
HM	2	0.907	0.955
PE	3	0.935	0.959
PR	2	0.890	0.948
PS	4	0.915	0.940
TT	2	0.902	0.953

Table 5. Fornell-Larcker criterion

	BI	EE	FC	HM	PE	PR	PS	SI	TT
BI	**0.955**								
EE	0.442	**0.946**							
FC	0.433	0.758	**0.803**						
HM	0.644	0.373	0.363	**0.956**					
PE	0.736	0.365	0.326	0.632	**0.941**				
PR	−0.476	−0.375	−0.414	−0.367	−0.346	**0.949**			
PS	0.482	0.191	0.169	0.427	0.485	−0.188	**0.892**		
SI	0.599	0.290	0.268	0.520	0.528	−0.238	0.496	**1.000**	
TT	0.644	0.454	0.446	0.572	0.610	−0.628	0.413	0.480	**0.954**

Note: The square root of AVE appears in bold type

Table 6. Collinearity statistics (VIF).

Factor	Item	VIF
BI	BI1	3.120
	BI2	3.120
EE	EE2	2.647
	EE4	2.647
FC	FC1	2.078
	FC2	1.711
	FC3	1.959
	FC4	1.486
HM	HM2	3.206
	HM3	3.206
PE	PE1	3.223
	PE3	4.874
	PE4	4.947
PR	PR2	2.809
	PR3	2.809
PS	PS1	2.866
	PS2	3.718
	PS4	3.258
	PS5	2.286
TT	TT1	3.072
	TT2	3.072

Table 7. Structural model results.

Path	B	t-statistic
EE → BI	0.034	0.596
FC → BI	0.079	1.519
HM → BI	0.162	2.492*
PE → BI	0.388	5.993**
PR → BI	−0.121	2.486*
PS → BI	0.051	1.238
SI → BI	0.179	3.118**
TT → BI	0.080	1.265
AGE → BI	0.020	0.539
EDU → BI	0.004	0.112
EMP → BI	0.052	1.527
GEN → BI	0.099	2.854**
HEB → BI	−0.045	1.111
INC → BI	−0.052	1.248

* $p < 0.05$; ** $p < 0.01$

Table 8. Hypotheses testing results.

Hypothesis	Relationship	Decision
H1	EE → BI	Not supported
H2	FC → BI	Not supported
H3	HM → BI	Supported
H4	PE → BI	Supported
H5	PR → BI	Supported
H6	PS → BI	Not supported
H7	SI → BI	Supported
H8	TT → BI	Not supported
H9	AGE → BI	Not supported
H10	EDU → BI	Not supported
H11	EMP → BI	Not supported
H12	GEN → BI	Supported
H13	HEB → BI	Not supported
H14	INC → BI	Not supported

4 Discussion and Conclusions

In this paper, we explored the end-user acceptance of last-mile delivery carried out by autonomous delivery vehicles, complementing the existing literature, where "an insufficient number of studies exist that focus explicitly on the acceptance of ADVs in the context of last-mile delivery" [15]. Moreover, Kapser and Abdelrahman [15] bring attention to the work of Hulse et al. [12], who write that "to date, there is limited research on the psychological factors that determine public acceptance of AVs from an outside vehicle perspective". While this technology holds great potential, "societal benefits will not be achieved unless these vehicles are accepted and used by a critical mass of people; thus, it will be important to understand consumers' acceptance" [20]. In particular, we built on the original work of Kapser and Abdelrahman [15] by exploring the topic from the cultural context of the United States.

Overall, consumers in the United States appear to hold a slightly favorable view of this technology, with a mean user acceptance (i.e., 'Behavioral Intention') score of 4.545 out of 7. This is in contrast to the findings of Kapser and Abdelrahman [15] who, for the German market, report that "respondents seem to hold neutral acceptance of towards the use of ADVs". Furthermore, we found that consumer perception of the perceived usefulness of this technology (i.e., 'Performance Expectancy') was the greatest determinant in consumer acceptance decisions. This finding was not surprising as it mirrors the findings of Venkatesh et al. [13], who note that "the performance expectancy construct within each individual model". Indeed, they state that it "is the strongest prediction of intention and remains significant at all points of measurement in both voluntary and mandatory settings". This finding also reaffirms the observations within the literature by Kapser and Abdelrahman [15], who write that this is "concurrent with previous AVs acceptance studies". However, one difference between our results and Kapser and Abdelrahman's [15] is with respect to the magnitude of the factor. On the contrary, they find that, for a German audience, price sensitivity is the greatest predictor of consumer acceptance of the technology, "indicating that the price for the delivery is more important to potential users than the usefulness of the technology itself". In contrast, in a United States context, price plays no statistically significant role in consumer acceptance decisions. This finding also provides insight to those offering such a service, suggesting that in the United States market a higher price could be charged, assuming that the price is within reasonable bounds, while there is an expectation that the product would give them value (i.e., be useful to them).

The second greatest predictor of end-user acceptance of last-mile delivery carried out by autonomous delivery vehicles was the opinion held by others (i.e., 'Social Influence'). Indeed, we find that "our respondents are likely to depend on their peers' opinion in regard to ADVs" [15]. The third greatest factor was the enjoyment experienced by interacting with the technology (i.e., Hedonic Motivation). This finding is again similar to what is reported by Kapser and Abdelrahman [15], who comment that "fun and entertainment derived from using ADVs seems important to determine user acceptance". Furthermore, it reflects what appears in the mainstream literature (see Madigan et al. [17] and Moták et al. [18]). However, there is one important difference that should be mentioned. In the German context (per Kapser and Abdelrahman's [15]), enjoyment plays the second greatest effect on consumer decisions and the opinion of others the third, whereas in the

United States context, the opinion of others is second and enjoyment is third. In other words, what others think is more important in consumer acceptance decisions in the United States, compared to Germany, than how much fun they have using it.

Gender was also found to influence acceptance, with males being more likely to accept the technology over females. This finding is contrary to two studies examining end-user acceptance of last-mile delivery carried out by autonomous delivery vehicles in Germany: the first by Kapser and Abdelrahman [15] and the second by Kapser et al. [14], where both studies find gender to play no statistically significant role. Lastly, we find that the perception of risk associated with the use of the technology (i.e., 'Perceived Risk') influences acceptance negatively. So, if a consumer perceives the technology to be risky, they are less likely to accept it. However, the average value for the construct was 2.675 out of 7, which indicates that, for the most part, the technology is not perceived as risky. Unexpectedly, support for using the technology did not have a statistically significant effect on consumers' behavioral intention to accept. This is in contrast to what was reported by Kapser and Abdelrahman [15], who conclude that "external resources like peer support plays an important aspect in user acceptance of ADVs". As well as what they note appears in the literature (e.g., Madigan et al. [17], Choi and Ji [6], and Buckley et al. [4]). Thus, in contrast to the German market, where consumers expect support if they are to accept this technology, in the United States market such support is not needed. Rather individuals have the expectation that they will figure it out – perhaps that is part of the enjoyment they expect to experience, or perhaps it adds a social element of working with peers to resolve the issue, giving a greater desire to figure things out on one's own.

4.1 Implications

Our research has both theoretical and practical implications. From the theoretical dimension, the work validates the model initially proposed by Kapser and Abdelrahman [15] for a United States cultural context. From the practical dimension, this study offers insight into the minds of the United States consumer with respect to end-user acceptance of last-mile delivery carried out by autonomous delivery vehicles. The findings can therefore inform both industry and governments as they move to promote the use of such innovative technology, affording society with a cleaner, more effective, and efficient solution to delivery. First, organizations know that the United States consumer sees the technology favorably and is concerned about quality rather than price when it comes to having access to this technology. This means that organizations should make sure that the technology is one that consumers find useful at the same time, knowing that they can charge for this service without worrying that it may lead to disenfranchisement on the part of the consumer. However, this is assuming prices are within reasonable bounds, and further research is warranted to truly understand how consumers will react to prices that go beyond such bounds. Second, consumers are influenced by the opinion of their peers when it comes to accepting this technology; consequently, "peer pressure can be taken into consideration for marketing purposes" [15]. Third, as the perception of the technology being fun to use leads to increased acceptance, efforts to gamify the experience are warranted. Fourth, those who identify as male have a greater affinity to accept the technology; this also informs marketers as they prepare campaigns. Fifth, while, for the most part, consumers do not perceive this technology as being risky, in those cases where it is perceived in that way (i.e., risky), interventions are necessary to inform. Lastly, consumers are not going to be seeking formalized support for using the technology. On the one hand, this may lead to fewer support staff; however, it does introduce other issues that need to be addressed. Specifically, efforts must be taken to help consumers that will resist contacting or interacting with technical support. It is possible that consumers appreciate the challenge of figuring out how to use such a novel technology on their own as fun. Consequently, there is a need to ensure the user interface is easy to understand and that there are alternative informal resources that can be used in lieu.

4.2 Limitations and Future Research

There are four limitations that should be mentioned that concurrently allow us to share ways through which this research can be further expanded in the future. The first has to do with the data for this study being collected during the Covid pandemic, which may have influenced consumer behavior during this period. This understandable change in consumer attitude is presented within the context of autonomous delivery vehicles in the work of Pani et al. [21], who write that "the ongoing COVID-19 pandemic has put a global spotlight on ADRs for contactless package deliveries". They explain that there has been "a surge in the public interest and demand for ADRs since it can provide contactless delivery, a highly sought-after service under the directives of social distancing". Pani et al. [21] conclude that "consumers, businesses, and governments have switched from being cautious beta testers into eager early adopters" [21]. Following the pandemic, it might be of value to investigate how, if at all, consumer behavior with respect to this technology changes.

The second limitation has to do with current consumer exposure to the technology being limited. Very few people have had actual access and thus experienced this technology. Hence the findings of this work are based on participants' imagination with respect to the operation of autonomous delivery vehicles and how they would carry out last-mile delivery to end-users. Subsequently, a study that exposed participants to the technology may yield different findings and would be of value to our community. The third is with respect to our study employing a generic perspective of autonomous delivery vehicles for last-mile delivery. Accordingly, brand may influence user acceptance and should be investigated in greater detail.

Lastly, we would point out that our study has presented participants only with the positive aspects of this technology. For example, with any introduction to technology that offers automation, there is the strong possibility of job loss. It is unclear how consumers would behave when knowing such tradeoffs.

Acknowledgments. This research was funded in part through the New York University School of Professional Studies Full-Time Faculty Professional Development Fund.

References

1. Abbey, J., Meloy, M.: Attention by design: using attention checks to detect inattentive respondents and improve data quality. J. Oper. Manag. **53–56**, 63–70 (2017). https://doi.org/10.1016/j.jom.2017.06.001
2. Al-Gahtani, S., et al.: Information technology (IT) in Saudi Arabia: culture and the acceptance and use of IT. Inf. Manag. **44**(8), 681–691 (2007). https://doi.org/10.1016/j.im.2007.09.002
3. Bandyopadhyay, K., Fraccastoro, K.: The effect of culture on user acceptance of information technology. Commun. Assoc. Inf. Syst. **19**, 522–543 (2007)
4. Buckley, L., et al.: Psychosocial factors associated with intended use of automated vehicles: a simulated driving study. Accid. Anal. Prev. **115**, 202–208 (2018). https://doi.org/10.1016/j.aap.2018.03.021
5. Chin, W.W.: The partial least squares approach to structural equation modeling. Mod. Methods Bus. Res. **295**(2), 295–336 (1998)
6. Choi, J.K., Ji, Y.G.: Investigating the importance of trust on adopting an autonomous vehicle. Int. J. Hum. Comput. Interact. **31**(10), 692–702 (2015). https://doi.org/10.1080/10447318.2015.1070549
7. Faqih, K.M.S., Jaradat, M.-I.R.M.: Assessing the moderating effect of gender differences and individualism-collectivism at individual-level on the adoption of mobile commerce technology: TAM3 perspective. J. Retail. Consum. Serv. **22**, 37–52 (2015). https://doi.org/10.1016/j.jretconser.2014.09.006
8. Figliozzi, M.A.: Carbon emissions reductions in last mile and grocery deliveries utilizing air and ground autonomous vehicles. Transp. Res. Part D Transp. Environ. **85**, 102443 (2020). https://doi.org/10.1016/j.trd.2020.102443
9. Gupta, K.P., et al.: Citizen adoption of e-government: a literature review and conceptual framework. Electron. Gov. Int. J. **12**(2), 160–185 (2016)
10. Hair, J.F., et al.: PLS-SEM: Indeed a silver bullet. J. Mark. Theory Pract. **19**(2), 139–152 (2011). https://doi.org/10.2753/MTP1069-6679190202
11. Hino, H.: Assessing factors affecting consumers' intention to adopt biometric authentication technology in e-shopping. J. Internet Commer. **14**(1), 1–20 (2015). https://doi.org/10.1080/15332861.2015.1006517
12. Hulse, L.M., et al.: Perceptions of autonomous vehicles: relationships with road users, risk, gender and age. Saf. Sci. **102**, 1–13 (2018). https://doi.org/10.1016/j.ssci.2017.10.001
13. Im, I., et al.: An international comparison of technology adoption: testing the UTAUT model. Inf. Manag. **48**(1), 1–8 (2011). https://doi.org/10.1016/j.im.2010.09.001
14. Kapser, S., et al.: Autonomous delivery vehicles to fight the spread of Covid-19 - how do men and women differ in their acceptance? Transp. Res. Part A Policy Pract. **148**, 183–198 (2021). https://doi.org/10.1016/j.tra.2021.02.020
15. Kapser, S., Abdelrahman, M.: Acceptance of autonomous delivery vehicles for last-mile delivery in Germany – extending UTAUT2 with risk perceptions. Transp. Res. Part C Emerg. Technol. **111**, 210–225 (2020). https://doi.org/10.1016/j.trc.2019.12.016
16. Kim, G., et al.: Understanding dynamics between initial trust and usage intentions of mobile banking. Inf. Syst. J. **19**(3), 283–311 (2009). https://doi.org/10.1111/j.1365-2575.2007.00269.x
17. Madigan, R., et al.: What influences the decision to use automated public transport? Using UTAUT to understand public acceptance of automated road transport systems. Transp. Res. F Traffic Psychol. Behav. **50**, 55–64 (2017). https://doi.org/10.1016/j.trf.2017.07.007
18. Moták, L., et al.: Antecedent variables of intentions to use an autonomous shuttle: moving beyond TAM and TPB? Eur. Rev. Appl. Psychol. **67**(5), 269–278 (2017). https://doi.org/10.1016/j.erap.2017.06.001

19. Mou, J., et al.: Trust and risk in consumer acceptance of e-services. Electron. Commer. Res. **17**(2), 255–288 (2017). https://doi.org/10.1007/s10660-015-9205-4
20. Panagiotopoulos, I., Dimitrakopoulos, G.: An empirical investigation on consumers' intentions towards autonomous driving. Transp. Res. Part C Emerg. Technol. **95**, 773–784 (2018). https://doi.org/10.1016/j.trc.2018.08.013
21. Pani, A., et al.: Evaluating public acceptance of autonomous delivery robots during COVID-19 pandemic. Transp. Res. Part D Transp. Environ. **89**, 102600 (2020). https://doi.org/10.1016/j.trd.2020.102600
22. Paolacci, G., et al.: Running experiments on Amazon Mechanical Turk. Judgm. Decis. Mak. **5**(5), 411–419 (2010)
23. Rajendran, S., Harper, A.: Simulation-based algorithm for determining best package delivery alternatives under three criteria: time, cost and sustainability. Transp. Res. Interdisc. Perspect. **12**, 100484 (2021). https://doi.org/10.1016/j.trip.2021.100484
24. Saravanos, A., Zervoudakis, S., Zheng, D., Stott, N., Hawryluk, B., Delfino, D.: The hidden cost of using Amazon Mechanical Turk for research. In: Stephanidis, C., et al. (eds.) HCII 2021. LNCS, vol. 13094, pp. 147–164. Springer, Cham (2021). https://doi.org/10.1007/978-3-030-90238-4_12
25. Srite, M., Karahanna, E.: The role of espoused national cultural values in technology acceptance. MIS Q. **30**(3), 679–704 (2006). https://doi.org/10.2307/25148745
26. Yu, C.S.: Factors affecting individuals to adopt mobile banking: empirical evidence from the UTAUT model. J. Electron. Commer. Res. **13**(2), 104–121 (2012)
27. Yuen, Y.: Internet banking acceptance in the United States and Malaysia: a cross-cultural examination. Mark. Intell. Plan. **33**(3), 292–308 (2015). https://doi.org/10.1108/MIP-08-2013-0126

Open Access This chapter is licensed under the terms of the Creative Commons Attribution 4.0 International License (http://creativecommons.org/licenses/by/4.0/), which permits use, sharing, adaptation, distribution and reproduction in any medium or format, as long as you give appropriate credit to the original author(s) and the source, provide a link to the Creative Commons license and indicate if changes were made.

The images or other third party material in this chapter are included in the chapter's Creative Commons license, unless indicated otherwise in a credit line to the material. If material is not included in the chapter's Creative Commons license and your intended use is not permitted by statutory regulation or exceeds the permitted use, you will need to obtain permission directly from the copyright holder.

Mobility Data Stories for a Better Understanding of Mobility Data

Tobias Steinert, Ulrike Große, Matthias Hirth, and Heidi Krömker[✉]

Technische Universität Ilmenau, PF 10 05 65, 98684 Ilmenau, Germany
{tobias.steinert,ulrike.grosse,matthias.hirth,
heidi.kroemker}@tu-ilmenau.de

Abstract. Numerous stakeholders are involved in mobility planning, such as citizens' initiatives, political decision-makers, and mobility consultants. Here, data and its linkage form an important building block for decision-making. However, the challenge is to process heterogeneous data sources in a problem-adequate and target group-specific manner. Therefore, this publication addresses how decision-relevant contexts can be visualized and developed into mobility data stories. First, the approaches and principles of Neifer, Freytag, and Field are presented. They show that data stories are formed from an intersection of the key components data, visualizations, and stories. After that, an example is used to show how Mobility Data Stories are developed, starting from the core question, through the selection of data, the conception of the story, to the visualization. The sample solution developed in the research process is then evaluated regarding usability and user experience with the stakeholders. Based on the evaluation results, a method for creating target-group-specific Mobility Data Stories is derived to support the stakeholders in the mobility sector with the visual and content-related preparation of the data. Further, the target-oriented mobility planning process is structured regarding the potential of mobility data stories. Finally, general guidelines for creating target-group-specific Mobility Data Stories are derived. The results show the potential of Mobility Data Stories.

Keywords: Mobility Data Story · Storytelling · Mobility data

1 Introduction

1.1 Mobility Data and Mobility Process

A solid and holistic data basis is an essential component for communication and decision-making by the stakeholders in the increasingly complex field of sustainable mobility planning. Today many new data collection methods are available to make decisions based on an expanded data basis. For example, forecasts for vehicle utilization can be developed based on real passenger numbers. A common data basis is essential for all stakeholders involved in the planning process. This includes planning in public transport and services, strategic local and regional infrastructure planning, and the integration of new and environmentally friendly forms of mobility.

© Springer Nature Switzerland AG 2022
M. Rauterberg et al. (Eds.): HCII 2022, LNCS 13520, pp. 533–546, 2022.
https://doi.org/10.1007/978-3-031-18158-0_38

At present, decision-relevant reports, analyses, and documentation are mainly compiled based on individual requests. This can result in deficits regarding the systematic and problem-oriented use of data or different degrees of processing. Data access can also exhibit different characteristics so that not all stakeholders involved in the planning process have access to the same data basis. Mobility Data Stories can provide a common basis for communication. Important correlations, results, and data are clearly visualized and communicated understandably through a story component. Mobility data can turn into stories.

1.2   Stakeholders in Mobility Planning

The mobility planning process is characterized by the participation of many stakeholders. These include mobility planners, mobility consultants, political decision-makers, transport companies, mobility service providers, and citizens' initiatives (Fig. 1). Citizens, residents, and mobility users are also increasingly involved in the mobility planning process through citizen referendums.

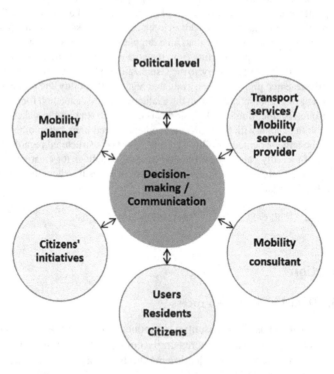

Fig. 1. Stakeholders in the mobility planning process

Decisions of mobility planners and consultants as well as mobility service providers and transport companies are made based on extensive data and associated comprehensive analyses. Political decision-makers, users, and citizens, on the other hand, rely on a reduced data basis. This is mainly due to the lack of accessibility of existing data sets, time restrictions, and a lack of basic understanding of the data.

2 State of the Art

2.1 Data Stories and Data Storytelling

Mobility Data Stories are fundamentally based on the principle of storytelling. Olivier Serrat defines storytelling as follows: *"Storytelling is the vivid description of ideas, beliefs, personal experiences, and life-lessons through stories or narratives that evoke powerful emotions and insights"* [1].

Thomas Neifer et al. describes data storytelling in their publication as "Process of preparing and presenting information from the results of a data analysis to motivate a decision or action in a language and visualization appropriate to the target group" [2]. Lutz Klaus summarizes data storytelling as follows: "Data storytelling is about communicating relevant developments in an understandable way with the aim of making necessary decisions" [3].

Storytelling is thus a method for directly conveying messages, knowledge, data, and insights by means of a vivid story. Using data stories, emotions and feelings can be evoked, which makes the story and thus the information more profound. In contrast to the communication of pure facts and figures, the narrative memory is addressed in this way. According to Jennifer Aaker, stories are *"22 times better captured than pure facts. A mixture of stories and facts is received about twice as well as pure facts or figures. (...)"* [4].

Data stories can take on different forms. The spectrum ranges from simple, static posters to interactive digital visualizations. The difference to classic infographics lies in the story content, although the boundaries between infographics and data stories are fluid.

2.2 Methodological Approaches

The approaches and principles of Neifer, Freytag, and Field are presented below. Based on a comprehensive literature analysis, Thomas Neifer et al. developed success factors for data storytelling and derived from them the storytelling process shown in Fig. 2.

Data must be carefully considered and selected. They form the basis for the development of a data story. Only data that relates directly or indirectly to the core topic should be included, redundant data should be avoided.

When *visualizing* the data, the focus is on the core question. In addition, the visualization is accompanied by a reduction in complexity. Extensive tables and diagrams may be difficult for a target group to grasp. Simple representations, conversely, can also be understood by people unfamiliar with the topic. It should be ensured that visualizations are as self-explanatory as possible.

Focus on the core idea refers to the fact that data and visualizations always serve to answer the question. Therefore, the development of the two elements must always be oriented to the core question.

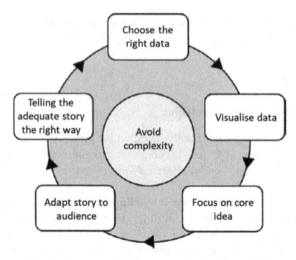

Fig. 2. Data storytelling process by Neifer et al. [2]

The story conveys the core topic and enables people to form an opinion. Neifer describes the step *Telling the adequate story the right way* as "Ability (…) to transform numbers into good stories" [2].

Adapt story to audience is also a focus. Stories may make sense in terms of the core topic but may not be suitable for the audience. Therefore, the story must be geared to the level of knowledge and understanding of the target group.

The *Avoid complexity* step applies to all data storytelling process steps. A Data Story should be easy to grasp and easy to follow. Visual aids also support this process. Unnecessarily complex visualizations and stories can have a negative impact on the attention of the target group or lead to misinterpretations [2].

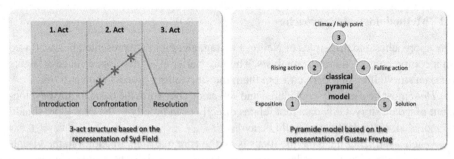

Fig. 3. 3-act structure [5] and classical pyramid model [6] in comparison

The content structure of a Data Story can be based on the principle of Syd Field's three-act system or on Gustav Freytag's classic pyramid model of drama. Figure 3 shows both principles. The basic structure of the two principles is similar. First, boundary conditions or current states are described. In this way, a comparable starting position is created regarding prior knowledge or prior information. In addition, the introduction facilitates the entry into the topic. In the following step a confrontation, a problem or an idea is introduced. An arc of suspense is created that conveys the core topic and sensitizes the target group. In conclusion, clear results, alternatives, or solution ideas are given and consolidated with the help of explanations.

In summary, it can be determined that data stories are basically formed from an intersection of the key elements data, visualizations, and stories, as shown in Fig. 4. A balanced ratio of the three key elements is required.

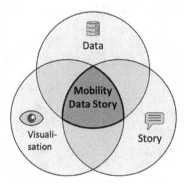

Fig. 4. Structural approach of data storytelling in accordance with [7]

3   Empirical Study

3.1   Development of Mobility Data Stories

The development of Mobility Data Stories was based on the above-mentioned principles of Field and Freytag, the data storytelling process by Neifer and the structural approach of data storytelling.

At the beginning of the development, selected core questions from the mobility sector were extracted, which can be assigned to different stages of the mobility planning process. To answer the core questions, it was possible to draw on extensive data sets on the topics of public passenger transport, individual transport, freight transport and electro mobility. The development process will be explained using the Mobility Data Story of the lack of parking spaces for trucks on German motorways as an example. The aim of the Mobility Data Story was to answer the core question: What is the current truck-parking situation along German motorways?

Within the process step *data component*, extensive data sets were analysed. The aim was to determine meaningful key figures and facts to answer the core question. This primarily concerned information on the share of freight traffic, the increase in transport volumes and legal regulations. During the analysis, care was taken to ensure that the data was transparent, unambiguous, and reliable.

Within the *visualization* component, first drafts and later digital prototypes were developed with the appropriate tools. In this way, a visualization of the core question was developed step by step. The focus was on the truck, which was highlighted by colour. In this way, the viewer's focus is directed to the core message.

The story component primarily addresses the text modules that serve to illustrate the data. During the study, a storyline has been developed using the three-act system. In this way, the stakeholders were introduced to the core question. In this example, the initial situation and the future development of transport services and traffic shares were described first. This should result in an arc of tension, which, due to the legally defined driving and rest times, leads to the conclusion that the number of trucks will also increase in the future. Finally, the current situation along the German motorways is presented and the lack of suitable parking spaces is described. The truck is the backbone of freight transport, nevertheless, one in four truck drivers cannot find a suitable parking space.

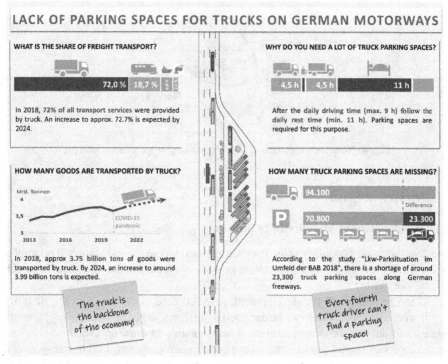

Fig. 5. Work in progress: Mobility Data Story *truck parking shortage on German motorways* based on the data [8–11]

The visualization of the data went hand in hand with the development of the story, so that a fusion between data, visualizations, and accompanying texts was created. This was to ensure consistency of content and to consolidate the connections. The Mobility Data Story was first developed as a rough framework. Afterwards, it was converted into paper prototypes and digital prototypes. The entire development process was iterative. Stakeholder feedback was constantly collected and incorporated. The sticky notes at the bottom of the image, which were intended as an aide memoire, were approved and were incorporated into the final version of the Mobility Data Story in this way, shown in Fig. 5. Finally, the Mobility Data Story was completed and converted into a format suitable for the usability and user experience tests.

3.2 Evaluation of Mobility Data Stories

The user-oriented evaluation of the Mobility Data Stories aimed to ensure the usability and user experience of the developed sample solutions in terms of completeness, comprehensibility, attractiveness, transparency, and stimulation. Ten Mobility Data Stories were tested in the topic areas of public passenger transport, motorised individual transport, freight transport, sharing transport, cycling transport, and walking transport.

Four to five test persons can identify more than 80% of the usability problems [12]. Therefore, five to seven test persons per Mobility Data Story were planned for the evaluation. Each participant evaluated four mobility data stories. The selection of the test persons was representative of the analysed stakeholders. Due to the current COVID19 restrictions, the evaluations could only be carried out via remote usability tests. For this purpose, a combination of a Webex meeting [13] and an accompanying questionnaire via the survey tool Unipark [14] was chosen. The evaluation participants received the link to the survey tool at the beginning of the evaluation and were asked to share their screen via Webex. In this way, the evaluator was able to recognise the answers of the participants and ask targeted questions.

In the process of the evaluation, it was first determined whether and to what extent the evaluation participants were in touch with data in their daily work, and whether they analyse and, if so, visualize data. All subsequent test objectives related directly or indirectly to the individual mobility data stories, and were selected to cover a broad spectrum of criteria and to receive as many comments as possible. The survey ended with the collection of demographic data. All answers were evaluated anonymously so that no conclusions can be drawn about individual evaluation participants.

Twenty participants, 10 female and 10 male, aged between 30 and 49 years, participated in the evaluation. Three participants of the evaluation participants stated that they worked in the mobility sector. Seven of the 20 respondents are partly employed in the mobility sector. These include politicians and project managers. 18 out of 20 evaluation participants stated that they always or often meet data during their activities. Only two male and two female evaluators work without having much contact to data. Figure 6 provides an overview of all the information collected.

Following the common questions about the data reference, the Mobility Data Stories were evaluated according to the criteria *selection of data*, *design of the Data Story* and *content of the Data Story* as well as the User Experience Questionnaire (UEQ) categories *attractiveness, transparency,* and *stimulation* [15]. The following is an example of the result of the evaluation of the Mobility Data Story "Lack of parking spaces for trucks on German motorways".

Overall, the Mobility Data Story received a consistently positive evaluation. All information and data could be easily grasped even by non-topic evaluation participants (Fig. 7). The selection of data and information scored an average of 4.3 out of a maximum of 5.0 points. The test persons also perceived the design of the Mobility Data Story positively, so that a score of 4.7 out of a possible 5.0 points was achieved here. The topic-related content was rated by the evaluation participants with an average of 4.5 out of a possible 5.0 points.

Participants of the evaluation

Sample: 20 participants

Age: 30 – 49 years

Gender: w10 | m10

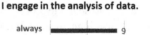

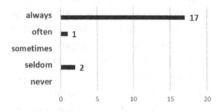

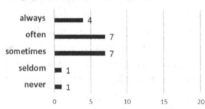

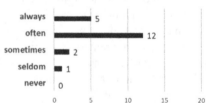

Fig. 6. Description of the acquired participants [own presentation]

Selection of data.

The data looks credible   Ø 4.4 / 5.0

The data could be collected quickly   Ø 4.0 / 5.0

The connection between the data is recognisable   Ø 4.6 / 5.0

Design of the data story.

The design of the Data Story is appealing   Ø 4.6 / 5.0

The design of the Data Story is clear   Ø 4.9 / 5.0

The data was illustrated in an appropriate form   Ø 4.7 / 5.0

Content of the data story.

No background knowledge is needed to follow the story   Ø 4.6 / 5.0

The story has a clear arc of tension   Ø 3.7 / 5.0

I was able to extract all relevant information from the Data Story   Ø 4.6 / 5.0

The core message became clear to me   Ø 5.0 / 5.0

Fig. 7. Evaluation results of the individual categories [own presentation]

Positive results were also achieved within the User Experience Questionnaire. These results are shown in Fig. 8. Attractiveness received an average score of 1.29 out of a maximum of 3.00 points. Transparency achieved an average score of 1.04 out of 3.00

points. In the category stimulation, the best result could be achieved with 1.43 out of a possible 3.00 points.

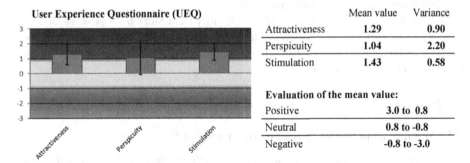

User Experience Questionnaire (UEQ)	Mean value	Variance
Attractiveness	1.29	0.90
Perspicuity	1.04	2.20
Stimulation	1.43	0.58

Evaluation of the mean value:	
Positive	3.0 to 0.8
Neutral	0.8 to -0.8
Negative	-0.8 to -3.0

Fig. 8. Results of the User Experience Questionnaire based on [15]

During the evaluations, all test persons were asked to mention their opinion and mood about the respective Mobility Data Story within the framework of the Thinking Aloud method. Both the clarity of the Mobility Data Story and the comprehensibility of the information received positive feedback. The uniformity and simplicity of the diagrams were mentioned positively several times. Finally, the visualization of the core statements

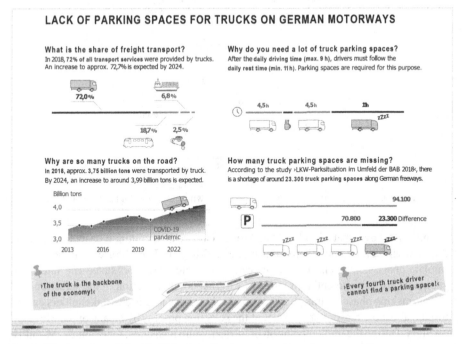

Fig. 9. Final version of the Mobility Data Story *truck parking shortage on German motorways* based on the data [8–11]

using sticky notes was mentioned positively, too. There is potential for improvement in the icon of a pipeline used in the diagram of the freight transport share. This was not recognised as a pipeline and should be replaced or revised. The Mobility Data Stories were finalised based on the evaluation results.

Figure 9 shows the final version of the Mobility Data Story *truck parking shortage on German motorways*. The Mobility Data Story was standardised using a predefined colour scheme. Due to design reasons, the separating element motorway has been moved to the lower edge of the picture.

4   Results

4.1   Mobility Data Stories in the Focused Planning Process

As a partial result of the interviews with the stakeholders, the potential of Mobility Data Stories along the goal-oriented planning process was also determined. For this purpose, the respective phases were identified in which Mobility Data Stories offer added value in terms of external project communication. External project communication refers, for example, to the communication between mobility planners, the political decision-making level and passenger associations.

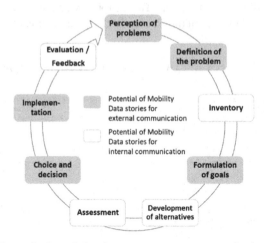

Fig. 10. Focused oriented planning process own representation based on [16]

Figure 10 shows that Mobility Data Stories can create a common basis for communication when defining problems. Furthermore, Mobility Data Stories can be used to formulate goals, i.e., to clarify the planned and theoretical target state. The interview participants also saw potential in terms of external communication in the selection and decision-making phase. In this phase, a project alternative is chosen. Stakeholders can be informed about the reasons and results of the selection process by means of the Mobility Data Story. During the implementation of infrastructure measures, for example, Mobility Data Stories can also make a positive contribution in terms of acceptance and provide information about the current implementation status.

According to the interview participants, the effects of Mobility Data Stories in external communication in the phases of inventory, alternative development, alternative assessment, and evaluation are rather low. Mobility Data Stories could support internal project communication in these phases.

4.2 Method for Mobility Data Stories

Based on the experiences from the research process and the evaluation results, a method for creating target-group-specific Mobility Data Stories was developed based on the process proposed by Neifer regarding data stories, shown in Fig. 11.

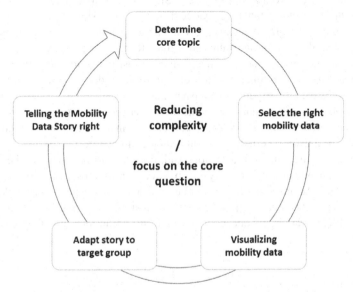

Fig. 11. Modified Mobility Data Story process own representation based on [2]

In Neifer's storytelling process, the selection of the right data was the first step. If the assumption was made, that extensive data sources are available and that facts information are available in sufficient quantity and quality, the focus on the core topic can move to the first place. In this way, the concern, the core topic, or the research question is fixed first. Then the required data are identified, selected, and analysed from an existing data pool. The rest of the process is analogous to Neifer's storytelling process: the data are visualized, the story adapted to the target group, and the story is adequately told. Neifer places the reduction of complexity in the middle of the cycle, as this affects all process steps. The empirical studies have shown that focussing on the core topic is highly relevant in all steps of the process, especially regarding the visualization and the structure of the story. It should therefore be at the centre of attention together with the reduction of complexity and thus receive continuous attention.

4.3 Guidelines for Mobility Data Stories

As part of this research work, guidelines for Mobility Data Stories have been derived based on the interview results, the experiences in the development process and based on a comprehensive literature review.

When *selecting data*, for example, one must take care to ensure that it is credible and verifiable. Insufficient, untrustworthy, and unseaworthy sources must be avoided, as these can have a negative influence on the authenticity of a Mobility Data Story. Another problem is the sometimes widely varying description and interpretation of data from different sources. For example, there are different data on how many private cars can be replaced by a Car-Sharing vehicle. Depending on the source, the range is from 4 to 20 vehicles. Data from a Mobility Data Story, which illuminate the problem area from different perspectives can, thus, lead to different conclusions in answering the core question, should be integrated in any case. Only a transparent and reliable Mobility Data Story can support democratic and balanced opinion forming. Typical examples of this are the costs, or also negative influences, of a planned infrastructure measure on the personal environment. Although in this sense it seems sensible to dispense with "unwelcome" information, this is at the expense of transparency.

Colours and colour concepts can evoke both intended and unintended associations. Although red colour formatting is often chosen as a means of drawing attention, the colour itself has a warning effect and signals danger, fire or stop.

During the evaluation, the illustrations and, thus, the core message of the Mobility Data Stories were perceived differently due to the chosen colour scheme. As an Example, see Fig. 12. The CO_2 emissions of a regular bus with approx. 80 g per passenger kilometre compared to a passenger car with 170 g per passenger kilometre appeared to be positive or ecological. This was largely due to the colour design of the corresponding illustrations.

Fig. 12. Example of colour association own representation based on [17]. (Color figure online)

The design of Mobility Data Stories must pay attention to the choice of colours, the associated colour effects, and colour associations. Even when using corporate colours and colours of a corporate identity, misinterpretations can occur in the worst case.

The *wording, formulation and expression* must also be adapted to the target group of a Mobility Data Story. The different stakeholders have different vocabularies. Technical terms are no problem for mobility planners, and employees in the transport and mobility sector. Yet, the vocabularies are not necessarily understood by users or residents. Examples of this are terms such as low-floor vehicle, individual traffic, block traffic or cycle frequency.

Reducing complexity applies to all areas of a Mobility Data Story. Complex and extensive texts should be avoided, as should multidimensional representations or confusing diagrams. Here, the later target group of the Mobility Data Story must be kept in mind. The complexity of diagrams, for example, can be reduced to a minimum without compromising the expressiveness of the presentation. Through the skilful use of colours, icons and markings, the focus can be placed on the core message. As an example, see Fig. 13. The diagram was simplified, unnecessary components removed and the focus was placed on the truck. The diagram below contains all the key statements that are important for the target group in an easy-to-grasp presentation.

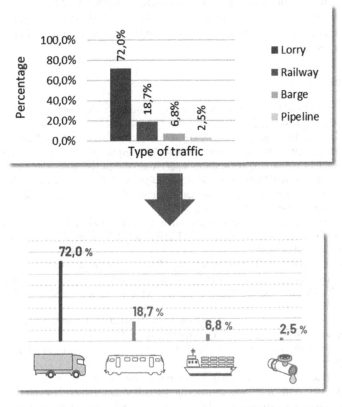

Fig. 13. Reduction of complexity own representation based on [9]

5 Discussion

Mobility Data Stories can support decisions in the mobility sector as a common basis for communication. The comprehensive existing mobility data can be used in a decision-relevant way. Depending on the scope and complexity of the core question, data analysts, designers, editors, and other experts are involved in the development of a Data Story. Smaller companies, municipalities, and planning bodies lack the resources to do this.

The main challenge is to reduce the effort required to create mobility data stories. One approach is generic Mobility Data Stories that provide sample solutions for Mobility Data

Stories for typical core questions. Typical core questions in mobility are, for example, the user-friendliness of cycle and footpath infrastructures, parking space utilisation or the citizen-focused development of rural areas. These can be further explored at any time regarding individual questions. An approach to this concept was tested for research purposes. However, further research work is needed here.

Furthermore, the interactive potential of digital Mobility Data Stories should be used. Clickable, transformable data stories or data stories that can adapted by the user are conceivable. In combination with automated analysis systems, data stories that autonomously adapt to new circumstances would be possible. In this way, permanently changing demand data or occupancy levels in public transport could still be output as a Mobility Data Story.

References

1. Serrat, O.: Storytelling. https://www.adb.org/sites/default/files/publication/27637/storytelling.pdf. Accessed 24 Feb 2022
2. Neifer, T., et al.: Data Storytelling als kritischer Erfolgsfaktor von Data Science. HMD **57**, 1033–1046 (2020). https://doi.org/10.1365/s40702-020-00662-3. https://link.springer.com/content/pdf/10.1365/s40702-020-00662-3.pdf. Accessed 24 Feb 2022
3. Lutz, K.: Data-Driven Marketing und der Erfolgsfaktor Mensch - Schlüsselfaktoren und Kernkompetenzen für das Marketing der Zukunft, 1st edn. Springer, Wiesbaden (2019). https://doi.org/10.1007/978-3-658-20821-9
4. Youtube.com. https://www.youtube.com/watch?v=9X0weDMh9C4. Accessed 24 Feb 2022
5. Duarte, N.: Data Story - Explain Data and Inspire Action Through Story, 2nd edn. IdeaPress Publishing, Canada (2019)
6. Kinateder, B.: Klassische Erzählformen. https://www.br-online.de/jugend/izi/deutsch/publikation/televizion/25-2012-2/Kinateder-Klassische_Erzaehlformen.pdf. Accessed 24 Feb 2022
7. Pyczak, T.: Tell me! Wie Sie mit Storytelling überzeugen, 1st edn. Rheinwerk Computing, Bonn (2017)
8. Irzik, M., et al.: Lkw-Parksituation im Umfeld der BAB 2018. Bundesanstalt für Straßenwesen Bergisch Gladbach (2019). https://www.bmvi.de/SharedDocs/DE/Anlage/StB/bast-erhebung-lkw-parksituation-im-umfeld-der-bab-2018.pdf?__blob=publicationFile. Accessed 22 Feb 2022
9. Statista: Modal-Split im deutschen Güterverkehr im Zeitraum von 2013 bis 2024 nach Landverkehrsträgern. https://de.statista.com/statistik/daten/studie/12149/umfrage/gueteraufkommen-nach-verkehrstraegern-in-deutschland/. Accessed 20 Feb 2022
10. Statista: Anteil der LKW an der Transportleistung im Güterverkehr in Deutschland in den Jahren von 2013 bis 2014. https://de.statista.com/statistik/daten/studie/12195/umfrage/anteil-der-lkw-am-gueterverkehr-in-deutschland/. Accessed 20 Feb 2022
11. arbeitsrecht.de: Lenkzeiten - Ruhezeiten – Arbeitszeiten. https://www.arbeitsrechte.de/wp-content/uploads/ebook-lenk-ruhezeiten.pdf. Accessed 20 Feb 2022
12. Nielsen, J.: Usability Engineering, 1st edn. Academic Press, San Diego (1993)
13. Webex by Cisco. https://www.webex.com/de/index.html. Accessed 25 Feb 2022
14. Enterprise Feedback Suite [Tivian]. https://ww2.unipark.de/www/front.php?controller=login&module=survey. Accessed 25 Feb 2022
15. UEQ - User Expérience Questionnaire. https://www.ueq-online.org/. Accessed 25 Feb 2022
16. Forschungsinformationssystem: Zielorientierter Planungsprozess. https://www.forschungsinformationssystem.de/servlet/is/415008/. Accessed 10 Feb 2022
17. Verband Deutscher Verkehrsunternehmen e.V.: Daten & Fakten zum Personen- und Schienengüterverkehr. https://www.vdv.de/daten-fakten.aspx. Accessed 10 Feb 2022

Correction to: New Energy Hybrid Environment Power Management System: Design and Test Based on DSpace High-Fidelity Simulation

Yuyang Tian, Han Ye, and Shaoyi (Stephen) Liao

Correction to:
Chapter "New Energy Hybrid Environment Power
Management System: Design and Test Based on DSpace
High-Fidelity Simulation" in: M. Rauterberg et al. (Eds.):
HCI International 2022 – Late Breaking Papers, **LNCS 13520,**
https://doi.org/10.1007/978-3-031-18158-0_27

In the original published version of this chapter, an acknowledgement was missing. This now has been added.

The updated original version of this chapter can be found at
https://doi.org/10.1007/978-3-031-18158-0_27

© Springer Nature Switzerland AG 2023
M. Rauterberg et al. (Eds.): HCII 2022, LNCS 13520, p. C1, 2023.
https://doi.org/10.1007/978-3-031-18158-0_39

Author Index